An Introduction to SOLIDWORKS® Flow Simulation 2026

John E. Matsson, Ph.D., P.E.

SDC Publications
P.O. Box 1334
Mission, KS 66222
913-262-2664
www.SDCpublications.com
Publisher: Stephen Schroff

ISBN 13: 978-1-63057-784-1
ISBN-10: 1-63057-784-7

Printed and bound in the United States of America.

Acknowledgements

I would like to thank Stephen Schroff of SDC Publications for his help in preparing this book for publication.

About the Author

Dr. John Matsson is a Professor of Engineering and Chair of the School of Engineering at Oral Roberts University in Tulsa, Oklahoma. He earned M.S. and Ph.D. degrees from the Royal Institute of Technology in Stockholm, Sweden, in 1988 and 1994, respectively and completed postdoctoral work at the Norwegian University of Science and Technology in Trondheim, Norway. His teaching areas include Aerodynamics, Finite Element Methods, Fluid Mechanics and Manufacturing Processes. He is a member of the American Society for Engineering Education ASEE and American Society of Mechanical Engineers ASME Mid-Continent Section. Please contact the author jmatsson@oru.edu with any comments, questions, or suggestions on this book.

Notes:

TABLE OF CONTENTS

Notes:

CHAPTER 1. INTRODUCTION

A. SOLIDWORKS® Flow Simulation

SOLIDWORKS® Flow Simulation 2026 is a fluid flow analysis add-in package that is available for SOLIDWORKS in order to obtain solutions to the full Navier-Stokes equations that govern the motion of fluids. Other packages that can be added to SOLIDWORKS include SOLIDWORKS Motion and SOLIDWORKS Simulation. A fluid flow analysis using Flow Simulation involves numerous basic steps that are shown in the following flowchart in figure 1.1.

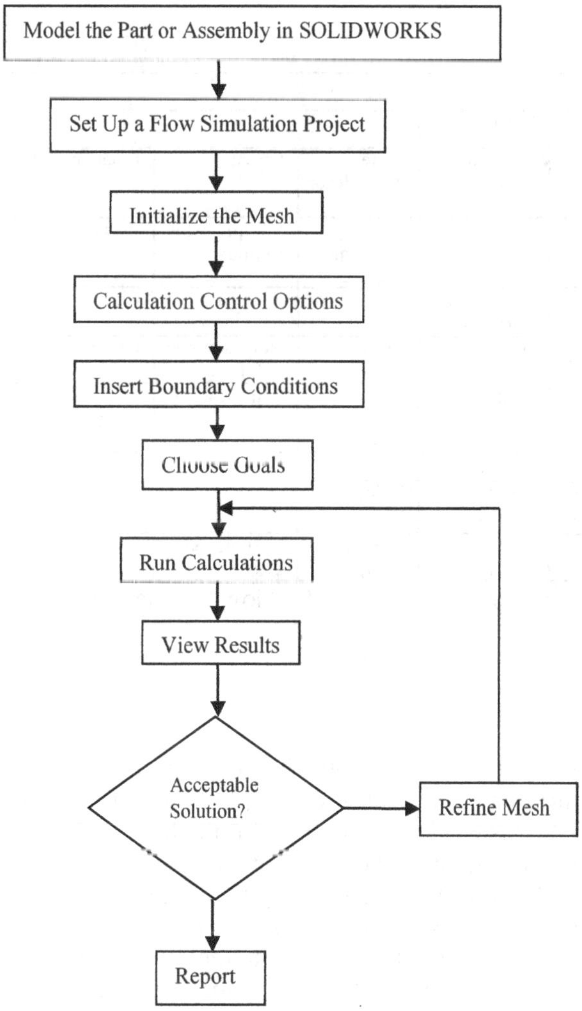

Figure 1.1 Flowchart for fluid flow analysis using SOLIDWORKS® Flow Simulation

B. Project

The process of setting up a Flow Simulation project includes the following general setting steps in order: choosing the analysis type, selecting a fluid and a solid and settings of wall condition and initial and ambient conditions. Any fluid flow problem that is solved using Flow Simulation must be categorized as either internal bounded or external unbounded flow. Examples of internal flows include flows bounded by walls such as pipe- and channel flows, heat exchangers and obstruction flow meters. External flow examples include flows around airfoils and fuselages of airplanes and fluid flow related to different sports such as flows over golf balls, baseballs and soccer balls. Furthermore, during the project setup process a fluid is chosen as belonging to one of the following six categories: gas, liquid, non-Newtonian liquid, compressible liquid, real gas or steam. Physical features include heat conduction in solids, radiation, time-varying flows, gravity and rotation. Roughness of surfaces can be specified and different thermal conditions for walls can be chosen including adiabatic walls or specified heat flux, heat transfer rate or wall temperature. For a more complete list of possible settings, see table 1.1.

General Settings						
Analysis type	Internal	External				
Physical Features	Heat Conduction in Solids	Radiation	Time-dependence	Gravity	Rotation	Free Surface
Fluids	General settings	Liquids	Non-Newtonian Liquids	Compressible Liquids	Real Gases	Steam
Flow Types	Laminar	Laminar and Turbulent	Turbulent			
Solids	Alloys	Glasses and Minerals	Metals	Non-Isotropic Solids	Polymers	Semi-conductors
Wall Thermal Condition	Adiabatic Wall	Heat Flux	Heat Transfer Rate	Temperature		
Thermodynamic Parameters	Pressure	Temperature	Density			
Velocity Parameters	Velocity in X direction	Velocity in Y direction	Velocity in Z direction			
Turbulence Parameters	Turbulence Intensity	Turbulence Length	Turbulence Energy	Turbulence Dissipation		

Table 1.1 List of different general settings in SOLIDWORKS® Flow Simulation

C. Meshing

The SOLIDWORKS® Flow Simulation mesh consists of cells in the form of rectangular parallelepipeds. The Flow Simulation mesh can contain basic cells of three different types: fluid cells, partial cells and solid cells, see figure 1.2. Basic cells can be split during the process of refinement. During refinement, each basic cell is split into eight smaller cells with the same volume, see figure 1.2. Therefore, the volume of each refined cell is only 1/8 of the original volume. A maximum of seven refinement levels can be set in the calculation control options. A table of the different available mesh settings is summarized in table 1.2. An essential part of any computational study of fluid flows is to vary the density of the computational mesh and study whether the solution converges as the mesh is refined. However, it should be remembered that a fine mesh in fluid flow simulations may require a substantial amount of RAM and that calculations can take a very long time to reach convergence.

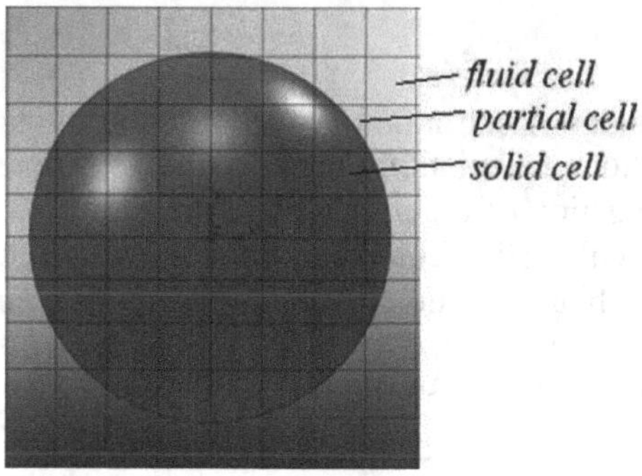

Figure 1.2 Different types of mesh cells

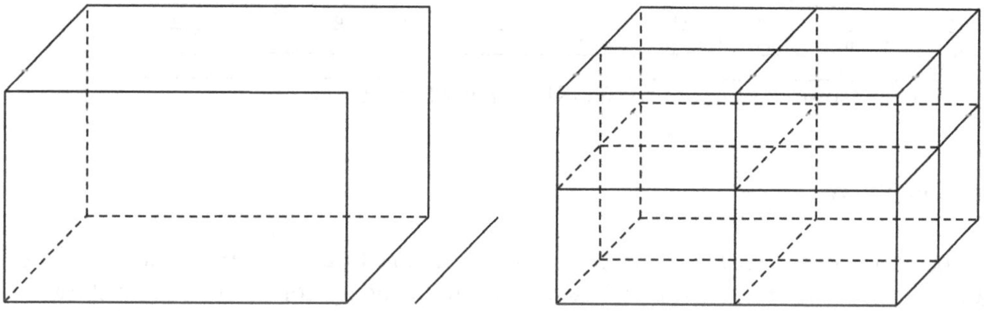

Figure 1.3 Refinement of a rectangular parallelepiped

Mesh Settings				
Automatic Settings	*Level of Initial Mesh*	*Minimum Gap Size*	*Minimum Wall Thickness*	
Manual Settings	*Basic Mesh*	*Solid/Fluid Interface*	*Refining Cells*	*Narrow Channels*
	Number of Cells per X <1001	Small Solid Features Refinement Level < 8	All Cells	Number of Cells
	Number of Cells per Y <1001	Curvature Refinement Level < 8	Fluid Cells	Refinement Level
	Number of Cells per Z <1001	Tolerance Refinement Level < 8	Partial Cells	Minimum Height
			Solid Cells	Maximum Height

Table 1.2 List of mesh settings in SOLIDWORKS® Flow Simulation

There are also six control planes available in Flow Simulation that can be used to optimally contract or expand the mesh in order to assure that details and features of the geometry will be captured by the computational mesh.

The computational mesh is recommended to be constructed in the following order:

a) Start by using the automatic mesh setting. Set the minimum gap size and minimum wall thickness to appropriate values.
b) Turn off automatic settings and set your own basic mesh values with both the small solid features refinement level and the curvature refinement level set to zero. Disable the narrow channel refinement.
c) Increase both the small solid features refinement level and the curvature refinement level in steps and enable the narrow channel refinement.

D. Calculation Control Options

There are many ways in which you can control your calculations, see table 1.3. As shown in the table the finishing conditions include refinement number, iterations, calculation time and travels. Travel is defined as the number of iterations related to the propagation of a perturbation through the computational domain. In the value drop down box of the calculation control options it is possible to choose whether calculations will stop when one of the finishing conditions is satisfied or when all of them are satisfied. The maximum number of travels depends on the specific goals that are used in the calculations, result resolution level and the type of problem that is studied.

Calculation Control Options			
Finish Conditions	*Saving*	*Refinement*	*Advanced*
Minimum Refinement Number	Save Before Refinement	Disabled	Flow Freezing
Maximum Iterations	Periodic Saving	Level = 1 - 7	Notify when calculation is finished
Maximum Calculation Time	Tabular Saving		
Maximum Travels			

Table 1.3 List of mesh settings in SOLIDWORKS® Flow Simulation

E. Boundary Conditions

Boundary conditions are required for both the inflow and outflow faces of internal flow regions except enclosures subjected to natural convection. Visualization of boundary conditions can be shown with arrows of different colors indicating the type and direction of the boundary condition. The boundary conditions are divided into three different types: flow openings, pressure openings and walls, see table 1.4.

Boundary Conditions								
Flow Openings	Inlet Mass Flow	Inlet Volume Flow	Inlet Velocity	Inlet Mach Number	Outlet Mass Flow	Outlet Volume Flow	Outlet Velocity	Outlet Mach Number
Pressure Openings	Environment Pressure	Static Pressure	Total Pressure					
Wall	Real Wall	Ideal Wall						

Table 1.4 List of available boundary conditions in SOLIDWORKS® Flow Simulation

Each boundary condition has parameters related to it that can be set to different values. The available parameters for each boundary condition are shown in Table 1.5.

Boundary Conditions							
	Flow Parameters	Thermodynamic Parameters	Turbulence Parameters	Boundary Layer	Wall Parameters	Wall Motion	Options
Inlet Mass Flow	√	√	√	√			√
Inlet Volume Flow	√	√	√	√			√
Inlet Velocity	√	√	√	√			√
Inlet Mach Number	√	√	√	√			√
Outlet Mass Flow	√						√
Outlet Volume Flow	√						√
Outlet Velocity	√						√
Outlet Mach Number	√						√
Environment Pressure		√	√	√			√
Static Pressure		√	√	√			√
Total Pressure		√	√	√			√
Real Wall					√	√	√
Ideal Wall							√

Table 1.5 List of available parameters for different boundary conditions in SOLIDWORKS® Flow Simulation

The flow parameter depends on the boundary condition but includes velocity, Mach number and mass and volume flow rate. The direction of the flow vector can be specified as normal to the face, as swirl or as a 3D vector. The thermodynamic parameters include temperature and pressure. For the turbulence parameters you can choose between specifying the turbulence intensity and length or the turbulence energy and dissipation (k-ε turbulence model). The boundary layer is set to either laminar or turbulent. You can also specify velocity and thermal boundary layer thickness for the inlet velocity boundary condition as well as specify the core velocity and temperature. For the real wall boundary condition, one can specify the wall roughness together with wall temperature and heat transfer coefficient. The real wall also has an option for motion in the form of translational or angular velocity.

F. Goals

Goals are criteria used to stop the iterative solution process. The goals are chosen from the physical parameters of interest to the user of Flow Simulation. The use of goals minimizes errors in the calculated parameters and shortens the total solution time for the solver. There are five different types of goals: global goals, point goals, surface goals, volume goals and equation goals. The global goal is based on parameter values determined everywhere in the flow field whereas a point goal is related to a specific point inside the computational domain. Surface goals are determined on specific surfaces, and volume goals are determined within a specific subset of the computational domain as specified by the user. Finally, equation goals are defined by mathematical expressions. Table 1.6 shows 48 different parameters that can be chosen by the different types of goals.

GG: Global Goal, SG: Surface Goal, VG: Volume Goal					***PG: Point Goal***
Parameter	*Minimum*	*Average*	*Maximum*	*Bulk Average*	*Value*
Static Pressure	*GG, SG, VG*	*GG, SG, VG*	*GG, SG, VG*	*GG, SG, VG*	*PG*
Total Pressure	*GG, SG, VG*	*GG, SG, VG*	*GG, SG, VG*	*GG, SG, VG*	*PG*
Dynamic Pressure	*GG, SG, VG*	*GG, SG, VG*	*GG, SG, VG*	*GG, SG, VG*	*PG*
Temperature of Fluid	*GG, SG, VG*	*GG, SG, VG*	*GG, SG, VG*	*GG, SG, VG*	*PG*
Density	*GG, SG, VG*	*GG, SG, VG*	*GG, SG, VG*	*GG, SG, VG*	*PG*
Mass Flow Rate			*GG, SG*		
Mass in Volume			*VG*		
Volume Flow Rate			*SG*		
Velocity	*GG, SG, VG*	*GG, SG, VG*	*GG, SG, VG*	*GG, SG, VG*	*PG*
X-Component of Velocity	*GG, SG, VG*	*GG, SG, VG*	*GG, SG, VG*	*GG, SG, VG*	*PG*
Y-Component of Velocity	*GG, SG, VG*	*GG, SG, VG*	*GG, SG, VG*	*GG, SG, VG*	*PG*
Z-Component of Velocity	*GG, SG, VG*	*GG, SG, VG*	*GG, SG, VG*	*GG, SG, VG*	*PG*
Mach Number	*GG, SG, VG*	*GG, SG, VG*	*GG, SG, VG*	*GG, SG, VG*	*PG*
Turbulent Viscosity	*GG, SG, VG*	*GG, SG, VG*	*GG, SG, VG*	*GG, SG, VG*	*PG*
Turbulent Time	*GG, SG, VG*	*GG, SG, VG*	*GG, SG, VG*	*GG, SG, VG*	*PG*
Turbulent Length	*GG, SG, VG*	*GG, SG, VG*	*GG, SG, VG*	*GG, SG, VG*	*PG*
Turbulent Intensity	*GG, SG, VG*	*GG, SG, VG*	*GG, SG, VG*	*GG, SG, VG*	*PG*
Turbulent Energy	*GG, SG, VG*	*GG, SG, VG*	*GG, SG, VG*	*GG, SG, VG*	*PG*
Turbulent Dissipation	*GG, SG, VG*	*GG, SG, VG*	*GG, SG, VG*	*GG, SG, VG*	*PG*
Heat Flux	*GG, SG*	*GG, SG*	*GG, SG*		
X-Component of Heat Flux	*GG, SG*	*GG, SG*	*GG, SG*		
Y-Component of Heat Flux	*GG, SG*	*GG, SG*	*GG, SG*		
Z-Component of Heat Flux	*GG, SG*	*GG, SG*	*GG, SG*		
Heat Transfer Rate			*GG, SG*		
X-Component of Heat Transfer Rate			*GG, SG*		
Y-Component of Heat Transfer Rate			*GG, SG*		
Z-Component of Heat Transfer Rate			*GG, SG*		
Normal Force			*GG, SG*		
X-Component of Normal Force			*GG, SG*		
Y-Component of Normal Force			*GG, SG*		
Z-Component of Normal Force			*GG, SG*		
Force			*GG, SG*		
X-Component of Force			*GG, SG*		
Y-Component of Force			*GG, SG*		
Z-Component of Force			*GG, SG*		
Shear Force			*GG, SG*		
X-Component of Shear Force			*GG, SG*		
Y-Component of Shear Force			*GG, SG*		
Z-Component of Shear Force			*GG, SG*		
X-Component of Torque			*GG, SG*		
Y-Component of Torque			*GG, SG*		
Z-Component of Torque			*GG, SG*		
Temperature of Solid	*GG, SG, VG*	*GG, SG, VG*	*GG, SG, VG*		*PG*
Melting Temperature Exceed	*SG, VG*	*SG, VG*	*SG, VG*		*PG*
Mass Fraction of Air	*GG, SG, VG*	*GG, SG, VG*	*GG, SG, VG*	*GG, SG, VG*	*PG*
Volume Fraction of Air	*GG, SG, VG*	*GG, SG, VG*	*GG, SG, VG*	*GG, SG, VG*	*PG*
Mass Flow Rate of Air			*SG*		
Volume Flow Rate of Air			*SG*		

Table 1.6 List of available parameters for different goals in SOLIDWORKS® Flow Simulation

G. Results

Results can be visualized in different ways as indicated by table 1.7.

Result Settings								
Results	Cut Plots	3D-Profile Plots	Surface Plots	Isosurfaces	Flow Trajectories	Particle Studies	XY Plots	Point Surface and Volume Parameters

Table 1.7 List of available results in SOLIDWORKS® Flow Simulation

H. References

1. Technical Reference SOLIDWORKS® Flow Simulation 2026
2. Tutorials SOLIDWORKS® Flow Simulation 2026
3. Validation Examples SOLIDWORKS® Flow Simulation 2026

Notes:

CHAPTER 2. FLAT PLATE BOUNDARY LAYER

A. Objectives

- Creating the SOLIDWORKS part needed for the Flow Simulation
- Setting up Flow Simulation projects for internal flow
- Setting up a two-dimensional flow condition
- Initializing the mesh
- Selecting boundary conditions
- Inserting global goals, point goals and equation goals for the calculations
- Running the calculations
- Using Cut Plots to visualize the resulting flow field
- Use of XY Plots for velocity profiles, boundary layer thickness, displacement thickness, momentum thickness and friction coefficients
- Use of Excel templates for XY Plots
- Comparison of Flow Simulation results with theories and empirical data
- Cloning of the project

B. Problem Description

In this chapter, we will use SOLIDWORKS Flow Simulation to study the two-dimensional laminar and turbulent flow on a flat plate and compare with the theoretical Blasius boundary layer solution and empirical results. The inlet velocity for the 1 m long plate is 5 m/s and we will be using air as the fluid for laminar calculations and water to get a higher Reynolds number for turbulent boundary layer calculations. We will determine the velocity profiles and plot the profiles using the well-known boundary layer similarity coordinate. The variation of boundary-layer thickness, displacement thickness, momentum thickness and the local friction coefficient will also be determined. We will start by creating the part needed for this simulation, see figure 2.0.

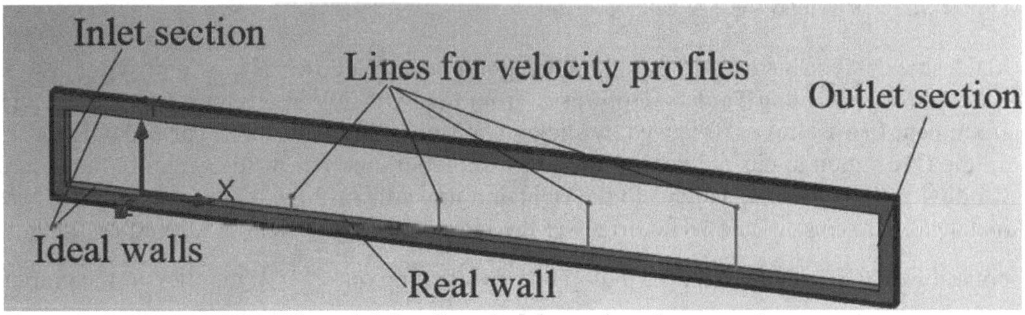

Figure 2.0 SOLIDWORKS model for flat plate boundary layer study

C. Creating the SOLIDWORKS Part

1. Start by creating a new part in SOLIDWORKS: select **File>>New...** from the menu and click on the **OK** button in the **New SOLIDWORKS Document** window. Click on **Front Plane** in the **FeatureManager design tree** and select **Front** from the **View Orientation** drop down menu in the graphics window.

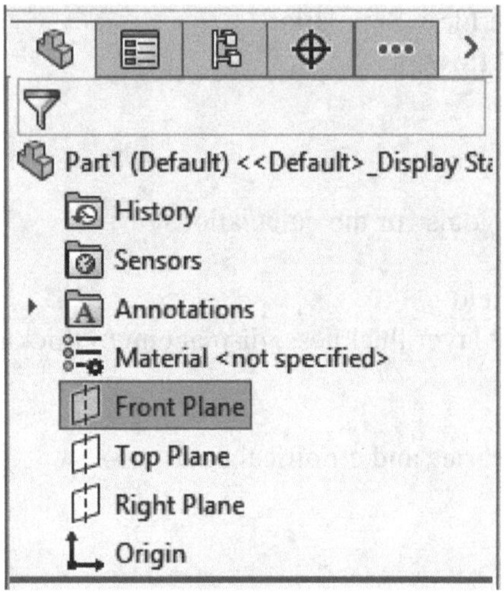

Figure 2.1a) Selection of front plane

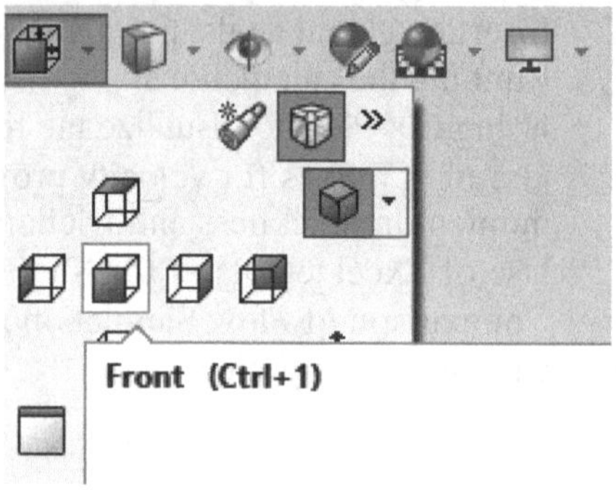

Figure 2.1b) Selection of front view

2. Click on the **Sketch** tab from under the menu and select **Corner Rectangle**.

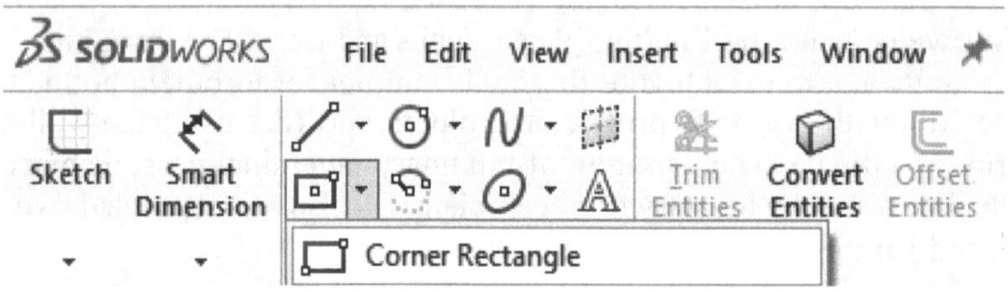

Figure 2.2 Selecting a sketch tool

3. Make sure that you have **MMGS** (millimeter, gram, second) chosen as your unit system. You can check this by selecting **Tools>>Options...** from the SOLIDWORKS menu and selecting the **Document Properties** tab followed by clicking on **Units**. Check the circle for **MMGS** and click on the **OK** button to close the window. Click to the left and below the origin in the graphics window and drag two rectangles to the right and upward. Add the dimensions for the two rectangles, see Figure 2.3a). The origin of the red coordinate system is located on the inner bottom wall. Close the Rectangle dialog box by clicking on ✓. Right click in the graphics window and select **Zoom/Pan/Rotate>> Zoom to Fit**.

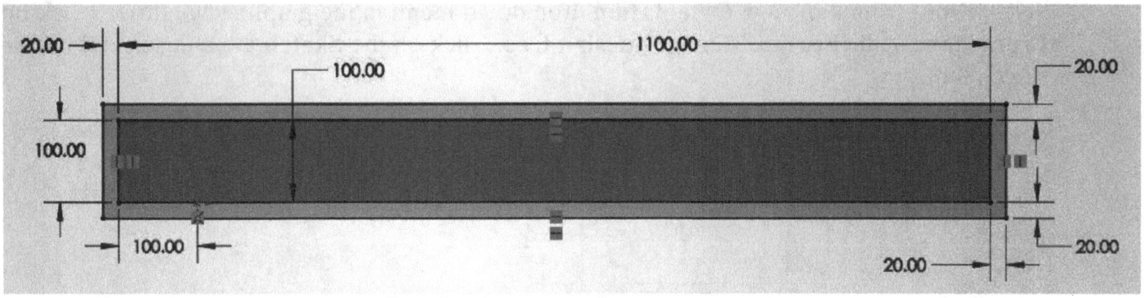

Figure 2.3a) Parameter settings for the rectangle

Figure 2.3b) Zooming in the graphics window

4. Select **Features** tab and **Extruded Boss/Base**. Check the box for **Direction 2** and click **OK** to exit the **Boss-Extrude Property Manager**.

Figure 2.4a) Selection of extrusion feature

Figure 2.4b) Closing the property manager

5. Select **Front** from the **View Orientation** drop down menu in the graphics window. Click on **Front Plane** in the **FeatureManager design tree.** Click on the **Sketch** tab and select the **Line** sketch tool.

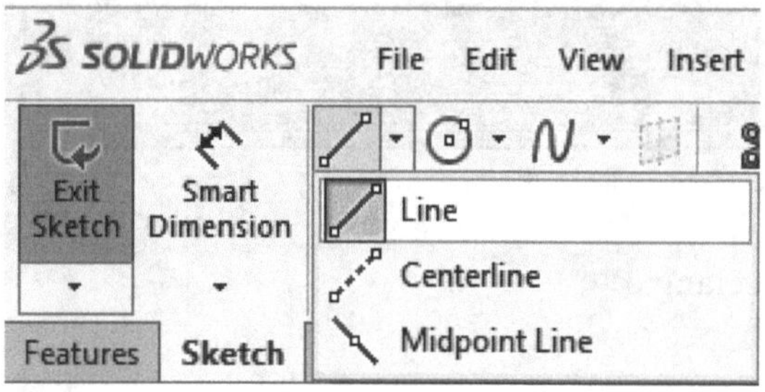

Figure 2.5 Selection of the line sketch tool

6. Draw a vertical line in the positive Y-direction in the front plane starting at the lower inner surface of the sketch. Set the **Parameters** and **Additional Parameters** to the values shown in figure 2.6. Close the **Line Properties** dialog and the **Insert Line** dialog.

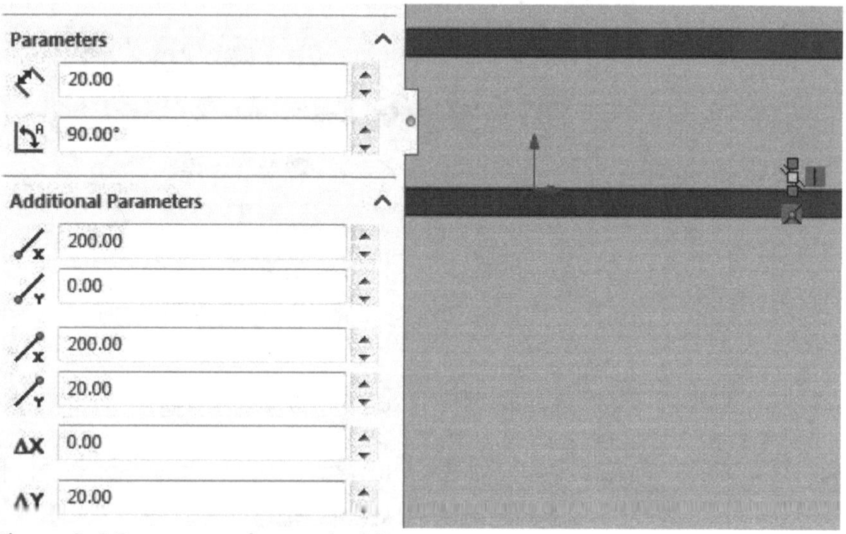

Figure 2.6 Parameters for vertical line

7. Repeat step **6** three more times and add three more vertical lines to the sketch, the second line at X = 400 mm with a length of 40 mm, the third line at X = 600 mm with a length of 60 mm and the fourth line at X = 800 mm with a length of 80 mm. These lines will be used to plot the boundary layer velocity profiles at different streamwise positions along the flat plate. Close the **Line Properties** dialog and the **Insert Line** dialog. Save the SOLIDWORKS part with the following name: **Flat Plate Boundary Layer Study 2026**. Rename the newly created sketch in the **FeatureManager design tree**, see figure 2.7. You will need to left click twice to rename the sketch.

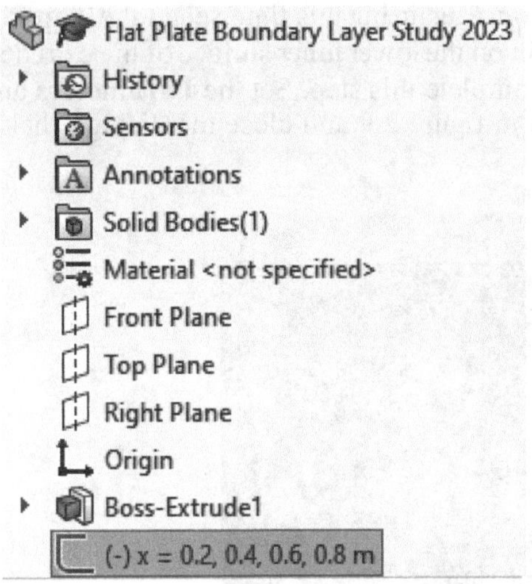

Figure 2.7 Renaming the sketch for boundary layer velocity profiles

8. Click on the **Rebuild** symbol in the SOLIDWORKS menu. Repeat step **6** and draw a horizontal line in the positive X-direction starting at the origin of the lower inner surface of the sketch. Set the **Parameters** and **Additional Parameters** to the values shown in figure 2.8 and close the **Line Properties** dialog and the **Insert Line** dialog. Click on the **Rebuild** symbol. Rename the sketch in the **FeatureManager design tree** and call it **x = 0 – 0.9 m**.

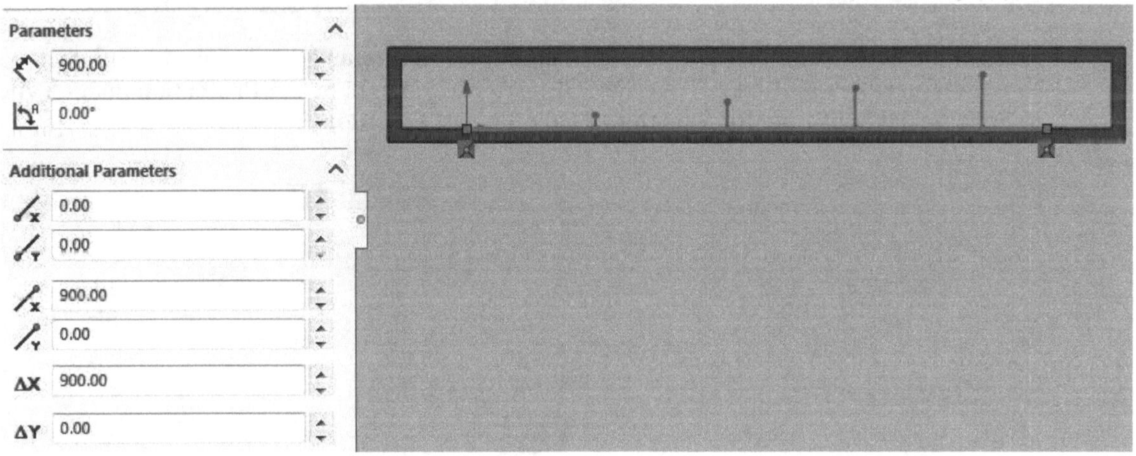

Figure 2.8 Sketch of a line in the X-direction

9. Next, we will create a split line. Repeat step **6** once again but this time select the **Top Plane** and draw a line in the Z-direction through the origin on the lower inner surface of the extruded part. It will help to zoom in and rotate the view to complete this step. Set the **Parameters** and **Additional Parameters** to the values shown in figure 2.9 and close the dialog. Click on the **Rebuild** symbol.

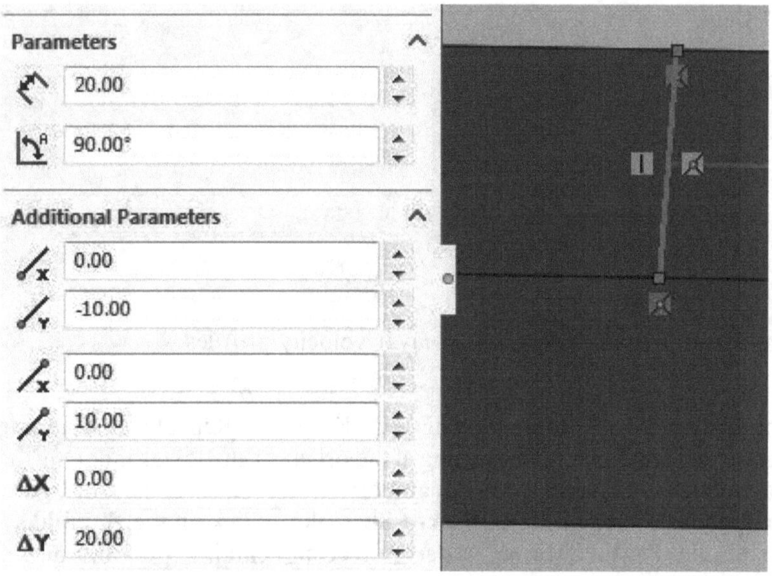

Figure 2.9 Drawing of a line in the Z-direction

10. Rename the new sketch in the **FeatureManager design tree** and call it **Split Line**. Select **Insert>>Curve>>Split Line...** from the SOLIDWORKS menu. Select **Projection** under **Type to Split**. Select **Split Line** for **Sketch to Project** under **Selections**.

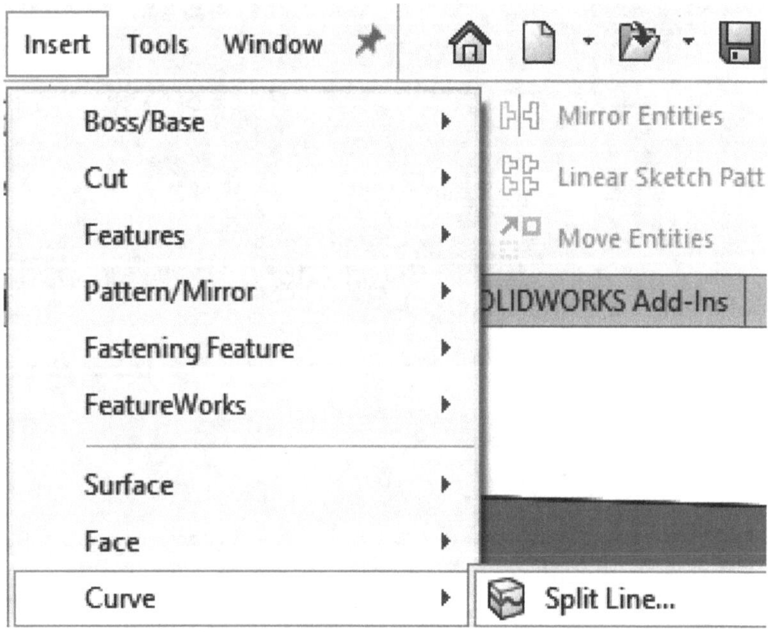

Figure 2.10 Creating a split line

11. For **Faces to Split**, select the surface where you have drawn your split line, see figure 2.11. Close the dialog ✓. You have now finished the part for the flat plate boundary layer. Select **File>>Save** from the SOLIDWORKS menu.

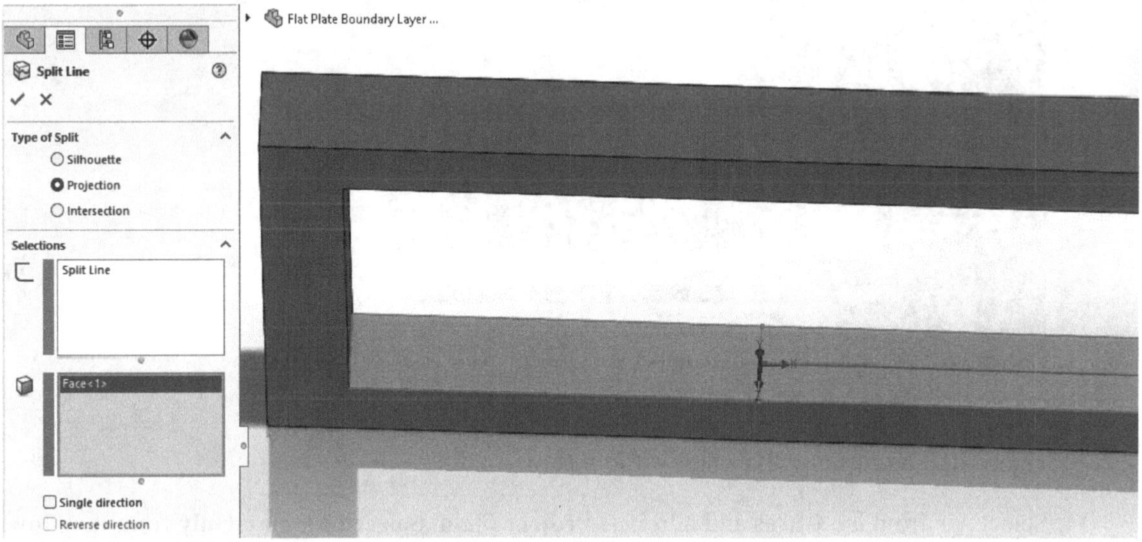

Figure 2.11 Selection of surface for the split line

D. Setting Up the Flow Simulation Project

12. If **Flow Simulation** is not available in the menu, you have to add it from SOLIDWORKS menu: **Tools>>Add Ins…** and check the corresponding **SOLIDWORKS Flow Simulation 2026** box under SOLIDWORKS Add-Ins and click OK to close the Add-Ins window. Select the tab **Flow Simulation>>Wizard** to create a new Flow Simulation project. Enter Project name: **Flat Plate Boundary Layer Study**. Click on the **Next>** button. Select the default **SI (m-kg-s)** unit system and click on the **Next>** button once again.

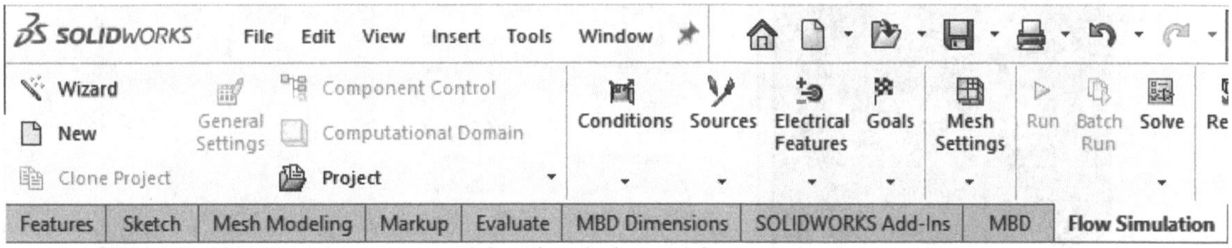

Figure 2.12a) Starting a new Flow Simulation project

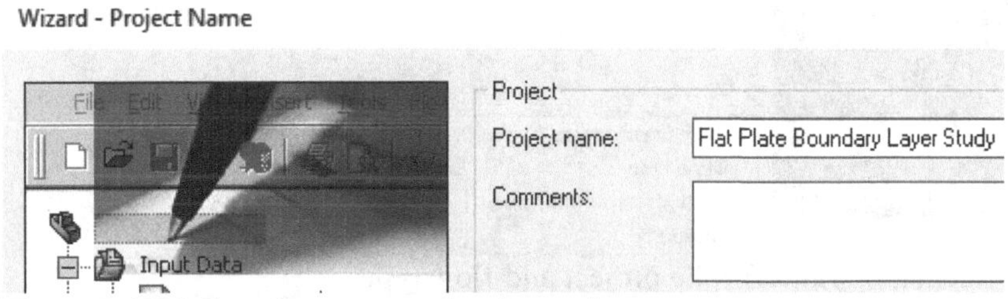

Figure 2.12b) Creating a name for the project

13. Use the **Internal Analysis type** and click on the **Next>** button once again.

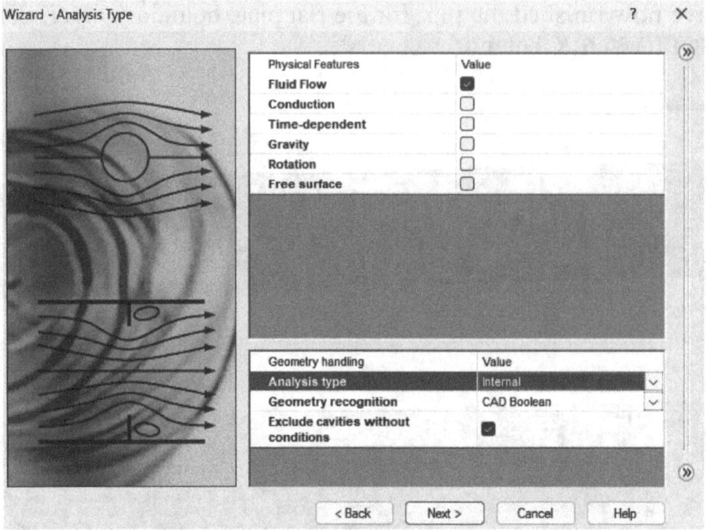

Figure 2.13 Exclusion of cavities without flow conditions

14. Select **Air** from the **Gases** and add it as **Project Fluid**. Select **Laminar Only** from the **Flow Type** drop down menu. Click on the **Next >** button. Use the default **Wall Conditions** and click on the **Next >** button. Insert **5 m/s** for **Velocity in X direction** as **Initial Conditions** and click on the **Finish** button. You will get a fluid volume recognition failure message. Answer **Yes** to this question and create a lid on each side of the model. Answer **Yes** to the questions about wanting to reset the mesh settings, fluid volume recognition and computational domain when you create the lids.

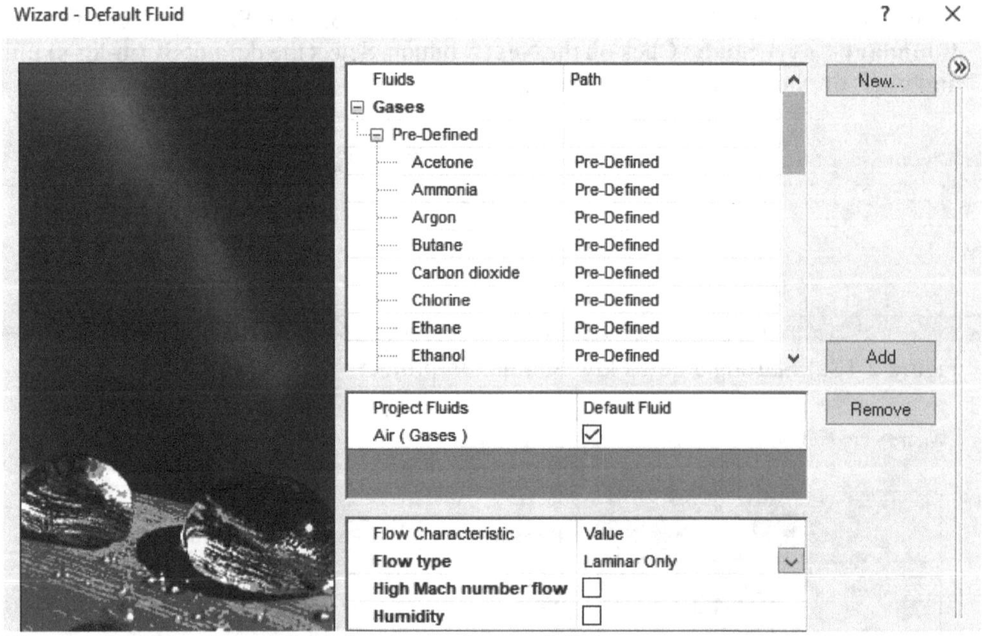

Figure 2.14 Selection of fluid for the project and flow type

15. Select the tab **Flow Simulation>>Computational Domain….** Click on the **2D simulation** button under **Type** and select **XY plane**. Close the **Computational Domain** dialog ✓.

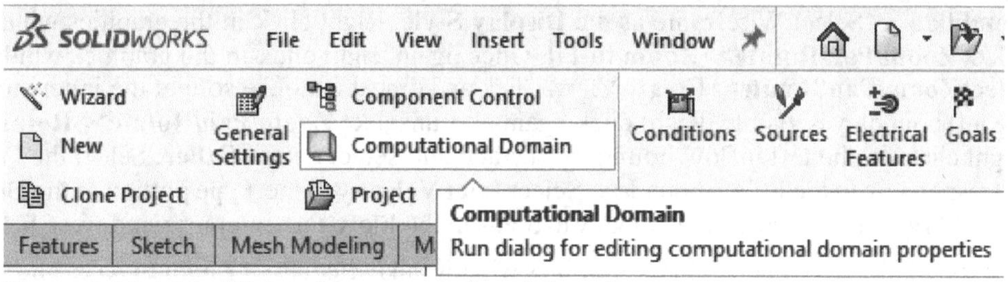

Figure 2.15a) Modifying the computational domain

16. Select the tab **Flow Simulation>>Mash Settings>>Global Mesh….** Select **Manual** under **Type**. Change **N**$_X$ to **300** and **N**$_Y$ to **200**. Click on the **OK** button (green check mark) to exit the **Initial Mesh** window.

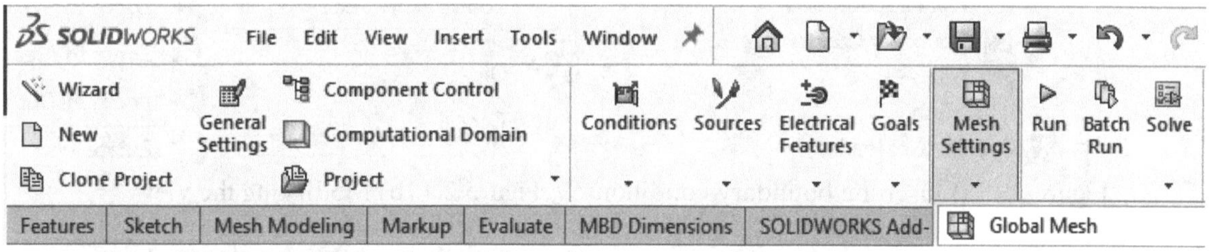

Figure 2.16a) Modifying the initial mesh

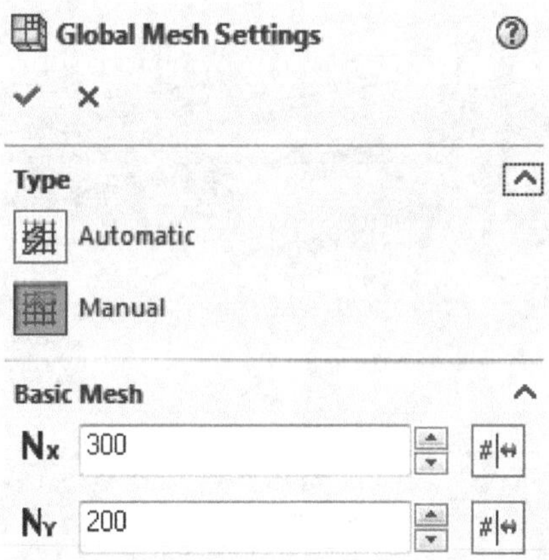

Figure 2.16b) Changing the number of cells in two directions

E. Selecting Boundary Conditions

17. Select the **Flow Simulation analysis tree** tab, open the **Input Data** folder by clicking on the plus sign next to it and right click on **Boundary Conditions**. Select **Insert Boundary Condition…**. Select Wireframe as the **Display Style**. Right click in the graphics window and select **Zoom/Pan/Rotate>>Zoom to Fit**. Once again, right click in the graphics window and select **Zoom/Pan/Rotate>>Rotate View**. Click and drag the mouse so that the inner surface of the left boundary is visible. Right click again and unselect **Zoom/Pan/Rotate>>Rotate View**. Right click on the left inflow boundary surface and select **Select Other**. Select the Face corresponding to the inflow boundary. Select **Inlet Velocity** in the **Type** portion of the **Boundary Condition** window and set the velocity to **5 m/s** in the **Flow Parameters** window. Click **OK** to exit the window. Right click in the graphics window and select **Zoom to Area** and select an area around the left boundary.

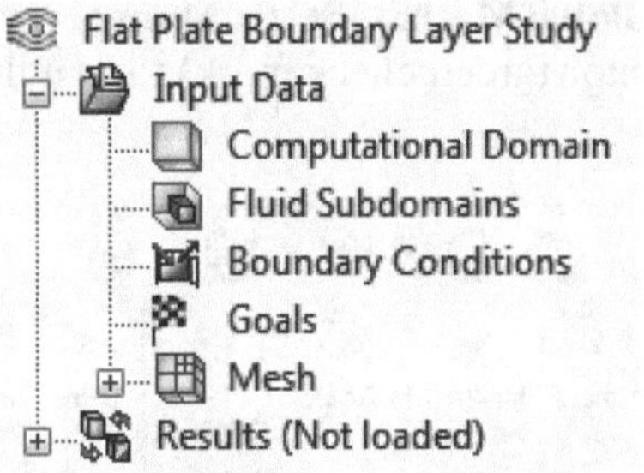

Figure 2.17a) Inserting boundary condition

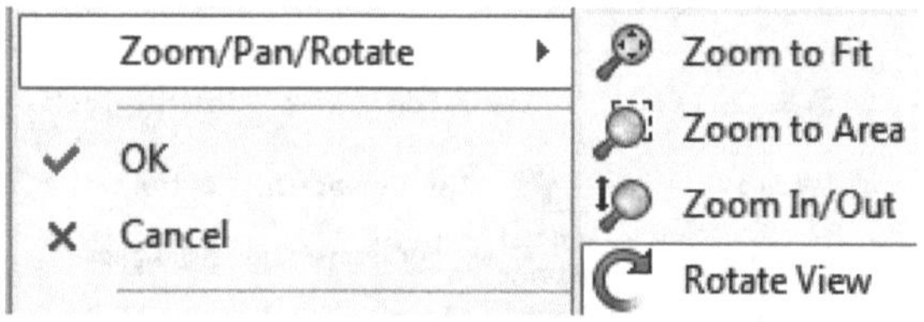

Figure 2.17b) Modifying the view

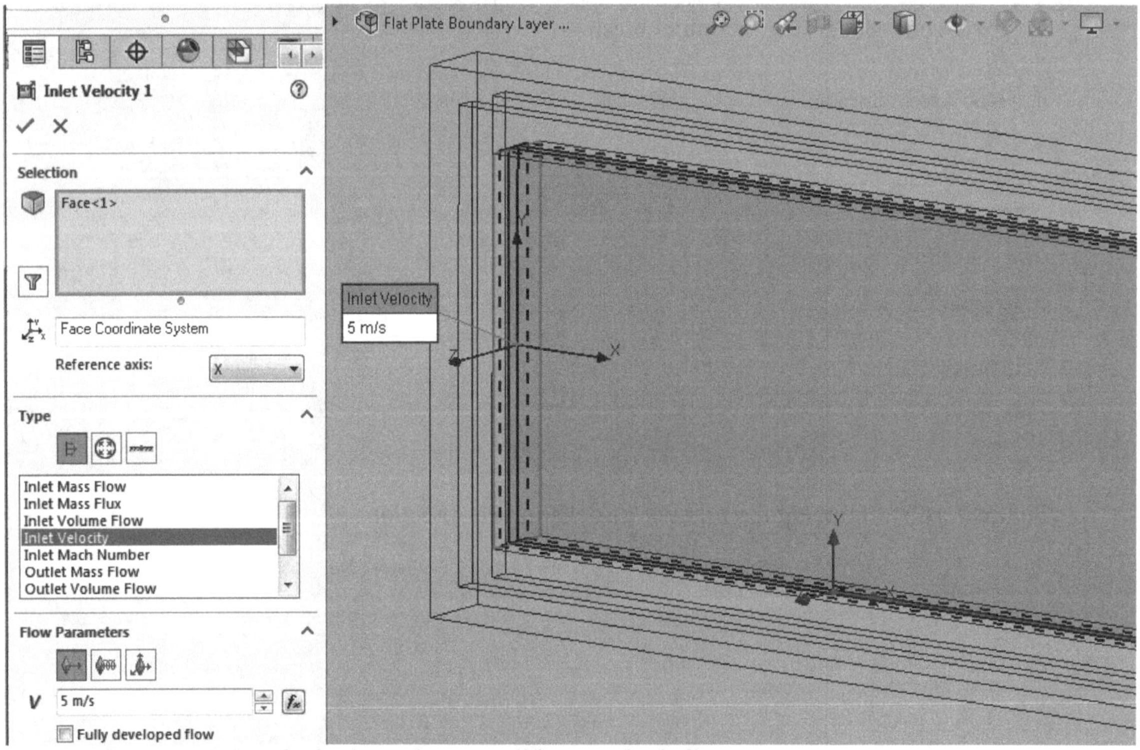

Figure 2.17c) Velocity boundary condition on the inflow

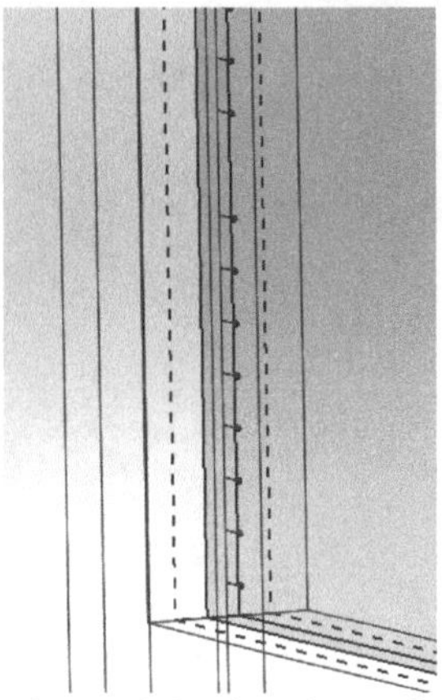

Figure 2.17d) Inlet velocity boundary condition indicated by arrows

18. Red arrows pointing in the flow direction indicate the inlet velocity boundary condition, see figure 2.17d). Right click in the graphics window and select **Zoom to Fit**. Right click again in the graphics window and select **Rotate View** once again to rotate the part so that the inner right outlet surface is visible in the graphics window. Right click and click on **Select**. Right click on **Boundary Conditions** in the **Flow Simulation analysis tree** and select **Insert Boundary Condition…**. Right click on the outflow boundary surface and select **Select Other**. Select the Face corresponding to the outflow boundary. Click on the **Pressure Openings** button in the **Type** portion of the **Boundary Condition** window and select **Static Pressure**. Click **OK** to exit the window. If you zoom in on the outlet boundary, you will see blue arrows in both directions indicating the static pressure boundary condition, see figure 2.18b).

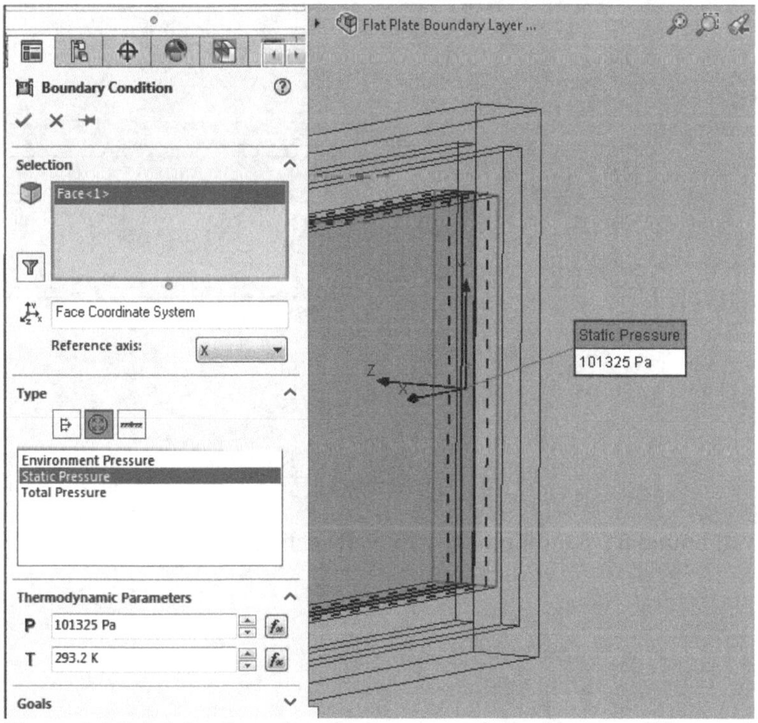

Figure 2.18a) Selection of static pressure as boundary condition at the outlet of the flow region

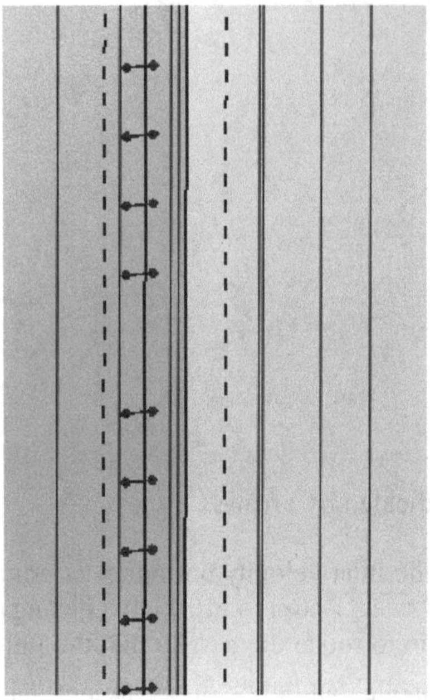

Figure 2.18b) Outlet static pressure boundary condition

19. Enter the following boundary conditions: **Ideal Wall** for upper wall and lower wall at the inflow region, see figures 2.19. These will be adiabatic and frictionless walls.

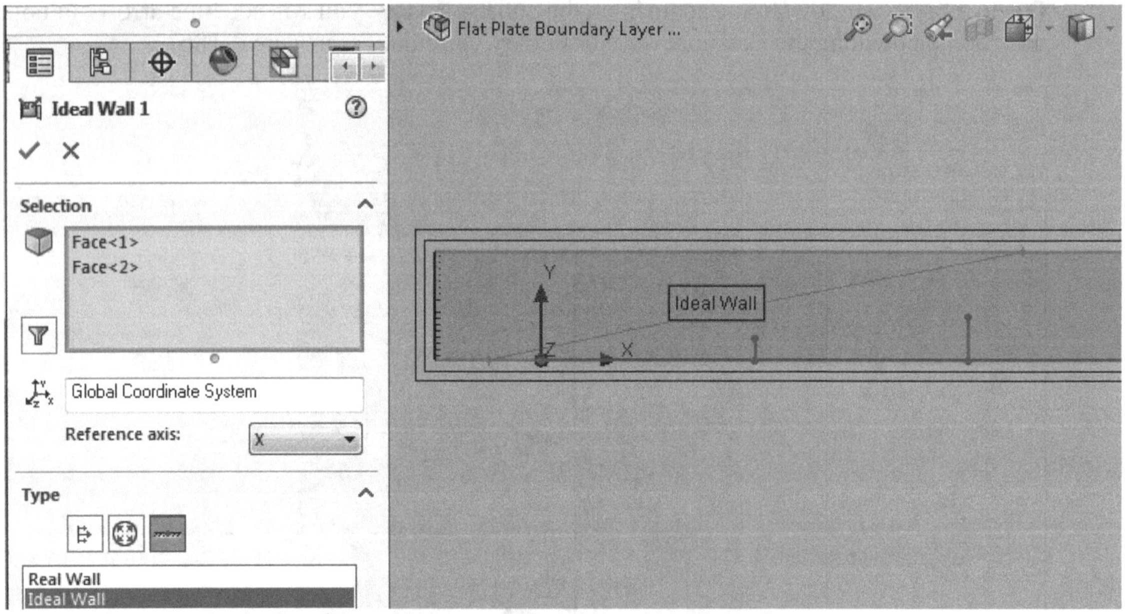

Figure 2.19 Ideal wall boundary condition for two wall sections

20. The last boundary condition will be in the form of a **Real Wall.** We will study the development of the boundary layer on this wall.

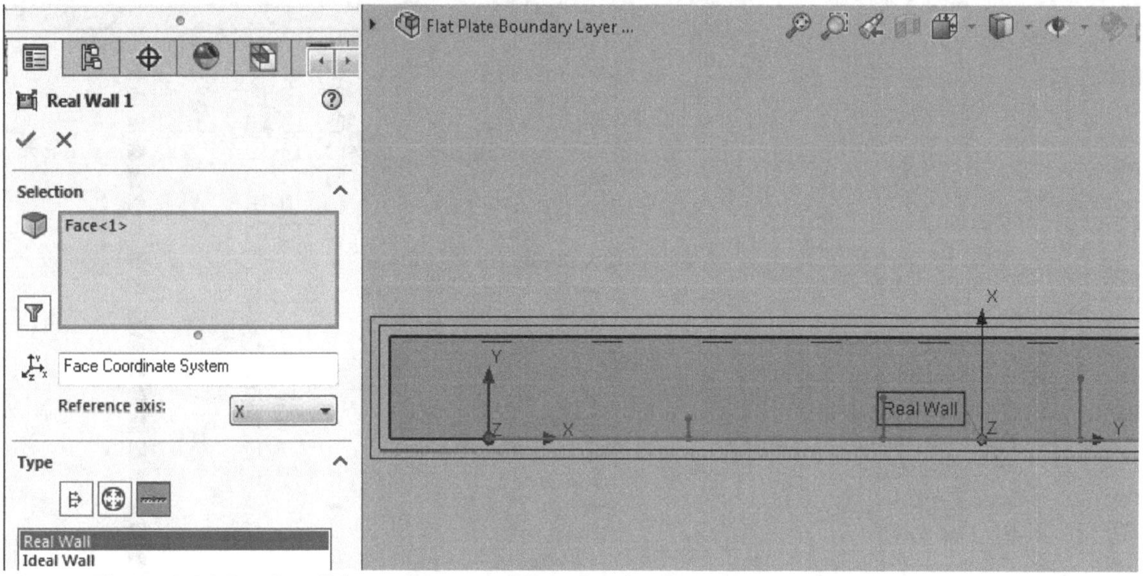

Figure 2.20 Real wall boundary condition for the flat plate

F. Inserting Global Goals and Calculation Controls

21. Right click on **Goals** in the **Flow Simulation analysis tree** and select **Insert Global Goals....** Select **Friction Force (X)** as a global goal. Exit the **Global Goals** window. Right click on **Goals** in the **Flow Simulation analysis tree** and select **Insert Point Goals....** Click on the **Point Coordinates** button. Enter **0.2 m** for X coordinate and **0.02 m** for Y coordinate and click on the **Add Point** button. Add three more points with the coordinates shown in figure 2.21e). Check the **Value** box for **Velocity (X)**. Exit the **Point Goals** window.

    Rename the goals as shown in figure 2.21f). Right click on **Goals** in the **Flow Simulation analysis tree** and select **Insert Equation Goal....** Click on **PG Velocity (X) at x = 0.2 m** goal in the **Flow Simulation analysis tree**, multiply by *0.2* (for x = 0.2 m) and divide by *1.516E-5* (kinematic viscosity of air at room temperature (ν = 1.516E-5 m^2/s) to get an expression for the Reynolds number in the **Equation Goal** window, see figure 2.21g). Select **No unit** from the dimensionality drop down menu. Rename the equation goal to **Reynolds number at x = 0.2 m.** Exit the **Equation Goal** window. Insert three more equation goals corresponding to the Reynolds numbers at the three other *x* locations. For a definition of the Reynolds number, see equation (2.15).

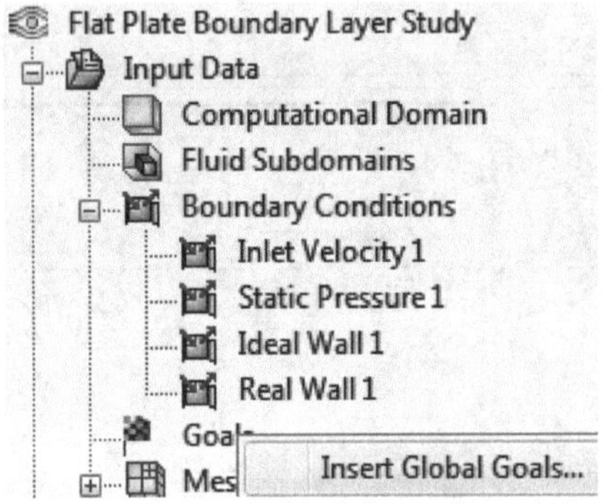

Figure 2.21a) Inserting global goals

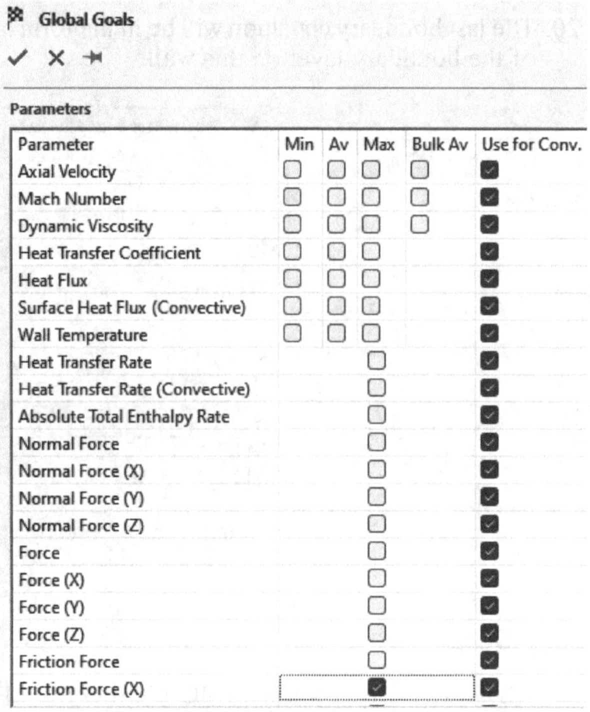

Figure 2.21b) Selection of friction force

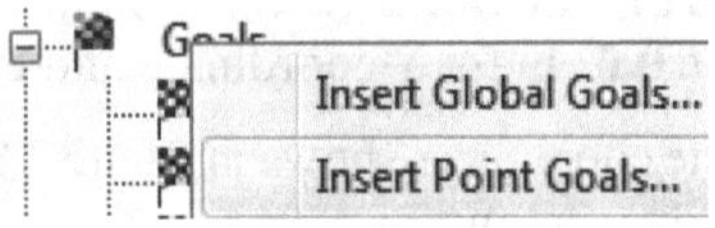

Figure 2.21c) Inserting point goals

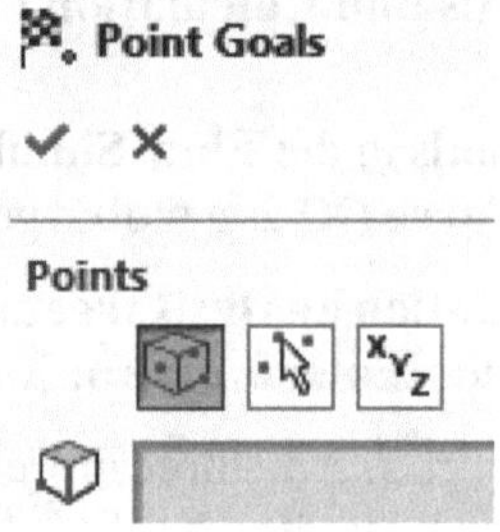

Figure 2.21d) Selecting point coordinates

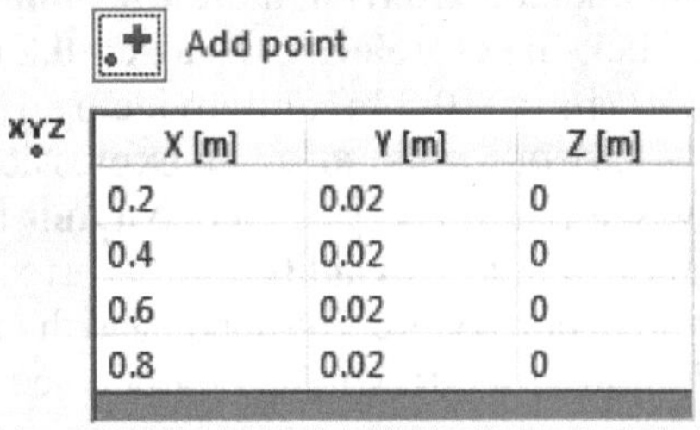

Figure 2.21e) Coordinates for point goals

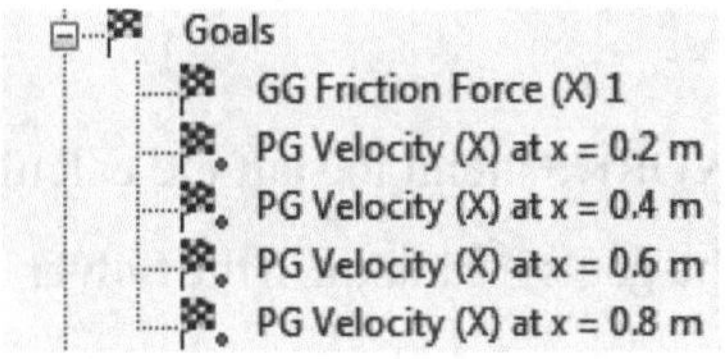

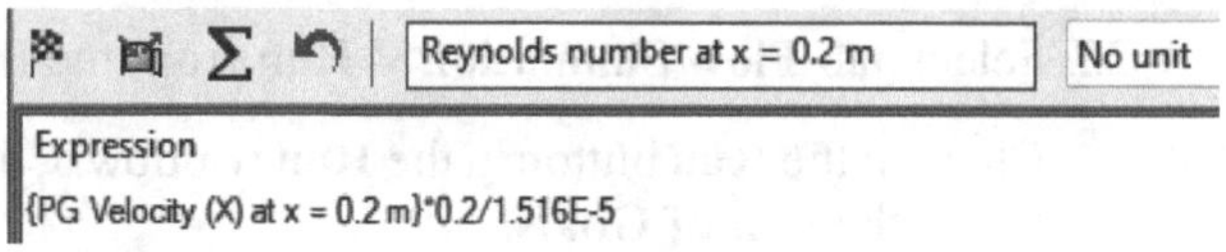

Figure 2.21f) Renaming the point goals   Figure 2.21g) Entering an equation goal

Select the tab **Flow Simulation>>Solve>>Calculation Control Options** from the menu. Select the **Refinement** tab. Set the **Value** to **level = 2** for **Global Domain**. Select **Goal Convergence** and **Iterations** as **Refinement strategy**. Click on [...] in the **Value** column for **Goals** and check all the boxes in the **Table**. Select the **Finishing** tab and uncheck the **Travels** box under **Finish Conditions**. Set the **Refinements Criteria** to **2**.

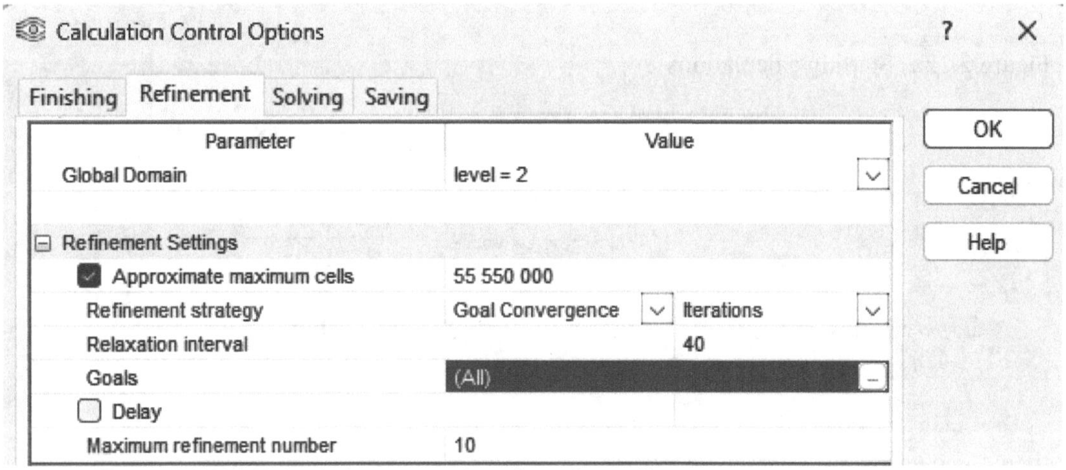

Figure 2.21h) Calculation control options for refinement

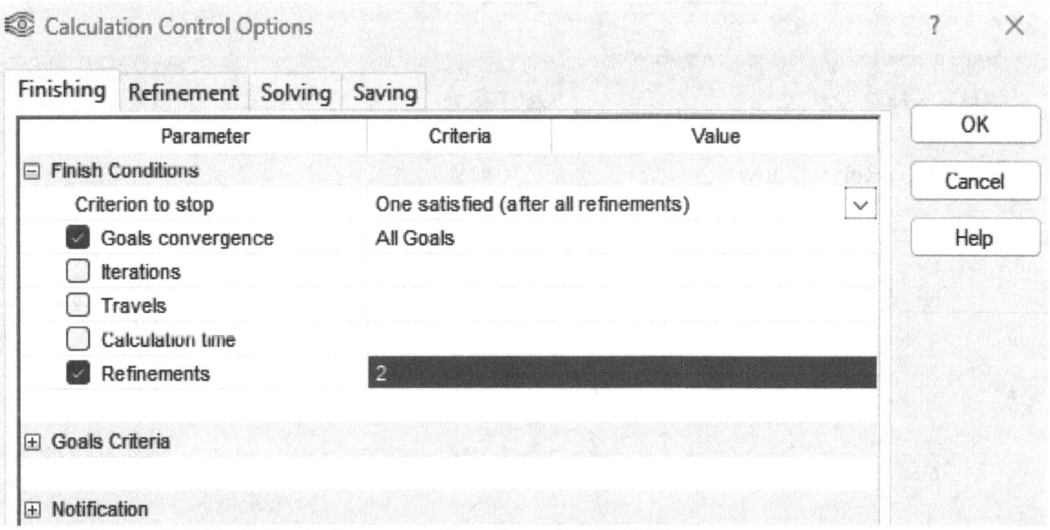

Figure 2.21i) Calculation control options for finishing

G. Running the Calculations

22. Select tab **Flow Simulation>>Run** from the SOLIDWORKS menu to start the calculations. Click on the **Run** button in the **Run** window. Click on the goals button in the **Solver** window to see the **List of Goals**.

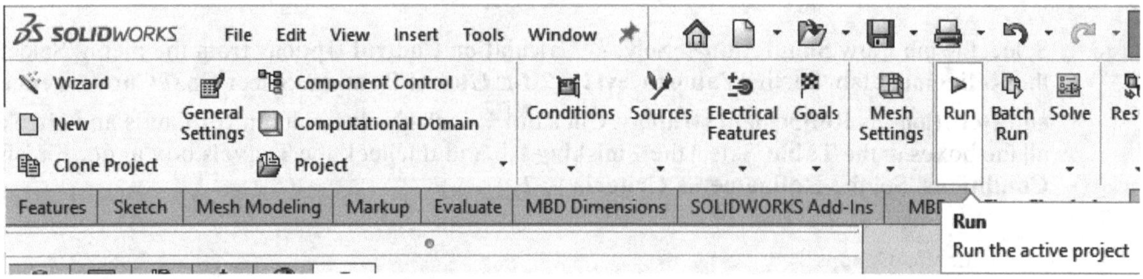

Figure 2.22a) Starting calculations

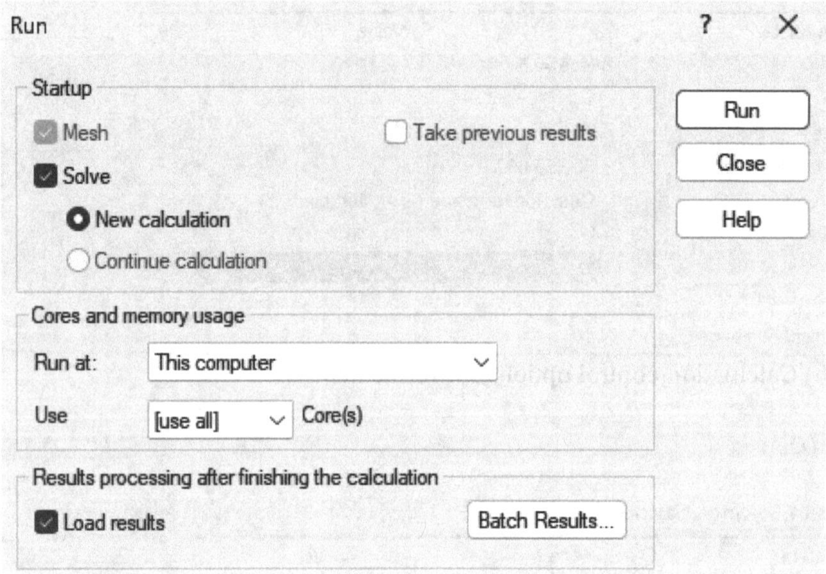

Figure 2.22b) Run window

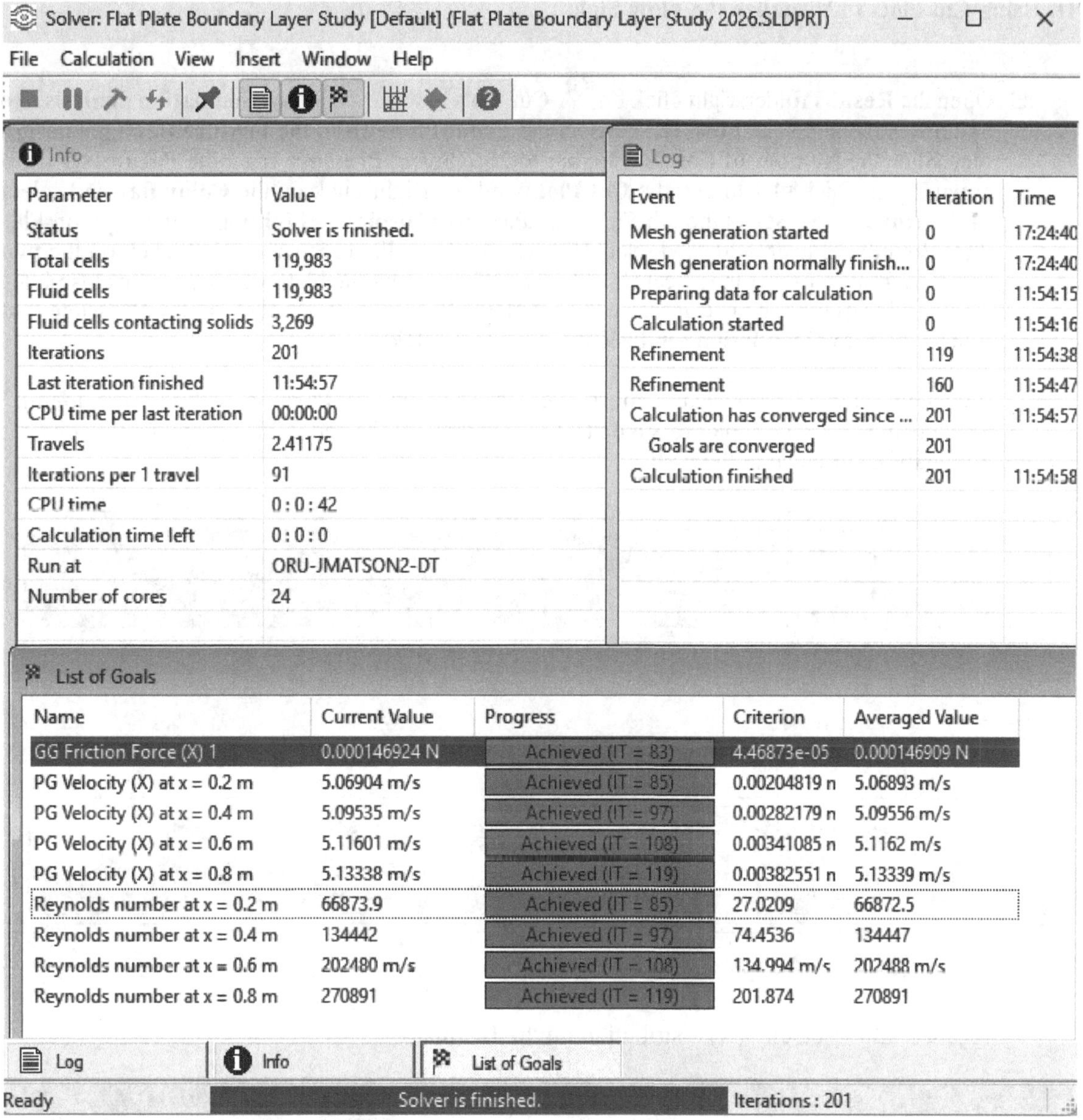

Figure 2.22c) Solver window

H. Using Cut Plots to Visualize the Flow Field

23. Open the **Results** folder, right click on Cut Plots in the **Flow Simulation analysis tree** under **Results** and select **Insert....** Select the **Front Plane** from the **FeatureManager design tree**. Slide the **Number of Levels** slide bar to **255**. Select **Pressure** from the **Parameter** drop down menu. Click **OK** to exit the **Cut Plot** window. Right-click on the **Color Bar** and select **Make Horizontal**. Select the tab **Flow Simulation>>Display>>Lighting**. Right click on Flat Plate Boundary Layer Study and select Hide Global Coordinate System. Right click on the two sketches from steps 8-9 and select Hide. Figure 2.23a) shows the high-pressure region close to the leading edge of the flat plate. Rename the cut plot to **Pressure**. Right click on the **Pressure Cut Plot** in the **Flow Simulation analysis tree** and select **Hide**.

    Repeat this step 23 but instead choose **Velocity (X)** from the **Parameter** drop down menu. Rename the second cut plot to **Velocity (X)**. Figures 2.23b) and 2.23c) show the velocity boundary layer close to the wall.

Figure 2.23a) Pressure distribution along the flat plate

Figure 2.23b) Velocity (X) distribution on the flat plate

Figure 2.23c) Close up view of the velocity boundary layer

I. Using XY Plots with Templates

24. Place the file **"graph 2.24c).xlsm"** on the desktop. This file and the other exercise files are available for download from the *SDC Publications* website. Click on the **FeatureManager design tree**. Select the sketch **x = 0.2, 0.4, 0.6, 0.8 m**. Click on the **Flow Simulation analysis tree** tab. Right click **XY Plot** and select **Insert....** Check the **Velocity (X)** box. Open the **Resolution** portion of the **XY Plot** window and slide the **Geometry Resolution** as far as it goes to the right. Click on the **Evenly Distribute Output Points** button and increase the number of points to **500**. Open the **Options** portion and check the **Display boundary layer** box. Select the **"Excel Workbook (*.xlsx)"** from the drop-down menu. Click **Export to Excel** to create the **XY Plot** window. An **Excel** file will open with a graph of the velocity in the boundary layer at different streamwise positions.

    Double click on the **graph 2.24c)** file to open the file. Click on **Enable Content** if you get a **Security Warning** that **Macros** have been disabled. If **Developer** is not available in the menu of the **Excel** file, you will need to do the following: Select **File>>Options** from the menu and click on the **Customize Ribbon** on the left-hand side. Check the **Developer** box on the right-hand side under **Main Tabs**. Click **OK** to exit the **Excel Options** window.

    Click on the **Developer** tab in the **Excel** menu for the **graph 2.24c)** file and select **Visual Basic** on the left-hand side to open the editor. Click on the plus sign next to **VBAProject (XY Plot 1.xlsx)** and click on the plus sign next to **Microsoft Excel Objects**. Right click on **Sheet2 (Plot Data)** and select **View Object**.

    Select **Module1** in the **Modules** folder under **VBAProject (graph 2.24c).xlsm)**. Select **Run>>Run Macro** from the menu of the **MVB for Applications** window. Click on the **Run** button in the **Macros** window. Figure 2.24c) will become available in **Excel** showing the streamwise velocity component ***u (m/s)*** versus wall normal coordinate ***y (m)***. Close the **XY Plot** window and the **graph 2.24c)** window in **Excel**. Exit the **XY Plot** window in **SOLIDWORKS Flow Simulation** and rename the inserted *xy*-plot in the **Flow Simulation analysis tree** to **Laminar Velocity Boundary Layer**.

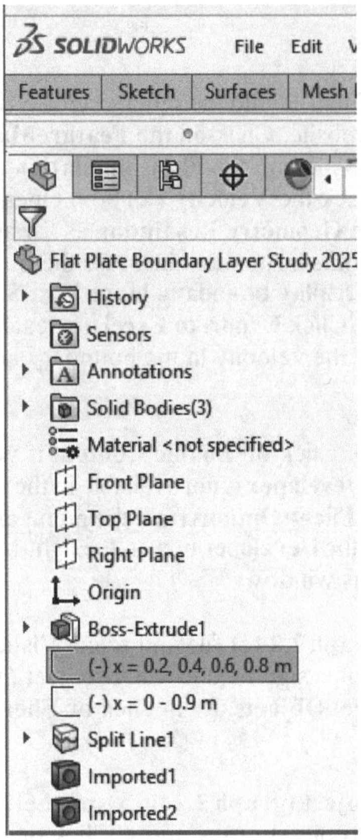

Figure 2.24a) Sketch for the XY Plot

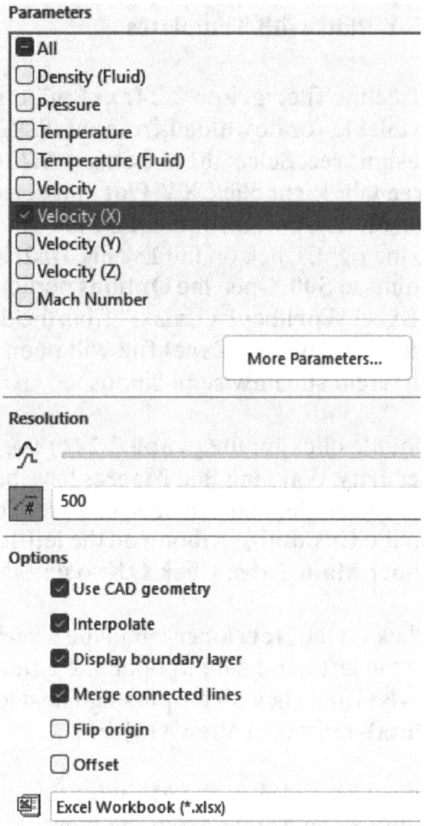

Figure 2.24b) Settings for the XY Plot

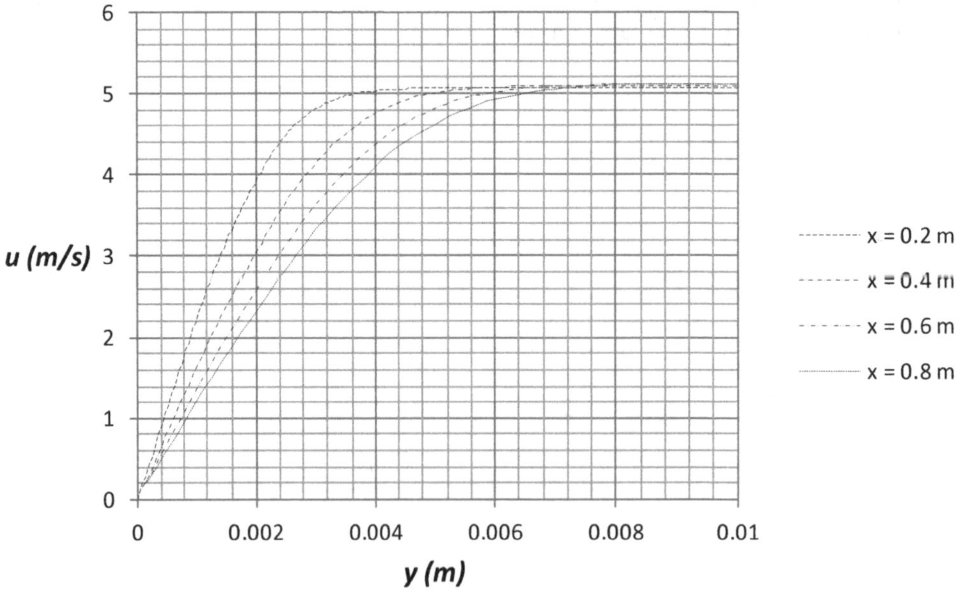

Figure 2.24c) Boundary layer velocity profiles on a flat plate at different streamwise positions

J. Comparison of Flow Simulation Results with Theory and Empirical Data

25. We now want to compare this velocity profile with the theoretical Blasius velocity profile for laminar flow on a flat plate. First, we have to normalize the streamwise Velocity (X) component with the free stream velocity. Secondly, we need to transform the wall normal coordinate into the similarity coordinate for comparison with the Blasius profile. The similarity coordinate is described by

$$\eta = y\sqrt{\frac{U}{\upsilon x}} \tag{2.1}$$

where y (m) is the wall normal coordinate, U (m/s) is the free stream velocity, x (m) is the distance from the leading edge and υ (m^2/s) is the kinematic viscosity of the fluid.

Place the file **graph 2.25a)** on the desktop. Repeat step **24** and replace the file **graph 2.24c)** with the file **graph 2.25a)** to plot Figure 2.25a). Rename the *xy*-plot to **Comparison with Blasius Profile**. We see in figure 2.25a) that all profiles at different streamwise positions collapse on the same Blasius curve when we use the boundary layer similarity coordinate.

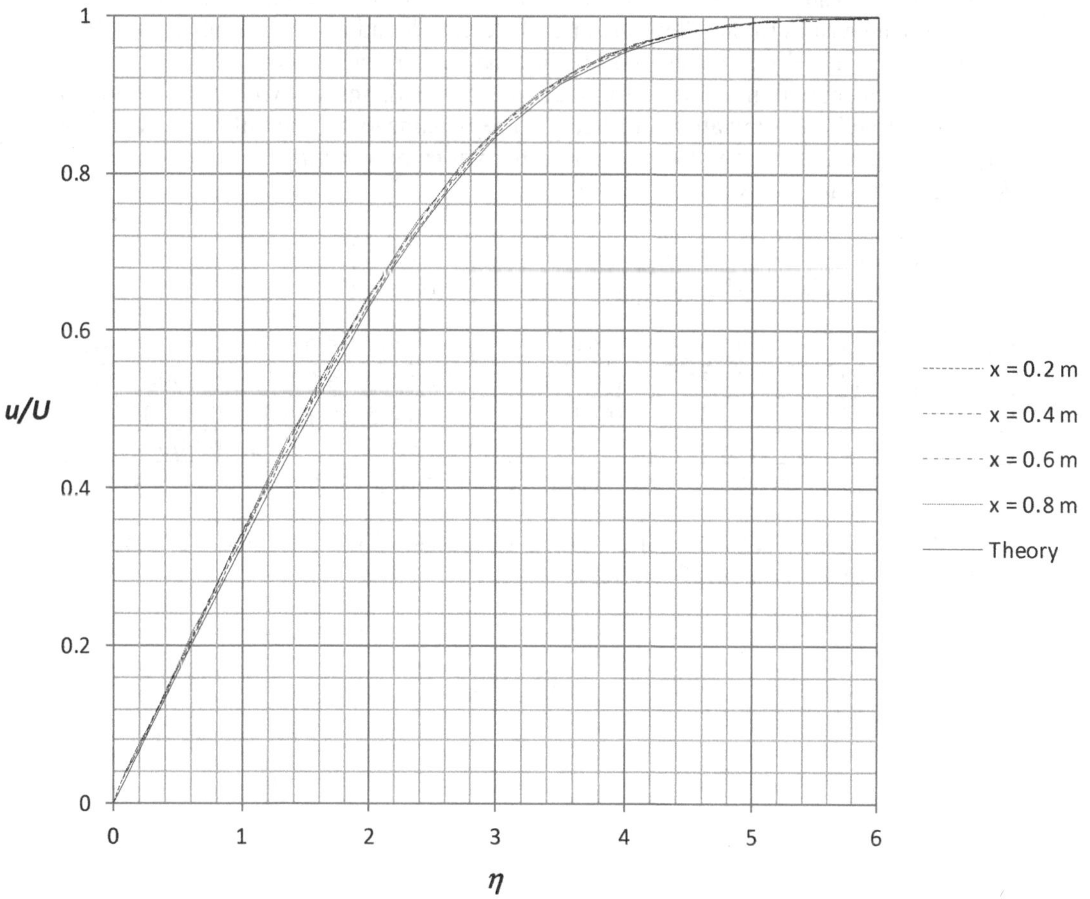

Figure 2.25a) Velocity profiles in comparison with the theoretical Blasius profile (full line)

The Reynolds number for the flow on a flat plate is defined as

$$Re_x = \frac{Ux}{\nu} \quad (2.2)$$

The boundary layer thickness δ is defined as the distance from the wall to the location where the velocity in the boundary layer has reached 99% of the free stream value. The theoretical expression for the thickness of the laminar boundary layer is given by

$$\delta = \frac{4.91x}{\sqrt{Re_x}} \quad (2.3)$$

, and the thickness of the turbulent boundary layer

$$\delta = \frac{0.16x}{Re_x^{1/7}} \quad (2.4)$$

From the data of figure 2.24c) we can see that the thickness of the laminar boundary layer is close to 3.80 mm at Re_x = 66,874 corresponding to x = 0.2 m. The free stream velocity at x = 0.2 m is U = 5.069 m/s, see figure 2.22c) for list of goals in solver window, and 99% of this value is U_δ = 5.018 m/s. The boundary layer thickness δ = 3.8 mm from Flow Simulation was found by finding the y position corresponding to the U_δ velocity. This value for δ at x = 0.2 m and corresponding values further downstream at different x locations are available in the Plot Data for Figure 2.25a). The different values of the boundary layer thickness can be compared with values obtained using equation (2.3). In Table 2.1 are comparisons shown between boundary layer thickness from Flow Simulation and theory corresponding to the four different Reynolds numbers shown in figure 2.24c). The Reynolds number varies between Re_x = 66,874 at x = 0.2 m and Re_x = 270,891 at x = 0.8 m.

x (m)	δ (mm) Simulation	δ (mm) Theory	Percent (%) Difference	U_δ (m/s)	U	$\nu\ (\frac{m^2}{s})$	Re_x
0.2	3.798	3.797	0.01	5.01835	5.06904	0.00001516	66,874
0.4	5.343	5.356	0.26	5.04440	5.09535	0.00001516	134,442
0.6	6.493	6.547	0.83	5.06485	5.11601	0.00001516	202,480
0.8	7.452	7.547	1.26	5.08205	5.13338	0.00001516	270,891

Table 2.1 Comparison between Flow Simulation and theory for laminar boundary layer thickness

Place the file **"graph 2.25b)"** on the desktop. Repeat step **24** to plot Figure 2.25b). Rename the *xy*-plot to **Boundary Layer Thickness.**

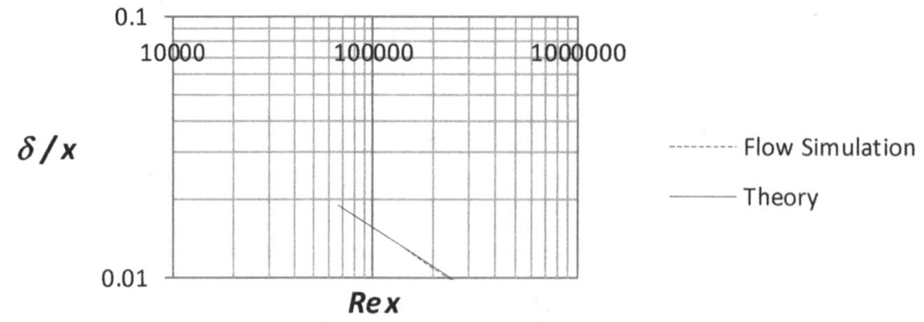

Figure 2.25b) Comparison between Flow Simulation and theory on boundary layer thickness

26. We now want to study how the local friction coefficient varies along the plate. It is defined as the local wall shear stress divided by the dynamic pressure:

$$C_{f,x} = \frac{\tau_w}{\frac{1}{2}\rho U^2} \tag{2.5}$$

The theoretical local friction coefficient for laminar flow is given by

$$C_{f,x} = \frac{0.664}{\sqrt{Re_x}} \qquad Re_x < 5 \cdot 10^5 \tag{2.6}$$

and for turbulent flow

$$C_{f,x} = \frac{0.027}{{Re_x}^{1/7}} \qquad 5 \cdot 10^5 \leq Re_x \leq 10^7 \tag{2.7}$$

Place the file **"graph 2.26"** on the desktop. Repeat step **24** but this time choose the sketch **x = 0 – 0.9 m**, uncheck the box for **Velocity (X)** and check the box for **Shear Stress**. Use the file **"graph 2.26"** to create Figure 2.26. Rename the *xy*-plot to **Local Friction Coefficient.** Figure 2.26 shows the local friction coefficient versus the Reynolds number compared with theoretical values for laminar boundary layer flow.

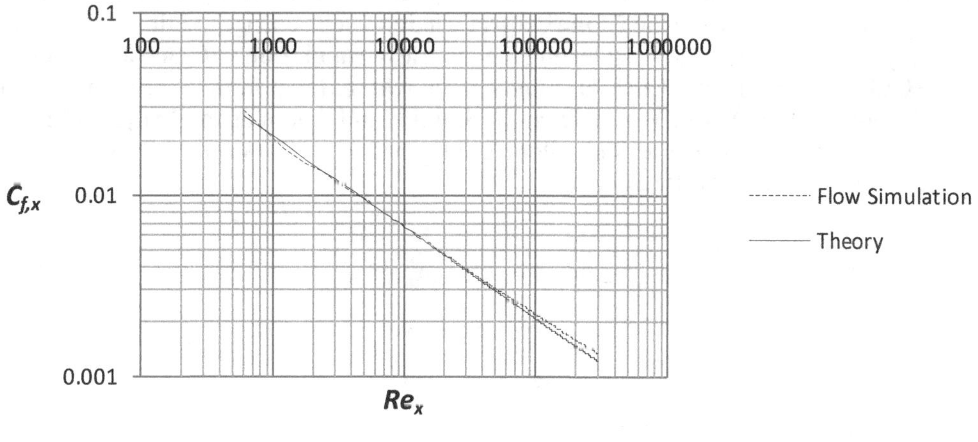

Figure 2.26 Local friction coefficient as a function of the Reynolds number

The average friction coefficient over the whole plate C_f is not a function of the surface roughness for the laminar boundary layer but a function of the Reynolds number based on the length of the plate Re_L, see figure E3 in Exercise 8 at the end of this chapter. This friction coefficient can be determined in Flow Simulation by using the final value of the global goal, the X-component of the Shear Force F_f, see figure 2.22c), and dividing it by the dynamic pressure times the area A in the X-Z plane of the computational domain related to the flat plate.

$$C_f = \frac{F_f}{\frac{1}{2}\rho U^2 A} = \frac{0.000146924N}{\frac{1}{2}\cdot 1.204kg/m^3 \cdot 5^2 m^2/s^2 \cdot 1m \cdot 0.004m} = 0.00244 \tag{2.8}$$

$$Re_L = \frac{UL}{\nu} = \frac{5m/s \cdot 1m}{1.516 \cdot 10^{-5} m^2/s} = 3.3 \cdot 10^5 \tag{2.9}$$

The average friction coefficient from Flow Simulation can be compared with the theoretical value for laminar boundary layers

$$C_f = \frac{1.328}{\sqrt{Re_L}} = 0.002312 \qquad Re_L < 5 \cdot 10^5 \tag{2.10}$$

This is a difference of 5.5 %. For turbulent boundary layers the corresponding expression is

$$C_f = \frac{0.0315}{{Re_L}^{1/7}} \qquad 5 \cdot 10^5 \leq Re_L \leq 10^7 \tag{2.11}$$

If the boundary layer is laminar on one part of the plate and turbulent on the remaining part, the average friction coefficient is determined by

$$C_f = \frac{0.0315}{{Re_L}^{1/7}} - \frac{1}{Re_L} \left(0.0315 {Re_{cr}}^{\frac{6}{7}} - 1.328\sqrt{Re_{cr}}\right) \tag{2.12}$$

where $\boldsymbol{Re_{cr}}$ is the critical Reynolds number for laminar to turbulent transition.

K. Cloning of the Project

27. In the next step, we will clone the project. Select the tab **Flow Simulation>> Clone Project....** Enter the Project Name **Flat Plate Boundary Layer Study Using Water**. Select **Create New Configuration** and exit the **Clone Project** window. Next, change the fluid to water to get higher Reynolds numbers. Start by selecting the tab **Flow Simulation>>General Settings...** from the SOLIDWORKS menu. Click on **Fluids** in the **Navigator** portion, select **Air** and click on the **Remove** button. Select **Water** from the **Liquids** and **Add** it as the **Project Fluid**. Change the **Flow type** to **Laminar and Turbulent**, see figure 2.27d). Click on **Apply** and the **OK** buttons to close the **General Settings** window.

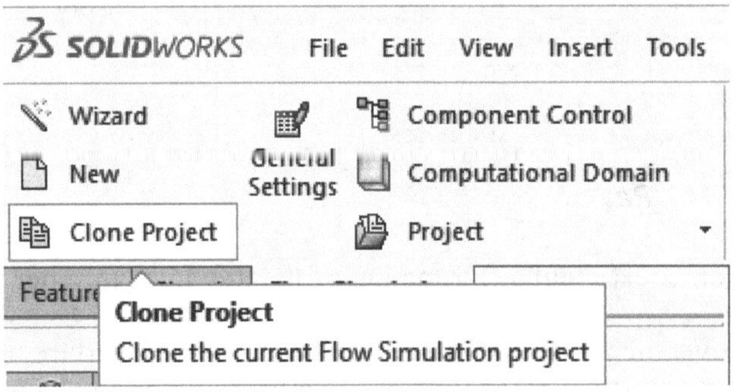

Figure 2.27a) Cloning the project

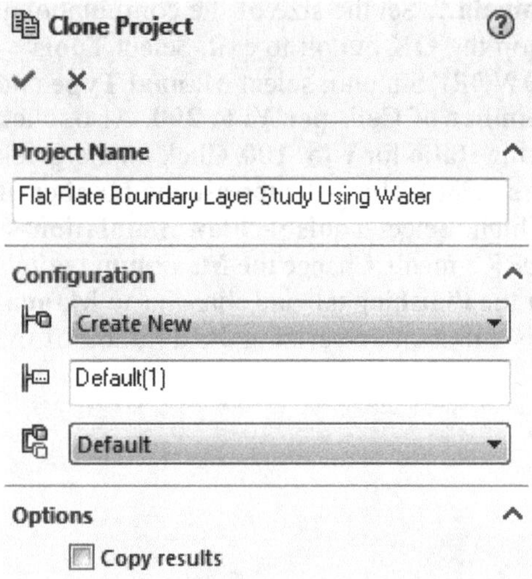

Figure 2.27b) Creating a new project

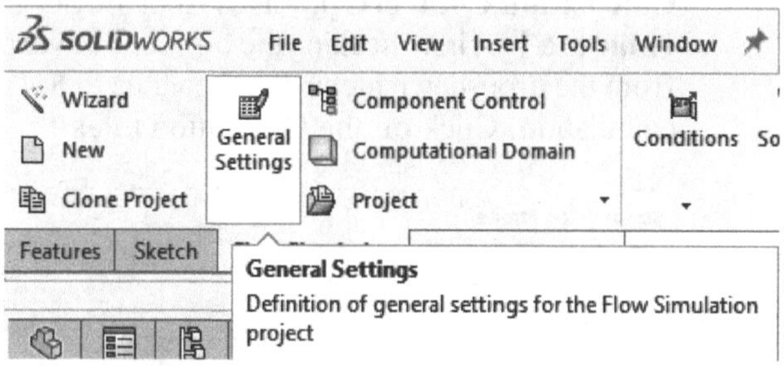

Figure 2.27c) Selection of general settings

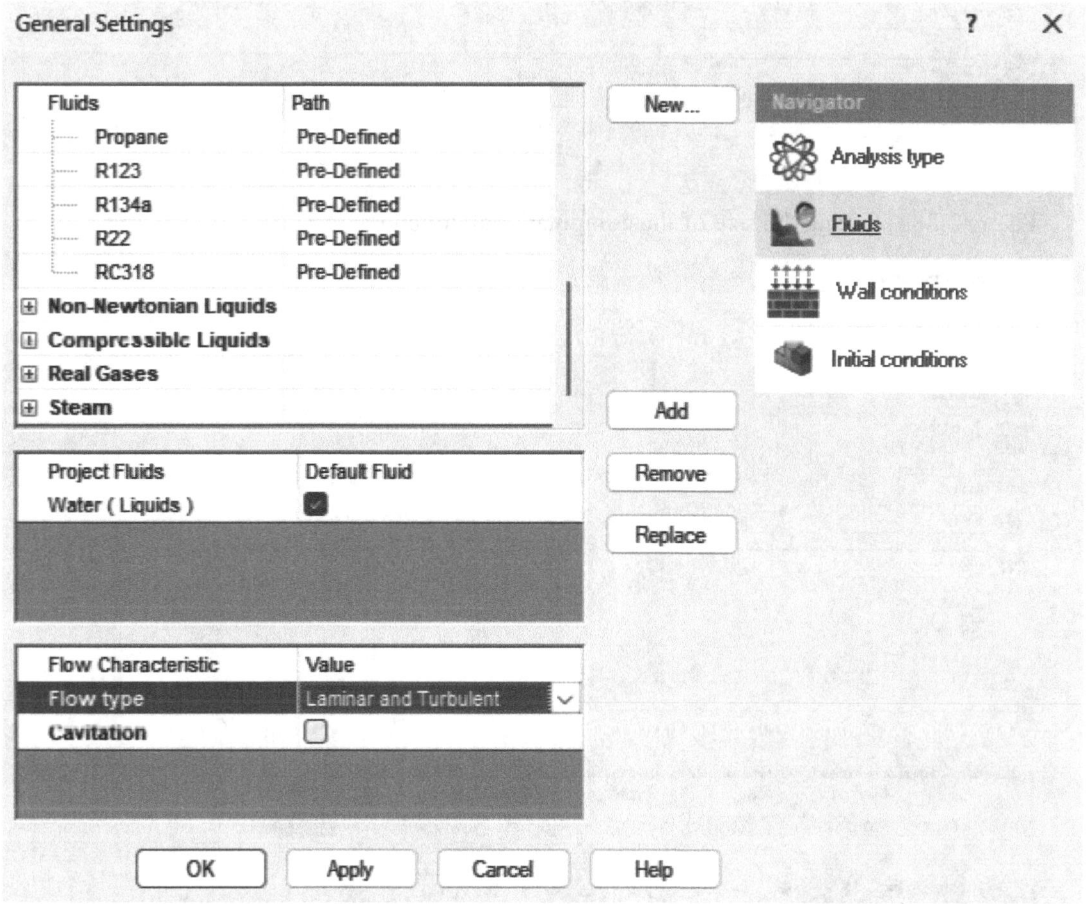

Figure 2.27d) Selection of fluid and flow type

28. Select the tab **Flow Simulation>>Computational Domain...** Set the size of the computational domain to the values shown in figure 2.28a). Click on the **OK** button to exit. Select **Tools>> Flow Simulation>> Global Mesh...** from the SOLIDWORKS menu, select **Manual Type** and change the **Number of cells per X:** to **400** and the **Number of Cells per Y:** to **200**. Also, click on **Control Planes**. Change the **Ratio** for **X** to **-5** and the **Ratio** for **Y** to **-100**. Click on the green check mark above Ratio for Y min – Y max, see Figure 2.28b). This will increase the number of cells close to the wall where the velocity gradient is high. Select **Tools>> Flow Simulation>> Calculation Control Options...** from the SOLIDWORKS menu. Change the **Maximum travels value** to **5** by first checking the box for **Travels** under the **Finishing** tab and changing to **Manual** from the drop-down menu. Set the value to **5**. Travel is a unit characterizing the duration of the calculation. Click on the **OK** button to exit.

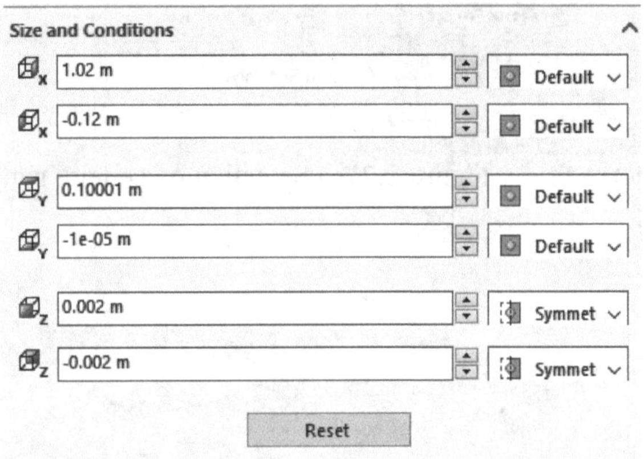

Figure 2.28a) Setting the size of the computational domain

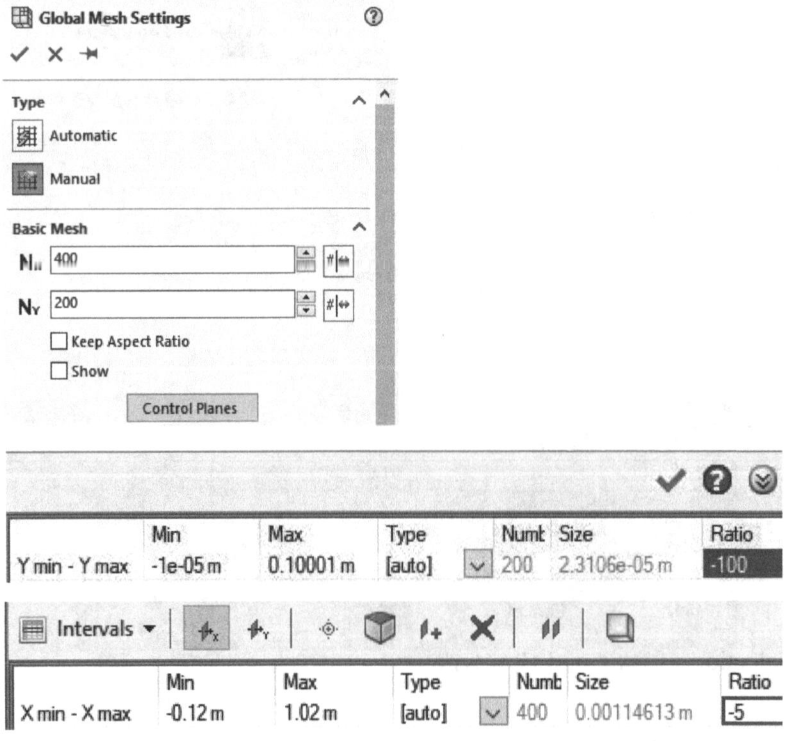

Figure 2.28b) Increasing the number of cells and changing the distribution of cells

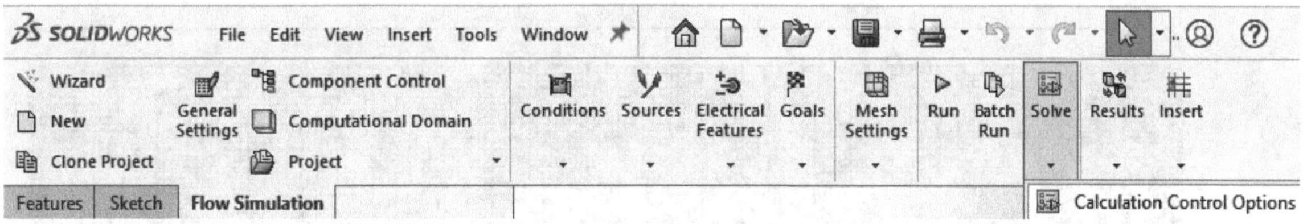

Figure 2.28c) Calculation control options

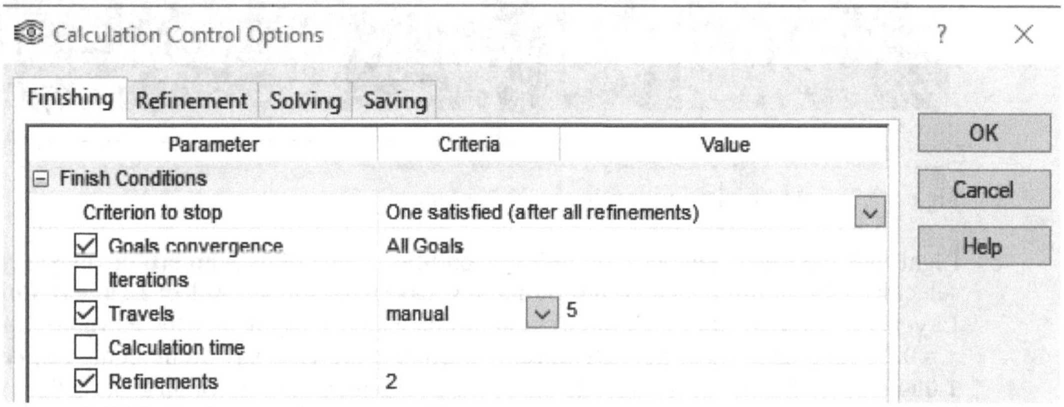

Figure 2.28d) Setting maximum travels

Select **Tools>>Flow Simulation>>Project>>Show Basic Mesh** from the SOLIDWORKS menu. We can see in figure 2.28f) that the density of the mesh is much higher close to the flat plate at the bottom wall as compared to the region further away from the wall.

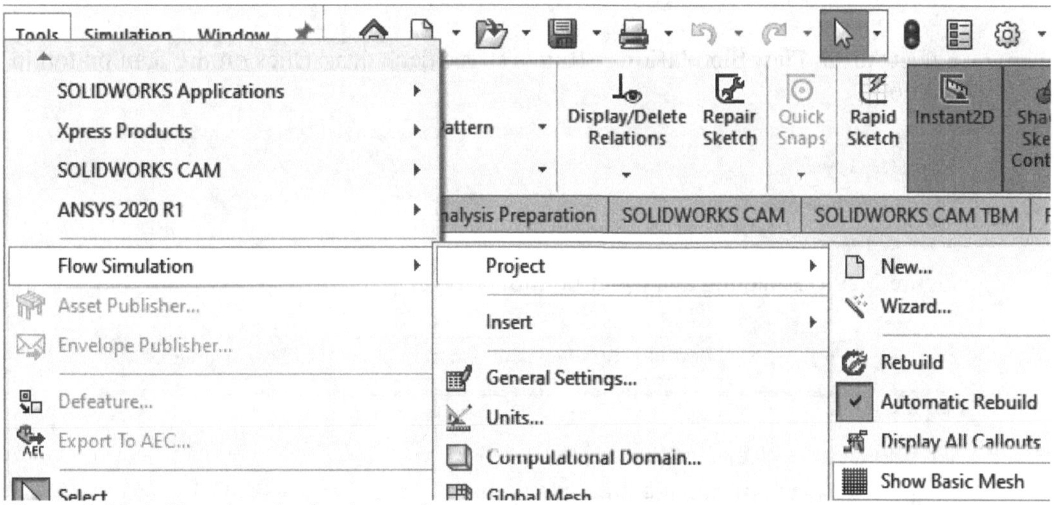

Figure 2.28e) Showing the basic mesh

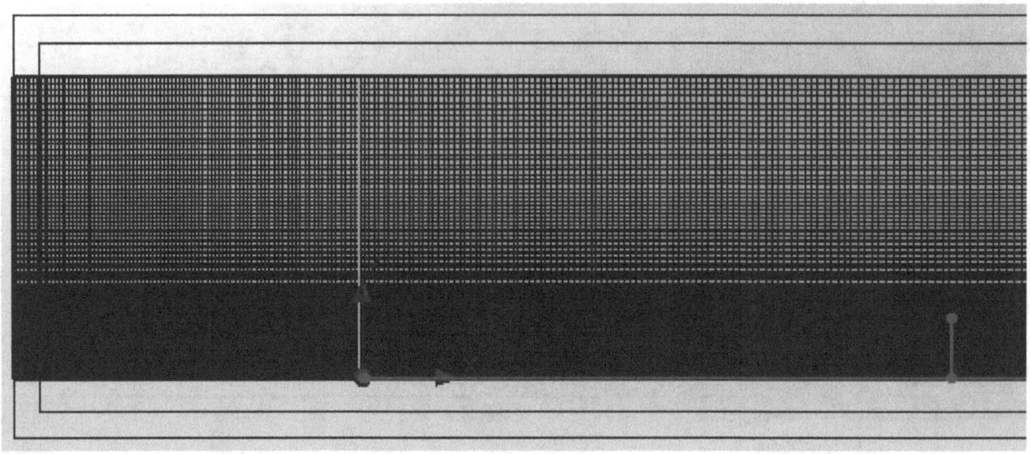

Figure 2.28f) Mesh distribution in the X-Y plane

29. Right click the **Inlet Velocity 1 Boundary Condition** in the **Flow Simulation analysis tree** and select **Edit Definition….** Open the **Boundary Layer** section and select **Laminar Boundary Layer**. Click **OK** to exit the **Boundary Condition** window. Right click the **Reynolds number at x = 0.2 m** goal and select **Edit Definition….** Change the viscosity value in the **Expression** to **1.004E-6**. Click on the **OK** button to exit. Change the other three equation goals in the same way.

    Select **Tools>>Flow Simulation>>Calculation Control Options** from the menu. Select the **Refinement** tab. Set the **Value** to **level = 2** for **Global Domain.** Select **Goal Convergence** and **Iterations** as **Refinement strategy**. Click on  in the **Value** column for **Goals** and check all the boxes in the **Table**. Select the **Finishing** tab and uncheck the **Travels** box under **Finish Conditions**. Set the **Refinements Criteria** to **2**.

    Select the tab **Flow Simulation>>Run** to start calculations. Click on the **Run** button in the **Run** window.

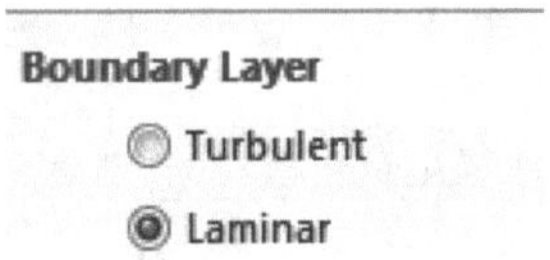

Figure 2.29a) Selecting a laminar boundary layer

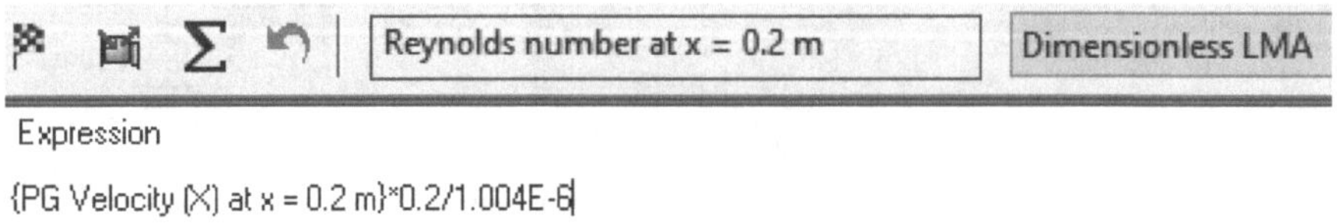

Figure 2.29b) Modifying the equation goals

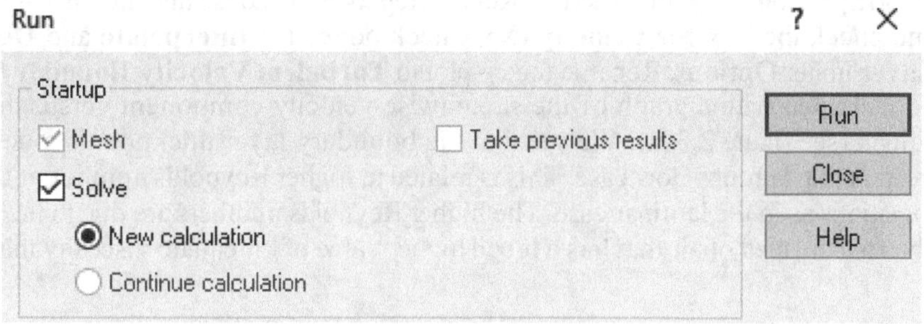

Figure 2.29c) Creation of mesh and starting a new calculation

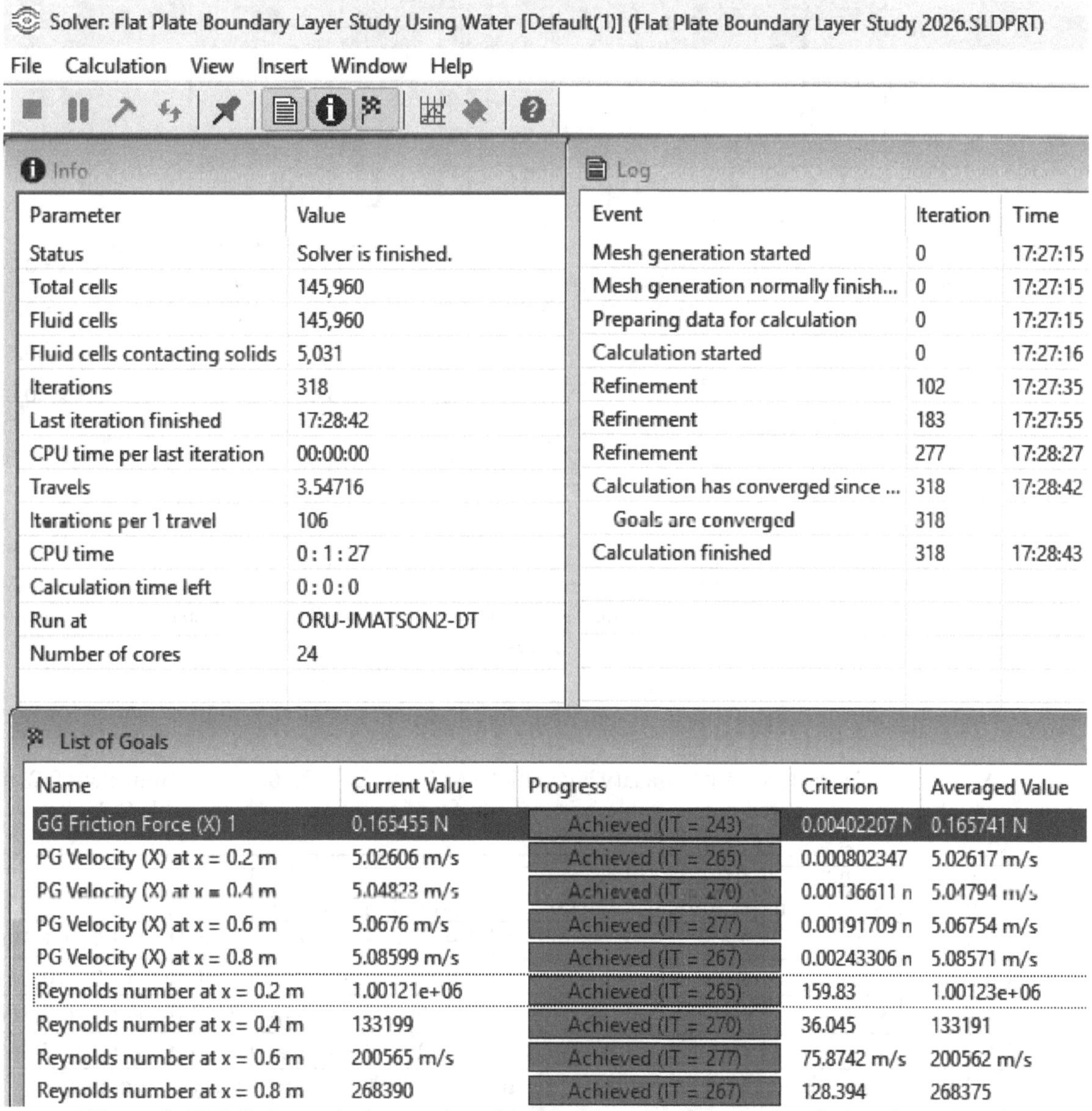

Figure 2.29d) Solver window and goals table for calculations of turbulent boundary layer

30. Place the file **"graph 2.30a)"** on the desktop. Repeat step **24** and choose the sketch **x = 0.2, 0.4, 0.6, 0.8 m** and check the box for **Velocity (X)**. Check boxes for **Interpolate** and **Display Boundary Layer** under **Options**. Rename the *xy*-plot to **Turbulent Velocity Boundary Layer**. An Excel file will open with a graph of the streamwise velocity component versus the wall-normal coordinate, see figure 2.30a). We see that the boundary layer thickness is much higher than the corresponding laminar flow case. This is related to higher Reynolds number at the same streamwise positions as in the laminar case. The higher Reynolds numbers are due to the selection of water as the fluid instead of air that has a much higher value of kinematic viscosity than water.

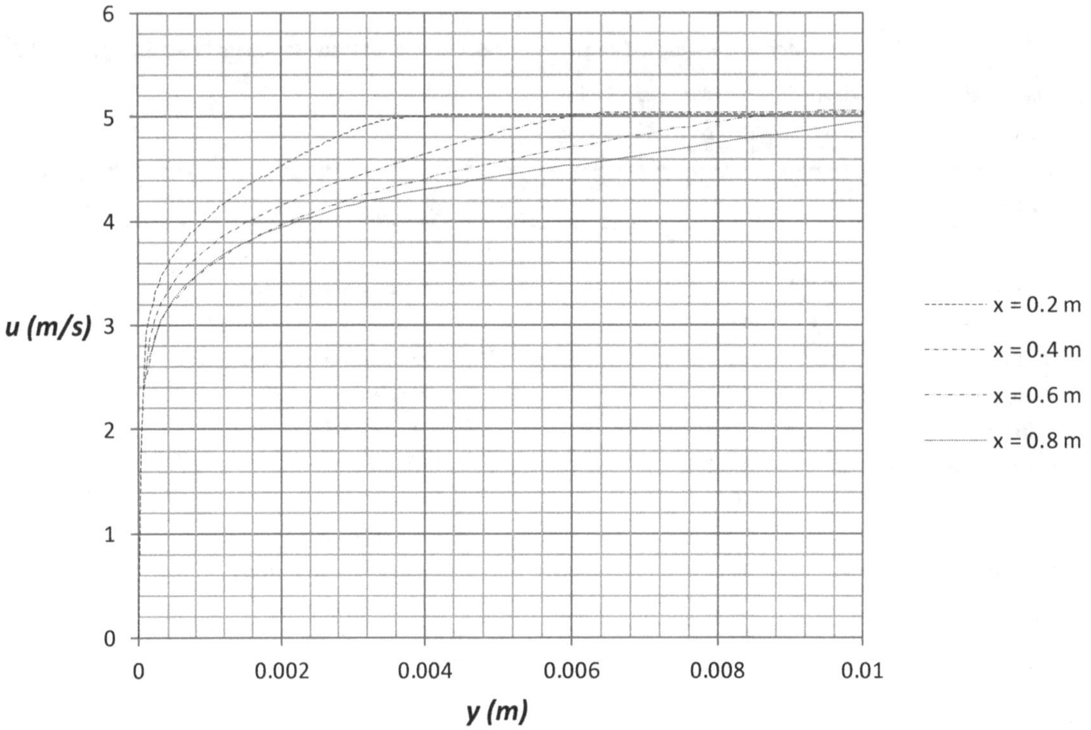

Figure 2.30a) Comparison of turbulent boundary layers at $Re_x = 10^6 - 4.04 \cdot 10^6$

As an example, the turbulent boundary layer thickness from figure 2.30a) is 3.49 mm at $x = 0.2$ m which can be compared with a value of 4.45 mm from equation (2.4), see table 2.2.

x (m)	δ (mm) Simulation	δ (mm) Empirical	% Difference	U_δ(m/s)	U (m/s)	ν (m²/s)	Re_x
0.2	3.49	4.45	21	4.977	5.02698	1.004E-06	1,001,390
0.4	5.89	8.05	27	4.995	5.04571	1.004E-06	2,010,243
0.6	8.70	11.39	24	5.016	5.06668	1.004E-06	3,027,896
0.8	11.03	14.57	24	5.029	5.07944	1.004E-06	4,047,363

Table 2.2 Flow Simulation and empirical results for turbulent boundary layer thickness

Place the file **"graph 2.30b)"** on the desktop. Repeat step **24** and choose the sketch **x = 0.2, 0.4, 0.6, 0.8 m** and check the box for **Velocity (X)**. Rename the *xy*-plot to **Turbulent Boundary**

Layer Thickness. An Excel file will open with a graph of the boundary layer thickness versus the Reynolds number, see figure 2.30b).

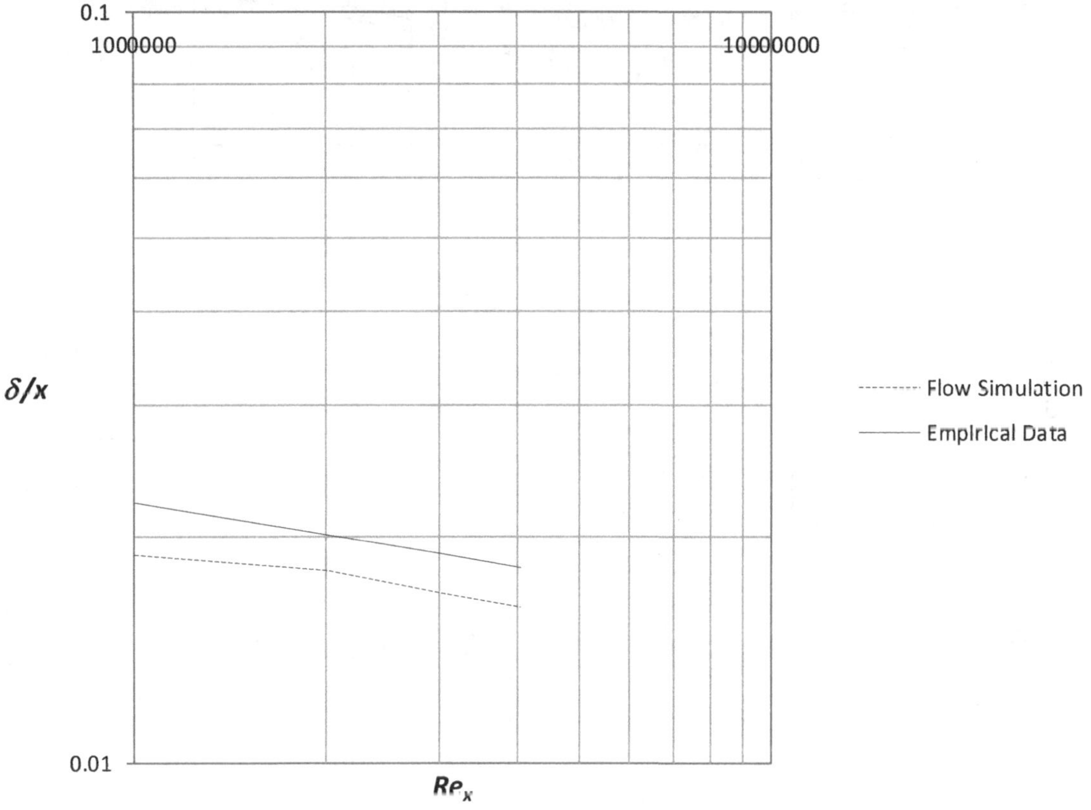

Figure 2.30b) Boundary layer thickness for turbulent boundary layers at $Re_x = 10^6 - 4.04 \cdot 10^6$

31. Place the file **"graph 2.31"** on the desktop. Repeat step **24** and choose the sketch **x = 0.2, 0.4, 0.6, 0.8 m** and check the box for **Velocity (X)**. Rename the *xy*-plot to **Comparison with One-Sixth Power Law**. An Excel file will open with Figure 2.31. In figure 2.31 we compare the results from Flow Simulation with the turbulent profile for $n = 7$. The power –law turbulent profiles suggested by Prandtl are given by

$$\frac{u}{U_\delta} = \left(\frac{y}{\delta}\right)^{1/n} \tag{2.13}$$

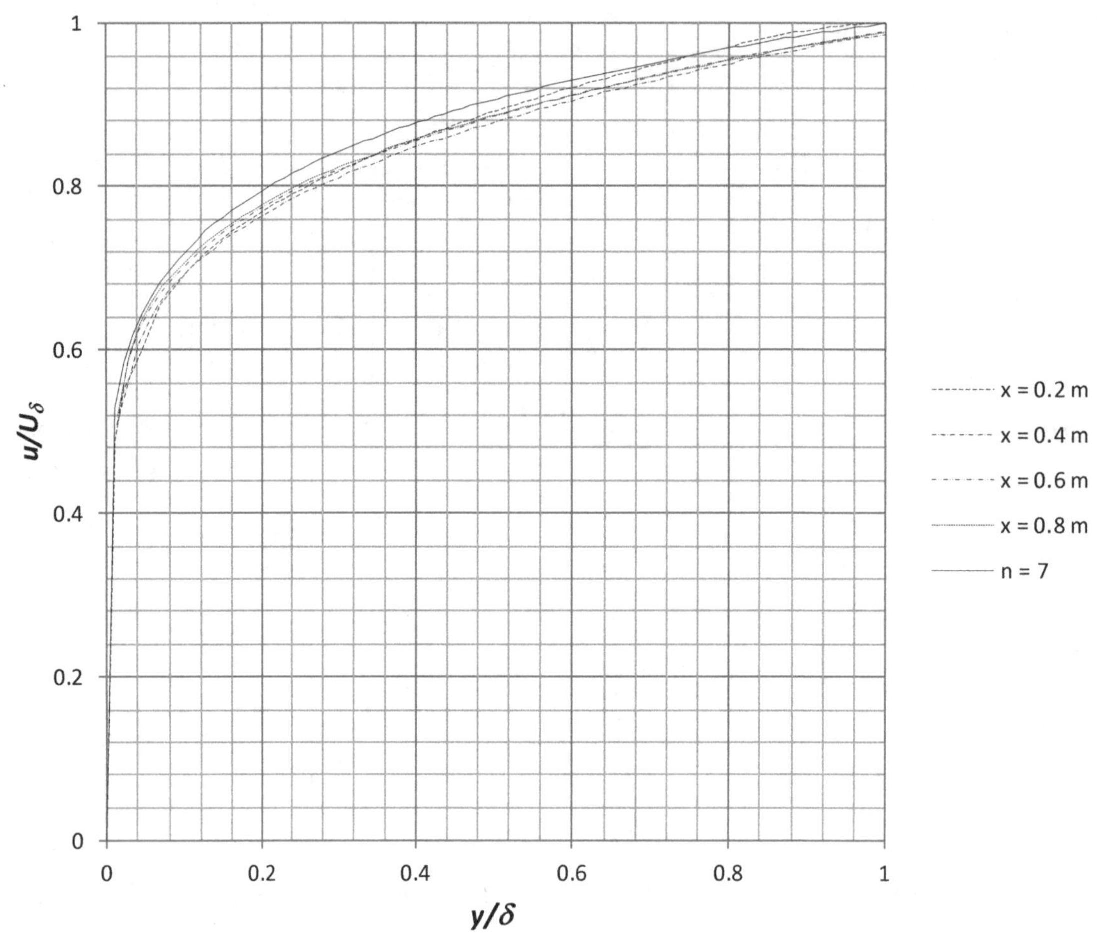

Figure 2.31 Velocity profiles compared with 1/6 power law for turbulent profile

32. Place the file **"graph 2.32"** on the desktop. Repeat step **24** and choose the sketch **x = 0 – 0.9 m**, uncheck the box for **Velocity (X)** and check the box for **Shear Stress**. Rename the *xy*-plot to **Local Friction Coefficient for Laminar and Turbulent Boundary Layer**. An Excel file will open with figure 2.32. Figure 2.32 shows the Flow Simulation is able to capture the local friction coefficient in the laminar region in the Reynolds number range 10,000 – 200,000. At Re slightly less than 200,000 there is an abrupt increase in the friction coefficient caused by laminar to turbulent transition. In the turbulent region the friction coefficient is decreasing again but the local friction coefficient from Flow Simulation is significantly lower than empirical data.

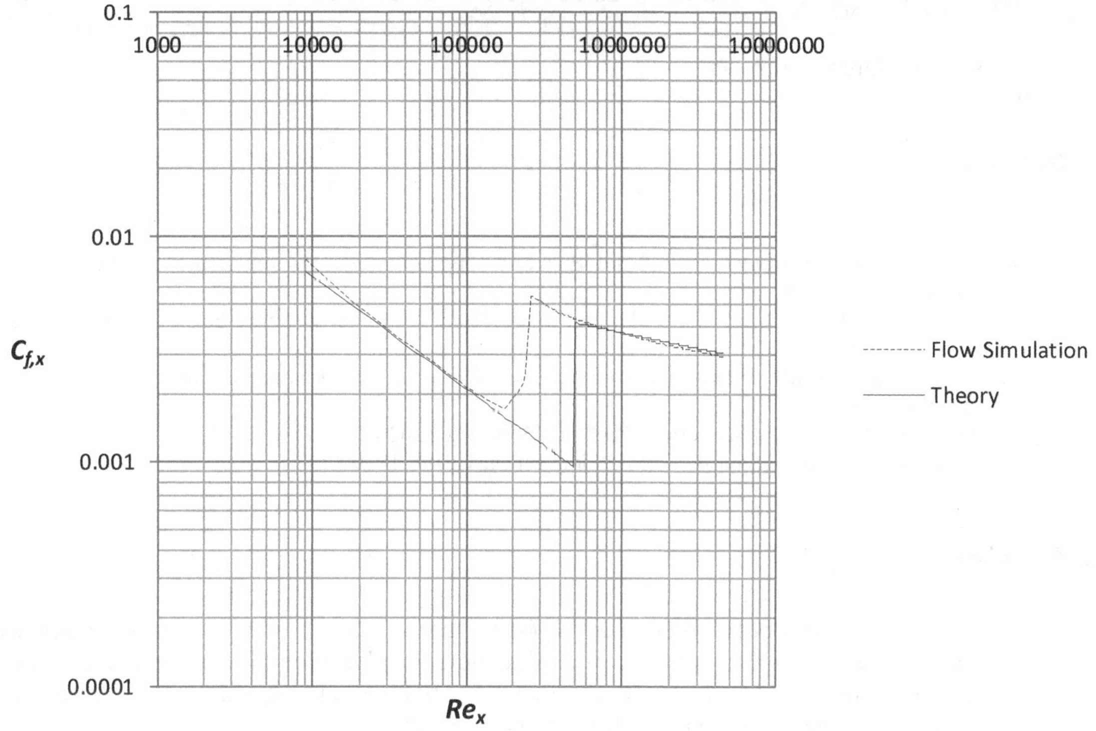

Figure 2.32 Flow Simulation (dashed line) and theoretical turbulent friction coefficients

The average friction coefficient over the whole plate C_f is a function of the surface roughness for the turbulent boundary layer and also a function of the Reynolds number based on the length of the plate Re_L, see figure E3 in Exercise 8. This friction coefficient can be determined in Flow Simulation by using the final value of the global goal, the X-component of the Shear Force F_f and dividing it by the dynamic pressure times the area A in the X-Z plane of the computational domain related to the flat plate, see figure 2.28a) for the size of the computational domain.

$$C_f = \frac{F_f}{\frac{1}{2}\rho U^2 A} = \frac{0.15729N}{\frac{1}{2}\cdot 998kg/m^3 \cdot 5^2 m^2/s^2 \cdot 1m \cdot 0.004m} = 0.003152 \tag{2.14}$$

$$Re_L = \frac{UL}{\nu} = \frac{5m/s \cdot 1m}{1.004 \cdot 10^{-6} m^2/s} = 4.98 \cdot 10^6 \tag{2.15}$$

The variation and final values of the goal can be found in the solver window during or after calculation by clicking on the associated flag, see figures 2.33 and 2.29d).

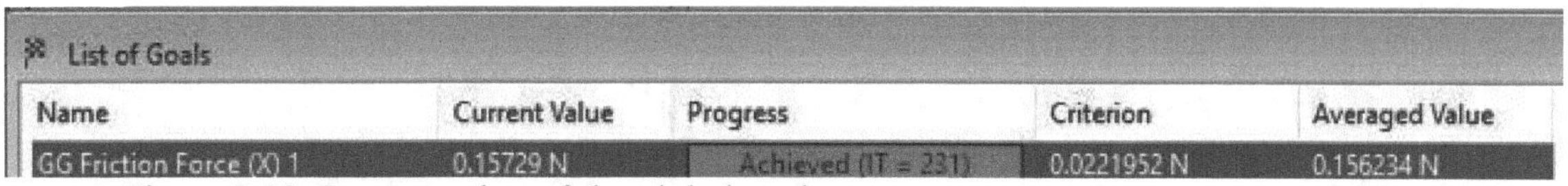
List of Goals

Name	Current Value	Progress	Criterion	Averaged Value
GG Friction Force (X) 1	0.15729 N	Achieved (IT = 231)	0.0221952 N	0.156234 N

Figure 2.33 Current value of the global goal

For comparison with Flow Simulation results we use equation (2.16) with $Re_{cr} = 200{,}000$

$$C_f = \frac{0.0315}{{Re_L}^{1/7}} - \frac{1}{Re_L}\left(0.0315{Re_{cr}}^{\frac{6}{7}} - 1.328\sqrt{Re_{cr}}\right) = 0.003378 \tag{2.16}$$

This is a difference of 6.7%.

L. References

1. Çengel, Y. A., and Cimbala J.M., Fluid Mechanics Fundamentals and Applications, 1st Edition, McGraw-Hill, 2006.
2. Fransson, J. H. M., Leading Edge Design Process Using a Commercial Flow Solver, Experiments in Fluids 37, 929 – 932, 2004.
3. Schlichting, H., and Gersten, K., Boundary Layer Theory, 8th Revised and Enlarged Edition, Springer, 2001.
4. SOLIDWORKS® Flow Simulation Technical Reference 2025.
5. White, F. M., Fluid Mechanics, 4th Edition, McGraw-Hill, 1999.

M. Exercises

2.1 Change the number of cells per *X* and *Y*, (see figure 2.16b), for the laminar boundary layer and plot graphs of the boundary layer thickness, displacement thickness, momentum thickness and local friction coefficient versus Reynolds number for different combinations of cells per X and Y. Compare with theoretical results.

2.2 Choose one Reynolds number and one value of number of cells per *X* for the laminar boundary layer and plot the variation in boundary layer thickness, displacement thickness and momentum thickness versus number of cells per *Y*. Compare with theoretical results.

2.3 Choose one Reynolds number and one value of number of cells per *Y* for the laminar boundary layer and plot the variation in boundary layer thickness, displacement thickness and momentum thickness versus number of cells per *X*. Compare with theoretical results.

2.4 Import the file "Leading Edge of Flat Plate". Study the air flow around the leading edge at 5 m/s free stream velocity and determine the laminar velocity boundary layer at different locations on the upper side of the leading edge and compare with the Blasius solution. Also, compare the local friction coefficient with figure 2.26. Use different values of the initial mesh to see how it affects the results.

Figure E1. Leading edge of asymmetric flat plate, see Fransson (2004)

2.5 Modify the geometry of the flow region used in this chapter by changing the slope of the upper ideal wall so that it is not parallel with the lower flat plate. By doing this you get a streamwise pressure gradient in the flow. Use air at 5 m/s and compare your laminar boundary layer velocity profiles for both accelerating and decelerating free stream flow with profiles without a streamwise pressure gradient.

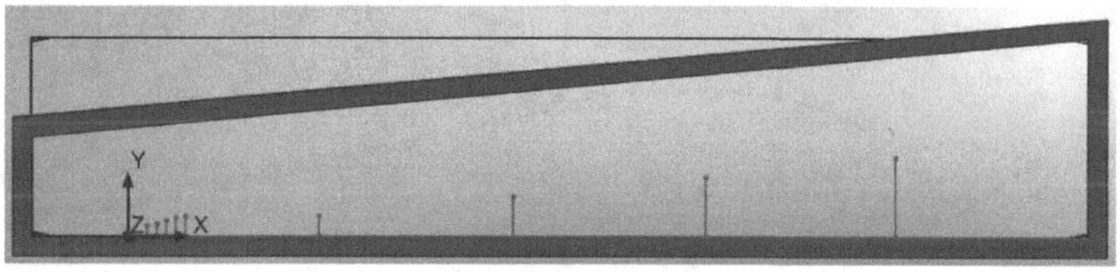

Figure E2. Example of geometry for a decelerating outer free stream flow.

2.6 Determine the displacement thickness, momentum thickness and shape factor for the turbulent boundary layers in figure 2.30a) and determine the percent differences as compared with empirical data.

2.7 Change the distribution of cells using different values of the ratios in the X and Y directions, see figure 2.28b), for the turbulent boundary layer and plot graphs of the boundary layer thickness, displacement thickness, momentum thickness and local friction coefficient versus Reynolds number for different combinations of ratios. Compare with theoretical results.

2.8 Use different fluids, surface roughness, free stream velocities and length of the computational domain to compare the average friction coefficient over the entire flat plate with figure E3.

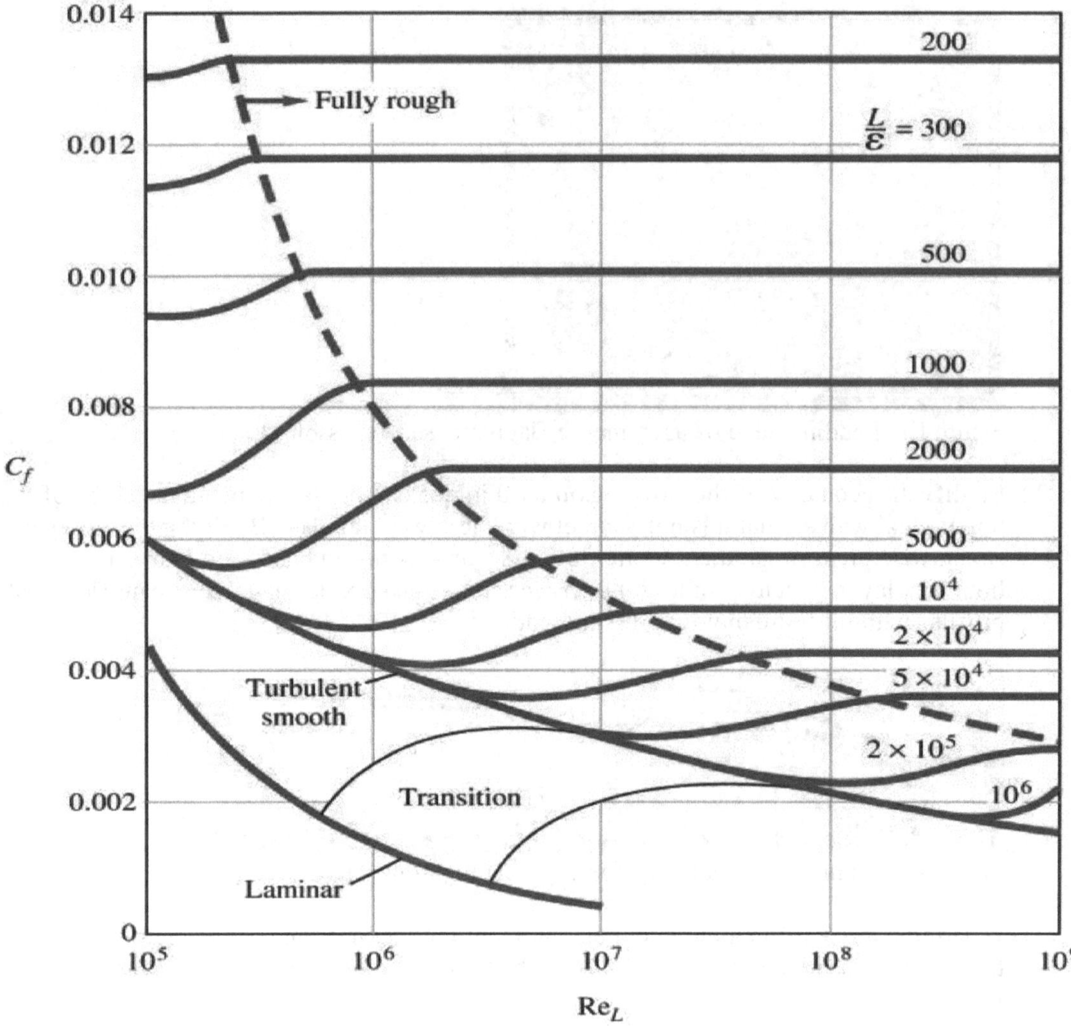

Figure E3. Average friction coefficient for flow over smooth and rough flat plates, White (1999)

CHAPTER 3. FLOW PAST A SPHERE AND A CYLINDER

A. Objectives

- Creating the sphere and cylinder needed for the SOLIDWORKS Flow Simulation
- Setting up Flow Simulation projects for external flow
- Running the calculations
- Using XY-Plots and Cut Plots to visualize the resulting flow fields
- Study values of surface parameters
- Cloning of the project
- Run time-dependent calculations to determine the vortex shedding frequency and the Strouhal number for the cylinder
- Compare with empirical results

B. Problem Description

In this chapter, we will use Flow Simulation to study the three-dimensional flow of air past a sphere with a diameter of 50 mm at different Reynolds numbers and compare with empirical results for the drag coefficient. The second part of this chapter covers the two-dimensional flow past a cylinder, and we will determine the Strouhal number related to vortex shedding from the cylinder. We will start by creating the sphere needed for this simulation, see figure 3.0a).

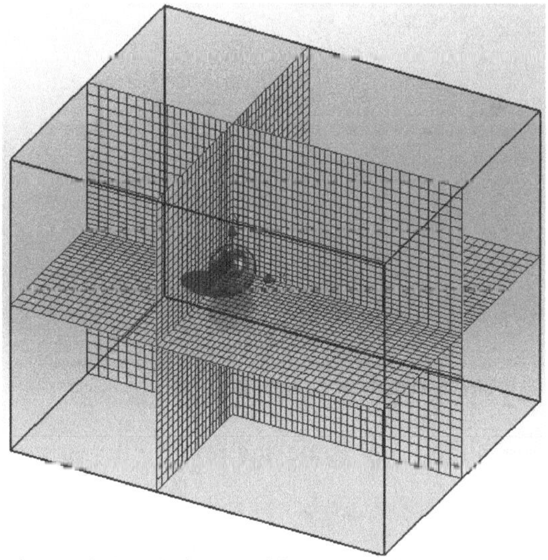

Figure 3.0a) Sphere with 3D mesh

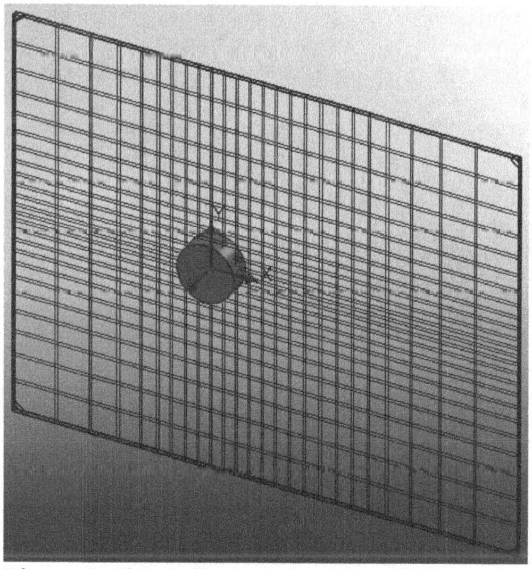

Figure 3.0b) Cylinder with 2D initial mesh

C. Creating the SOLIDWORKS Part for the Sphere

In this exercise we will analyze the flow around a sphere. First, we will create a model of the sphere in SOLIDWORKS and export the part to Flow Simulation. Follow these steps to create a solid model of a sphere with 50mm diameter and perform a 3D simulation of the flow field.

1. Start SOLIDWORKS and create a **New Document**. Select **File>>New...** from the SOLIDWORKS menu.

Figure 3.1 New document in SOLIDWORKS

2. Select **Part** in the **Welcome** window.

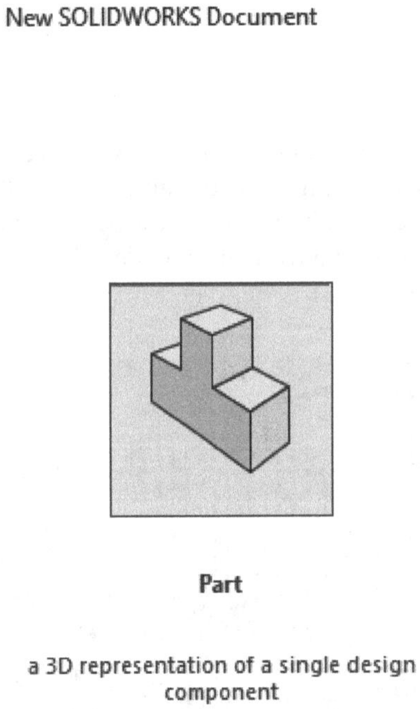

Figure 3.2 New SOLIDWORKS document selection window

To model the sphere, we will sketch a half circle in the Front Plane and revolve it. We start this process by making a new sketch.

3. Click on the **Front Plane** to select **Normal To**.

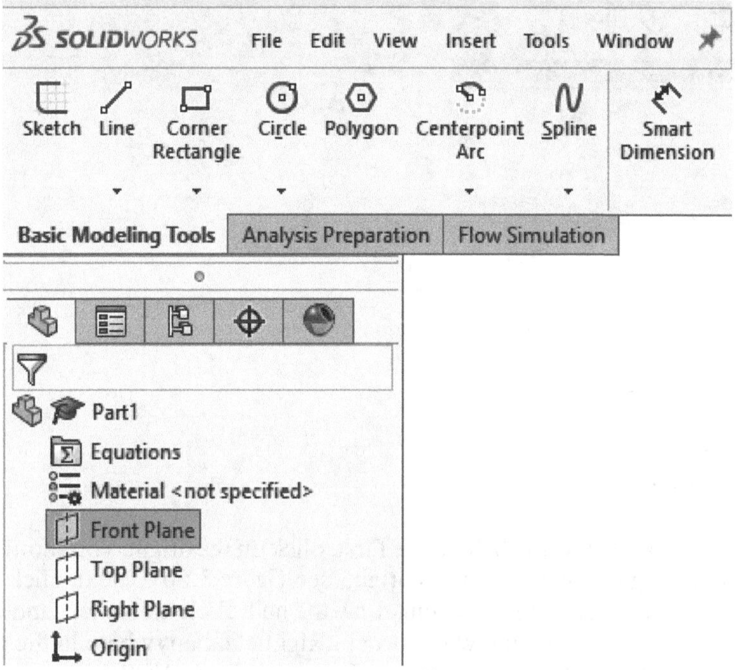

Figure 3.3 Selection of front plane and normal to

We start sketching by drawing a vertical symmetry line in the sketch plane. This centerline will be used to create the sphere as a revolved feature.

4. Select the **Sketch** tab and **Line>>Centerline...**

Figure 3.4 Selection of the centerline sketch tool

5. Next, draw the vertical centerline in the sketch window. Start above the vertical coordinate axis and make sure that you get the blue dashed helpline, see figure 3.5a). Click and draw the line downward through the origin and end the line approximately the same distance below the origin as shown in figure 3.5b). Right click anywhere in the graphics window and click on **Select**. You have now finished the vertical centerline.

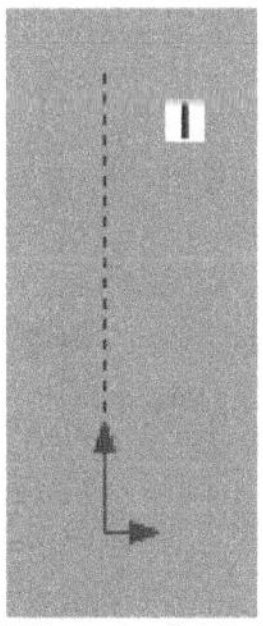
Figure 3.5a) Vertical dashed helpline

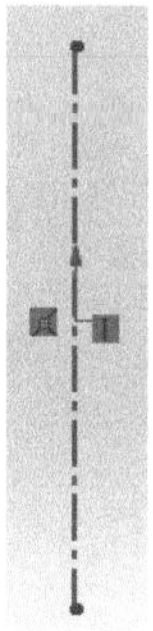
Figure 3.5b) Drawing a vertical centerline

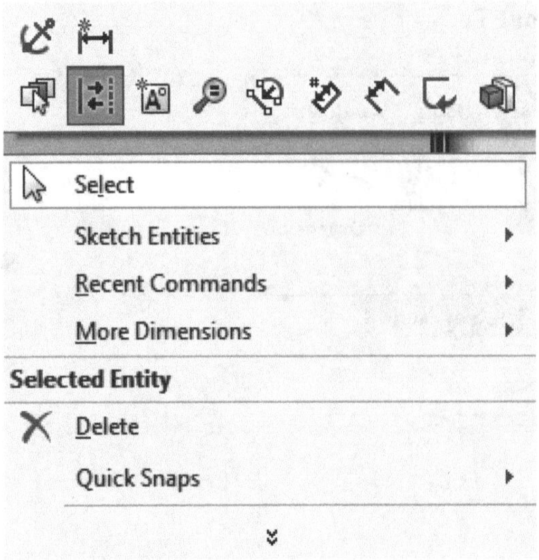

Figure 3.5c) Clicking on select

6. Select the **Centerpoint Arc** and draw the half circle. First, click on the origin; you should see an orange filled circle indicating that you are at the origin, see figure 3.6b). Next, click on the centerline above the origin of the coordinate system, draw the half circle to the left and click on the centerline once again but this time below the origin. Right click anywhere in the graphics window and click on **Select**. Select **Tools>>Options...** from the SOLIDWORKS menu and click on the **Document Properties** tab. Click on **Units** and select **MMGS** (millimeter, gram, second) as Unit system. Click OK to close the window.

Figure 3.6a) Selecting centerline arc

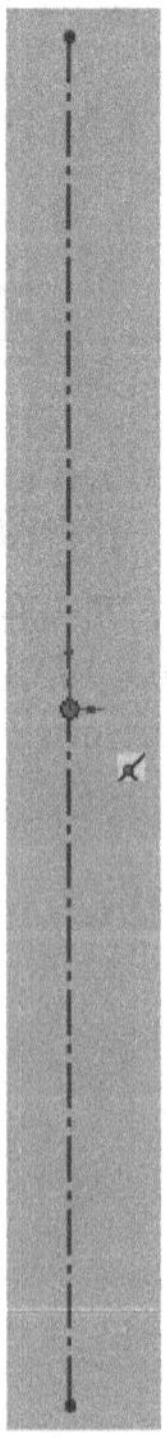

Figure 3.6b) Starting at the origin

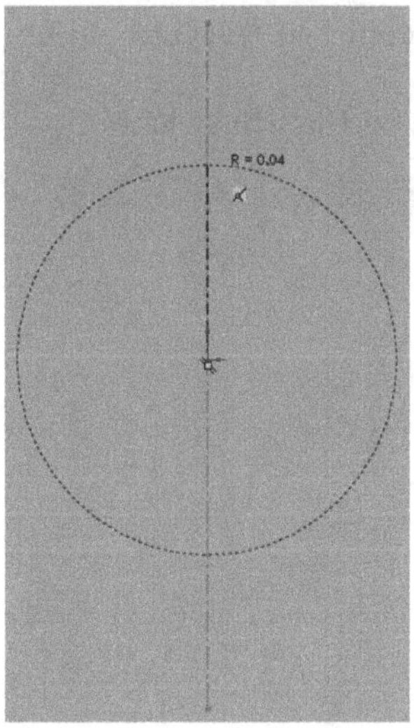

Figure 3.6c) Click above the origin

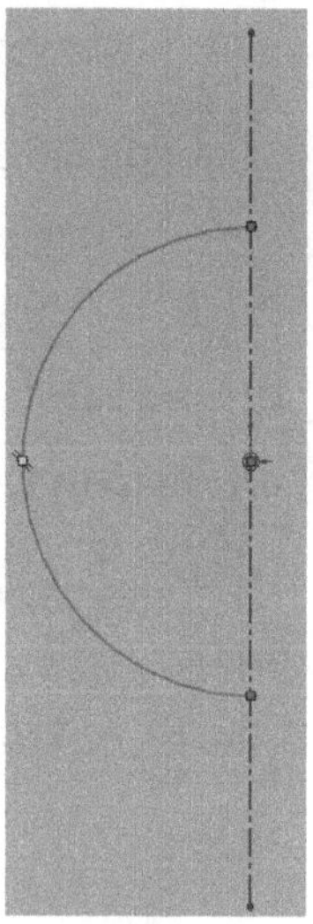

Figure 3.6d) Finished half circle

7. Next, select the **Smart Dimension** tool

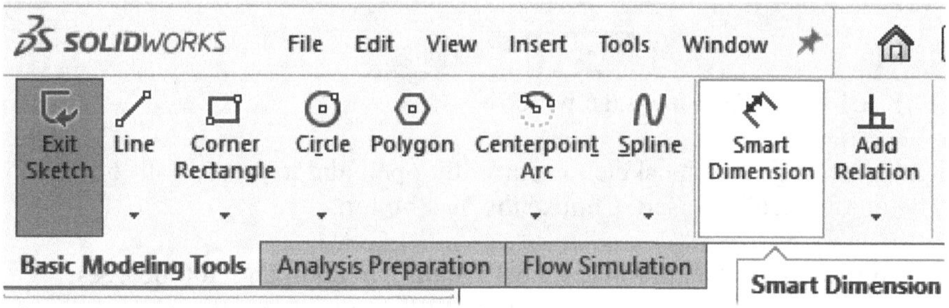

Figure 3.7 Selecting the Smart Dimension tool

8. Create a radius of 25.00 mm for the half-circle by clicking on the half-circle twice and enter the numerical value as shown in Figure 3.8. Save the value and exit the dialog.

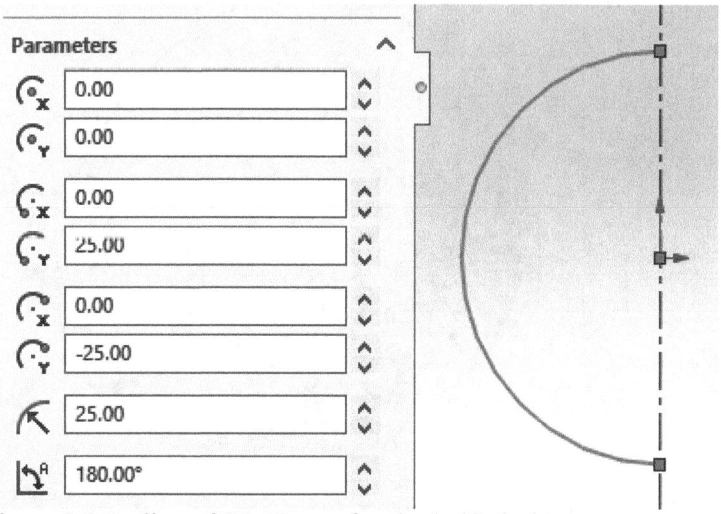

Figure 3.8 Radius of 25.00 mm for the half-circle

The next step is to make the sphere by using the Revolve feature in SOLIDWORKS.

9. Click on the Analysis Preparation tab and select the **Revolved Boss/Base** icon.

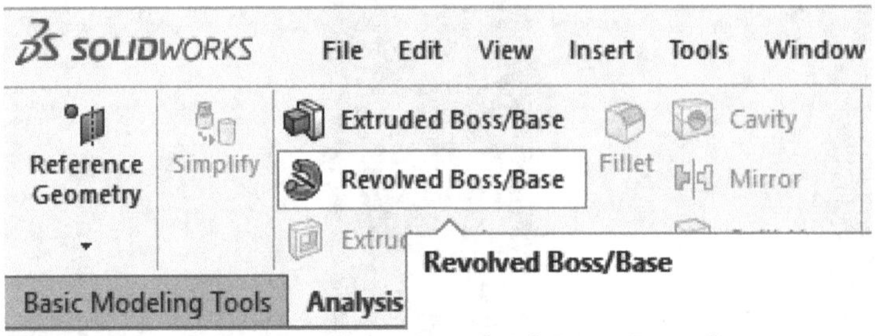

Figure 3.9a) Selection of the Revolved Boss-Base feature

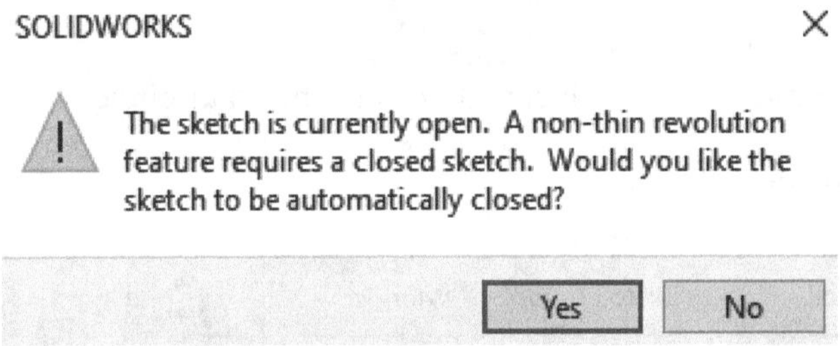

Figure 3.9b) SOLIDWORKS message window

You will get a message that the sketch is currently open and a question if you would like the sketch to be automatically closed. Choose the **Yes** button.

10. Use the default **Revolve Parameters**: Line 1, Blind Direction and 360 degrees. Click on the OK button with the green symbol ✔ to exit the **Revolve** window.

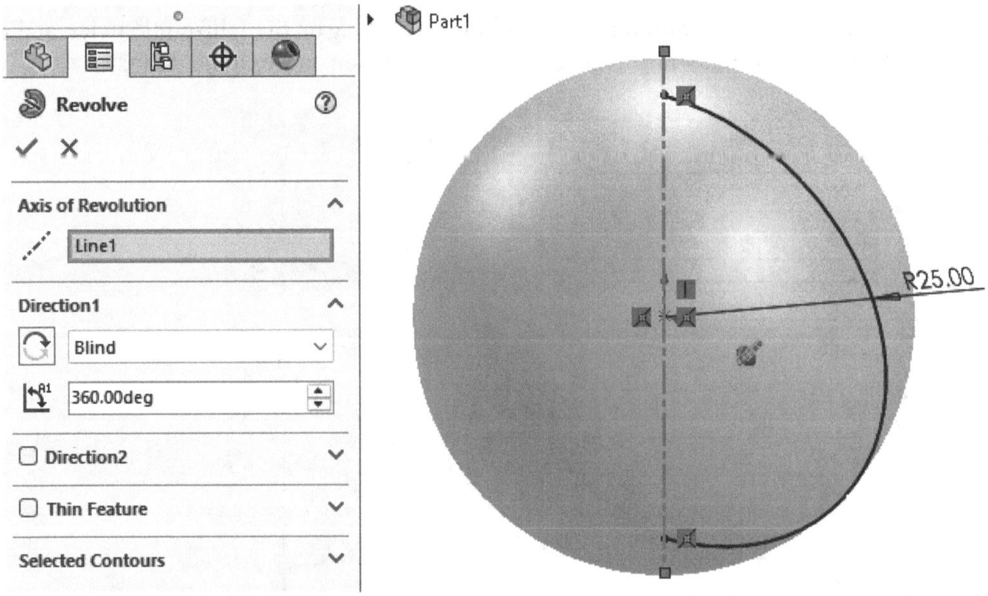

Figure 3.10 Selection of default revolve parameters

11. Move the cursor to the **File** menu and select **Save As...**
    Enter **Sphere 2026** as File name and click on the **Save** button.

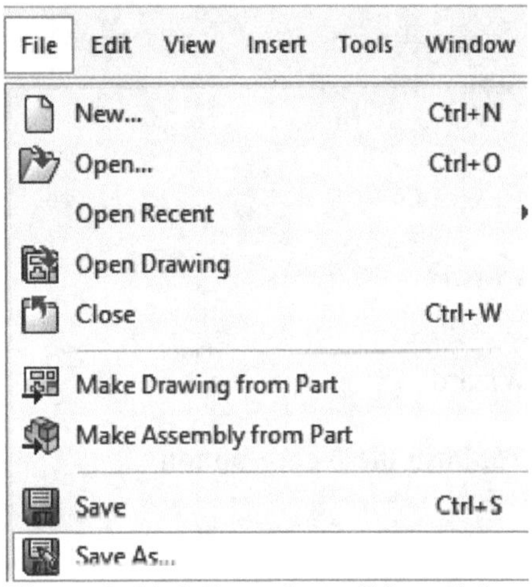

Figure 3.11a) Save the solid model

Figure 3.11b) Finished model

12. Select **Tools>>Add-Ins...**from menu and check **SOLIDWORKS Flow Simulation 2026** box.

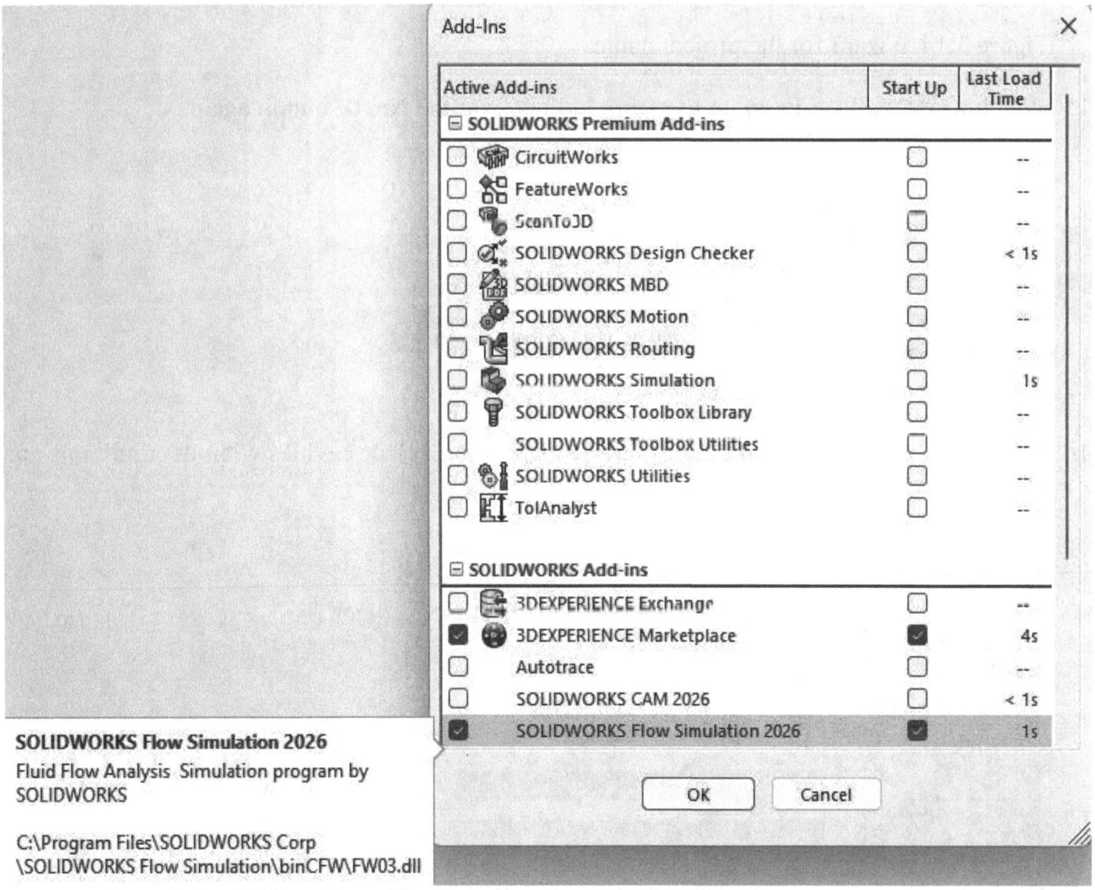

Figure 3.12 Adding Flow Simulation to the SOLIDWORKS menu

D. Setting Up the Flow Simulation Project for the Sphere

13. We create a project by selecting tab **Flow Simulation>>Wizard...** from the menu.

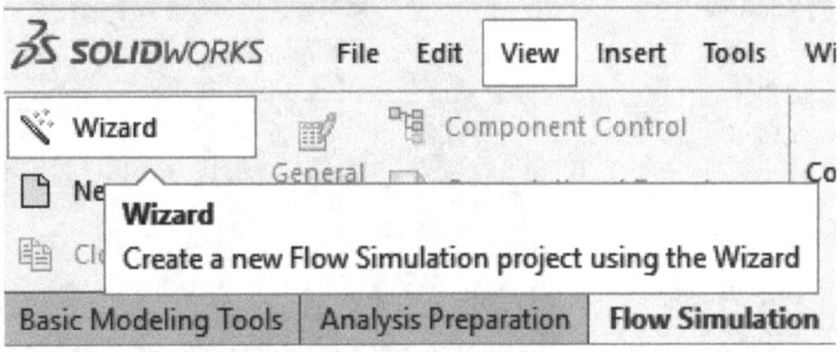

Figure 3.13 Using the Flow Simulation Project Wizard

14. Enter Project Name: **Flow around a Sphere 2026**. Push the **Next>** button.

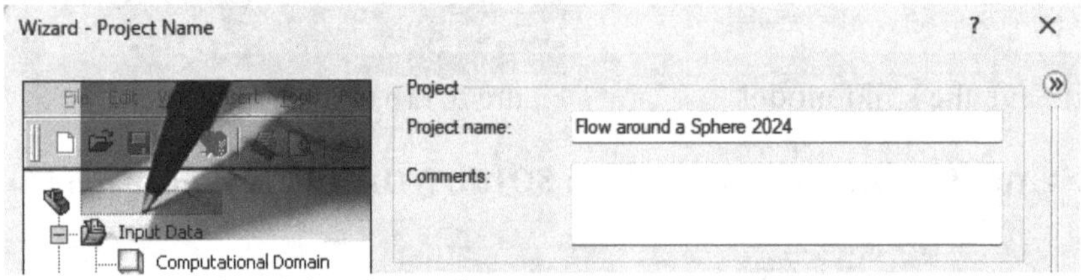

Figure 3.14 Wizard for the project name

15. We choose the **SI (m-kg-s)** unit system and click on the **Next>** button again.

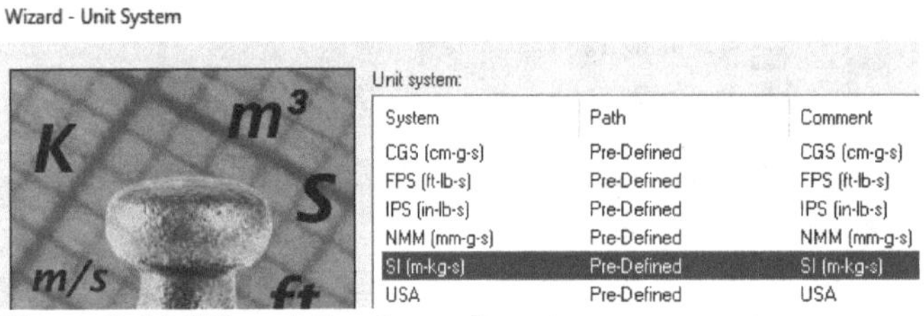

Figure 3.15 Wizard for the unit system

16. Select the **External** option for **Analysis type**. Uncheck Exclude cavities without conditions and click the **Next>** button.

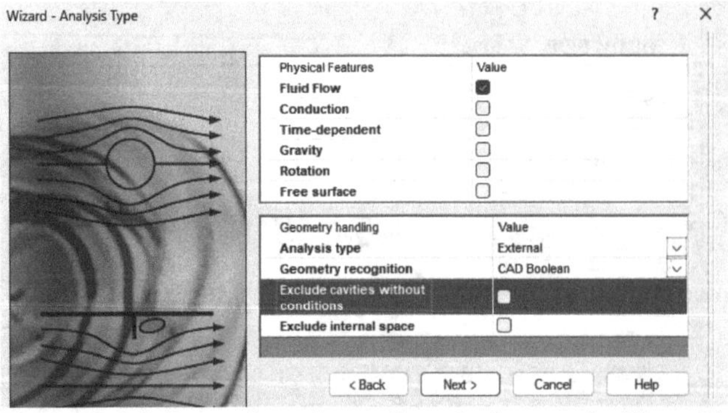

Figure 3.16 General settings of analysis type in Flow Simulation

17. Choose **Air** as the **Default Project Fluid** by clicking on the plus sign next to the **Gases** and selecting **Air**. Next, select the **Add** button. Click on the **Next>** button.

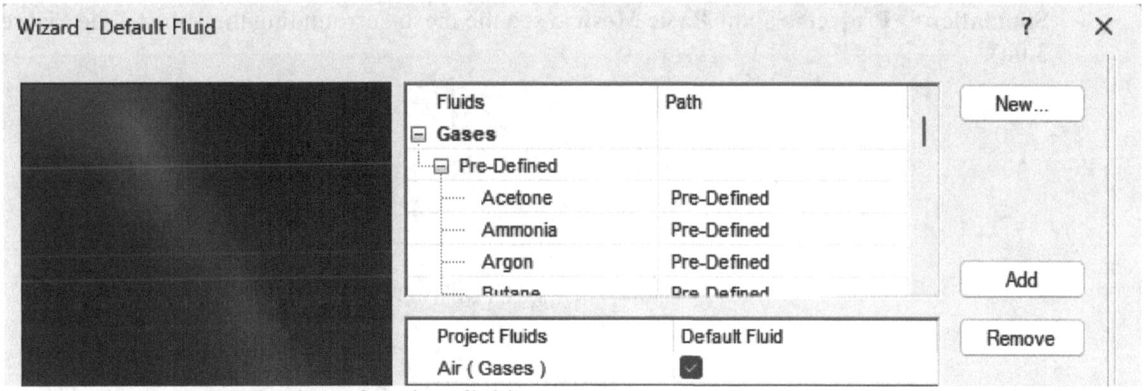

Figure 3.17 Selection of project fluid

The next part of the wizard is about **Wall Conditions**. We will use an **Adiabatic wall** for the sphere and use zero roughness on the surface of the same sphere. Next, we get the **Initial and Ambient Conditions** in the Wizard.

18. Click on the **Next>** button.

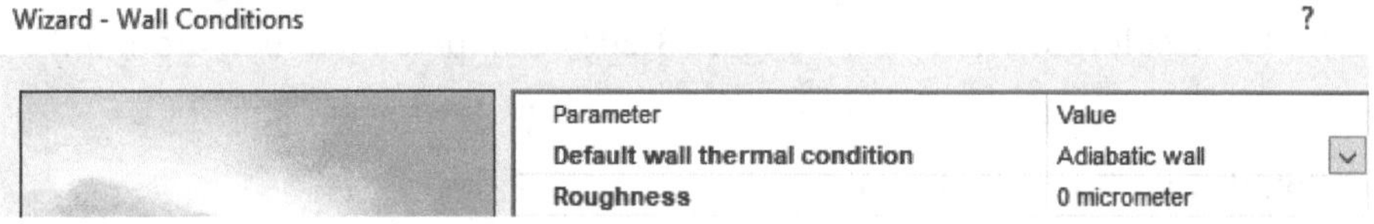

Figure 3.18 Wall conditions wizard

19. Enter **0.003 m/s** as the **Velocity in X-direction** and push the **Finish** button.

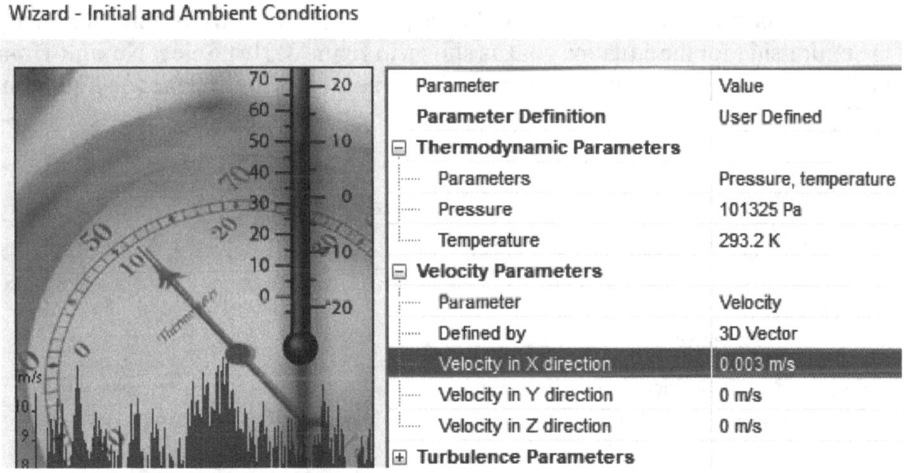

Figure 3.19 Initial and ambient conditions wizard

20. Select **Tools>> Flow Simulation>>Global Mesh** from the menu. Slide the **Level of Initial Mesh** to **4** and close the Dialog. Right click anywhere in the graphics window and select **Zoom In/Out** to see computational domain surrounding the sphere. Select **Tools>>Flow Simulation>>Project>>Show Basic Mesh** to see the mesh surrounding the sphere, see Figure 3.0a).

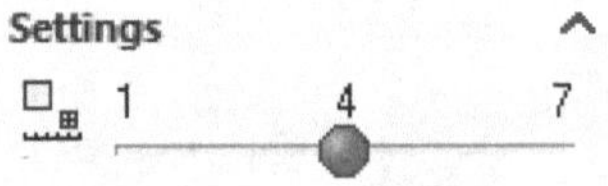

Figure 3.20a) Result resolution

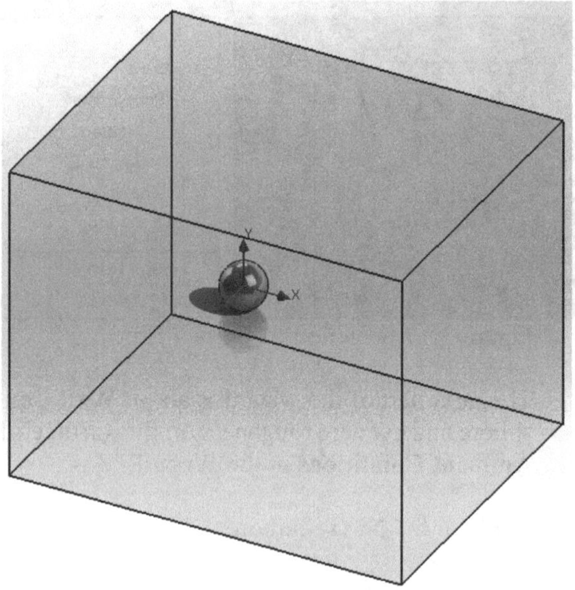

Figure 3.20b) Computational box around the sphere

E. Inserting Global Goal for Calculations

21. We create global goals for the project by selecting the tab **Flow Simulation>>Goals>>Global Goals…** from the SOLIDWORKS menu and check the box for **Force (X) Max**. Exit the global goals by clicking on OK ✔. Right click on **Goals** in the **Flow Simulation analysis tree** and select **Insert Equation Goal….** Select **GG Force (X) 1** from the **Flow Simulation analysis tree**. Enter the expression for the equation goal as shown in figure 3.21e). Select **No unit** from the top of **Dimensionality** drop down menu and enter the name **Drag Coefficient** for Equation Goal 1. Exit the **Equation Goal** window.

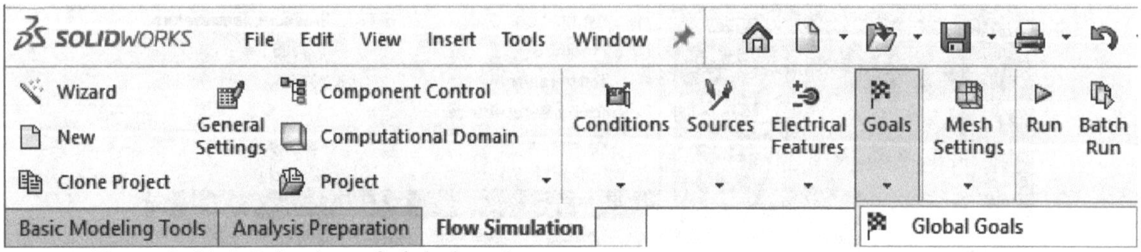

Figure 3.21a) Selection of global goals

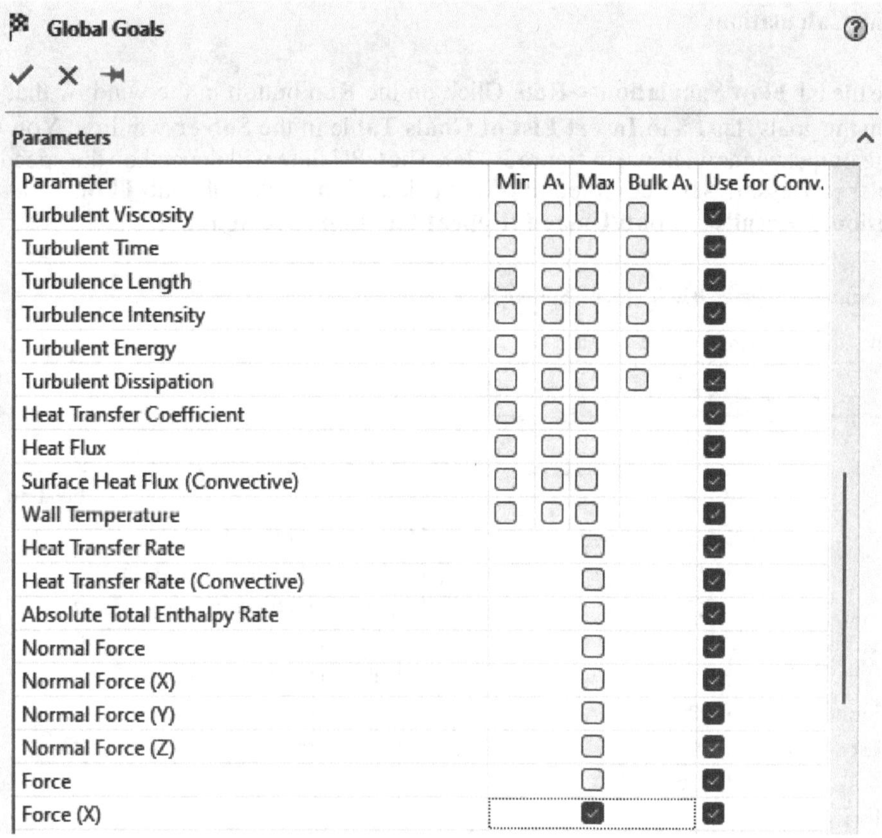

Figure 3.21b) Selection of X - Component of Force

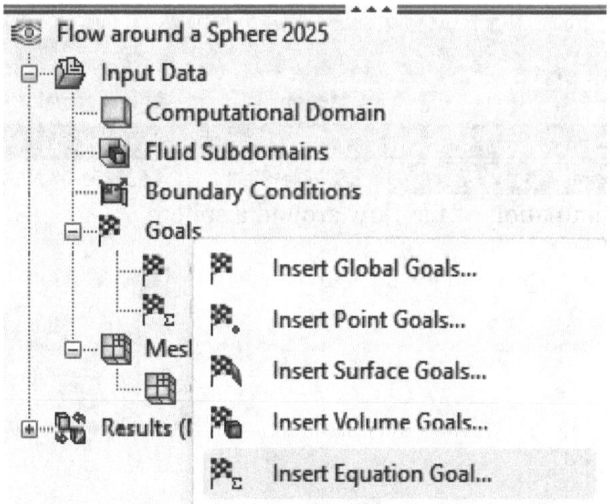

Figure 3.21c) Inserting equation goal

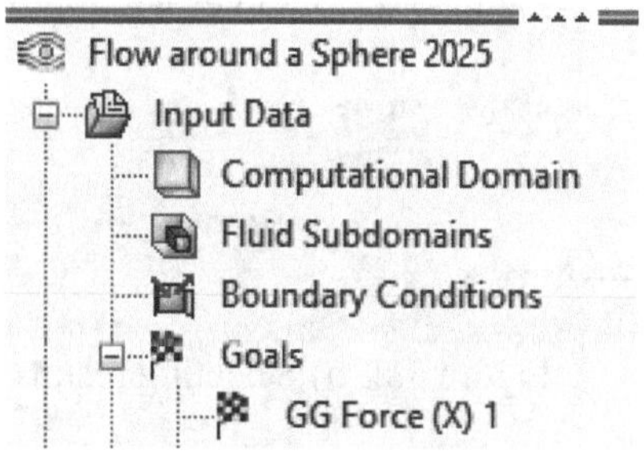

Figure 3.21d) X - Component of Force

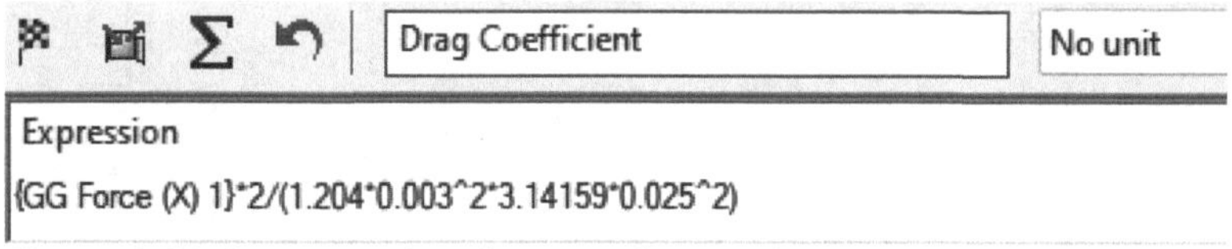

Figure 3.21e) Expression for equation goal

F. Running the Calculations

22. Choose the tab **Flow Simulation>>Run**. Click on the **Run** button in the window that appears. Click on the goals flag to **Insert List of Goals Table** in the **Solver** window. You will now have the output window shown in figure 3.22a). The CPU time will depend on the speed of your computer processor. After completion of the calculations, select the tab **Flow Simulation>>Results>>Load/Unload. Repeat this step once again.**

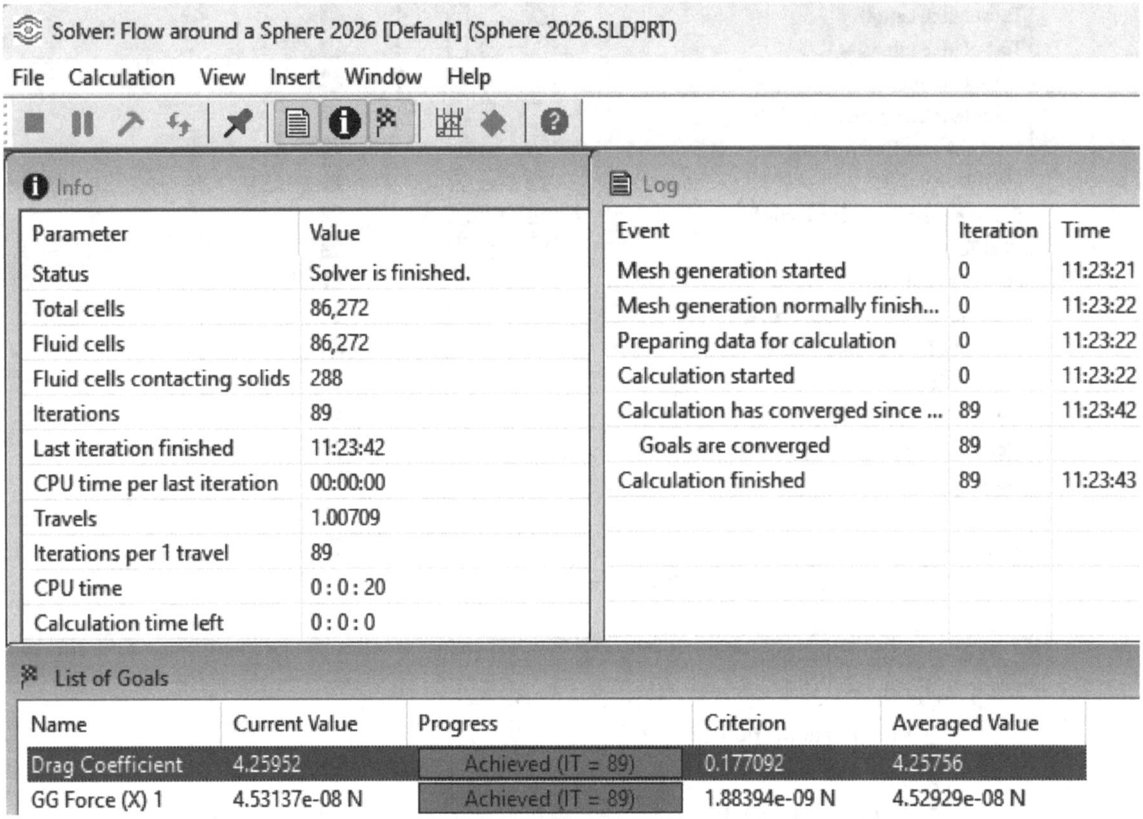

Figure 3.22a) Solver window for simulation of the flow around a sphere

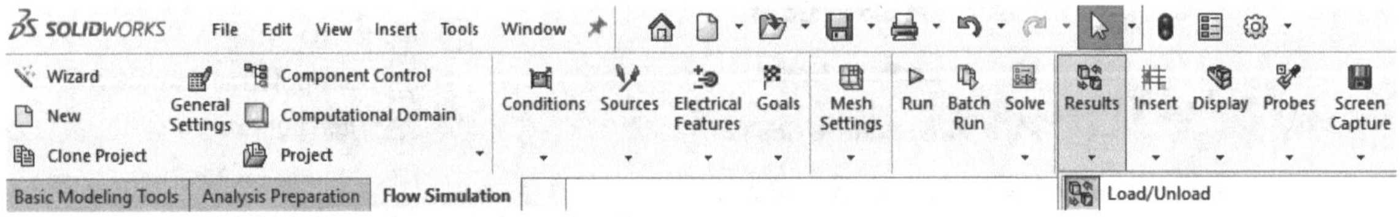

Figure 3.22b) Selecting results to load

G. Using Cut Plots

23. Select the **Flow Simulation analysis tree** tab.

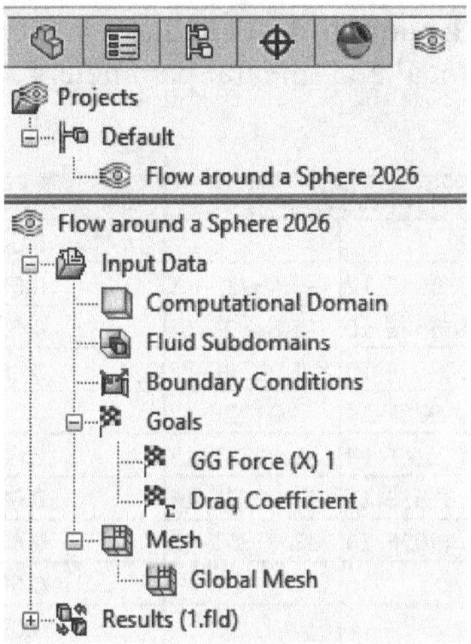

Figure 3.23 Selecting the Flow Simulation analysis tree

24. Open the Results folder, right click on the **Cut Plots** in the Results folder of the **Flow Simulation analysis tree** and select **Insert…** Click on the **Vectors** button in the **Display** section. Choose **Velocity** from the **Contours** section drop down menu. Slide **Number of Levels** to **255**. Exit the **Cut Plot** window. Rename **Cut Plot 1** to **Velocity around Sphere**. Select the scale in the graphics window, right click and select **Make Horizontal**. Select **Tools>>Flow Simulation>>Results>>Display>>Lighting** from the menu.

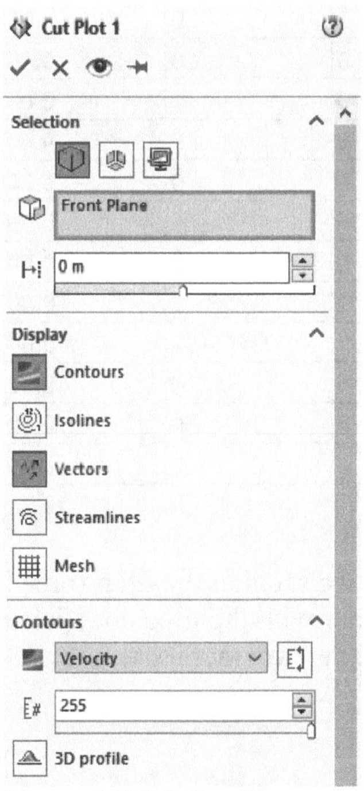

Figure 3.24a) Cut Plot

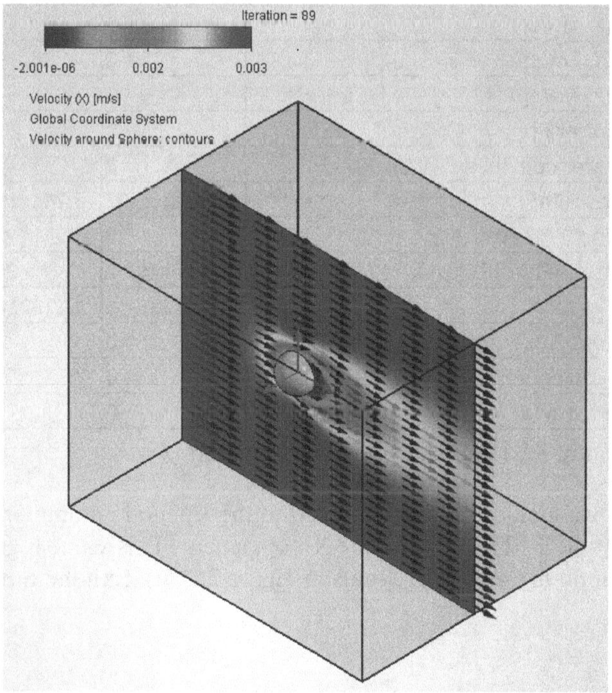

Figure 3.24b) Velocity distribution around sphere

H. Inserting Surface Parameters

25. Right-click on **Surface Parameters** in the **Flow Simulation analysis tree** and select **Insert....** Open the **FeatureManager design tree** in the graphics window and select the **Revolve1** feature. Check the **All** box in the **Parameters** window. Push the **Export to Excel** button in the **Surface Parameters** window. An Excel file is generated with local and integral parameters.

Integral Parameters					
Integral Parameter	Value	X-componen	Y-componen	Z-componen	Surface Area [m^2]
Heat Transfer Rate [W]	0				0.007736455
Normal Force [N]	1.78707E-08	1.78707E-08	5.03691E-12	-9.4921E-13	0.007736455
Friction Force [N]	2.74432E-08	2.7443E-08	1.14968E-10	-5.8682E-14	0.007736455
Force [N]	4.53138E-08	4.53137E-08	1.20005E-10	-1.0079E-12	0.007736455
Torque [N*m]	3.01342E-12	-2.6369E-14	-2.4938E-14	-3.0132E-12	0.007736455
Surface Area [m^2]	0.007736455	-1.5988E-19	2.48816E-19	-1.0673E-19	0.007736455
Torque of Normal Force [N*m]	1.03871E-15	1.00751E-15	-3.6199E-17	2.50077E-16	0.007736455
Torque of Friction Force [N*m]	3.01368E-12	-2.7377E-14	-2.4902E-14	-3.0135E-12	0.007736455
Heat Transfer Rate (Convective) [W]	0				0.007736455
Uniformity Index [ ]	1				0.007736455
Area (Fluid) [m^2]	0.007853982				0.007853982

Figure 3.25a) Integral surface parameters

Local Parameters				
Local Parameter	Minimum	Maximum	Average	Surface Area [m^2]
Pressure [Pa]	101325	101325	101325	0.007736455
Density (Fluid) [kg/m^3]	1.203705624	1.203705624	1.203705624	0.007736455
Velocity [m/s]	0	0	0	0.007736455
Velocity (X) [m/s]	0	0	0	0.007736455
Velocity (Y) [m/s]	0	0	0	0.007736455
Velocity (Z) [m/s]	0	0	0	0.007736455
Mach Number [ ]	0	0	0	0.007736455
Heat Transfer Coefficient [W/m^2/K]	0	0	0	0.007736455
Shear Stress [Pa]	2.22256E-07	7.74104E-06	4.11E-06	0.007736455
Surface Heat Flux [W/m^2]	0	0	0	0.007736455
Temperature (Fluid) [K]	293.2	293.2	293.2	0.007736455
Relative Pressure [Pa]	-3.6829E-05	1.21971E-05	-9.0846E-07	0.007736455
Surface Heat Flux (Convective) [W/m^2]	0	0	0	0.007736455
Acoustic Power Level [dB]	0	0	0	0.007736455
Acoustic Power [W/m^3]	0	0	0	0.007736455

Figure 3.25b) Local surface parameters

If we look at the Force related to the Integral parameters, we see that the drag force is $D = 4.53137\text{E-}08$ N for the X-component. This value together with the drag coefficient can be found in the **List of Goals** in figure 3.22a). Exit the **Surface Parameters** window.

I. Theory

The drag coefficient can be determined from the following formula

$$C_D = \frac{D}{\frac{1}{2}\rho U^2 A} = \frac{4.53137E-8}{\frac{1}{2}1.204 \cdot 0.003^2 \cdot \pi \cdot 0.025^2} = 4.25952 \quad (3.1)$$

, where ρ ($\frac{kg}{m^3}$) is the free-stream density, U (m/s) is the free-stream velocity and A (m^2) is the frontal area of the sphere. The Reynolds number is determined by

$$Re = \frac{Ud\rho}{\mu} = \frac{0.003 \cdot 0.05 \cdot 1.204}{1.825 \cdot 10^{-5}} = 9.9 \quad (3.2)$$

where μ ($\frac{kg}{ms}$) is the dynamic viscosity of air in the free-stream and d is the diameter of the sphere. The drag coefficient can be compared with the following curve-fit from experimental data

$$C_{D,Experiment} = \frac{24}{Re} + \frac{6}{1+\sqrt{Re}} + 0.4 = 4.273 \qquad 0 \leq Re \leq 200{,}000 \quad (3.3)$$

and we see that the difference in the Flow Simulation result is only 0.3 %.

J. Cloning the Project

26. We now want to run the simulations for different Reynolds numbers. Select the tab **Flow Simulation>>Clone Project...** from the SOLIDWORKS drop down menu. Create a new project with a different configuration name than the first project, see Figure 3.26b). Exit the **Clone Project** window.

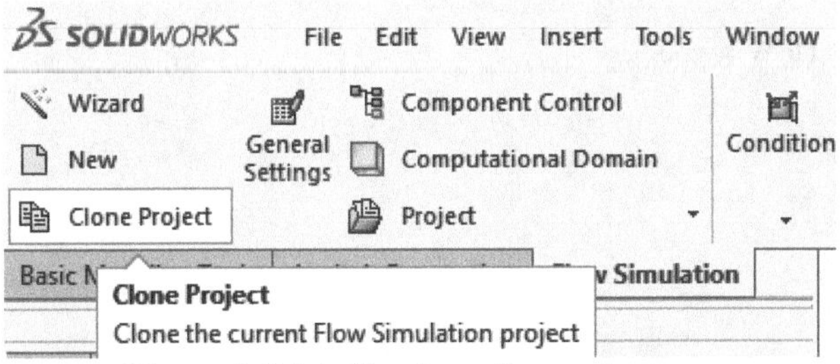

Figure 3.26a) Cloning of a project

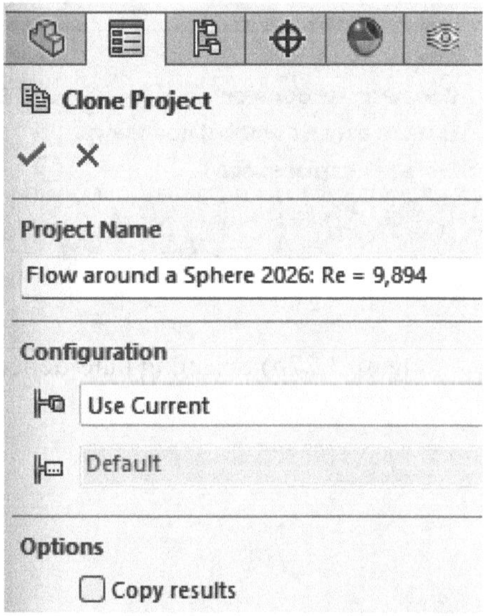

Figure 3.26b) name for cloned project

K. Time-Dependent Calculations

27. Select the tab **Flow Simulation>>General Settings...** Check the box for Time-dependent flow under **Physical Features** for this higher Reynolds number. The flow past a sphere is time dependent for *Re* above 200. Select **Apply**.

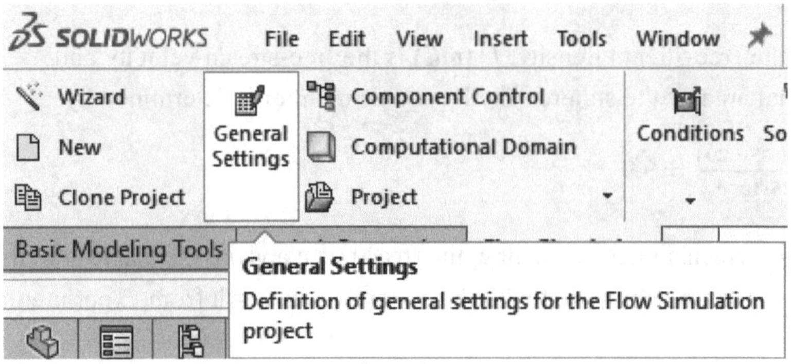

Figure 3.27a) Selecting General Settings

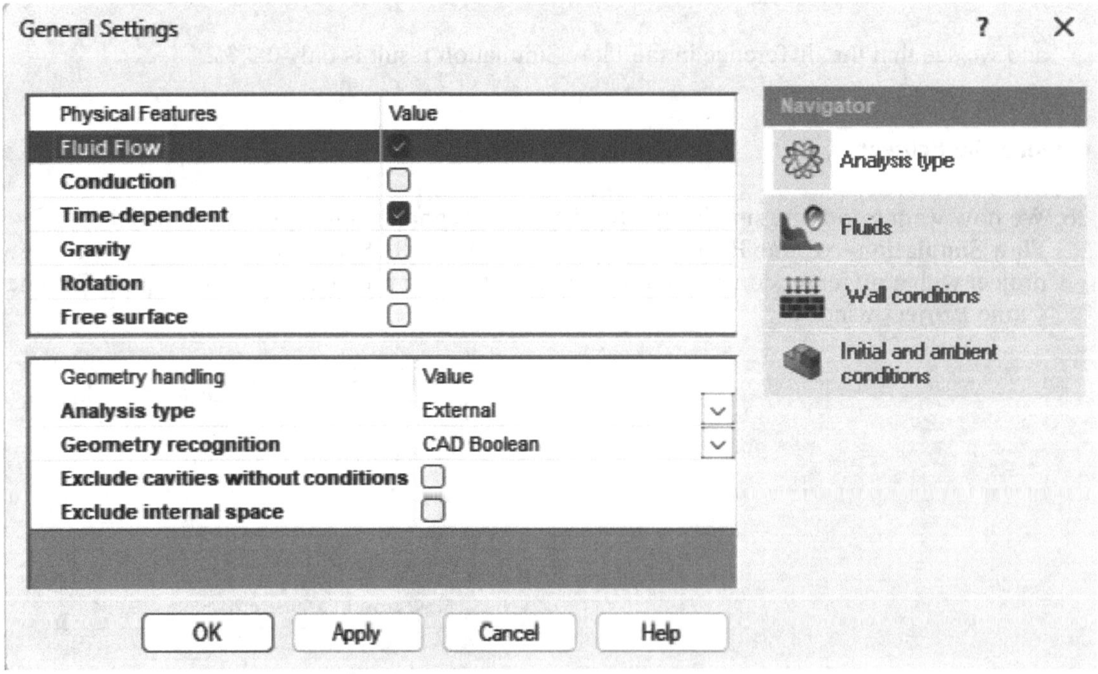

Figure 3.27b) Selecting time-dependent flow

28. Select **Initial and ambient conditions** in the **Navigator** and enter the **Velocity in X direction** to **3 m/s**. Click on the **Apply** and **OK** buttons to exit the **General Settings** window.

    Right click on the **Drag Coefficient Goal** in the **Flow Simulation analysis tree** and select **Edit Definition....** Change the velocity in the **Expression** from 0.003 m/s to **3 m/s,** see Figure 3.28b). Exit the **Equation Goal** window. You are now ready to run the calculations for this higher Reynolds number. Cloning of the project can be repeated and results from different Reynolds numbers are shown in Table 3.1. You can use the tab **Flow Simulation>>Batch Run** to start a batch run for all the different Reynolds numbers.

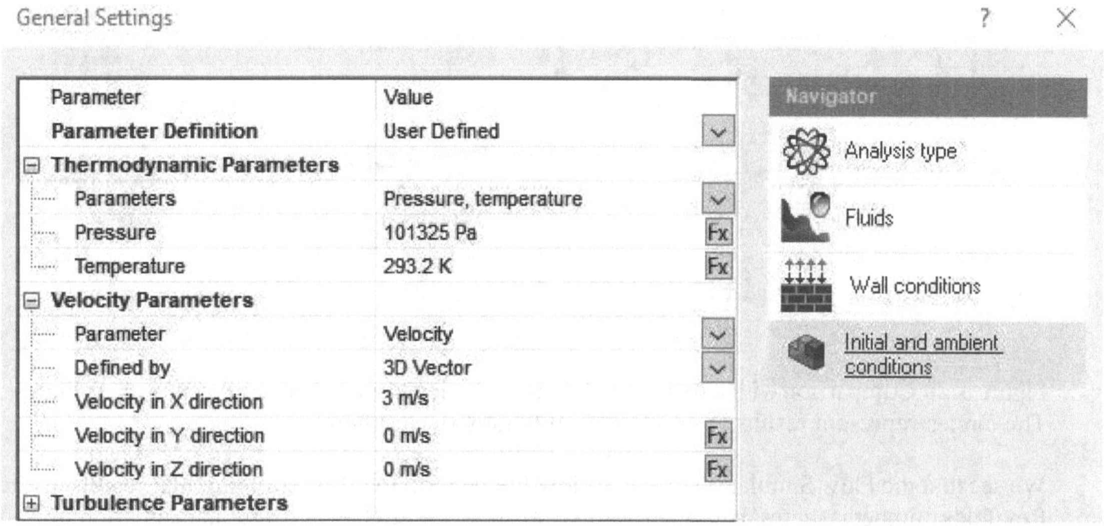

Figure 3.28a) Enter velocity in X direction

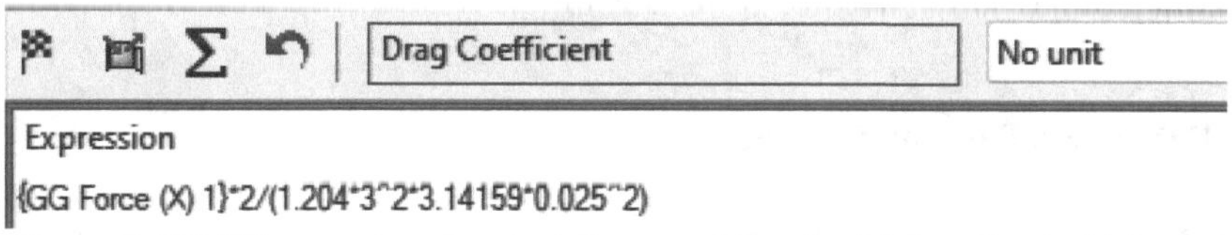

Figure 3.28b) Expression for equation goal for the higher Reynolds number

29. The following table shows a comparison between the computations and experiments at different Reynolds numbers including the percent difference for the drag coefficient:

U (m/s)	Re	$C_{D,Simulation}$	$C_{D,Experiment}$	Difference (%)
0.00003	0.1	222.424	247	9.9
0.0003	1.0	27.0636	27.7	2.3
0.003	9.9	4.25952	4.273	0.3
0.03	99	0.974893	1.191	18
0.3	990	0.370854	0.609	39
3	9,894	0.227332	0.462	51
30	99,000	0.18374	0.419	56

Table 3.1 Comparison of drag coefficient for a sphere at various Reynolds numbers

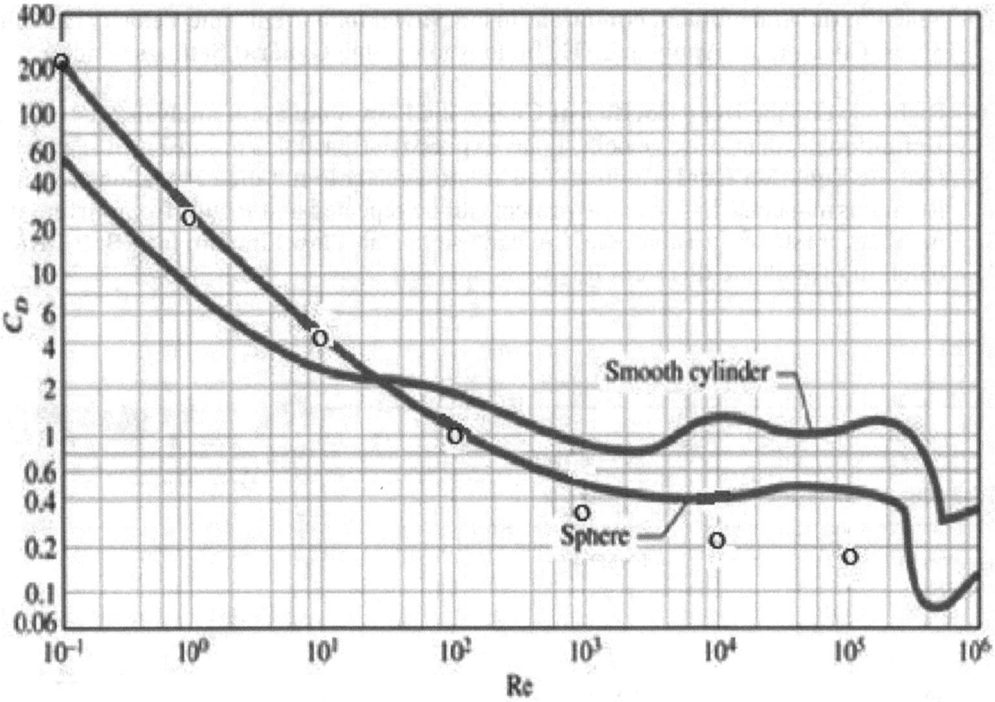

Figure 3.29 Comparison with experimental drag coefficient for a sphere and a smooth cylinder[1]. The circles represent results from Flow Simulations for a sphere.

We see that the Flow Simulation results follow the general trend of experimental results as the Reynolds number is increasing. A finer initial mesh and several levels of refinement are required to get results closer to experimental results at higher Reynolds numbers. You have now completed your simulation of the flow around a sphere.

L. Creating SOLIDWORKS Part for Cylinder

30. Select **File>>New...** from the SOLIDWORKS menu. Select a new **Part** and click on the **OK** button. Click on the **Front Plane** in the graphics window and select the Front Plane in the FeatureManager Design Tree. Select Front view from the **View Orientation** drop down menu in the graphics window.

    Select **Tools>>Options...** from the SOLIDWORKS menu and click on the **Document Properties** tab. Click on **Units** and select **MMGS** (millimeter, gram, second) as Unit system. Click OK to close the window.

    Select the Front Plane in the FeatureManager Design Tree. Select the **Circle** sketch tool from **Tools>>Sketch Entities** in the SOLIDWORKS menu.

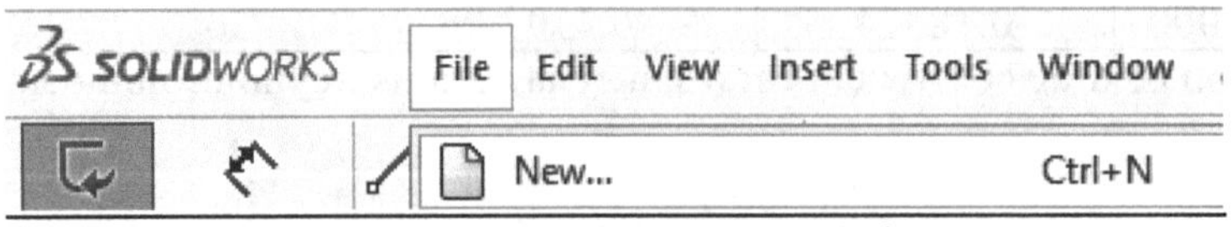

Figure 3.30a) Creating a new SOLIDWORKS document

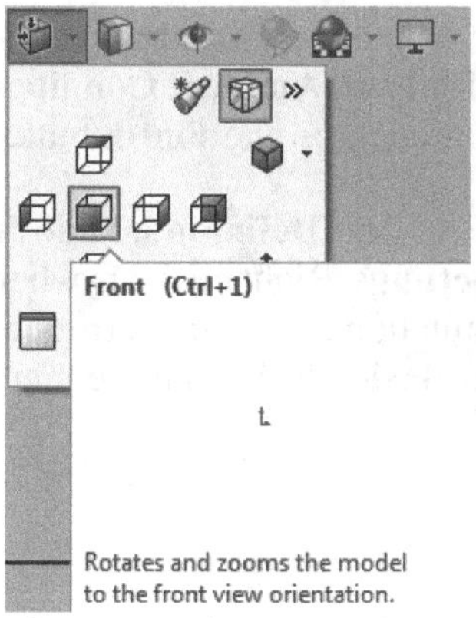

Figure 3.30b) Front view orientation

31. Draw a circle centered at the origin with a radius of **25.00 mm**. Close the **Circle** dialog box. Select **Insert>>Boss/Base>>Extrude** from the SOLIDWORKS menu. Check the **Direction 2** box and exit the **Extrude** dialog box. Select **File>>Save As** and enter the name **Cylinder 2026** as the name for the SOLIDWORKS part.

Figure 3.31a) Sketch of a circle

Figure 3.31b) Finished cylinder

M. Setting Up Flow Simulation Project for Cylinder

32. We create a project by selecting the tab **Flow Simulation>> Wizard** from the menu. Enter **Flow around a Cylinder 2026** as project name. Push the **Next>** button. We choose the **SI (m-kg-s)** unit system and click on the **Next>** button again.

    In the next step we select **External** as analysis type, check the box for **Time-dependent** flow and then click on the **Next>** button. The **Default Fluid Wizard** will now appear. We are going to add **Air** as the **Project Fluid**. Start by clicking on the plus sign next to the **Gases** in the **Fluids** column. Scroll down the different gases and select **Air.** Next, click on the **Add** button so that air will appear as the **Default Fluid**. Click on the **Next>** button.

The next part of the wizard is about **Wall Conditions**. We will use an **Adiabatic wall** for the cylinder and use zero surface roughness. Next, we get the **Initial and Ambient Conditions** in the Wizard. We set the **Velocity in X-direction** to **0.06 m/s** and click on the **Finish** button.

Right click on **Global Mesh** in the **Input Data** folder and select **Edit Definition**. Slide the **Level of Initial Mesh** under **Settings** to **7.** Exit the **Global Mesh Settings.** Right click anywhere in the graphics window and select **Zoom In/Out** to see the computational domain surrounding the cylinder. Select **Tools>>Flow Simulation>>Project>>Show Basic Mesh** from the menu to see the mesh surrounding the cylinder.

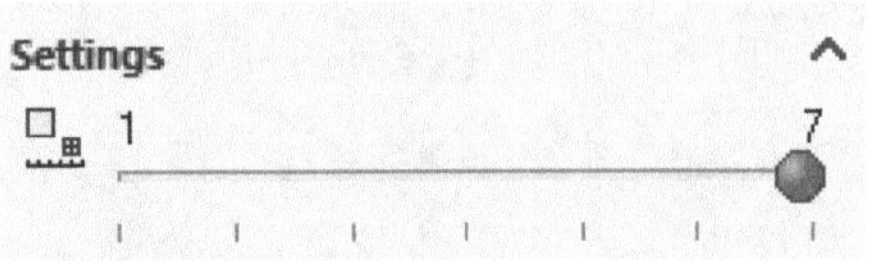

Figure 3.32 Setting for level of initial mesh for cylinder

N. Inserting Global Goals for Calculations and Selecting 2D Flow

33. We create global goals for the project by selecting the tab **Flow Simulation>>Goals>>Global Goals...** from the SOLIDWORKS menu and check the boxes for **Force (X) Max** and **Force (Y) Max**. Exit the global goals.

    Select the tab **Flow Simulation>>Goals>>Equation Goal...** from the menu and select **GG Force (X) 1** from the **Flow Simulation analysis tree**. Enter the expression for the equation goal as shown in figure 3.33a). Select **No unit** from the **Dimensionality** drop down menu. Enter **Drag Coefficient** as name. Exit the **Equation Goal** window. Repeat this step and create an equation goal for the lift coefficient, see figure 3.33b).

    Select the tab **Flow Simulation>>Computational Domain...** from the SOLIDWORKS menu. Select **2D Simulation** and **XY plane**, see figure 3.33c). Exit the **Computational Domain** window.

    Right click on Mesh in the Input Data folder and select Global Mesh. Select **Manual** as **Type.** Set the **Number of Cells Per X:** to **101** and the **Number of Cells Per Y:** to **100**. Click on the **OK** button.

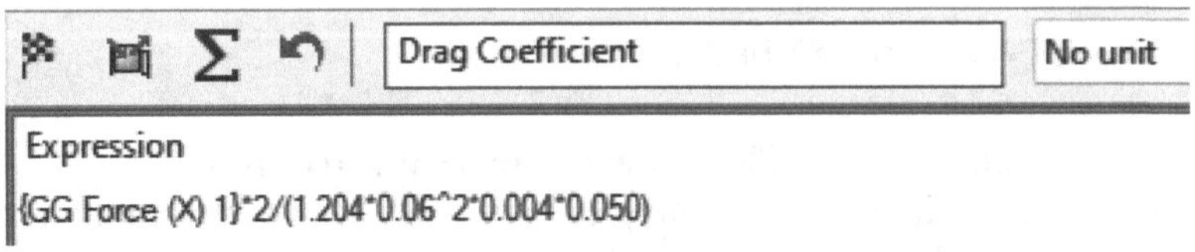

Figure 3.33a) Expression for equation goal for drag coefficient

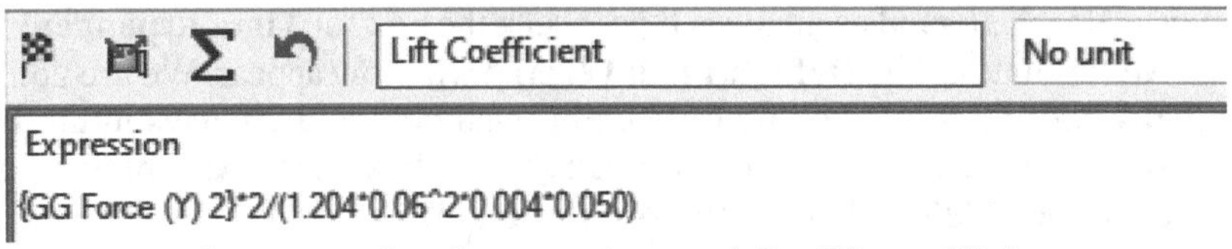

Figure 3.33b) Expression for equation goal for lift coefficient

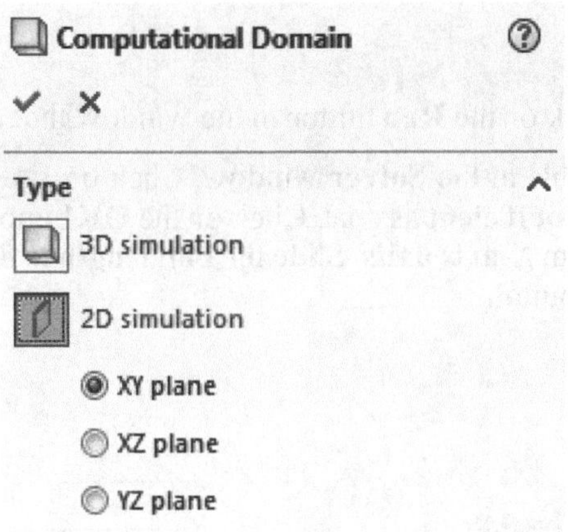

Figure 3.33c) Computational domain

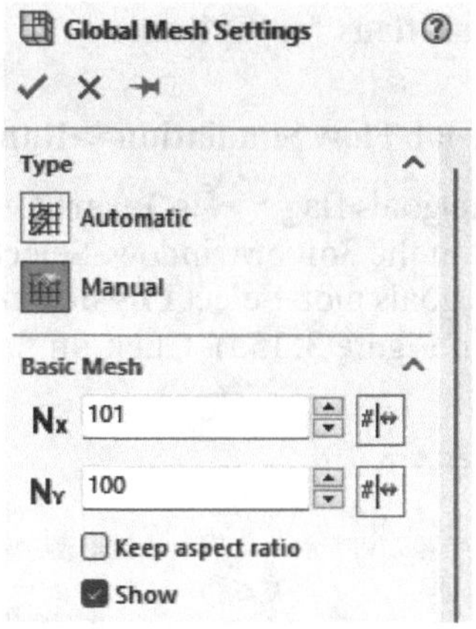

Figure 3.33d) Global mesh settings

O. Tabular Saving

34. We would like to save the calculations at different times so that we can capture the vortex shedding motion. We start by selecting the tab **Flow Simulation>>Solve>>Calculation Control Options...** from the SOLIDWORKS menu. Select the **Saving** tab and check the box next to **Periodic**. Set the **Start Value** to Iteration number **300** and the **Period Value** to **1**, see Figure 3.34. Select the **Finishing** tab and set the **Criteria** for **Physical time** to 200 s. Click on **OK** to exit the **Calculation Control Options** window.

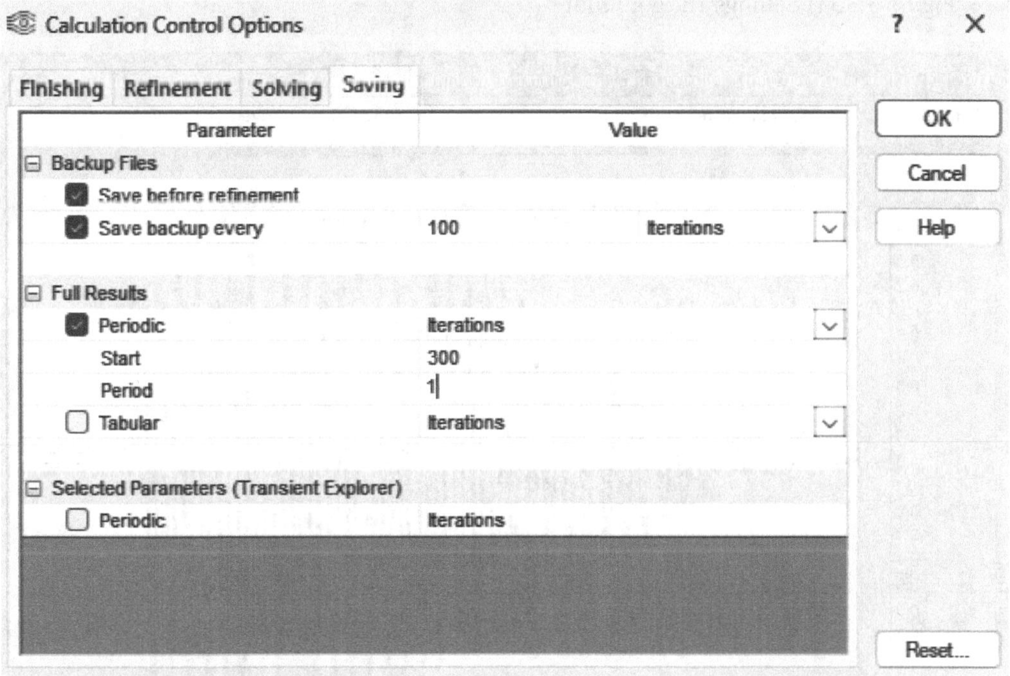

Figure 3.34 Calculation control options

P. Running Calculations for Cylinder

35. Choose the tab **Flow Simulation>>Run...** Click on the **Run** button in the window that appears. Click on the goals flag to **Insert Goals Table** in the **Solver** window. Click on **Insert Goals Plot** in the **Solver** window. Select **Lift Coefficient** as goal. Click on the **OK** button. Right click in the goals plot. Select **Physical time** from **X-axis units**. Slide the **Plot length** to the value as shown in Figure 3.35a). Click on the **OK** button.

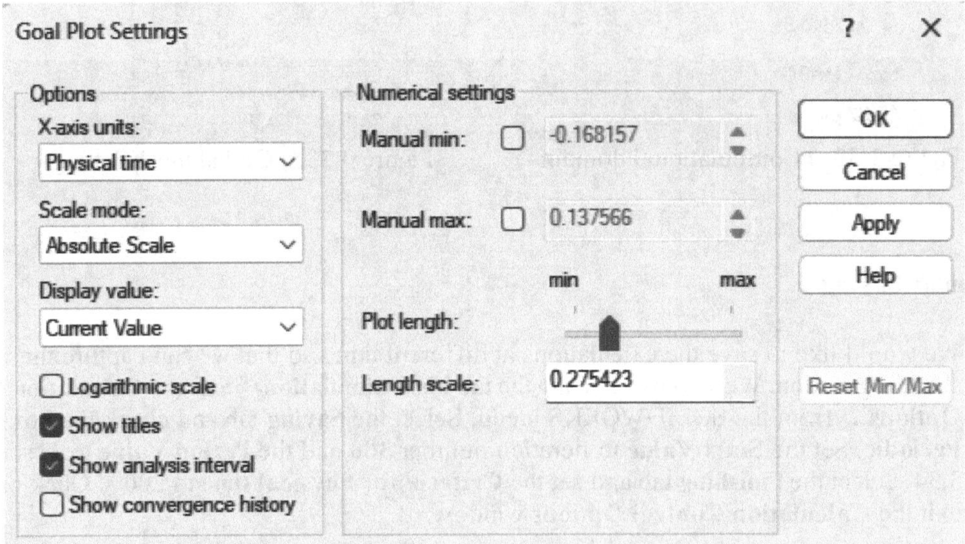

Figure 3.35a) Settings for goal plot

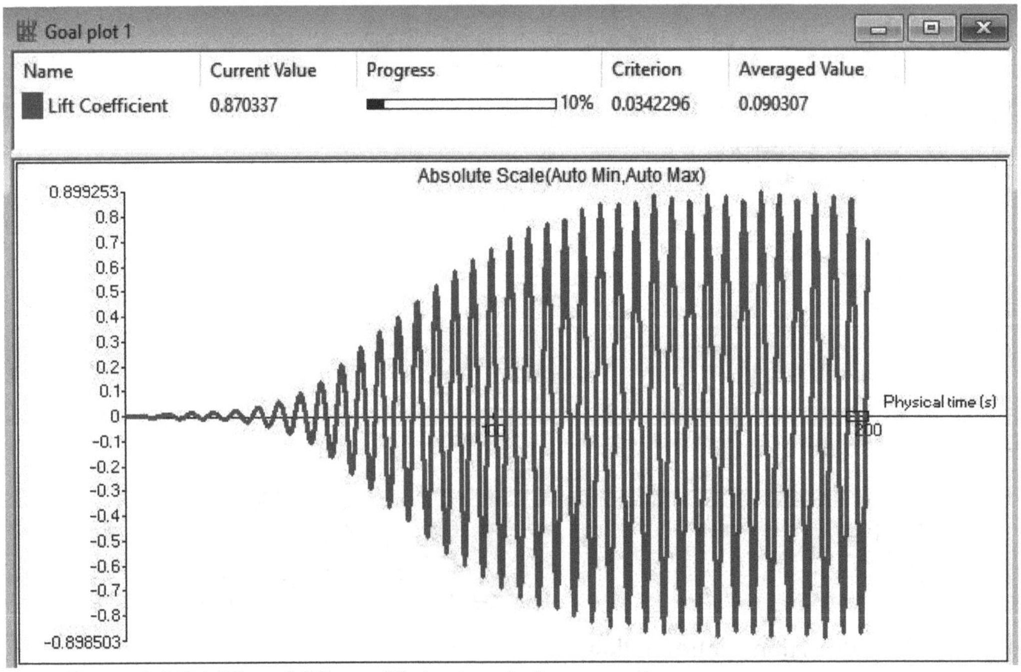

Figure 3.35b) Plot of lift coefficient variation over time

Q. Using Excel for Frequency Analysis

36. We are interested in determining the frequency of the time signal in Figure 3.35b). To use FFT (Fast Fourier Transform) calculations in **Excel**, we will add the analysis tool packages. Select **File>>Options** from the menu in Excel. Select Add-ins on the left-hand side and select **Excel Add-Ins** from the **Manage:** drop down menu and click on the **Go…** button. Check the boxes for **Analysis ToolPak** and **Analysis ToolPak – VBA**. Click on the **OK** button. You will now install the add-ins. Place the files **"graph 3.37b)"** and **"graph 3.37c)"** on the desktop. These files can be downloaded from *sdcpublications.com*.

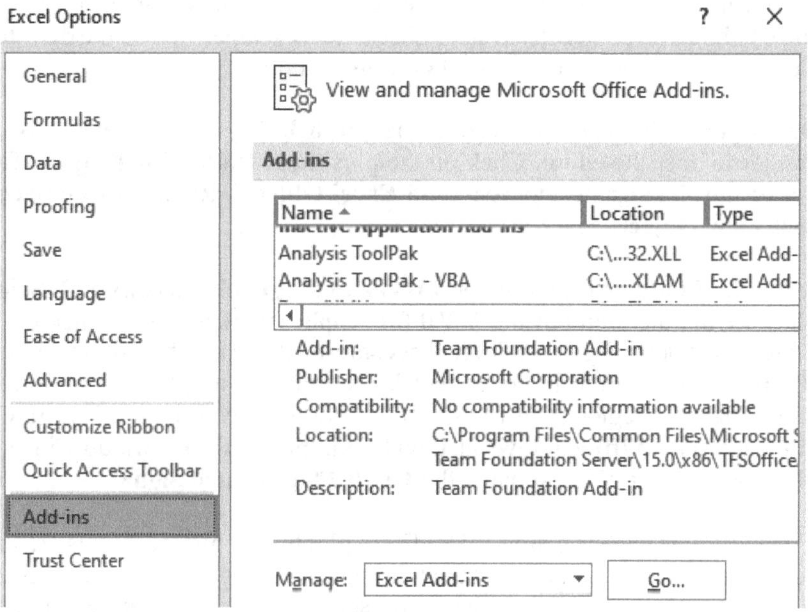

Figure 3.36a) Using Excel to add analysis

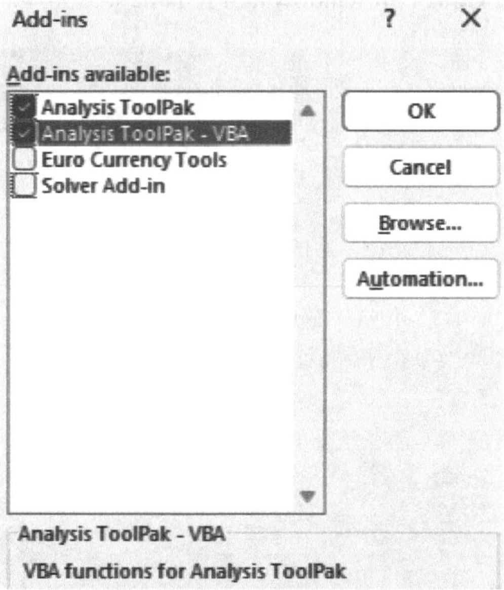

Figure 3.36b) Adding analysis tools

R. Inserting XY Plots

37. Right click and select **Insert...** on **Goal Plots** in the **Results** section of the **Flow Simulation analysis tree**. Check the box for **Lift Coefficient**, see Figure 3.37a). Select **Physical time** from the **Abscissa** drop down menu. Select **Excel Workbook (*.xlsx)** from the **Options** drop down menu. Click on the **Export to Excel** button. An Excel file will open with a summary sheet, a lift coefficient sheet, and a plot data sheet.

    Double click on the **graph 3.37b)** file to open the file. Click on **Enable Content** if you get a **Security Warning** that **Macros** have been disabled. If **Developer** is not available in the menu of the **Excel** file, you will need to do the following: Select **File>>Options** from the menu and click on the **Customize Ribbon** on the left-hand side. Check the **Developer** box on the right-hand side under **Main Tabs**. Click **OK** to exit the **Excel Options** window.

    Click on the **Developer** tab in the **Excel** menu for the **graph 3.37b)** file and select **Visual Basic** on the left-hand side to open the editor. Click on the plus sign next to **VBAProject (Goal Plot 1.xlsx)** and click on the plus sign next to **Microsoft Excel Objects**. Right click on **Sheet3 (Plot Data)** and select **View Object**.

    Select **Module2** in the **Modules** folder under **VBAProject (graph 3.37b).xlsm)**. Select **Run>>Run Macro** from the menu of the **MVB for Applications** window. Click on the **Run** button in the **Macros** window. Figure 3.37b) will become available in **Excel** showing the regular oscillation of the time signal for the lift coefficient. We see that the amplitude and period of the time signal is constant in the region from 140 s – 180 s, compare with Figure 3.35b). Close the **Goal Plot** and the **graph 3.37b)** windows in **Excel**. Exit the **Goal Plot** window in **SOLIDWORKS Flow Simulation**. Rename the **Goals Plot** to **Time Signal**.

    Repeat step **37** but this time use the **graph 3.37c)** file to plot the amplitude versus frequency of the power spectrum from the FFT analysis of the time signal, see Figure 3.37c). The spectrum is a result of using Fourier analysis on the time signal. We see that there is a clear peak in amplitude at a frequency between 0.2 Hz and 0.3 Hz. A more exact value of the frequency can be found from plot data to be 0.22896 Hz. Exit the **Goal Plot** window and rename it to **FFT**.

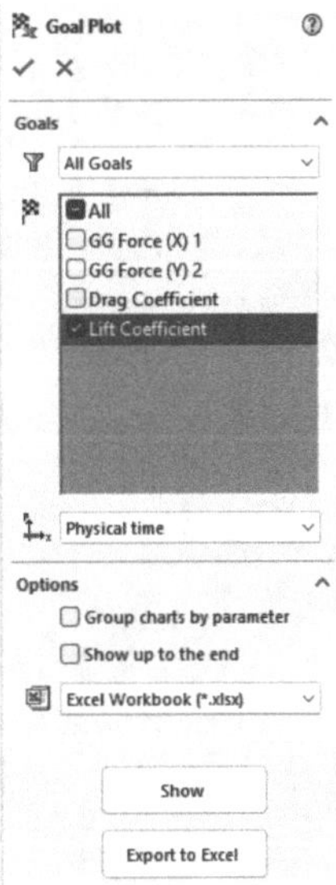

Figure 3.37a) Goal plot

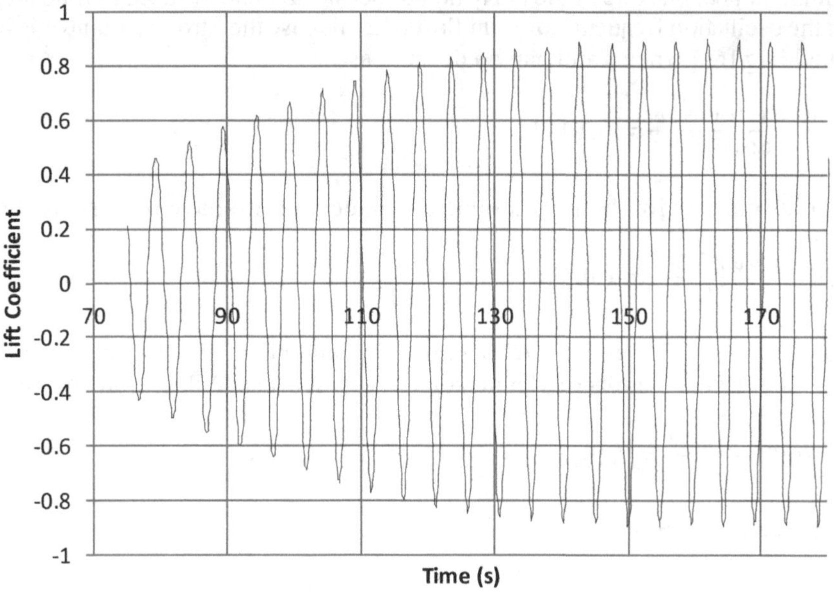

Figure 3.37b) Time signal

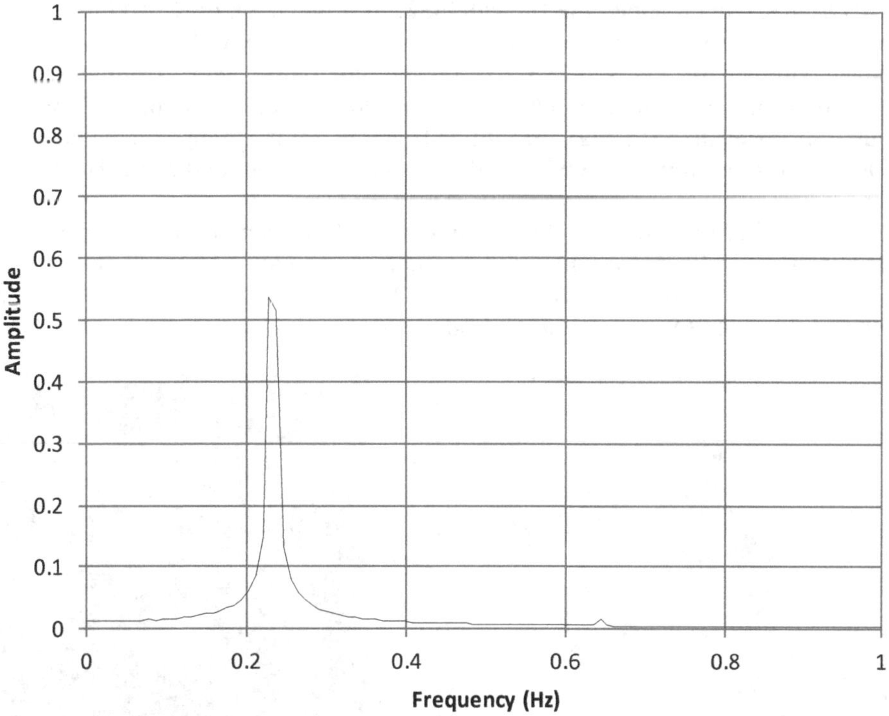

Figure 3.37c) Waveform in the frequency domain

S. Strouhal number

38. The Strouhal number S is one of the many non-dimensional numbers used in fluid mechanics and based on the oscillation frequency of fluid flows. In this case the Strouhal number is based on the vortex shedding frequency f and can be defined as

$$S = \frac{fd}{U} = \frac{0.2331\ Hz \cdot 0.050\ m}{0.06\ m/s} = 0.1942 \tag{3.4}$$

The Reynolds number for the flow around a cylinder that we have been studying is

$$Re = \frac{Ud\rho}{\mu} = \frac{0.06 \cdot 0.05 \cdot 1.204}{1.825 \cdot 10^{-5}} = 198 \tag{3.5}$$

This value of the Strouhal number from Flow Simulation can be compared with DNS (Direct Numerical Simulations) results of Henderson (1997), see also Williamson and Brown (1998).

$$S_{DNS} = 0.2698 - \frac{1.0272}{\sqrt{Re}} = 0.1968 \tag{3.6}$$

The difference is 1.3 %.

T. Inserting Cut Plots

1. We now want to plot the X-velocity component, and vorticity at the different instants that we tabulated in step **34**. Select the tab **Flow Simulation>>Results>>Load from File...** from the SOLIDWORKS menu. Open the file **r000652.fld**. Right click on **Cut Plots** in the **Flow Simulation analysis tree** and select **Insert...** and select **Velocity (X)** from the **Contours** section. Slide the **Number of Levels** to **255**. Exit the cut plot dialog. Select front view from the view orientation drop down menu in the graphics window. Select the **Tools>>Flow Simulation>>Results>>Display>>Lighting** from the menu. Change the name of Cut Plot 1 to **Velocity (X) (mps) Iteration 652**. Right click on the cut plot and select Hide.

   Right click on **Flow around a Cylinder 2026** in the **Flow Simulation analysis tree** and select **Hide Global Coordinate System**. Insert one more cut plot and plot **Vorticity**. Change the name of the cut plot to **Vorticity (1ps) Iteration 652**. Load the remaining four files **r_000664.fld**, **r_000674.fld**, **r_000685.fld**, **r_000695.fld** and plot **Velocity (X)** and **Vorticity** for each file.

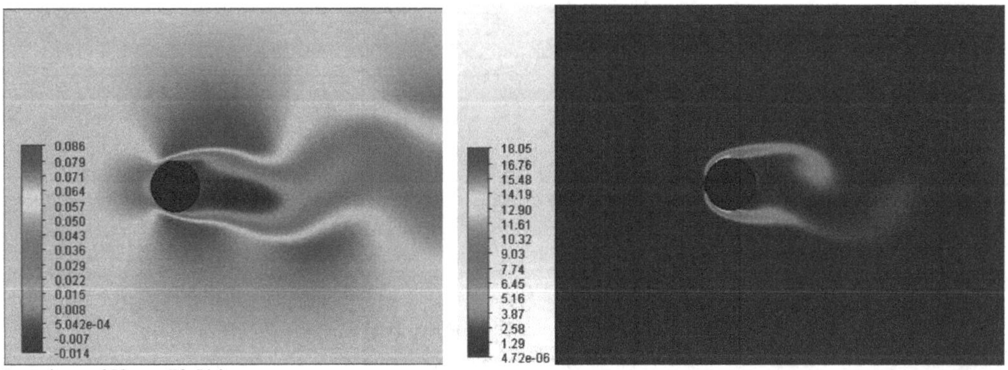

Iteration = 652, t = 73.514 s

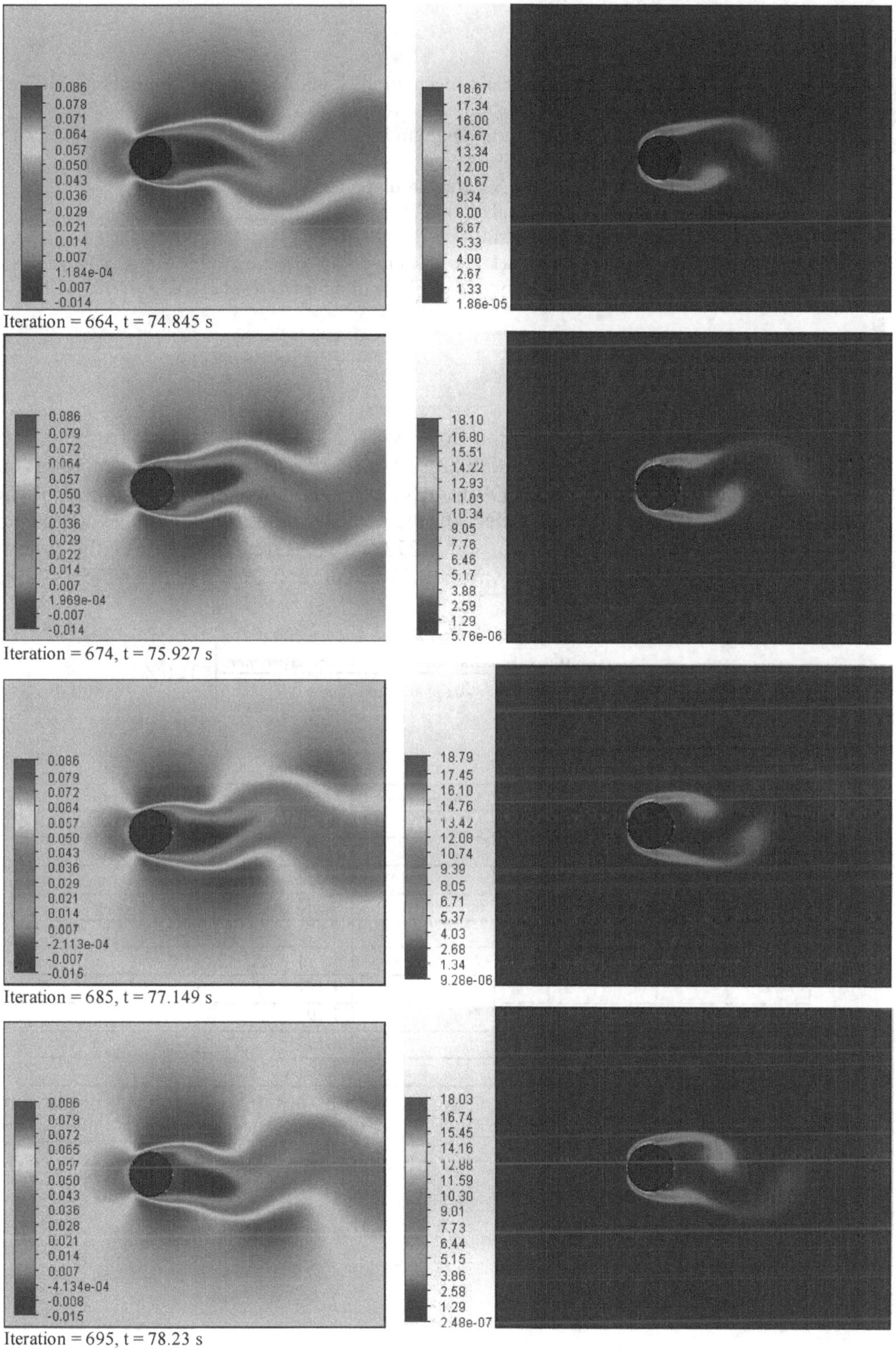

Figure 3.38 Velocity (X) in left column and vorticity in right column during vortex shedding

U. References

1. Çengel, Y. A., and Cimbala, J.M., Fluid Mechanics: Fundamentals and Applications, McGraw-Hill, 2006.
2. Henderson, R., Nonlinear dynamics and pattern formation in turbulent wake transition, J. of Fluid Mech., 352, (65-112), 1997.
3. Technical Reference SOLIDWORKS Flow Simulation 2025.
4. Tutorial SOLIDWORKS Flow Simulation 2025.
5. White, F. M., Viscous Fluid Flow, McGraw-Hill, 1991.
6. Williamson, C. H. K., and Brown G.L., A series in $1/\sqrt{Re}$ to represent the Strouhal-Reynolds number relationship of the cylinder wake, Journal of Fluids and Structures, 12, (1073 – 1085), 1998.

V. Exercises

3.1 Run the steady calculations for the flow over a 25 mm radius sphere for Re = 9.9, 99 and use different levels of initial mesh: 1, 2, 3, 4 and 5. Plot the drag coefficient versus mesh level using Excel. Include both SOLIDWORKS Flow Simulation results and empirical data in the same plot. Fill out Table 3.2. Determine the percent difference variation as compared with the experimental values $C_{D,Sphere\ Experiment} = 4.273$ and 1.191, respectively. Use the following size of the computational domain: Xmin: -0.175, Xmax: 0.275, Ymin: -0.175, Ymax: 0.175, Zmin: -0.175, Zmax: 0.175

$$Percent\ Difference = \left|\frac{C_{D,Sphere\ Simulation} - C_{D,Sphere\ Experiment}}{C_{D,Sphere\ Experiment}}\right| * 100\%$$

Discuss your results.

Initial Mesh	U (m/s)	Re	$C_{D,\ Simulation}$	$C_{D,\ Experiment}$	Difference (%)
1		9.9		4.273	
2		9.9		4.273	
3		9.9		4.273	
4		9.9		4.273	
5		9.9		4.273	
1		99		1.191	
2		99		1.191	
3		99		1.191	
4		99		1.191	
5		99		1.191	

Table 3.2 Drag coefficient for a sphere at various initial mesh and Reynolds numbers

3.2 Run the steady calculations for the flow around a 25 mm radius sphere for Re = 9.9 for an initial mesh level of 4 and use different sizes a) – d) of the computational domain. Plot the drag coefficient versus length of computational domain. Include flow simulations and empirical data in the same plot.

a) Xmin: -0.05, Xmax: 0.05, Ymin: -0.05, Ymax: 0.05, Zmin: -0.05, Zmax: 0.05
b) Xmin: -0.1, Xmax: 0.1, Ymin: -0.1, Ymax: 0.1, Zmin: -0.1, Zmax: 0.1
c) Xmin: -0.15, Xmax: 0.15, Ymin: -0.15, Ymax: 0.15, Zmin: -0.15, Zmax: 0.15
d) Xmin: -0.2, Xmax: 0.2, Ymin: -0.2, Ymax: 0.2, Zmin: -0.2, Zmax: 0.2
e) Xmin: -0.25, Xmax: 0.25, Ymin: -0.25, Ymax: 0.25, Zmin: -0.25, Zmax: 0.25

How does the drag coefficient vary with the size of the computational domain? Determine percent difference variation as compared with empirical results. Discuss your results.

Comp. Domain Length	U (m/s)	Re	$C_{D,\ Simulation}$	$C_{D,\ Experiment}$	Difference (%)
0.1		9.9		4.273	
0.2		9.9		4.273	
0.3		9.9		4.273	
0.4		9.9		4.273	
0.5		9.9		4.273	

Table 3.3 Drag coefficient for a sphere at various computational domain lengths.

3.3 Use SOLIDWORKS Flow Simulation to determine the drag coefficient for a cylinder with a radius of 25 mm. Use 2D-plane, XY-plane flow boundary condition for the calculations at Re = 0.1, 1, 10, 100, 1000, 10000, 100000 (initial mesh level of 6) and compare with experimental results using the following curve-fit formula:

$$C_{D,CylinderExperiment} = 1 + \frac{10}{Re^{2/3}} \qquad 0 \le Re \le 250{,}000$$

Determine the percentage difference from experiments in Table 3.3 for the different Reynolds numbers. Use the following size of the computational domain:
Xmin: -0.175, Xmax: 0.275, Ymin: -0.175, Ymax: 0.175, Zmin: -0.002, Zmax: 0.002

$$Percent\ Difference = \left|\frac{C_{D,Cylinder\ Simulation} - C_{D,Cylinder\ Experiment}}{C_{D,Cylinder\ Experiment}}\right| * 100\%$$

Plot drag coefficient versus Reynolds number for flow simulation results and empirical data in the same graph. Use time dependent calculation for Re ≥ 50. Discuss your results.

U (m/s)	Re	$C_{D,Simulation}$	$C_{D,Experiment}$	Difference (%)
	0.1			
	1			
	10			
	100			
	1,000			
	10,000			
	100,000			

Table 3.4 Comparison of drag coefficient for a cylinder at various Reynolds numbers

Notes:

CHAPTER 4. FLOW PAST AN AIRFOIL

A. Objectives

- Creating the wing section needed for the SOLIDWORKS Flow Simulation
- Inserting a curve through given coordinates
- Setting up a Flow Simulation project for external flow
- Inserting global goals and equation goal
- Running the calculations
- Using Cut Plots to visualize the resulting flow field
- Creating a custom visualization parameter
- Cloning of the project
- Create a batch run
- Compare with experimental results

B. Problem Description

In this exercise we will analyze the flow around a Selig/Donovan SD 2030 airfoil section. We will study the flow at a Reynolds number $Re = 100{,}000$ and determine the lift coefficient versus the angle of attack and compare with experimental data. First, we have to create a model of the airfoil in SOLIDWORKS and export the part to Flow Simulation. The chord length of the airfoil is 305 mm and the thickness is 26.1 mm. Follow the different steps in this chapter to create a solid model of the airfoil, see figure 4.0 and perform a 2D plane Flow Simulation of the flow field.

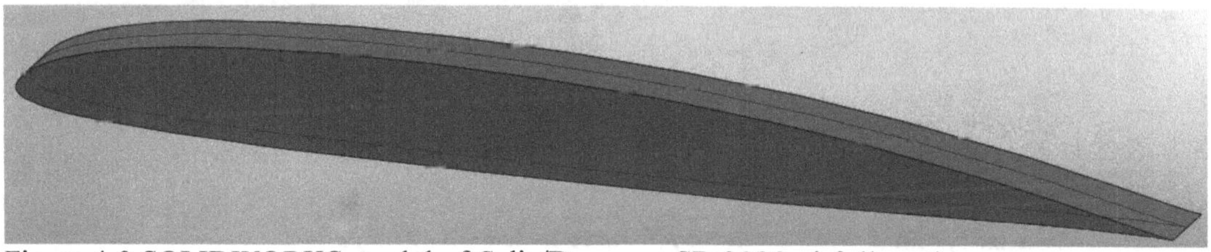

Figure 4.0 SOLIDWORKS model of Selig/Donovan SD 2030 airfoil section.

C. Creating the SOLIDWORKS Part

1. Start SOLIDWORKS and create a New Part. Select the **Front** view from the drop down menu in the graphics window. Select **Tools>>Options...** from the SOLIDWORKS menu. Click on the Document Properties tab and select **Units**. Select **MMGS** as your **Unit system**.

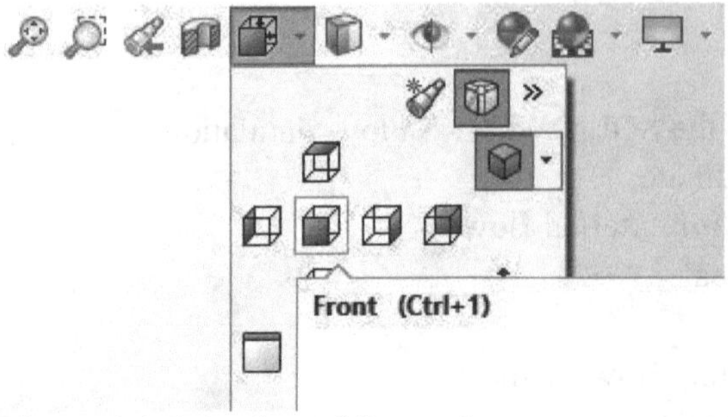

Figure 4.1 Selection of front view

2. Select **Insert>>Curve>>Curve Through XYZ Points...** from the menu.

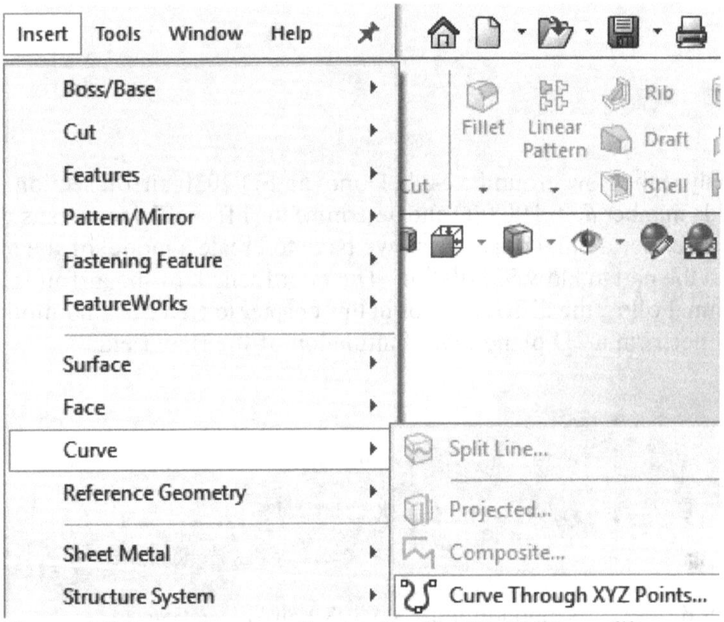

Figure 4.2 Importing coordinates for the SD 2030 profile

3. In the **Curve File** window, you select **Browse** and open the file **SD2030.sldcrv** that can be downloaded from ***sdcpublications.com*** website. The Curve File window appears with the X and Y coordinates shown for the airfoil. Click **OK**. Right click in the graphics window and **Zoom/Pan/Rotate>>Zoom to Fit.**

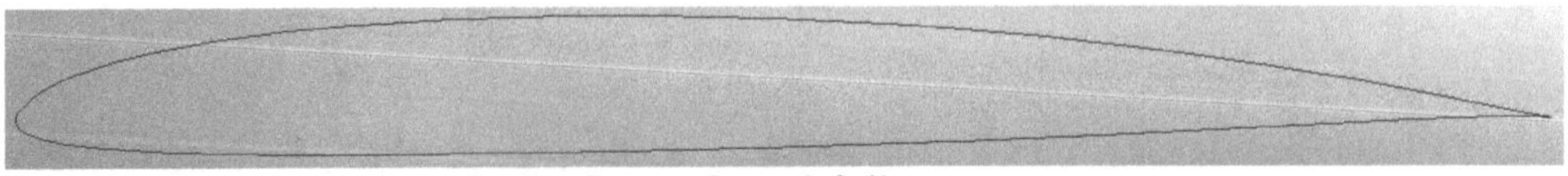

Figure 4.3 Imported curve in the form of an airfoil

4. Next, we select the **Front Plane** in the **FeatureManager design tree**, select the **Analysis Preparation** tab and click on the **Extruded Boss/Base** feature.

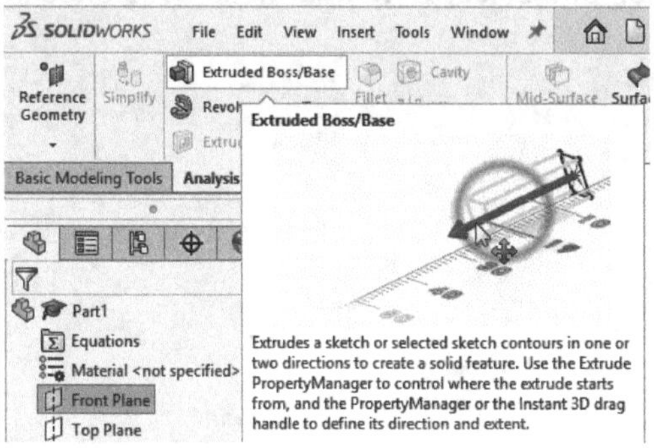

Figure 4.4 Selection of front plane and extruded boss/base feature

5. Click on **Curve1** in the **FeatureManager design tree** and select **Tools>>Sketch Tools>>Convert Entities** from the SOLIDWORKS menu.

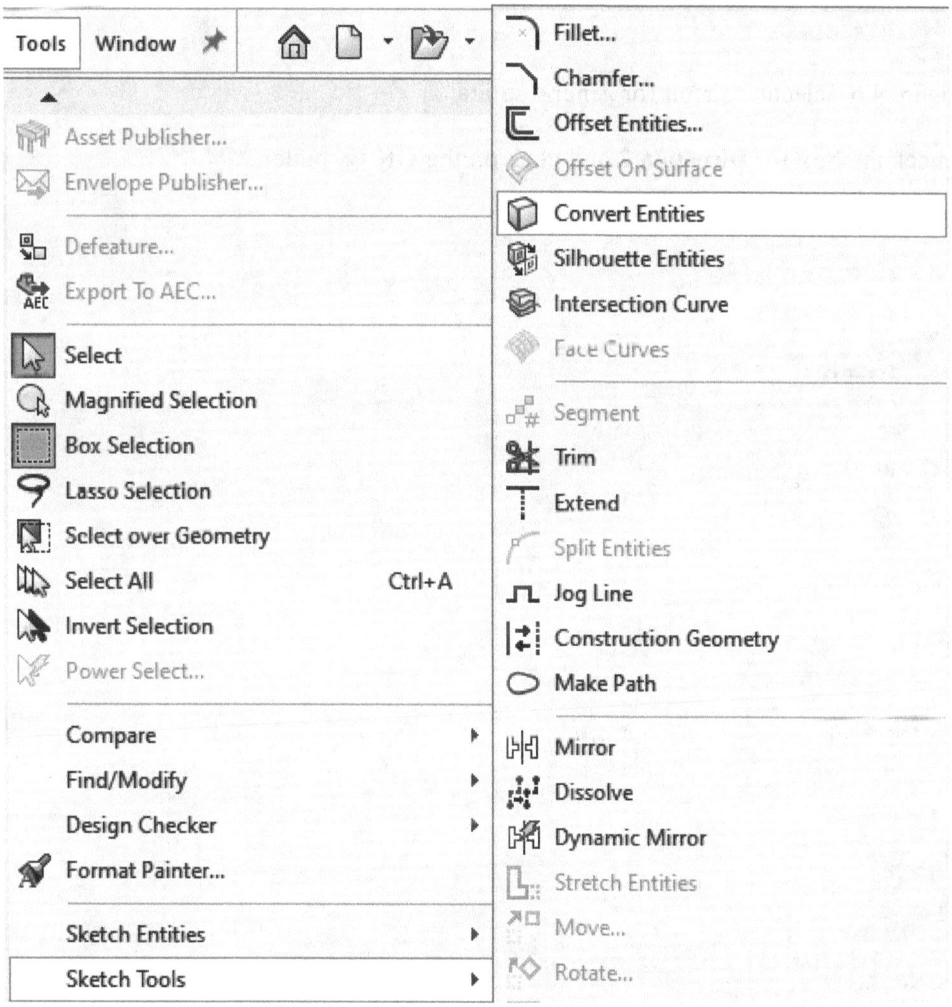

Figure 4.5 Convert entities sketch tool

6. Select the airfoil in the graphics window and click on the **OK** ✓ button in the **Generic Spline** section. Select the **Analysis Preparation** tab and select **Extruded Boss/Base** once again.

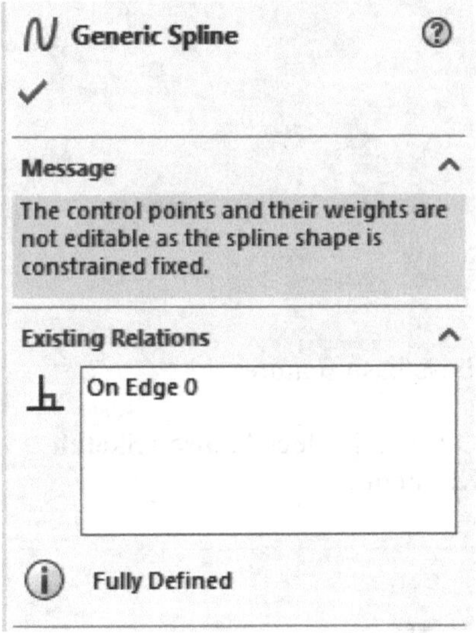

Figure 4.6 Selecting airfoil for generic spline

7. Check the box for **Direction 2** and click on the **OK** ✓ button.

Figure 4.7 Entering the direction of the extrusion

8. Select the **Front** view from the drop-down menu in the graphics window. Right click in the graphics window and select **Zoom/Pan/Rotate>>Zoom to Fit**. Save your airfoil as **SD 2030**.

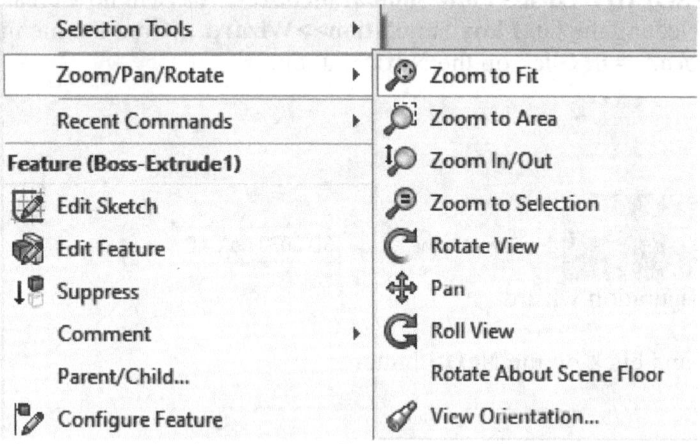

Figure 4.8 Selecting zoom to fit

9. Click on the arrow next to the **Boss-Extrude1** symbol in the **FeatureManager design tree** and rename the sketch to **Airfoil Sketch** and the extrusion to **Extruded Airfoil Sketch**. You have now finished your **SD 2030** section. Save the part.

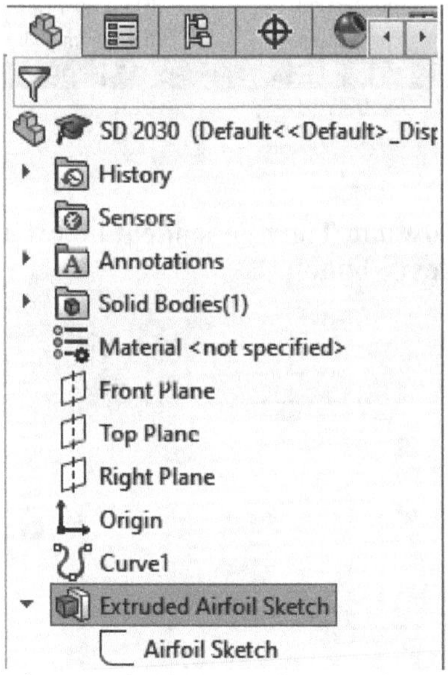

Figure 4.9 Change of name for the extrusion

D. Setting Up Flow Simulation Project

10. If Flow Simulation is not available in the SOLIDWORKS menu, select **Tools>>Add Ins...** and check the corresponding **SOLIDWORKS Flow Simulation** boxes. We will now create a Flow Simulation project by selecting the tab **Flow Simulation>>Wizard...** from the menu. Enter Project name: **SD 2030 AoA = 0**. Click on the **Next>** button.

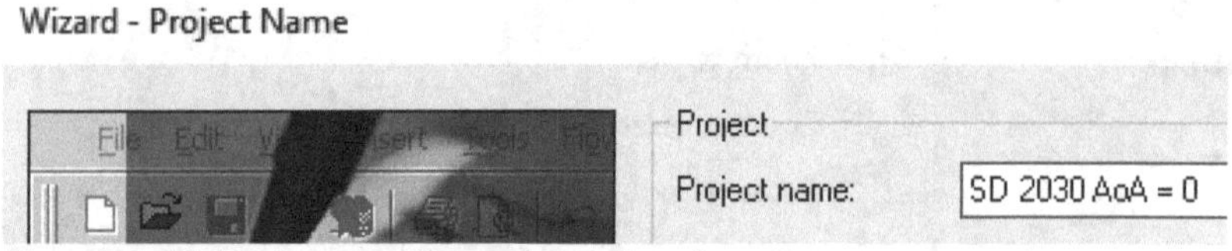

Figure 4.10 Project configuration wizard

11. Choose **SI Unit system** and click on the **Next>** button

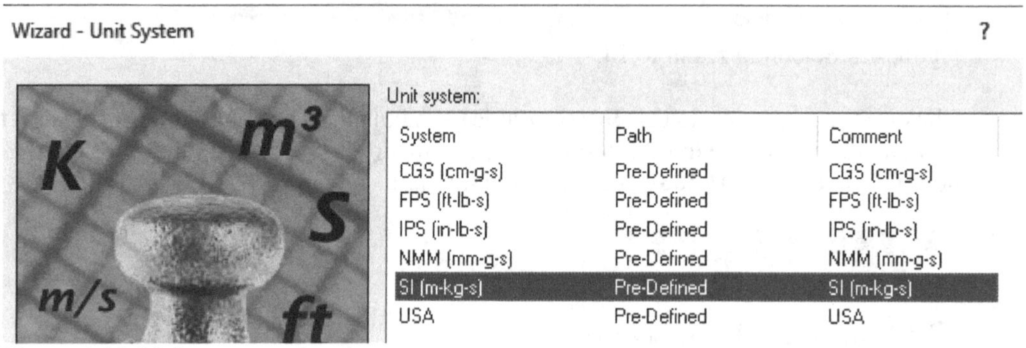

Figure 4.11 Unit system wizard

12. Select the **External Analysis type**, check the **Fluid Flow** and **Time-dependent** boxes, uncheck Exclude cavities without conditions and click the **Next>** button.

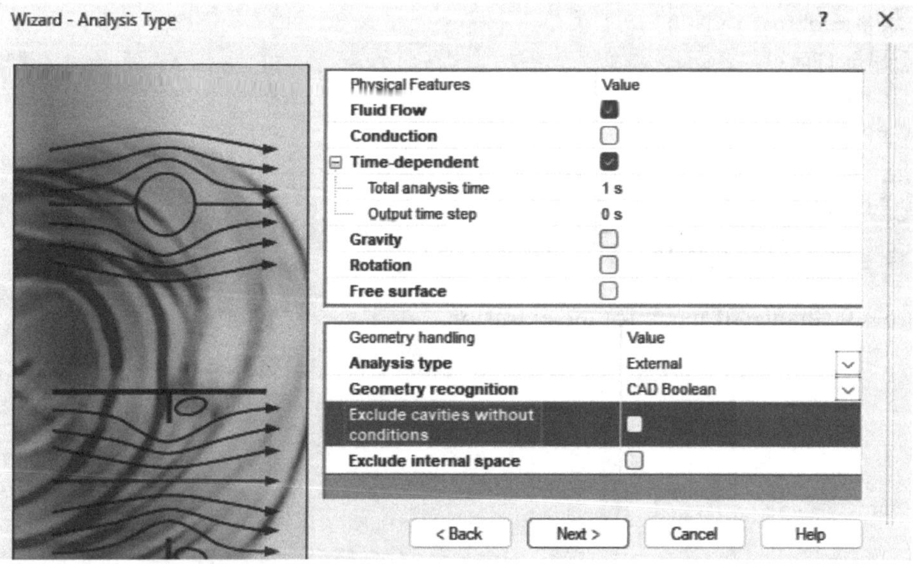

Figure 4.12 External time-dependent flow

13. Choose **Air** from the gases in the **Fluids** window and push the **Add** button. Air will now appear as the **Default Project Fluid**. Click on the **Next>** button.

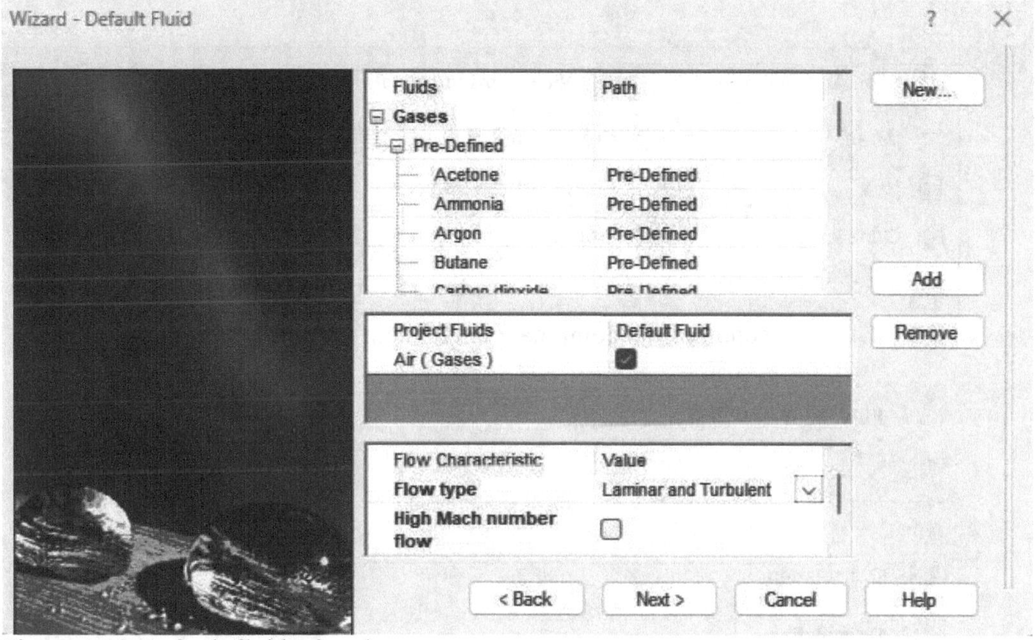

Figure 4.13 Default fluid wizard

14. In the next step we will leave the default value of the surface roughness as **Wall Condition** and click on the **Next>** button. Enter **4.9 m/s** as the **Velocity in X direction** and **0.12%** as **Turbulence intensity** from the **Turbulence Parameters** section. Click on the **Finish** button.

    Select **Tools>>Flow Simulation>>Global Mesh** from the menu. Slide the **Level of Initial Mesh** to **6.** Exit the **Global Mesh Settings**. Select **Tools>>Flow Simulation>>Project>>Show Basic Mesh**.

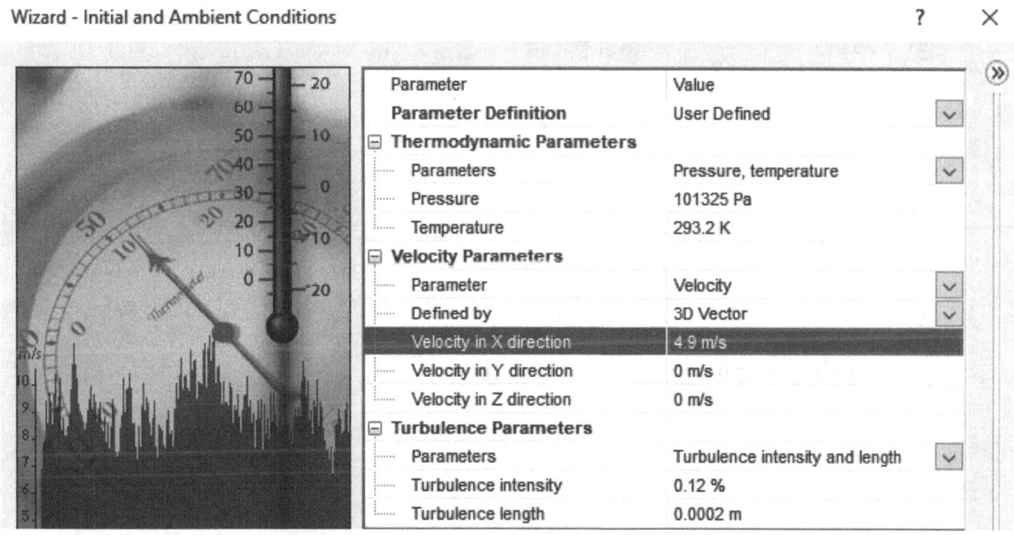

Figure 4.14 Adding velocity and turbulence intensity

15. Select the tab **Flow Simulation>>Computational Domain...** from the menu. Select **2D simulation** and **XY plane** from the **Type** section. Enter the values as shown in figure 4.15b). Select the **OK** button.

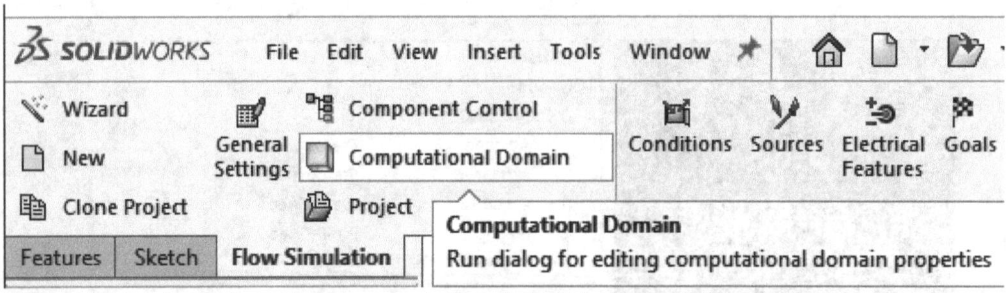

Figure 4.15a) Selection of the computational domain in Flow Simulation

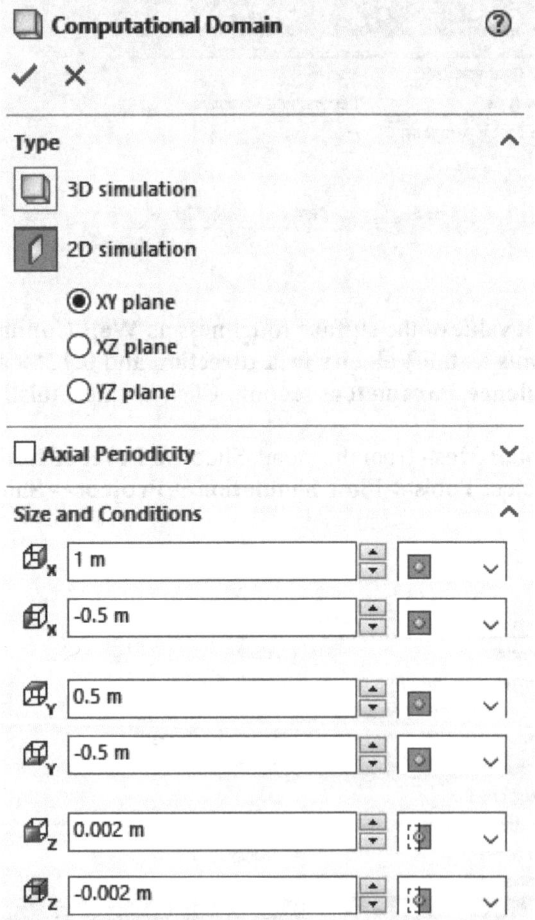

Figure 4.15b) Computational domain settings

E. Inserting Global Goals

16. Click on the **Flow Simulation analysis tree** tab and open the **Input Data** folder by clicking on the plus sign next to it. Right click on **Goals** and select **Insert Global Goals....** Check the box for **Force (X)**, **Force (Y)** and click on the **OK** button to exit the **Global Goals** window.

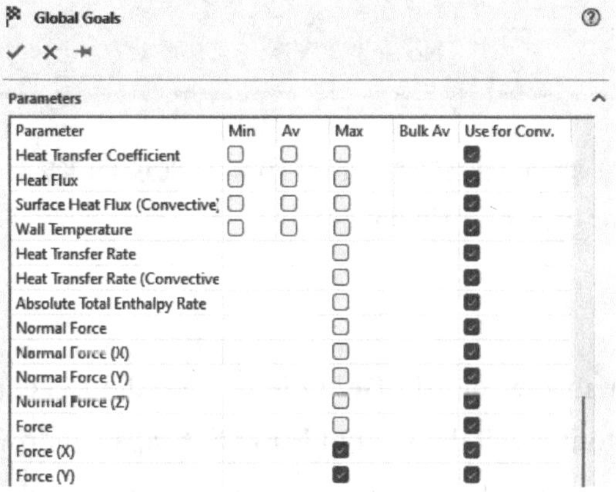

Figure 4.16 Selecting global goal

F. Inserting Equation Goals

17. Right-click on **Goals** under **Input Data** in the **Flow Simulation analysis tree** and select **Insert Equation Goal....** Enter the expression for the lift coefficient by clicking on the **GG Force (Y) 2** goal under **Goals** in the **Flow Simulation analysis tree**. Complete the expressions as shown below, in figure 4.17b) and in equation (4.1) in the theory section. You will also select **GG Force (X) 1** when you enter this expression:

({GG Force (Y) 2}*cos(0*3.14159265/180)-{GG Force (X) 1}*sin(0*3.14159265/180))/(0.5*1.204*4.9^2*0.004*0.305)

Select **No unit** from the **Dimensionality:** drop down menu. Enter the name **Lift Coefficient** and click on the **OK** button to exit the **Equation Goal** window. Repeat this step for the **Drag Coefficient.**

({GG Force (X) 1}*cos(0*3.14159265/180)+{GG Force (Y) 2}*sin(0*3.14159265/180))/(0.5*1.204*4.9^2*0.004*0.305)

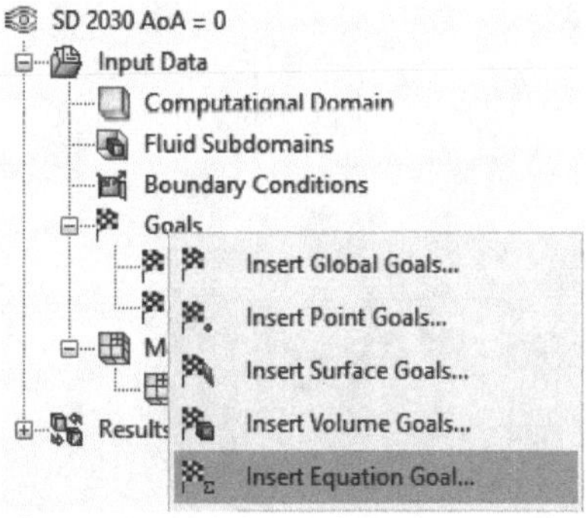

Figure 4.17a) Inserting an equation goal

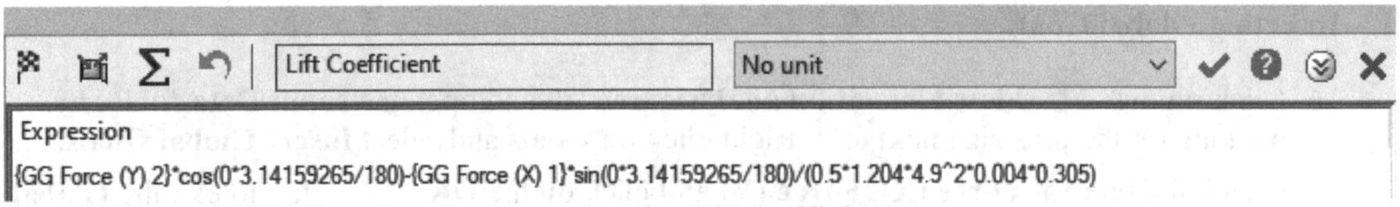

Figure 4.17b) Entering the expression for lift coefficient

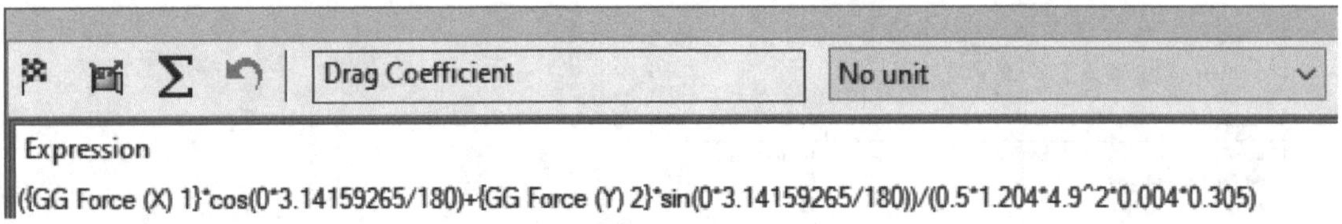

Figure 4.17c) Entering the expression for drag coefficient

G. Global and Local Mesh

18. Right click on **Global Mesh** under **Mesh** and select **Edit Definition…**. Set the **Level of initial mesh** to **4** and click on the **OK** button to exit the **Global Mesh Settings** window. Select **Tools>>Flow Simulation>>Insert>>Local Mesh** from the menu. Select **Region** under **Selection** and check **Cuboid**. Enter **0.35**, **-0.05** as **Xmax, Xmin, 0.04**, **-0.03** as **Ymax, Ymin** and **0.001**, **-0.001** as **Zmax, Zmin**. Set **Level of Refining Fluid Cells** to **1** and **Level of Refining Cells at Fluid/Solid Boundary** to **3**. Uncheck the boxes for **Channels**, **Advanced Refinement** and **Close Thin Slots**. Click on the **OK** button to exit the **Local Mesh Settings** window.

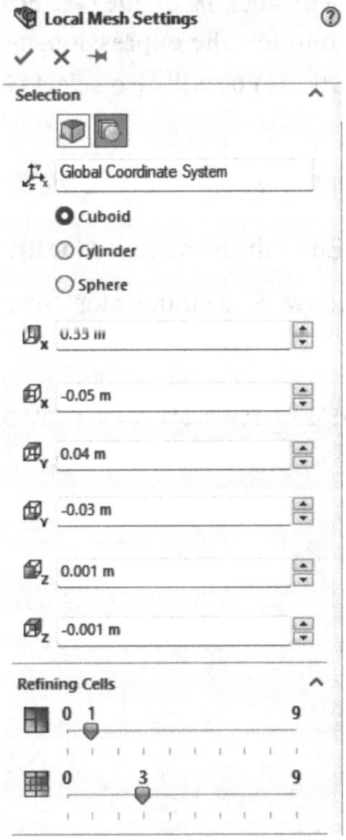

Figure 4.18a) Local mesh settings

Right click in the graphics window and select **Zoom In/Out** and zoom out until you can see the entire computational domain around the airfoil. Select **Tools>>Flow Simulation>>Project>>Show Basic Mesh** to see the mesh surrounding the airfoil.

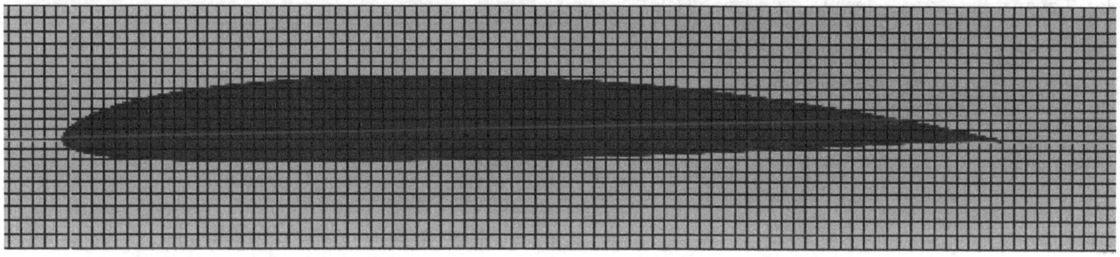

Figure 4.18b) Mesh around the airfoil

H. Running Simulations

19. Select the tab **Flow Simulation>>Run**. Push the **Run** button in the Run window.

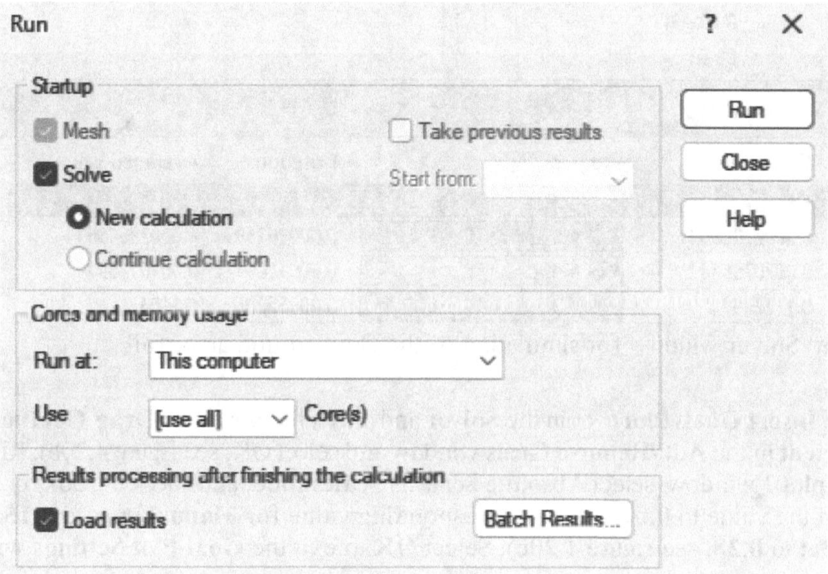

Figure 4.19 Calculations of the flow field

20. Select **Insert Goal Table...** from the menu of the **Solver**.

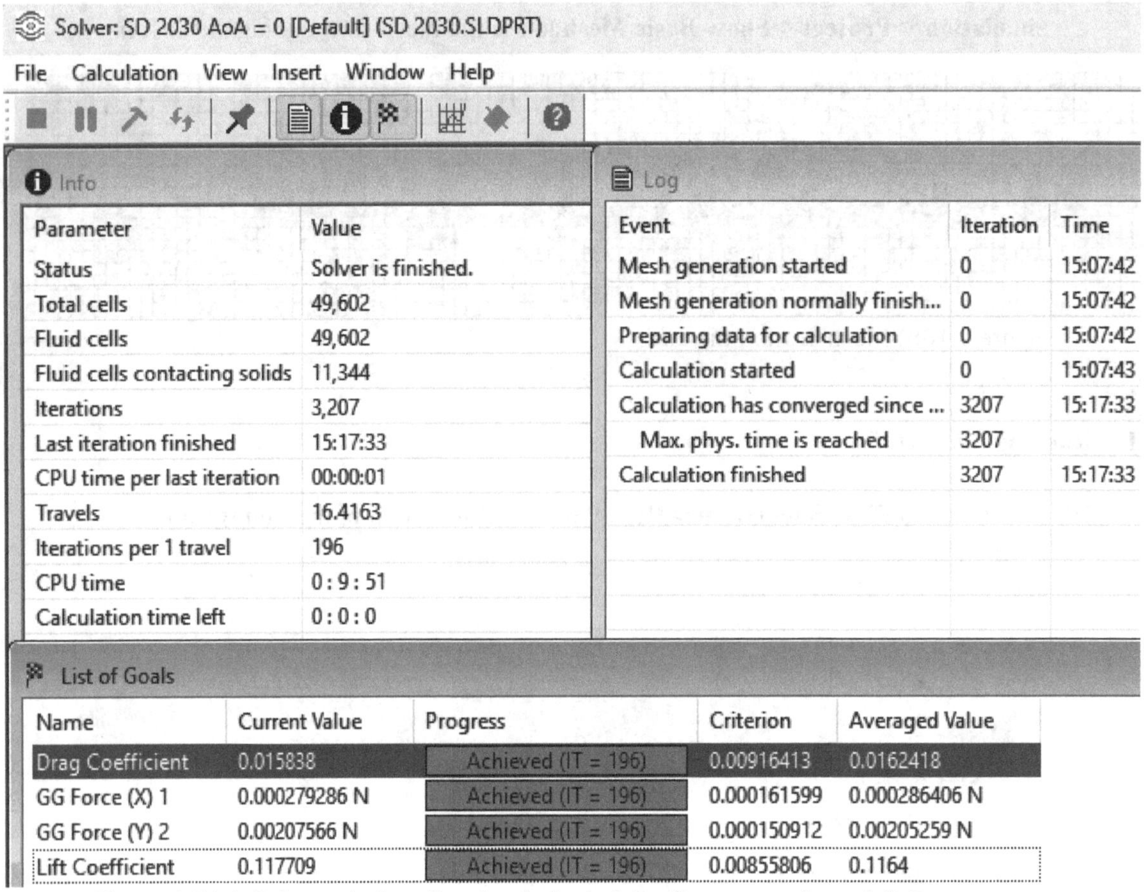

Figure 4.20a) Solver window for simulation of the flow around an airfoil

Click on the **Insert Goals Plot** in the **Solver** and check the boxes for **Drag Coefficient** and **Lift Coefficient** in the **Add/Remove Goals** window and select OK, see figure 4.20b). Right click in the **Goal plot 1** window, select **Absolute Scale** as **Scale mode:** and check the box for **Manual min:** and set the value to **0.01**. Set the corresponding value for **Manual max** to **0.15**. Set the **Length scale:** to **0.28**, see figure 4.20c). Select **OK** to exit the **Goal Plot Settings** window.

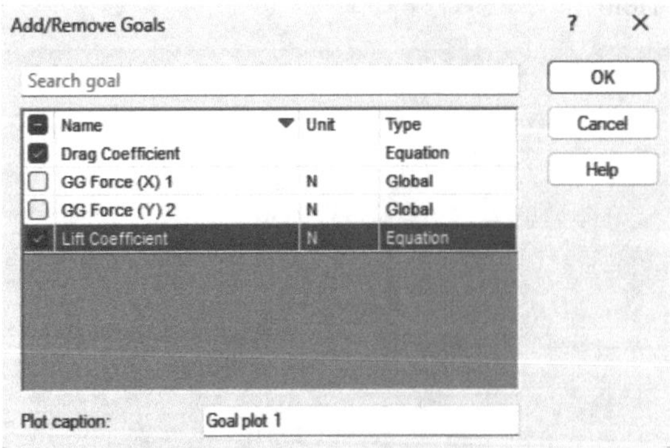

Figure 4.20b) Solver window

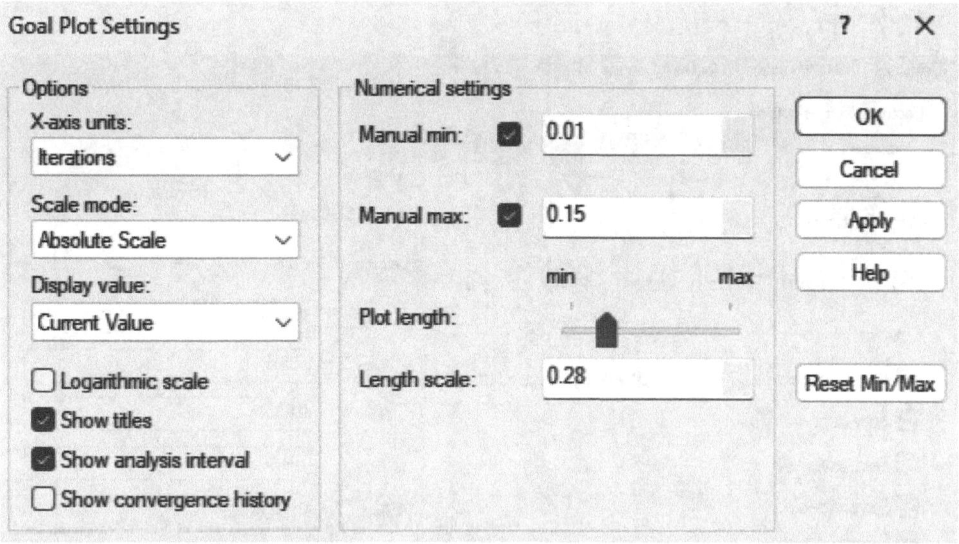

Figure 4.20c) Goal Plot settings

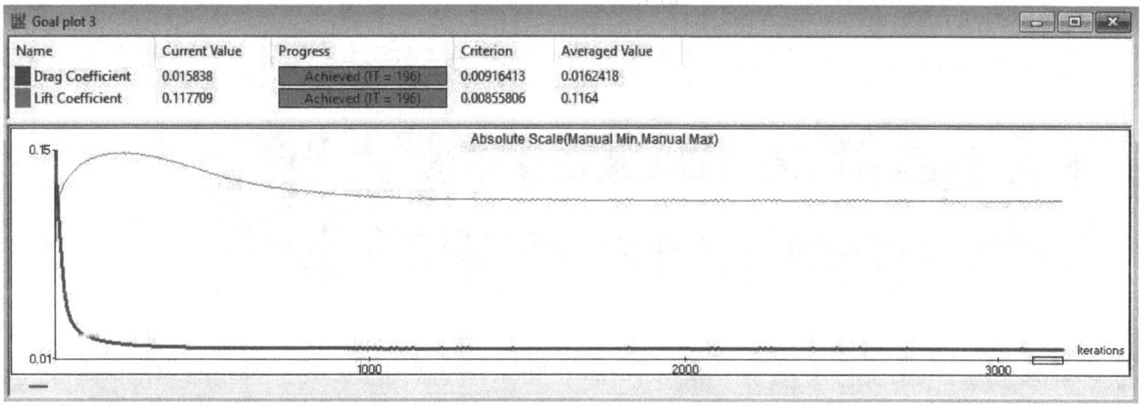

Figure 4.20d) Goal plot window

During the simulation, click on the **Insert Preview** in the **Solver** and select the **Definition** tab and the **Front Plane** and **Contours** as **Mode**, see Figure 4.20f). Select the **Settings** tab and select **Velocity** as **Parameter:** under **Contours/Isolines options**. Select the **Options** tab and check the box for **Display mesh**. Select the **Region** tab and set values as shown in Figure 4.20f).

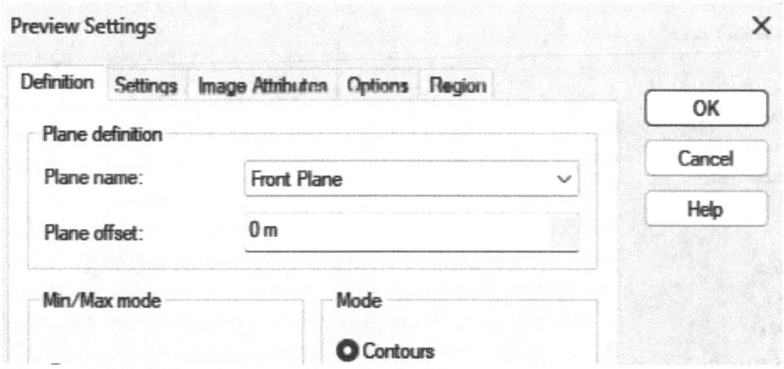

Figure 4.20e) Preview settings definition

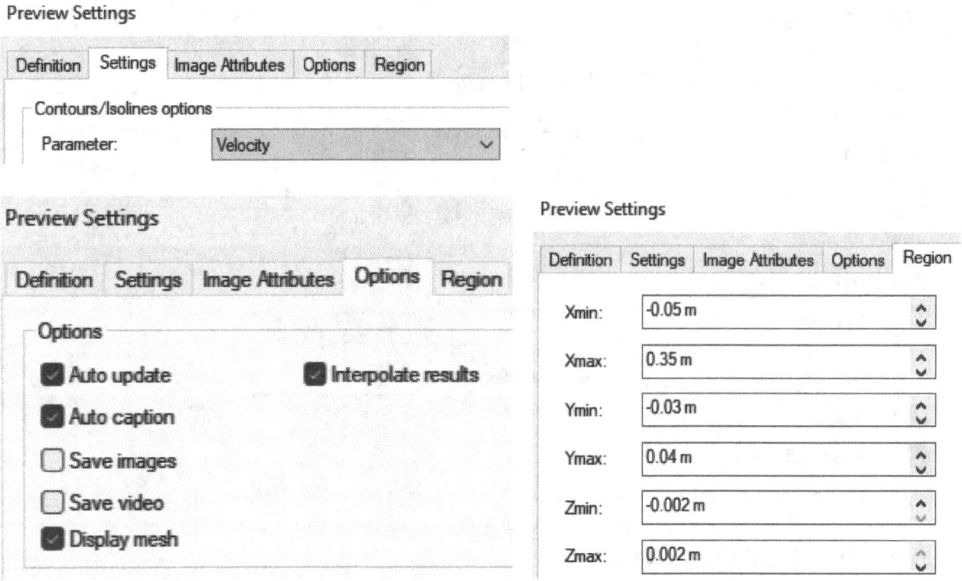

Figure 4.20f) Preview setting windows

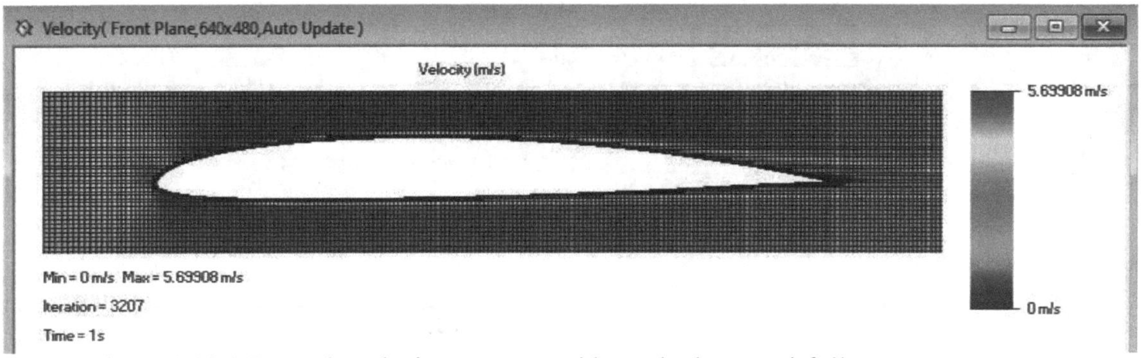

Figure 4.20g) Example velocity contours with mesh close to airfoil

I. Using Cut Plots

21. Select the **Flow Simulation** tab connected to the **Flow Simulation analysis tree**. Right click on **Mesh** and select **Hide Basic Mesh**.

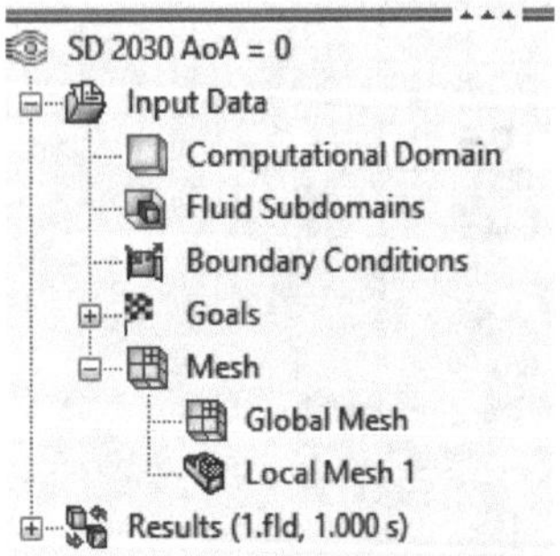

Figure 4.21 Flow Simulation analysis tree

22. Open the **Results** folder and right-click on the **Cut Plots** in the **Flow Simulation analysis tree** and select **Insert....** Slide the **Number of Levels** in the **Contours** section to **255** and exit the cut plot window. Select from the menu **Tools>>Flow Simulation>>Results>>Display>>Lighting.** Select the scale in the graphics window, right click and select **Make Horizontal.** Right click on **SD 2030 AoA = 0** and select Hide Global Coordinate System. Rename the **Cut Plot** in the **Flow Simulation analysis tree** to **Pressure.** Select **Tools>>Flow Simulation>>Results>>Screen Capture>>Save Image...** and click Save to save the image.

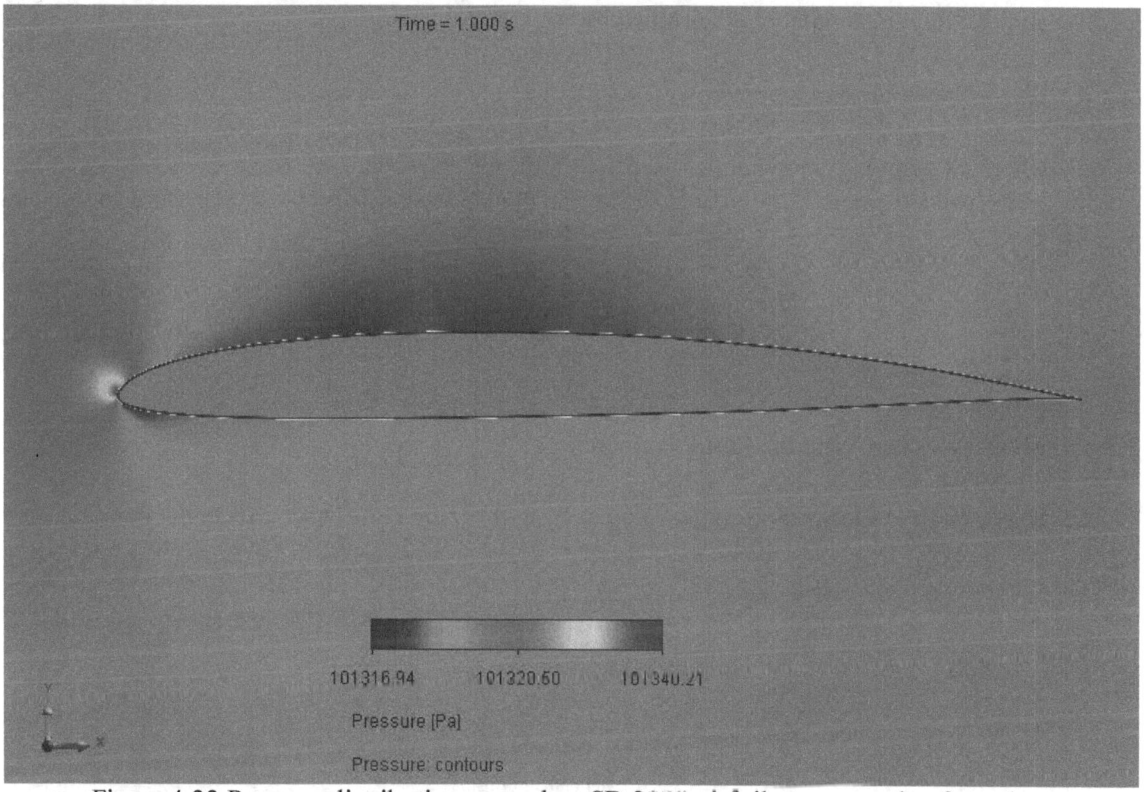

Figure 4.22 Pressure distribution around an SD 2030 airfoil at zero angle of attack

J. Theory

23. If we look at the Current Value for the force in the Solver window, we see that the lift force is L = 0.00207566 N for the Y-component and the drag force is D = 0.000279286 N for the X-component. The lift and drag coefficients can for positive angles of attack be determined from

$$C_L = \frac{L \cdot Cos\alpha - D \cdot Sin\alpha}{\frac{1}{2}\rho U^2 bc} \tag{4.1}$$

$$C_D = \frac{D \cdot Cos\alpha + L \cdot Sin\alpha}{\frac{1}{2}\rho U^2 bc} \tag{4.2}$$

The drag polar can be expressed as

$$C_D = C_{D0} + K(C_L - C_{L0})^2 = K{C_L}^2 - 2KC_{L0}C_L + \left(C_{D0} + K{C_{L0}}^2\right) = K{C_L}^2 - AC_L + B \qquad (4.3)$$

where ρ (kg/m^3) is the free-stream density, U (m/s) is the free-stream velocity, b (m) is the airfoil wingspan, c (m) is the chord length of the airfoil, α is the angle of attack and C_{D0},C_{L0},K are constants. The value for b used is the difference between $Z\,max$ and $Z\,min$ in the computational domain. The lift coefficient has been determined using Flow Simulation at zero angle of attack and at a Reynolds number determined by

$$Re = \frac{Uc\rho}{\mu} = \frac{4.9 \cdot 0.305 \cdot 1.204}{1.8 \cdot 10^{-5}} = 100{,}000 \qquad (4.4)$$

where μ (kg/ms) is the dynamic viscosity of air in the free-stream. Next, we want to plot the pressure distribution on the airfoil expressed in dimensionless form by the pressure coefficient

$$C_p = \frac{p_i - p}{\frac{1}{2}\rho U^2} \qquad (4.5)$$

where p_i (Pa) is the surface pressure at location i and p (Pa) is the pressure in the free-stream.

K. Creating a Custom Visualization Parameter

24. Select **Tools>>Flow Simulation>>Tools>>Engineering Database...** from the menu.

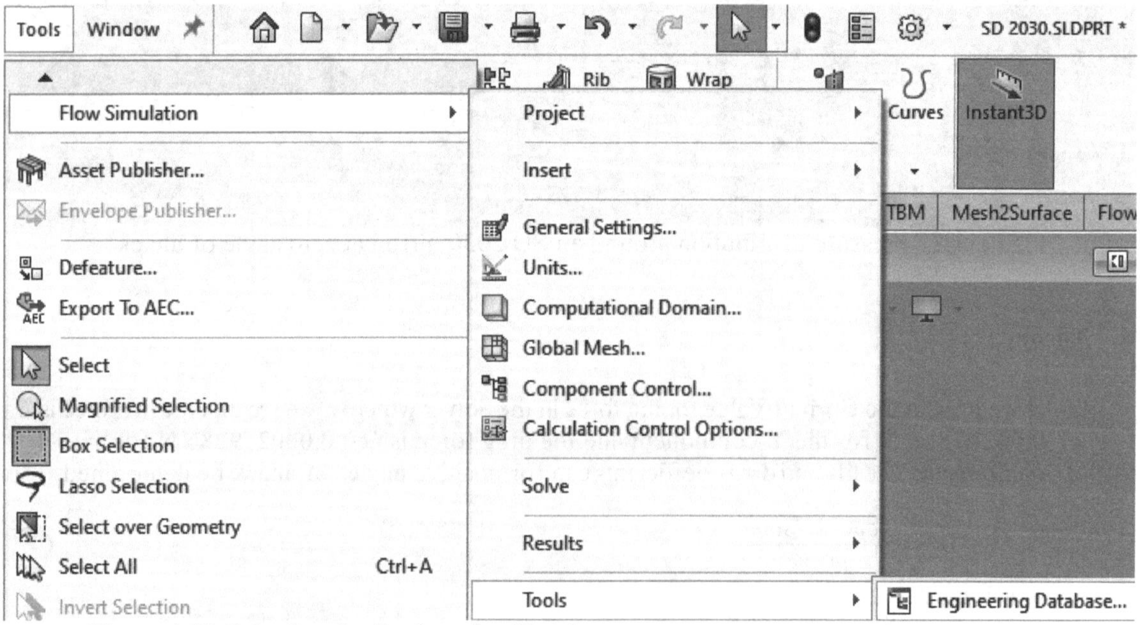

Figure 4.23 Selecting the Engineering Database

25. In the **Database tree** expand the **Custom Visualization Parameters** item, right-click the **User Defined** item and select **New Item.**

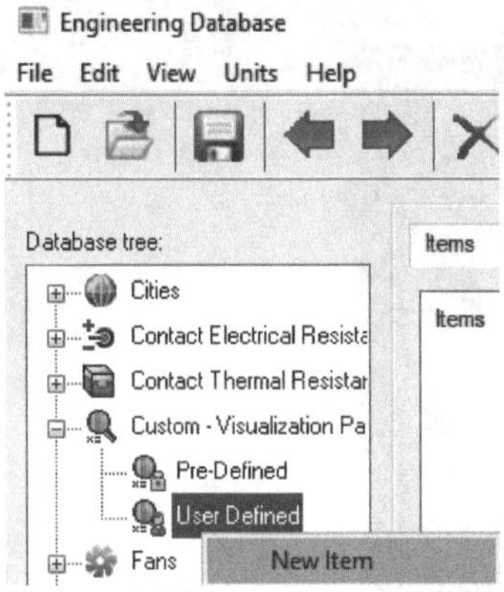

Figure 4.24 Creating a New Visualization Parameter

26. Under the **Item Properties** tab, type the parameter's **Name** as **Pressure Coefficient**.

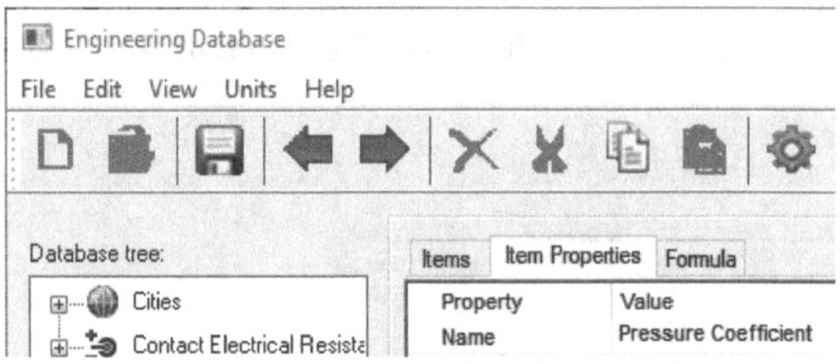

Figure 4.25 Enter a name for the new parameter

27. In the **Formula** row under Item Properties tab, click on **...** and specify the parameter definition as **Pressure**, see figure 4.26. The formula that you enter will be the following: ({Pressure}-101324)/(0.5*1.204*4.9^2). Select **File, Save** from the **Engineering Database** menu and exit the engineering database window.

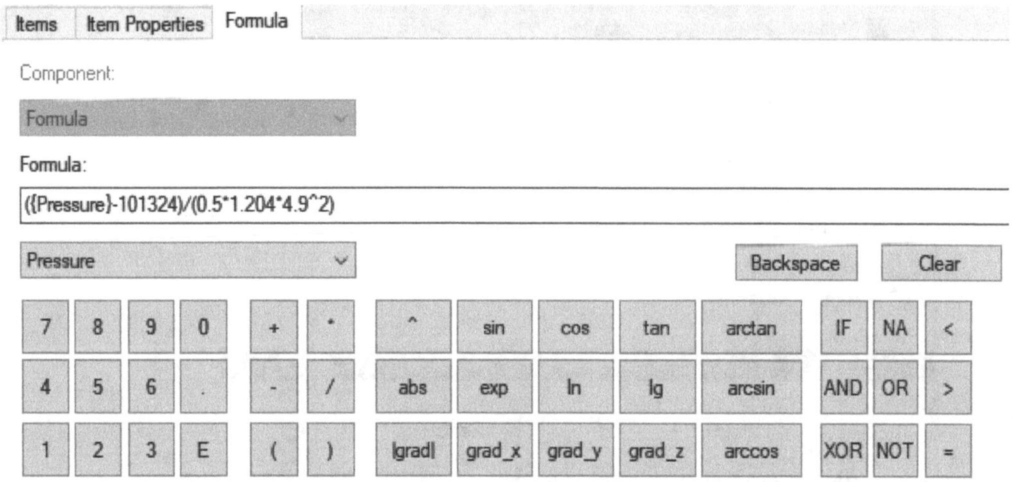

Figure 4.26 Entering a formula for the new parameter

28. Right-click on the **XY Plots** and select **Insert...** from the **Flow Simulation analysis tree**. Click on the **FeatureManager design tree** tab and select the **Airfoil Sketch** under the **Extruded Airfoil Sketch**.

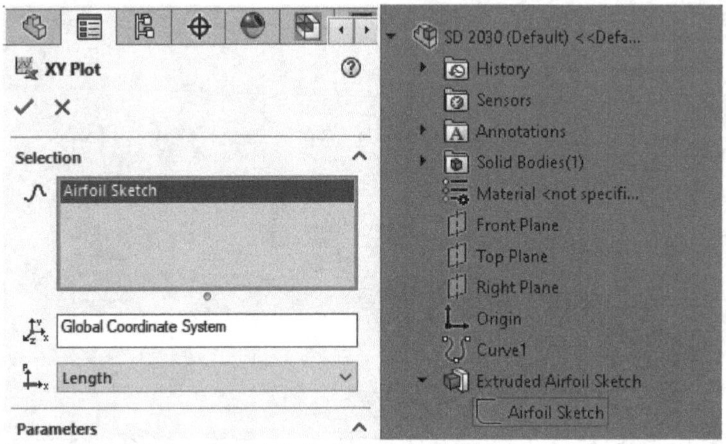

Figure 4.27 Selecting airfoil sketch for XY Plot

29. Click on **More Parameters...** and check the box for **Pressure Coefficient** under **Custom**.

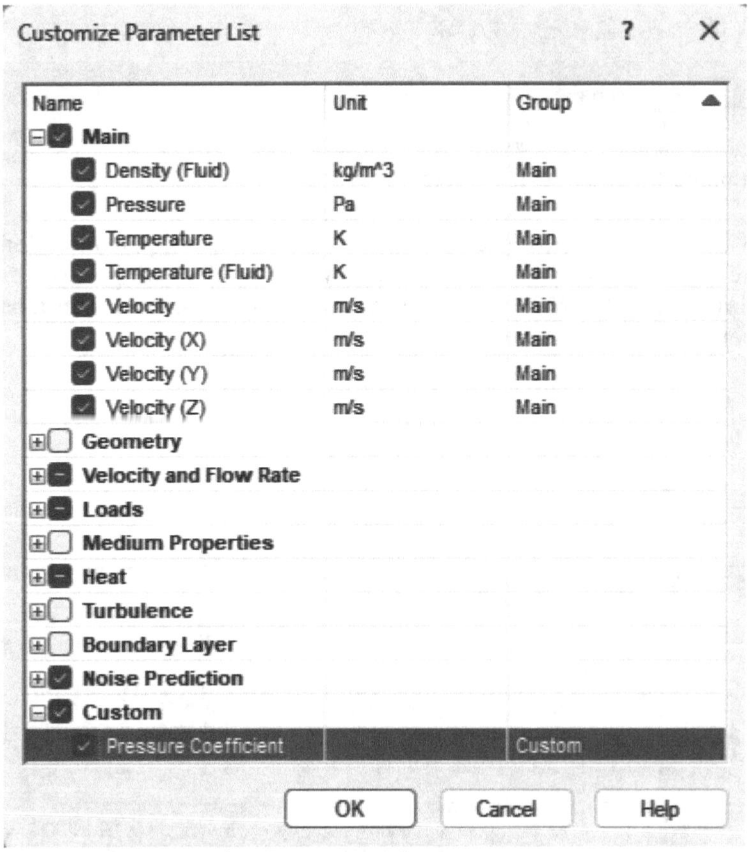

Figure 4.28 Customize Parameter List

30. Next, check **Pressure Coefficient** in the **Parameter** list of the **XY Plot window** and choose **Model X** for the **Abscissa** in the same window. Open the **Options** portion of the **XY Plot** window and select **Excel Workbook (*.xlsx)** from the drop-down menu.

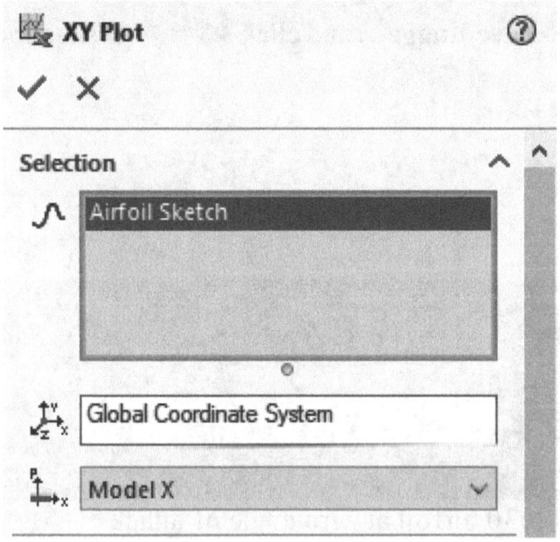

Figure 4.29 Selecting Sketch X for the abscissa

31. Click on the **Export to Excel** button and an Excel graph will be generated showing the variation of the pressure coefficient over the airfoil. Rename the **XY Plot** in the **Flow Simulation analysis tree** to **Pressure Coefficient**.

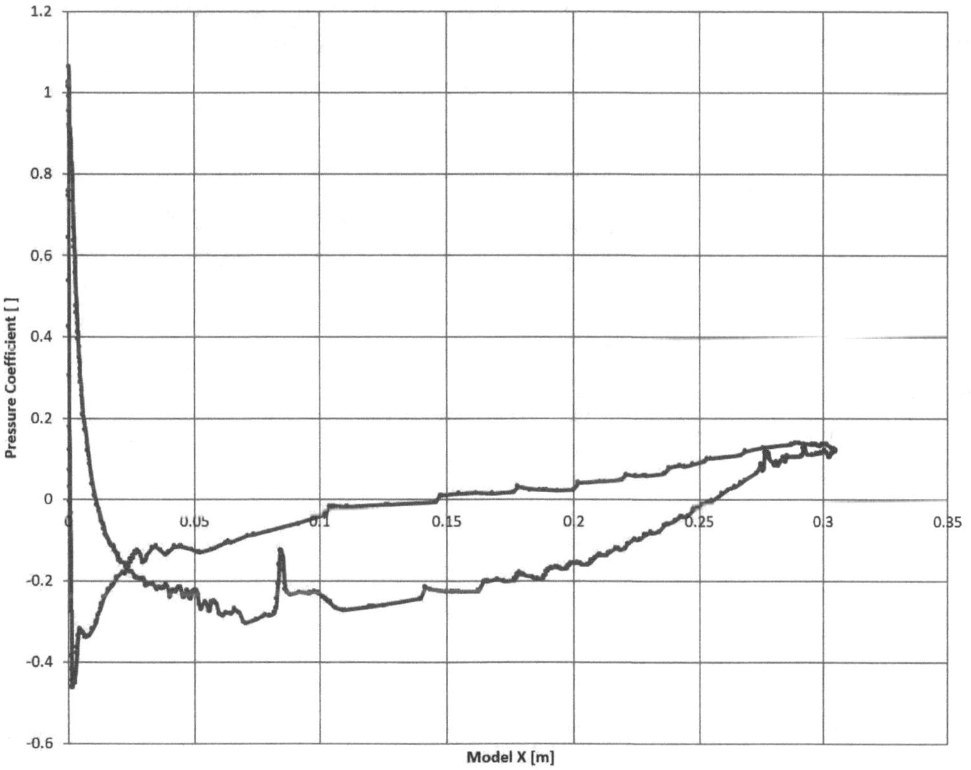

Figure 4.30 Variation of pressure coefficient on SD 2030 airfoil at zero angle of attack

32. Insert a new **Cut Plot** in the **Flow Simulation analysis tree**. Choose **Velocity** from the **Parameter Settings** drop down menu in the **Contours** section. Exit the **Cut Plot** window to display the velocity field over the airfoil. You will need to right click on the Pressure cut plot and select Hide. Rename the new **Cut Plot** as **Velocity**. Select **Tools>>Flow Simulation>>Results>>Screen Capture>>Save Image...** and click Save to save the image.

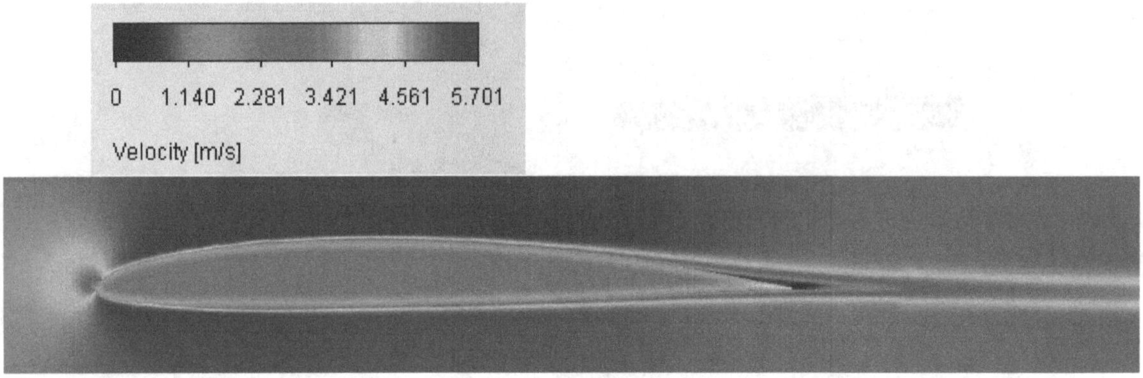

Figure 4.31 Velocity field around the SD 2030 airfoil at zero angle of attack

L. Cloning of Project

33. Select **Tools>>Flow Simulation>>Project>>Clone Project....** Create a cloned project with the name **SD 2030 AoA = 1 degree**. Exit the **Clone Project** window.

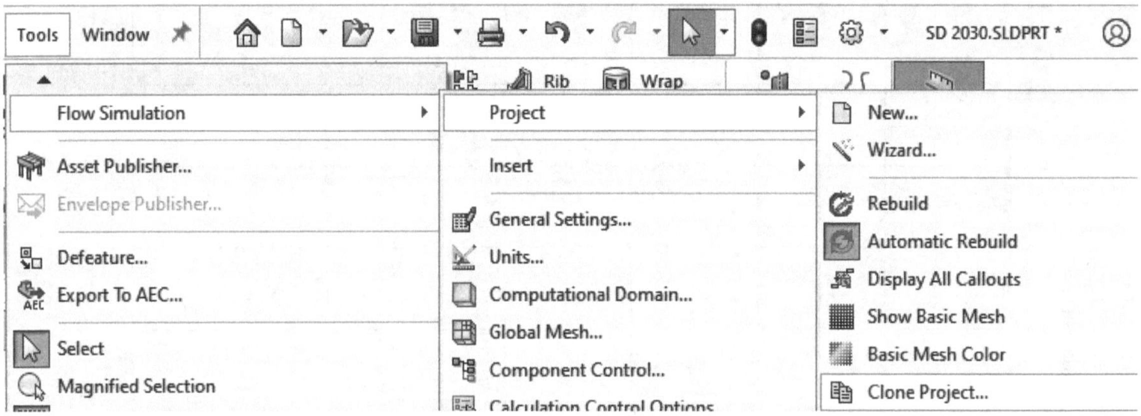

Figure 4.32 Cloning of the project

34. Select **Tools>>Flow Simulation>>General Settings….** Click on **Initial and ambient conditions** in the **Navigator**. Enter **4.8993 m/s** as **Velocity in X-direction** and **0.0855 m/s** as **Velocity in Y-direction** corresponding to an angle of attack of **1°**. Click on **Apply** and the **OK** button to exit the window. Also, change the angle of attack in Lift and Drag Coefficient Goals in line with equations (4.1) – (4.4). You will replace the 0 degree inside the sine and cosine expressions with the new angle 1 degree. Repeat steps **33** and **34** nineteen more times and change the angles of attack and corresponding velocity components as shown in Table 4.1.

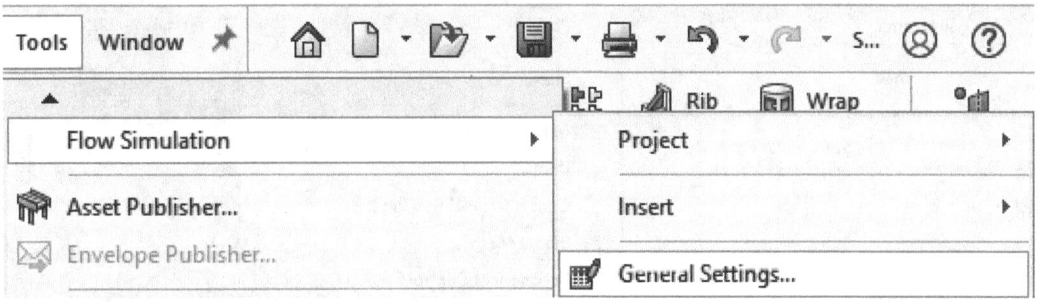

Figure 4.33 Selection of general settings

Number	Angle of Attack	X – Velocity (m/s)	Y – Velocity (m/s)
1	-7°	4.8635	-0.5972
2	-6°	4.8732	-0.5122
3	-5°	4.8814	-0.4271
4	-4°	4.8881	-0.3418
5	-3°	4.8933	-0.2564
6	-2°	4.8970	-0.1710
7	-1°	4.8993	-0.0855
8	0°	4.9000	0.0000
9	1°	4.8993	0.0855
10	2°	4.8970	0.1710
11	3°	4.8933	0.2564
12	4°	4.8881	0.3418
13	5°	4.8814	0.4271
14	6°	4.8732	0.5122
15	7°	4.8635	0.5972
16	8°	4.8523	0.6819
17	9°	4.8397	0.7665
18	10°	4.8256	0.8509
19	11°	4.8100	0.9350
20	12°	4.7929	1.0188

Table 4.1 Velocity component for different angles of attack

M. Creating a Batch Run

35. Select **Tools>>Flow Simulation>>Solve>>Batch Run…**. Make sure to check all boxes as shown in figure 4.34b). Click on the **Run** button to start the calculations.

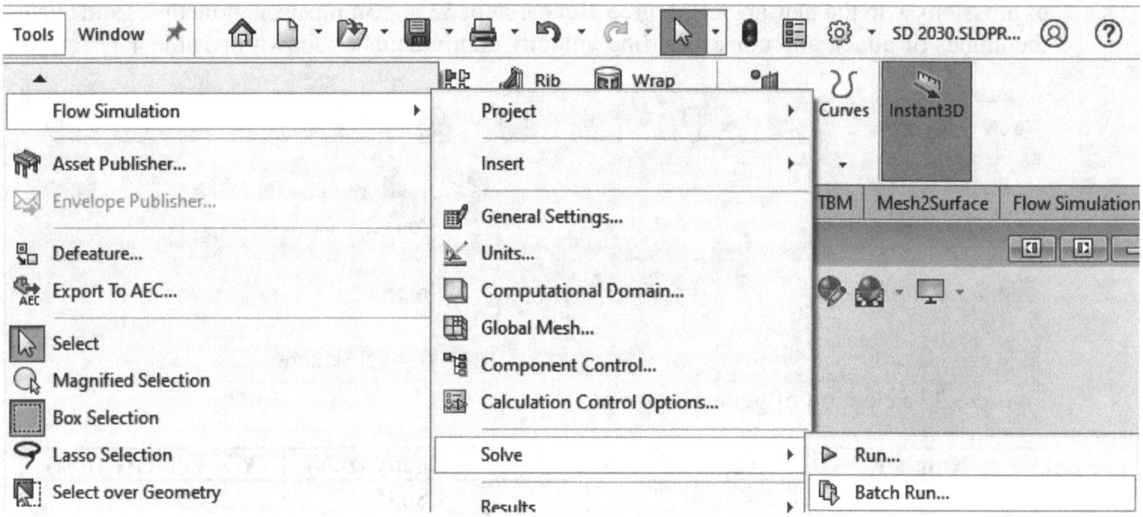

Figure 4.34a) Starting the batch run for different angles of attack

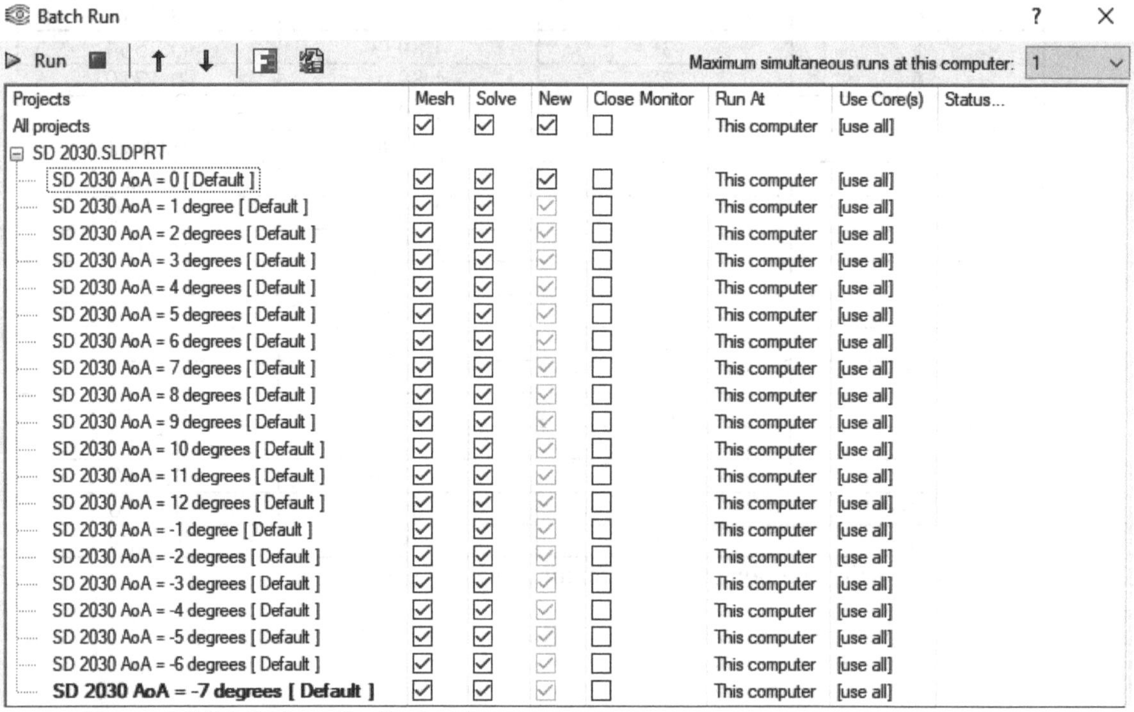

Figure 4.34b) Settings for the batch run

Angle of Attack (deg.) Flow Simulation	Lift Coefficient Flow Simulation	Drag Coefficient Flow Simulation	Angle of Attack (deg.) Experiment	Lift Coefficient Experiment	Drag Coefficient Experiment
-7	-0.392367	0.0548807			
-6	-0.330221	0.034464	-6.02	-0.414	0.0531
-5	-0.240997	0.0294073	-4.95	-0.339	0.0321
-4	-0.177137	0.0240633	-3.98	-0.262	0.0238
-3	-0.0926524	0.0191533	-2.99	-0.17	0.0189
-2.12	0	0.0168121	-1.9	-0.074	0.0136
-2	0.012134	0.0165055	-0.93	0.011	0.0138
-1	0.0910754	0.0160251	0.11	0.122	0.0154
0	0.1163	0.0161858	1.14	0.231	0.0163
1	0.262546	0.0178499	2.17	0.403	0.0188
2	0.362112	0.0201438	3.17	0.574	0.0171
3	0.461066	0.0226007	4.26	0.693	0.0154
4	0.553026	0.0254549	5.29	0.784	0.0147
5	0.665671	0.0287641	6.32	0.873	0.017
6	0.656815	0.0259	7.33	0.945	0.0215
7	0.839739	0.0426503	8.34	1	0.0269
8	0.89976	0.0553698	9.36	1.051	0.0351
9	0.976069	0.0852295	10.34	1.09	0.0437
10	0.97896	0.0891607	11.39	1.105	0.0679
11	0.909934	0.125812			
12	0.921958	0.1304			

Table 4.2 Lift coefficient for different angles of attack, experimental results from Selig and McGranaham (2004), $Re = 100{,}000$

The figure below shows a comparison of experimental results and Flow Simulation calculations for $Re = 100{,}000$. It is seen that Flow Simulation values for the lift coefficient have a linear trendline. The lift slope $a_0 = 0.0879$. The zero-lift angle of attack is $\alpha_{L=0} = -2.12°$. The drag coefficient is shown in figure 4.34d) and the drag polar in 4.35e).

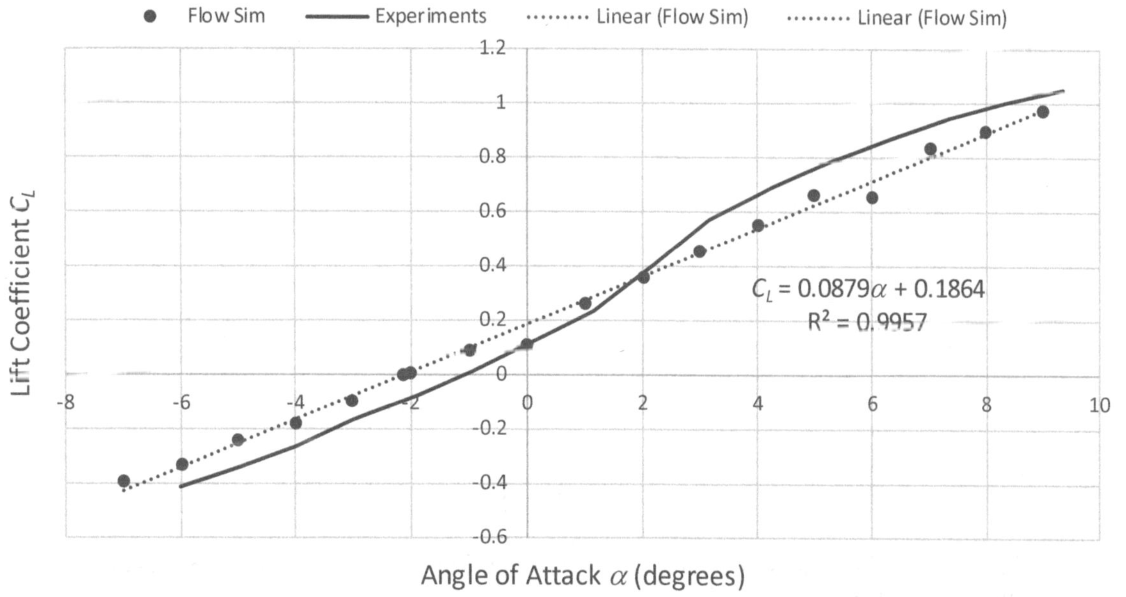

Figure 4.34c) Comparison of lift coefficient for experiments (line) with Flow Simulation results

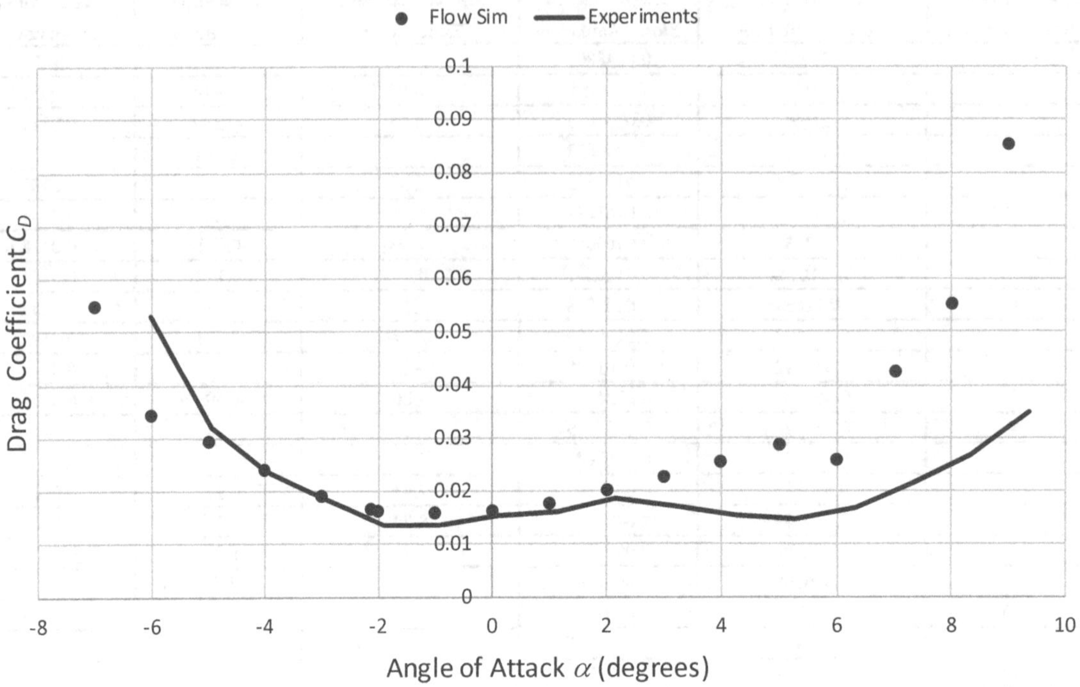

Figure 4.34d) Comparison of drag coefficient for experiments (line) with Flow Simulation results (filled circles)

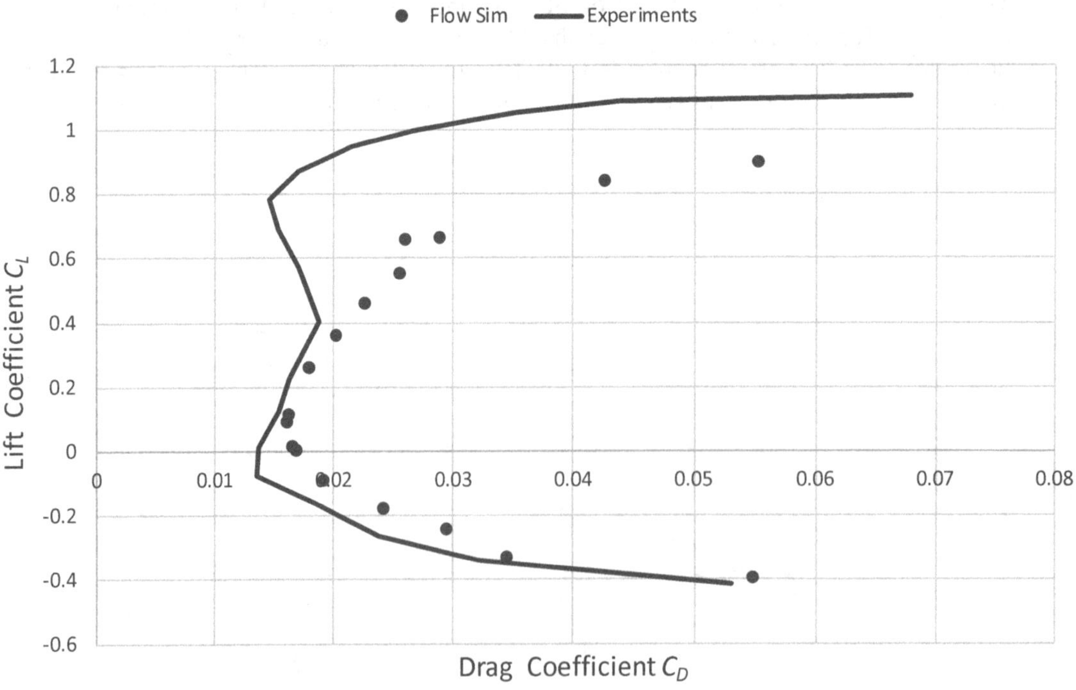

Figure 4.34e) Comparison of drag polar for experiments (line) with Flow Simulation results (filled circles).

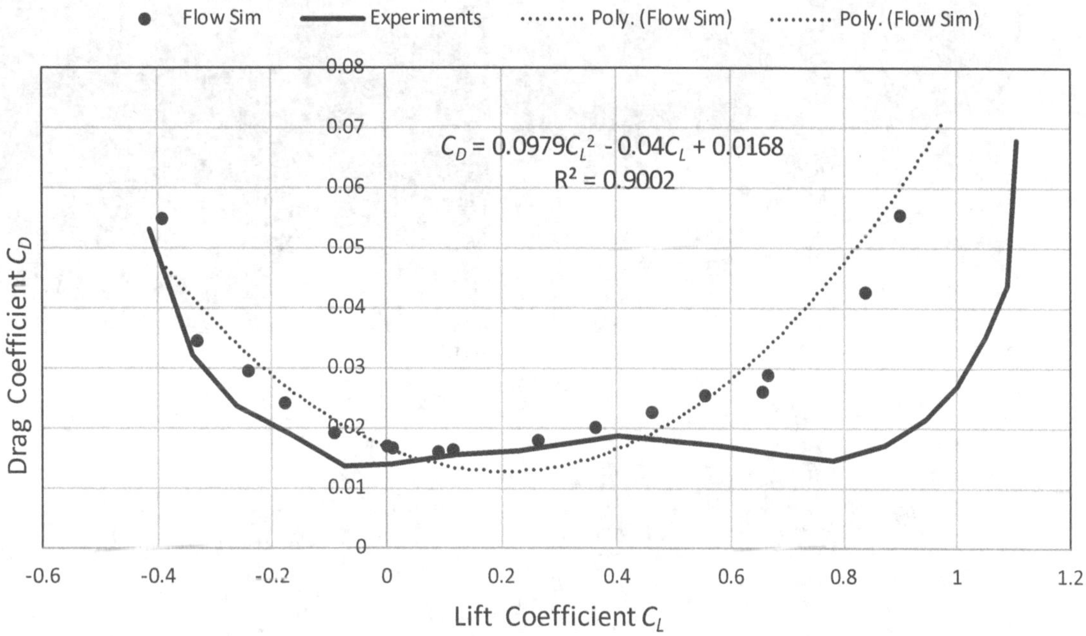

Figure 4.34f) Comparison of drag polar for experiments (line) with Flow Simulation results (filled circles). From Flow Simulation results: $C_{D0} = 0.0127,\ C_{L0} = 0.2043, K = 0.0979$.

$$C_D = C_{D0} + K(C_L - C_{L0})^2 = KC_L{}^2 - 2KC_{L0}C_L + \left(C_{D0} + KC_{L0}{}^2\right) = KC_L{}^2 - AC_L + B \quad (4.3)$$

From the second order polynomial trendline in Figure 4.35f) we find that

$K = 0.0979$

$A = 0.04 = 2KC_{L0} = 2 \cdot 0.0979 \cdot C_{L0}$

$C_{L0} = 0.2043$

$B = 0.0168 = C_{D0} + KC_{L0}{}^2 = C_{D0} + 0.0979 \cdot 0.2043^2$

$C_{D0} = 0.0127$

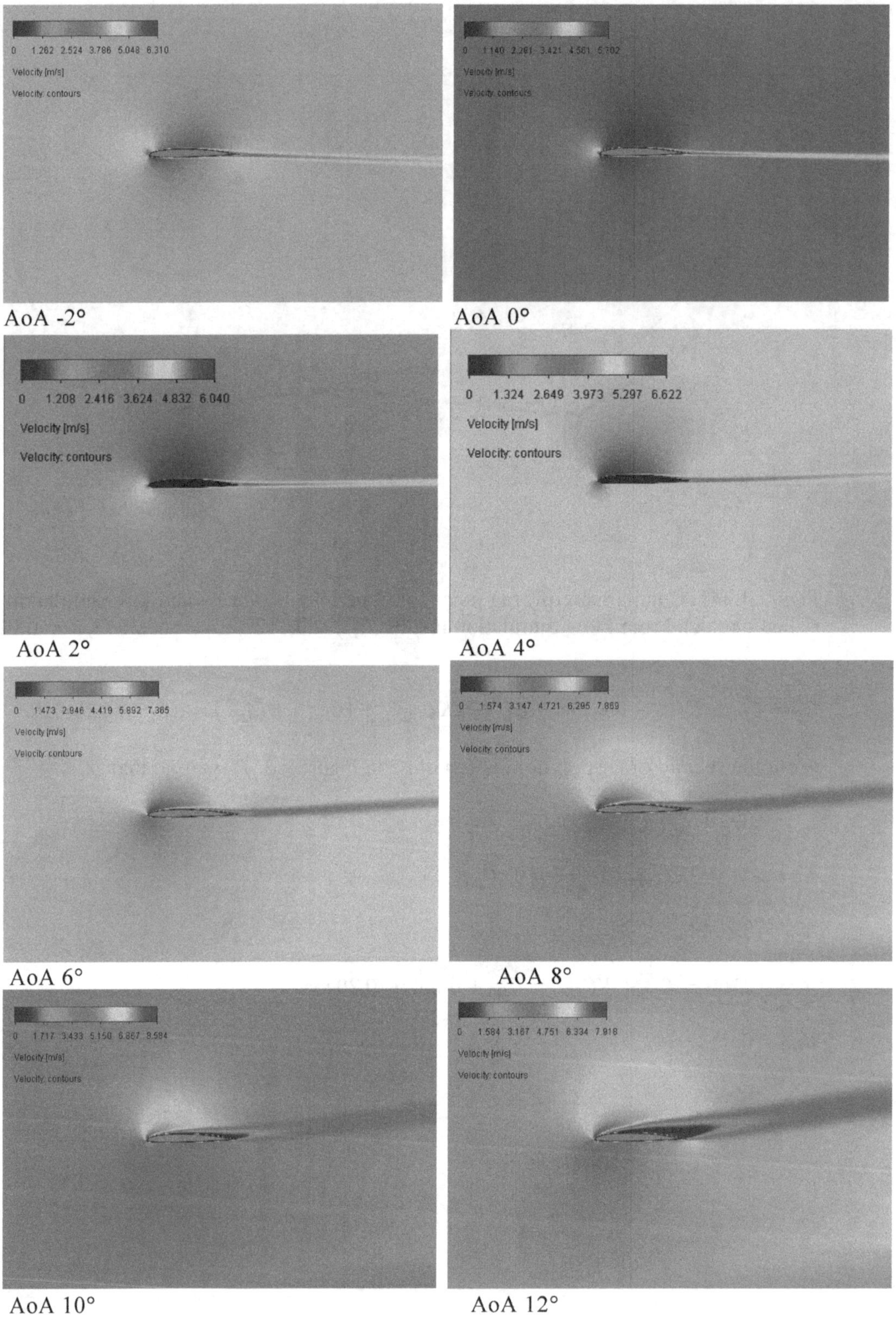

Figure 4.34g) Velocity field around SD 2030 airfoil at different angles of attack

N. Reference

1. Selig M.S. and McGranaham B., Wind Tunnel Aerodynamics Tests of Six Airfoils for Use on Small Wind Turbines, NREL/SR-500-34515, National Renewable Energy Laboratory, 2004.

O. Exercises

4.1 Run the calculations for the flow over a SD 2030 airfoil for *Re* = 200,000 and use different levels of initial mesh. Plot the lift coefficient versus mesh level and study the percent difference variation as compared with the experimental values. Discuss your results.

Angle of Attack	Lift Coefficient
0.15	0.252
1.17	0.391
2.23	0.499
3.21	0.593
4.22	0.690
5.26	0.784
6.30	0.869
7.34	0.945
8.35	1.012
9.34	1.070
10.37	1.112
11.38	1.138

Table E1 Experimental values of lift coefficient for SD 2030 and *Re* = 200,000, from Selig and McGranaham (2004)

4.2 Run the calculations for the flow over a SD 2030 airfoil for *Re* = 500,000 for an initial mesh level of 6 and use different sizes of the computational domain:

a) Xmin: -0.2 m, Xmax: 0.4 m, Ymin: -0.2 m, Ymax: 0.2 m
b) Xmin: -0.4 m, Xmax: 0.6 m, Ymin: -0.4 m, Ymax: 0.4 m
c) Xmin: -1 m, Xmax: 2 m, Ymin: -1 m, Ymax: 1 m

How does the lift coefficient vary with the size of the computational domain? Compare your results with the following experimental results as shown in table 4.3. Include solver windows and goal values for each case. Discuss your results.

Angle of Attack Experiment	Lift Coefficient Experiment
0.20	0.291
1.16	0.410
2.23	0.525
3.24	0.628
4.28	0.725
5.28	0.814
6.30	0.909
7.34	0.993
8.36	1.012
9.34	1.068
10.42	1.176
11.4	1.199

Table 4.3 Experimental values of lift coefficient for SD 2030 and *Re* = 500,000, from Selig and McGranaham (2004)

Notes:

CHAPTER 5. RAYLEIGH-BENARD CONVECTION & TAYLOR-COUETTE FLOW

A. Objectives

- Creating the SOLIDWORKS models needed for Flow Simulations
- Setting up Flow Simulation projects for internal flows
- Creating lids for boundary conditions and setting up boundary conditions
- Use of gravity as a physical feature and running the calculations
- Using cut plots and surface plots to visualize the resulting flow field
- Compare results with linear stability theory

B. Problem Description

In this chapter we will study roll cell instabilities in two simple geometries. We will start by looking closer at the flow caused by natural convection between a hot bottom wall and an upper colder wall, see figure 5.0a). This flow case is known as Rayleigh-Bénard convection. We will use water as the fluid and only a very small temperature difference is required to get the primary instability in this flow. The lower hot wall will be set to 295 K and the upper cold wall to 293 K. The depth of the fluid layer is 4.793 mm and the inner diameter of the enclosure is 100 mm. The second flow case that will be studied in this chapter is Taylor-Couette flow, see figure 5.0b), the flow between two vertical and rotating cylinders. In this chapter, we will rotate the inner cylinder at 5 rad/s and keep the outer cylinder stationary. The inner and outer cylinders have radii of 30 mm and 35 mm, respectively, and the height of the cylinders is 100 mm. A centrifugal instability will cause the appearance of counter-rotating vortices at low rotation speed of the inner cylinder. For both flow cases, comparisons will be made with linear stability theory.

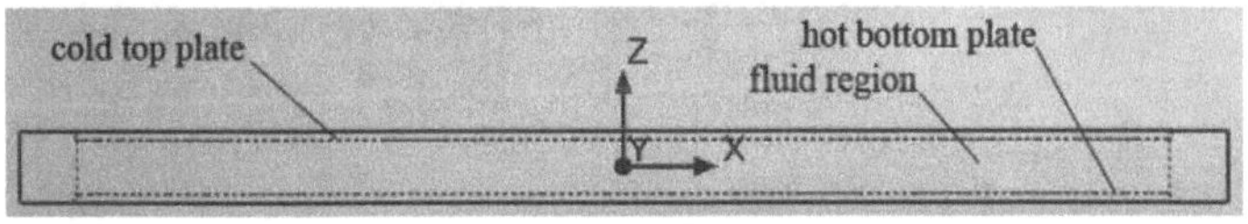

Figure 5.0a) Model of Rayleigh-Bénard convection cell

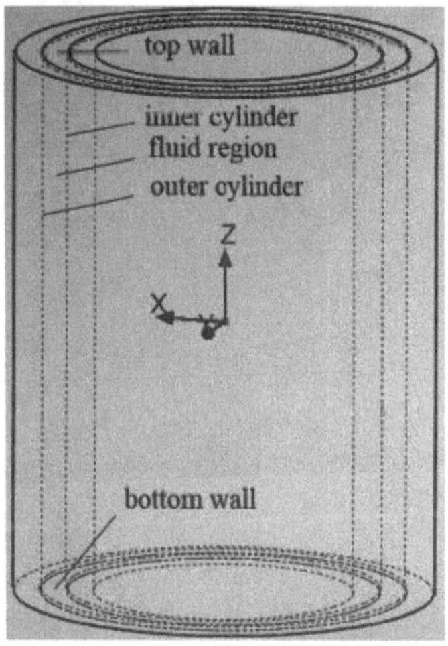

Figure 5.0b) Taylor-Couette cell

C. Creating the SOLIDWORKS Part for Rayleigh-Benard Convection

1. Start SOLIDWORKS and create a New Part. Select **Tools>>Options...** from the SOLIDWORKS menu. Click on the Document Properties tab and select **Units**. Select **MMGS** as your **Unit system**. Select the **Front** view from the **View Orientation** drop down menu in the graphics window and click on the **Front Plane** in the **FeatureManager design tree**. Next, select the **Circle** sketch tool from the Basic Modeling Tools tab.

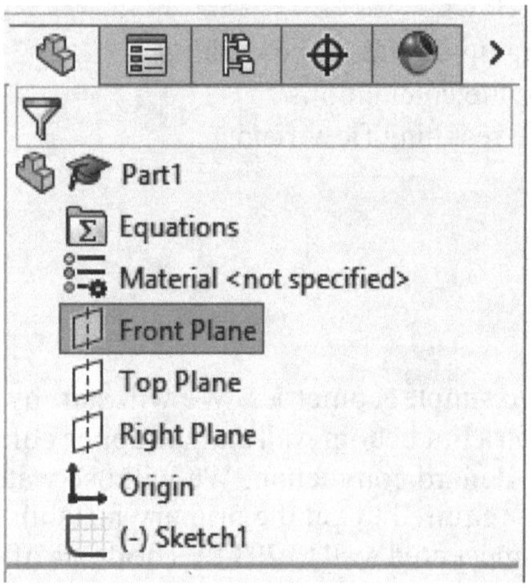

Figure 5.1a) Front Plane

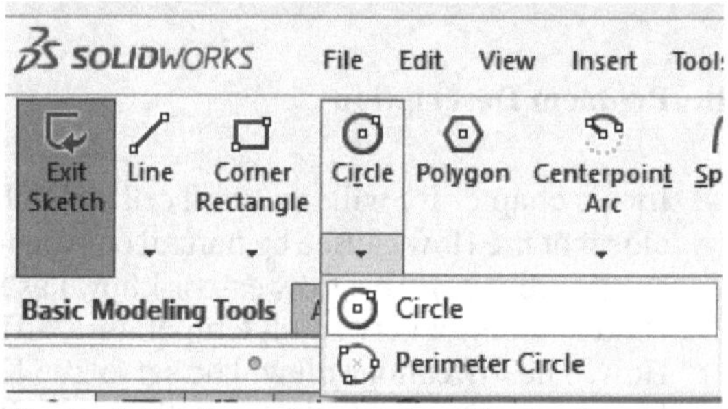

Figure 5.1b) Selection of the **Circle** sketch tool

2. Click on the origin in the graphics window and create a circle. Enter **50 mm** for the radius of the circle in the **Parameters** box. Close the dialog box.

Figure 5.2 Drawing of a circle with 50 mm radius

3. Draw another larger circle concentric with the first circle and enter **55 mm** for the radius. Close the dialog box.

Figure 5.3 Drawing of a second circle with 55 mm radius

4. Next, make an extrusion by selecting the tab **Analysis Preparation>>Extruded Boss/Base.** Enter 3.175mm in **Direction 1** and the same depth in **Direction 2**. Close the dialog box. Save the part with the name **Rayleigh-Benard Cell 2026.**

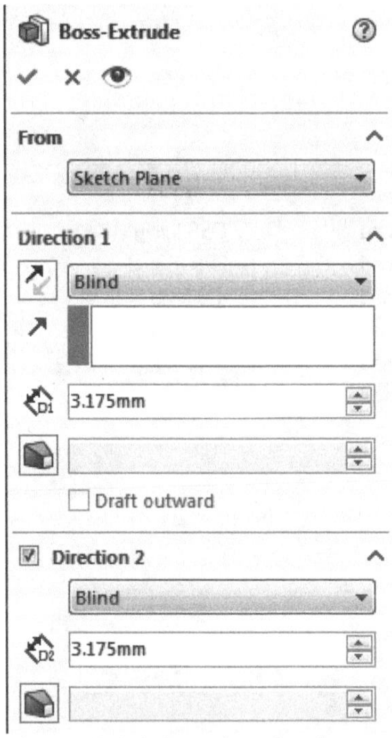

Figure 5.4a) Entering depth

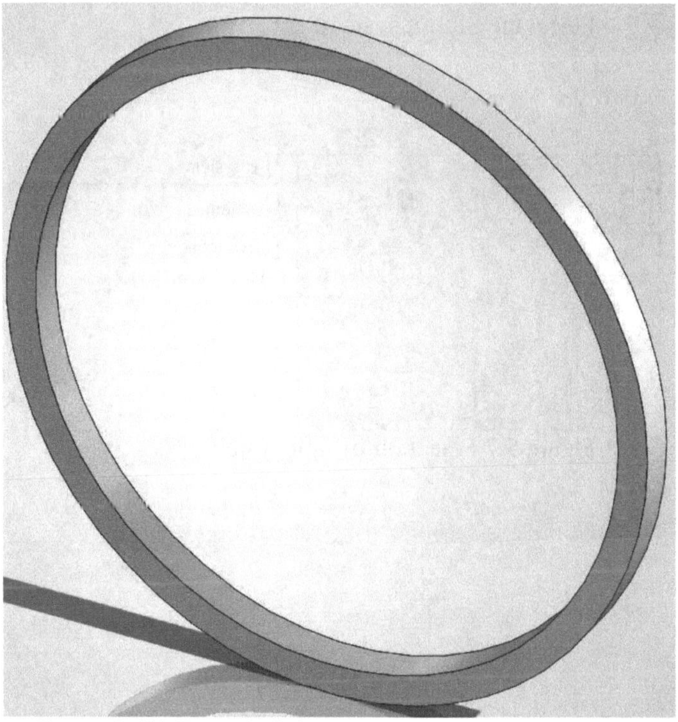

Figure 5.4b) Extruded ring

D. Setting Up Flow Simulation Project for Rayleigh-Benard Convection

5. If Flow Simulation is not available in the SOLIDWORKS menu, select **Tools>>Add Ins...** and check the corresponding **SOLIDWORKS Flow Simulation** box. Start the **Flow Simulation Wizard** by selecting **Tools>>Flow Simulation>>Project>>Wizard...** from the SOLIDWORKS menu.

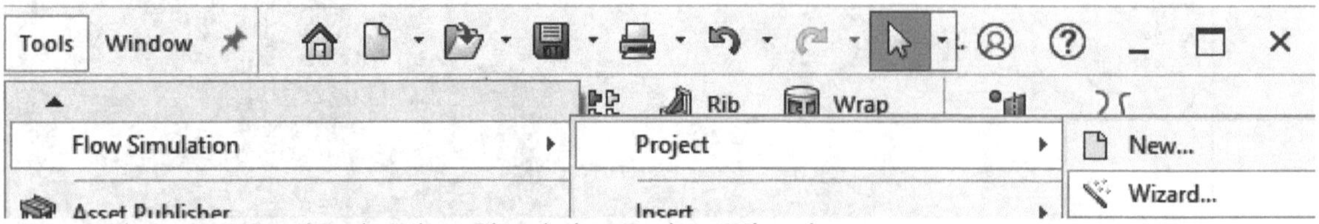

Figure 5.5 Starting the Flow Simulation Project Wizard

6. Enter Project name: **Convection in Rayleigh-Benard Cell**.

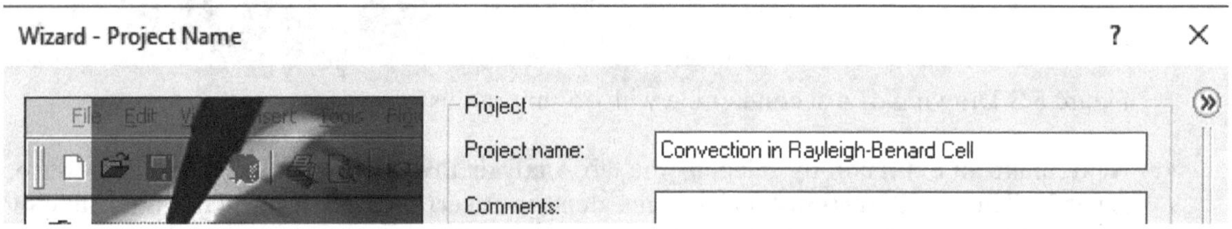

Figure 5.6 Entering configuration name

7. Select the SI unit system

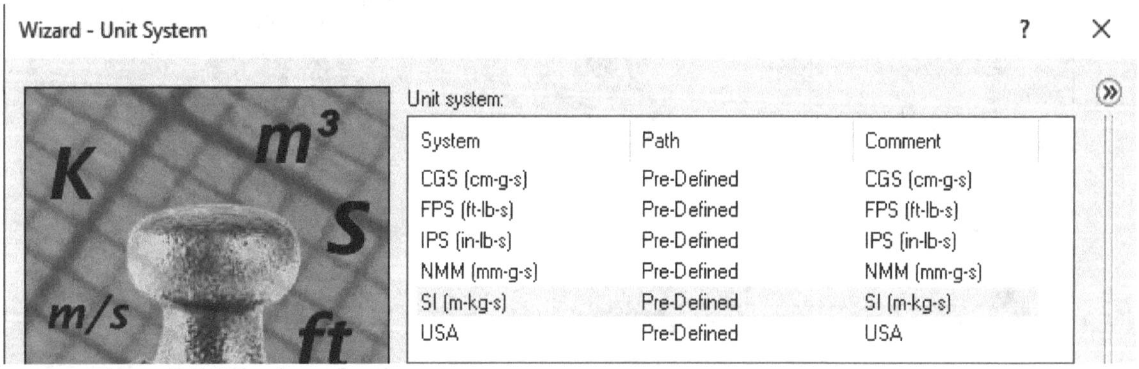

Figure 5.7 Selection of unit system

8. Select **Internal Analysis type** and enter **-9.81 m/s^2** as **Gravity** for the **Z component** in **Physical Features**.

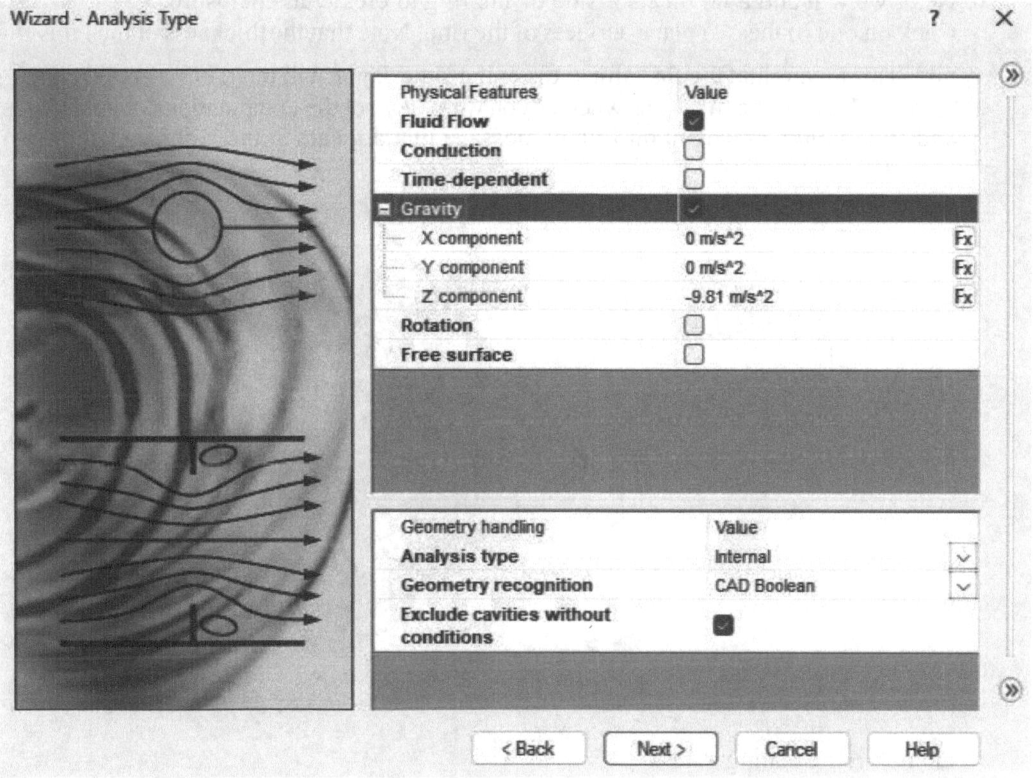

Figure 5.8 Enter gravity as physical feature

9. Add **Water** as the default **Project Fluid** by selecting it from **Liquids**. Choose default values for **Wall Conditions** and **Initial Conditions.**

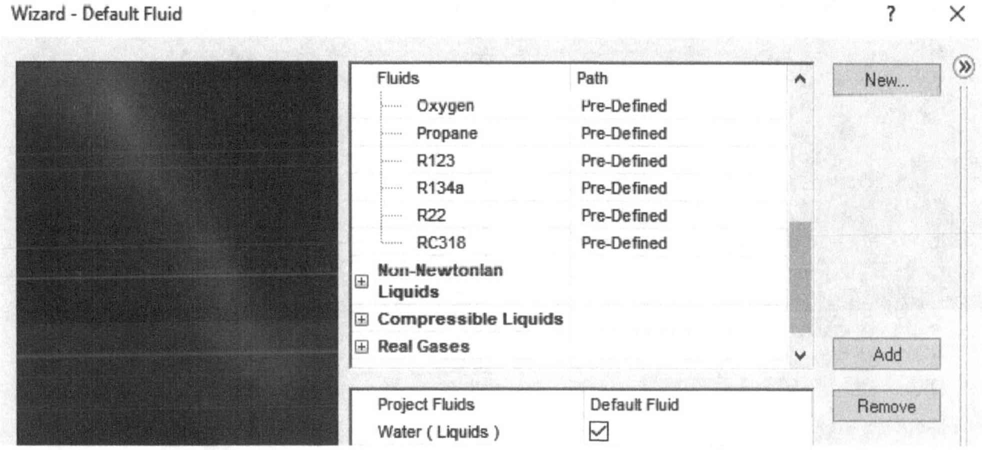

Figure 5.9 Default fluid

You will get a fluid volume recognition failure message. Answer **Yes** to this question and create a lid on each side of the model as described in the next section.

E. Creating Lids

10. Next, we will add a lid on each side of the ring to create an enclosure. Click on one of the two plane surfaces of the ring. Note that the thickness of the lid is 0.7784652 mm. This means that the final thickness of the fluid layer will be 4.793 mm. Click ✓ **OK** and answer "**Yes**" to the questions whether you want to reset the computational domain, mesh setting, and fluid volume recognition failure message that appears in the graphics window.

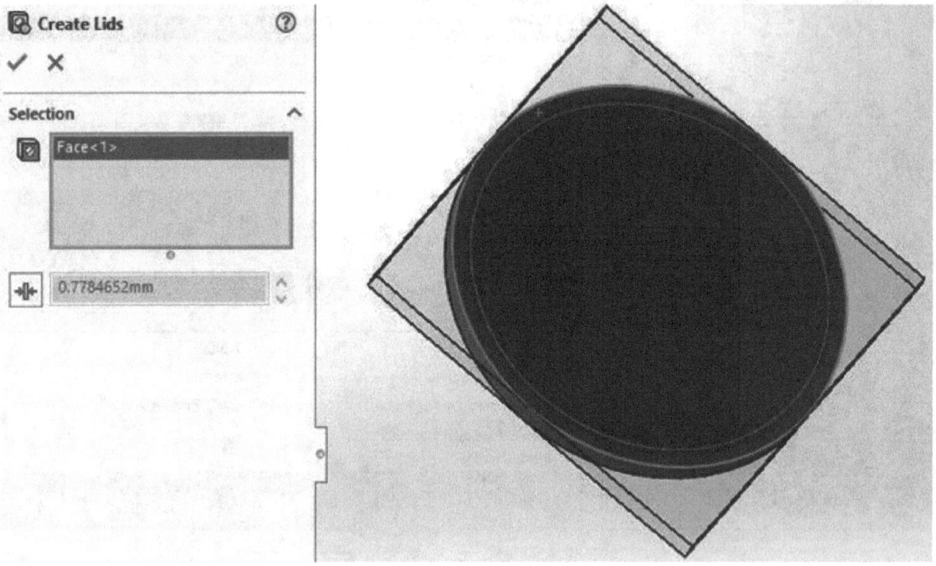

Figure 5.10 Creating a lid

11. Next, right click in the graphics window and select **Zoom/Pan/Rotate>>Rotate View**. Rotate the ring with a lid. Right click and click on **Rotate View** to deselect the view. Select the other plane surface of the ring and create the second lid with the same thickness as the first lid. Answer "**Yes**" when asked to reset the computational domain and mesh settings. Select **Hidden Lines Visible** from the **Display Style** drop down menu in the graphics window.

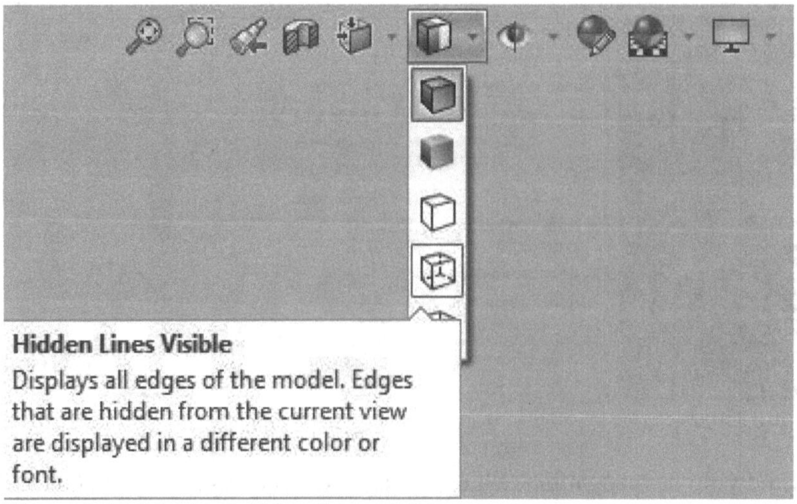

Figure 5.11 Making hidden lines visible

F. Boundary Conditions for Rayleigh-Benard Convection

12. Click on the **Flow Simulation analysis tree** tab and click on the plus sign next to the **Input Data** folder. Right click on **Boundary Conditions** and select **Insert Boundary Condition…**

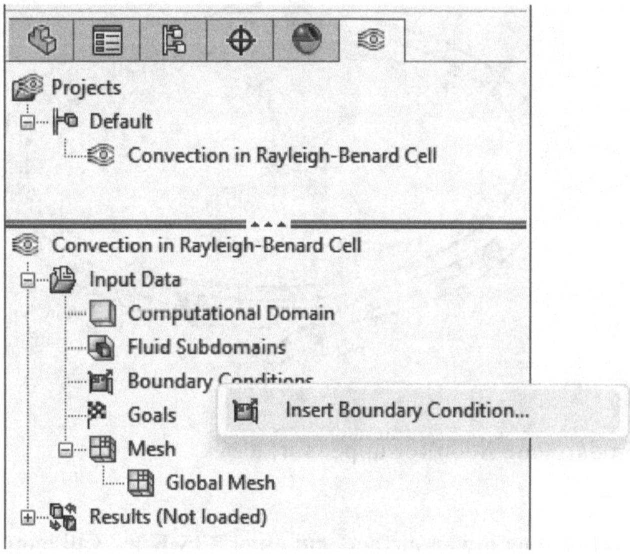

Figure 5.12 Selecting boundary conditions

13. Right click in the graphics window and select **Zoom/Pan/Rotate>>Rotate View**. Rotate the enclosure so that it has the same view as in Figure 5.13a), right click and click on **Rotate View** to deselect Rotate View. Move the cursor over the top lid, right-click again and click on **Select Other**. Select the face for the inner upper surface of the enclosure. Select the **Wall** button and select **Real Wall** boundary condition. Set the value of **293 K** for the wall temperature in the **Wall Parameters** window. Click **OK** to finish the first boundary condition. Rename the boundary condition from **Real Wall 1** to **Top Wall.**

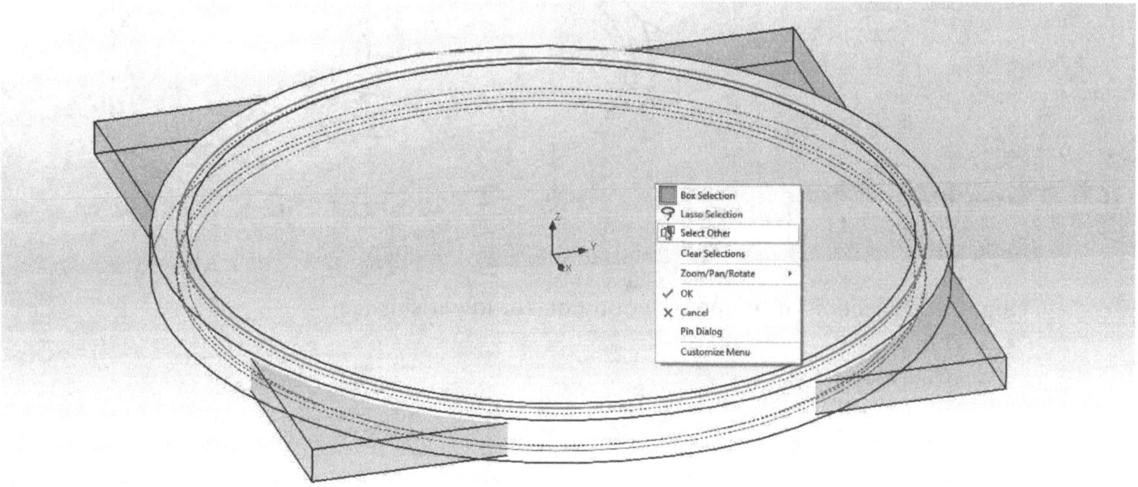

Figure 5.13a) View of enclosure for upper boundary condition

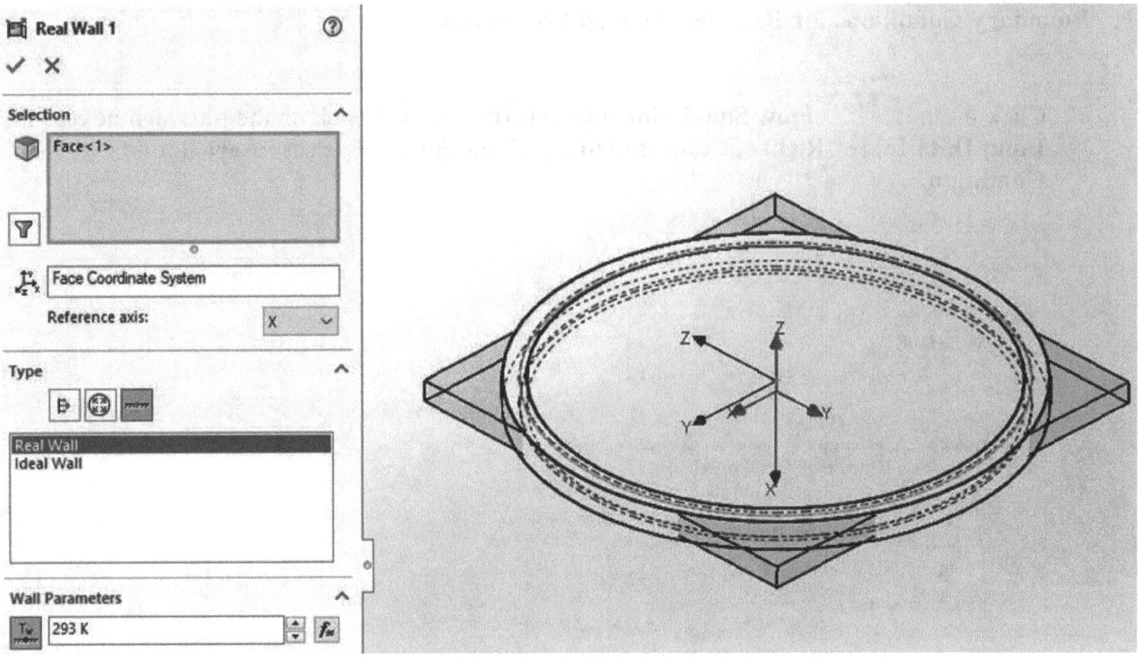

Figure 5.13b) Selection of boundary condition for upper surface

14. Repeat steps **12** and **13** but select the inner lower surface and enter **295 K** as wall temperature. Rename the boundary condition from **Real Wall 2** to **Bottom Wall**.

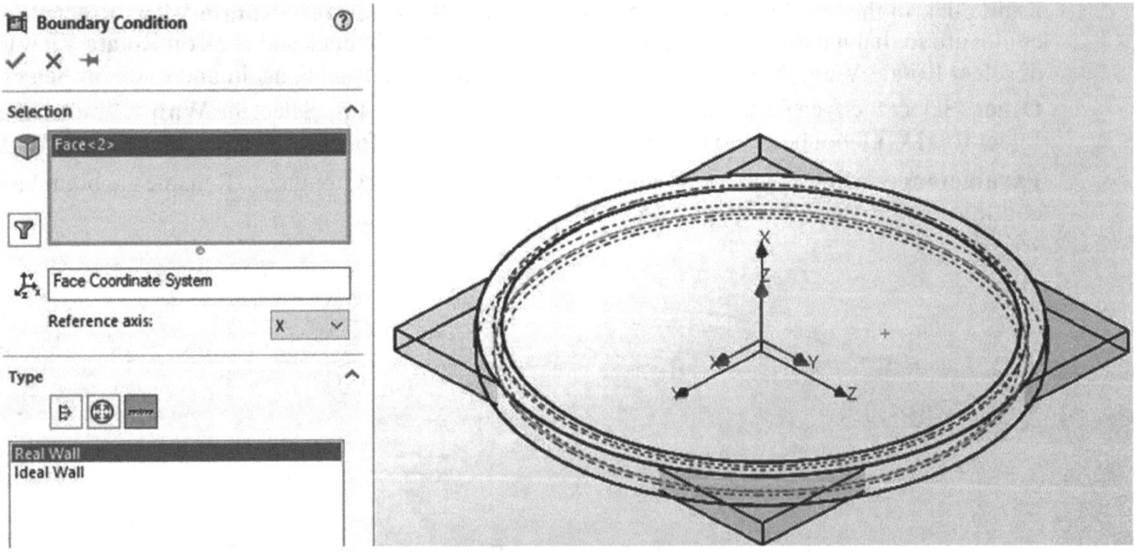

Figure 5.14 Selection of boundary condition for lower surface

15. Select **Bottom** view from the **View Orientation** drop down menu in the graphics window. Right click on **Boundary Conditions** and select **Display Callouts** to label the boundary conditions.

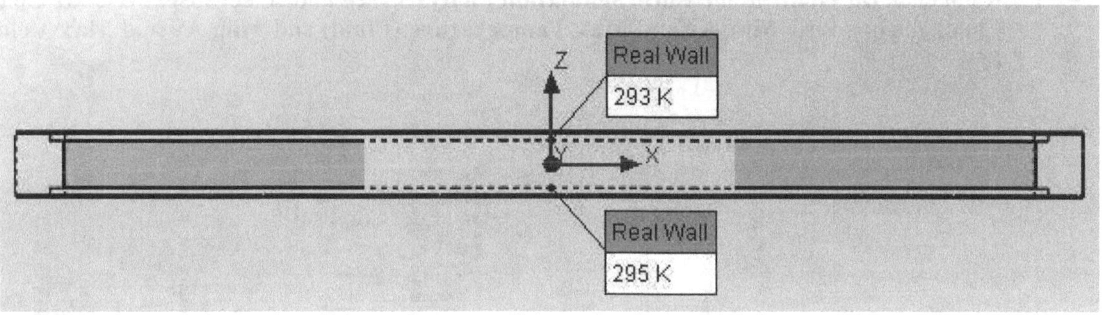

Figure 5.15 Two real wall boundary conditions for the Rayleigh-Benard Convection Cell

G. Setting Up 2D Flow

16. Choose **Tools>>Flow Simulation>>Computational Domain…**. Select **2D simulation** and **XZ-Plane Flow**. Exit the **Computational Domain** window. Choose **Tools>>Flow Simulation>>Global Mesh…**. Set the level of initial mesh to **5**.

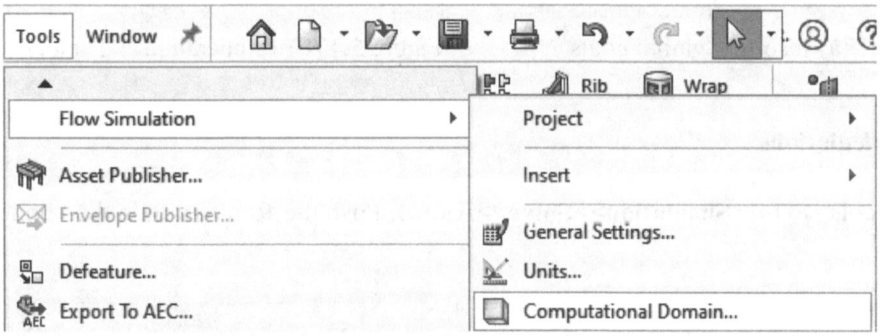

Figure 5.16a) Modifying the computational domain

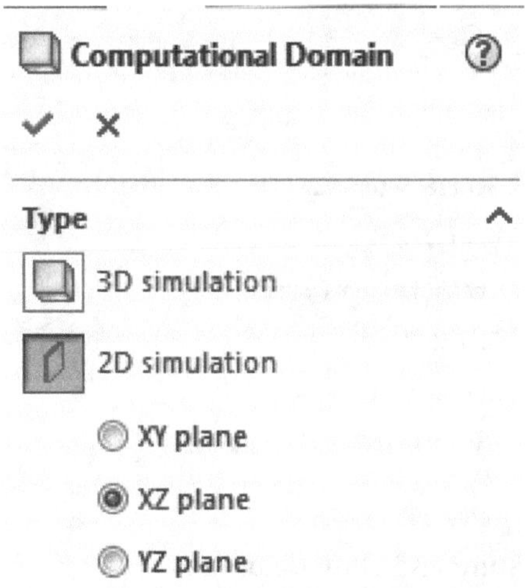

Figure 5.16b) Selecting XZ-Plane Flow

H. Global Goal for Rayleigh-Benard Convection

17. Right click on **Goals** in the **Flow Simulation analysis tree** and select **Insert Global Goals...** Check the boxes for **Min, Av** and **Max Temperature (Fluid)** and **Min, Av** and **Max Velocity (Z)**.

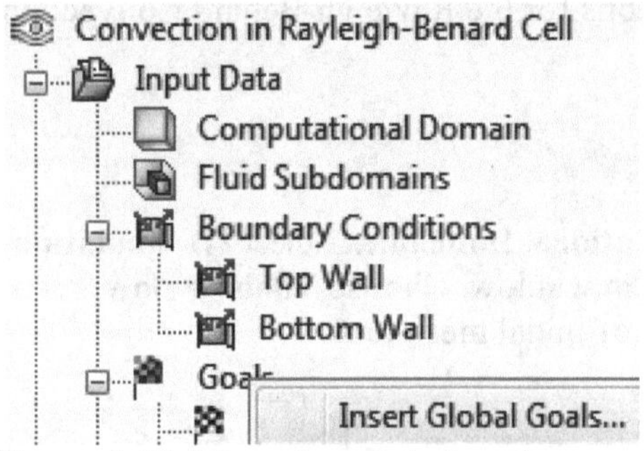

Figure 5.17a) Inserting global goals

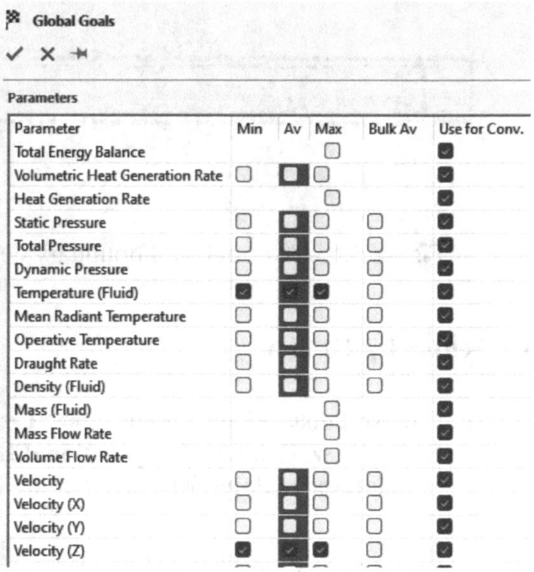

Figure 5.17b) Temperature and velocity as goals

I. Running Calculations

18. Select **Tools>>Flow Simulation>>Solve>>Run....** Push the **Run** button in the window that appears.

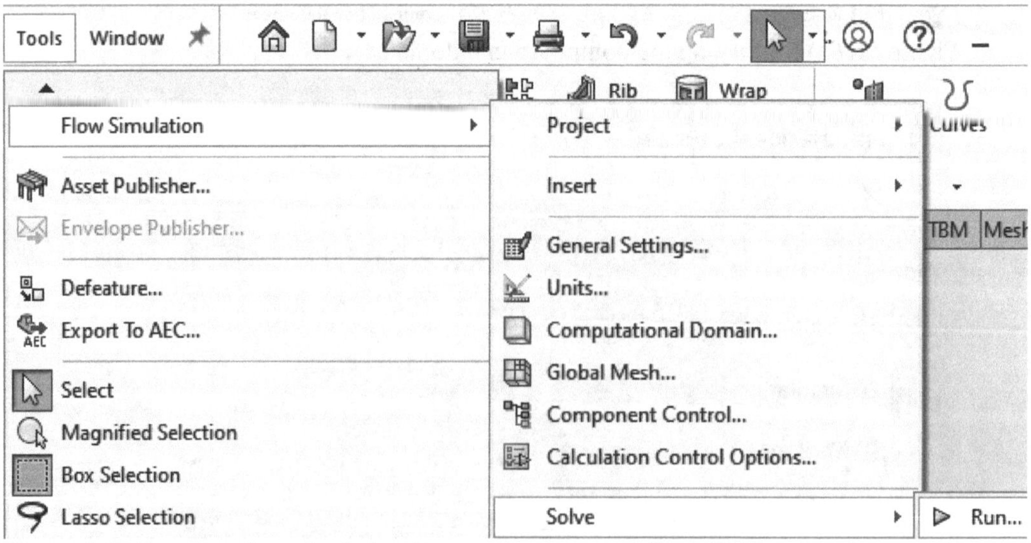

Figure 5.18 Running the calculation for temperature and flow fields

19. Insert the goals table by clicking on the flag in the **Solver** as shown in figure 5.19.

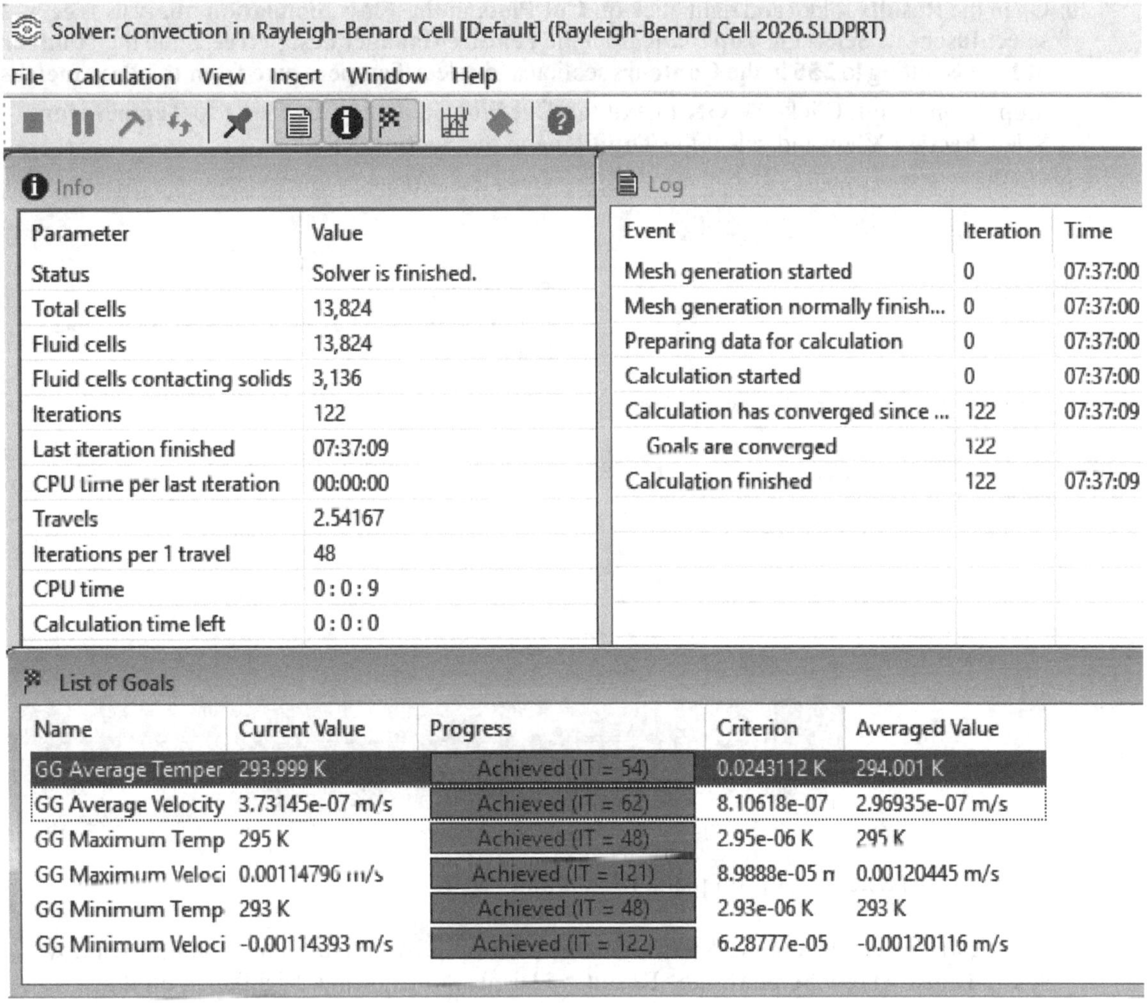

Figure 5.19 Solver window with list of goals.

J. Inserting Cut-Plots

20. Open the **Results** folder and right click on **Cut Plots** in the **Flow Simulation analysis tree** and select **Insert…**. Select the **Top Plane** from the **FeatureManager design tree**. Slide the **Number of Levels** setting to **255** in the **Contours** section and select **Temperature** from the **Parameters** drop down menu. Click **OK** to exit the **Cut Plot**. Rename **Cut Plot 1** to **Temperature**. Select **Section View** and select the **Top Plane** in the **Section View**.

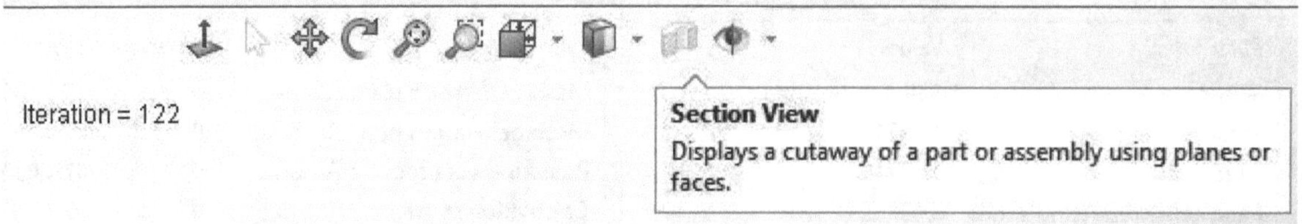

Figure 5.20a) Section View selection

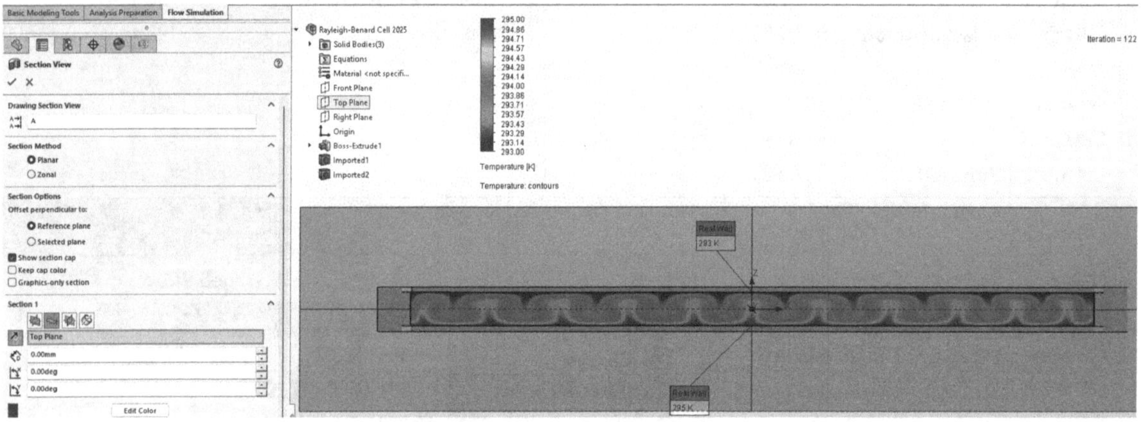

Figure 5.20b) Selection of top plane for cut plot

21. Select **Bottom** view from the **View Orientation** drop down menu in the graphics window. Select **Tools>>Flow Simulation>>Results>>Display>>Lighting**. Right click on the temperature scale in the graphics window and select **Make Horizontal**. In Figure 5.21 is the temperature field shown with the hot bottom wall and the colder upper wall. Plumes of water are rising from the hot bottom wall.

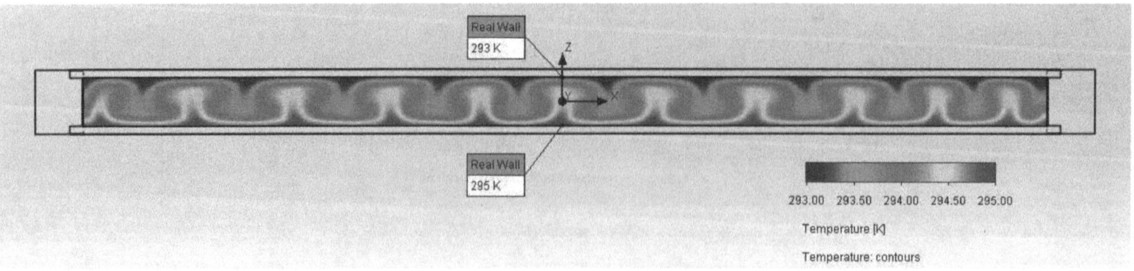

Figure 5.21 Temperature field for Rayleigh-Benard cell

22. Repeat step **20** and select the **Top Plane** in the **Selection** section of the **Cut Plot** window. Select **Velocity (Z)** from the **Parameters** drop down menu in the **Contours** section. Also, click on the **Vectors** button and Static Vectors button in the **Cut Plot** settings and exit the **Cut Plot** window. Right-click on the **Temperature Cut Plot** and **Hide** it. You can see alternating regions of positive and negative z-velocity indicate the presence of counter-rotating vortices in the cell. The counter-rotating motion of the vortices is shown by vectors.

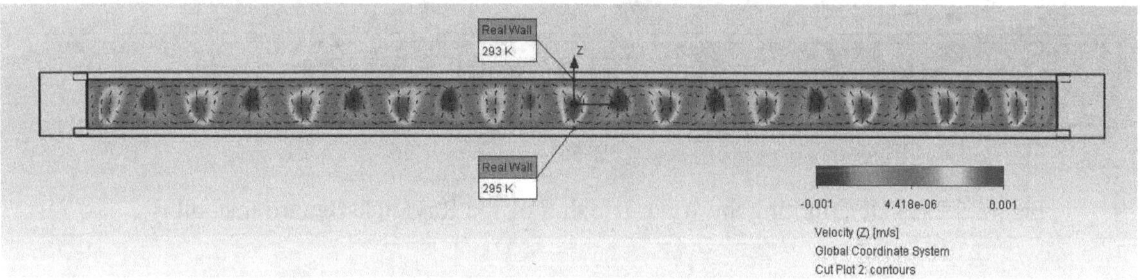

Figure 5.22a) Velocity (Z) field in Rayleigh-Benard cell

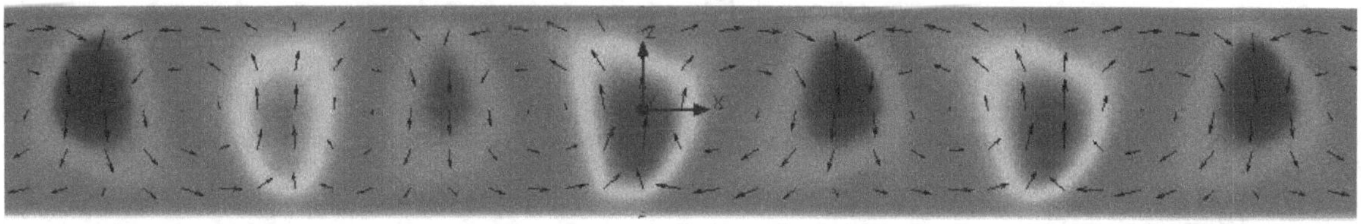

Figure 5.22b) Enlargement of cell regions

K. Comparison with Neutral Stability Theory

23. The instability of the flow between two parallel plates heated from below is governed by the so-called Rayleigh number *Ra*.

$$Ra = \frac{g\beta(T_1 - T_2)L_c^3}{\nu^2} Pr \tag{5.1}$$

where g is acceleration due to gravity, β is the coefficient of volume expansion, T_1 and T_2 are the temperatures of the hot and cold surfaces respectively, L_c is the distance between the surfaces (fluid layer thickness). Pr is the Prandtl number and ν is the kinematic viscosity of the fluid. Below the critical $Ra_{crit} = 1715$ for a rigid upper surface, the flow is stable but convective currents will develop above this Rayleigh number. For the case of a free upper surface, the theory predicts a lower critical Rayleigh number. Unfortunately, Flow Simulation is not able to model free surface boundary conditions. The non-dimensional wave number α of this instability is determined by

$$\alpha = \frac{2\pi L_c}{\lambda} \tag{5.2}$$

where λ is the wave-length of the instability. The critical wave numbers are $\alpha_{crit} = 3.12$, 2.68 for rigid and free surface boundary conditions, respectively. From figure 5.22b) the wave number can be determined to be

$$\alpha = \frac{2\pi \cdot 0.004793}{0.009444} = 3.19 \tag{5.3}$$

The wave-length from the simulation is determined by measuring the length of 10 wave lengths as shown in Figure 5.23a). The 10λ length is a fraction of the 100 mm diameter of the Rayleigh-Benard cell and can be determined using a ruler. In this case 10λ corresponds to 94.44 mm in Figure 5.23a) which gives $\lambda = 9.444$ mm.

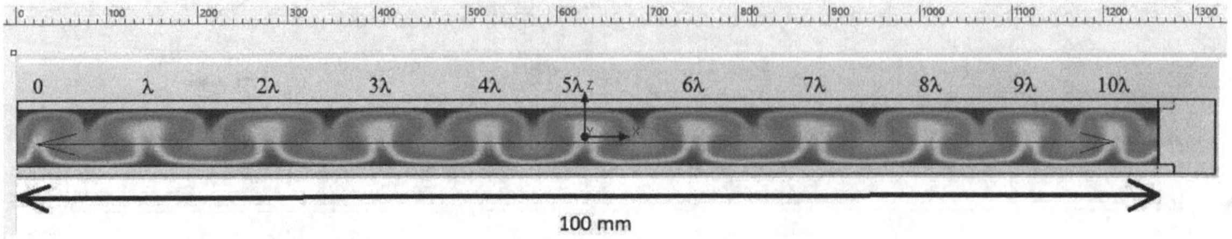

Figure 5.23a) Determining the wave-length λ of the Rayleigh-Benard instability

The Rayleigh number in the Flow Simulation is

$$Ra = \frac{9.81*0.000195*2*0.004793\text{^}3}{10\text{^}(-12)} * 6.84 = 2881 \tag{5.4}$$

The neutral stability curve can be given to the first approximation, see figure 5.23b).

$$Ra = \frac{(\pi^2+\alpha^2)^3}{\alpha^2\left\{1-16\alpha\pi^2 cosh^2(\frac{\alpha}{2})/[(\pi^2+\alpha^2)^2(sinh\alpha+\alpha)]\right\}} \tag{5.5}$$

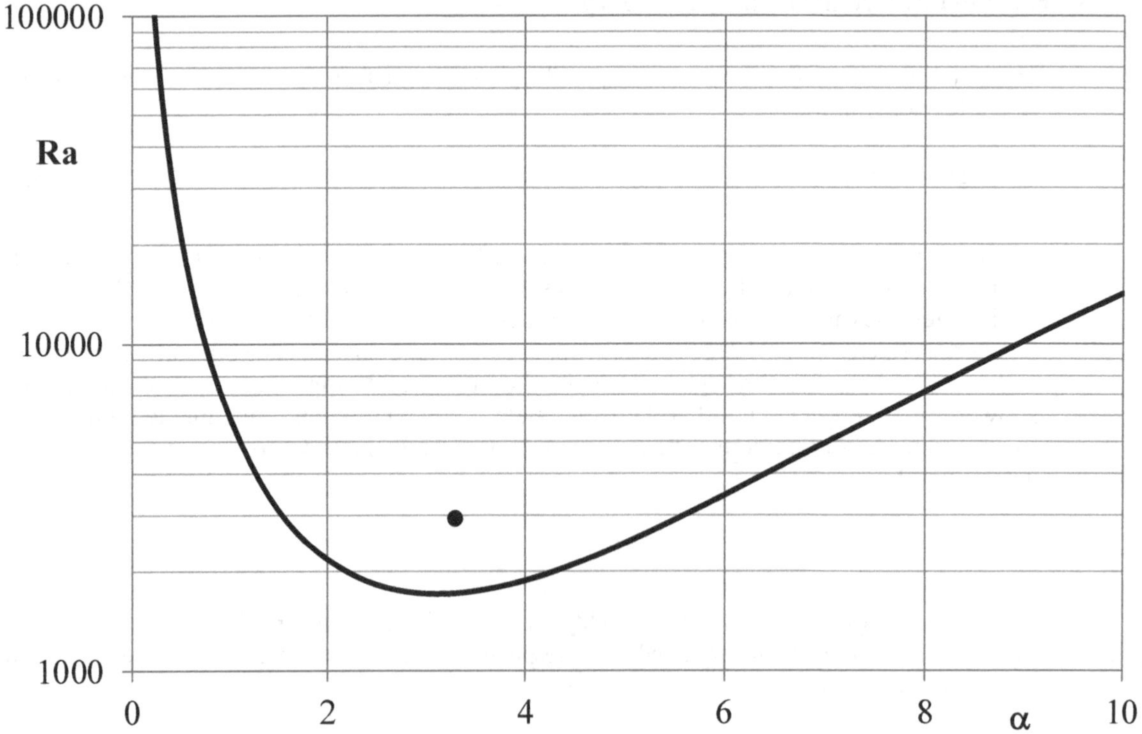

Figure 5.23b) Neutral stability curve for Rayleigh-Benard convection. The filled circle represents result from Flow Simulation.

L. Creating SOLIDWORKS Part for Taylor-Couette Flow

The second flow-case that we will run in this chapter is Taylor-Couette flow, the flow between vertical rotating cylinders. This flow is sometimes called the twin to Rayleigh-Beard convection. In this case, we will have an inner rotating cylinder and a stationary outer cylinder. We start by creating the part using SOLIDWORKS.

24. Start by repeating steps **1** – **3** from the beginning of this chapter: Start SOLIDWORKS and create a New Part. Select **Tools>>Options…** from the SOLIDWORKS menu. Click on the Document Properties tab and select **Units**. Select **MMGS** as your **Unit system**. Select the **Top** view from the **View Orientation** drop down menu in the graphics window and click on the **Top Plane** in the **FeatureManager design tree**. Next, select the **Circle** sketch tool from the **Basic Modeling Tools** tab in the menu. Click on the origin in the graphics window and create a circle. Enter **25 mm** for the radius of the circle in the **Parameters** box. Close the dialog box. Draw another larger circle concentric with the first circle and enter **30 mm** for the radius. Close the dialog box.

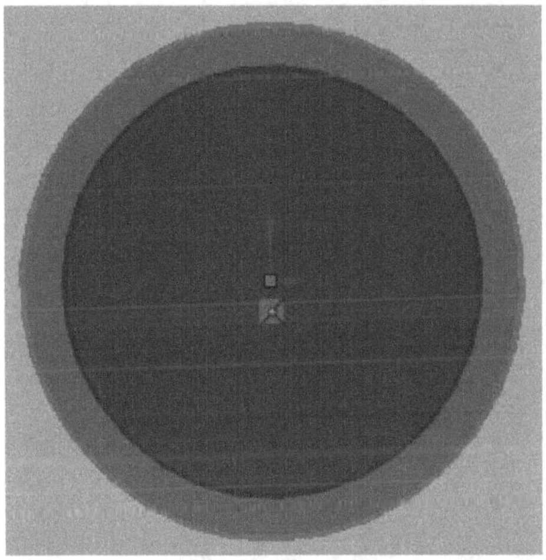

Figure 5.24 Two circles for the inner cylinder

25. The two circles for the outer cylinder are drawn in the next step. The radii for these two circles are **35 mm** and **40 mm**.

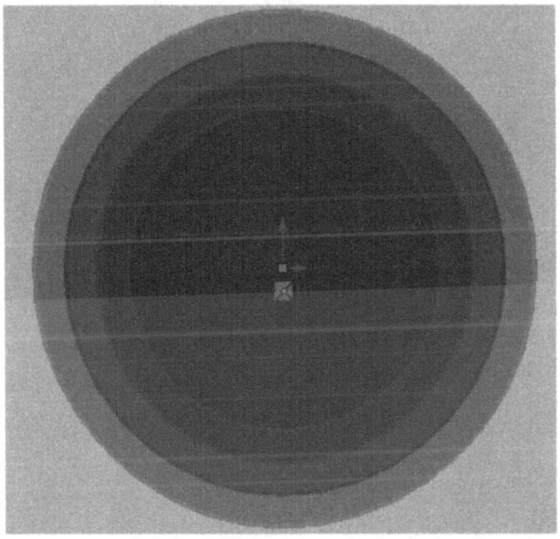

Figure 5.25 Adding two more circles for the outer cylinder.

26. Click on **Sketch 1** in the **FeatureManager design tree** followed by the selection of **Extruded Boss/Base** from the **Analysis Preparation** tab in the menu. Right click in Selected Contours and select Clear Selections. Select the inner and outer sketch regions for extrusion and enter a depth of **50 mm** in both **Direction 1** and **Direction 2**, see Figures 5.26b) and c). Click on OK ✓. Save the part with the name **Taylor-Couette Cell 2026**.

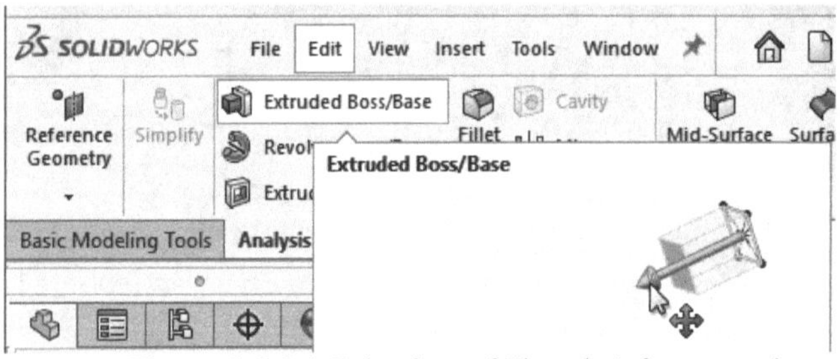

Figure 5.26a) Selection of Sketch 1 for extrusion

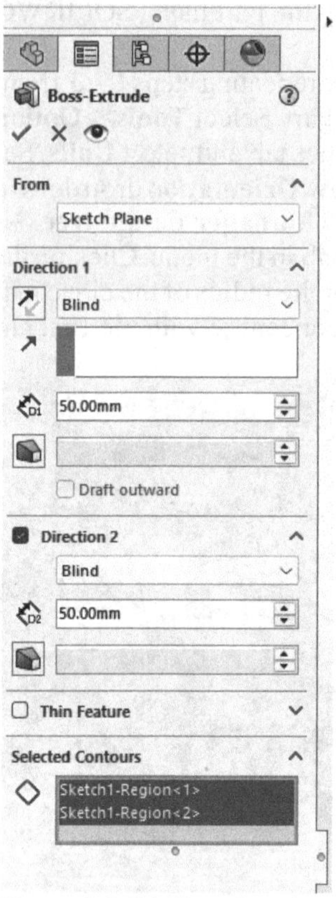

Figure 5.26b) Entering depth of extrusion

Figure 5.26c) Inner and outer sketch regions

Figure 5.26d) Finished extrusion

M. Flow Simulation Project for Taylor-Couette Flow

27. If Flow Simulation is not available in the SOLIDWORKS menu, select **Tools>>Add Ins...** and check the corresponding **SOLIDWORKS Flow Simulation** box. Start the Flow Simulation Wizard by selecting **Tools>>Flow Simulation>>Project>>Wizard....** Enter Project name: **Instabilities in Taylor-Couette Flow.**

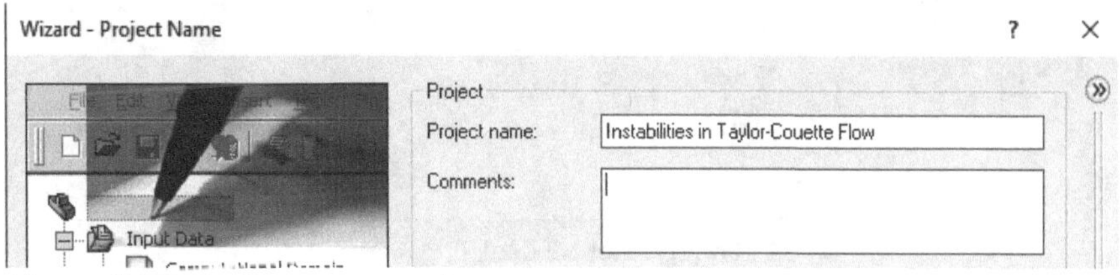

Figure 5.27 Create a new project name

28. Select the **SI unit system** in the next step followed by selection of the **Internal Analysis type**. Add **Water** as the **Project Fluid** and use default values of wall conditions and initial conditions. You will get a fluid volume recognition failure message. Answer **Yes** to this question and create lids on top and bottom of the model. Select the outer and inner rings as the faces for the lid and click OK ✓. Answer **Yes** to the questions whether you want to reset the computational domain, mesh settings and the Create Lids tool will open. Next, right click in the graphics window and select **Zoom/Pan/Rotate>>Rotate View**. Rotate the Taylor-Couette model around and deselect **Rotate View**. Select the outer and inner rings and create the second lid. Answer "**Yes**" when asked to reset the computational domain and mesh settings.

Select **Tools>>Flow Simulation>>Global Mesh...** from the SOLIDWORKS menu. Select **Manual settings**. Set the number of cells in all three directions X, Y and Z to **35**. Click on the **OK** button to exit the **Global Mesh Settings** window. Select **Tools>>Flow Simulation>>Calculation Control Options...** from the SOLIDWORKS menu. Click on the **Refinement** tab and select **level = 1** for the **Value** of the **Refinement Parameter**. Click on the **OK** button to exit the **Calculation Control Options** window.

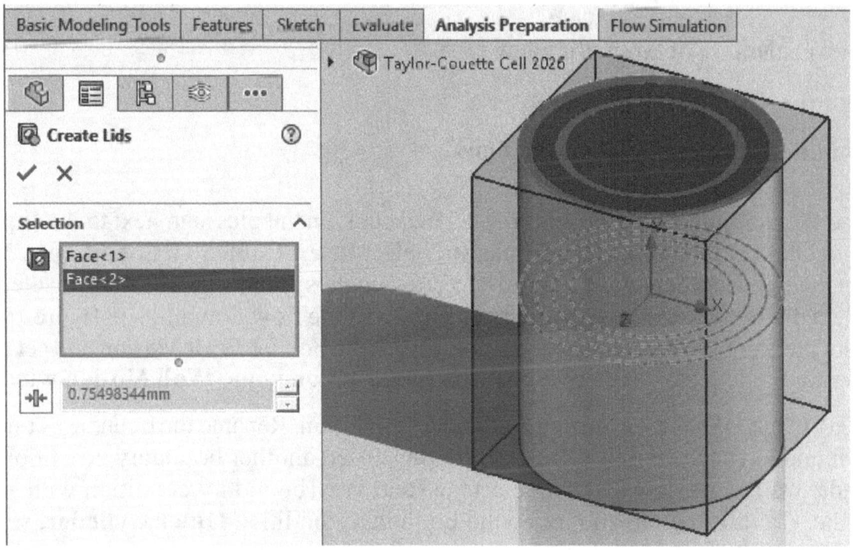

Figure 5.28 Lids added to the Taylor-Couette cell

29. Select **Hidden Lines Visible** from the **Display Type** drop down menu in the graphics window and **Isometric** view from the **View Orientation** drop down menu.

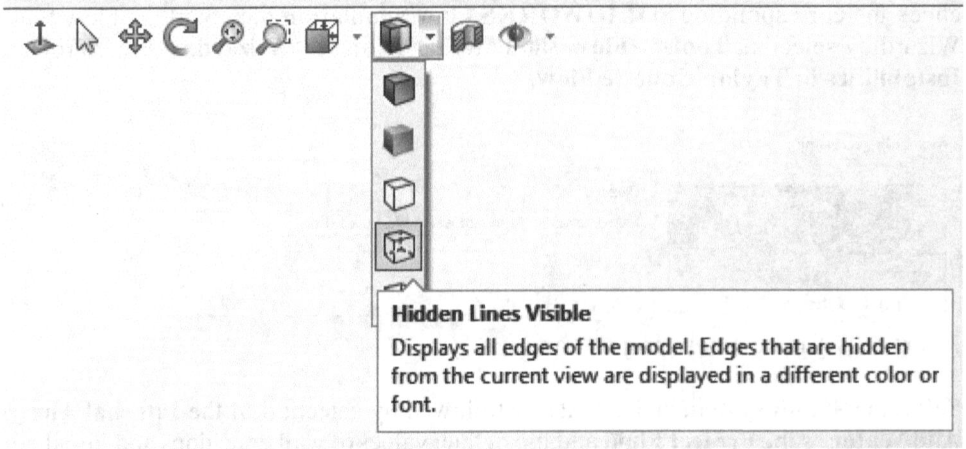

Figure 5.29a) Showing hidden lines

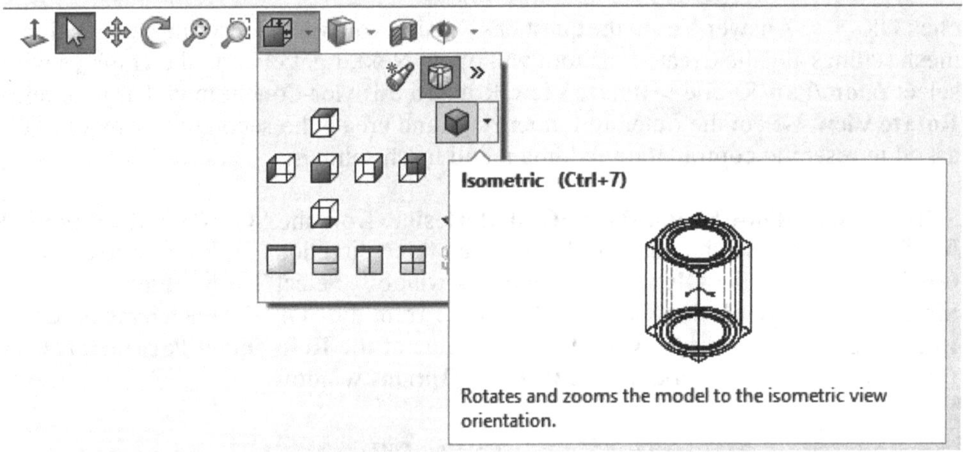

Figure 5.29b) Selection of isometric view

N. Boundary Conditions for Taylor-Couette Flow

30. Click on the **Flow Simulation analysis tree** tab and click on the plus sign next to the **Input Data** folder. Right click on **Boundary Conditions** and select **Insert Boundary Condition…** Move the cursor over the cylinders near the origin of the coordinate system, right click and select **Select Other**. Select the face for the inner cylindrical surface of the flow domain, see figures 5.30 and 5.0b). Select the **Real Wall** boundary condition, check the box for **Wall Motion** and set the value of **1.5 rad/s** for the angular velocity in the **Y Axis direction** in the **Wall Motion** window, see figure 5.30a). Click OK  to finish the boundary condition. Rename the boundary condition in the Flow Simulation analysis tree to **Inner Cylinder**. Insert another boundary condition for the outer cylinder wall of the flow domain, select the **Real Wall** boundary condition with zero wall motion in the Y axis direction and name the boundary condition **Outer Cylinder**, see Figure 5.30b).

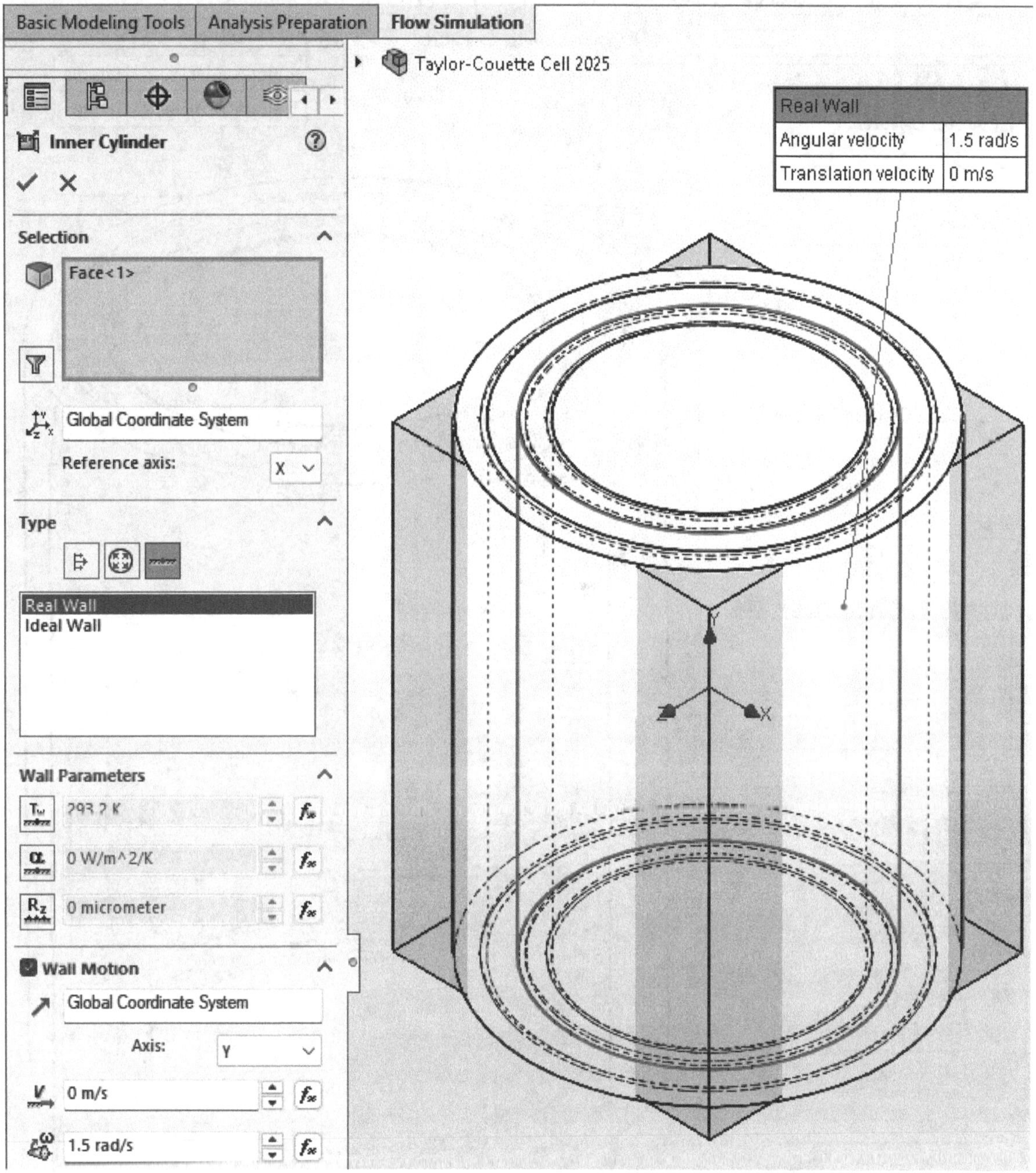

Figure 5.30a) Selection of boundary condition for rotating inner cylinder

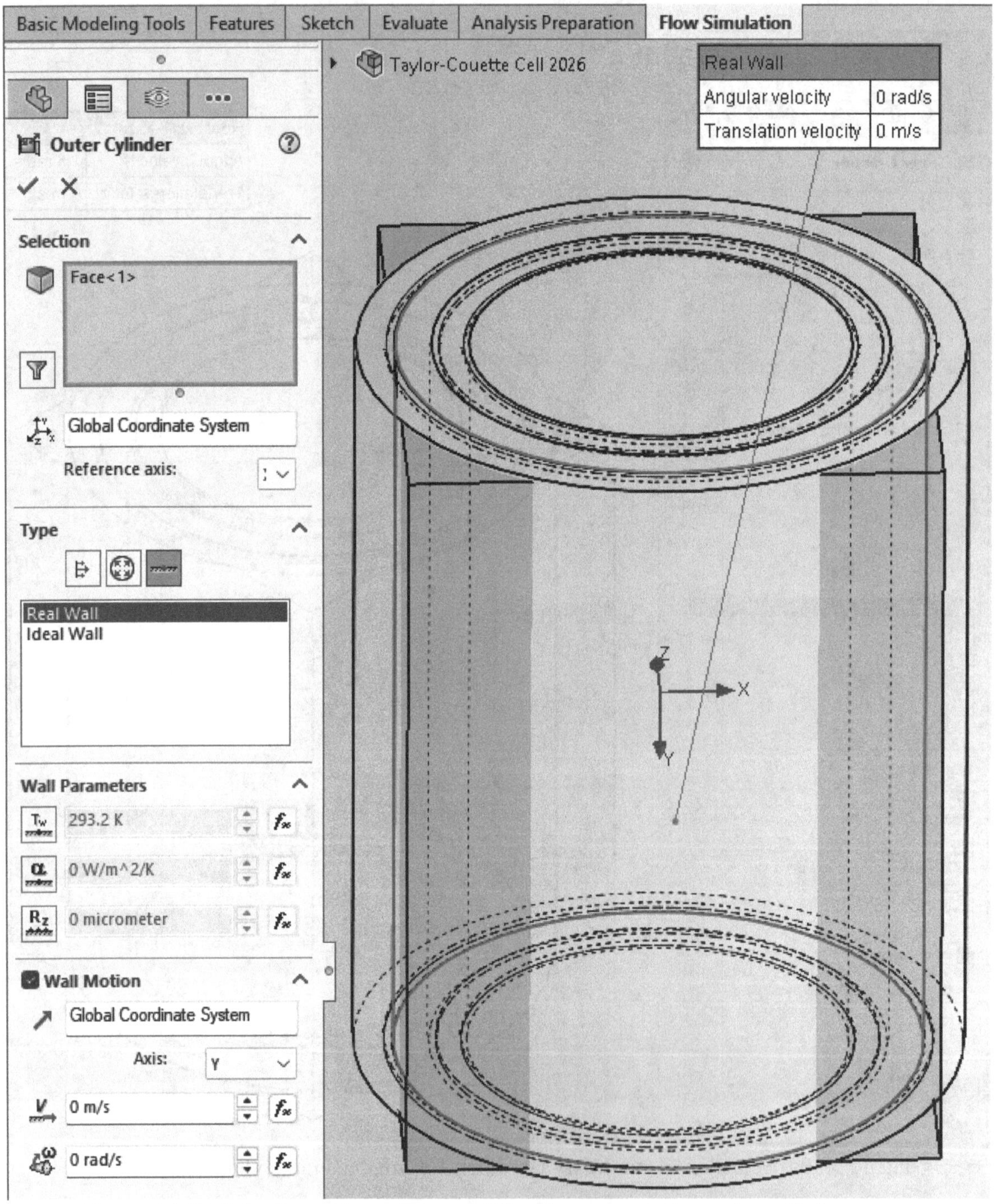

Figure 5.30b) Selection of boundary condition for non-rotating outer cylinder

O. Global Goal and Simulations for Taylor-Couette Flow

31. Right click on **Goals** in the **Flow Simulation analysis tree** and select **Insert Global Goals...** Check the boxes for **Min**, **Av** and **Max Velocity** and exit the window. Select **Tools>>Flow Simulation>>Solve>>Run....** Push the **Run** button in the window that appears.

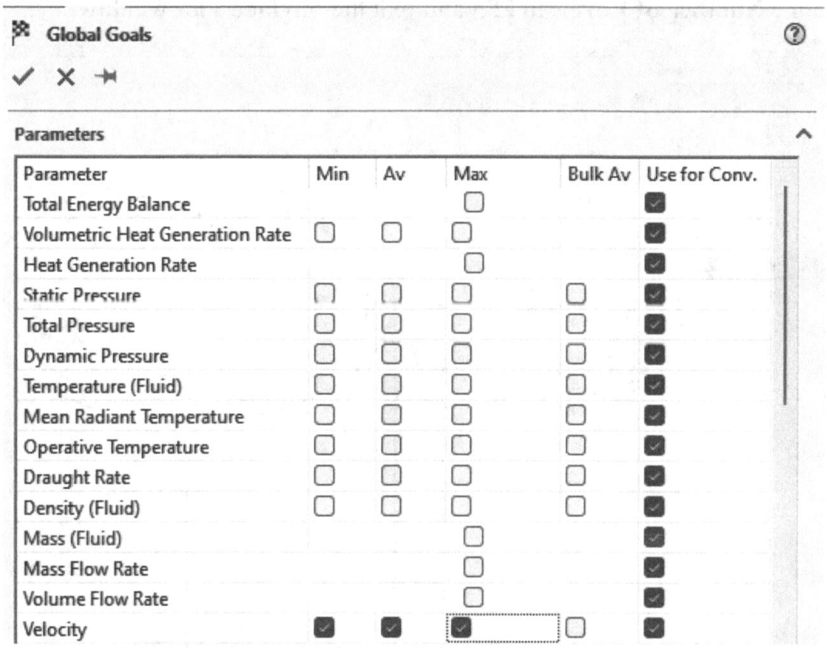

Figure 5.31a) Selecting velocity as global goal

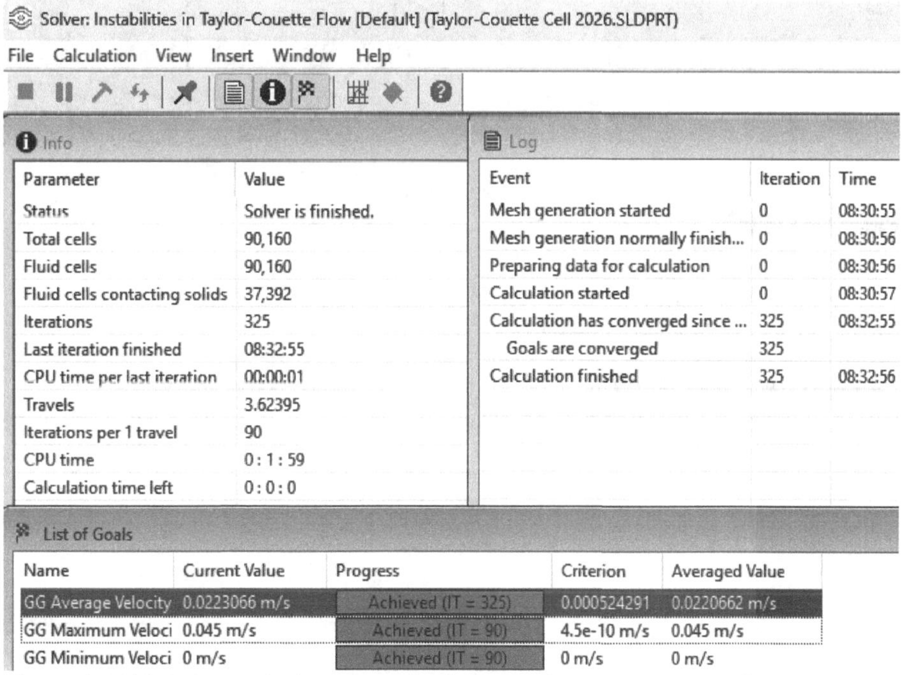

Figure 5.31b) Solver window for calculations of Taylor-Couette flow

P. Inserting Surface Plots

32. Select **Tools>>Flow Simulation>>Results>>Load/Unload**. Repeat this step. Open the **Results** folder and right click on **Surface Plots** in the **Flow Simulation analysis tree** and select **Insert…**. Select the face of the inner rotating cylinder in the graphics window. Expand **Options** and check the **Offset** box. Select **Velocity (Y)** from the **Parameter** drop down menu in the **Contours** section. Slide the **Number of Levels** to **255** and exit the **Surface Plot** window.

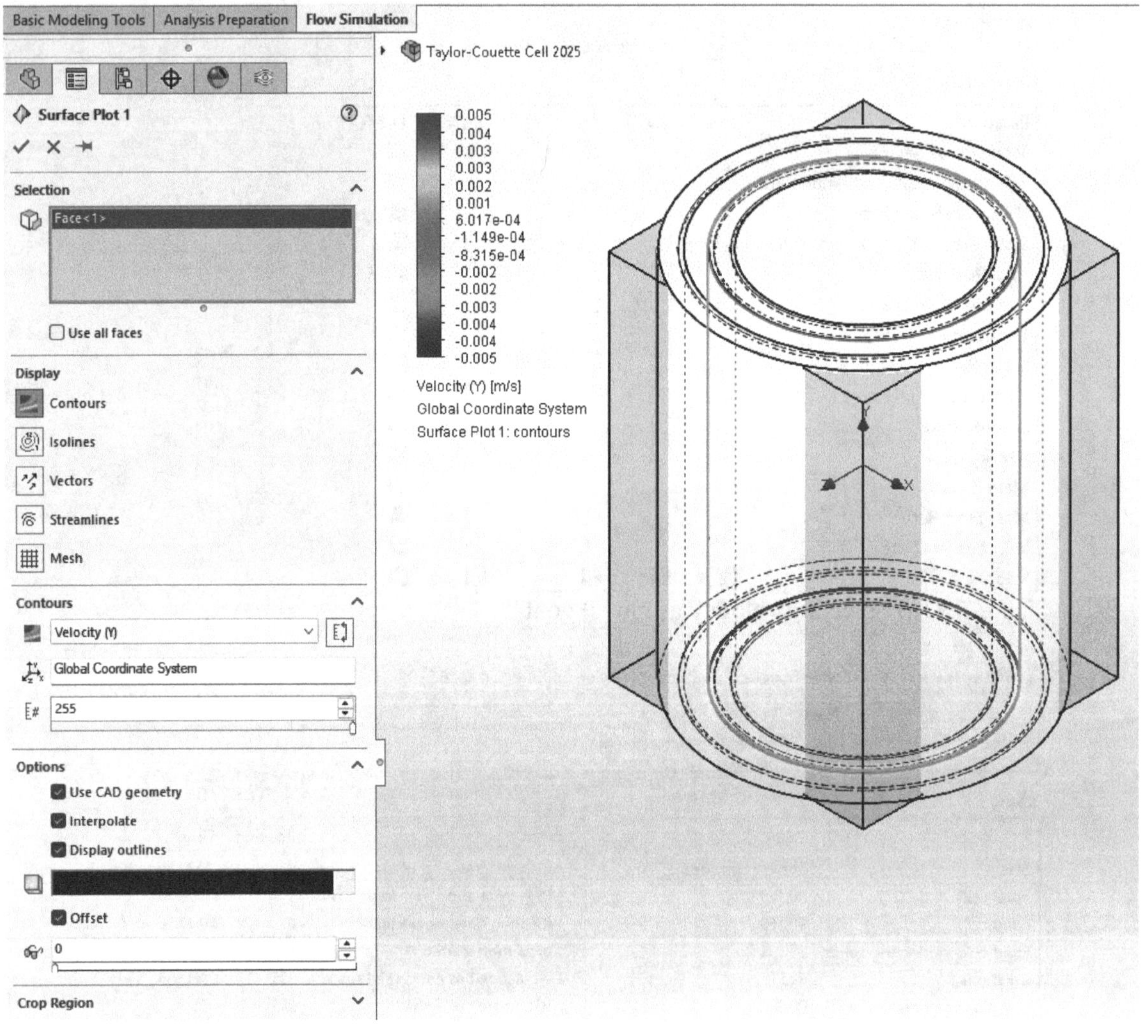

Figure 5.32 Surface plot settings.

33. Select **Tools>>Flow Simulation>>Results>>Display>>Lighting** from the SOLIDWORKS menu. Select **Isometric** view from the **View Orientation** drop down menu in the graphics window. Rename the surface plot to **Velocity (Y)**. Click on **Section View** and select the **Top Plane** for **Section 1**. Check the box for **Section 2** and select **Top Plane, Reverse Section Direction**  . Exit the **Section View** window. Select **Create the section view with the current settings** when you get a message window. The velocity field is shown in figure 5.33. Alternating bands of high and low velocity are shown in the spanwise *Y* direction indicating the presence of Taylor vortices. It should be emphasized that the surface plot is not located on the rotating cylinder but offset in the radial direction towards the outer cylinder. Right click on **Computational Domain** in the **Input Data** folder and select **Hide**. Right click on **Instabilities in Taylor-Couette Flow** and select **Hide Global Coordinate System**.

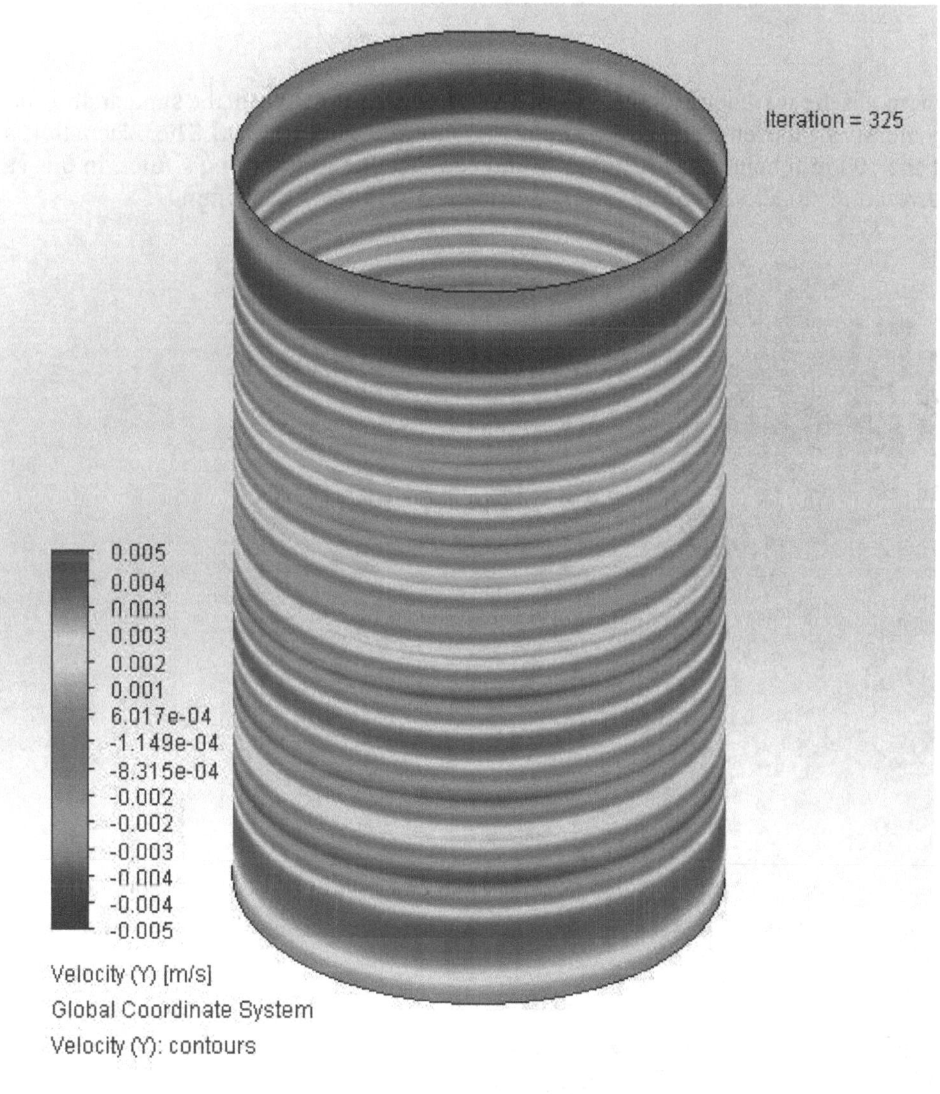

Figure 5.33 Surface plot for Taylor-Couette flow: Velocity (Y)

Q. Comparison with Neutral-Stability Theory

34. The instability of the flow between two vertical rotating cylinders is governed by the Taylor number *Ta*.

$$Ta = \frac{4\Omega_i^2 d^4}{\nu^2} \tag{5.6}$$

where Ω_i is the rotation rate of the inner cylinder, d is the distance between the cylinders and ν is the kinematic viscosity of the fluid. Below the critical $Ta_{crit} = 3430$ for a non-rotating outer cylinder, the flow is stable, but instabilities will develop above this Taylor number. The non-dimensional wave number α of this instability is determined by

$$\alpha = \frac{2\pi d}{\lambda} \tag{5.7}$$

where λ is the wave length of the instability. The wave-length from the simulation is determined by measuring the length of 6 wave lengths as shown in Figure 5.34a). The 6λ length is a fraction of the 100 mm height of the cylinder and can be determined using a ruler. In this case 6λ corresponds to 72.9 mm in Figure 5.34a) which gives $\lambda = 12.15$ mm.

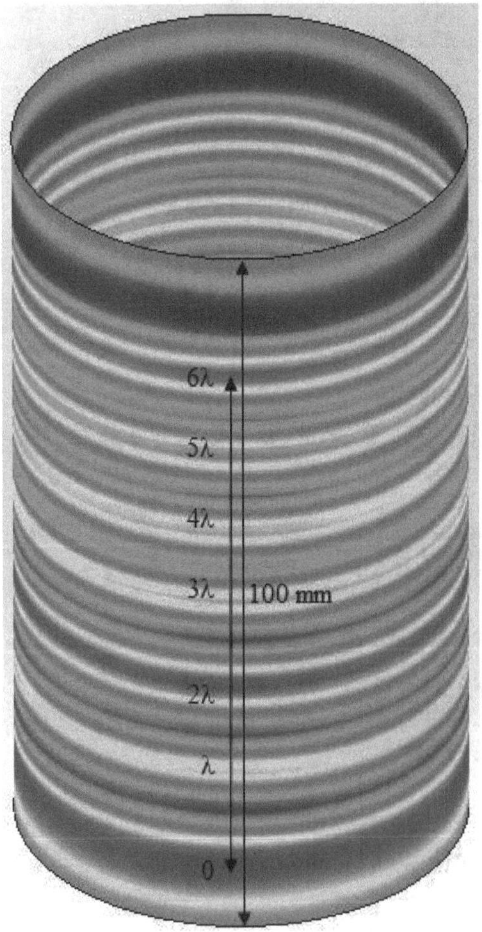

Figure 5.34a) Determining the wave-length λ of the Taylor-Couette instability

The critical wave number is $\alpha_{crit} = 3.12$ in the narrow gap limit: $\eta \rightarrow 1$. The radius ratio is defined as $\eta = r_i/r_o$ where r_i and r_o is the radius of the inner and outer cylinder, respectively. The wave number can be determined to be

$$\alpha = \frac{2\pi \cdot 0.005}{0.01215} = 2.585 \tag{5.8}$$

The Taylor number in the calculations is

$$Ta = \frac{4 \cdot 1.5^2 \cdot 0.005^4}{(1.004 \cdot 10^{-6})^2} = 5580 \tag{5.9}$$

The neutral stability curve to the first approximation can be seen in Figure 5.34b).

$$Ta = \frac{2(\pi^2+\alpha^2)^3}{(1+\mu)\alpha^2\left\{1-16\alpha\pi^2 cosh^2(\frac{\alpha}{2})/[(\pi^2+\alpha^2)^2(\sinh\alpha+\alpha)]\right\}} \tag{5.10}$$

where $\mu = \Omega_o/\Omega_i$ and Ω_o is the rotation rate of the outer cylinder.

Create an Excel sheet and enter 0.1 and 0.2 in cells A2 and A3, respectively. Select the two cells and drag the column downward to a maximum value of 10 in cell A101. Label the column as α. Enter the following equation in cell B2:

=2*(PI()^2+A2^2)^3/(A2^2*(1-16*A2*PI()^2*COSH(A2/2)^2/((PI()^2+A2^2)^2*(SINH(A2)+A2))))

Drag cell B2 downward all the way to cell B101 corresponding to $\alpha = 10$. Label the column as *Ta*. Select the two columns and select Insert>>Charts>>Scatter with Smooth Lines. Set the *y*-axis to a logarithmic scale with Minimum and Maximum Bounds set to 1000 and 100000, respectively. Enter 2.585 in cell C2 and 5580 in cell D2. Label columns C and D as α and *Ta*, respectively.

Select the curve in the chart, right click and choose Select Data.... Select Add in the Select Data Source window. Enter Flow Simulation as Series name:, =Sheet1!$C$2:$C$2 as Series X values: and =Sheet1!$D$2:$D$2 as Series Y values:. Select OK to close the Edit Series window.

Check the box for Legend associated with the chart by selecting the plus sign that becomes available when you move the cursor to the upper right corner of the chart and left click. Select Flow Simulation Legend in the chart, right click and select Change Series Chart Type.... Select Scatter as Chart Type for Flow Simulation.

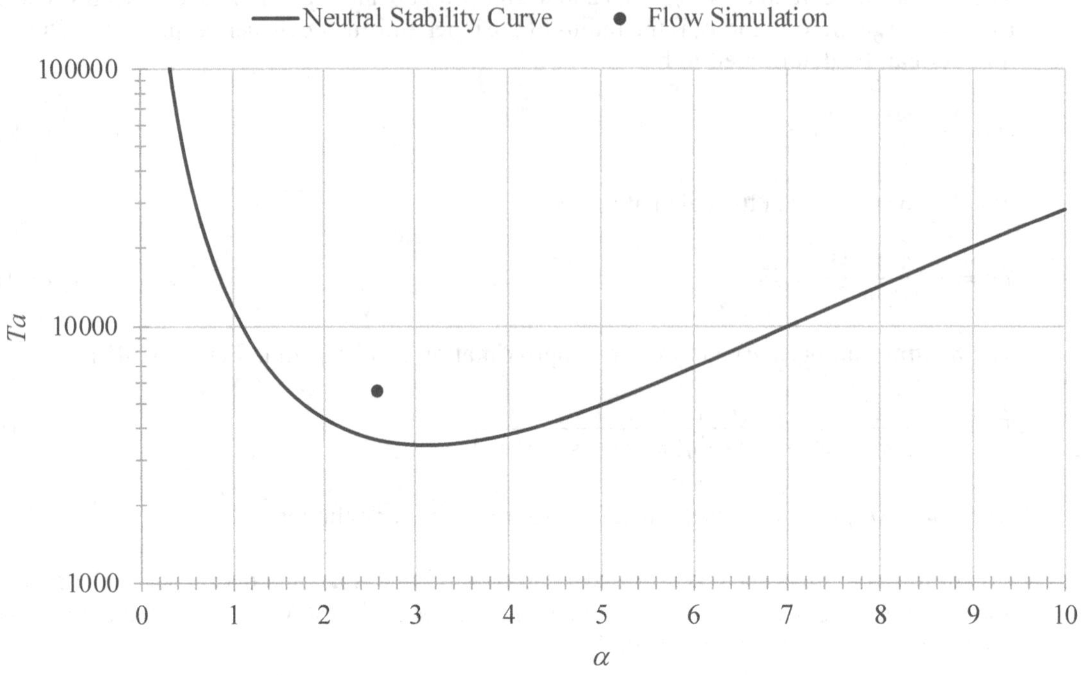

Figure 5.34b) Neutral stability curve for Taylor-Couette flow with stationary outer cylinder, $\mu = 0$. The circle represents result from Flow Simulation. The radius ratio is $\eta = 6/7$ in the Flow Simulation calculations and $\eta = 1$ for the stability curve.

R. References

1. Chandrasekhar, S., Hydrodynamic and Hydromagnetic Stability, Dover, 1981.
2. Koschmieder, E.L., Benard Cells and Taylor Vortices, Cambridge, 1993.

S. Exercises

5.1 Run the calculations for the flow in the Taylor-Couette apparatus with only the inner cylinder rotating $\mu = 0$ for Taylor numbers $Ta = 10000$, 20000 and 30000 and compare the spanwise wave numbers with the one determined in this chapter for $Ta = 5580$. Include your results in figure 5.34 for comparison with the neutral stability curve.

5.2 Run the calculations for the flow in the Taylor-Couette apparatus with both cylinders rotating $\mu = 1$ and for Taylor numbers $Ta = 3000$, 5000 and 10000 and determine the spanwise wave numbers. Include your results in a graph and compare with the neutral stability curve corresponding to $\mu = -1/2$, see equation 10.

5.3 Run the calculations for the flow in a Rayleigh-Bénard cell for Rayleigh numbers $Ra = 5000$, 10000 and 20000 and compare the wave numbers with the one determined in this chapter for $Ra = 2953$. Include your results in figure 5.23 for comparison with the neutral stability curve.

CHAPTER 6. PIPE FLOW

A. Objectives

- Creating the SOLIDWORKS model of the pipe needed
- Setting up Flow Simulation projects for internal flows
- Creating a fluid with a certain value of dynamic viscosity
- Creating lids for boundary conditions
- Setting up boundary conditions
- Running the calculations
- Using cut plots and XY plots to visualize the resulting flow field
- Compare results with theory and empirical data

B. Problem Description

In this chapter, we will use Flow Simulation to study flows in pipes and compare with the theoretical solutions and empirical data. First, we will model the laminar flow with a mean velocity of 0.5 m/s corresponding to a Reynolds number *Re* = 100 for a 5 m long pipe with an inner diameter of 200 mm. Next, we will consider turbulent flow in the same pipe extended to a length of 10 m and a higher Reynolds number *Re* = 100,000. We start by creating the part needed for this simulation.

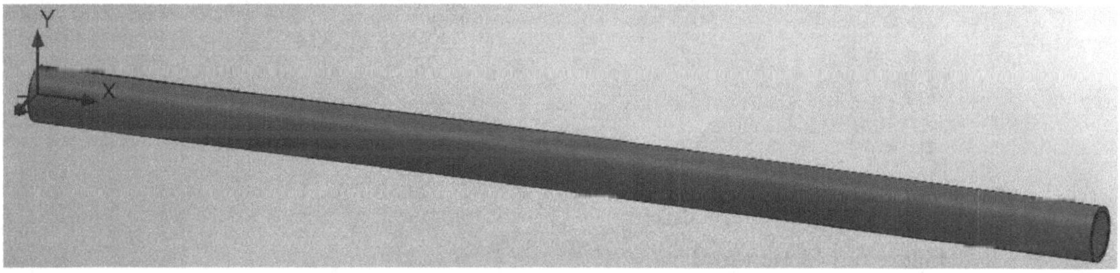

Figure 6.0 SOLIDWORKS model of pipe section

C. Creating the SOLIDWORKS Part

1. Start by creating a new part in SOLIDWORKS: select **File>>New** and click on the **OK** button in the **New SOLIDWORKS Document** window. Select **Tools>>Options...** from the SOLIDWORKS menu. Click on the Document Properties tab and select **Units**. Select **MMGS** as your **Unit system**. Click on **Right Plane** in the **FeatureManager design tree** and select **Right** from the **View Orientation** drop down menu in the graphics window.

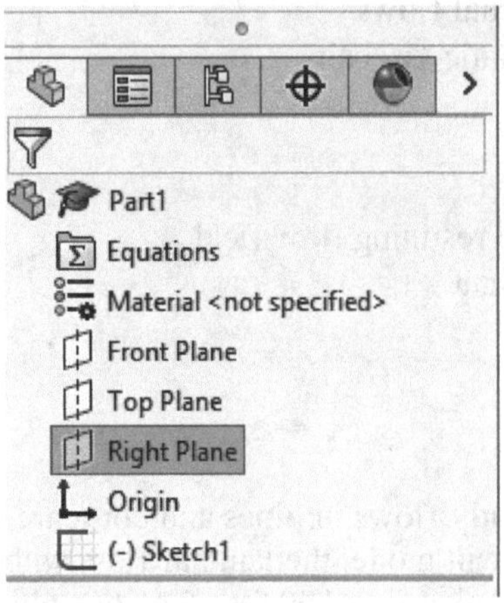

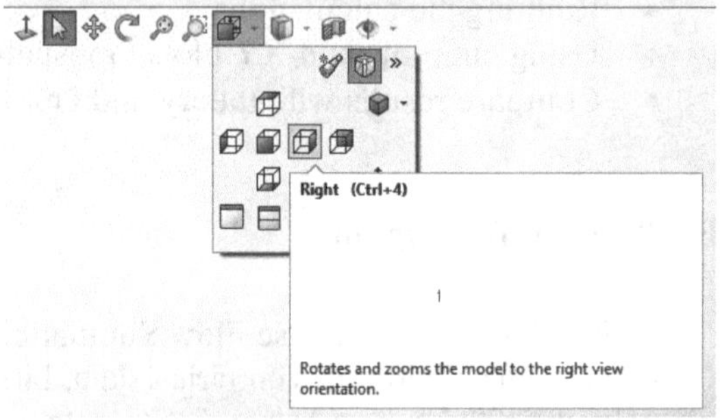

Figure 6.1a) Selection of right plane Figure 6.1b) Selection of right view

2. Click on the **Basic Modeling Tools** tab and **Circle**.

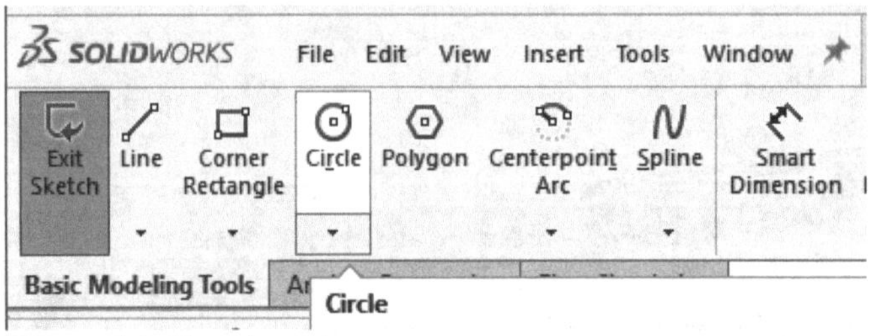

Figure 6.2 Sketch tool

3. Click on the origin in the graphics window and create a circle. Fill in the **Parameters** for the circle: **100 mm** radius. Close the **Circle** dialog box by clicking on ✓ . Repeat this step and create another concentric circle with a larger radius of **120 mm**.

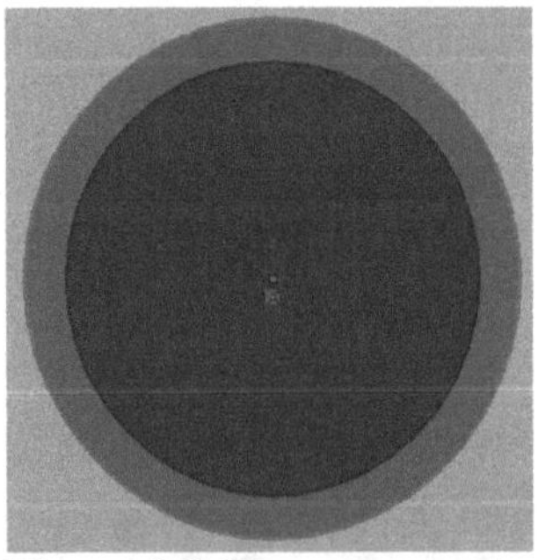

Figure 6.3 Two concentric circles with radii 100 mm and 120 mm

4. Select the **Analysis Preparation** tab and **Extruded Boss/Base**. Enter a **Depth D1** of **5000 mm** in **Direction 1**. Next, click **OK** to exit the **Extrude Property Manager**.

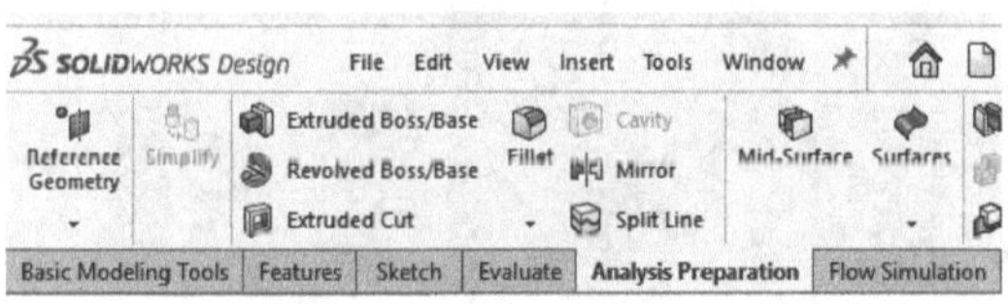

Figure 6.4a) Selection of extrusion feature

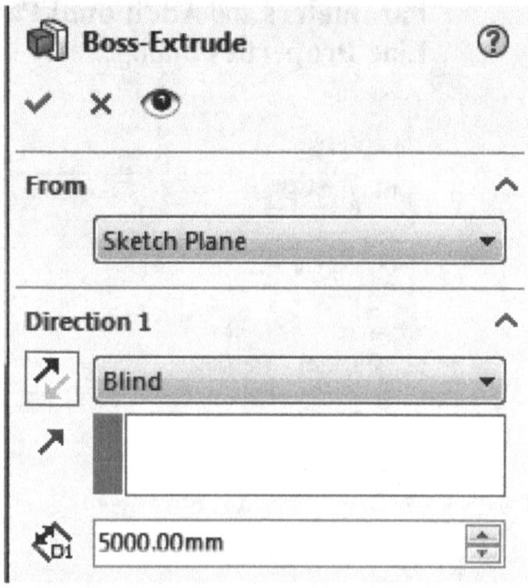

Figure 6.4b) Entering depth of extrusion

5. Select **Wireframe** from the **Display Style** drop down menu in the graphics window. Select **Front** from the **View Orientation** drop down menu in the graphics window. Click on **Front Plane** in the **FeatureManager design tree.** Right click in the graphics window and select **Zoom/Pan/Rotate>>Zoom to Area** and zoom in around the left end of the pipe.

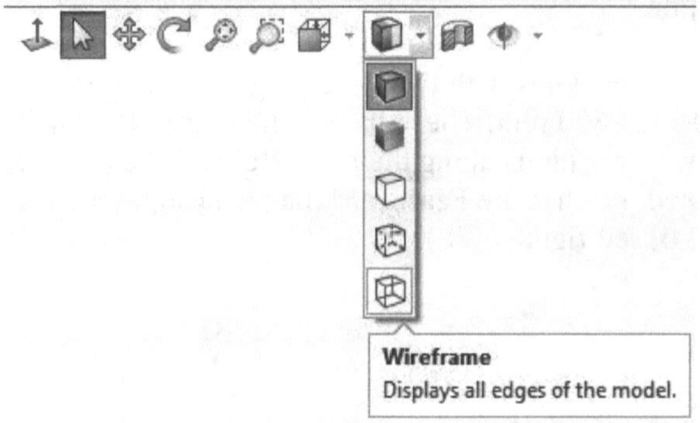

Figure 6.5a) Displaying the wireframe style

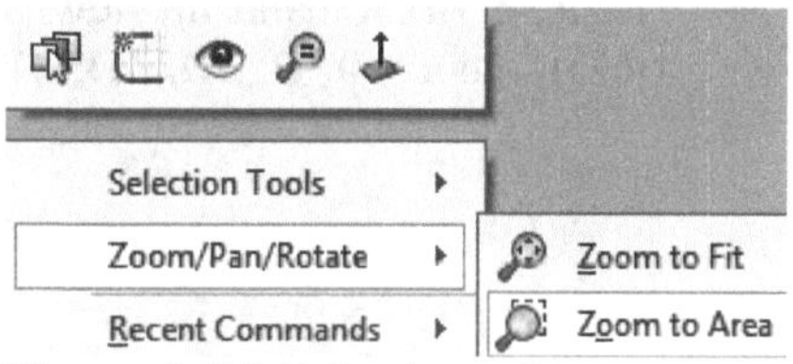

Figure 6.5b) Selection of zoom to area

6. Select the **Front** plane and **Line** sketch tool. Draw a vertical line in the Y-direction starting at the origin in the center of the pipe and end at the inner surface of the pipe. Right click in the graphics window and click on **Select.** Click on the new line and set the **Parameters** and **Additional Parameters** to the values shown in Figure 6.6. Close the **Line Properties** dialog.

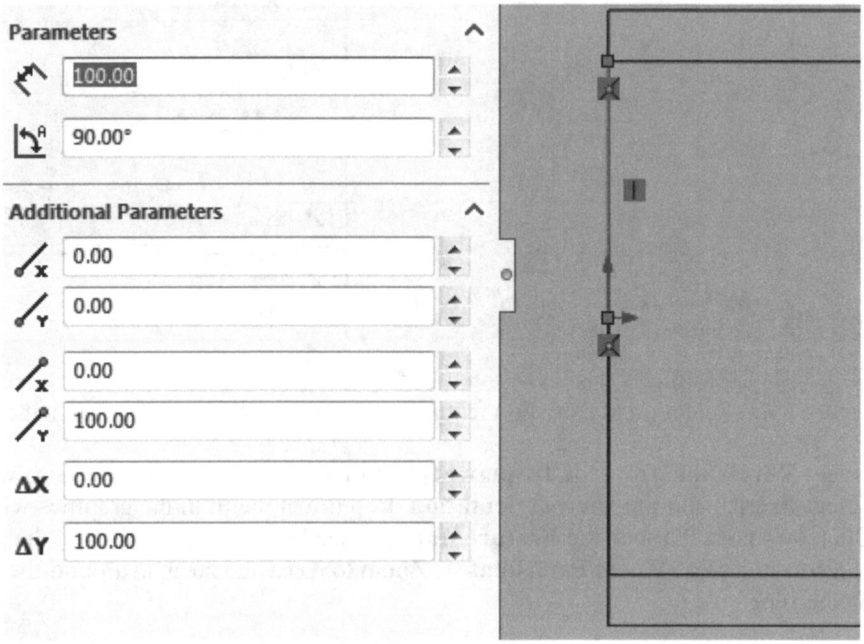

Figure 6.6 Parameters for vertical line

7. Repeat step **6** and draw five more vertical lines with the same length and the lines positioned at $x = 200$, 400, 600, 800 and 4600 mm. These lines will be used to plot the velocity profiles at different streamwise positions along the pipe. Rebuild the part, see figure 6.7a). Rename the newly created sketch in the **FeatureManager design tree** with the name **x = 0, D, 2D, 3D, 4D, 23D**, see figure 6.7b).

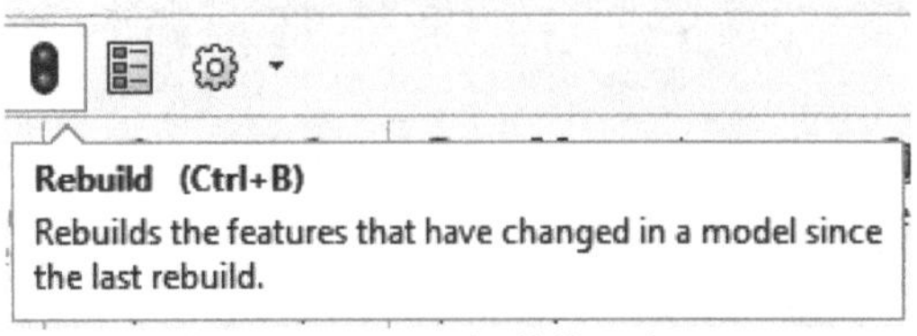

Figure 6.7a) Rebuilding the part

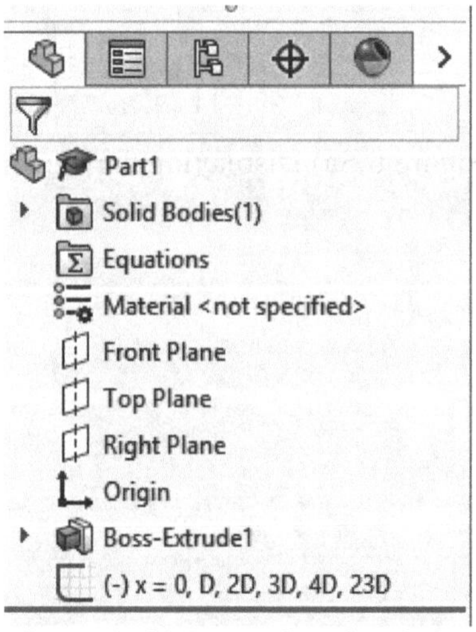

Figure 6.7b) Renaming sketch for pipe flow

8. Create a new sketch by clicking on **Front Plane** in the **FeatureManager design tree** and selecting **Insert>>Sketch** from the menu. Draw a **4600 mm** long horizontal line in the *x*-direction starting at the origin of the pipe. Rebuild the part. Rename the sketch in the **FeatureManager design tree** and call it **x = 0 – 4.6 m (centerline)**. Repeat this step but draw the line along the wall of the pipe and name the sketch **x = 0 – 4.6 m (wall)**. Save the SOLIDWORKS part with the following name: **Pipe Flow 2026.**

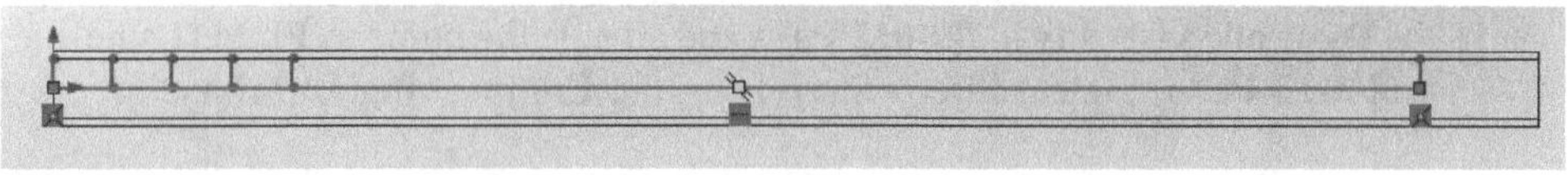

Figure 6.8a) Adding a line in the x-direction along the centerline of the pipe

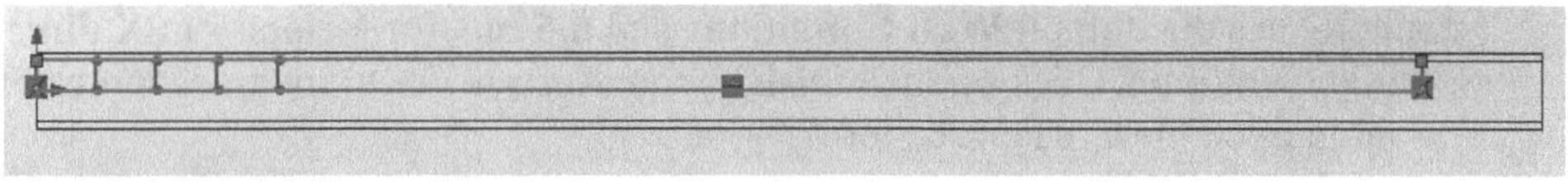

Figure 6.8b) Adding a line in the x-direction along the wall of the pipe

D. Flow Simulation Project

9. If Flow Simulation is not available in the menu, you can add it from the SOLIDWORKS menu: **Tools>>Add Ins…** and check the corresponding **SOLIDWORKS Flow Simulation** box. Select **Tools>>Flow Simulation>>Project>>Wizard…** from the SOLIDWORKS menu to create a new Flow Simulation project. Create a new project named **Pipe Flow Study**. Click on the **Next >** button. Select the default **SI (m-kg-s)** unit system and click on the **Next>** button once again.

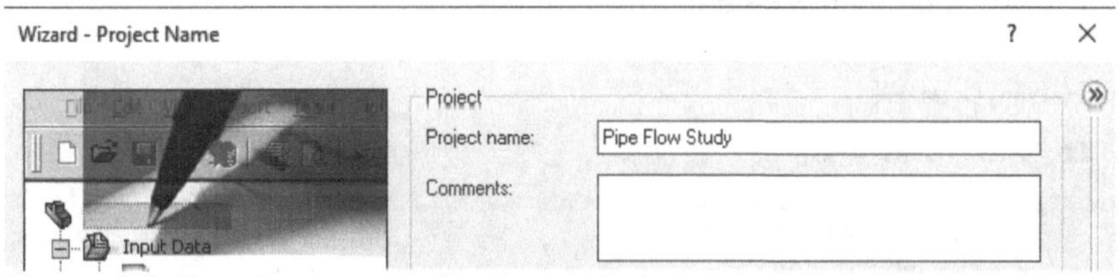

Figure 6.9 Creating a name for the project

10. Use the **Internal Analysis type**. Click on the **Next >** button.

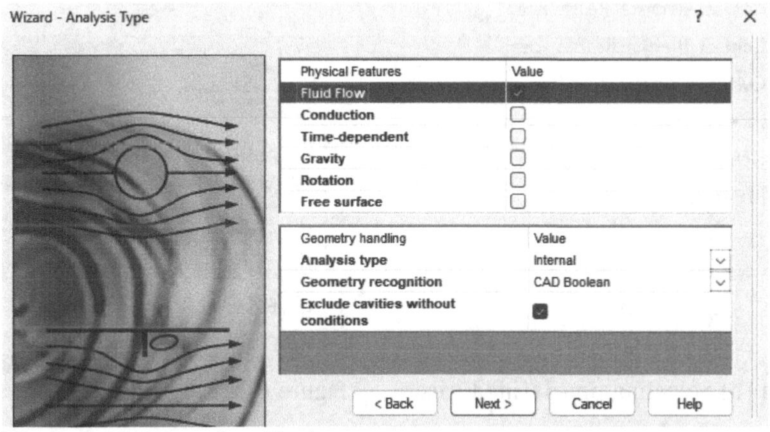

Figure 6.10 Internal analysis

11. Click on the **New...** button in the **Default Fluid** window to open the **Engineering Database**. Expand **Materials** in the **Database tree** by clicking on the plus sign next to the materials folder. Expand **Gases** and click on **Pre-Defined.** Select **Air** from the list of **Pre-Defined Items**, right click and select **Copy**.

    Click on **User Defined Gases** in the **Database tree**, right click in the field under the **Items** tab and **Paste.** Right click on the pasted **Air** and select **Item Properties**. Change the **Dynamic viscosity** to **0.0012 Pa*s** and change the name to **Fluid (Dynamic viscosity = 0.0012 Pa*s)**. Select **File>>Save** from the **Engineering Database** menu.

    Close the **Engineering Database** window and add the new fluid under **Gases** as **Project Fluid**. Select **Laminar Only** from the **Flow Type** drop down menu. Click on the **Next >** button. Use the default **Wall Conditions** and **0.5 m/s** for **Velocity in X direction** as **Initial Condition**. Click on the **Finish** button. Answer Yes to the question whether you want to open the Create Lids tool?

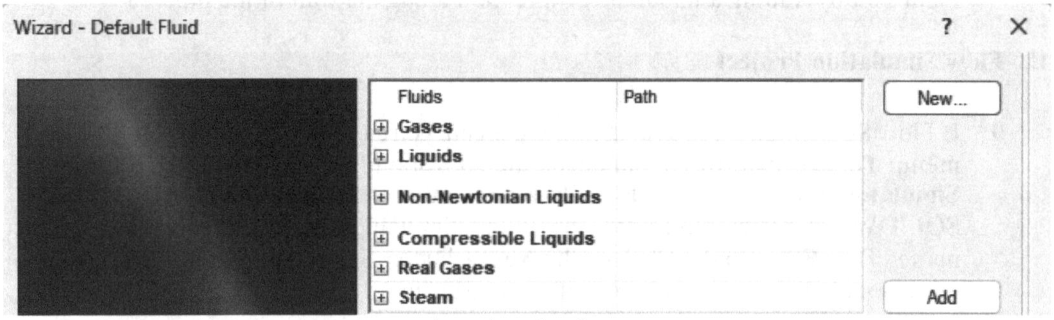

Figure 6.11a) Opening the engineering database

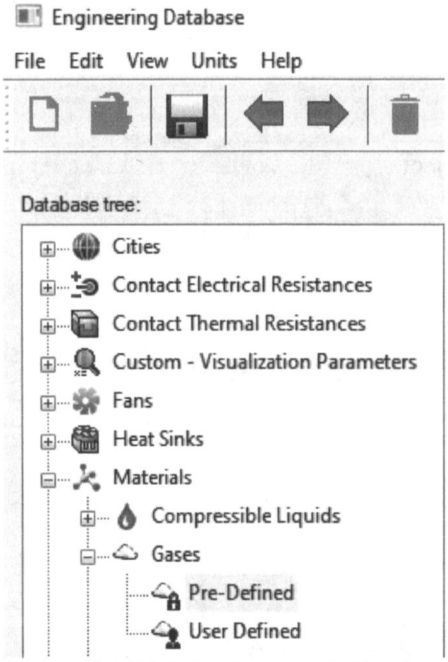

Figure 6.11b) Selecting pre-defined gases

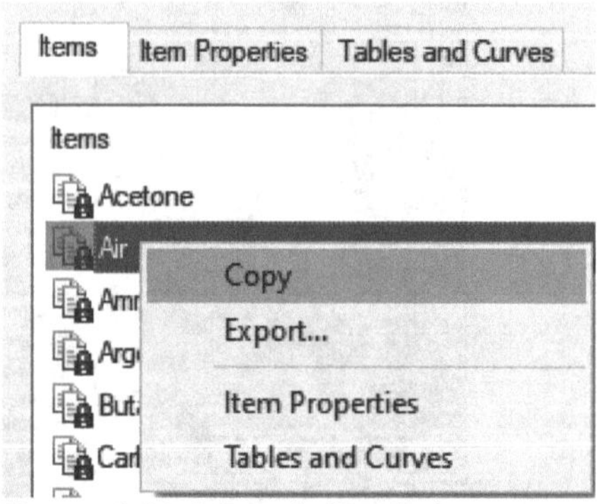

Figure 6.11c) Pre-defined air

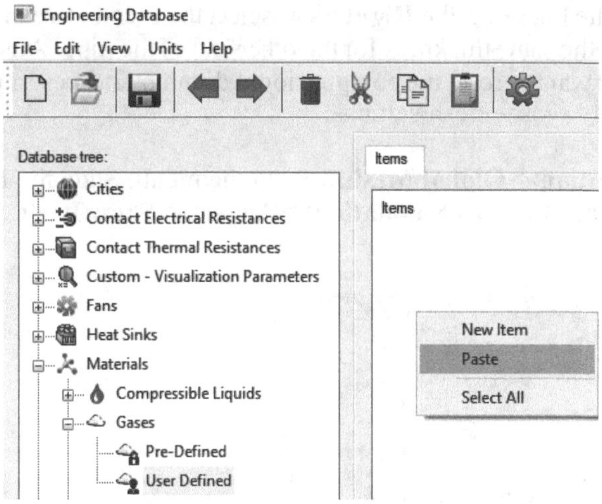

Figure 6.11d) Pasting air to user defined gases

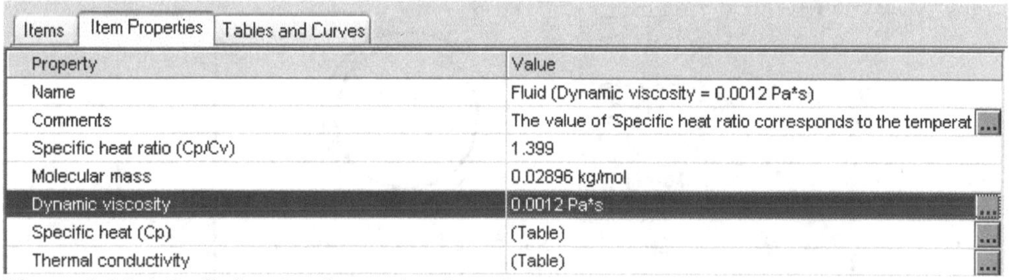

Figure 6.11e) Defining the dynamic viscosity

E. Lids for the Pipe

12. Rotate the pipe a little bit or select Left view so that you can access the outer left end surface of the pipe and click on the face between the two circles. Click on the **Adjust Thickness** button and adjust the thickness of the lid to **1.00 mm**. Close the **Create Lids** dialog . Answer **yes** to the questions whether you want to reset the computational domain and mesh settings. Answer **Yes** to the question whether you want to open the Create Lids tool?

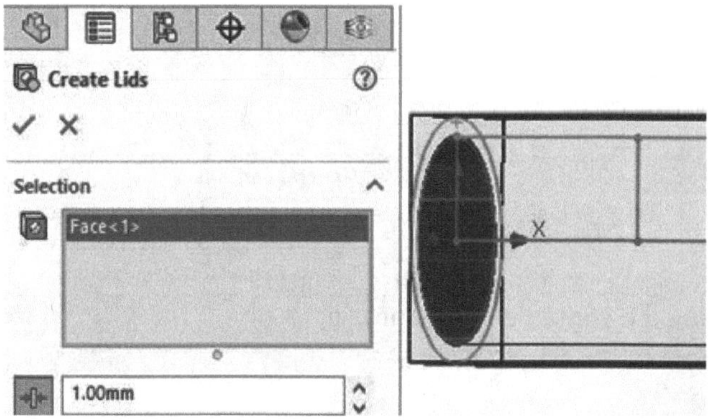

Figure 6.12 Creating a lid for the pipe

13. Repeat step **12** one more time but select the **Right** view, select the face between the two circles and create a lid with the same thickness for the other end of the pipe. Answer **yes** to the question whether you want to reset the computational domain and **yes** to the next question whether you want to reset mesh settings.

    Select **Tools>>Flow Simulation>>Global Mesh...** from the menu. Slide the **Level of Initial Mesh** to **7.** Select **Tools>>Flow Simulation>>Project>>Show Basic Mesh** to see the mesh.

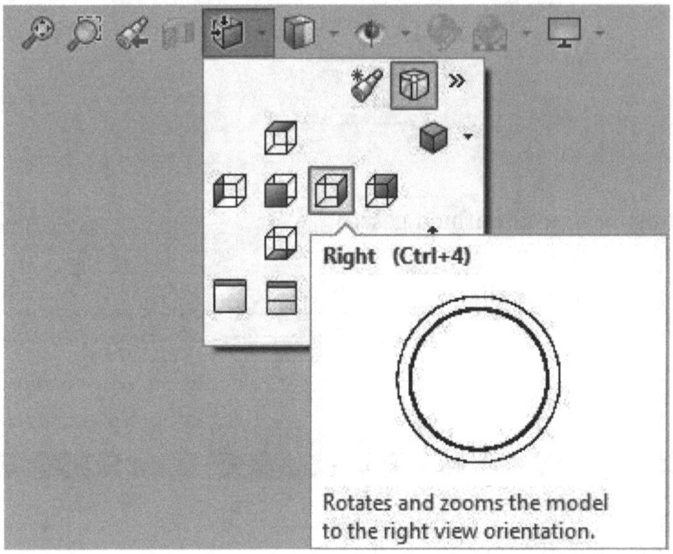

Figure 6.13 Selection of right view for the second lid

F. Computational Domain and Mesh

14. Select **Tools>>Flow Simulation>>Computational Domain...**. Select **Symmetry** boundary conditions at **Y min** and **Z min**, see figure 6.14b). Set both **Y min** and **Z min** to **0 m**. Exit the **Computational Domain** window.

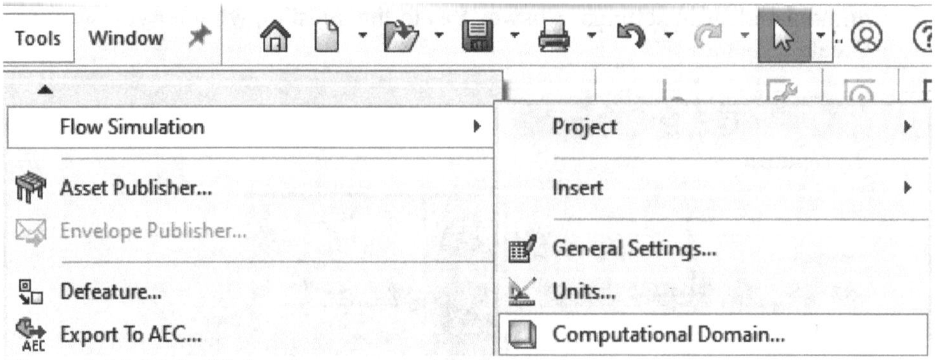

Figure 6.14a) Modifying the computational domain

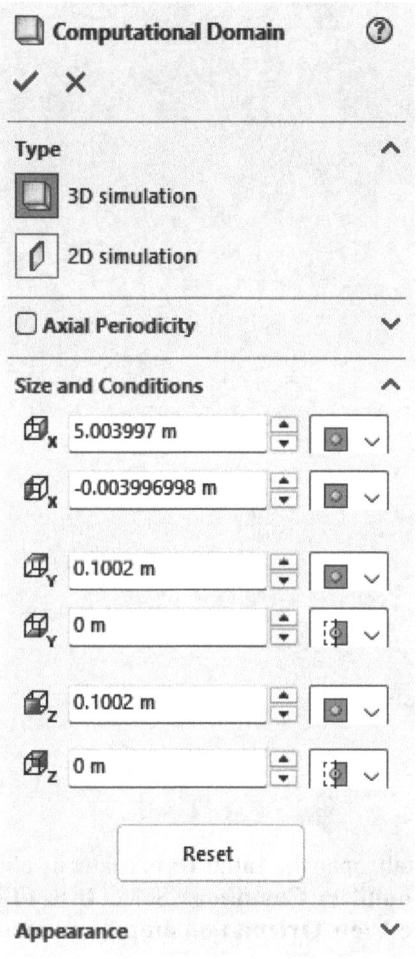

Figure 6.14b) Symmetry boundary conditions and size of the domain

15. Select **Tools>>Flow Simulation>>Global Mesh…**. Check the **Manual setting** as Type. Change the **Number of cells per X:** to **100** and set both **Number of cells per Y:** and **Number of cells per Z:** to **15**. Click on the **OK** button to exit the **Global Mesh Settings** window.

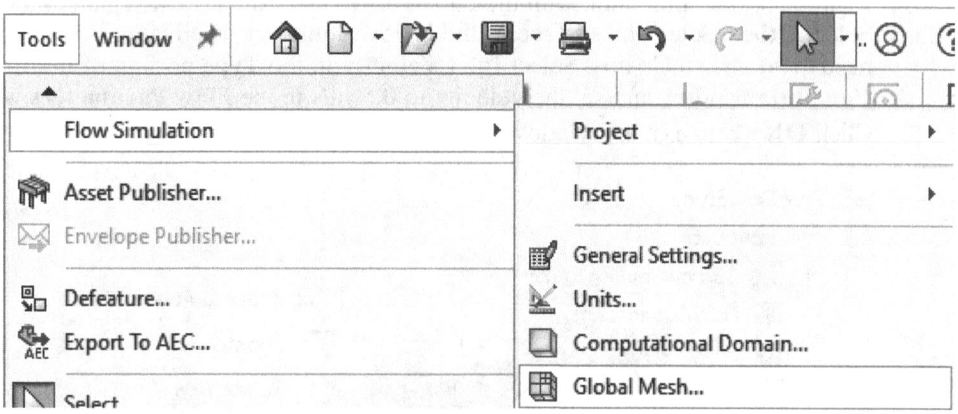

Figure 6.15a) Modifying the initial mesh

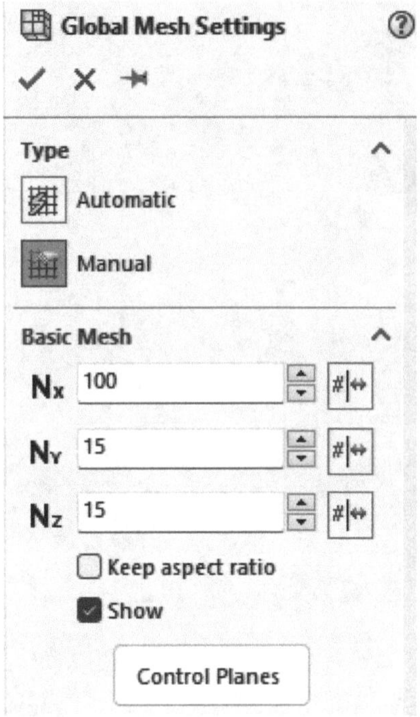

Figure 6.15b) Changing the number of cells

G. Boundary Conditions

16. Select the **Flow Simulation analysis tree** tab, open the **Input Data** folder by clicking on the plus sign next to it and right click on **Boundary Conditions**. Select **Insert Boundary Condition….** Select **Front View** from the **View Orientation** drop down menu in the graphics window.

    Right click in the graphics window and select **Zoom/Pan/Rotate>>Zoom to Area**. Zoom in on the left end of the pipe, right click in the graphics window and select **Zoom/Pan/Rotate>>Rotate View**. Click and drag the mouse wheel to the left so that the inner surface of the inflow boundary is visible. Right click and deselect **Rotate View**.

    Right click one more time with the cursor arrow over the inflow region and click on **Select Other**. Select the surface of the inflow boundary, see Figure 6.16c). You may need to zoom in to do this. Select **Inlet Velocity** in the **Type** portion of the **Boundary Condition** window and set the velocity to **0.5 m/s** in the **Flow Parameters** window. Click **OK** to exit the window.

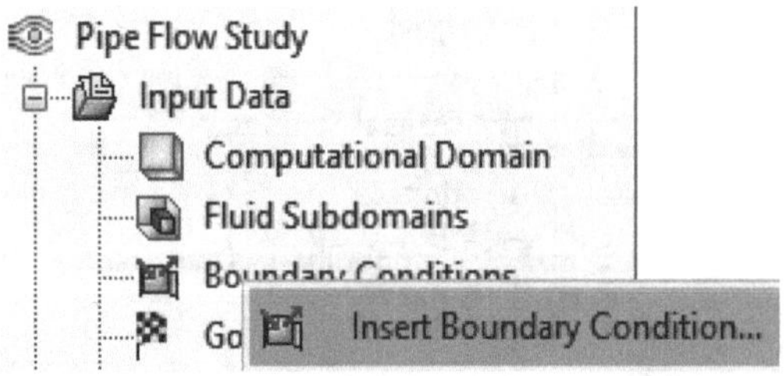

Figure 6.16a) Inserting boundary condition

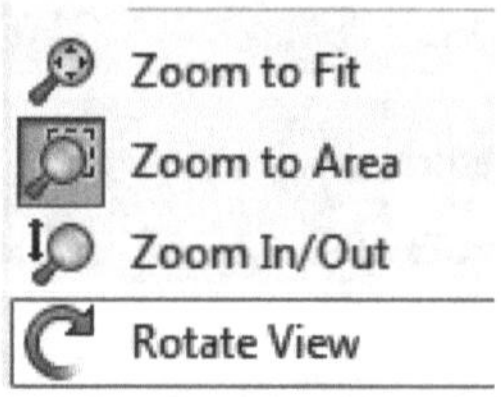

Figure 6.16b) Modifying the view

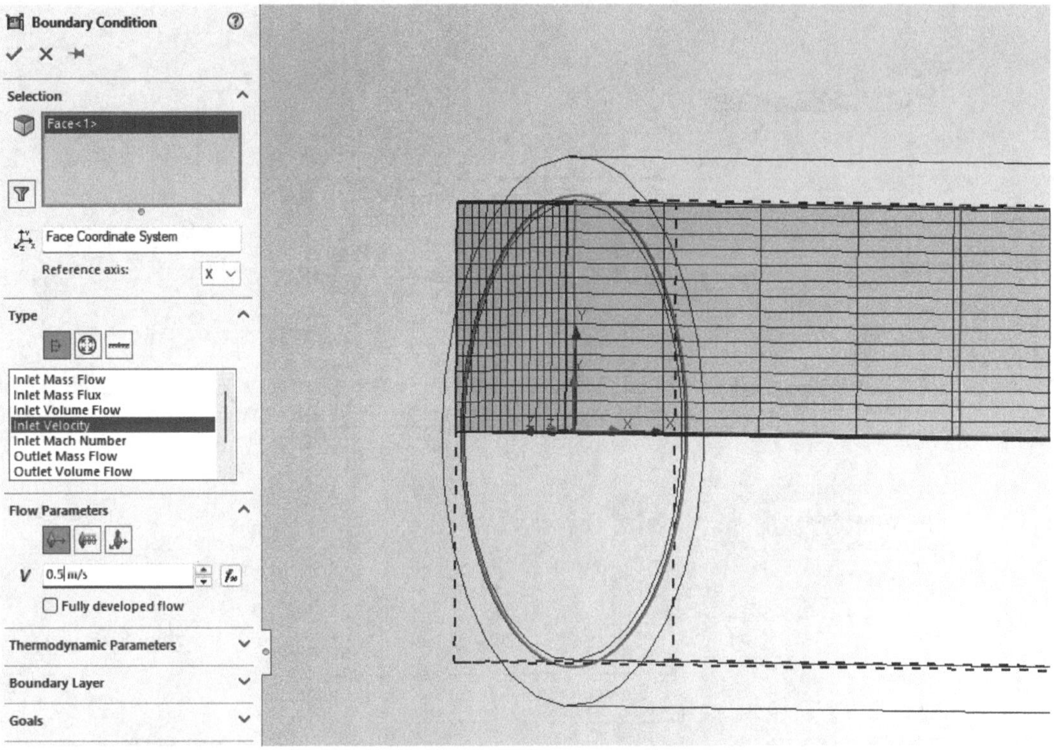

Figure 6.16c) Velocity boundary condition for the inflow

17. Right click in the graphics window and select **Zoom to Fit**. Select **Front View** from the **View Orientation** drop down menu in the graphics window. Right click in the graphics window and select **Zoom to Area**. Zoom in on the right end of the pipe.

    Right click again in the graphics window and select **Rotate View** once again to rotate the pipe so that the inner outlet surface is visible in the graphics window. Right click and click on **Select**.

    Right click on **Boundary Conditions** in the **Flow Simulation analysis tree** and select **Insert Boundary Condition…**. Right click one more time over the outflow region and click on **Select Other**. Select the surface of the outflow boundary, see Figure 6.17. Click on the **Pressure Openings** button in the **Type** portion of the **Boundary Condition** window and select **Static Pressure**. Click OK to exit the window.

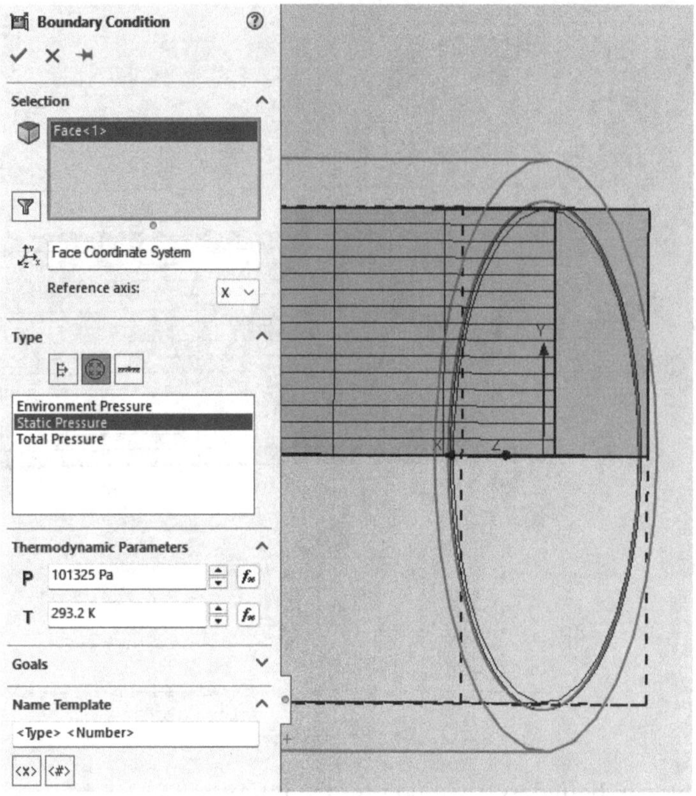

Figure 6.17 Selection of static pressure as boundary condition at the outlet of the flow

H. Global Goal and Calculation Control Options

18. Right click on **Goals** in the **Flow Simulation analysis tree** and select **Insert Global Goals…**. Select **Max Velocity (X)** as a global goal. Exit the **Global Goals** window.

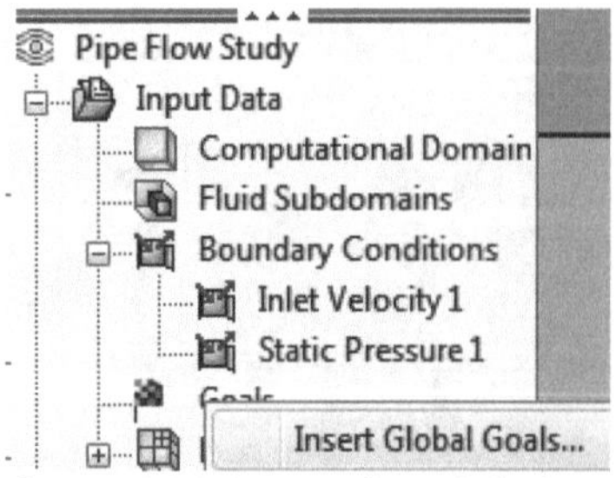

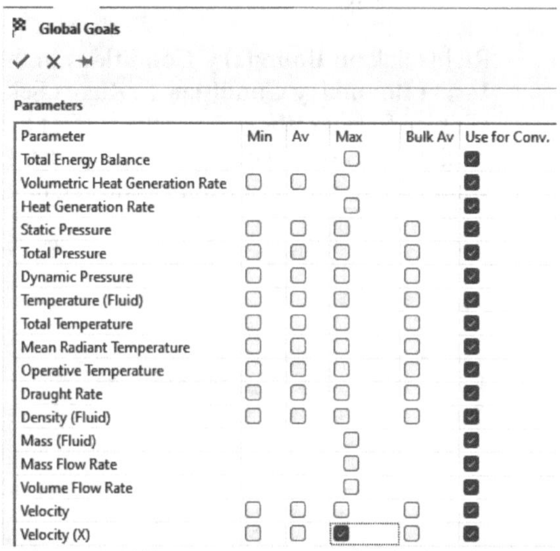

Figure 6.18a) Inserting global goals Figure 6.18b) X–component of velocity global goal

Select **Tools>>Flow Simulation>>Calculation Control Options...**. Select the **Refinement** tab. Set the refinement **level = 2** for **Global Domain**. Select **Goal Convergence** and **Iterations** as **Refinement strategy** under **Refinement Settings**. Click on  in the **Value** column for **Goals** and check the box for **GG Maximum Velocity (X) 1**. Select the **Finishing** tab in the Calculations Control Options window and uncheck the **Travels** check box under **Finish Conditions**. Set the **Refinements** to **2**.

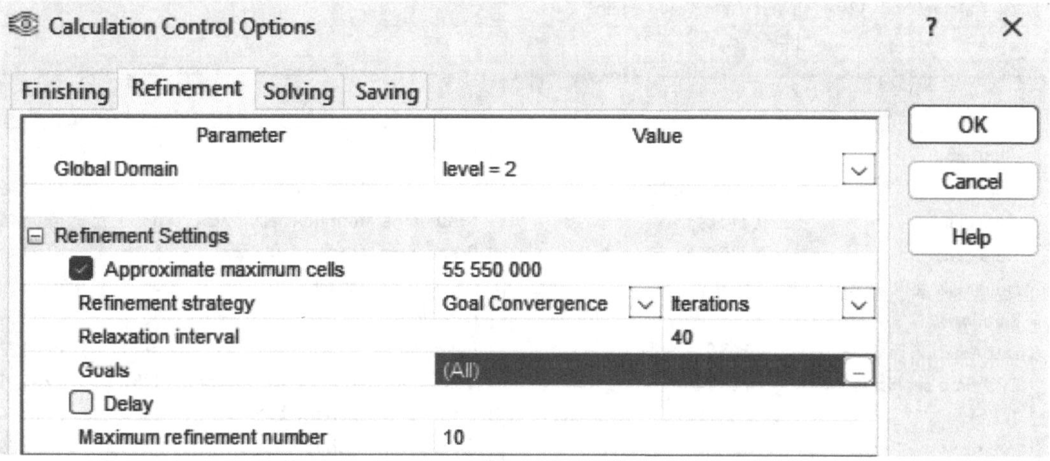

Figure 6.18c) Refinement settings for Calculation Control Options

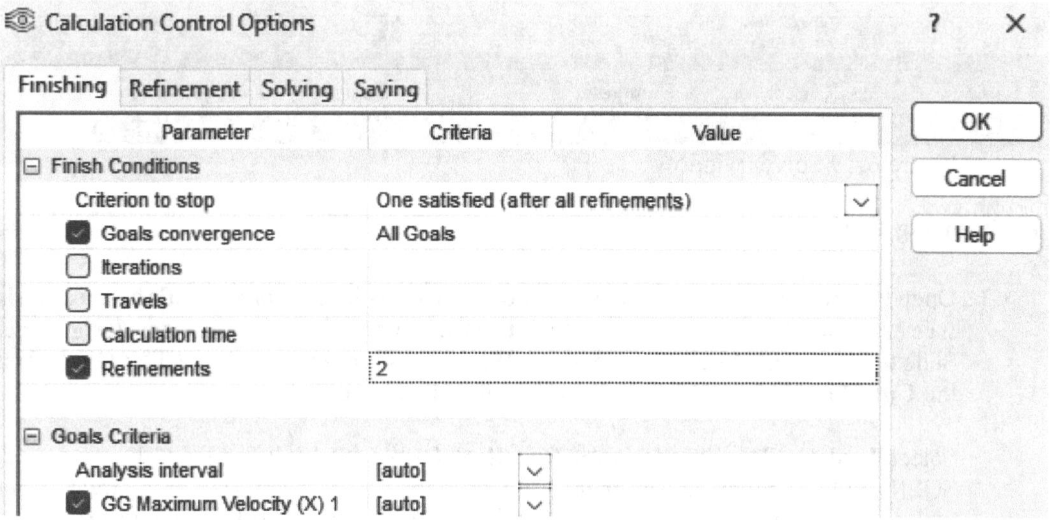

Figure 6.18d) Finishing settings for Calculation Control Options

I. Flow Simulations for Laminar Pipe Flow

19. Select **Tools>>Flow Simulation>>Solve>>Run...** to start calculations. Click on the **Run** button in the **Run** window.

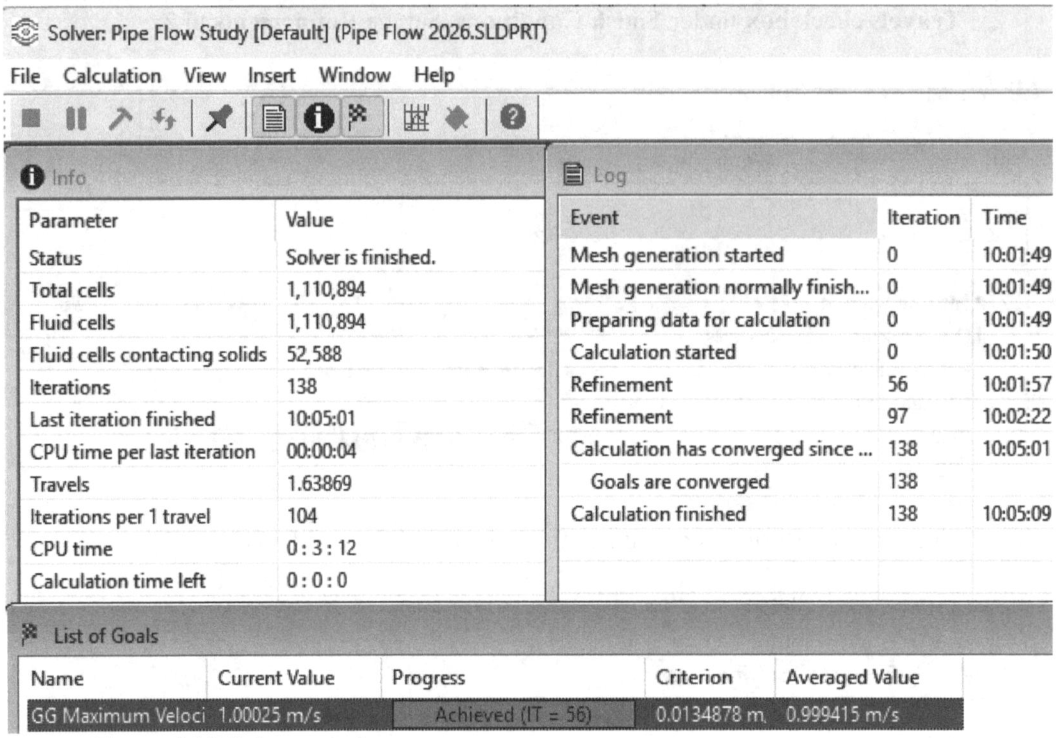

Figure 6.19 Solver window

J. Inserting Cut Plots

20. Open the **Results** folder and right click on **Cut Plots** in the **Flow Simulation analysis tree** and select **Insert…**. Select the **Front Plane** from the **FeatureManager design tree**. Slide the **Number of Levels** slide bar to **255** in the **Contours** section. Click OK to exit the **Cut Plot** window. Rename the cut plot to **Pressure**.

    Select **Tools>>Flow Simulation>>Results>>Display>>Lighting** from the SOLIDWORKS menu. Select **Front View** from the **View Orientation** drop down menu in the graphics window. Right click on the scale and select **Make Horizontal**. Select **Section View** for the **Front Plane**. In the **Flow Simulation analysis tree**, right-click on **Pipe Flow Study** and select **Hide Global Coordinate System**. In the **FeatureManager design tree**, control select the three sketches, right click and select hide.

    Repeat this step but select **Velocity (X)** from the **Parameter** drop down menu in the **Contours** section. Rename the cut plot to **Velocity (X)**. Right-click on the **Pressure Cut Plot** and select **Hide** to display the **Velocity (X) Cut Plot**. Double click on the scale for Velocity (X) in the graphics window and set the minimum to 0. Figure 6.20a) shows the pressure gradient along the length of the pipe. Figure 6.20b) shows the velocity distribution for the fluid in the pipe (a quarter of the pipe).

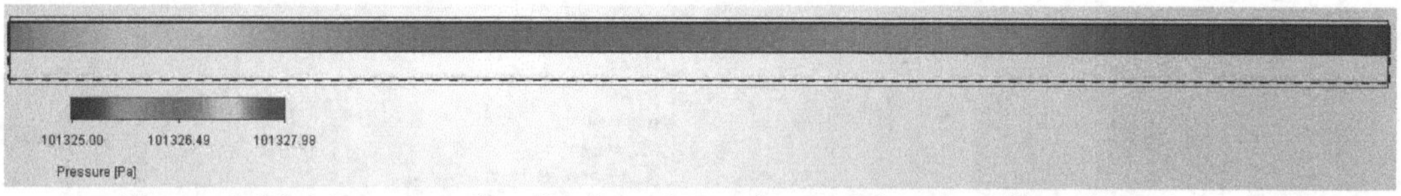

Figure 6.20a) Pressure distribution along the straight pipe (flow from left to right)

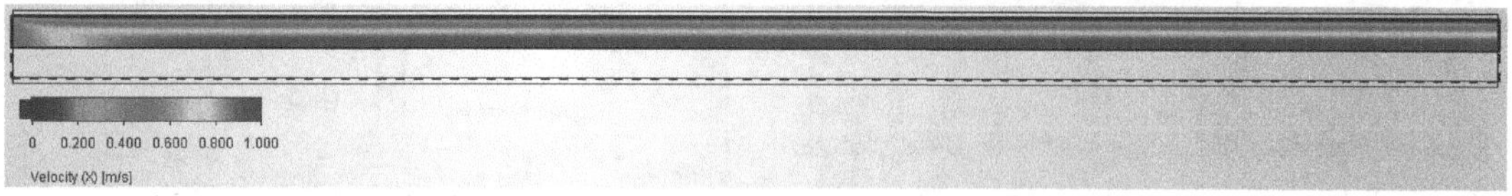

Figure 6.20b) Velocity (X) development along the straight pipe (flow from left to right)

K. Inserting XY Plots for Laminar Pipe Flow Using Templates

21. Place the files "**graph 6.21c)**", "**graph 6.22**", and "**graph 6.23**" on the desktop. These files are available for download from *sdcpublications.com.*

    Click on the **FeatureManager design tree**. Click on the sketch **x = 0, D, 2D, 3D, 4D, 23D**. Click on the **Flow Simulation analysis tree** tab. Right click **XY Plot** and select **Insert….** Check the **Velocity (X)** box. Open the **Resolution** portion of the **XY Plot** window and slide the **Geometry Resolution** as far as it goes to the right. Click on the **Evenly Distribute Output Points** button and increase the number of points to **500.**

    Open the **Options** portion of the **XY Plot** window and select **Excel Workbook (*.xlsx)** from the drop-down menu. Click **Export to Excel** to generate an Excel file that will open a graph of the velocity in the pipe at different streamwise positions.

    Double click on the **graph 6.21c)** file to open the file. Click on **Enable Editing** and **Enable Content** if you get a **Security Warning** that **Macros** have been disabled. If **Developer** is not available in the menu of the **Excel** file, you will need to do the following: Select **File>>Options** from the menu and click on the **Customize Ribbon** on the left-hand side. Check the **Developer** box on the right-hand side under **Main Tabs.** Click **OK** to exit the **Excel Options** window.

    Click on the **Developer** tab in the **Excel** menu for the **graph 6.21c)** file and select **Visual Basic** on the left-hand side to open the editor. Click on the plus sign next to **VBAProject (XY Plot 1.xlsx)** and click on the plus sign next to **Microsoft Excel Objects**. Right click on **Sheet2 (Plot Data)** and select **View Object.**

    Select **Macro** in the **Modules** folder under **VBAProject (graph 6.21c).xlsm)**. Select **Run>>Run Macro** from the menu of the **MVB for Applications** window. Click on the **Run** button in the **Macros** window. **Figure 6.21c)** will become available in **Excel** showing the streamwise velocity component ***u (m/s)*** versus wall normal coordinate *y* ***(m).*** Close the **XY Plot** window and the **graph 6.21c)** window in **Excel.** Exit the **XY Plot** window in **SOLIDWORKS Flow Simulation** and rename the inserted *xy*-plot in the **Flow Simulation analysis tree** to **Laminar Pipe Flow Velocity Profiles.**

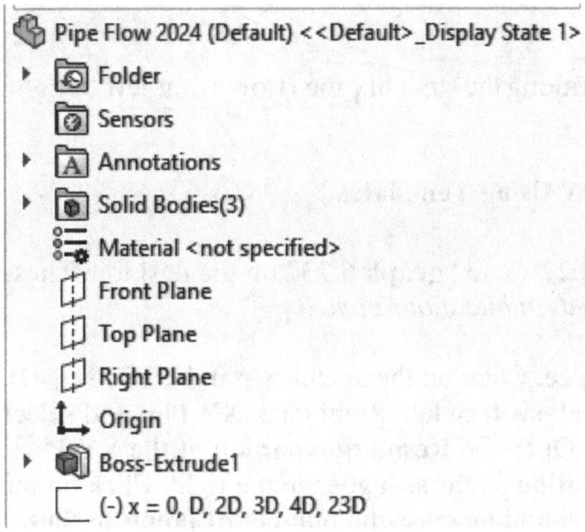

Figure 6.21a) Selecting the sketch

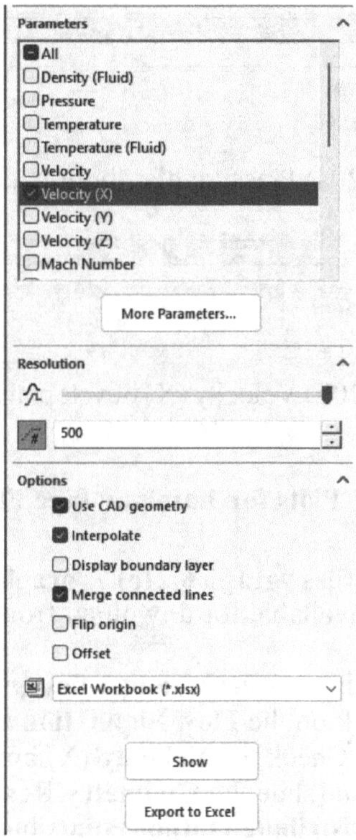

Figure 6.21b) Different settings for the XY Plot

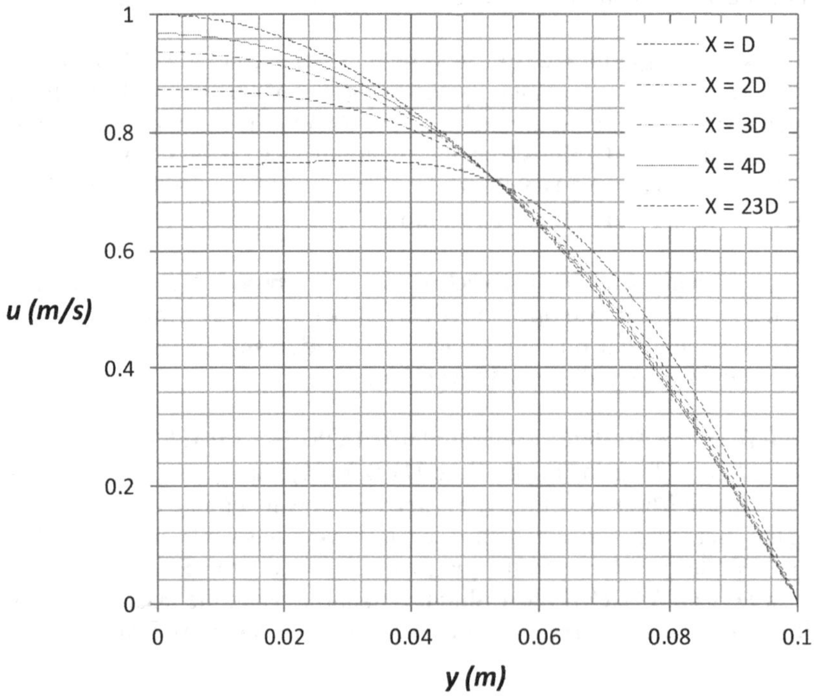

Figure 6.21c) Velocity profiles at different positions, Reynolds number $Re = 100$

The different velocity profiles are compared with the theoretical Hagen-Poiseuille velocity profile for laminar flow in a straight pipe:

$$u_{laminar} = U_{max}(1 - (\frac{2y}{D})^2) \quad (6.1)$$

where y (m) is the radial coordinate, u (m/s) is the velocity in the X-direction, and D (m) is the inner diameter of the pipe. We see in figure 6.21c) that the profiles at different streamwise positions further away from the inlet get closer to the fully developed theoretical profile. The theoretical ratio between maximum velocity U_{max} (m/s) and mean velocity U_m (m/s) for fully developed laminar pipe flow is

$$(\frac{U_{max}}{U_m})_{laminar} = 2 \quad (6.2)$$

22. Repeat step **21** but this time choose the sketch **x = 0 – 4.6 m (centerline)** and use the file "**graph 6.22**". This results in figure 6.22 that shows the streamwise development of the centerline velocity. It takes approximately ten pipe diameters for the flow to become fully developed. Rename the inserted *xy*-plot in the **Flow Simulation analysis tree** to **Velocity (X) along Centerline.**

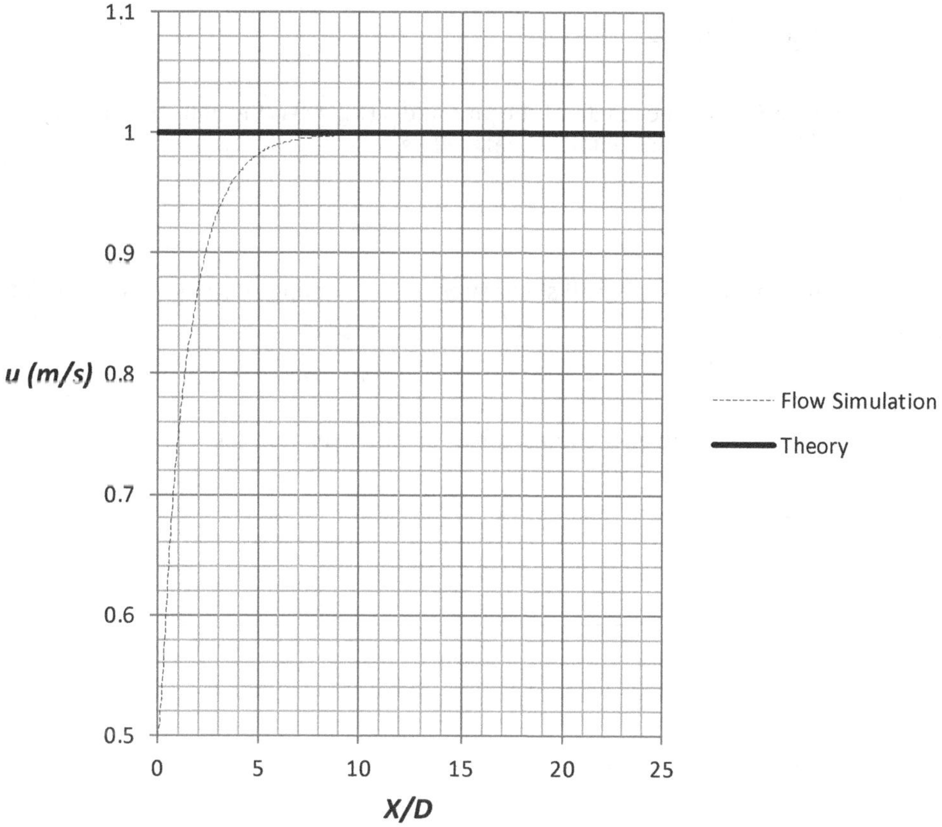

Figure 6.22 X-velocity along the centerline of the pipe at Re = 100, full line is showing theoretical value for fully developed flow.

L. Theory for Laminar Pipe flow

The Reynolds number for the flow in a straight pipe is defined as

$$Re = \frac{U_m D}{\nu} \tag{6.3}$$

where ν is the kinematic viscosity of the fluid. The hydrodynamic entry length L_h (m) is the distance between the pipe entrance and the location where the flow is fully developed. The entry length is approximately given by the following expression for laminar flow in a pipe:

$$\frac{L_{h,laminar}}{D} = 0.05Re \tag{6.4}$$

In our case, $D = 0.2$ m and $Re = 100$ gives an entry length of 1 m. If we define the entry length as the distance from the entrance to where the streamwise velocity maximum is within 2% of the fully developed value, Flow Simulation results in figure 6.22 gives a value of 0.959 m, a 4.1 % difference from theoretical results.

We now want to study pressure loss and how the friction factor varies along the pipe. The pressure loss is defined by

$$\Delta P = f \frac{L}{D} \frac{\rho U_m^2}{2} \tag{6.5}$$

where L (m) is the length of the pipe and ρ (kg/m^3) is the density of the fluid. The Darcy-Weisbach friction factor f is defined as:

$$f = \frac{8\tau_w}{\rho U_m^2} \tag{6.5}$$

where τ_w (Pa) is the wall shear stress. The Fanning friction factor is defined as:

$$C_f = \frac{2\tau_w}{\rho U_m^2} = \frac{f}{4} \tag{6.6}$$

For laminar flow in a circular pipe it can be shown that

$$C_{f,laminar} = \frac{16}{Re} \tag{6.7}$$

23. Repeat step **21** once again but this time choose the sketch **x = 0 – 4.6 m (wall)** and check the box for **Shear Stress**. Use the file **"graph 6.23"**. An Excel file will open with a graph of the Fanning friction factor versus the *X/D* –coordinate in comparison with theoretical values for laminar pipe flow, see figure 6.23. Rename the inserted *xy*-plot in the **Flow Simulation analysis tree** to **Fanning Friction Factor**.

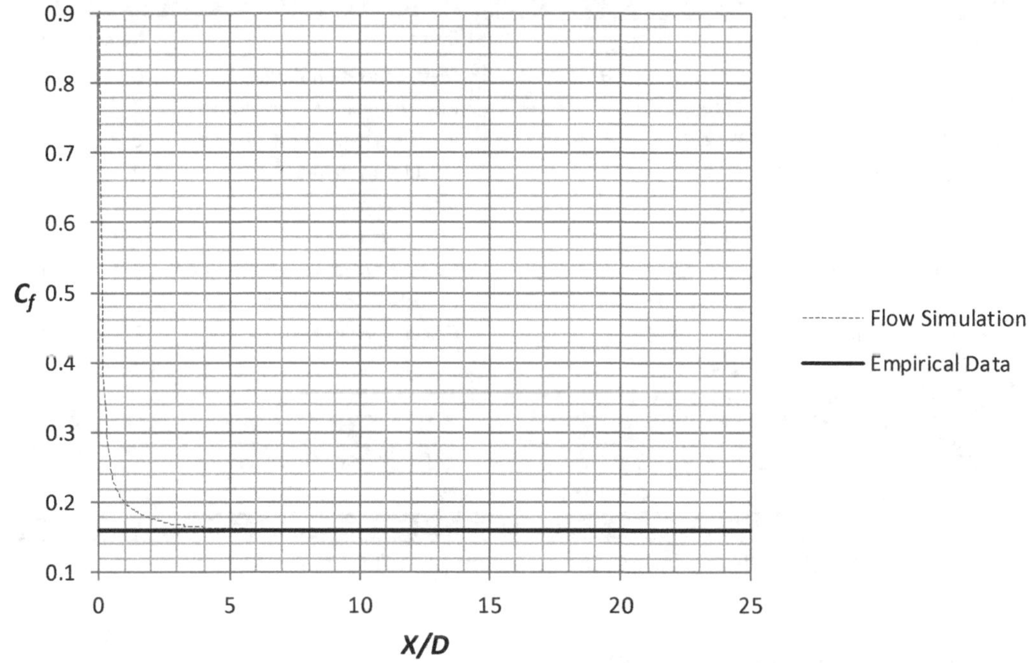

Figure 6.23 Fanning friction factor as a function of the streamwise coordinate at *Re* = 100, full line is showing theoretical value for fully developed flow

M. Flow Simulations for Turbulent Pipe Flow

24. In the next step, we will study turbulent pipe flow. Open the file **Turbulent Pipe Flow 2026**. This file can be downloaded from *sdcpublications.com*. Skip the feature recognition when you open the file. Select **Tools>>Flow Simulation>>Solve>>Run...** to start calculations. Check the **Mesh** box and select **New Calculation**. Click on the **Run** button in the **Run** window.

Figure 6.24a) Creation of mesh and starting a new calculation for turbulent pipe flow

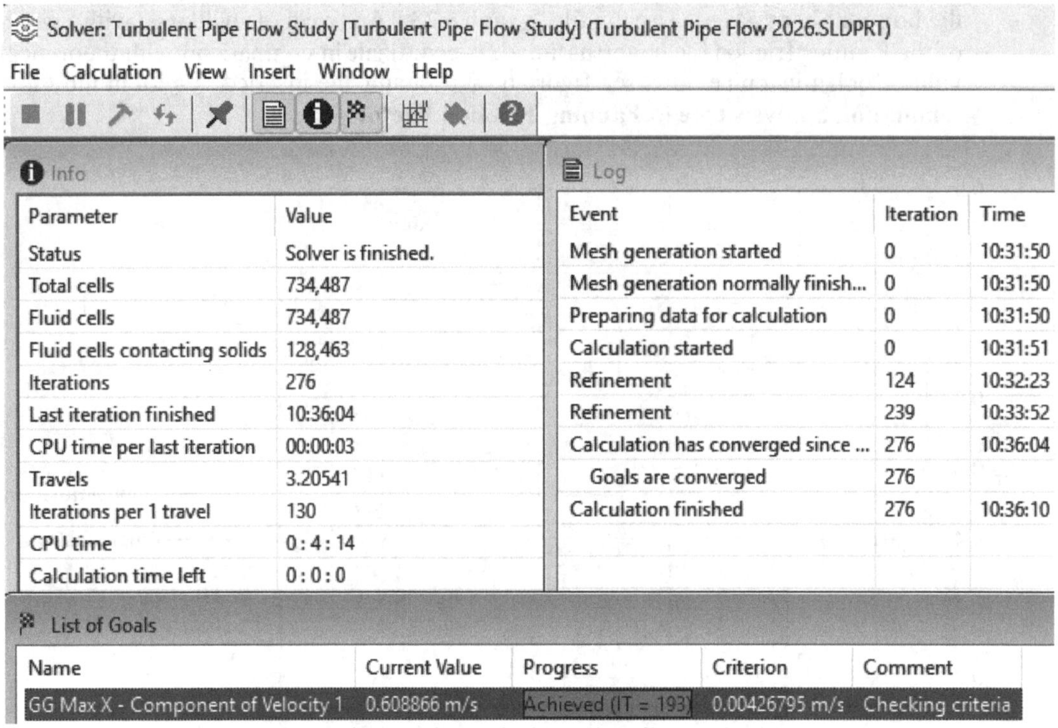

Figure 6.24b) Solver window for turbulent pipe flow calculations

N. Theory for Turbulent Pipe Flow

An approximate relation for the Darcy-Weisbach friction factor as a function of Reynolds number for turbulent pipe flow is given by Blasius:

$$f_{turbulent} = \frac{0.316}{Re^{1/4}} \qquad 4000 < Re < 10^5 \tag{6.8}$$

and the Fanning friction factor

$$C_{f,turbulent} = \frac{0.079}{Re^{1/4}} \qquad 4000 < Re < 10^5 \tag{6.9}$$

The pressure drop is given by

$$\Delta P_{turbulent} = 0.158 L \rho^{3/4} \mu^{1/4} U_m^{7/4} / D^{5/4} \tag{6.10}$$

where μ is the dynamic viscosity of the fluid. A formula can also be obtained relating max velocity to mean velocity for fully developed turbulent pipe flow:

$$\left(\frac{U_{max}}{U_m}\right)_{turbulent} = 1 + 2.66\sqrt{C_{f,turbulent}} \tag{6.11}$$

O. XY Plots for Turbulent Pipe Flow Using Templates

25. Place the files **graph 6.25a)**, **graph 6.25b)**, **graph 6.25c)** and **graph 6.25d)** on the desktop. Click on the **FeatureManager Design Tree**. Click on the sketch **x = 0 – 10 m (centerline)**. Click on the **Flow Simulation analysis tree** tab. Open the **Results** folder, right click **XY Plot** and select **Insert…**. Check the **Velocity (X)** box. Open the **Resolution** portion of the **XY Plot** window and slide the **Geometry Resolution** as far as it goes to the right. Select **Excel Workbook (*.xlsx)** from the drop-down menu under **Options**. Click on **Export to Excel**. An Excel file will open with a graph of the velocity along the centerline of the pipe.

    Double click on the **graph 6.25a)** file to open the file. Click on **Enable Content** and **Enable Editing** if you get a **Security Warning** that **Macros** have been disabled. If **Developer** is not available in the menu of the **Excel** file, you will need to do the following: Select **File>>Options** from the menu and click on the **Customize Ribbon** on the left-hand side. Check the **Developer** box on the right-hand side under **Main Tabs**. Click **OK** to exit the **Excel Options** window.

    Click on the **Developer** tab in the **Excel** menu for the **graph 6.25a)** file and select **Visual Basic** on the left-hand side to open the editor. Click on the plus sign next to **VBAProject (XY Plot 5.xlsx)** and click on the plus sign next to **Microsoft Excel Objects**. Right click on **Sheet2 (Plot Data)** and select **View Object**.

    Select **Macro** in the **Modules** folder under **VBAProject (graph 6.25a)).xlsm)**. Select **Run>>Run Macro** from the menu of the **MVB for Applications** window. Click on the **Run** button in the **Macros** window. **Figure 6.25a)** will become available in **Excel** showing the streamwise velocity component ***u (m/s)*** versus streamwise coordinate ***X/D***. Close the **XY Plot** window and the **graph 6.25a)** window in **Excel**. Exit the **XY Plot** window in **SolidWorks Flow Simulation** and rename the inserted *xy*-plot in the **Flow Simulation analysis tree** to **Figure 6.25a)**.

    Figure 6.25a) is showing the X-velocity along the centerline including a comparison between turbulent pipe flow and the empirical value for fully developed flow. The centerline velocity from Flow Simulation has an overshoot before attaining a level lower than the value given from empirical data. Flow Simulation is under predicting the fully developed maximum velocity.

    The Fanning friction factor is shown in figure 6.25b). Repeat the steps above to create this graph. Select the sketch **x = 0 – 10 m (wall)** and check the **Shear Stress** box. Select the file **"graph 6.25b)"**. An Excel file will open with a graph of the friction coefficient along the wall of the pipe, see figure 6.25b). The Fanning factor from Flow Simulation is higher than the empirical.

    Repeat the same steps above once again. Select the sketch **x = 45D**. Check the **Velocity (X)** box. Click on the  **Evenly Distribute Output Points** button and increase the number of points to **500**. Select the file **"graph 6.25c)"**. In figure 6.25c) is the fully developed velocity profile from Flow Simulation compared with the power-law profile for $n = 8$.

$$u_{turbulent} = U_{max}(1 - \frac{y}{0.1})^{1/n} \qquad (6.12)$$

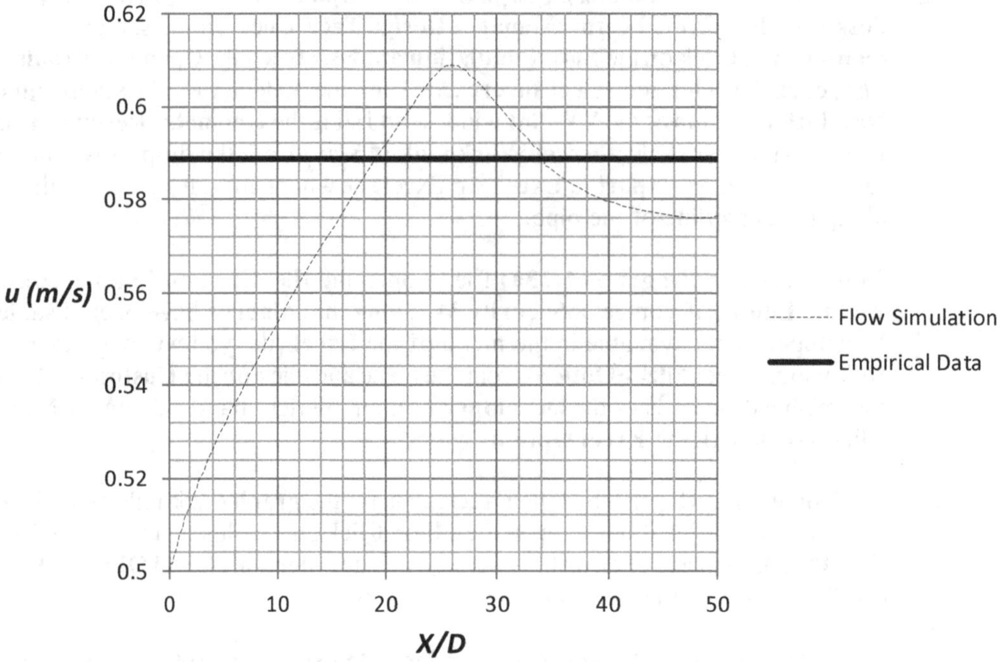

Figure 6.25a) X-velocity along the centerline of the pipe at Re = 100000, full line is showing empirical value for fully developed turbulent pipe flow

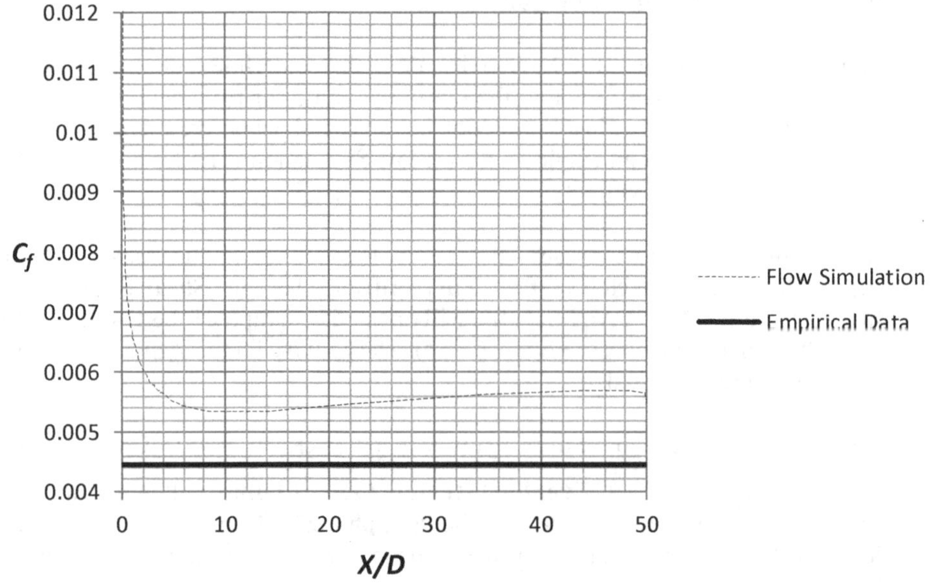

Figure 6.25b) Fanning friction factor as a function of the streamwise coordinate at Re = 100000, full line is showing empirical value for fully developed turbulent pipe flow

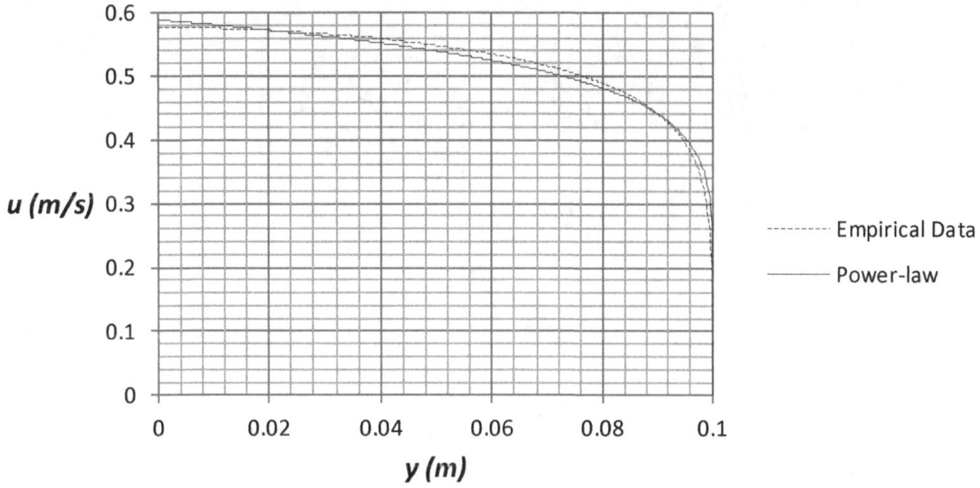

Figure 6.25c) Fully developed straight pipe turbulent velocity profile (dashed line) at *X/D* = 45, *Re* = 100000, compared with power-law velocity profile for $n = 8$

There are four different layers of the turbulent velocity profile: viscous sublayer, buffer layer, overlap layer and turbulent layer. If we start with the viscous sublayer located closest to the wall, the velocity profile in this region is described by the law of the wall:

$$u^+ = \frac{u}{u_*} = \frac{(\frac{D}{2}-y)u_*}{\nu} = y^+ \quad (6.13)$$

where the friction velocity $u_* = \sqrt{\tau_w/\rho}$. The thickness of the viscous sublayer is

$$\delta = \frac{5\nu}{u_*} \quad (6.14)$$

The velocity profile in the overlap layer is known as the logarithmic law

$$u^+ = 2.5 ln y^+ + 5.0 \quad (6.15)$$

and the profile in the outer turbulent layer is called the velocity defect law.

$$\frac{U_{max}-u}{u_*} = 2.5 ln \frac{D}{D-2y} \quad (6.16)$$

Click on the **FeatureManager design tree**. Click on the sketch **x = 45D**. Click on the **Flow Simulation analysis tree** tab. Right click **XY Plot** and select **Insert…**. Check the **Velocity (X)** box. Open the **Resolution** portion of the **XY Plot** window and slide the **Geometry Resolution** as far as it goes to the right. Click on the **Evenly Distribute Output Points** button and increase the number of points to **10000**. Select **Excel Workbook (*.xlsx)** from the drop-down menu under **Options**. Click on **Export to Excel**. Repeat the steps as outlined above and use file "**graph 6.25d)**" to create **Figure 6.25d)**.

In figure 6.25d) it is seen that result from Flow Simulation is over predicting the velocity in the viscous sublayer close to the wall.

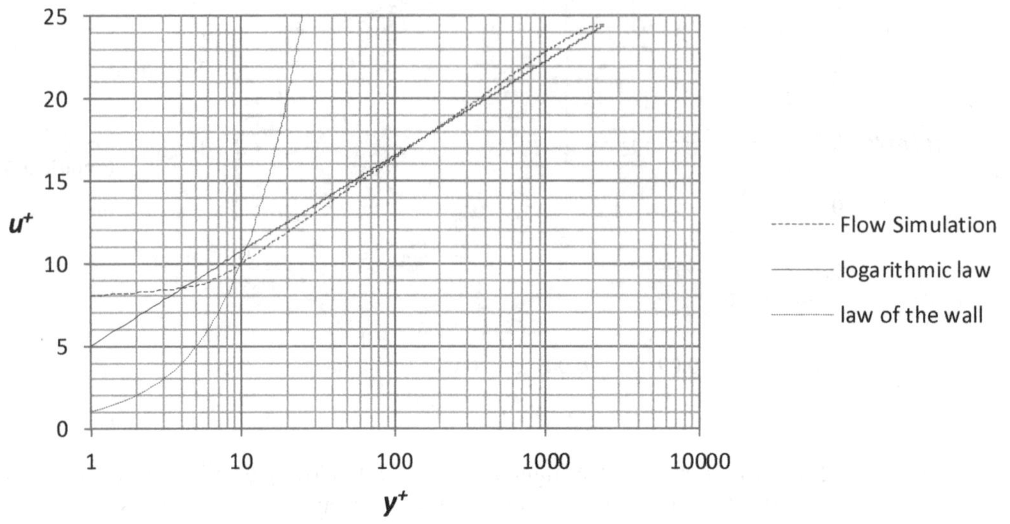

Figure 6.25d) Comparison of Flow Simulation, law of the wall and logarithmic law for fully developed turbulent flow in a pipe at *X/D = 45* and *Re* = 100,000

P. References

1. Technical Reference SOLIDWORKS Flow Simulation 2025.
2. White, F. M., Fluid Mechanics, 4th Edition, McGraw-Hill, 1999.

Q. Exercises

6.1 Run the laminar flow case for *Re* = 300, 500 and compare X-velocity and friction factor with *Re* = 100 as shown in figures 6.21c), 6.22 and 6.23, respectively. Discuss your results.

6.2 Run the laminar flow case for *Re* = 100 and change the number of cells in the *X*, *Y*, and *Z* directions to see how it affects the results for X-velocity and friction factor. Discuss differences in results. Use the following number of cells:

X	Y	Z
33	5	5
67	10	10
100	15	15
133	20	20
167	25	25

6.3 Run the turbulent flow case for *Re* = 100000 and change the number of cells in the *X*, *Y*, and *Z* directions to see how it affects the results. Discuss and compare the results.

CHAPTER 7. FLOW ACROSS A TUBE BANK

A. Objectives

- Creating the SOLIDWORKS model of the tube bank
- Setting up Flow Simulation projects for external flow
- Inserting boundary condition
- Running the calculations
- Using cut plots and XY plots to visualize the resulting flow field
- Compare results with theory and empirical data

B. Problem Description

In this chapter, we will use Flow Simulation to study the two-dimensional flow across a tube bank. We will use a total of twelve 20 mm diameter cylinders in an in-line arrangement. The cylinders will have a temperature of 373.2 K and the free stream velocity of the air will be 4 m/s. The temperature and velocity fields will be shown inside the tube bank and the development of both temperature and velocity profiles after the tube bank. The exit temperature of the fluid from Flow Simulation calculations will be compared with theoretical and empirical results.

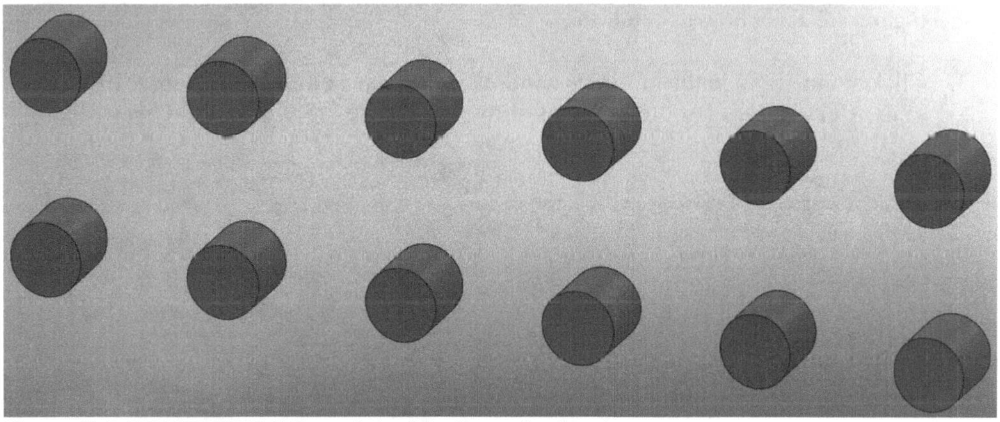

Figure 7.0 SOLIDWORKS model of in-line tube bank

C. Creating a SOLIDWORKS Part

1. Start by creating a new part in SOLIDWORKS: select **File>>New** and click on the **OK** button in the **New SOLIDWORKS Document** window. Select **Tools>>Options...** from the SOLIDWORKS menu. Click on the Document Properties tab and select **Units**. Select **MMGS** as your **Unit system**. Click on **Front Plane** in the **FeatureManager design tree** and select **Front** from the **View Orientation** drop down menu in the graphics window.

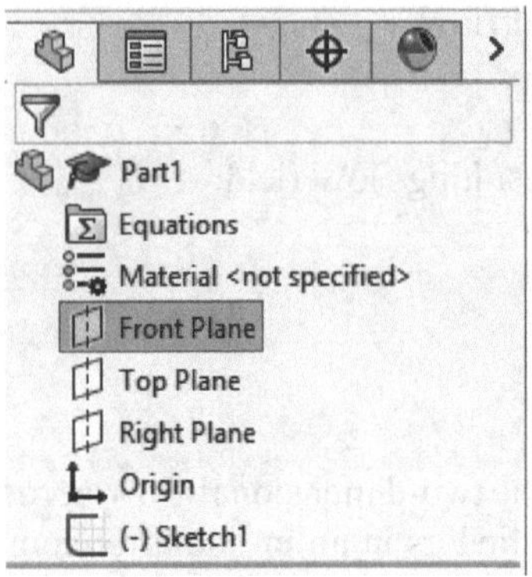

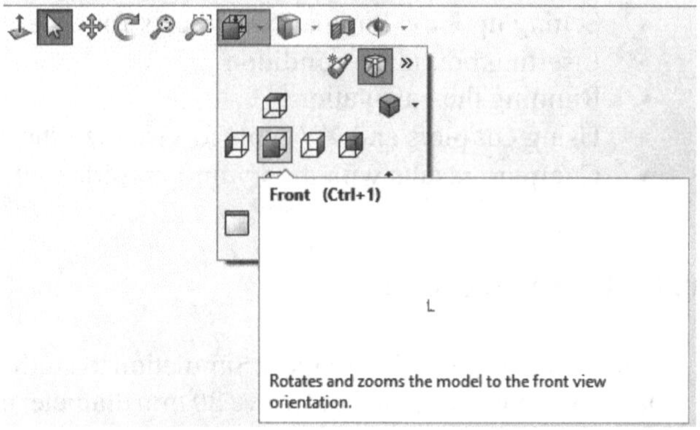

Figure 7.1a) Selection of front plane Figure 7.1b) Selection of front view

2. Select the **Basic Modeling Tools** tab and click on **Circle**.

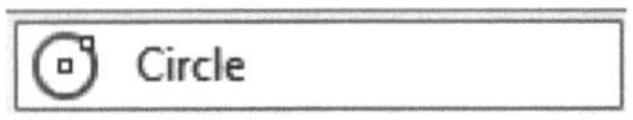

Figure 7.2 Selecting a sketch tool

3. Click at the origin in the graphics window and create a circle with a radius of 10 mm. Fill in the **Parameters** for the circle as shown in Figure 7.3. Close the **Circle** dialog box.

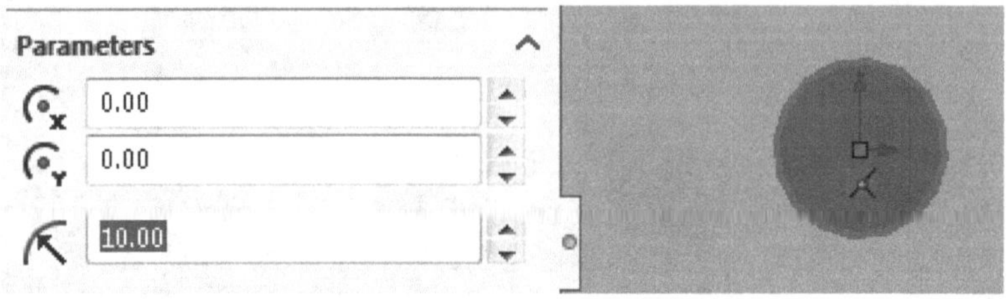

Figure 7.3 A circle with a radius of 10 mm

4. Create five more circles with the same radii and their centers located at $(X, Y) = (50,0)$, (100,0), (150,0), (200,0) and (250,0). Next, create another line of six more identical circles with their centers at $(X, Y) = (0,50)$, (50,50), (100,50), (150,50), (200,50) and (250,50). All dimensions in millimeter.

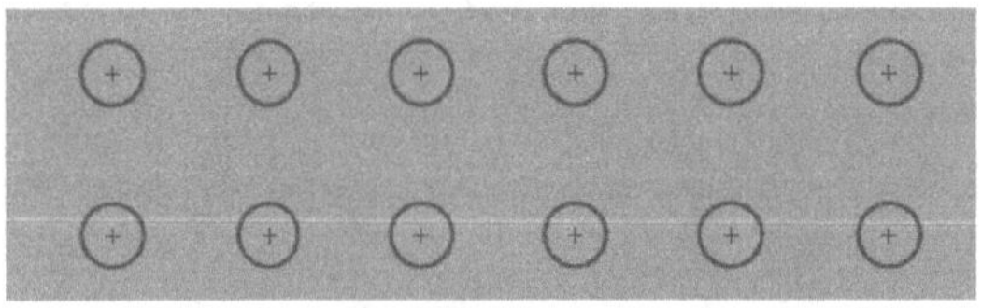

Figure 7.4 Sketch of in-line tube bank with six rows of cylinders

5. Select the **Analysis Preparation** tab and **Extruded Boss/Base**. Click on **Direction 2** check box and click OK to exit the **Extrude** dialog box. Select **File>>Save As...** and save the part with the name **In-Line Tube Bank 2026.**

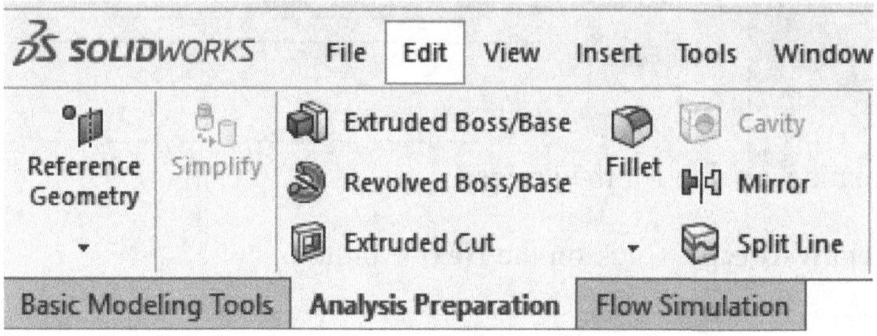

Figure 7.5a) Selection of extruded boss/base feature

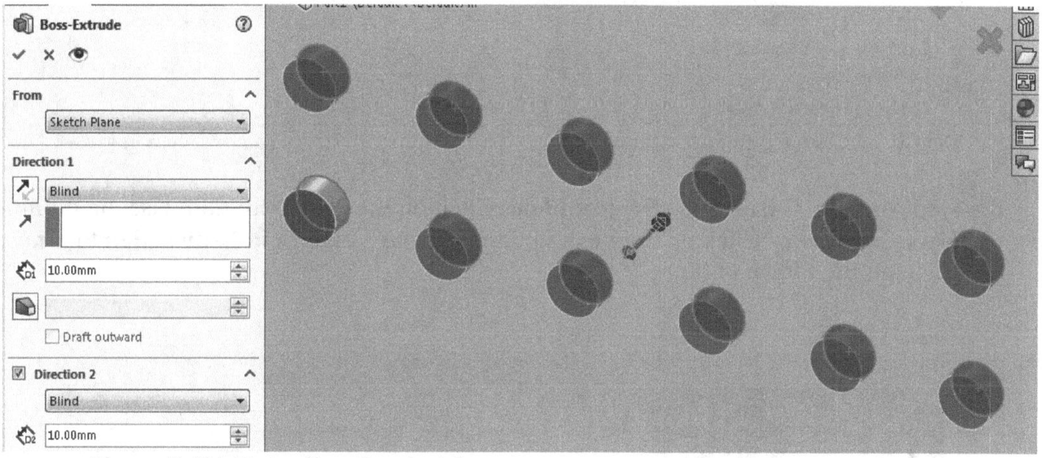

Figure 7.5b) Extruding the sketch

D. Flow Simulation Project

6. If Flow Simulation is not available in the menu, you can add it from the SOLIDWORKS menu: **Tools>>Add Ins...** and check the corresponding **SOLIDWORKS Flow Simulation** box. Select **Tools>>Flow Simulation>>Project>>Wizard...** to create a new Flow Simulation project. Create a new project named **In-Line Tube Bank Study**. Click on the **Next >** button. Select the default **SI (m-kg-s)** unit system and click on the **Next>** button once again.

Figure 7.6a) Starting a new Flow Simulation project

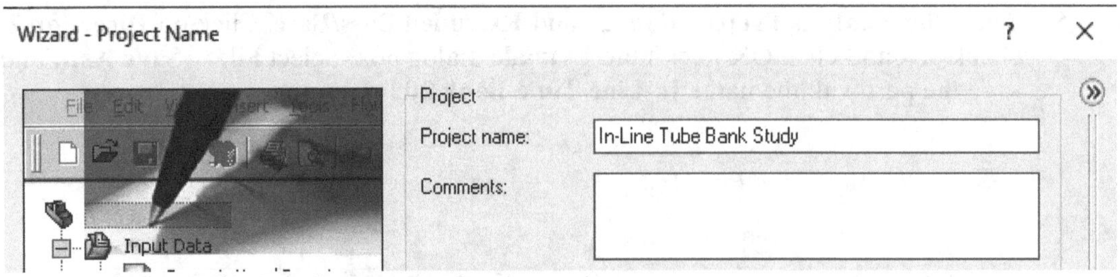

Figure 7.6b) Creating a name for the project

7. Use **External Analysis type**. Click on the **Next >** button.

Geometry handling	Value
Analysis type	External
Geometry recognition	CAD Boolean
Exclude cavities without conditions	☑
Exclude internal space	☐

Figure 7.7 External analysis type

8. Add **Air** from **Gases** as the **Project Fluid**. Click on the **Next >** button. Use the default **Wall Conditions**. Click on the **Next>** button. Set the **Velocity in X-direction** to **4 m/s**. Click on the **Finish** button.

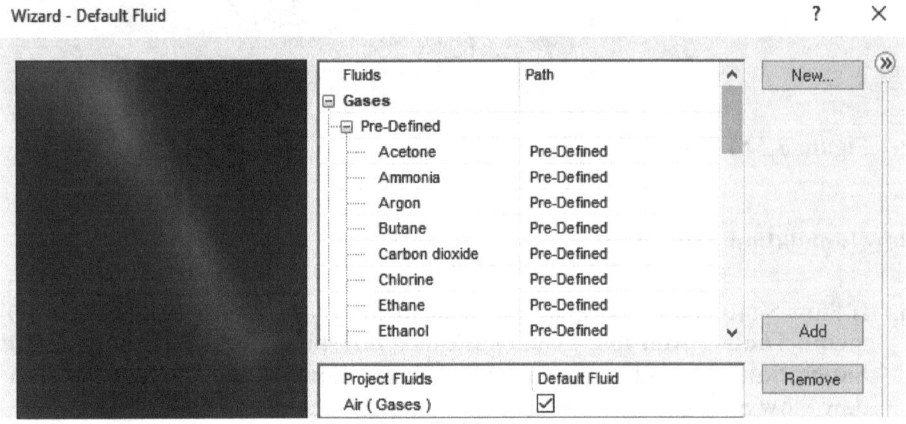

Figure 7.8a) Adding air as the project fluid

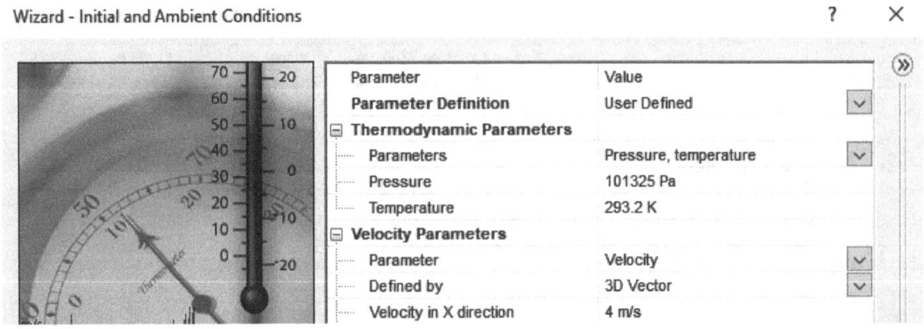

Figure 7.8b) Setting the velocity in the X-direction

E. Computational Domain and Mesh

9. Select **Tools>>Flow Simulation>>Computational Domain….** Select **2D simulation** and **XY plane** from the **Type** section. Exit the **Computational Domain** window. Select **Tools>>Flow Simulation>>Global Mesh….** Check the **Manual Type**. Change the **Number of cells per X:** to **198** and set **Number of cells per Y:** to **300**. Click on the **OK** button to exit the **Global Mesh** window.

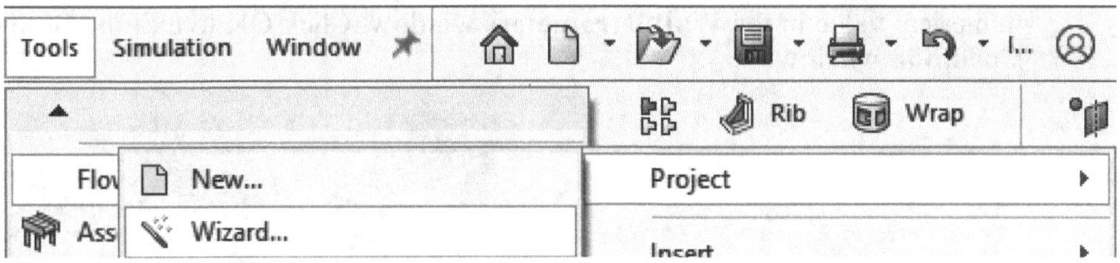

Figure 7.9a) Modifying the computational domain

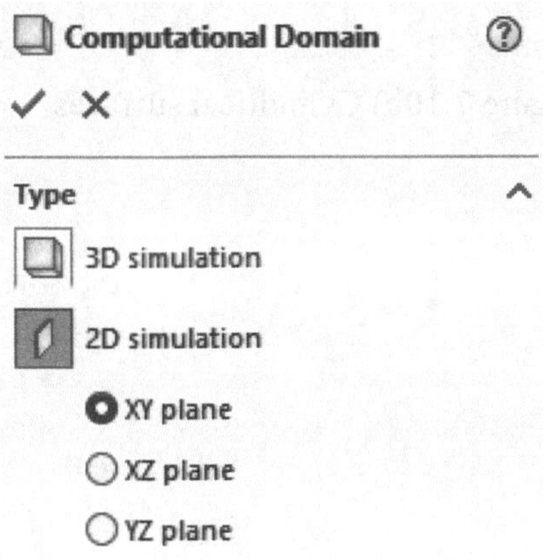

Figure 7.9b) Selecting 2D plane flow

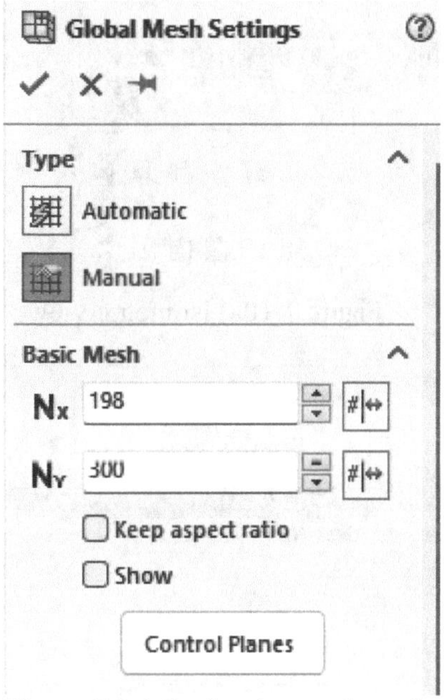

Figure 7.9c) Setting the number of cells

F. Boundary Conditions

10. Select **Isometric** view from the **View Orientation** drop down menu in the graphics window. Select **Tools>>Flow Simulation>>Insert>>Boundary Condition...** from the SOLIDWORKS menu. Select the twelve cylindrical surfaces. Click on the **Wall** button in the **Type** portion of the **Boundary Condition** window and select **Real Wall.** Adjust the **Wall Temperature** to **373.2 K** by clicking on the button and entering the numerical value in the **Wall Parameters** window. Click OK to exit the **Boundary Condition** window.

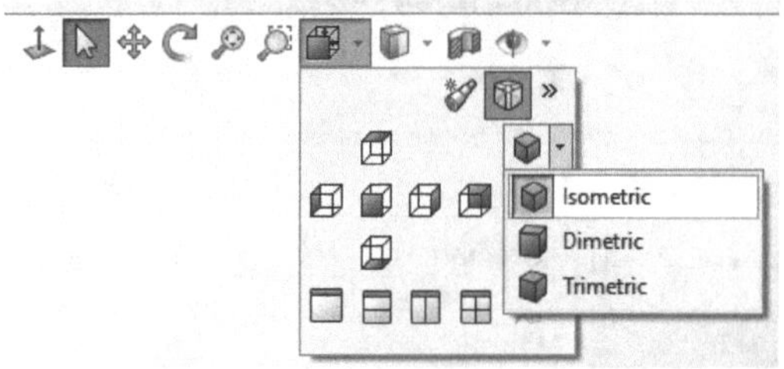

Figure 7.10a) Isometric view

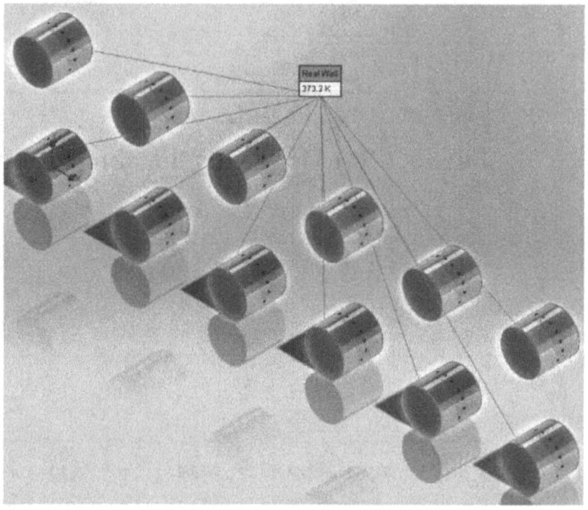

Figure 7.10b) Cylindrical surfaces

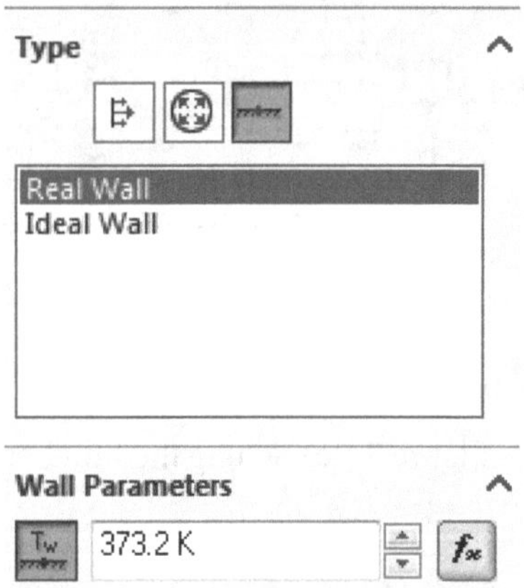

Figure 7.10c) Selecting wall temperature for in-line tube bank

G. Global Goals

11. Right click on **Goals** in the **Flow Simulation analysis tree** and select **Insert Global Goals….** Select **Max Velocity (X)** as a global goal. Also, select **Min, Av** and **Max Temperature (Fluid)** as global goals. Click OK to exit the **Global Goals** window.

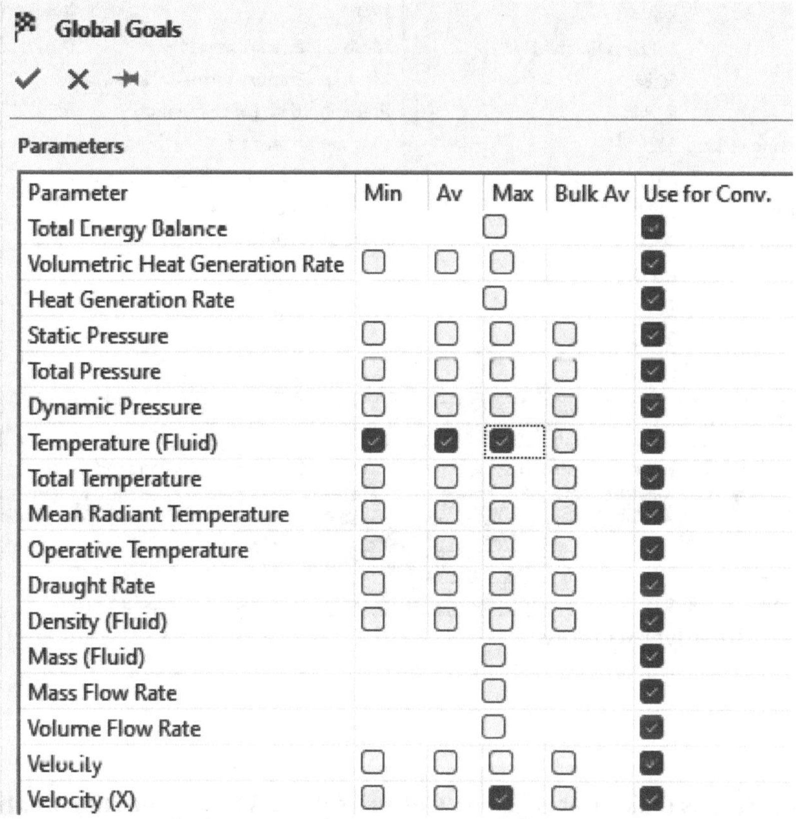

Figure 7.11 Velocity (X) and temperature of fluid as global goals

H. Flow Simulations for Tube Bank Flow

12. Select **Tools>>Flow Simulation>>Solve>>Run** to start calculations. Click on the **Run** button in the **Run** window.

Figure 7.12a) Run window

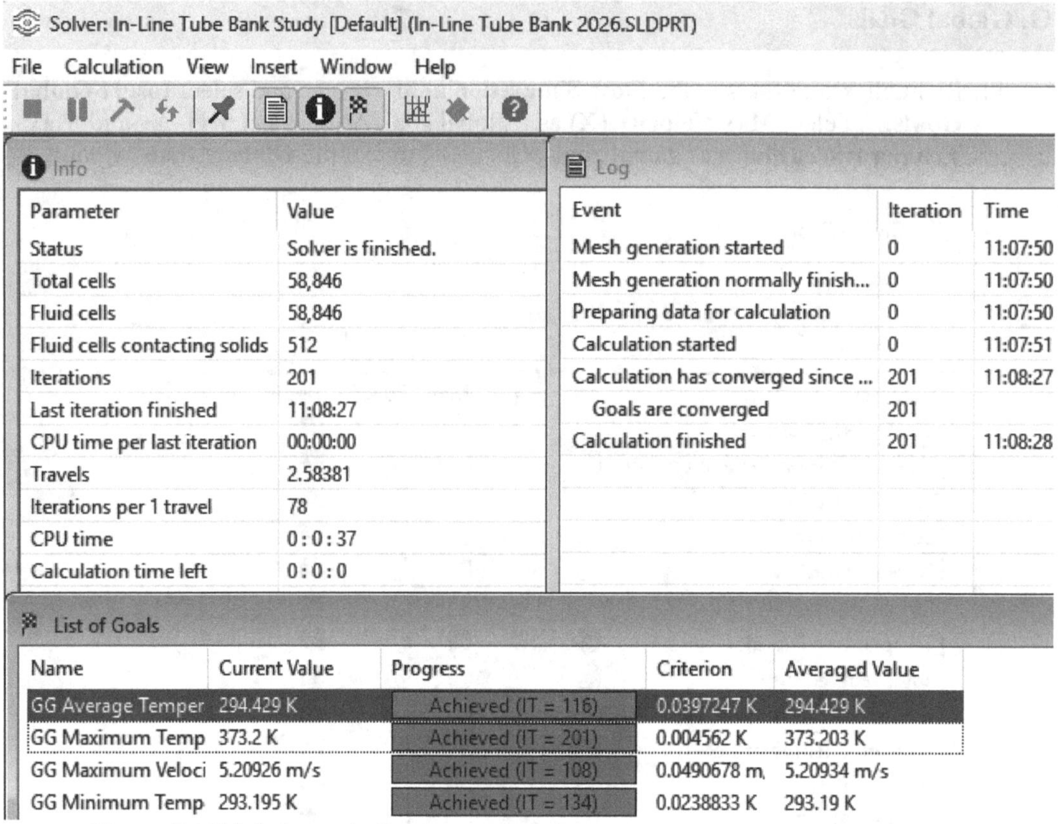

Figure 7.12b) Solver window

I. Inserting Cut Plots

13. Open the **Results** folder, right click on **Cut Plots** in the **Flow Simulation analysis tree** and select **Insert…**. Select the **Front Plane** from the **FeatureManager design tree**. Slide the **Number of Levels** slide bar to **255** in the **Contours** section. Exit the **Cut Plot** window. Name the cut plot as **Pressure**. Select **Front** from the **View Orientation** drop down menu in the graphics window. Select **Tools>>Flow Simulation>>Results>>Display>>Lighting** from the SOLIDWORKS menu. Right click on the Color Bar in the graphics window and select Make Horizontal.

    Repeat this step two more times but select **Velocity (X)** and **Temperature (Fluid)** as parameters. You will need to right-click on the cut plot in the FeatureManager design tree and hide it to display the next plot. Figure 7.13 shows the pressure gradient along the tube bank along with the velocity distribution in the same cross section and the temperature distribution.

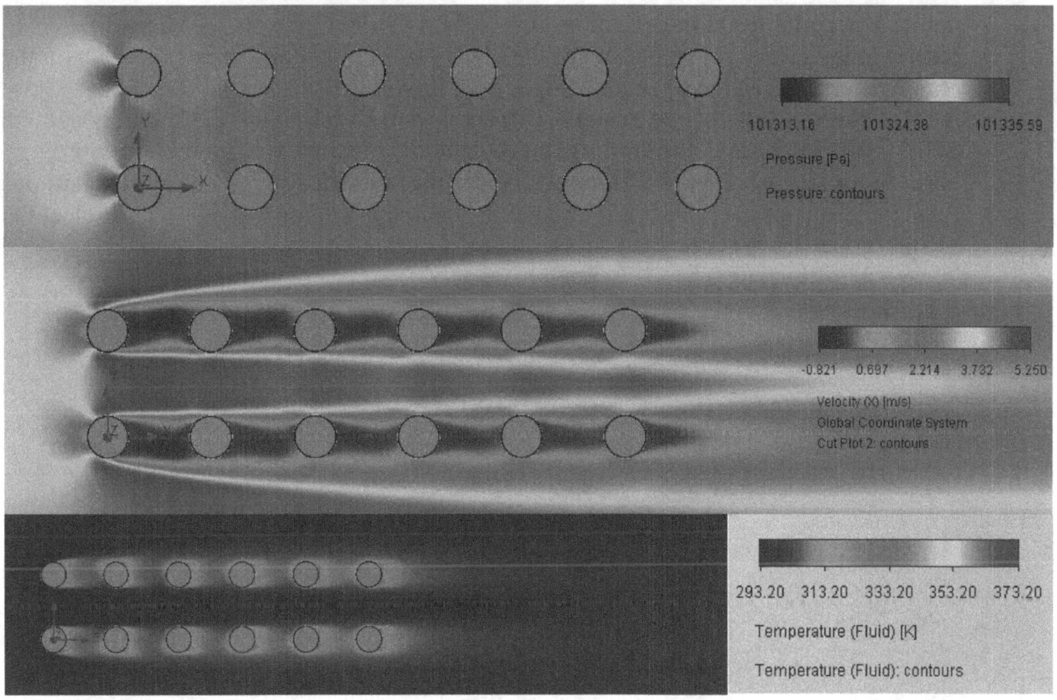

Figure 7.13 Pressure, velocity and temperature distributions along the tube bank

J. Sketches for XY Plots

14. Click on the **FeatureManager Design Tree,** select the **Front Plane**, select the **Basic Modeling Tools** tab and select **Line**. Draw a 50 mm long vertical line starting at (X, Y) = (275 mm, 0), see Figure 7.14a). Exit the **Line Properties** window and draw two more vertical lines with the same length starting at (X, Y) = (300 mm, 0) and (X, Y) = (325 mm, 0). Close the windows (use green check marks) and select **Rebuild** from the SOLIDWORKS Menu. Rename the new sketch to **x = 275, 300, 325 mm** as shown in Figure 7.14d).

    Place the files "**graph 7.14f)**" and "**graph 7.14g)**" on the desktop. Click on the **Flow Simulation analysis tree** tab. Right click **XY Plot** and select **Insert….** Check the **Temperature (Fluid)** box. Open the **Resolution** portion of the **XY Plot** window and slide the **Geometry Resolution** as far as it goes to the right. Open the **Options** portion of the **XY Plot** window and select **Excel Workbook (*.xlsx)** from the template drop down menu. Click on the **FeatureManager design tree** and select the sketch **x = 275, 300, 325 mm**. Click on **Export to Excel** to generate a plot.

    Double click on the **graph 7.14f)** file to open the file. Click on **Enable Content** if you get a **Security Warning** that **Macros** have been disabled. If **Developer** is not available in the menu of the **Excel** file, you will need to do the following: Select **File>>Options** from the menu and click on the **Customize Ribbon** on the left-hand side. Check the **Developer** box on the right-hand side under **Main Tabs**. Click **OK** to exit the **Excel Options** window. Click on the **Developer** tab in the **Excel** menu for the **graph 7.14f)** file and select **Visual Basic** on the left-hand side to open the editor. Click on the plus sign next to **VBAProject (XY Plot 1.xlsx)** and click on the plus sign next to **Microsoft Excel Objects**. Right click on **Sheet2 (Plot Data)** and select **View Object**.

Select **Macro** in the **Modules** folder under **VBAProject (graph 7.14f).xlsm)**. Select **Run>>Run Macro** from the menu of the **MVB for Applications** window. Click on the **Run** button in the **Macros** window. **Figure 7.14f)** will become available in **Excel**. Close the **XY Plot** window and the **graph 7.14f)** window in **Excel**. Exit the **XY Plot** window in **SOLIDWORKS Flow Simulation** and rename the inserted *xy*-plot in the **Flow Simulation analysis tree** to **Temperature profiles at different streamwise positions**. Repeat these steps once again but choose to check the **Velocity (X)** box and select the **graph figure 7.14g)** file.

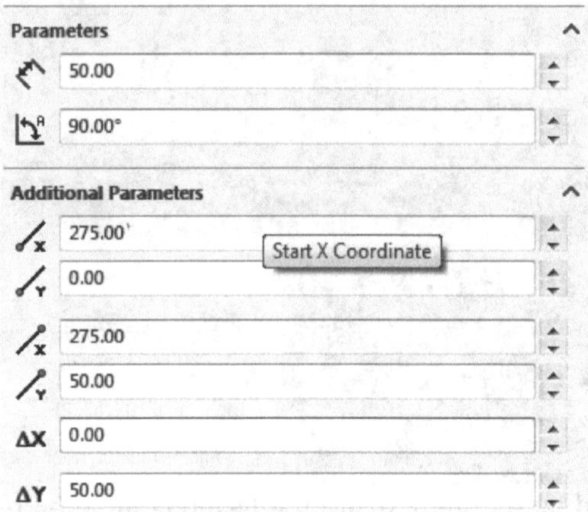

Figure 7.14a) Vertical line for the XY-plot

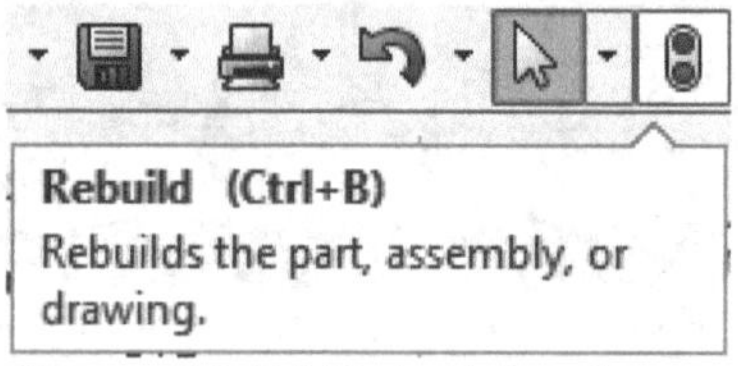

Figure 7.14b) Rebuilding the new sketch

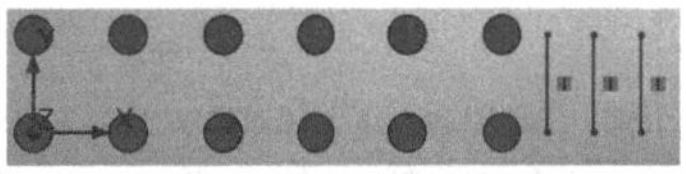

Figure 7.14c) Sketch with three lines

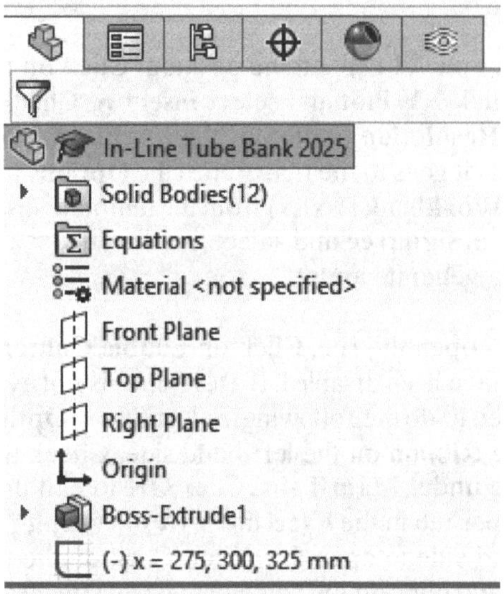

Figure 7.14d) Rename the new sketch

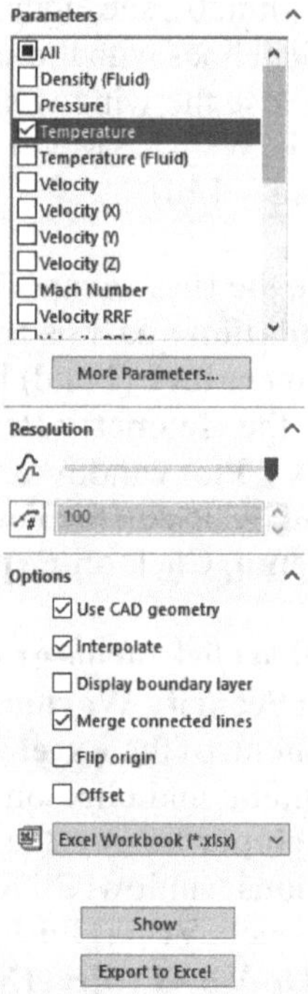

Figure 7.14e) Settings XY Plot

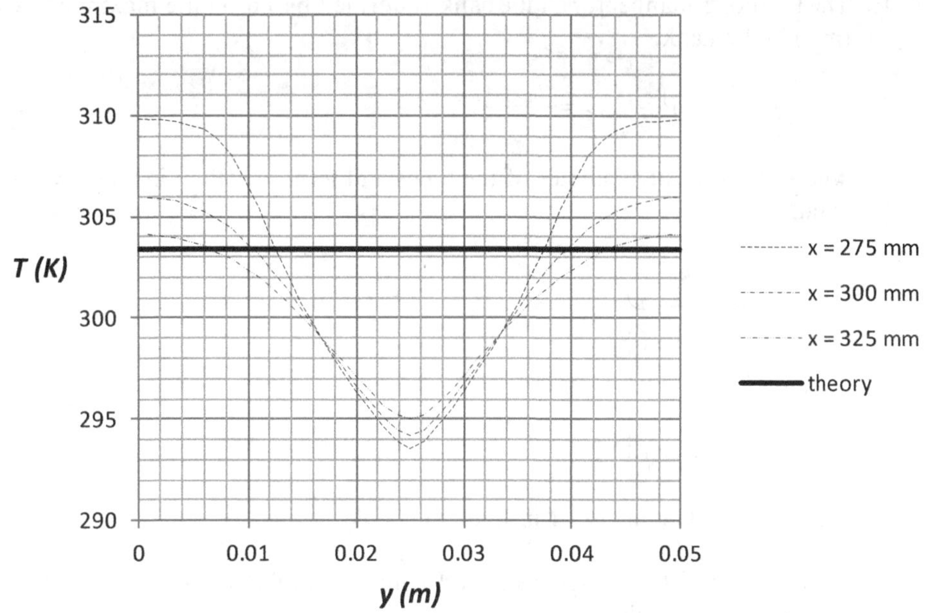

Figure 7.14f) Exit temperatures for tube bank for Flow Simulation compared with theory

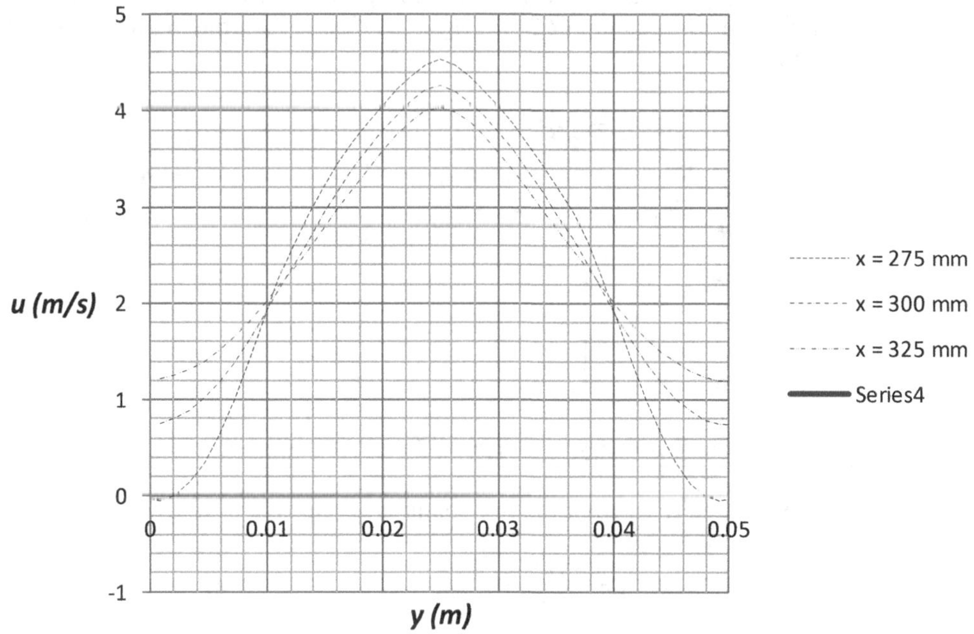

Figure 7.14g) Exit velocities for the tube bank from Flow Simulation

K. Theory and Empirical Data

1. The Reynolds number for a tube bank is defined based on the maximum velocity U_{max} (m/s) in the bank:

$$Re_{D,max} = \frac{U_{max}D}{\nu} \tag{7.1}$$

where D (m) is the diameter of the tubes and ν (m/s) is the kinematic viscosity of the fluid.

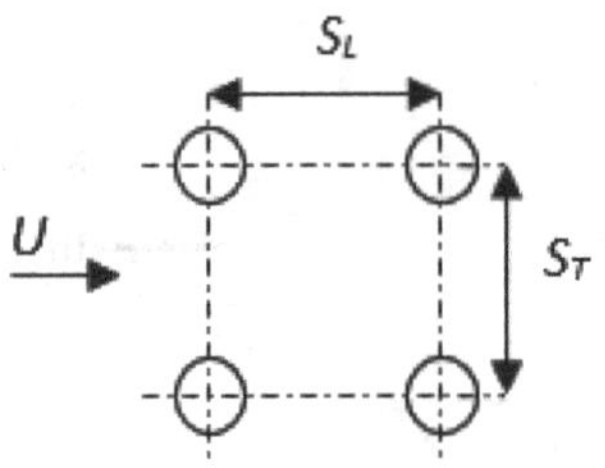

Figure 7.15a) Geometry of in-line tube bank

For the in-line tube arrangement, see figure 7.15a), the maximum velocity is related to the approach velocity U:

$$U_{max} = \frac{S_T U}{S_T - D} \tag{7.2}$$

For the staggered tube arrangement, see figure 7.15b), the maximum velocity is determined by equation (7.2) if $2A_D > A_T$. If $2A_D < A_T$, the maximum velocity is determined by

$$U_{max} = \frac{S_T U}{2(S_D - D)} \tag{7.3}$$

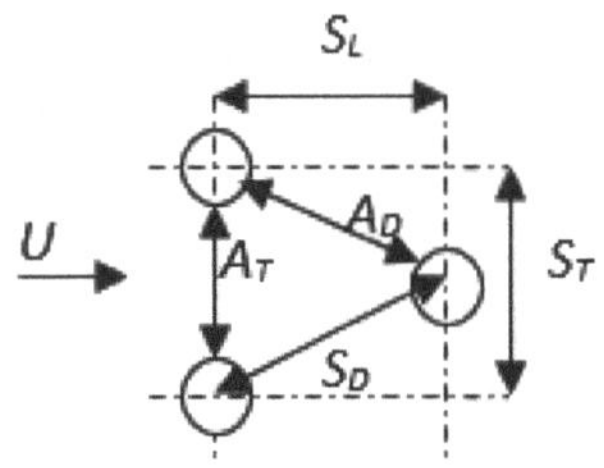

Figure 7.15b) Geometry of staggered tube bank

The pressure drop across the tube bank is given by the following equation:

$$\Delta P = \frac{N_L f \chi \rho U_{max}^2}{2} \tag{7.4}$$

where N_L is the number of rows of tubes in the flow direction, f is the friction factor, χ is a correction factor and ρ (kg/m^3) is the density of the fluid.

The friction-factor for in-line and staggered tube banks can be determined from figures 7.15c) and 7.15d), respectively.

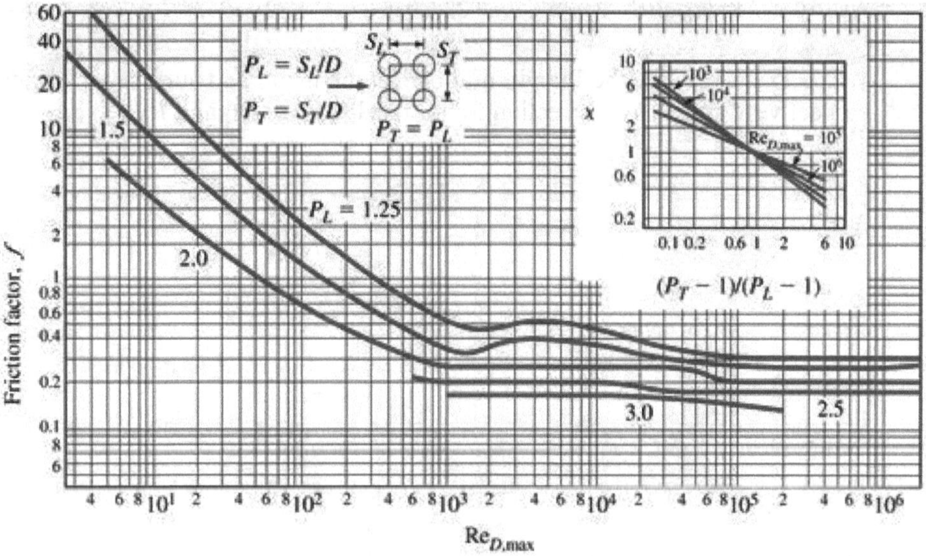

Figure 7.15c) Friction factors for in-line tube bank, from Cengel (2003)

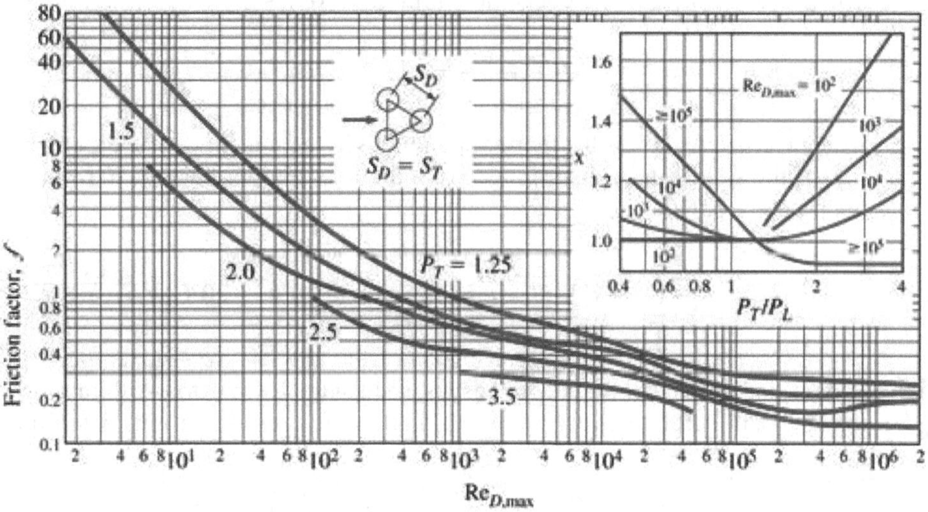

Figure 7.15d) Friction factors for staggered tube bank, from Cengel (2003)

In this case we are using a square in-line tube bank so the correction factor $\chi = 1$. The maximum velocity is

$$U_{max} = \frac{S_T U}{S_T - D} = \frac{0.050m \cdot 4\text{m/s}}{0.050m - 0.020m} = 6.67\ m/s \tag{7.5}$$

The Reynolds number can be determined based on an assumed mean temperature of 25°C based on the average of the inlet and outlet temperatures:

$$Re_{D,max} = \frac{U_{max} D}{\nu} = \frac{6.67m/s \cdot 0.020\text{m}}{1.562 \cdot 10^{-5} m^2/s} = 8536 \tag{7.6}$$

The average Nusselt number Nu for six rows of in-line tubes in the flow direction

$$Nu = 0.27F\,Re_{D,max}^{0.63}Pr^{0.36}\left(\frac{Pr}{Pr_s}\right)^{0.25} = 0.27\cdot 0.945\cdot 8536^{0.63}\cdot 0.7296^{0.36}\left(\frac{0.7296}{0.7073}\right)^{0.25} = 68.8$$

where Pr and Pr_s are the Prandtl numbers at the mean and surface temperature, respectively and F is a correction factor used for $N_L < 16$ and $Re_{D,max} > 1000$.

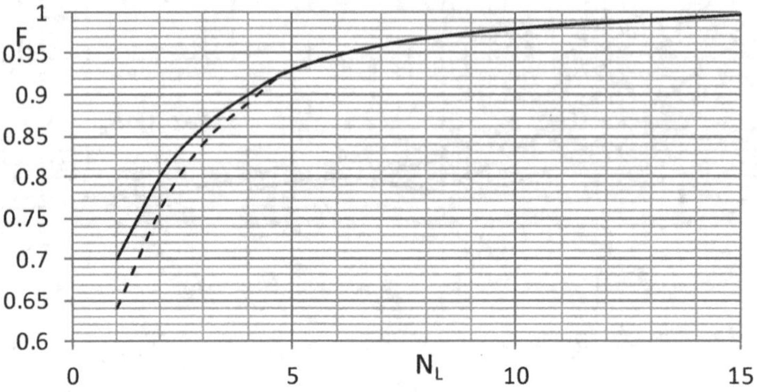

Figure 7.15e) Correction factors for in-line (full line) and staggered (dashed line) tubes
The average heat transfer coefficient h then becomes

$$h = \frac{kNu}{D} = \frac{0.02551 W/(m\cdot°C)\cdot 68.8}{0.02\ m} = 87.75\ W/(m^2\cdot°C) \tag{7.7}$$

where k $(W/(m^2\cdot°C))$ is the thermal conductivity of the fluid. The exit temperature T_e (°C) of the fluid can be determined from the inlet temperature T_i (°C) and the surface temperature T_s (°C)

$$T_e = T_s - (T_s - T_i)e^{\frac{-hN_L\pi D}{\rho U S_T C_p}} = 100°C - (100°C - 20°C)\,e^{\frac{-87.75\cdot 6\pi\cdot 0.02}{1.204\cdot 4\cdot 0.05\cdot 1007}} = 30.2\ °C$$

where C_P $(J/(kg\cdot°C))$ is the specific heat of the air. The average temperature as determined from Flow Simulation results, see figure 7.14f) at x = 300 mm is 27.46 °C, that is 9% different the result above. Finally, the pressure drop is determined to be

$$\Delta P = \frac{N_L f\chi\rho U_{max}^2}{2} = \frac{6\cdot 0.2\cdot 1\cdot 1.184\left(\frac{kg}{m^3}\right)\cdot 6.67^2\frac{m^2}{s}}{2} = 31.6\ Pa \tag{7.8}$$

L. References

1. Çengel, Y. A., Heat Transfer: A Practical Approach, 2nd Edition, McGraw-Hill, 2003. Granger, R.A., Experiments in Fluid Mechanics, Dryden Press, 1988.

M. Exercises

7.1 Change the mesh resolution in the flow simulations and see how the mesh size affects the maximum velocity and temperature profiles as shown in figures 7.14f) and 7.14g). Discuss your results.

7.2 Use an in-line five rows, $N_L = 5$, tube grid for flow simulations with a rectangular arrangement $S_L = 2S_T$, see figure 7.15a) and compare exit temperatures with corresponding calculations. The diameter of each cylinder is $D = 20$ mm, $S_T = 30\,mm$, and $N_T = 2$.

The coordinates for the centers of all cylinders will be (*X (mm)*, *Y (mm)*) = (0,0), (60,0), (120,0), (180,0), (240,0), (0,30), (60,30), (120,30), (180,30), (240,30). Use air as the project fluid and the velocity in the *X*-direction is 8 m/s. For the calculation of the Reynolds number, assume a mean temperature of $T_m = 25$ °C based on the average of the inlet and outlet temperatures. The surface temperature of the cylinders is $T_s = 100$ °C and the inlet temperature is $T_i = 20$ °C. Fill out Table 7.1 and discuss your results.

D (mm)	$S_L\ (mm)$	$S_T\ (mm)$	N_L	N_T	$U\ (m/s)$	$U_{max}\ (m/s)$
20	60	30	5	2	8	
T_m (°C)	ν (m²/s)	$Re_{D,max}$	F	Pr	Pr_s	Nu
25						
k (W/m-°C)	h (W/m²-°C)	T_s (°C)	T_i (°C)	ρ (kg/m³)	C_p (J/kg-°C)	T_e (°C)
		100	20			
T_e (°C) @ X = 265mm	% difference	T_e (°C) @ X = 290 mm	% difference	T_e (°C) @ X = 315 mm	% difference	
P_L	P_T	f	$(P_T-1)/(P_L-1)$	χ	ΔP (Pa)	
No. of Cells per X	No. of Cells per Y	No. of Cells per Z				

Table 7.1 Data for Exercise 7.2

7.3 Use a staggered grid for flow simulations with $S_L = S_T$, see figure 7.15b) and compare exit temperature profiles with corresponding calculations as shown in this chapter for in-line arrangement. For a staggered arrangement the Nusselt number in the range of Reynolds numbers *Re* = 1,000 – 200,000 is given by

$$Nu = 0.35F(S_T/S_L)^{0.2} Re_{D,max}^{0.6} Pr^{0.36} \left(\frac{Pr}{Pr_s}\right)^{0.25} \tag{7.9}$$

7.4 Use a staggered grid for flow simulations with $S_L = 2S_T$, see figure 7.15b), and compare exit temperature profiles with corresponding calculations.

Notes:

CHAPTER 8. HEAT EXCHANGER

A. Objectives

- Creating the SOLIDWORKS model of the heat exchanger
- Setting up Flow Simulation projects for internal flow
- Creating lids for the model
- Inserting boundary conditions
- Running the calculations
- Inserting surface parameters
- Using cut plots to visualize the resulting flow field
- Compare Flow Simulation results with effectiveness – NTU method

B. Problem Description

In this chapter, we will use SOLIDWORKS Flow Simulation to study the flow in a stainless-steel parallel flow shell and tube heat exchanger. Heat transfer will occur between the hot inner tube flow and the colder outer flow in the shell. The shell has a wall thickness of 10 mm and an inner diameter of 32 mm whereas the tube is 2 mm thick and has an outer diameter of 19 mm. The mass flow rate of water in the shell is 0.8 kg/s with an inlet temperature of 283.2 K and the mass flow rate of water in the tube is 0.2 kg/s at an inlet temperature of 343.2 K. The temperature distributions along the shell and tube will be shown from Flow Simulation results and the temperature of the hot water at the tube outlet will be used in comparison with the effectiveness – NTU method for calculation of the effectiveness of the parallel flow shell and tube heat exchanger.

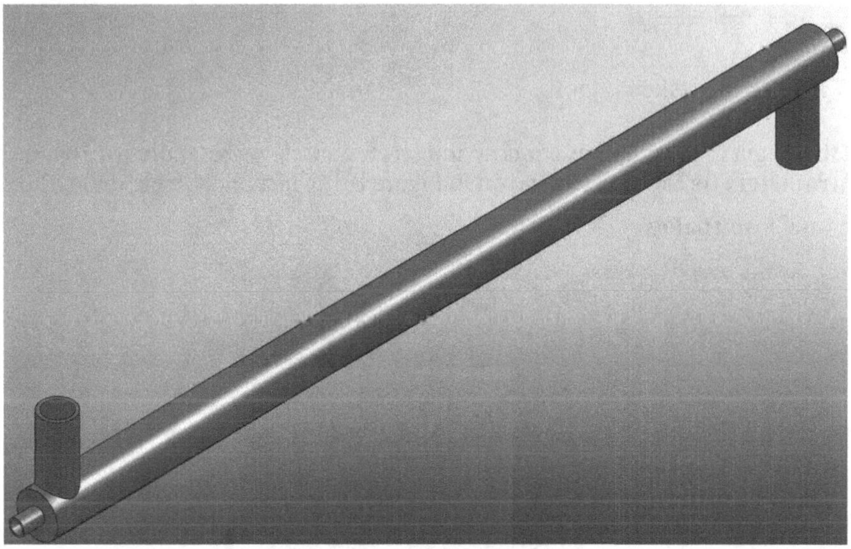

Figure 8.0 SOLIDWORKS model of shell and tube heat exchanger

C. Creating the SOLIDWORKS Part

1. Start by creating a new part in SOLIDWORKS: select **File>>New** and click on the **OK** button in the **New SOLIDWORKS Document** window. Select **Tools>>Options...** from the SOLIDWORKS menu. Click on the Document Properties tab and select **Units**. Select **MMGS** as your **Unit system**. Click on **Front Plane** in the **FeatureManager design tree** and select **Front** from the **View Orientation** drop down menu in the graphics window.

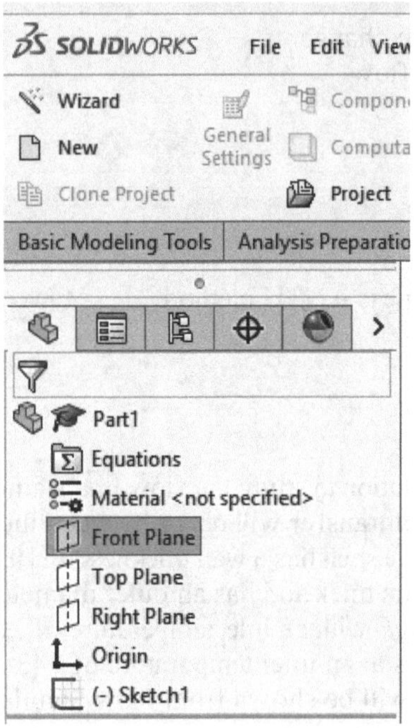

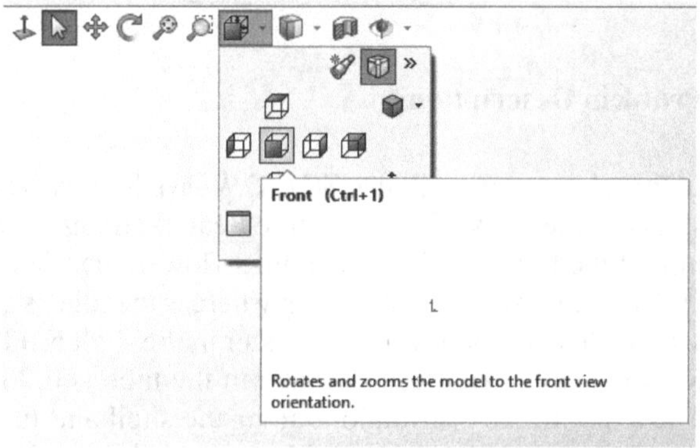

Figure 8.1a) Selection of front plane Figure 8.1b) Selection of right view

2. Select the **Basic Modeling Tools** tab and click on **Circle**.

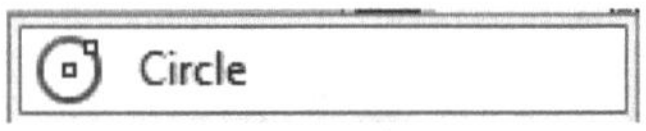

Figure 8.2 Selecting a sketch tool

3. Click at the origin in the graphics window and create a circle with a radius of 16 mm. Fill in the **Parameters** for the circle as shown in Figure 8.3. Close the **Circle** dialog box by clicking on **Close Dialog** ✓.

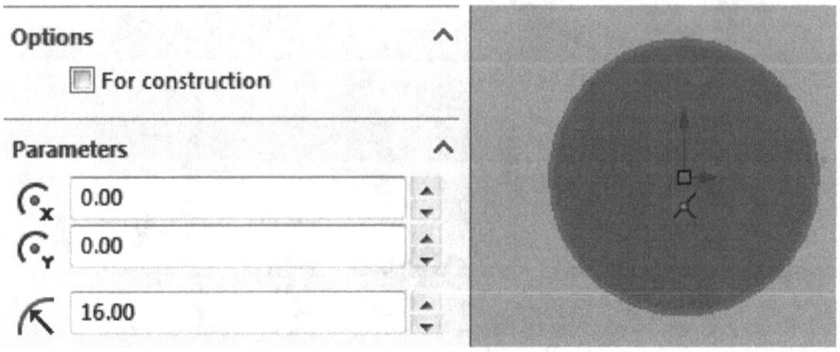

Figure 8.3 Circle with a radius of 16 mm

4. Select the **Analysis Preparation** tab and the **Extruded Boss/Base**. Enter **1000.00mm** for **Depth D1** of the extrusion in **Direction 1**. Check the **Thin Feature** box and check the **Cap ends** box. Close the Boss-**Extrude** dialog box by clicking on **OK** . Right click in the graphics window and select **Zoom/Pan/Rotate>>Zoom to Fit**. Select **Left** view from **View Orientation** in the graphics window, see Figure 8.4c). Select **Top Plane** from **Featuremanager design tree**. Insert a new plane from the SOLIDWORKS menu by selecting **Insert>>Reference Geometry>>Plane…**. Set the **Offset Distance** to **26.00mm** and exit the **Plane** dialog box. Select **Top** view from **View Orientation** in the graphics window, see Figure 8.4g).

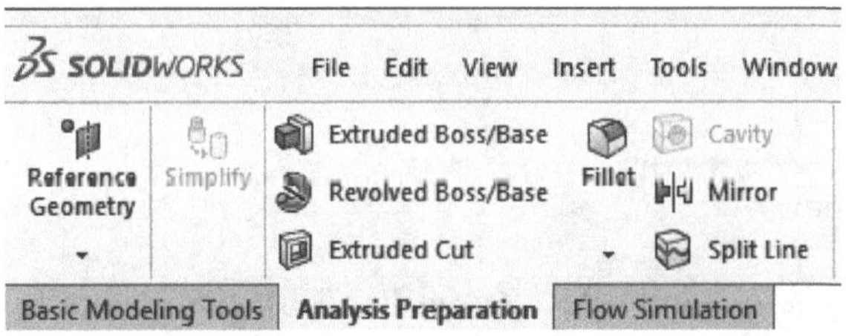

Figure 8.4a) Selection of extruded boss/base feature

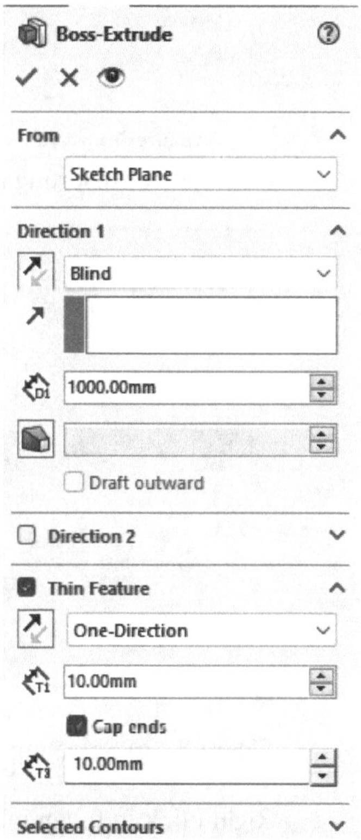

Figure 8.4b) Extruding a sketch

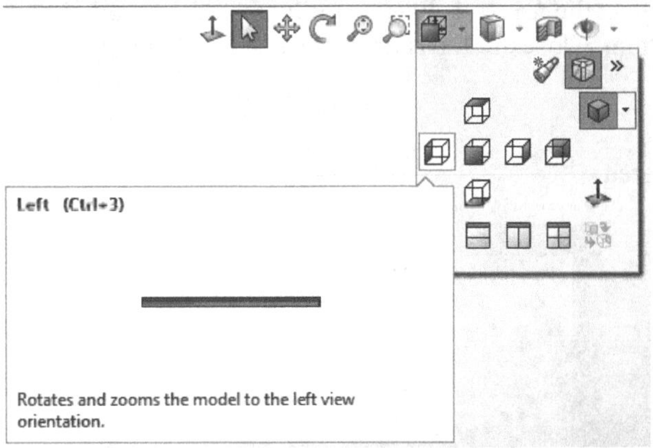

Figure 8.4c) Selecting a left view

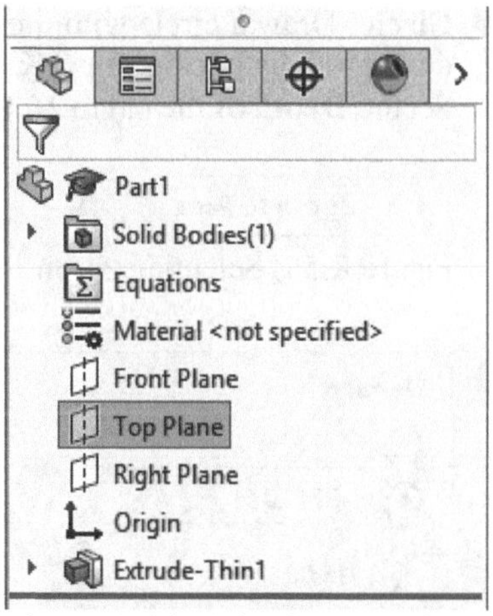

Figure 8.4d) Selecting top plane

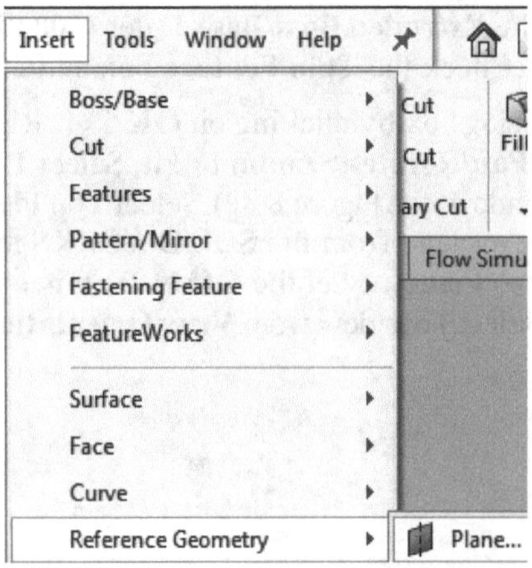

Figure 8.4e) Inserting a plane

Figure 8.4f) Setting the location of the plane

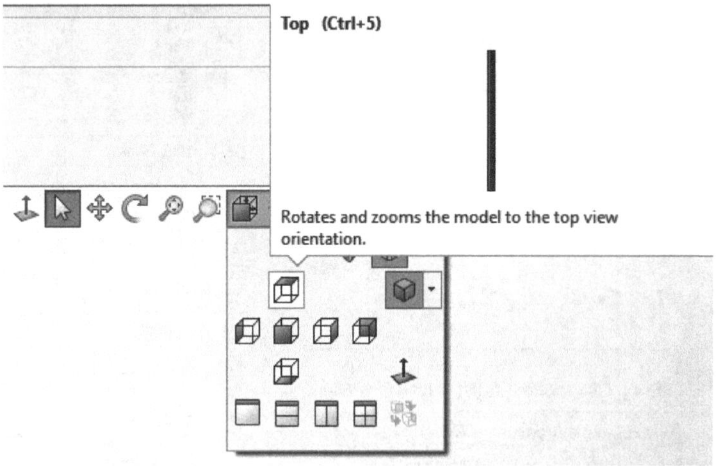

Figure 8.4g) Selecting top view

5. Right click in the graphics window and select **Zoom/Pan/Rotate>>Zoom to Area**. Select a region in the graphics window around the lower end of the tube. Click on **Plane 1** in the **Featuremanager design tree** and select the **Basic Modeling Tools** tab and **Circle**. Draw a circle with the parameters as given in Figure 8.5b). Close the **Circle** dialog box by clicking on **OK**. Select the **Analysis Preparation** tab and **Extruded Cut**. Set the **Depth** of the cut to **26.00mm**. Close the **Extrude** dialog box by clicking on **OK**.

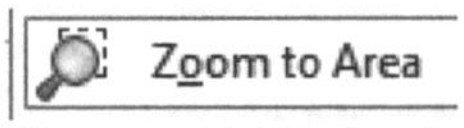

Figure 8.5a) Selecting zoom to area

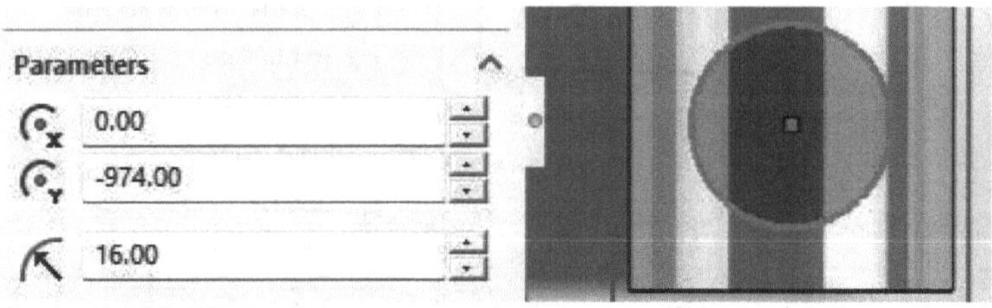

Figure 8.5b) Circle for cut-extrusion

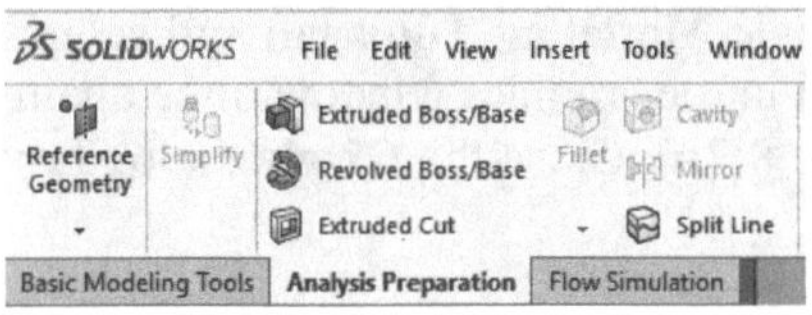

Figure 8.5c) Extruded cut tool

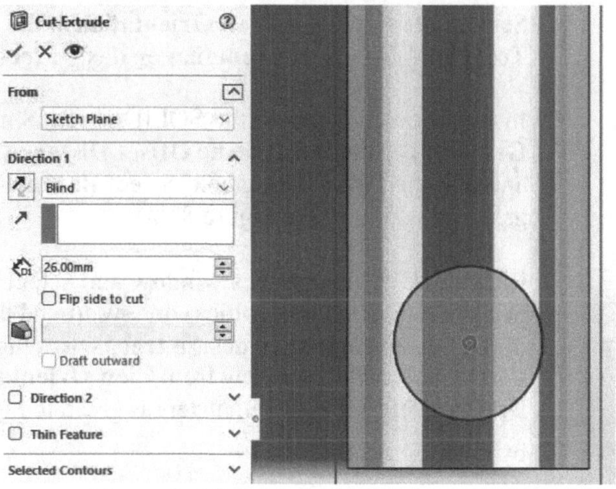

Figure 8.5d) Extruded cut

6. Click on the arrow next to **Cut-Extrude 1**, select **Sketch 2** in the **Featuremanager design tree**, select the **Analysis Preparation** tab and click on **Extruded Boss/Base**. Set **Depth D1** of the extrusion in **Direction 1** to **75.00mm**. Check the **Direction 2** box and enter **10.00mm** for **Depth**. Check the **Thin Feature** box and enter **4.00mm** for the **Thickness**. Close the **Boss-Extrude** dialog box.

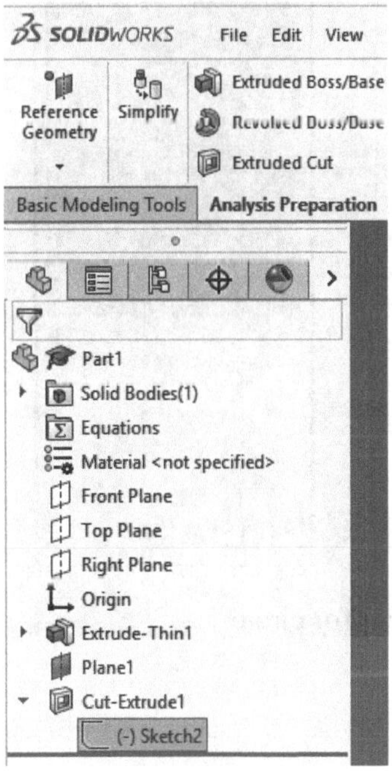

Figure 8.6a) Sketch 2

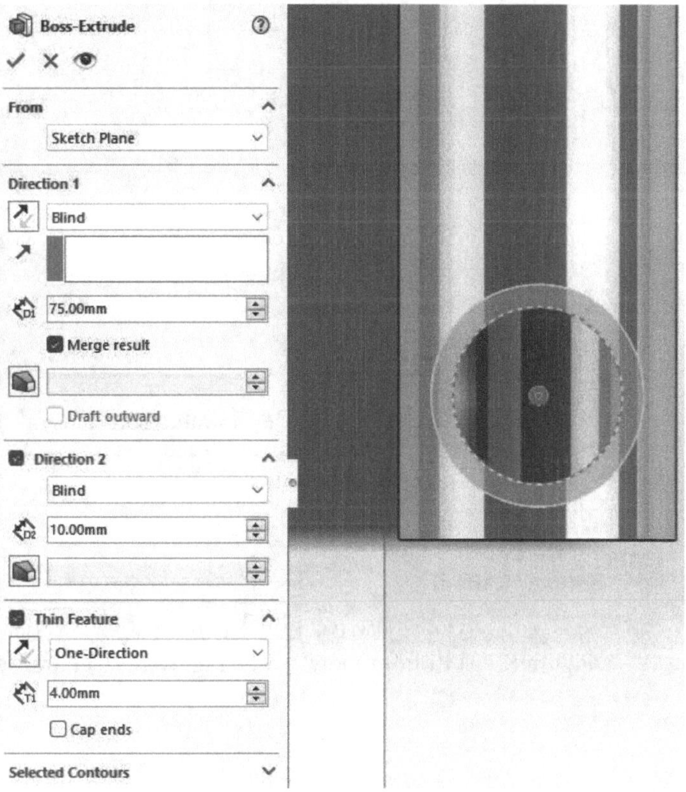

Figure 8.6b) Dimensions of the extrusion

7. Select **Left** view from **View Orientation** in the graphics window, see Figure 8.4c). Select **Top Plane** from **Featuremanager design tree**.

   Insert a new plane from the SOLIDWORKS menu by selecting **Insert>>Reference Geometry>>Plane….** Set the **Offset Distance** to **26.00mm**, check the **Flip offset** box and exit the **Plane** dialog box. Select **Bottom** view from **View Orientation** in the graphics window, see Figure 8.7a).

   Right click in the graphics window and select **Zoom/Pan/Rotate>>Zoom to Area**. Select a region in the graphics window around the lower end of the tube. Select **Plane 2** in the **Featuremanager design tree**, select the **Basic Modeling Tools** tab and select **Circle**. Select **Bottom** view from **View Orientation** in the graphics window once again. Draw a circle with the parameters as given in Figure 8.7b). Close the **Circle** dialog box by clicking on **OK** .

   Select the **Analysis Preparation** tab and the **Extruded Cut**. Set the **Depth** of the cut to **26.00mm**. Close the **Cut-Extrude** dialog box by clicking on **OK** .

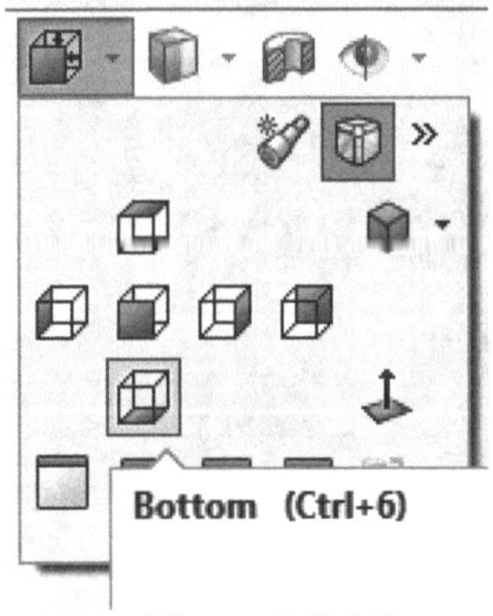

Figure 8.7a) Bottom view

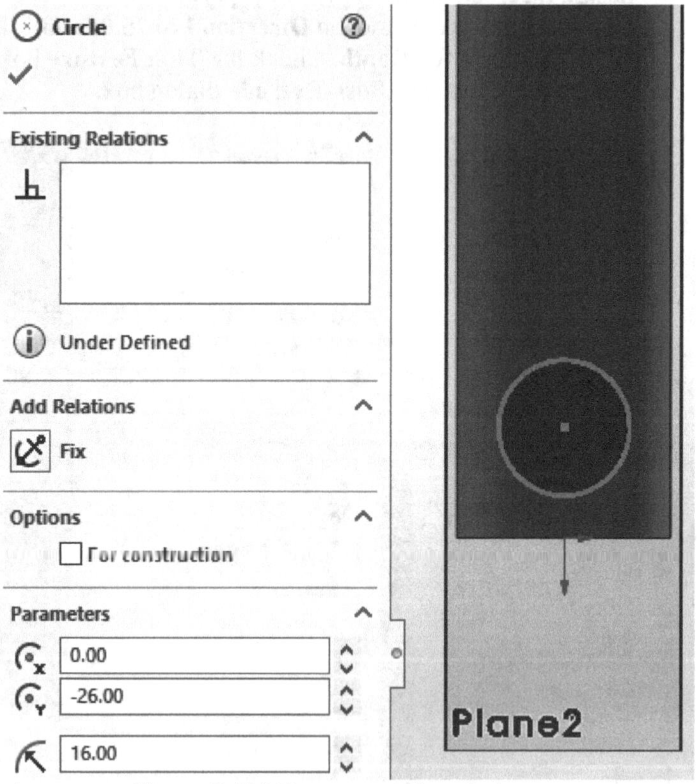

Figure 8.7b) Parameters for circle

8. Click on the arrow next to **Cut-Extrude 2**, select **Sketch 3** in the **Featuremanager design tree** and click on **Extruded Boss/Base**. Enter **10.00mm** as the **Depth** for **Direction 1**. Check the **Direction 2** box and enter **75.00mm** for the **Depth**. Check the **Thin Feature** box and enter **4.00mm** for the **Thickness**. Close the **Boss-Extrude** dialog box by clicking on **OK** .

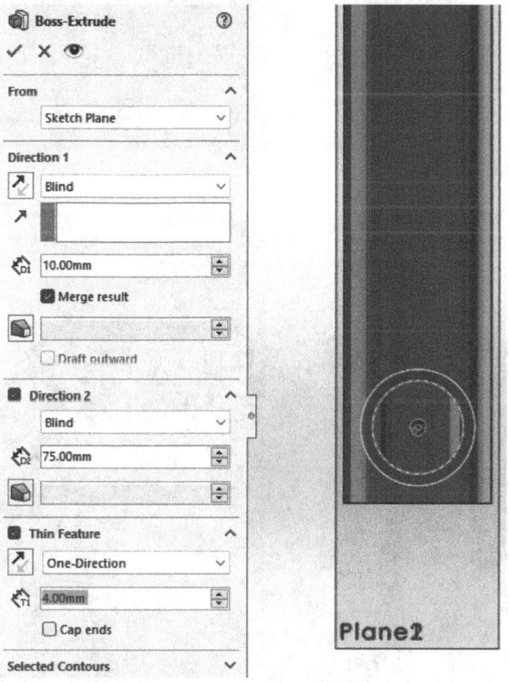

Figure 8.8 Extrusion from plane 2

9 Select **Back** view from **View Orientation** in the graphics window, see Figure 8.9a). Select **Front Plane** from **Featuremanager design tree**. Select the **Basic Modeling Tools** tab and **Circle**. Draw a circle with the parameters as given in Figure 8.9b). Close the **Circle** dialog box by clicking on **OK**. Select the **Analysis Preparation** tab and **Extruded Cut**. Set the **Depth** of the cut to **1000.00mm** and click on the **Reverse Direction** button. Close the **Extrude** dialog box by clicking on **OK**.

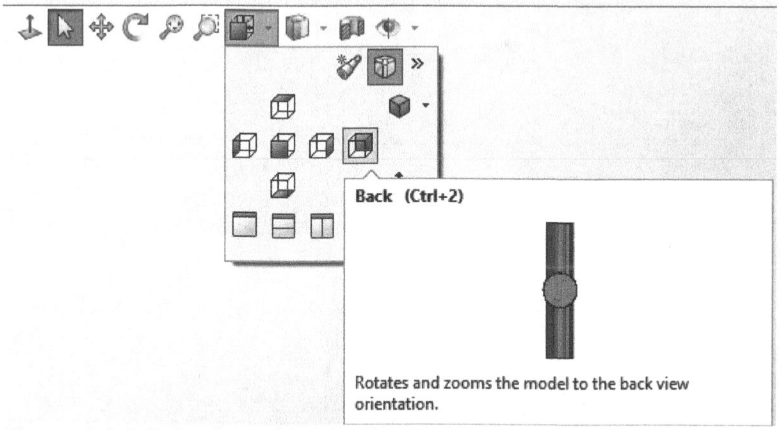

Figure 8.9a) Selection of back view

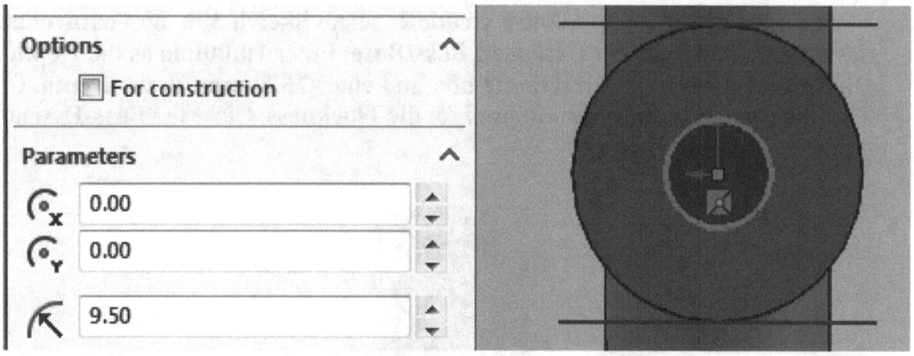

Figure 8.9b) Parameters for circle

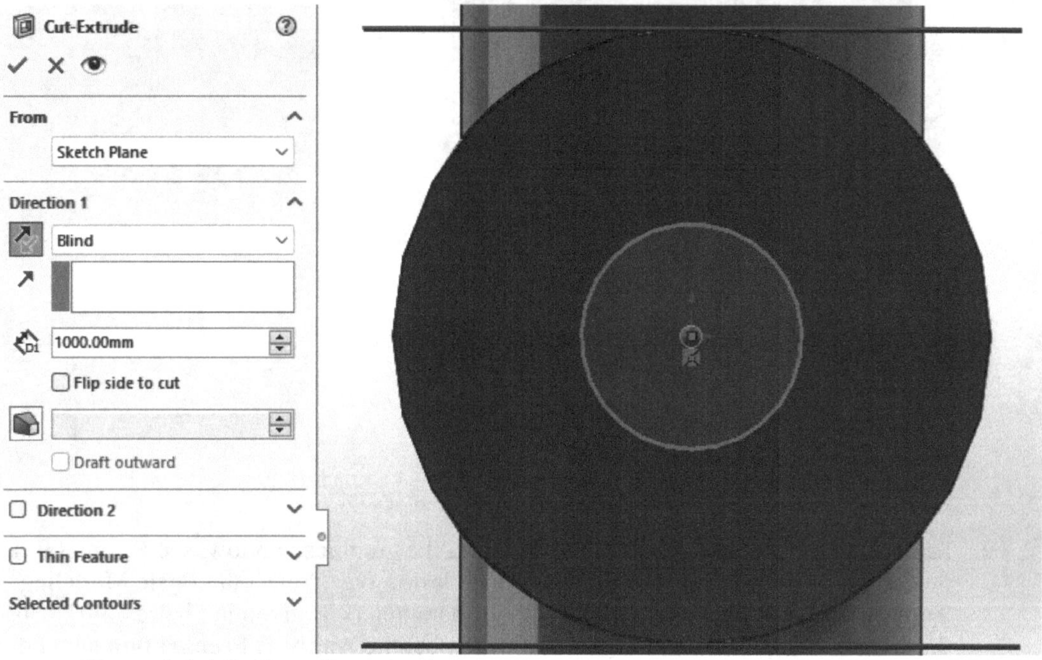

Figure 8.9c) Settings for extruded cut

10. Click on the arrow next to **Cut-Extrude 3**, select **Sketch 4** in the **Featuremanager design tree** and click on **Extruded Boss/Base**. Enter **1026.00mm** as the **Depth** for **Direction 1**. Check the **Direction 2** box and enter **26.00mm** for the **Depth**. Check the **Thin Feature** box, click on the **Reverse Direction** button and enter **2.00mm** for **Thickness**. Close the **Boss-Extrude** dialog box by clicking on **OK**. Right click on **Plane 1** in the **Featuremanager design tree** and select **Hide**. Repeat this step for **Plane 2**. Select **Left** view from **View Orientation** in the graphics window, see Figure 8.4c). Save the part with the name **Heat Exchanger Shell and Tube 2026**.

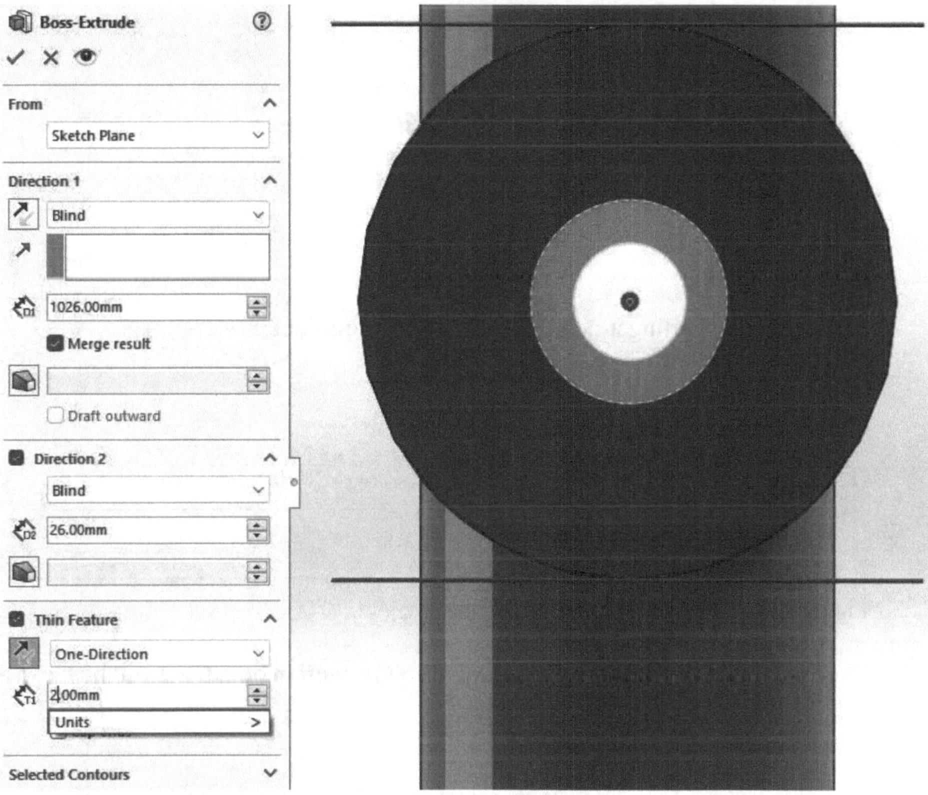

Figure 8.10a) Settings for extrusion from front plane

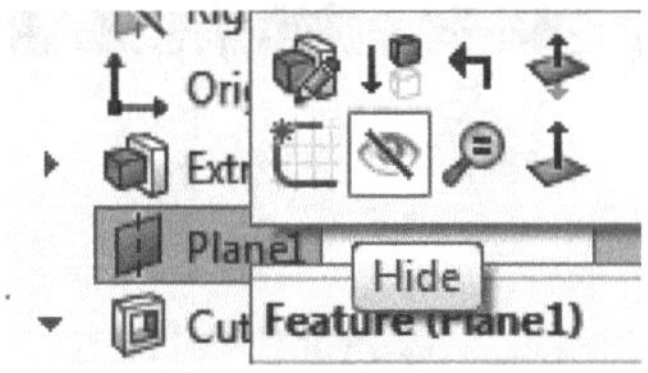

Figure 8.10b) Hiding plane 1

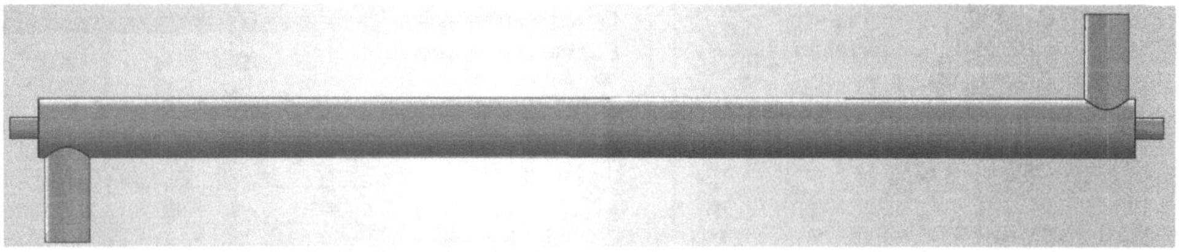
Figure 8.10c) Finished shell and tube heat exchanger

D. Flow Simulation Project

11. If Flow Simulation is not available in the menu, you need to add it from SOLIDWORKS menu: Select **Tools>>Add Ins…** and check the corresponding **SOLIDWORKS Flow Simulation** box. Select **Tools>>Flow Simulation>>Project>>Wizard…** to create a new Flow Simulation project. Create a new project named **Shell and Tube Heat Exchanger Study**. Click on the **Next >** button. Select the default **SI (m-kg-s)** unit system and click on the **Next>** button once again.

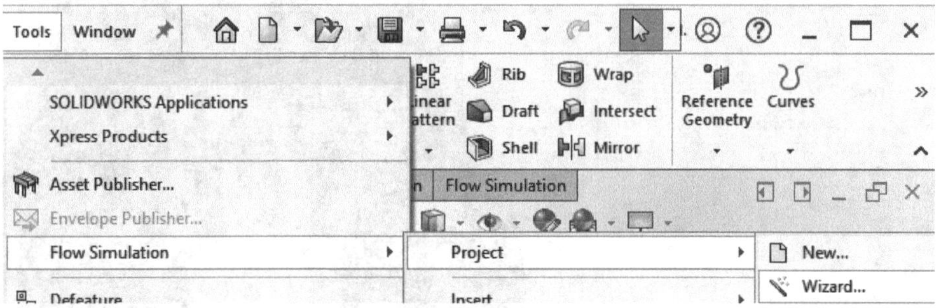

Figure 8.11a) Starting a new Flow Simulation project

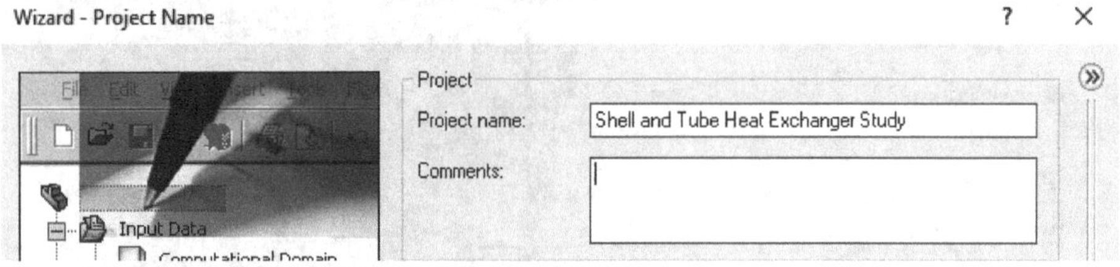

Figure 8.11b) Creating a name for the project

12. Use **Internal Analysis type** and check the **Conduction** box. Click on the **Next >** button.

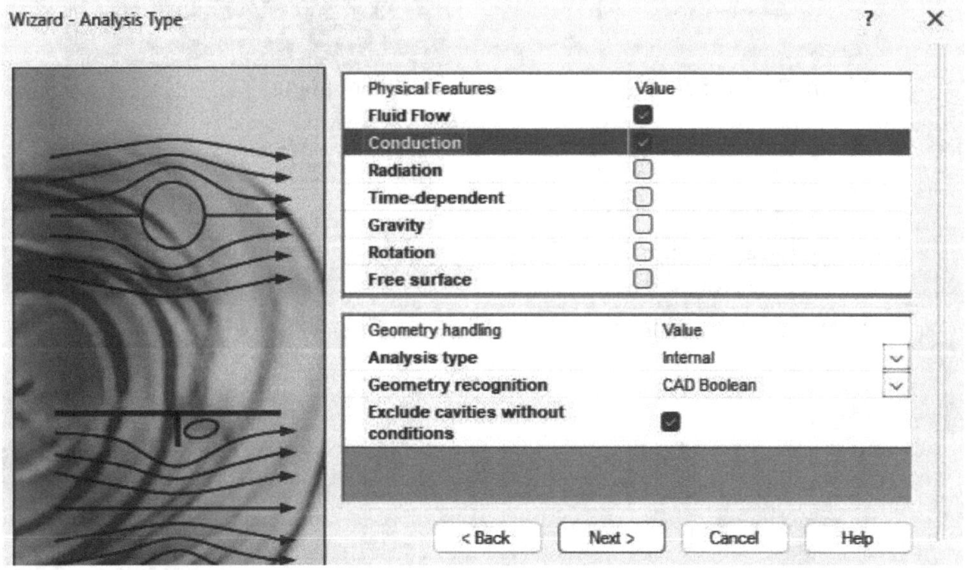

Figure 8.12 Internal analysis type with heat conduction in solids

13. Add **Water** from **Liquids** as the **Project Fluid**. Click on the **Next >** button. Select **Alloys>> Stainless Steel 321** as the **Default Solid**. Click on the **Next >** button. Use the default **Wall Conditions** and default **Initial Conditions**. Click on the **Finish** button. Answer Yes to the question whether you want to open the Create Lids tool.

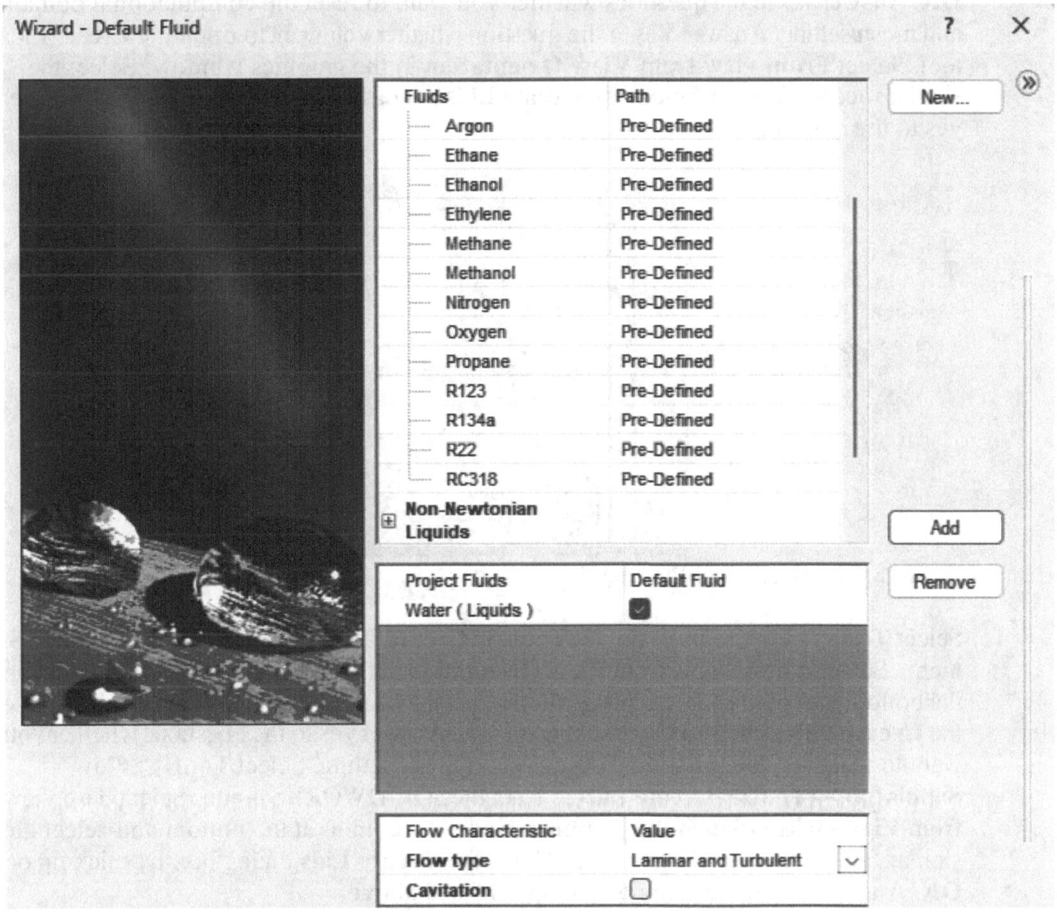

Figure 8.13a) Adding water as the project fluid

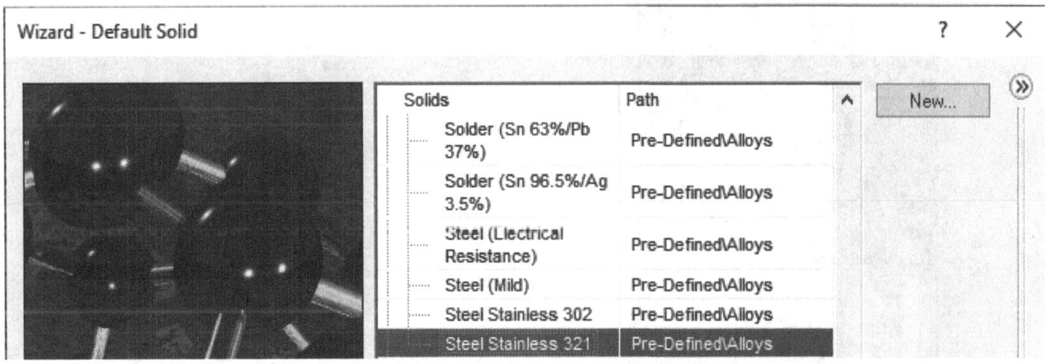

Figure 8.13b) Selecting stainless steel as the default solid

E. Creating Lids

14. Select **Back** view from **View Orientation** in the graphics window, see Figure 8.9a). Select the face as shown in Figure 8.14. Close the **Create Lids** dialog box by clicking on **OK**. Answer yes to the questions whether you want to reset the computational domain and mesh setting. Answer Yes to the question whether you want to open the Create Lids tool. Select **Front** view from **View Orientation** in the graphics window. Select the similar face as above and close the **Create Lids** dialog box by clicking on **OK**. Answer yes to the questions.

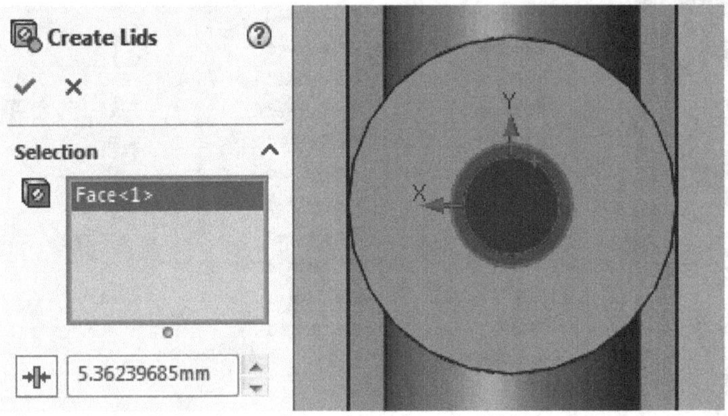

Figure 8.14 Selection of the face for the lid

15. Select **Tools>>Flow Simulation>>Tools>>Create Lids...** from the SOLIDWORKS menu. Select **Bottom** view from **View Orientation** in the graphics window. Zoom in on the bottom part of the heat exchanger and select the face as shown in Figure 8.15. Close the **Create Lids** dialog box by clicking on **OK**. Answer yes to the questions whether you want to reset the computational domain and mesh setting. Select **Tools>>Flow Simulation>>Tools>>Create Lids...** from the SOLIDWORKS menu. Select **Top** view from **View Orientation** in the graphics window. Zoom in at the bottom and select the similar face as shown in Figure 8.15. Close the **Create Lids** dialog box by clicking on **OK**. Answer yes to the same questions as listed above.

Figure 8.15 Selection of face for third lid

F. Boundary Conditions

16. Select **Left** view from **View Orientation** in the graphics window. Right click in the graphics window and select **Zoom/Pan/Rotate>>Rotate View**. Rotate the view a little bit and select **Zoom to Area**. Zoom in at the left end of the heat exchanger, see Figure 8.16b). Click on the plus sign next to the **Input Data** folder in the **Flow Simulation analysis tree**. Right click on **Boundary Conditions** and select **Insert Boundary Condition…**. Right click on the tube and select **Select Other**. Select the inner surface of the lid, see Figure 8.16b). Set the **Inlet Mass Flow** to **0.2 kg/s** and the **Temperature** to **343.2 K**. Click OK to exit the **Boundary Condition** window. Rename the created boundary condition in the **Flow Simulation analysis tree** to **Inlet Mass Flow for Tube**.

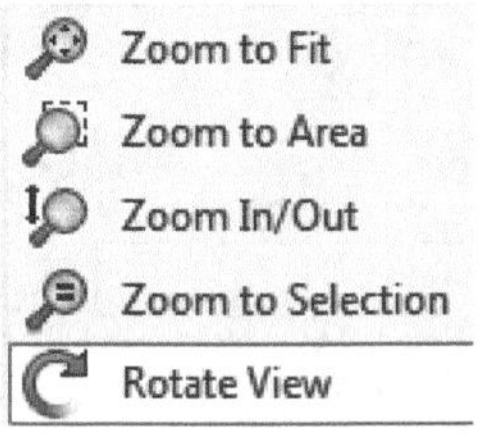

Figure 8.16a) Selection of rotate view

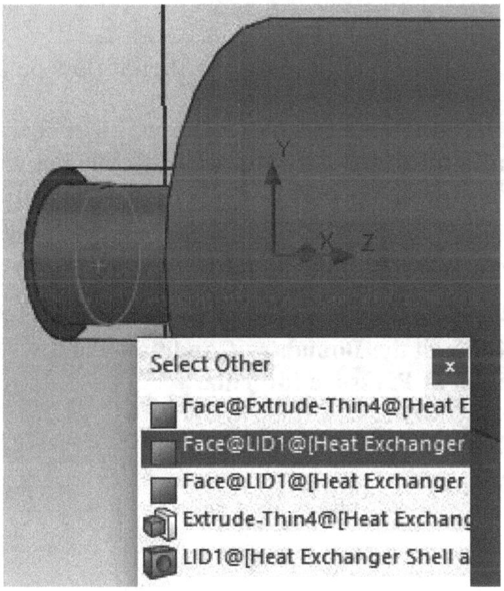

Figure 8.16b) Face for tube inflow region

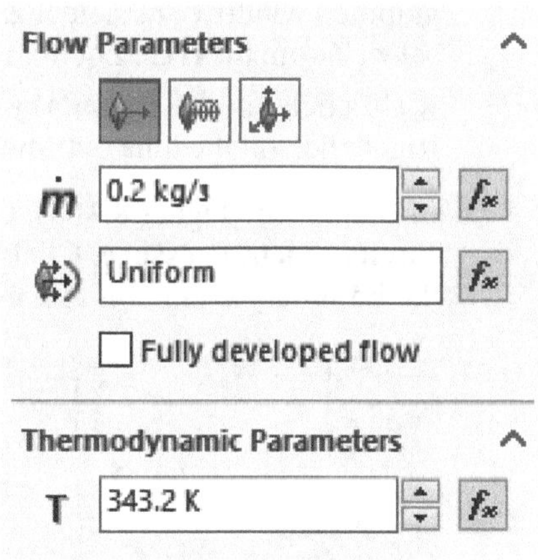

Figure 8.16c) Tube inflow

17. Zoom out a little bit and rotate the view a little bit, see Figure 8.17a). Right click on **Boundary Conditions** and select **Insert Boundary Condition….** Right click on the shell and select the inner surface of the shell inflow lid, see Figure 8.17a). Set the **Inlet Mass Flow** to **0.8 kg/s** and the **Temperature** to **283.2 K**. Click OK to exit the **Boundary Condition** window. Rename the boundary condition to **Inlet Mass Flow for Shell.**

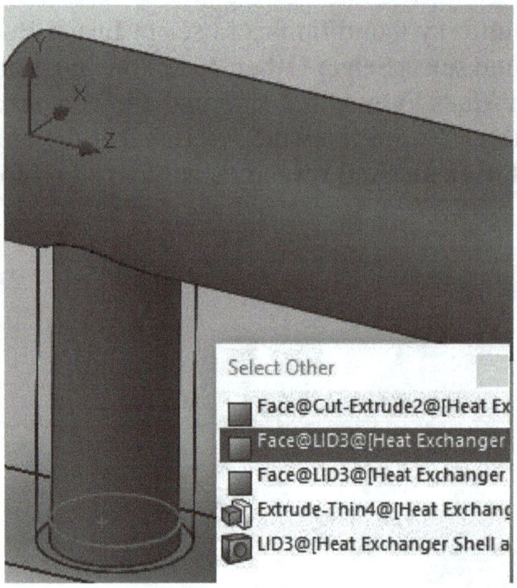

Figure 8.17a) Shell inflow region

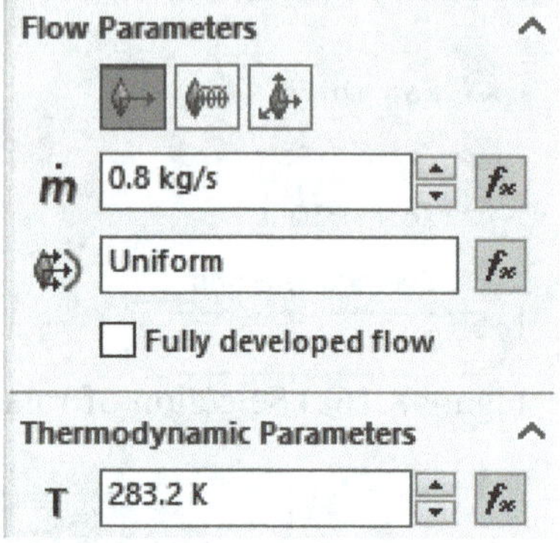

Figure 8.17b) Shell inflow parameters

18. Select **Left** view from **View Orientation** in the graphics window. Right click in the graphics window and select **Zoom/Pan/Rotate>>Rotate View**. Rotate the view and select **Zoom to Area**. Zoom in at the right end of the heat exchanger, see Figure 8.18a). Right click on **Boundary Conditions** and select **Insert Boundary Condition….** Right click on the tube outflow region and click on **Select Other**. Select the inner surface of the lid, see Figure 8.18a). Click on the **Pressure Openings** button and select **Environment Pressure**. Click OK to exit the **Boundary Condition** window. Rename the boundary condition to **Environment Pressure for Tube.**

Figure 8.18a) Face for tube outflow

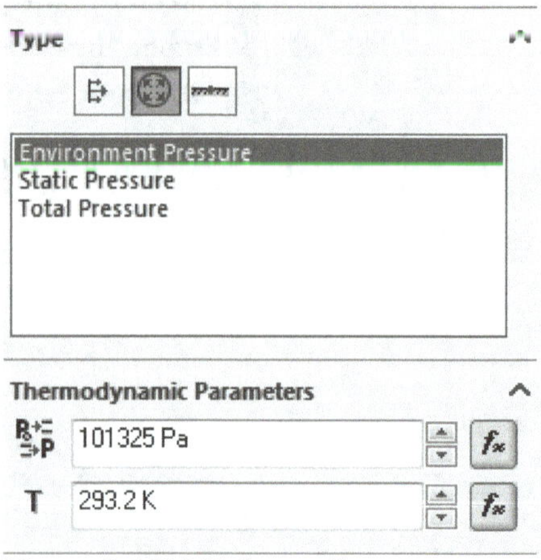

Figure 8.18b) Tube outflow parameters

19. Right click in the graphics window and select **Zoom/Pan/Rotate>>Rotate View**. Rotate the view a little bit and zoom out a little bit, see Figure 8.19a). Right click on **Boundary Conditions** and select **Insert Boundary Condition….** Right click on the shell outflow region and click on **Select Other**. Select the inner surface of the lid, see Figure 8.19b). Click on the **Pressure Openings** button. Select **Environment Pressure** and click OK to exit the **Boundary Condition** window. Rename the boundary condition to **Environment Pressure for Shell.**

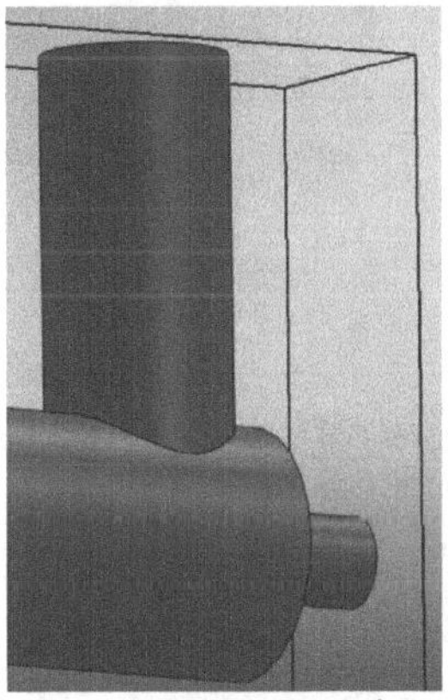

Figure 8.19a) Rotating the view

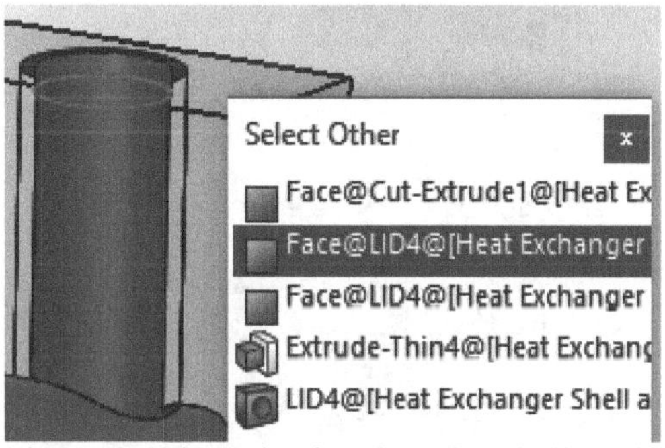

Figure 8.19b) Selecting face for shell outflow

G. Inserting Goals

20. Right click on **Goals** in the **Flow Simulation analysis tree** and select **Insert Global Goals….** Select **Min**, **Av** and **Max Temperature (Fluid)** and scroll down to select **Min**, **Av** and **Max Temperature (Solid)** as global goals. Click OK to exit the **Global Goals** window.

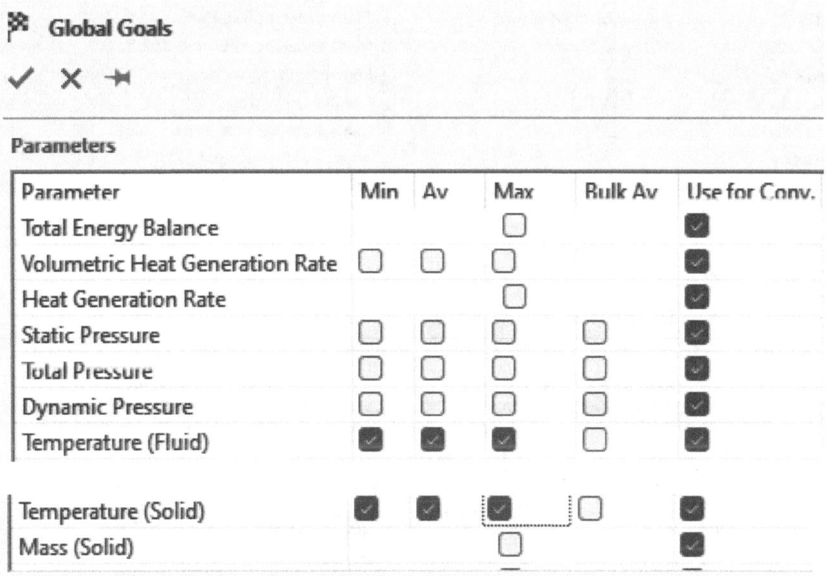

Figure 8.20 Selection of global goals

H. Simulations for Heat Exchanger

21. Select **Tools>>Flow Simulation>>Solve>>Run…** to start calculations. Click on the **Run** button in the **Run** window.

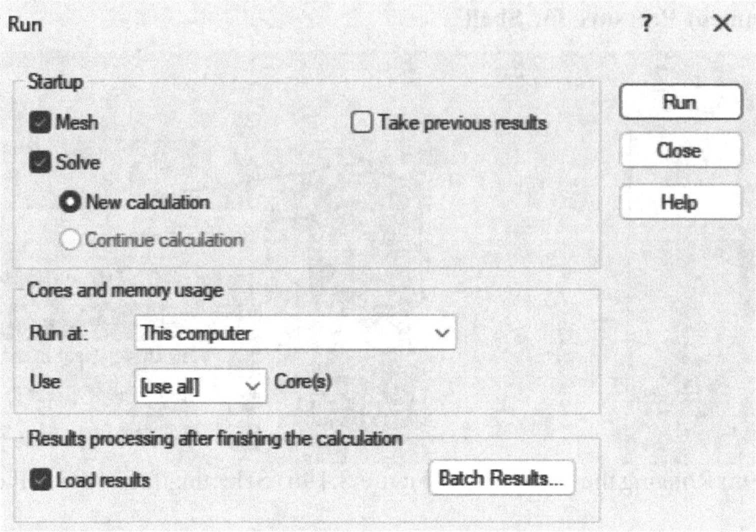

Figure 8.21a) Run window

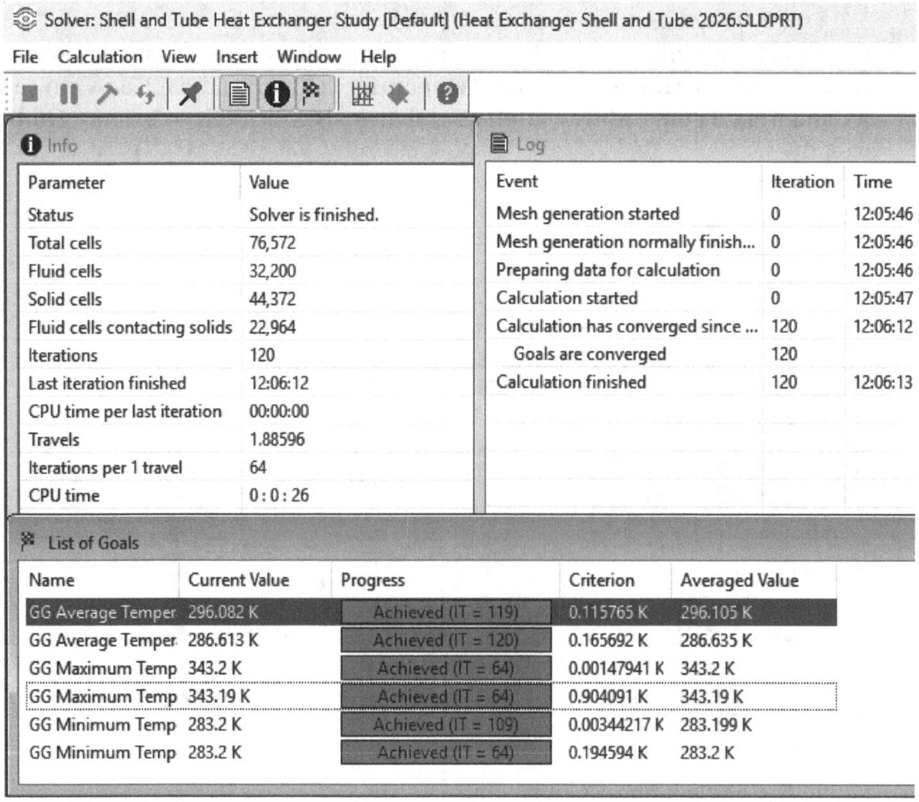

Figure 8.21b) Solver window

I. Surface Parameters

22. Open the **Results** folder, right click on **Surface Parameters** in the **Flow Simulation analysis tree** and select **Insert....** Select the **Environment Pressure for Tube Boundary Condition** in the **Flow Simulation analysis tree**. Check the **All Parameters** box and click on the **Export to Excel** button in the **Surface Parameters** window. Select the **Local parameters.** The minimum fluid temperature at the tube outflow region is **335.758 K** and the average value at the same outflow region is **336.336 K**.

    Select the **Environment Pressure for Shell Boundary Condition** in the **Flow Simulation analysis tree**. Click on the **Export to Excel** button once again in the **Surface Parameters** window. Select the **Local parameters**. The average fluid temperature at the shell outflow region is **285.035 K**. Exit the **Surface Parameters** window.

Local Parameters					
Local Parameter	Minimum	Maximum	Average	Bulk Average	Surface Area [m^2]
Pressure [Pa]	101325	101325	101325	101325	0.000169852
Density (Fluid) [kg/m^3]	980.9817145	981.6139355	981.3233421	981.311503	0.000169852
Velocity [m/s]	1.058497676	1.303400899	1.199917386	1.204346365	0.000169852
Velocity (X) [m/s]	-1.78E-05	2.17463E-05	-1.1831E-06	-1.22593E-06	0.000169852
Velocity (Y) [m/s]	-1.1332E-05	2.93635E-05	9.41423E-06	9.49153E-06	0.000169852
Velocity (Z) [m/s]	1.058497676	1.303400899	1.199917386	1.204346365	0.000169852
Temperature (Fluid) [K]	335.7580286	337.0159501	336.3361054	336.359663	0.000169852
Temperature (Solid) [K]	335.8580509	336.094718	335.9419152		0.000169852

Figure 8.22a) Values of local parameters at the tube outflow region

Local Parameters					
Local Parameter	Minimum	Maximum	Average	Bulk Average	Surface Area [m^2]
Pressure [Pa]	101323.9786	101325	101324.9872	101324.9995	0.000798803
Density (Fluid) [kg/m^3]	997.5617393	999.4360743	999.376104	999.3997864	0.000798803
Velocity [m/s]	0.026968244	1.776410005	1.004315919	1.375803397	0.000798803
Velocity (X) [m/s]	-0.03610223	0.036275598	0.000376623	0.000582045	0.000798803
Velocity (Y) [m/s]	-0.04525347	1.775771213	1.002194421	1.37491566	0.000798803
Velocity (Z) [m/s]	-0.10587966	0.009078658	-0.02943426	-0.03315496	0.000798803
Temperature (Fluid) [K]	284.7424039	293.2	285.0346799	284.9293172	0.000798803
Temperature (Solid) [K]	284.9063251	285.1724557	285.021142		0.000798803

Figure 8.22b) Values of local parameters at the shell outflow region

J. Cut-Plots

23. Right click on **Cut Plots** in the **Flow Simulation analysis tree** and select **Insert…**. Select the **Right Plane** from the **FeatureManager design tree**. Slide the **Number of Level** slide bar to **255** in the **Contours** section. Select **Temperature** from the **Parameter** dropdown menu. Click on **Adjust Minimum and Maximum** . Set the **Min:** temperature to **335.758 K**. Exit the **Cut Plot** window. Rename the cut plot to **Tube Temperature**. Select **Tools>>Flow Simulation>>Results>>Display>>Model Geometry** and **Section View** and select the **Right Plane** in **Section 1** settings to display the cut plot. Select **Left** view from **View Orientation** in the graphics window. Right click on scale in the graphics window and select Make Horizontal. Right click on Computational Domain under Input Data in Flow Simulation analysis tree and select Hide. Right click on Shell and Tube Heat Exchanger Study in the Flow Simulation analysis tree and select Hide Global Coordinate System. Select **Tools>>Flow Simulation>>Results>>Display>>Lighting.**

    Repeat this step and insert another cut plot but set the minimum temperature to **283.2 K** and the maximum temperature to **285.035 K** to see the temperature variation of the shell, see Figure 8.23b). Rename the cut plot to **Shell Temperature**. Right-click on the Tube Temperature Cut Plot in the Flow Simulation analysis tree and select **Hide** to display the shell temperature.

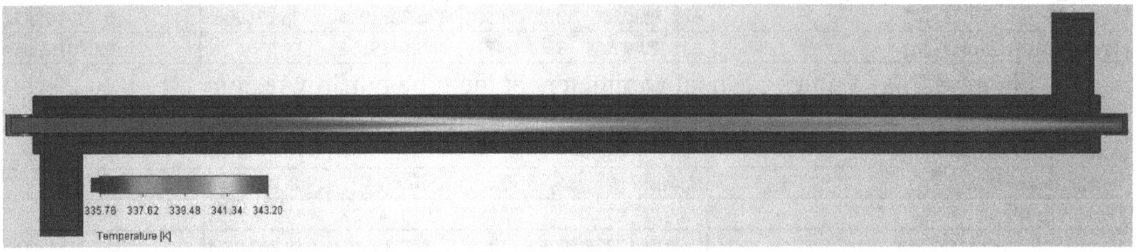

Figure 8.23a) Temperature distribution along the tube

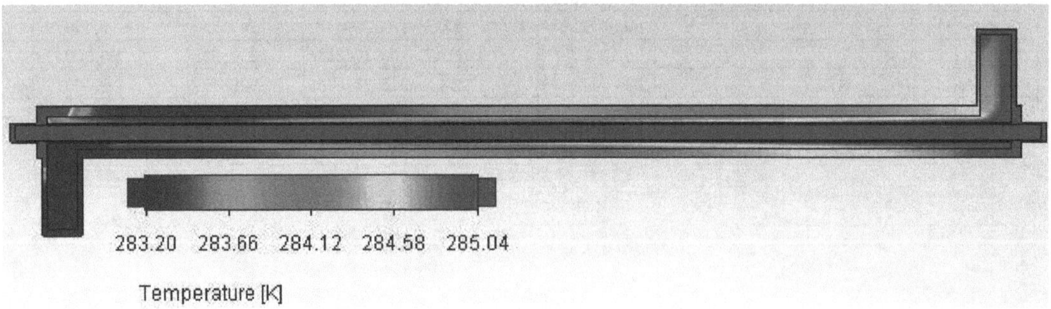

Figure 8.23b) Temperature distribution along the shell

K. Theory for Effectiveness-NTU Method

24. We will now use the effectiveness –NTU method for comparison of outlet temperatures with Flow Simulation results for the shell and tube heat exchanger. First, we determine the heat capacity rates of the shell and the tube fluids, respectively. The heat capacity rate of the shell C_s and tube C_t fluids are

$$C_s = \dot{m}_s C_{ps} = 0.8kg/s \cdot 4194J/(kg \cdot K) = 3355.2\ W/K \tag{8.1}$$

$$C_t = \dot{m}_t C_{pt} = 0.2kg/s \cdot 4190J/(kg \cdot K) = 838\ W/K \tag{8.2}$$

where $\dot{m}$ is the mass flow rate and C_p is the specific heat. The maximum heat transfer rate is given by

$$\dot{Q}_{max} = C_{min}(T_{max,in} - T_{min,in}) = C_t(T_{t,in} - T_{s,in}) = 838\frac{W}{K} \cdot (343.2 - 283.2)K = 50.28\ kW$$

where $T_{t,in}$ and $T_{s,in}$ are the tube and shell inflow temperatures, respectively. The heat transfer surface area is

$$A = \pi D_{it} L = \pi \cdot 0.015m \cdot 0.98m = 0.046m^2 \tag{8.3}$$

where D_{it} is the inner diameter of the tube and L is the length. The number of transfer units *NTU* is given by

$$NTU = \frac{UA}{C_{min}} \tag{8.4}$$

where U is the overall heat transfer coefficient. The mean velocities U_m in the tube is

$$U_{mt} = \frac{4\dot{m}_t}{\pi \rho_t D_{it}^2} = \frac{4 \cdot 0.2kg/s}{\pi \cdot 977.5\frac{kg}{m^3} \cdot 0.015^2 m^2} = 1.158m/s \tag{8.5}$$

where ρ_t is the density of the tube fluid. The Reynolds number Re_t for the tube flow is given by

$$Re_t = \frac{\rho_t U_{mt} D_{it}}{\mu_t} = \frac{977.5\frac{kg}{m^3} \cdot 1.158\frac{m}{s} \cdot 0.015m}{0.404 \cdot 10^{-3}\frac{kg}{m \cdot s}} = 42{,}021 \tag{8.6}$$

where μ_t is the dynamic viscosity of the tube fluid. The flow is turbulent and for smooth tubes the friction factor f can be determined from the Petukhov equation (for laminar tube flow $f = 64/Re$)

$$f = \frac{1}{(0.79 lnRe - 1.64)^2} \qquad 10^4 < Re < 10^6 \tag{8.7}$$

For the fluid in the tube the friction factor $f_t = 0.0218$. The Nusselt number *Nu* for turbulent pipe flow is a function of the friction factor, Reynolds number and Prandtl number (Pr_t=2.55) according to the Gnielinski equation (for laminar smooth tube flow *Nu* = 3.66

$$Nu = \frac{(\frac{f}{8})(Re-1000)Pr}{1+12.7(\frac{f}{8})^{\frac{1}{2}}(Pr^{\frac{2}{3}}-1)} \qquad 3 \cdot 10^3 < Re < 5 \cdot 10^6,\ 0.5 \le Pr \le 2000 \qquad (8.8)$$

For the fluid in the tube the Nusselt number $Nu_t = 181.16$. The convection heat transfer coefficient h_t for the tube flow can then be determined from

$$h_t = \frac{k_t Nu_t}{D_{it}} = \frac{0.663\frac{W}{m \cdot K} \cdot 181.16}{0.015m} = 8{,}007.13 \frac{W}{m^2 \cdot K} \qquad (8.9)$$

where k_t is the thermal conductivity of the tube fluid. For the shell the mean velocity

$$U_{ms} = \frac{4\dot{m}_s}{\pi \rho_s (D_{is}^2 - D_{ot}^2)} = \frac{4 \cdot 0.8kg/s}{\pi \cdot 999.7\frac{kg}{m^3} \cdot (0.032^2 m^2 - 0.019^2 m^2)} = 1.537m/s \qquad (8.10)$$

where D_{is} is the inner diameter of the shell and D_{ot} is the outer diameter for the tube. The Reynolds number for the shell is given by

$$Re_s = \frac{\rho_s U_{ms}(D_{is} - D_{ot})}{\mu_s} = \frac{999.7\frac{kg}{m^3} \cdot 1.537\frac{m}{s} \cdot 0.013m}{1.307 \cdot 10^{-3}\frac{kg}{m \cdot s}} = 15{,}281 \qquad (8.11)$$

This flow is also turbulent since $Re_s > 10{,}000$ and from eq. (7) we get the friction factor $f_s = 0.0280$. The Nusselt number $Nu_s = 122.57$ from eq. (8) multiplied with the Petukhov and Roizen correction factor $0.86(D_{ot}/D_{is})^{-0.16}$ for the annular shell flow using $Pr_s = 9.45$. If the flow in the annulus is laminar, the Nusselt number according to Kays and Perkins can be found for the inner surface by interpolation from Table 8.1.

D_{ot}/D_{is}	Nu_s
0	---
0.05	17.46
0.10	11.56
0.25	7.37
0.50	5.74
1.00	4.86

Table 8.1 Nusselt number for fully developed laminar flow in an annulus

The convection heat transfer coefficient for the shell flow

$$h_s = \frac{k_s Nu_s}{D_{is} - D_{ot}} = \frac{0.58\frac{W}{m \cdot K} \cdot 131.09}{0.013m} = 5{,}848.74 \frac{W}{m^2 \cdot K} \qquad (8.12)$$

The thermal resistance R for the shell and tube heat exchanger becomes

$$R = \frac{1}{UA} = \frac{1}{\pi L}\left(\frac{1}{h_i D_{it}} + \frac{\ln\left(\frac{D_{ot}}{D_{it}}\right)}{2k_{ss}} + \frac{1}{h_o D_{ot}}\right) = 0.00817K/W \qquad (8.13)$$

where $k_{ss} = 15.1\ W/(m \cdot K)$ is the thermal conductivity of stainless steel. Equation (4) can now be used to determine $NTU = 0.1426$. The capacity ratio c is given by

$$c = \frac{C_{min}}{C_{max}} = \frac{C_t}{C_s} = 0.25 \qquad (8.14)$$

Finally, the effectiveness of a parallel-flow shell and tube heat exchanger can be determined

$$\epsilon_{parallel-flow} = \frac{1-e^{-NTU(1+c)}}{1+c} = 0.1306 \qquad (8.15)$$

Using results from Flow Simulation, we get the following effectiveness

$$\epsilon = \frac{T_{max,in}-T_{max,out}}{T_{max,in}-T_{min,in}} = \frac{T_{t,in}-T_{t,out}}{T_{t,in}-T_{s,in}} = \frac{343.2K-335.780K}{343.2K-283.2K} = 0.1237 \qquad (8.16)$$

This is a difference of 5.3 % as compared with the effectiveness – NTU method. Figure 8.24 shows an effectiveness comparison between parallel-flow and counter-flow heat exchangers. We see that difference is very small for low NTU values and for low C_{min}/C_{max} values. The NTU value can be increased for example by increasing the length of the heat exchanger and/or decrease the mass flow rate of the tube flow.

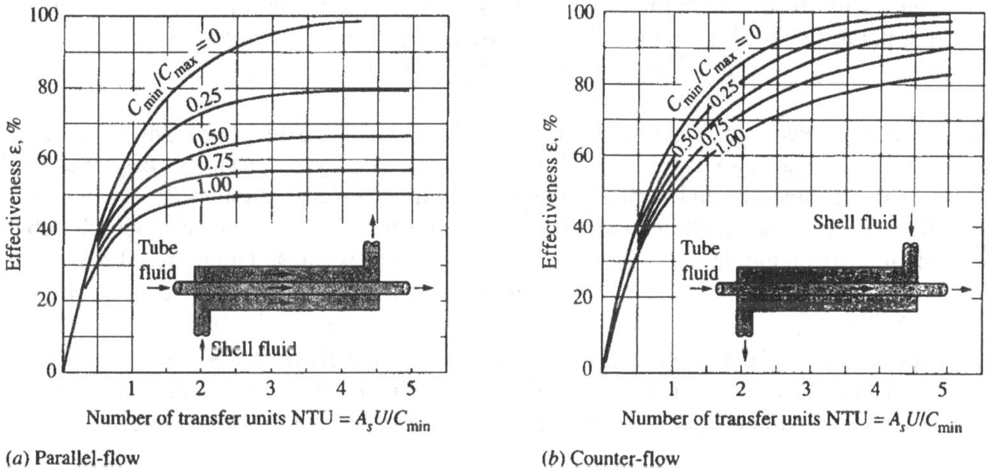

Figure 8.24 Effectiveness for parallel-flow and counter-flow heat exchangers, from Cengel (2003)

L. References

1. Çengel, Y. A., Heat Transfer: A Practical Approach, 2nd Edition, McGraw-Hill, 2003.
2. Tutorials SOLIDWORKS Flow Simulation 2025.

M. Exercises

8.1 Change the mesh resolution in flow simulations and see how the mesh size affects the effectiveness of the parallel-flow shell and tube heat exchanger.

8.2 Use counter-flow instead of parallel-flow for flow simulations and compare effectiveness with corresponding calculations as shown above for parallel-flow. For a counter-flow shell and tube heat exchanger the effectiveness in equation (15) is replaced by

$$\epsilon_{counter-flow} = \frac{1-e^{-NTU(1-c)}}{1-ce^{-NTU(1-c)}}$$

Discuss your results in comparison with figure 8.24. The difference in effectiveness between parallel and counter flow will be very small for this case.

8.3 Open the file Effectiveness-NTU Method for Exercise 8.3.xls. Calculations are shown related to the SOLIDWORKS model for this exercise. Open the two files SOLIDWORKS Model for Exercise 8.3 corresponding to both parallel flow and counter-flow cases. Run both cases and compare the effectiveness from SOLIDWORKS Flow Simulation results with the effectiveness-NTU method. Include cut plots of the temperature distributions for the two cases. Files can be downloaded from https://www.sdcpublications.com/book/978-1-63057-784-1/.

8.4 Open the Excel file Effectiveness-NTU Method.xls. This file can be downloaded from https://www.sdcpublications.com/book/978-1-63057-784-1/. Use the Excel file to design a parallel flow tube and shell heat exchanger with an effectiveness of 70%. The input data that can be varied are tube inner and outer diameter, shell inner diameter, length, tube and shell inflow temperatures, and tube and shell mass flow rates. The material that the heat exchanger is made of can also be changed. The tube and shell fluids are both water. The inflow temperatures must be in the region 273.3K $\leq T \leq$ 373.2K. Create a model of your design and determine the effectiveness using SOLIDWORKS Flow Simulation for both parallel flow and counter flow. Compare with results from the effectiveness-NTU method. Include cut plots of the temperature distributions for the two cases.

CHAPTER 9. BALL VALVE

A. Objectives

- Creating the SOLIDWORKS parts and assembly for the ball valve, housing and pipe
- Setting up Flow Simulation projects for internal flow
- Creating lids for the assembly
- Inserting boundary conditions
- Creating surface goals
- Running the calculations
- Using cut plots to visualize the resulting flow field
- Determine hydraulic resistance for the ball valve

B. Problem Description

SOLIDWORKS Flow Simulation will be used to study the flow through a ball valve. The pipe has an inner diameter of 50 mm and the length of the pipe is 600 mm on each side of the ball valve. Air will be used as the fluid, and the inlet velocity will be set to 10 m/s. The velocity and the pressure distribution at the ball valve will be shown and the hydraulic resistance of the valve will be determined for an opening angle of 20 degrees.

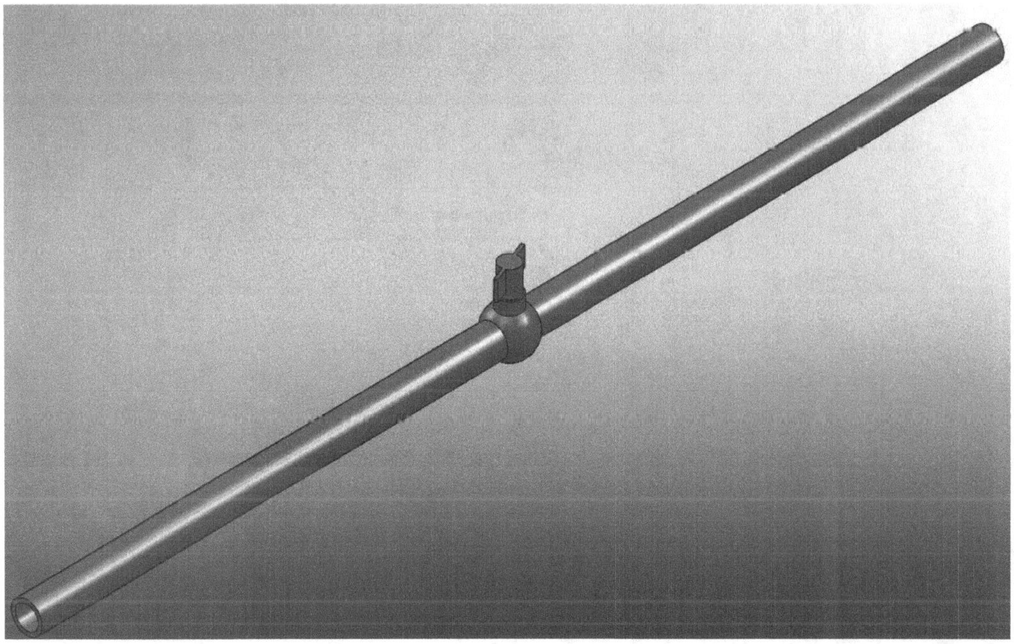

C. Creating the Ball Valve

1. Start by creating a new part in SOLIDWORKS: select **File>>New** and click on the **OK** button in the **New SOLIDWORKS Document** window. Select **Tools>>Options...** from the SOLIDWORKS menu. Click on the Document Properties tab and select **Units**. Select **MMGS** as your **Unit system**. Select **OK** to close the Document Properties – Units window. Click on **Front Plane** in the **FeatureManager design tree** and select **Front** from the **View Orientation** drop down menu in the graphics window.

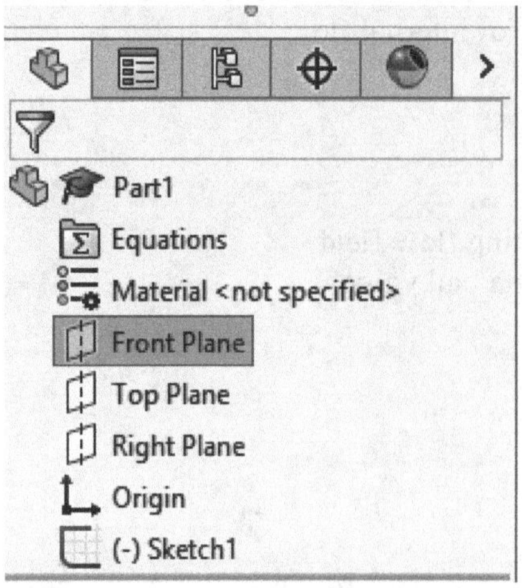

Figure 9.1a) Selection of front plane

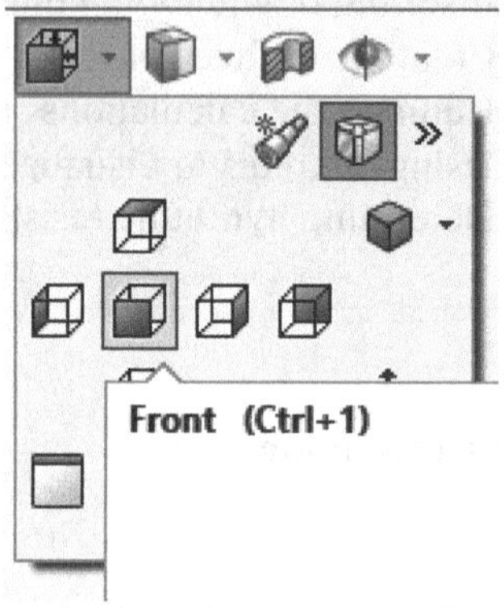

Figure 9.1b) Selection of front view

2. Select the **Basic Modeling Tools** tab and select **Centerline**. Draw a 70.00 mm long vertical centerline from below the origin and upward through the origin with Additional Parameters as shown in Figure 9.2b). Close the **Line Properties** and **Insert Line** dialogs.

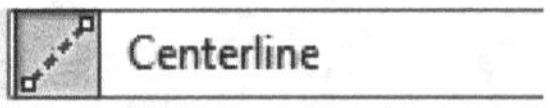

Figure 9.2a) Centerline

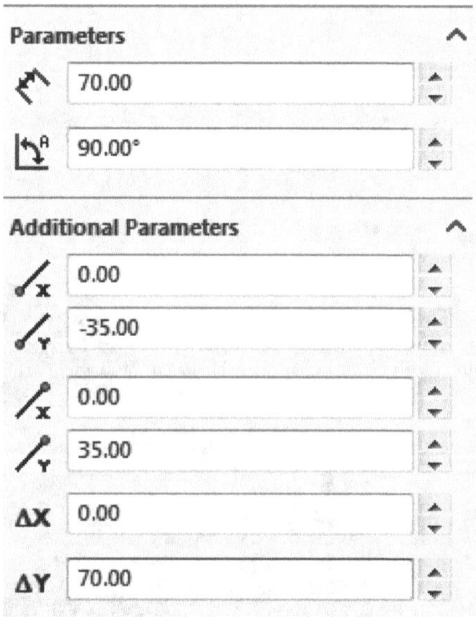

Figure 9.2b) Vertical centerline

3. Select the **Basic Modeling Tools** tab and select **Centerpoint Arc**. Click at the origin in the graphics window, then click anywhere on the vertical center line above the origin and complete the half-circle finally clicking on the vertical center line below the origin. Fill in the **Parameters** for the half-circle as shown in Figure 9.3b). Close the **Arc** dialog box.

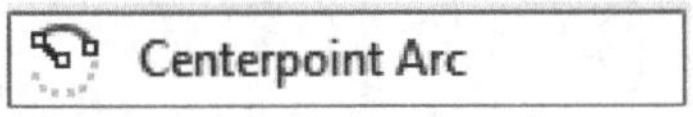

Figure 9.3a) Selecting the center point arc sketch tool

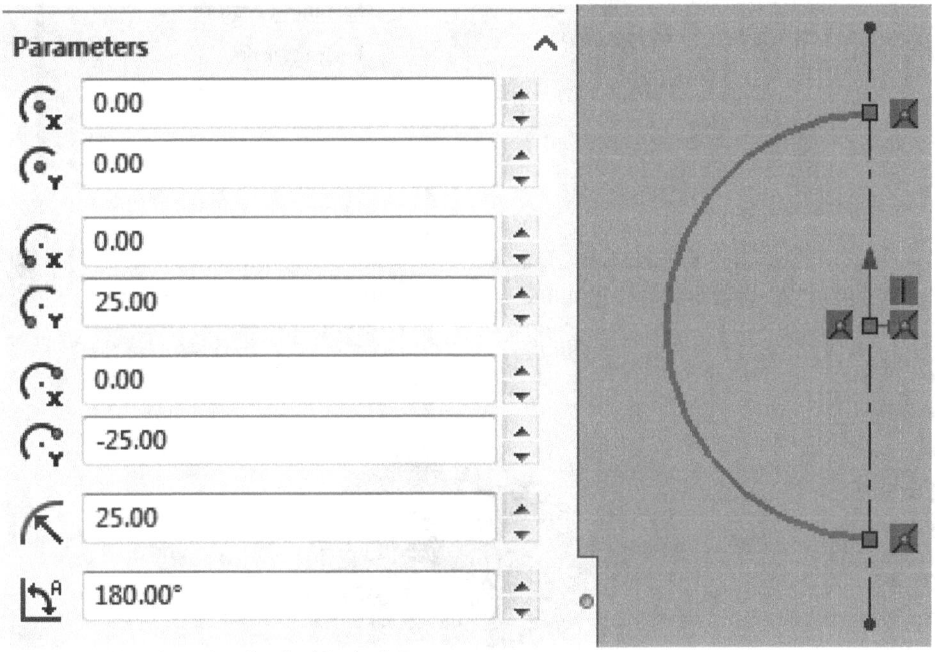

Figure 9.3b) Sketch of a half-circle

4. Select the **Analysis Preparation** tab and **Revolved Boss/Base**, see figure 9.4a). Answer Yes to the question if you want the sketch to be automatically closed. Close the **Revolve** dialog box by clicking **OK**. Right click in the graphics window and select **Zoom/Pan/Rotate>>Zoom to Fit**. Select **Front** view from **View Orientation** in the graphics window, see Figure 9.1b). Select **Top Plane** from the **Featuremanager design tree**. Insert a new plane from the SOLIDWORKS menu by selecting **Insert>>Reference Geometry>>Plane….** Set the **Offset Distance** to **25.00 mm** and exit the **Plane** dialog box. Select **Top** view from **View Orientation** in the graphics window, see Figure 9.4e).

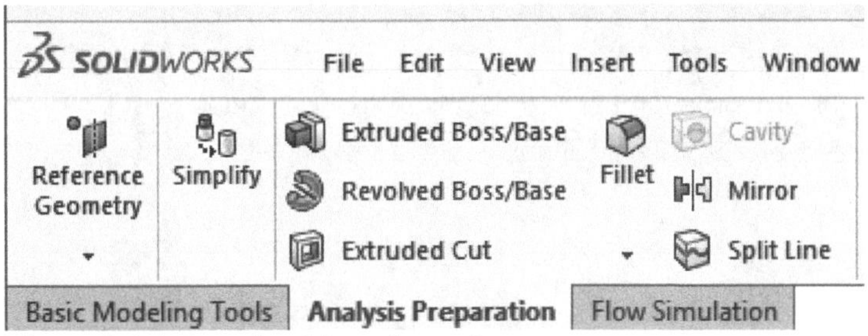

Figure 9.4a) Revolved boss/base feature

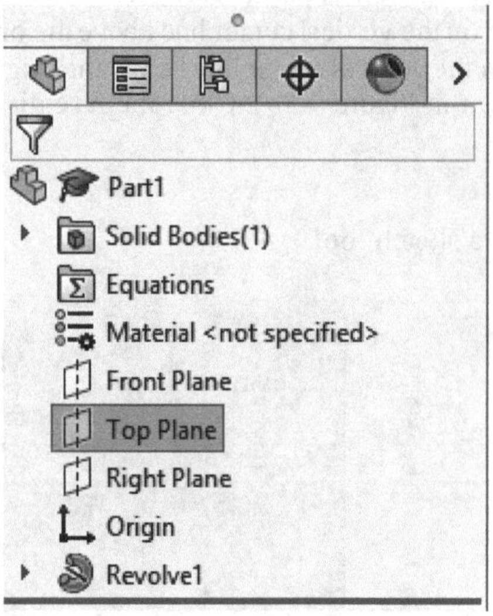

Figure 9.4b) Selecting top plane

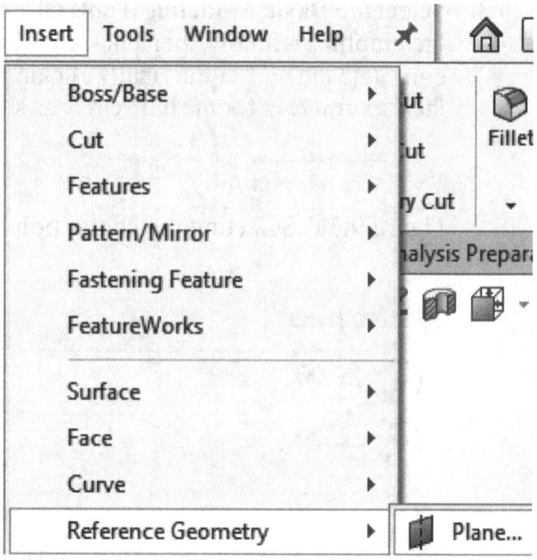

Figure 9.4c) Inserting a plane

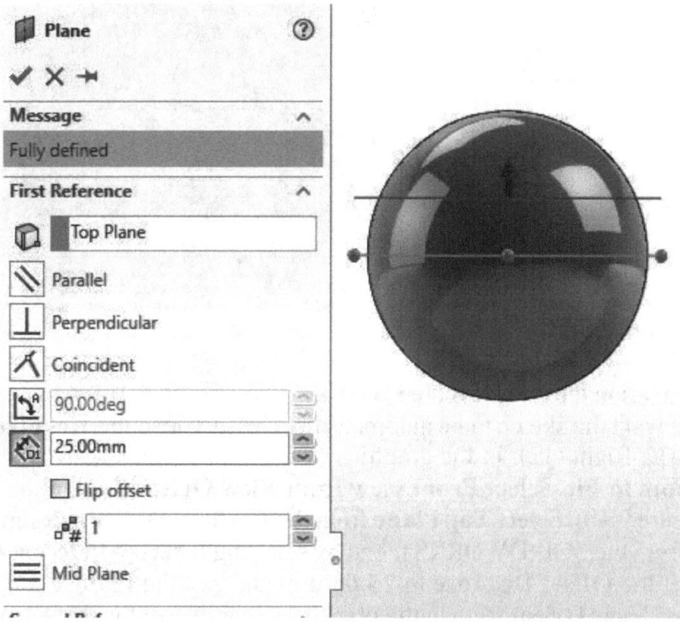

Figure 9.4d) Setting the location of the plane

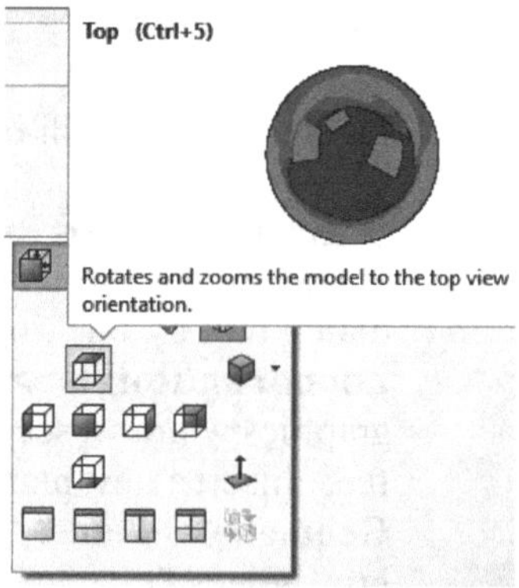

Figure 9.4e) Selecting top view

5. Click on **Plane 1** in the **Featuremanager design tree**, select the **Basic Modeling Tools** tab and select **Circle** from the **Sketch** tools. Draw a circle from the origin with a radius of **12.5 mm**. Close the **Circle** dialog box by clicking **OK**. Select the **Analysis Preparation** tab and **Extruded Boss/Base**. Set the **Depth** of the extrusion to **50.00mm**. Check the **Direction 2** box and select **Up To Next** from the drop-down menu, see Figure 9.5b). Close the **Extrude** dialog box by clicking **OK**.

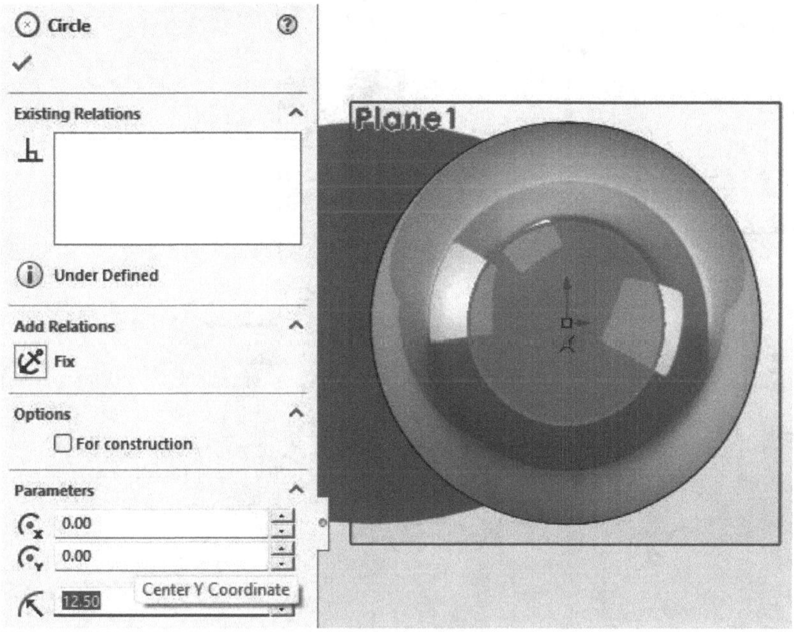

Figure 9.5a) Drawing of a circle for the extrusion

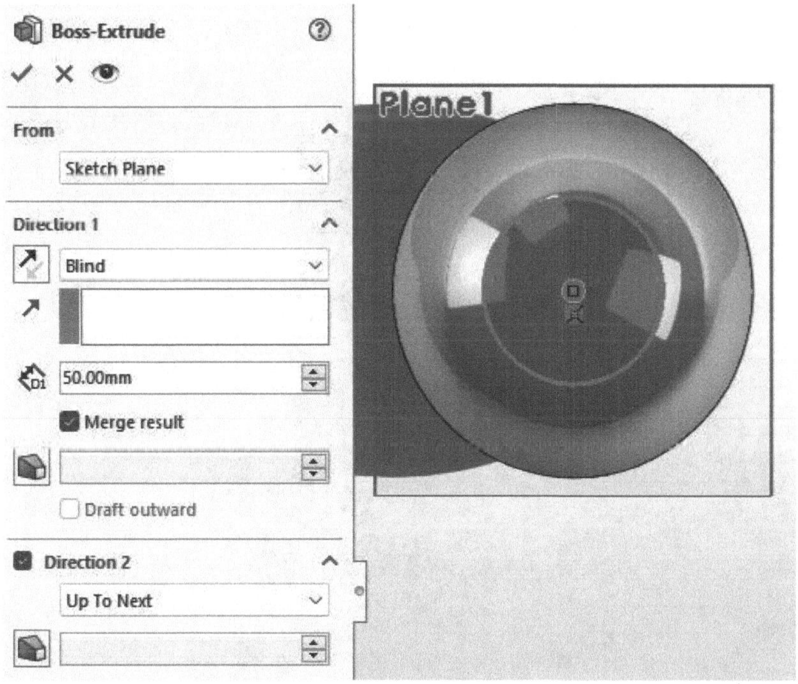

Figure 9.5b) Settings for extrusion

6. Select **Front** view from **View Orientation** in the graphics window, see Figure 9.1b). Click on **Front Plane** in the **Featuremanager design tree** and select the **Basic Modeling Tools** tab and **Circle**. Draw a circle with the parameters as given in Figure 9.6a). Close the **Circle** dialog box by clicking **OK**. Select the **Analysis Preparation** tab and **Extruded Cut**. Select **Through All** from the drop-down menu for both directions, see Figure 9.6b). Close the **Extrude** dialog box by clicking **OK**.

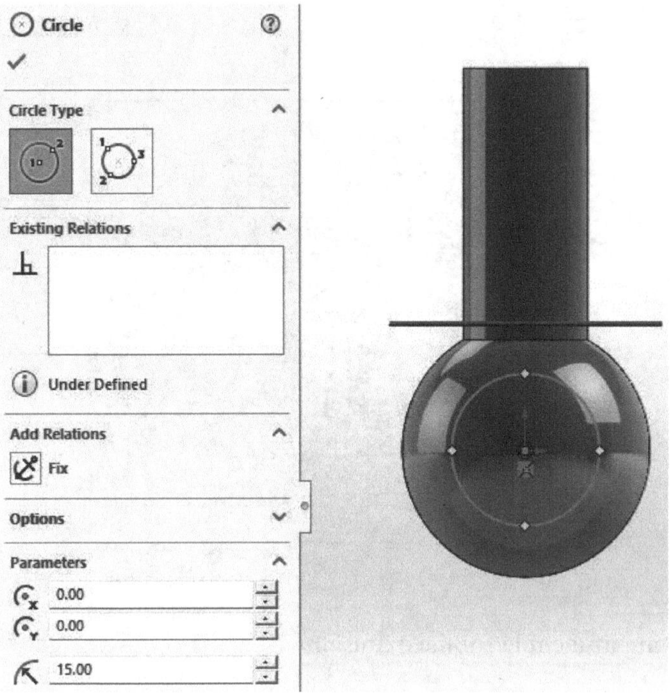

Figure 9.6a) Settings for dimensions of a circle

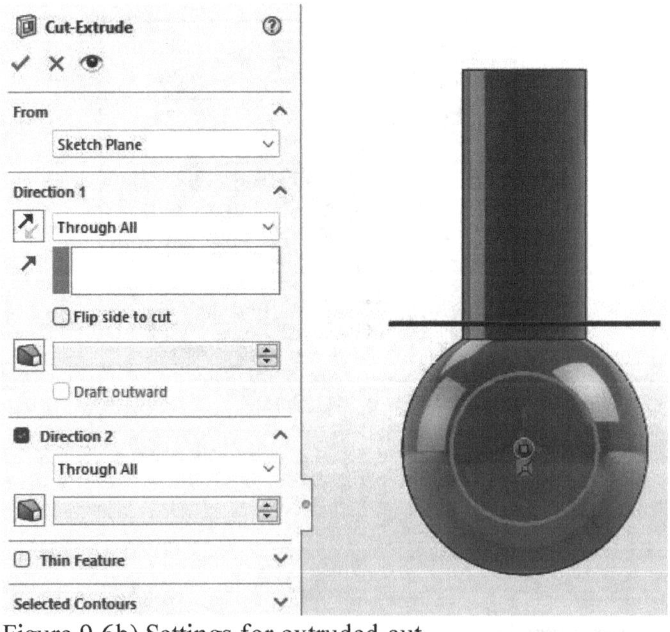

Figure 9.6b) Settings for extruded cut

7. Click on **Front Plane** in the **Featuremanager design tree** and select the **Basic Modeling Tools** tab and **Circle**. Draw a circle with the parameters as given in Figure 9.7a). Close the **Circle** dialog box by clicking **OK**. Select the **Analysis Preparation** tab and **Extruded Boss/Base**. Select **Blind** from the drop-down menu for both directions, see Figure 9.7b). Set the **Depth** of the extrusion to **30.00mm** in both directions. Close the **Extrude** dialog box by selecting **OK**. Save the part with the name **Ball Valve 2026**.

Figure 9.7a) Parameter settings for circle

Figure 9.7b) Directions setting for extrusion

D. Ball Valve Housing and Pipe Sections

8. Create another part in SOLIDWORKS: select **File>>New** and click on the **OK** button in the **New SOLIDWORKS Document** window. Select **Tools>>Options...** from the SOLIDWORKS menu. Click on the Document Properties tab and select **Units**. Select **MMGS** as your **Unit system**. Select **OK** to close the Document Properties – Units window. Click on **Front Plane** in the **FeatureManager design tree** and select **Front** from the **View Orientation** drop down menu in the graphics window, see step **1**. Repeat step **2** by selecting the **Basic Modeling Tools** tab and the **Centerline**. Draw a 70.00 mm long vertical centerline through the origin. Close the **Line Properties** dialog box and the **Insert Line** dialog.

   Select **Centerpoint Arc**. Click at the origin in the graphics window, then click somewhere on the vertical centerline below the origin and complete the arc at an angle of 150°. Set the angle to 150.00° and fill in the other **Parameters** for the arc section as shown in Figure 9.8a). Close the **Arc** dialog box. Repeat this process and create another arc section, see Figure 9.8b). Next, use the **Line** sketch tool and complete the closed contour as shown in Figure 9.8c). Start by completing the vertical line on the centerline. Next, draw the inner vertical line with a length of 20 mm, see Figure 9.8c). Continue with the short horizontal line and close the contour with the outer vertical line. Close the **Line Properties** dialog box and the **Insert Line** dialog.

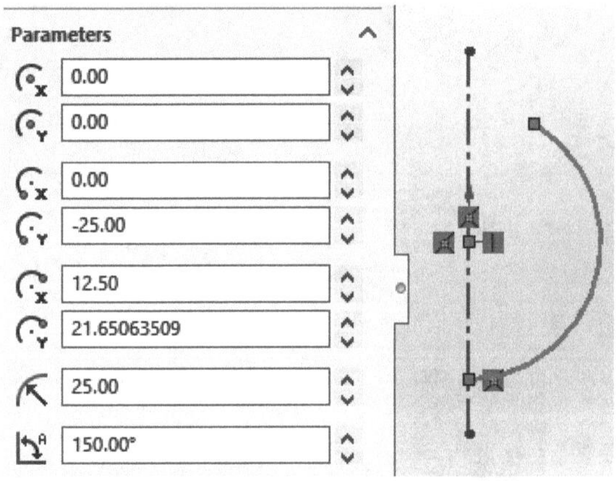

Figure 9.8a) Parameters for first arc section

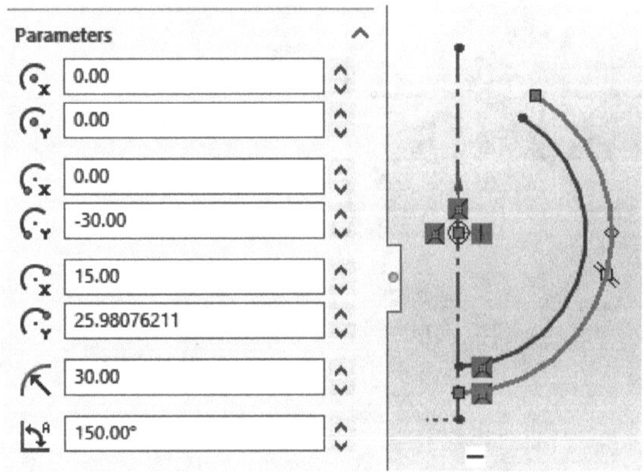

Figure 9.8b) Parameters for second arc section

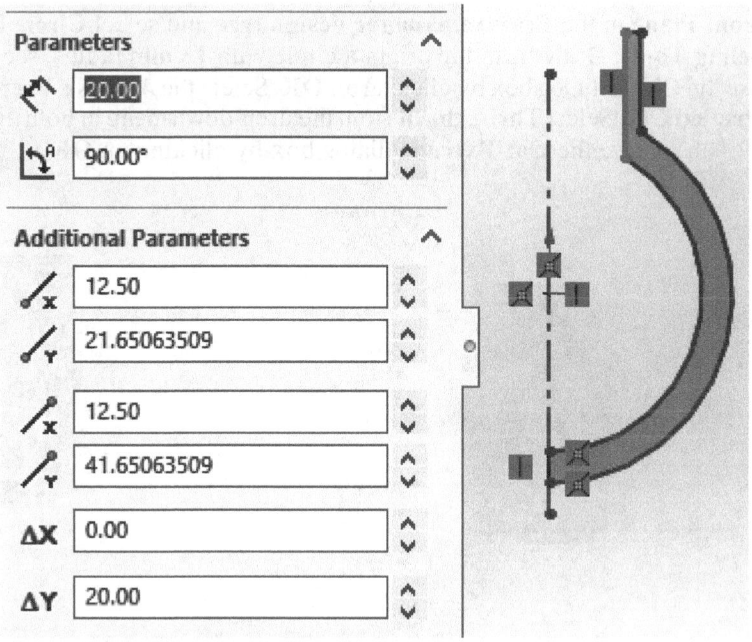

Figure 9.8c) Completed closed contour

9. Select the **Analysis Preparation** tab and **Revolved Boss/Base**. Click on the vertical centerline in the graphics window. Close the **Revolve** dialog box by clicking on **OK**. Right click in the graphics window and select **Zoom/Pan/Rotate>>Zoom to Fit**. Select **Front** view from **View Orientation** in the graphics window, see Figure 9.1b).

Figure 9.9 Housing for the ball valve

10. Click on **Front Plane** in the **Featuremanager design tree** and select **Circle** from the **Basis Modeling Tools**. Draw from the origin a circle with **15 mm** radius, see Figure 9.10a). Close the **Circle** dialog box by clicking on **OK**. Select the **Analysis Preparation** tab and **Extruded Cut**. Select **Through All** from the drop-down menu in both directions, see Figure 9.10b). Close the **Cut-Extrude** dialog box by clicking on **OK**.

Figure 9.10a) Dimensions of the circle

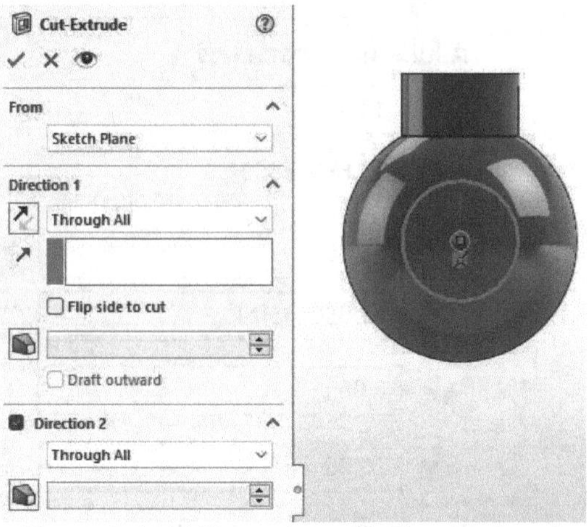

Figure 9.10b) Extrusion of ball valve housing

11. Select **Front Plane** from **Featuremanager design tree**. Insert a new plane from the SOLIDWORKS menu by selecting **Insert>>Reference Geometry>>Plane....** Set **At angle** to **90.00 deg** and the **Offset Distance** to **30.00mm** (see Figure 9.11a) and exit the **Plane** dialog box. Select **Plane 1** in the **FeatureManager design tree** and select **Circle** from the **Basic Modeling Tools**. Draw from the origin a circle with a radius of **15.00 mm**, see Figure 9.11b). Close the **Circle** dialog box by clicking on **OK**. Select **Analysis Preparation** tab and **Extruded Boss/Base**. Set **Direction 1** to **Blind** and **Depth D1** for the extrusion in **Direction 1** to **600.00mm**. Check the **Direction 2** box and select **Up To Next** from the drop-down menu. Check the **Thin Feature** box and set the thickness **T1** to **5.00mm**, see Figure 9.11c). Close the **Extrude** dialog box by clicking on **OK**.

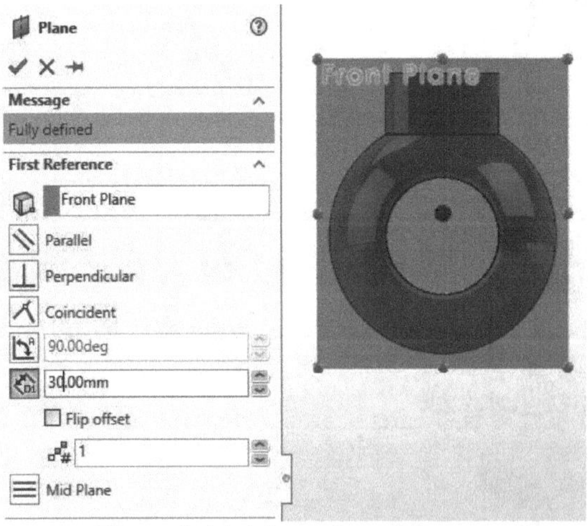

Figure 9.11a) Location of the new plane

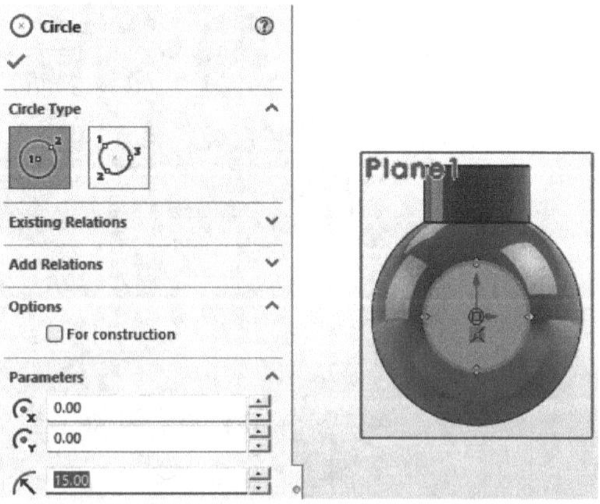

Figure 9.11b) Drawing of a circle

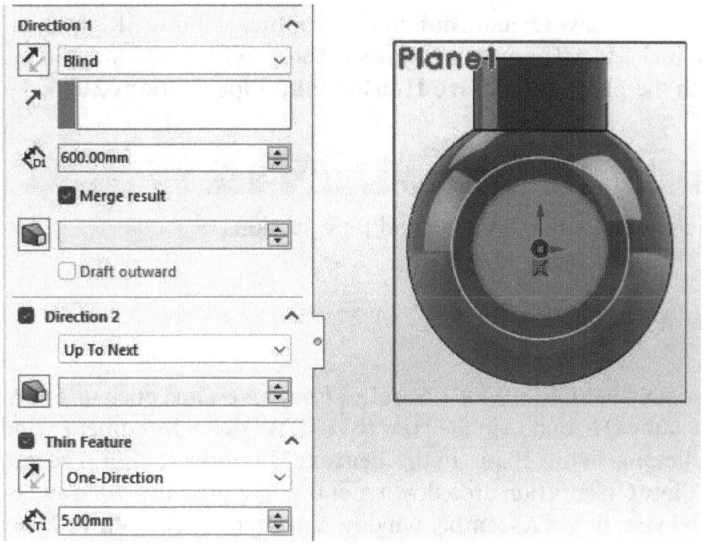

Figure 9.11c) Settings for the pipe extrusion

12. Repeat step **11** by selecting **Front Plane** from **Featuremanager design tree**. Insert a new plane from the SOLIDWORKS menu by selecting **Insert>>Reference Geometry>>Plane…**. Set the **Offset Distance** to **30.00mm** and check the **Flip offset** box, see Figure 9.12a), and exit the **Plane** dialog box. Select **Plane 2** in the **FeatureManager design tree** and select **Circle** from **Basic Modeling Tools**. Draw from the origin a circle with a radius of **15.00mm**. Close the **Circle** dialog box by clicking on **OK**. Select the **Analysis Preparation** tab and **Extruded Boss/Base**. Click on the **Reverse Direction** button for **Direction 1**. Check the **Thin Feature** box and set the thickness **T1** to **5.00mm**. Check the **Direction 2** box and select **Up To Next** from the drop-down menu, see Figure 9.12b). Close the **Extrude** dialog box by clicking on **OK**.

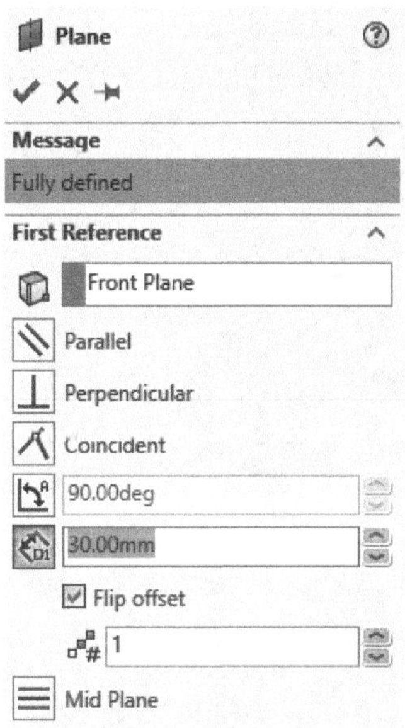

Figure 9.12a) New plane

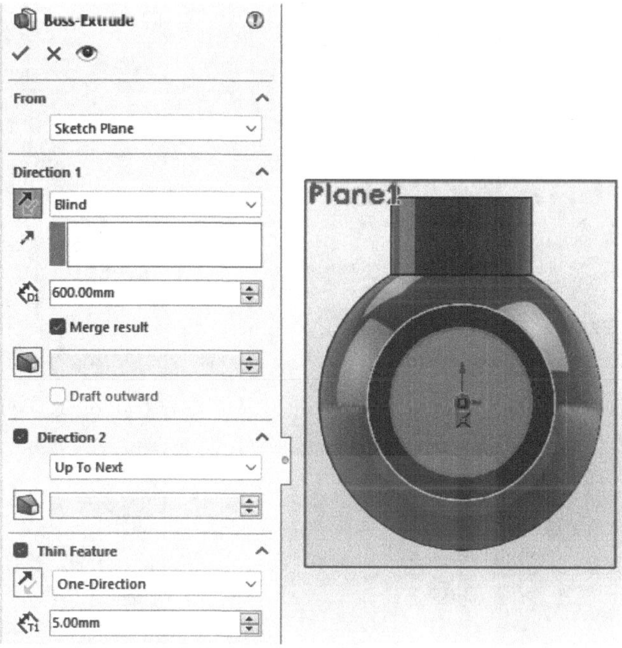

Figure 9.12b) Settings for the pipe extrusion

13. Select **Left** view from **View Orientation** in the graphics window. Right click in the graphics window and select **Zoom/Pan/Rotate>>Zoom to Fit.** Hide the two planes and save the part with the name **Ball Valve Housing and Pipe Sections 2026**.

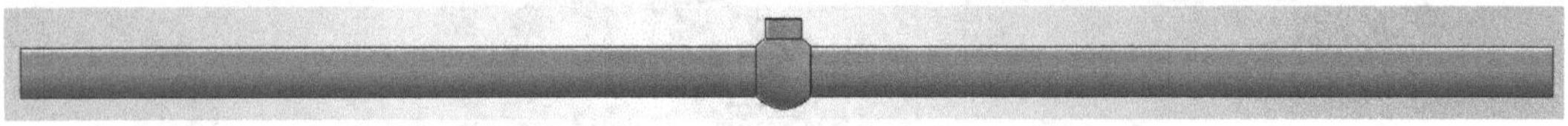

Figure 9.13 Finished ball valve housing and pipe sections

E. Ball Valve and Pipe Assembly

14. Create a new assembly in SOLIDWORKS: select **File>>New** and click on the **Assembly** button followed by the **OK** button in the **New SOLIDWORKS Document** window, see Figure 9.14a). Click on **Front Plane** in the **FeatureManager design tree** and select **Front** from the **View Orientation** drop down menu in the graphics window. Select the **Browse...** button in the **Begin Assembly** window and open the **Ball Valve Housing and Pipe Sections 2026** part. Click in the graphics window. Select **Isometric** view from **View Orientation** in the graphics window. Select **Insert>>Component>>Existing Part/Assembly...** from the menu. Select the **Browse...** button in the **Insert Component** window and open the **Ball Valve 2026** part. Click in the graphics window above the other part. Select **Insert>>Mate...** from the SOLIDWORKS menu. Click on the cylindrical face of the ball valve and the inner cylindrical face of the ball valve housing. Select the **Concentric** standard mate and exit the **Concentric 1** window. Exit the **Mate** window.

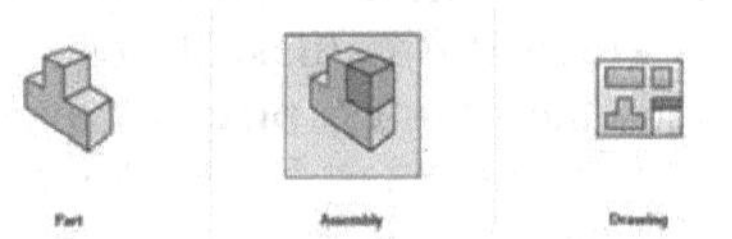

Figure 9.14a) Creating a new assembly

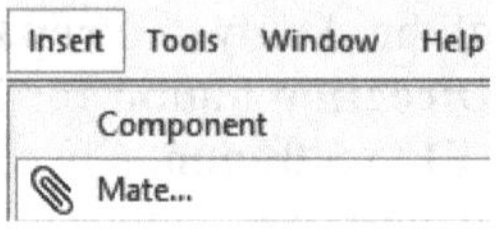

Figure 9.14b) Inserting a mate

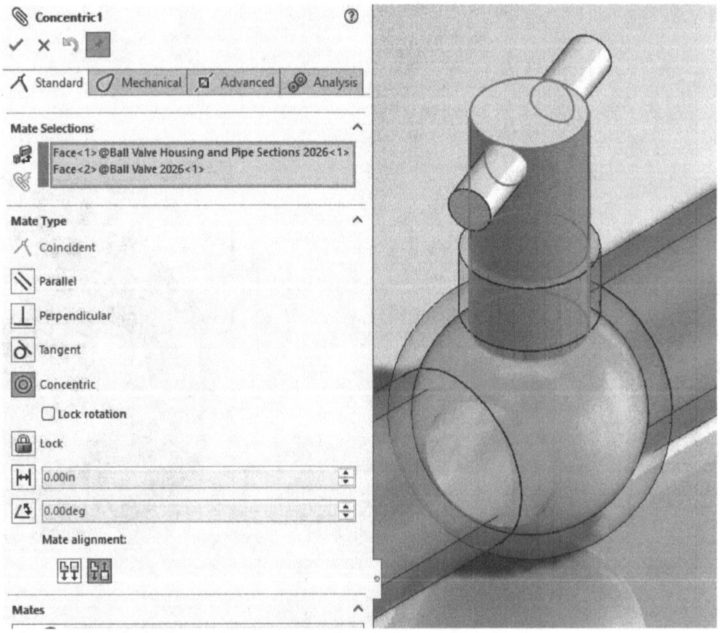

Figure 9.14c) Creating a concentric mate

15. Select **Insert>>Mate...** from the SOLIDWORKS menu. Right click in the **Mate Selections** portion of the **Mate** window and select **Clear Selections**. Select the spherical face of the ball valve and the inner spherical face of the ball valve housing, see Figure 9.15a). You select the inner spherical face of the ball valve housing by right clicking on the housing and selecting Select Other. Select the **Concentric** standard mate and exit the **Concentric2** and **Mate** windows. You will have Figure 9.15b) in the graphics window.

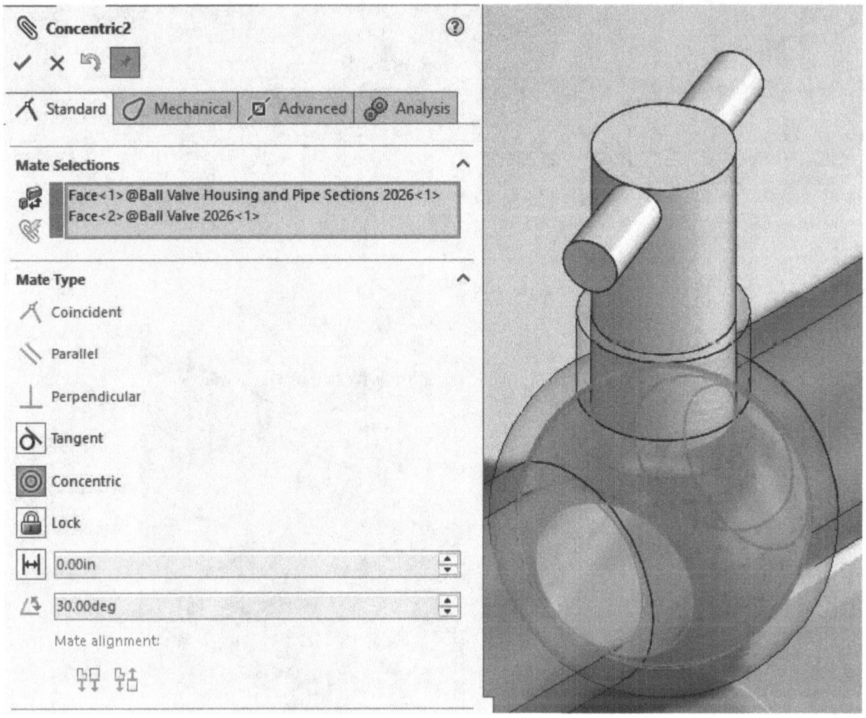

Figure 9.15a) Selecting the valve housing

Figure 9.15b) Ball valve and housing

16. Select **Insert>>Mate...** from the SOLIDWORKS menu. Select the **Front Plane** from the **Ball Valve Housing** on the fly-out assembly and select the corresponding **Front Plane** from the **Ball Valve.** Select the **Angle** button from **Standard Mates** and enter **20.00 deg.** Exit the angle and mate windows.

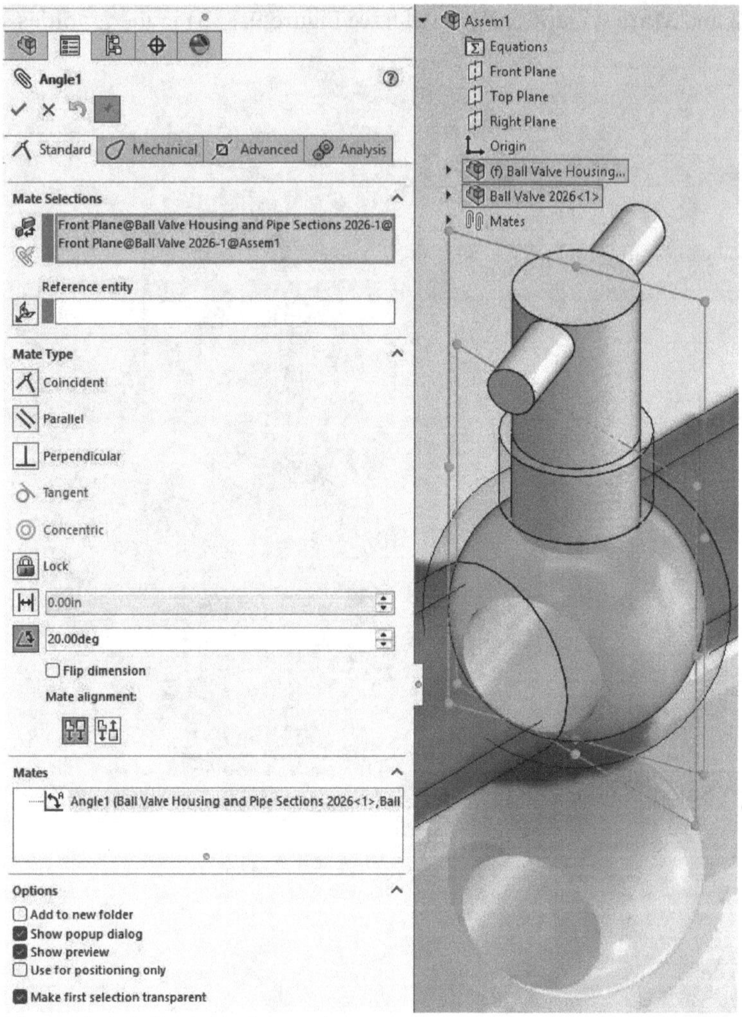

Figure 9.16) Settings for angle mate

17. Select **Front** view from **View Orientation** in the graphics window. You have now finished the Ball Valve Assembly and in Figure 9.17 you can see the partially open ball valve. Save the assembly with the name **Ball Valve and Pipe Assembly 2026**.

Figure 9.17 Ball valve assembly with partially open valve

F. Flow Simulation Project for Ball Valve

18. If Flow Simulation is not available in the menu, you can add it from SOLIDWORKS menu: **Tools>>Add Ins...** and check the corresponding **SOLIDWORKS Flow Simulation** box. Select **Tools>>Flow Simulation>>Project>>Wizard...** to create a new Flow Simulation project. Create a new project named **Ball Valve Study**. Click on the **Next >** button. Select the default **SI (m-kg-s)** unit system and click on the **Next>** button once again. Use the **Internal Analysis type**. Click on the **Next >** button.

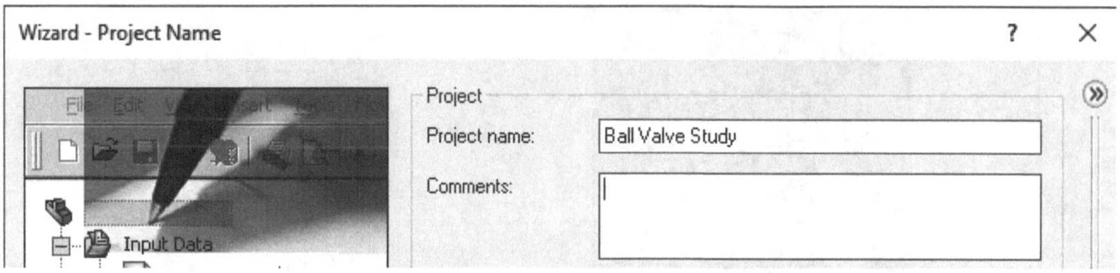

Figure 9.18 Name for the project

19. Add **Air** from **Gases** as the **Project Fluid**. Click on the **Next >** button. Use the default **Wall Conditions**. Click on the **Next >** button. Use the default **Initial Conditions** and click on the **Finish** button. Answer Yes to the question whether you want to open the Create Lids tool.

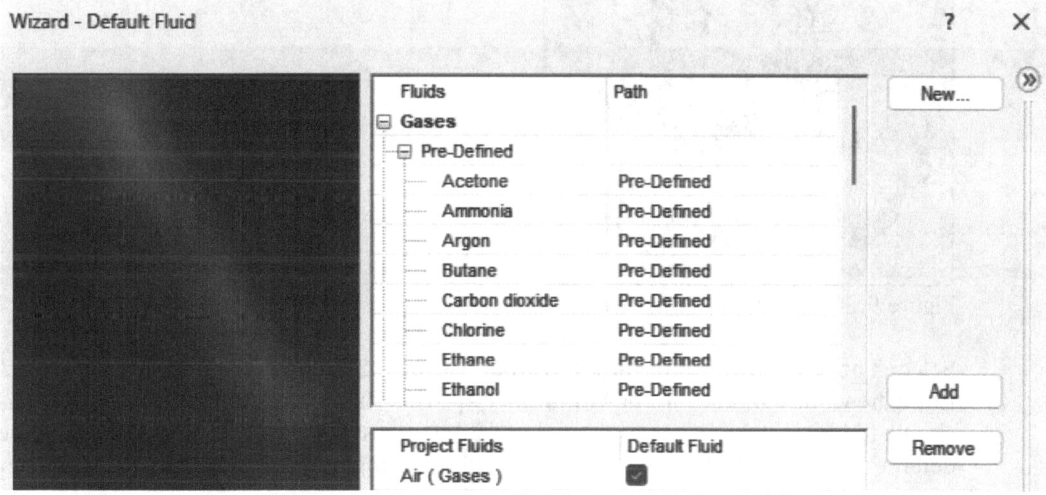

Figure 9.19 Adding air as the project fluid

G. Creating Lids, Maximum Gap Size and Number of Cells

20. Select **Front** view from **View Orientation** in the graphics window. Select the face as shown in Figure 9.20. Close the **Create Lids** dialog box by clicking on **OK**. Answer yes to the questions. Select **Back** view from **View Orientation** in the graphics window. Select the similar face as described above and close the **Create Lids** dialog box by clicking on **OK**. Answer yes to the questions if you want to reset the computational domain and the mesh setting.

Figure 9.20 Selection of surface for lid

Select **Tools>>Flow Simulation>>Global Mesh...**. Slide the **Result resolution** to **6**. Enter the value **0.022255 m** for **Minimum gap size**. This is the size d of the opening as shown in Figure 9.17 for a valve angle of 20 degrees. The size of the opening can be determined from the valve angle θ, the closed valve angle $\theta_c = 73.74°$ and the diameter of the ball $D_b = 50\,mm$.

$$d = \sqrt{D_b^2 Sin^2\left(\frac{\theta_c - \theta}{2}\right) - \frac{D_b^2}{4}\left(Cos\left(\frac{\theta_c}{2} - \theta\right) - Cos\left(\frac{\theta_c}{2}\right)\right)^2} \tag{9.1}$$

, where $\theta_c = 2\,Sin^{-1}(D_p/D_b)$ and $D_p = 30$ mm is the inner diameter of the pipe section. Check the box for **Manual settings** under **Type**. Set the **Number of cells per X:** to **8**, the **Number of cells per Y:** to **6** and the **Number of cells per Z:** to **236**. Click on the OK button to exit the window.

H. Boundary Conditions

21. Select **Left** view from **View Orientation** in the graphics window. Right-click in the graphics window and select **Zoom to Area**. Zoom in on the left end of the pipe, right click in the graphics window and select **Rotate View**. Rotate the view a little bit, see Figure 9.21. Click on the plus sign next to the **Input Data** folder in the **Flow Simulation analysis tree**. Right click on **Boundary Conditions** and select **Insert Boundary Condition…**. Right click on the end section of the pipe and select **Select Other**. You may first need to right-click and select **Clear Selections** and hide the computational domain. To hide the computational domain, right click on **Computational Domain** under the **Input Data** folder in the **Flow Simulations analysis tree** and select **Hide**. Select the inner surface of the lid, see Figure 9.21. Select **Inlet Velocity** in the **Type** portion of the boundary condition window. Set the inlet velocity to **10 m/s**. Click OK to exit the **Boundary Condition** window.

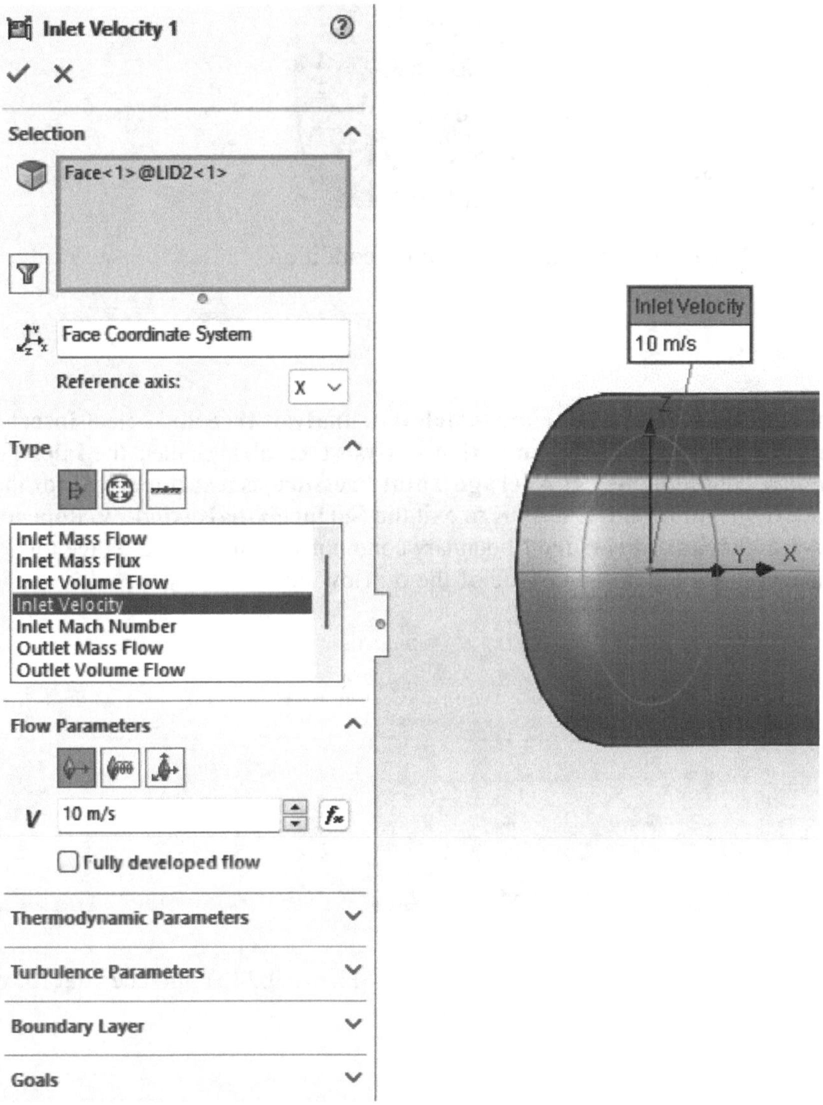

Figure 9.21 Selection of inflow boundary condition

22. Select **Left** view from **View Orientation** in the graphics window. Select **Zoom to Area** and zoom in on the right end of the pipe, right click in the graphics window and select **Rotate View**. Rotate the view a little bit. Right click on **Boundary Conditions** and select **Insert Boundary Condition….** Select (-) LID1<1> . Select **Pressure Openings** in the **Type** portion of the **Boundary Condition** window. Select **Static Pressure**. Click OK to exit the **Boundary Condition** window.

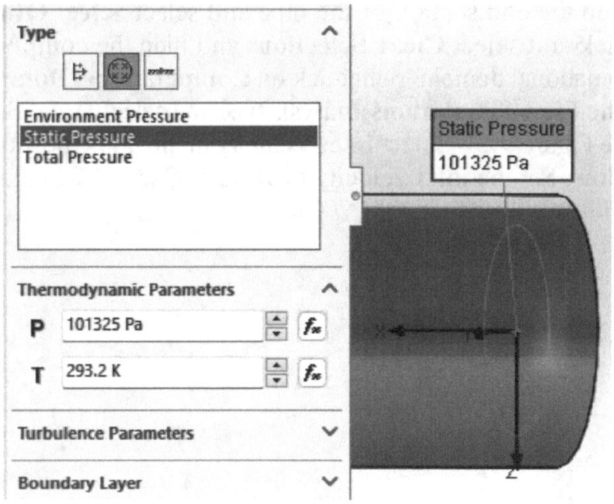

Figure 9.22 Selection of outflow boundary condition

I. Goals

23. Right click on **Goals** in the **Flow Simulation analysis tree** and select **Insert Surface Goals….** Click on the **Flow Simulation analysis tree** tab and select the **Inlet Velocity 1** boundary condition. Select **Average Total Pressure** as a surface goal for the inner surface of the inflow lid. Click OK to exit the **Surface Goals** window. Repeat this step and select the **Static Pressure 2** boundary condition and insert an average total pressure surface goal for the inner surface of the outflow lid.

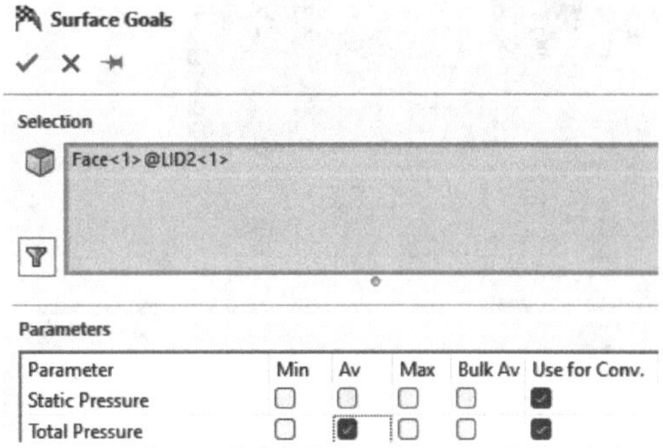

Figure 9.23a) Surface goal for inlet

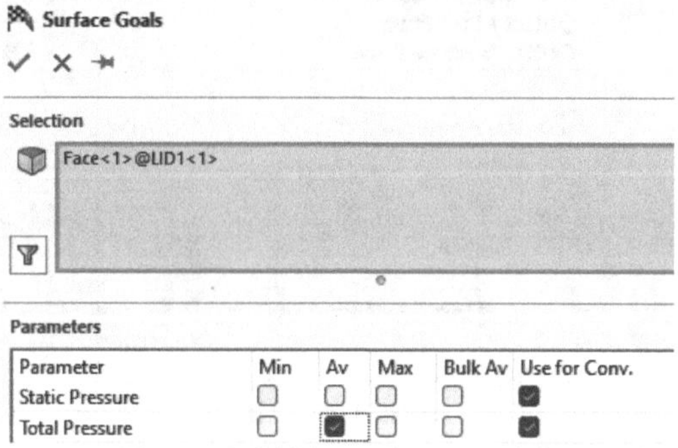

Figure 9.23b) Surface goal for outlet

J. Simulation for Ball Valve

24. Select **Tools>>Flow Simulation>> Calculation Control Options…** from the SOLIDWORKS menu, click on the **Refinement** tab and **Disable** the refinement from the **Value** drop down menu. Click on the **OK** button to exit the window. Select **Tools>>Flow Simulation>>Solve>>Run…** to start calculations. Click on the **Run** button in the **Run** window.

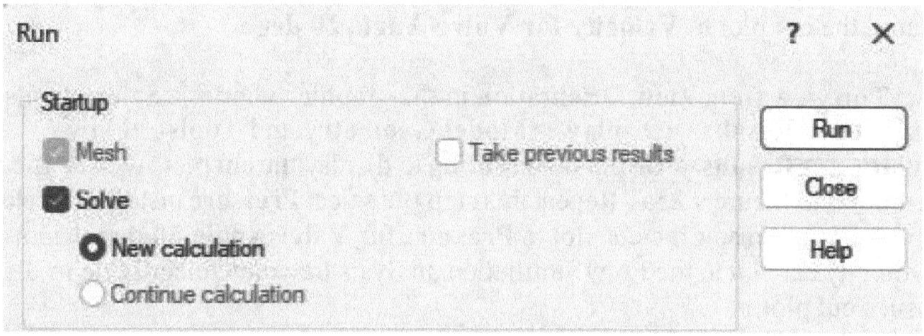

Figure 9.24a) Run window

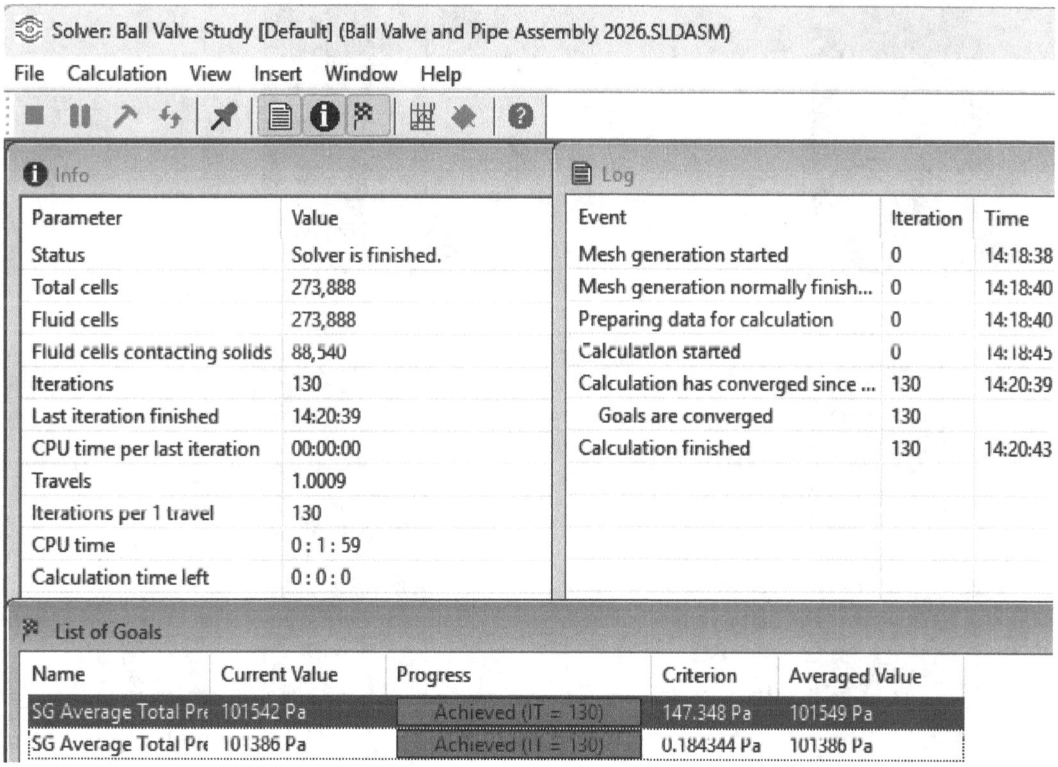

Figure 9.24b) Solver window, valve angle $\theta = 20$ deg

K. Cut-Plots

25. Open the **Results** folder, right click on **Cut Plots** in the **Flow Simulation analysis tree** and select **Insert…**. Select the **Top Plane** from the **FeatureManager design tree** for the **Ball Valve and Pipe Assembly 2026.** Click on the **Vectors** button in the **Display** portion of the **Cut Plot** window. Click on the **Static Vectors** button in the **Vectors** portion of the **Cut Plot** window. Slide the **Number of Levels** slide bar to **255** in the **Contours** section. Select **Velocity** from the **Parameter** drop down menu. Exit the **Cut Plot** window. Rename the cut plot to **Velocity for Valve Angle 20 deg**.

    Select **Top** view from **View Orientation** in the graphics window. Select **Tools>>Flow Simulation>>Results>>Display>>Model Geometry** and **Tools>>Flow Simulation>>Results>>Display>>Lighting** to display the cut plot. We see the velocity distribution in Figure 9.25a). Repeat this step but select **Pressure** instead of **Velocity**, see Figure 9.25b). Rename the cut plot to **Pressure for Valve Angle 20 deg**. Right-click on the velocity cut plot in the Flow Simulation analysis tree and select **Hide** to display the pressure cut plot.

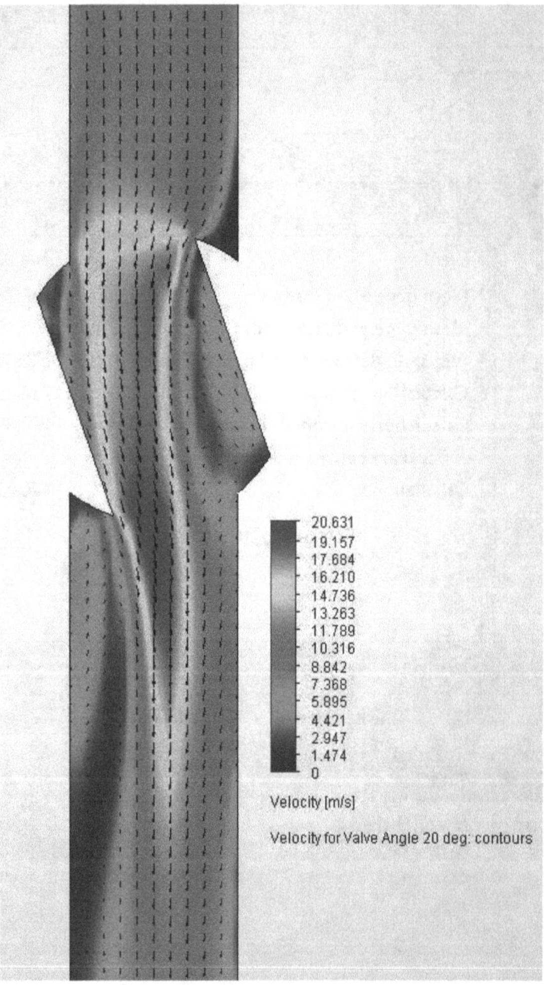

Figure 9.25a) Ball valve velocity

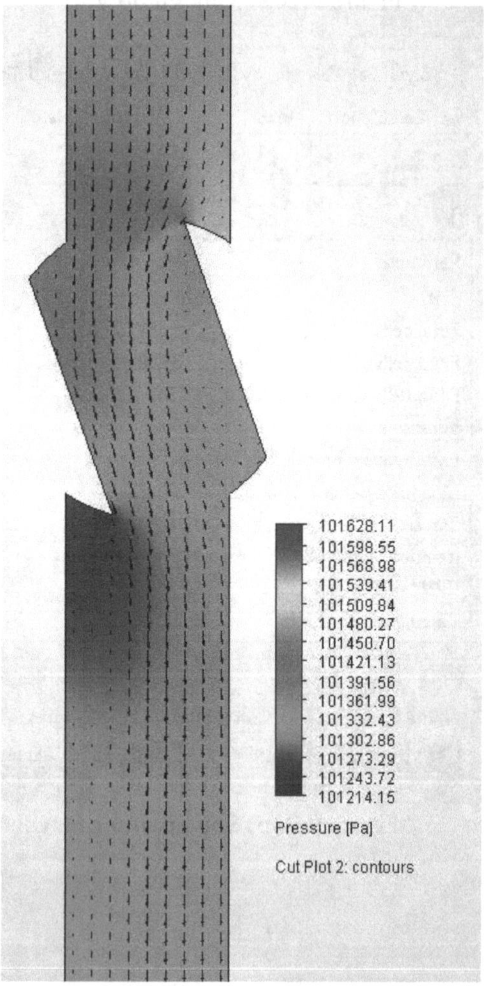

Figure 9.25b) Ball valve pressure distribution

L. Hydraulic Resistance

26. In the next step, we want to determine the hydraulic resistance of the ball valve. To complete this we will determine the total pressure drop without the valve. Click on the arrow next to **Mates** in the **Featuremanager Design Tree**. Right click on **Angle1** and select **Edit Feature** and set the angle θ to **0.00deg**. Exit the **Angle1** window. Answer **Yes** to the question if you want to reset the computational domain. Select **Tools>>Flow Simulation>>Global Mesh….** Check the box for **Automatic settings** under **Type**. Enter the value **0.03 m** for **Minimum Gap Size**. This value is the inside diameter of the pipe. Click on the **OK** button to exit the **Global Mesh Settings** window. Select **Tools>>Flow Simulation>>Global Mesh…** and check the **Manual settings** box. Set the **Number of cells per X** to **6**, **Number of cells per Y** to **6** and **Number of cells per Z** to **240**. Click on the **OK** button to exit. Select **Tools>>Flow Simulation>>Solve>>Run…** to start calculations. Click on the **Run** button in the **Run** window. Repeat step **25** and create a cut plot with the velocity distribution for the ball valve at zero valve angle θ.

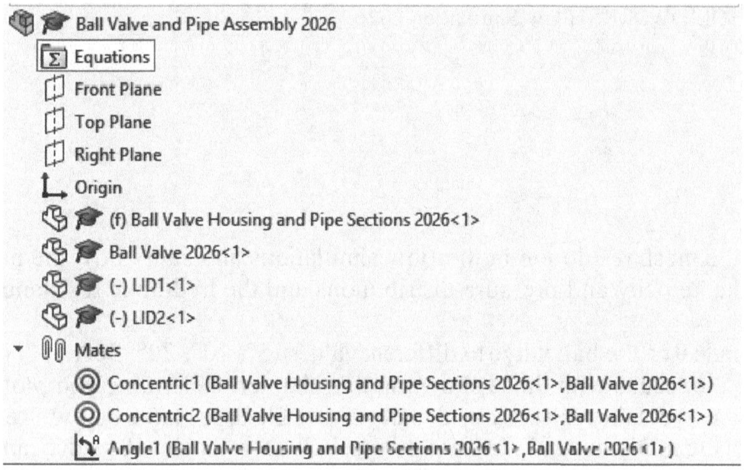

Figure 9.26a) Changing the angle of the ball valve

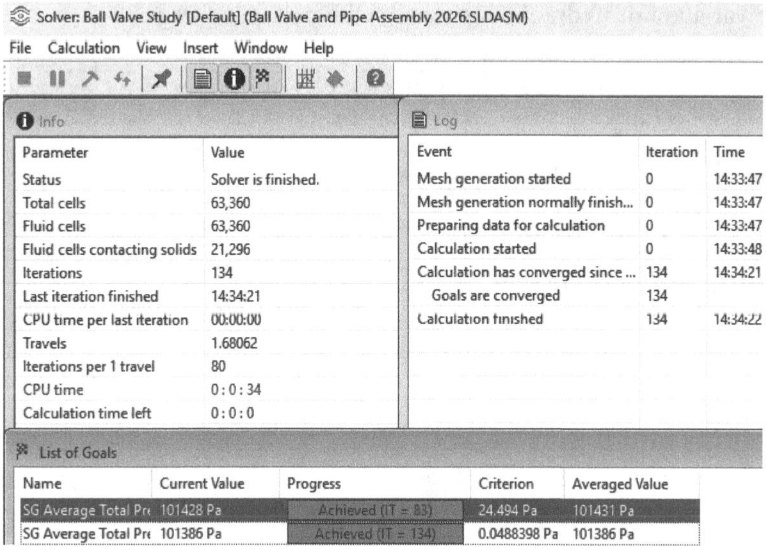

Figure 9.26b) Solver window, valve angle $\theta = 0$ deg

From Figure 9.26b) in the list of goals, we see that the total pressure difference between inlet and outlet based on average values is 101,428 Pa – 101,386 Pa = 42 Pa. This value will be subtracted from the pressure difference value that we determine from Figure 9.24b). The final total pressure difference over the valve is 114 Pa for 20 degrees valve angle. We can now determine the hydraulic resistance ξ of the valve to be

$$\xi = \frac{2\Delta P}{\rho U^2} = \frac{2 \cdot 114\text{Pa}}{1.204\frac{kg}{m^3} \cdot 10^2 m^2/s^2} = 1.89 \quad (9.2)$$

where ρ is the density of air, ΔP is the difference in total pressure over the valve and U is the average velocity in the pipe.

M. References

1. Idelchik, I.E., Handbook for Hydraulic Resistance, Jaico Publishing House, 2005.
2. Tutorials SOLIDWORKS Flow Simulation 2026.

N. Exercises

9.1 Change the mesh resolution in the flow simulations and study how the mesh size affects the velocity and pressure distributions and the hydraulic resistance.

9.2 Set the angle θ of the ball valve to different values (5°, 10°, 20°, 30°, 40°, 45°) and compare the results with those shown in this chapter. Determine and plot the variation in hydraulic resistance with ball valve angle θ, see table below. Remember to change the minimum gap size for different ball valve angles. Use the same result resolution (6) for all calculations. Include copies of solver windows and velocity and pressure plots for each angle. Discuss results and determine the exponential equation for the variation of hydraulic resistance with ball valve angle.

θ (deg.)	*d* (m)	*No of cells per X*	*No of cells per Y*	*No of cells per Z*	*ξ*
5	0.03	6	6	240	
10	0.0263	6	6	236	
20	0.022255	8	6	236	1.89
30	0.01799	8	6	236	
40	0.013635	8	6	236	
45	0.009321	8	6	236	

Table 9.1 Data for exercise 9.2

CHAPTER 10. ORIFICE PLATE AND FLOW NOZZLE

A. Objectives

- Creating the SOLIDWORKS part for the orifice plate
- Setting up Flow Simulation projects for internal flow
- Inserting boundary conditions
- Creating point goals
- Running the calculations
- Using cut plots, XY plots and flow trajectories to visualize the resulting flow fields
- Determine discharge coefficients for orifice plate and flow nozzle

B. Problem Description

We will use Flow Simulation to study the flow through an orifice plate and a long radius flow nozzle. Obstruction flow meters are commonly in use to measure flow rates in pipes. Both the orifice and nozzle are modeled inside a pipe with an inner diameter of 50 mm and a length of 1 m. Water in the pipe flows with a mean velocity of 1 m/s corresponding to a Reynolds number *Re* = 50,000. The opening in the orifice is 20 mm in diameter. The long radius nozzle has a length of 33.6 mm and the opening is 21 mm in diameter. We will study how the centerline velocity varies along the length of the pipe for both cases and plot both pressure and velocity fields. The discharge coefficients will be determined and compared with experimental values.

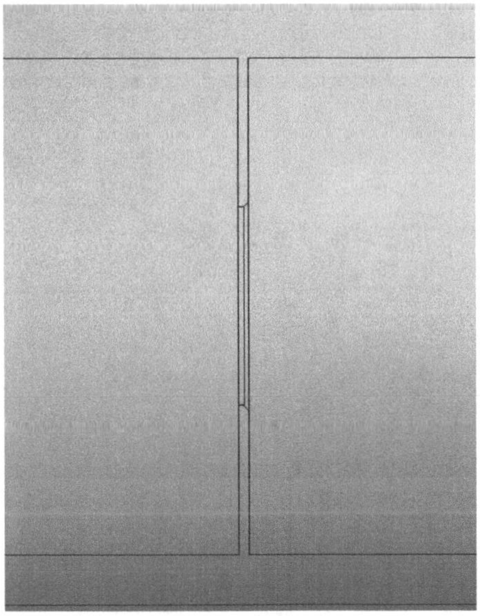

Figure 10.0a) Orifice plate

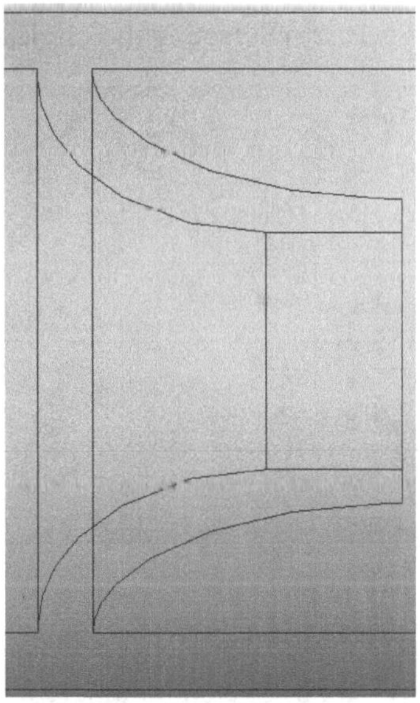

Figure 10.0b) Nozzle

C. Modeling an Orifice Plate in a Pipe

1. Start by creating a new part in SOLIDWORKS: select **File>>New**, select **Part** and click on the **OK** button in the **New SOLIDWORKS Document** window. Select **Tools>>Options...** from the SOLIDWORKS menu. Click on the Document Properties tab and select **Units**. Select **MMGS** as your **Unit system**. Click on **Front Plane** in the **FeatureManager design tree** and select **Front** from the **View Orientation** drop down menu in the graphics window.

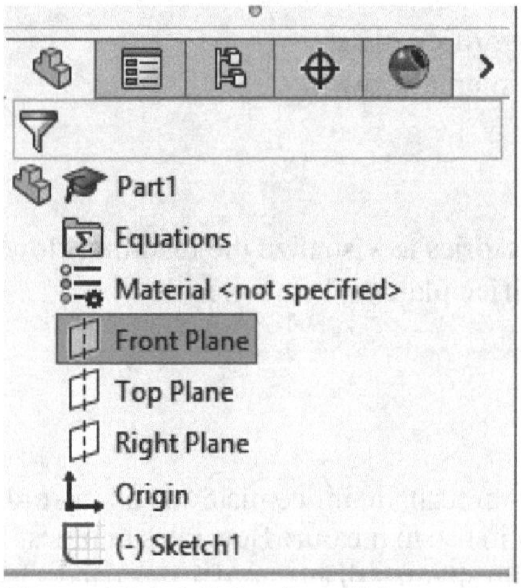

Figure 10.1a) Selection of front plane

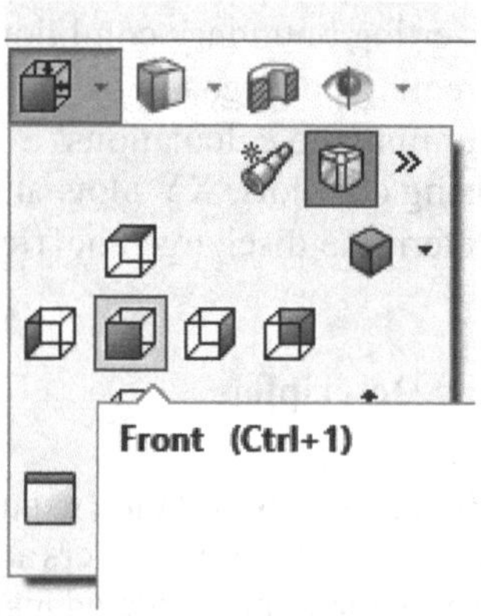

Figure 10.1b) Selection of front view

2. Select the **Basic Modeling Tools** tab and **Circle** from the sketch tools. Draw a circle from the origin with a **25.00mm** radius. Close the **Circle** dialog box.

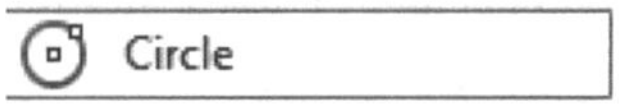

Figure 10.2a) Selecting the circle sketch tool

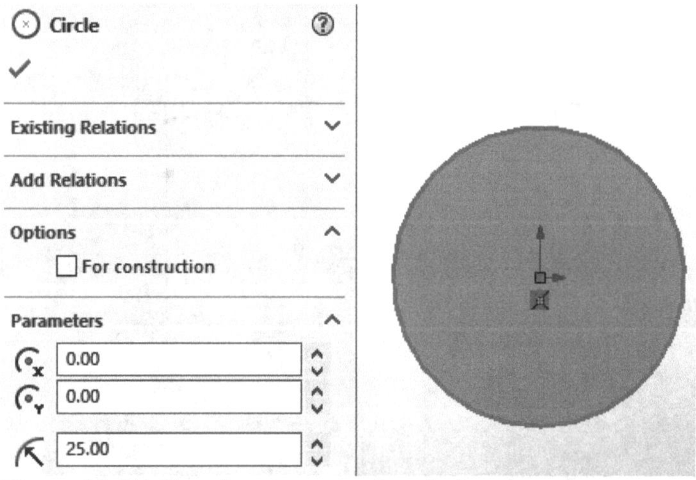

Figure 10.2b) Sketch parameters for circle

3. Select the **Analysis Preparation** tab and the **Extruded Boss/Base** feature. Set the **Depth** of the extrusion to **500.00mm** in both directions. Check the **Thin Feature** box and enter a **Thickness** value of **5.00mm**. Check the **Cap ends** box and enter **5.00 mm** for the thickness. Close the **Boss-Extrude** dialog box by clicking on **OK**.

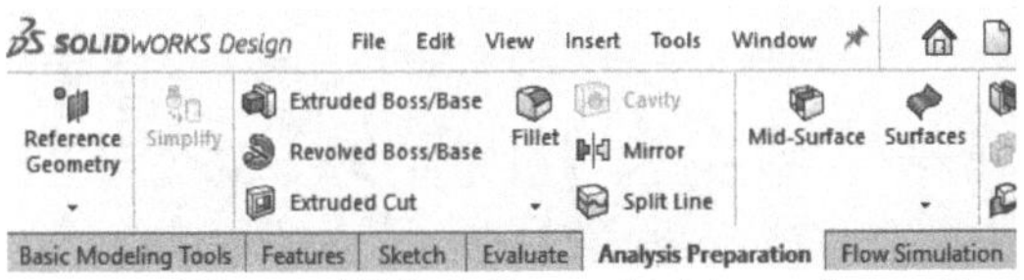

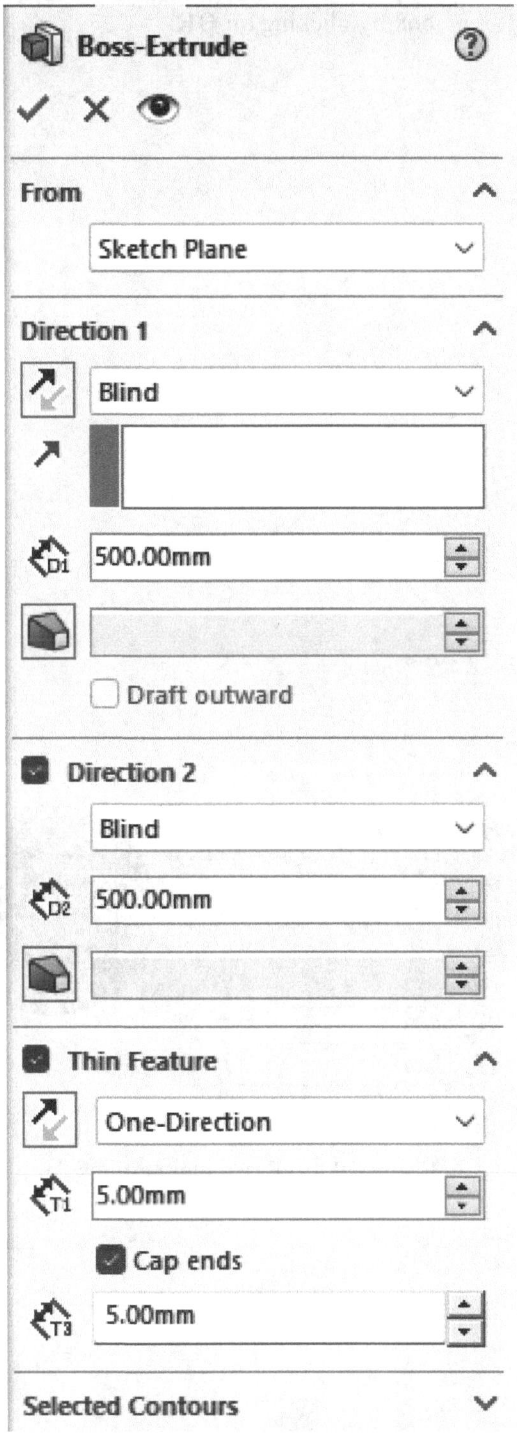

Figure 10.3a) Extruded boss/base feature Figure 10.3b) Settings for extrusion

4. Select **Front** view from **View Orientation** in the graphics window. Click on **Front Plane** in the **Featuremanager design tree** and select **Circle** from **Basic Modeling Tools**. Draw a circle centered at the origin with a **25 mm** radius, see Figure 10.4a). Close the **Circle** dialog box by clicking on **OK**. Select the **Extruded Boss/Base** feature. Set the **Depth** of the extrusion to **0.50 mm** in both directions. Close the **Boss-Extrude** dialog box by clicking on **OK**.

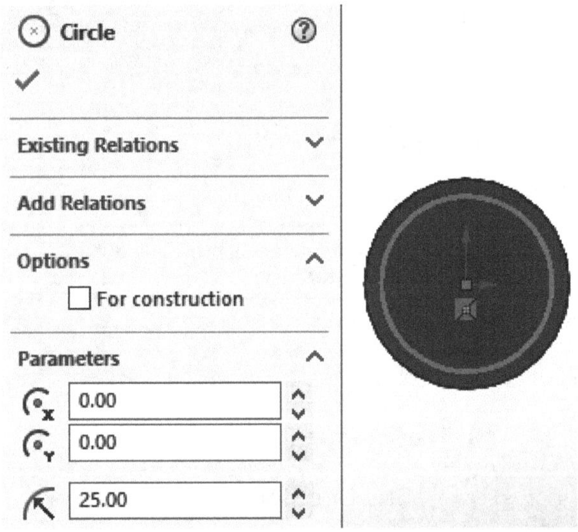

Figure 10.4a) Parameter settings for a circle

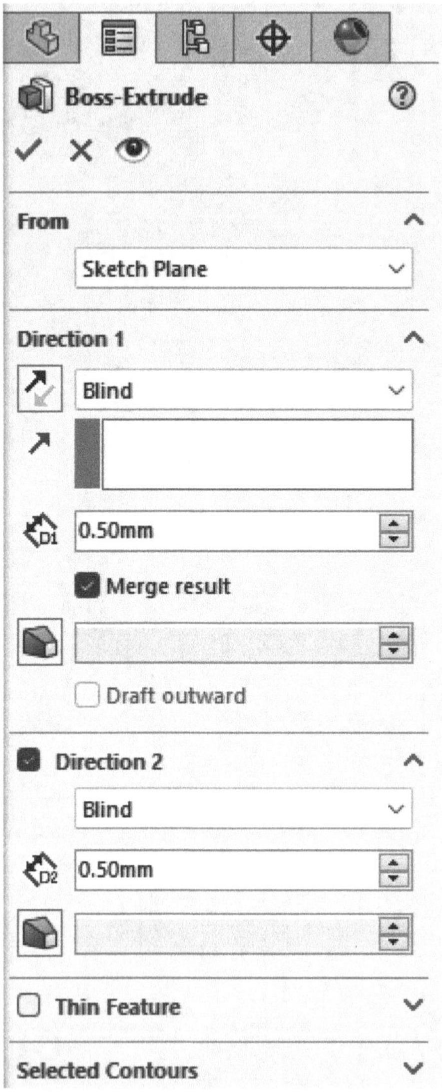

Figure 10.4b) Extrusion

5. Click on **Front Plane** in the **Featuremanager design tree** and select **Circle** from the sketch tools. Draw a circle centered at the origin with a **10 mm** radius. Close the **Circle** dialog box by clicking on **OK**. Select the **Extruded Cut** feature. Set the **Depth** of the cut to **0.50mm** in both directions. Click on the **Draft** button for **Direction 2** and enter **45.00deg**. Check the **Draft outward** box, see Figure 10.5. Exit the cut-extrude window.

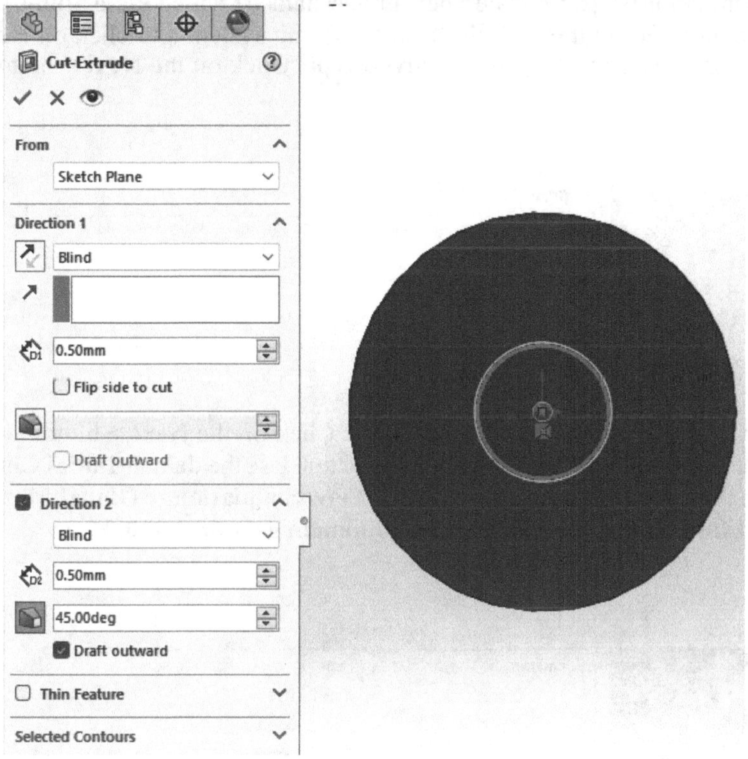

Figure 10.5 Extruded cut parameters

6. Select **Left** view from **View Orientation** in the graphics window. Select **Wireframe** display style from the drop-down menu in the graphics window. Select **Zoom/Pan/Rotate>>Zoom to Area** and zoom in on the middle section of the pipe, right click in the graphics window and select **Rotate View**. Rotate the view a little bit to get Figure 10.6b). You have now completed your orifice plate inside a pipe. Save the part as **Orifice Plate 2026**.

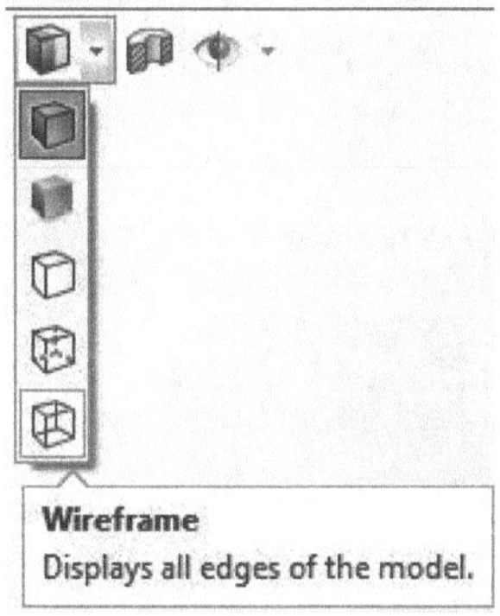

Figure 10.6a) Wireframe display style

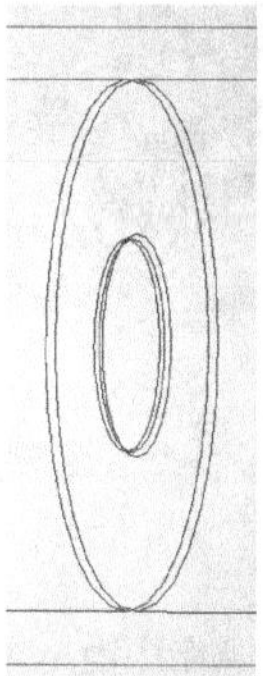
Figure 10.6b) Orifice plate

D. Flow Simulation Project for Orifice Plate

7. If Flow Simulation is not available in the menu, you can add it from SOLIDWORKS menu: **Tools>>Add Ins...** and check the corresponding **SOLIDWORKS Flow Simulation** box. Select **Tools>>Flow Simulation>>Project>>Wizard...** to create a new Flow Simulation project. Create a new project named **Orifice Plate Study**. Click on the **Next >** button. Select the default **SI (m-kg-s)** unit system and click on the **Next>** button once again. Use the **Internal Analysis type**. Click on the **Next >** button.

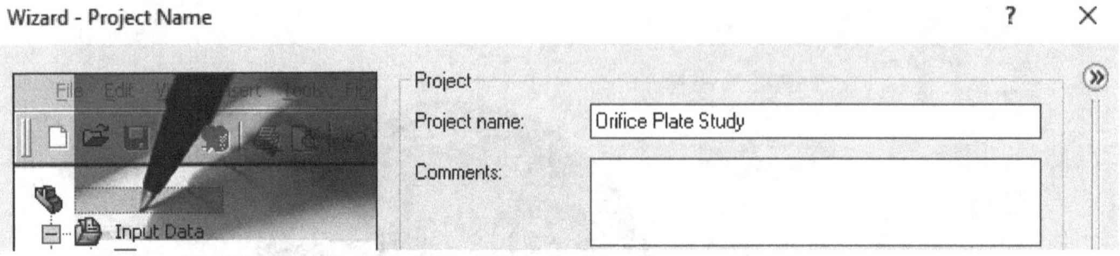

Figure 10.7 Name for the project

8. Add **Water** from **Liquids** as the **Project Fluid**. Click on the **Next >** button. Use the default **Wall Conditions**. Click on the **Next >** button. Use the default **Initial Conditions** and click on the **Finish** button. Select **Tools>>Flow Simulation>>Global Mesh....** Set the **Level of Initial Mesh** to **5** and set the **Minimum gap size:** to **0.02 m**.

Figure 10.8 Adding water as the project fluid

E. Boundary Conditions

9. Select **Left** view from **View Orientation** in the graphics window. Select **Zoom to Area** and zoom in on the left end of the pipe, right click in the graphics window and select **Zoom/Pan/Rotate>>Rotate View**. Rotate the view a little bit, see Figure 10.9. Click on the plus sign next to the **Input Data** folder in the **Flow Simulation analysis tree**. Right click on **Computational Domain** and select **Hide**. Right click on **Boundary Conditions** and select **Insert Boundary Condition...**. Right click on the end of the pipe and choose **Select Other**. Select the inner surface of the end cap. Select **Inlet Velocity** in the **Type** portion of the boundary condition window. Set the inlet velocity to **1 m/s** and check the box for **Fully developed flow**, see Figure 10.9. Click OK to exit the **Boundary Condition** window.

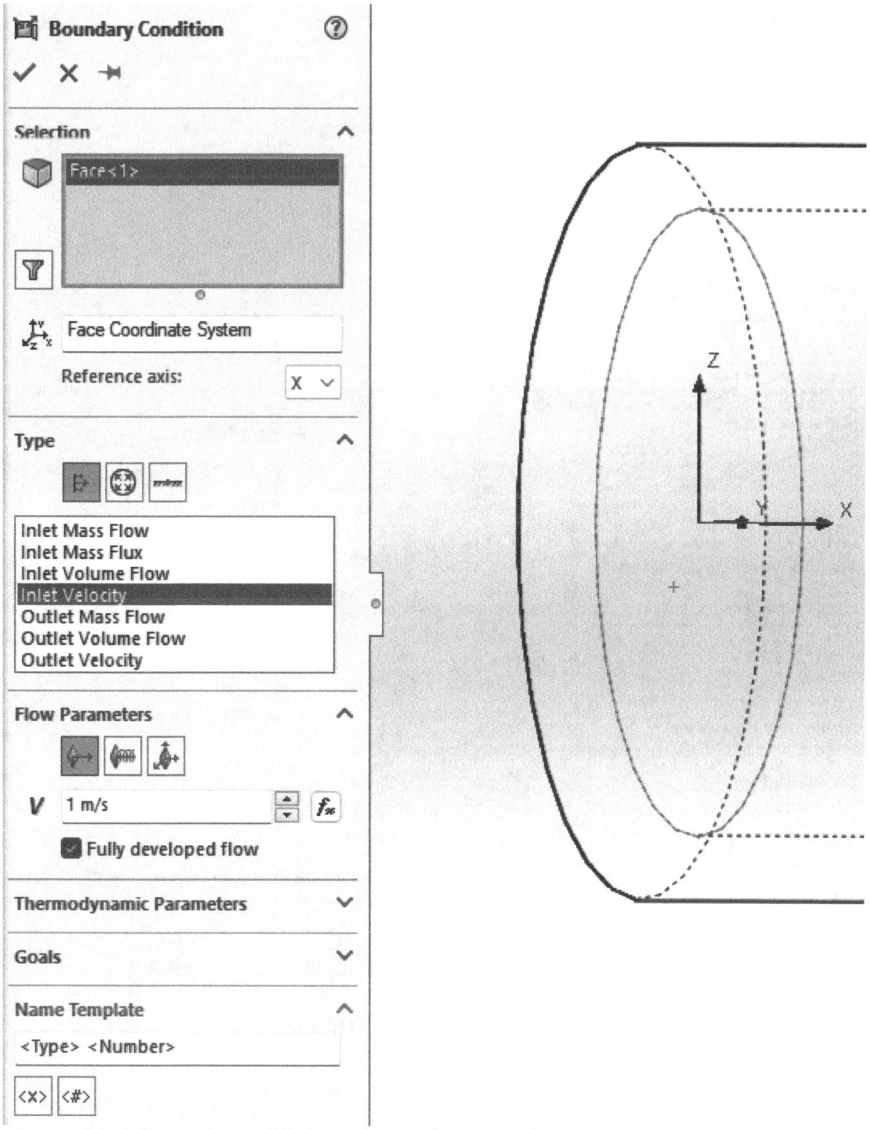

Figure 10.9 Selection of inflow boundary condition

10. Select **Left** view from **View Orientation** in the graphics window. Select **Zoom to Area** and zoom in on the right end of the pipe, right click in the graphics window and select **Rotate View**. Rotate the view a little bit, see Figure 10.10. Right click on **Boundary Conditions** and select **Insert Boundary Condition....** Right click on the end of the pipe and select **Select Other**. Select the inner surface of the pipe outflow cap. Select **Pressure Openings** in the **Type** portion of the **Boundary Condition** window. Select **Static Pressure**. Click **OK** to exit the **Boundary Condition** window.

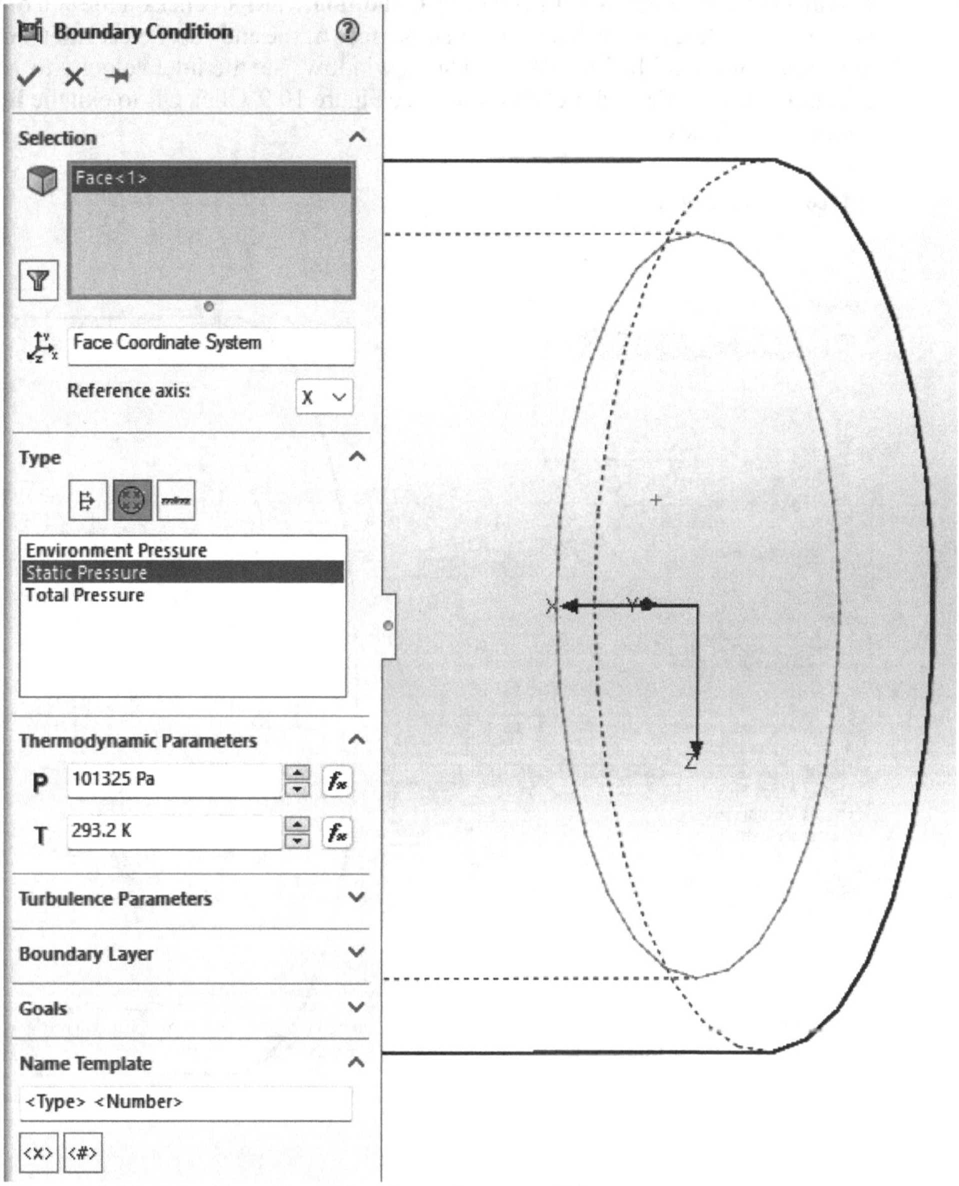

Figure 10.10 Selection of outflow boundary condition

F. Goals

11. Right click on **Goals** in the **Flow Simulation analysis tree** and select **Insert Point Goals....** Click on the Point Coordinates button and enter the coordinates (X 0 m, Y 0.025, Z -0.05) as shown in Figure 10.11. Check the **Static Pressure** box as a point goal for the coordinate. Click on the **Add Point** button to add the point to the table. Add another point (X 0 m, Y 0.025, Z 0.025) to the table of point goals as shown in Figure 10.11 and make sure that the **Static Pressure** box is checked. Click **OK** to exit the **Point Goals** window.

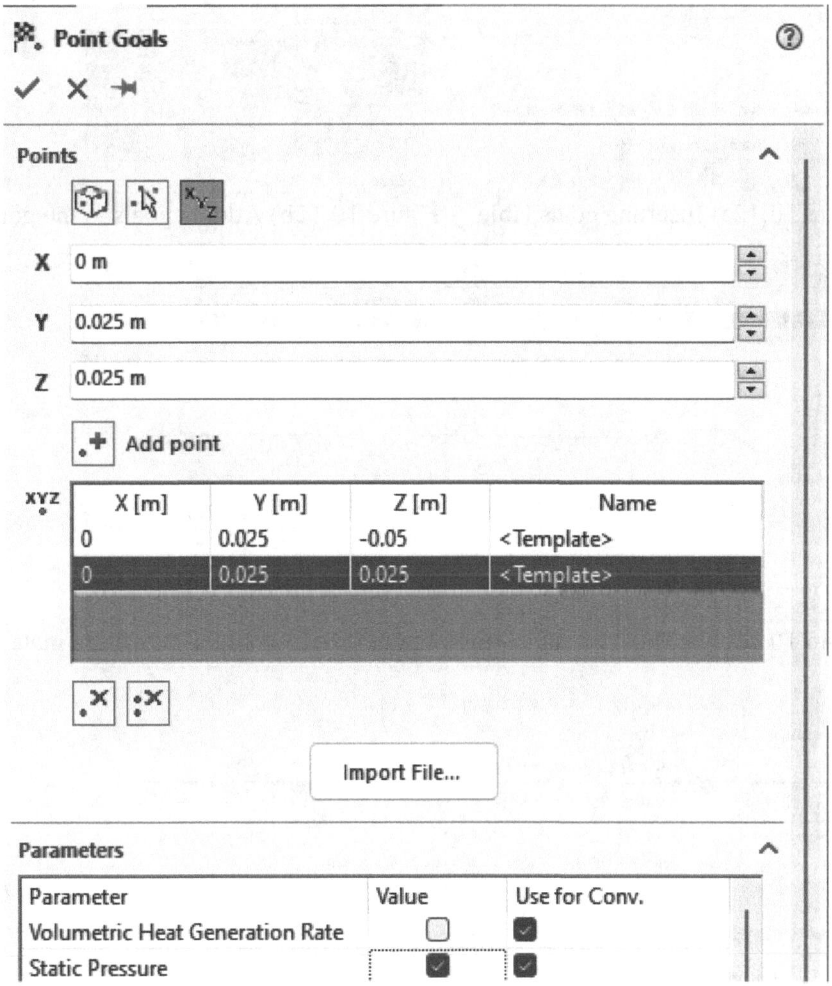

Figure 10.11 Selection of points for point goals

G. Flow Simulation for Orifice Plate

12. Select **Tools>>Flow Simulation>>Solve>>Run...** to start calculations. Click on the **Run** button in the **Run** window. Click on **Insert Goals Table** to view the static pressure goals in a table. Click on **Insert Goals Plot** to view a graph of the pressure goals. Check the two-point goals in the **Add/Remove Goals** window and click on the **OK** button to exit the window.

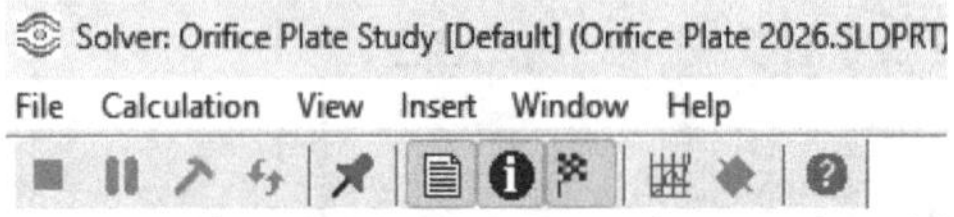

Figure 10.12a) Inserting goals table

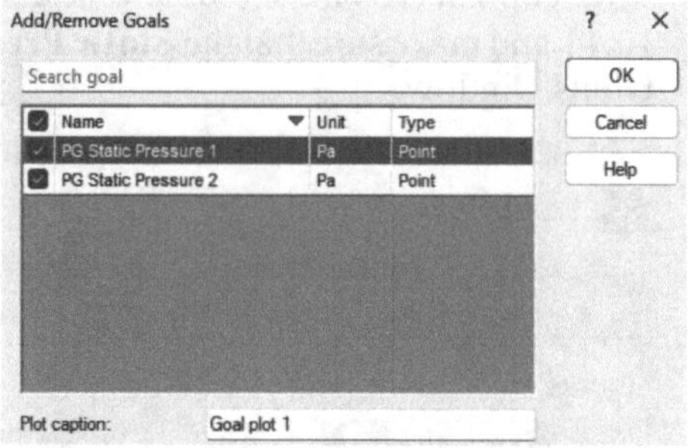

Figure 10.12b) Adding goals to the goals plot

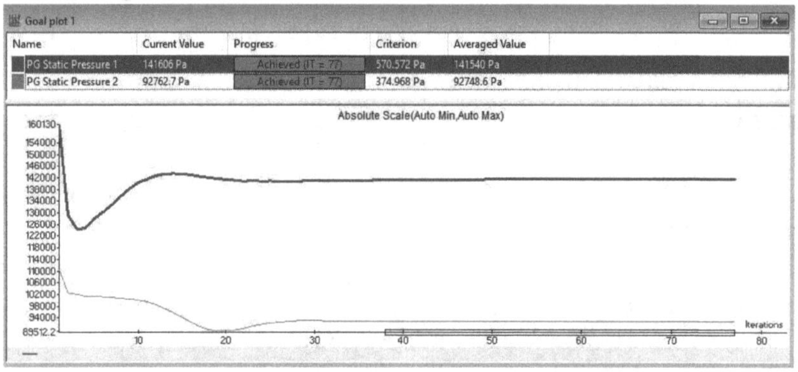

Figure 10.2c) Variation of static pressure goals before and after orifice plate

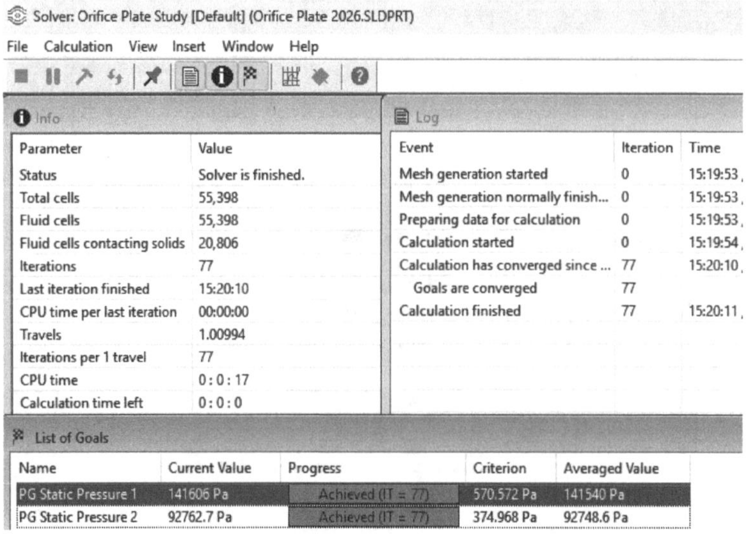

Figure 10.12d) Solver window for orifice plate flow

H. Cut-Plots for Orifice Plate

13. Open the **Results** folder, right click on **Cut Plots** in the **Flow Simulation analysis tree** and select **Insert....** Select the **Right Plane** from the **FeatureManager design tree**. Slide the **Number of Levels:** slide bar to **255**. Select **Velocity (Z)** from the **Parameter:** dropdown menu. Click **OK** to exit the **Cut Plot** window. Rename the cut plot to **Velocity (Z)**. Select **Left** view from **View Orientation** in the graphics window. Select **Section View** and select the **Right Plane** for **Section 1**. Select **Tools>>Flow Simulation>>Results>>Display>>Lighting** to display the cut plot. Right click on the scale in the graphics window and select Make Horizontal. Repeat this cut plot but select **Pressure** from the **Parameter:** dropdown menu. Click OK to exit the **Cut Plot** window, see Figure 10.13b). Rename the cut plot to **Pressure**.

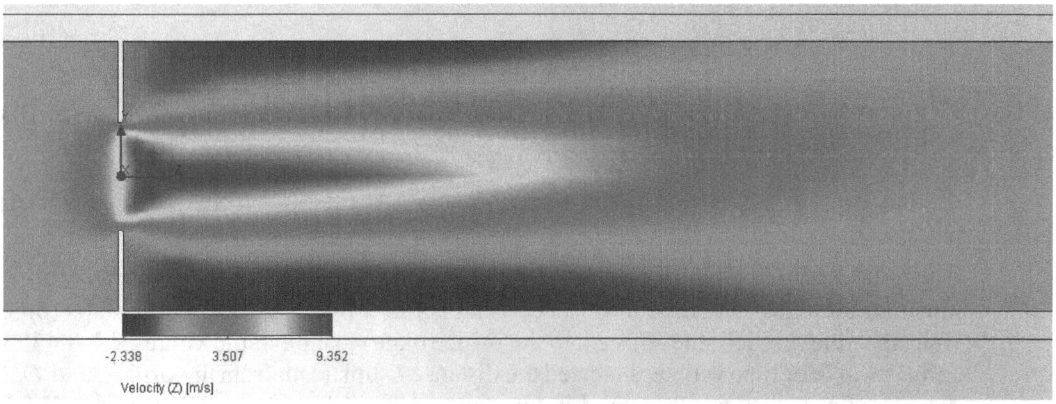

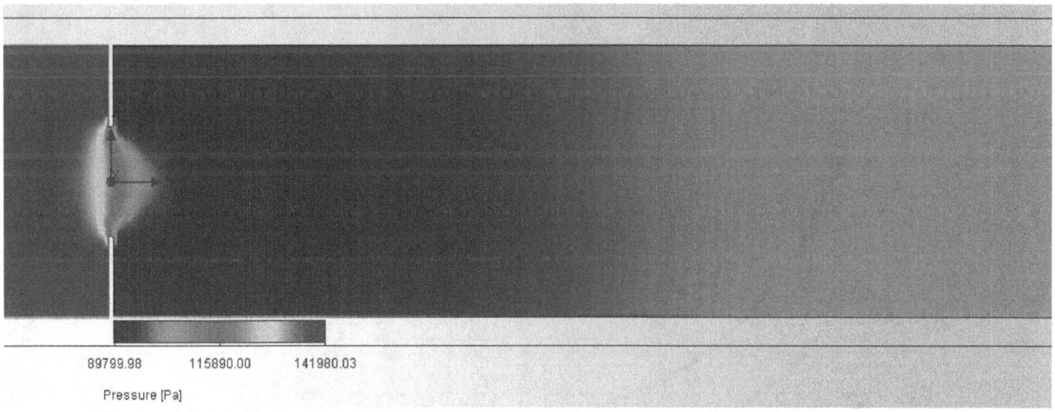

Figure 10.13 Velocity (Z) and pressure distribution before and after the orifice plate

I. Discharge Coefficient, XY Plots and Flow Trajectories for Orifice Plate

14. From a mass balance and from Bernoulli equation we can derive an expression for the velocity at the orifice V_o

$$V_o = \sqrt{\frac{2\Delta P}{\rho(1-\beta^4)}} \tag{10.1}$$

where $\Delta P = P_1 - P_2$ is the pressure difference between the pressure P_1 before and P_2 after the orifice, ρ is the density of the fluid and $\beta = d/D$ is the ratio of the orifice diameter d and the inner pipe diameter D. Due to frictional effects and the vena contracta, we have to incorporate a correction factor known as the discharge coefficient C_d in order to determine the volume flow rate $\dot{V}$ in the pipe

$$\dot{V} = C_d A_o V_o \tag{10.2}$$

where A_o is the area of the orifice opening. The discharge coefficient has been experimentally determined for orifice flow meters as

$$C_d = 0.5959 + 0.0312\beta^{2.1} - 0.184\beta^8 + 91.71\frac{\beta^{2.5}}{Re^{0.75}} + 0.09A\frac{\beta^4}{1-\beta^4} - 0.0337B\beta^3 \tag{10.3}$$

where the Reynolds number $Re = V_1 D/\nu$ is based on the approach velocity V_1 and kinematic viscosity ν of the fluid. The constants A and B are zero for corner taps (pipe wall taps, one on each side adjacent to the orifice plate) that have the values $A = 0.4333$ and $B = 0.47$ for pipe wall taps located the distance D upstream from the orifice and $D/2$ downstream. Equation (3) is valid in the region $10^4 < Re < 10^7$, $0.25 < \beta < 0.75$.

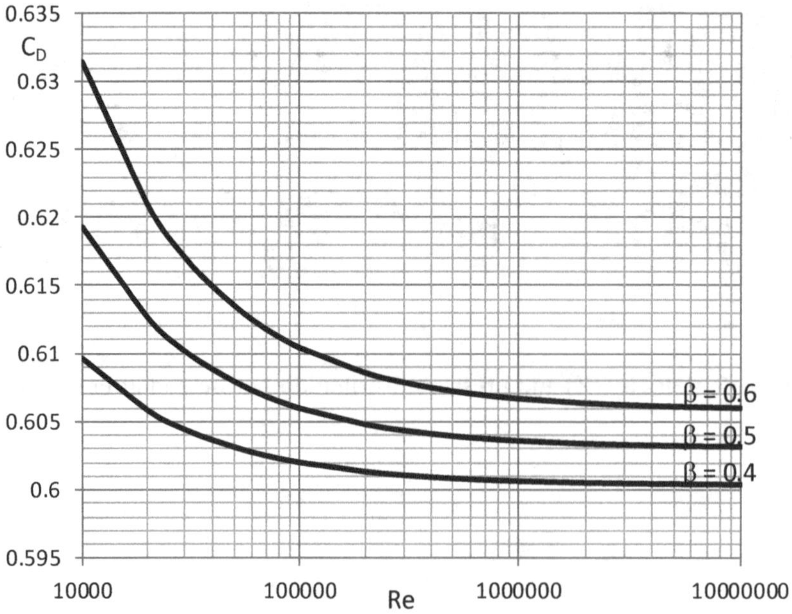

Figure 10.14a) Discharge coefficient versus Reynolds number for three different β ratios, pipe wall taps located distance D upstream and $D/2$ downstream from orifice plate

The diameter ratio β = 20mm/50mm = 0.4 in the Flow Simulation calculations and the Reynolds number is

$$Re = \frac{V_1 D}{\nu} = \frac{1m/s \cdot 0.050m}{1 \cdot 10^{-6} m^2/s} = 50{,}000 \qquad (10.4)$$

The pressure difference can be determined from data in Figure 10.12d) as $\Delta P = 141606\ Pa - 92762.7\ Pa = 48843.3\ Pa$. The discharge coefficient from Flow Simulation is

$$C_D = \frac{\dot{V}}{A_O V_O} = \frac{A_1 V_1}{A_O}\sqrt{\frac{\rho(1-\beta^4)}{2\Delta P}} = \frac{V_1}{\beta^2}\sqrt{\frac{\rho(1-\beta^4)}{2\Delta P}} = \frac{1m/s}{0.4^2}\sqrt{\frac{998kg/m^3(1-0.4^4)}{2 \cdot 48843.3\ \text{Pa}}} = 0.62359 \qquad (10.5)$$

The corresponding value from experiments, equation (3), is 0.603, which is 3.4 % difference. We are interested in the velocity and pressure variation along the pipe. Click on the **Featuremanager design tree** tab and select the **Right Plane**. Select **Line** from the **Basic Modeling Tools**. Select **Left** view from **View Orientation** in the graphics window. Draw a horizontal **990.00 mm** long line along the pipe wall from left to right, see Figure 10.14b). Exit the **Line Properties** window and the **Insert Line** window. Click on **Rebuild** from the SOLIDWORKS menu. Rename the sketch and call it "**Wall**". Repeat this step and sketch another horizontal line with the same length along the centerline of the pipe from left to right, see figure 10.14c), and name the sketch "**Centerline**".

Figure 10.14b) Drawing of a horizontal line along the pipe wall

Figure 10.14c) Drawing of a horizontal line along the pipe centerline

Click on the **Flow Simulation analysis tree** tab and right click on **XY Plots** and select **Insert….** Click on the **Featuremanager design tree** tab and select the sketch named **Centerline**. Choose **Model Z** from the **Abscissa:** drop down menu. Check the **Velocity** box in the **Parameters** portion of the **XY Plot** window. Slide the **Resolution** to the maximum value and set the number of evenly distributed output points to **200.** Open the **Options** portion of the **XY Plot** window and select the template Excel Workbook (*.xlsx), see Figure 10.14d). Click on the button **Export to Excel.** An Excel file will open. The maximum velocity along the centerline is around nine times higher than the approach velocity, see Figure 10.14e). Rename the XY Plot in the Flow Simulation analysis tree to **Velocity along Centerline.** Repeat this step but select the sketch named "**Wall**" and check the box for **Pressure**. Rename the XY Plot to **Pressure along Wall.** We can see in Figure 10.14f) that there is a partial recovery in pressure after the orifice.

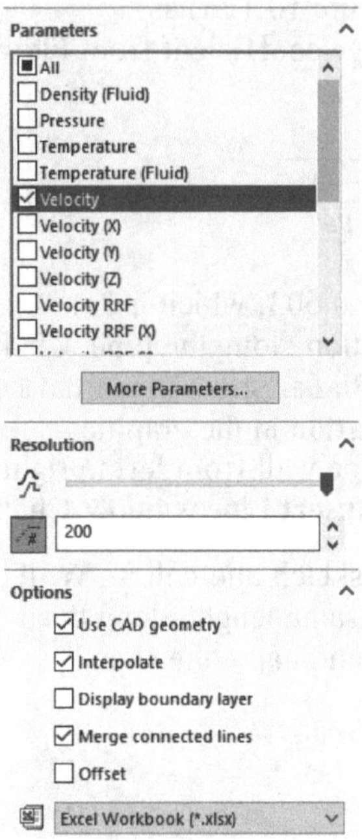

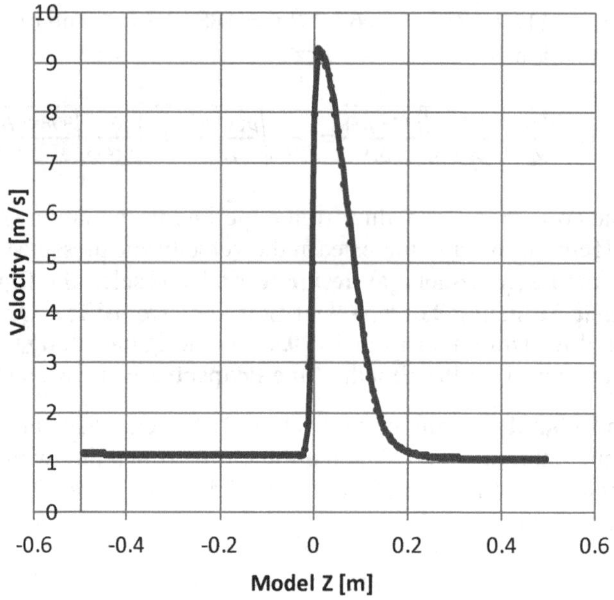

Figure 10.14d) Settings for XY plot   Figure 10.14e) Velocity along the centerline

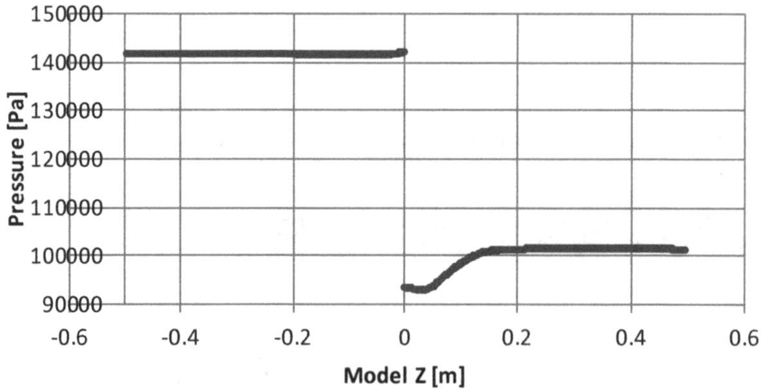

Figure 10.14f) Pressure variation along the pipe wall

Flow trajectories show the streamlines of the flow and we will now insert these for the orifice plate flow. Right click on the **Pressure** cut plot in the Flow Simulation analysis tree and select **Hide**. Right click on the **Velocity (Z)** cut plot in the Flow Simulation analysis tree and select **Hide**. Right click on **Flow Trajectories** in the Flow Simulation analysis tree and select **Insert…**. Go to the FeatureManager design tree and click on the **Front Plane.** The front plane will be listed as the **Reference** plane in the **Flow Trajectories** window. Set the **Number of Points** to **100**. Select the **Static Trajectories** button and select **Lines** from the **Draw Trajectories As** drop-down menu in the **Appearance** section. Select **Velocity** from the **Color by** drop-down menu. Click on the **OK** button to exit the **Flow Trajectories** window. Select **Section View** and select the **Right Plane** and **Reverse Section Direction** for **Section 1**.

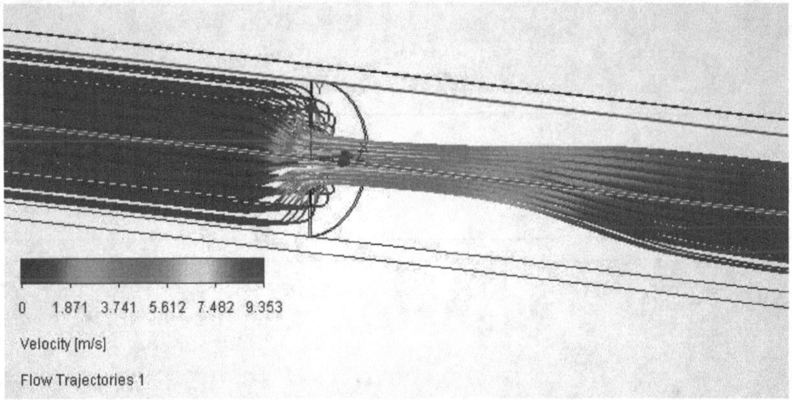

Figure 10.14g) Flow trajectories for orifice plate flow

J. Simulation and Discharge Coefficient for Long Radius Nozzle

15. Next, we will study the long radius flow nozzle meter. Open the file **Long Radius Nozzle 2026**. Select **Tools>>Flow Simulation>>Solve>>Run...**. Check the **Mesh** box in the **Run** window and check **New calculation** in the same window. Click on the **Run** button. Select **Tools>>Flow Simulation>>Results>>Load from File...**. Click on the Open button. Insert cut plots of **Velocity (Z)** and **Pressure** in the same way as was shown in step **13**. The cut plots for the long radius nozzle are shown in Figures 10.15b) and 10.15c). Insert an XY-Plot of centerline velocity. Also, copy plot data and include centerline velocity for the orifice plate in the same graph, see Figure 10.15e) for the result. We see that the maximum velocity is 66 % higher for the orifice plate as compared with the long radius nozzle.

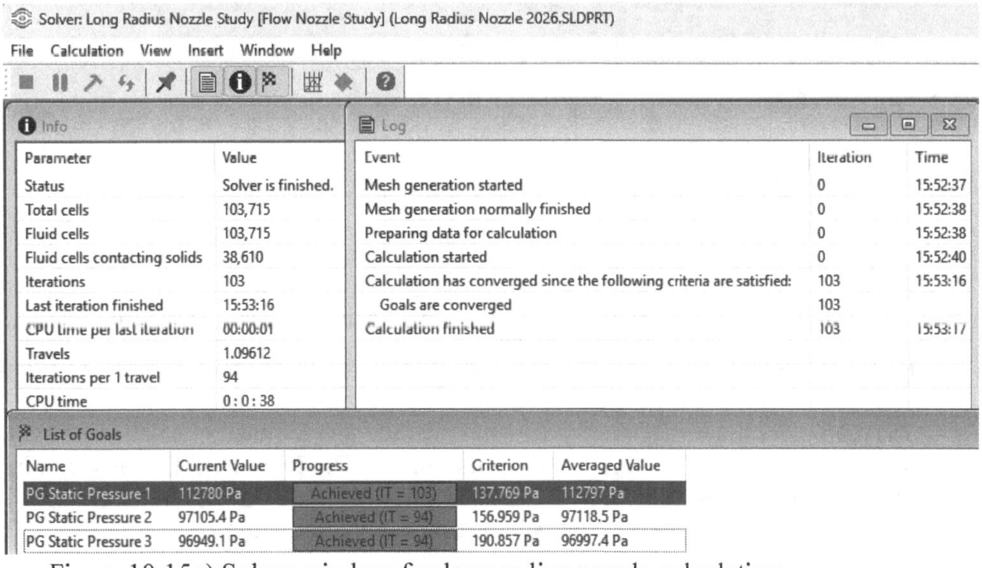

Figure 10.15a) Solver window for long radius nozzle calculation

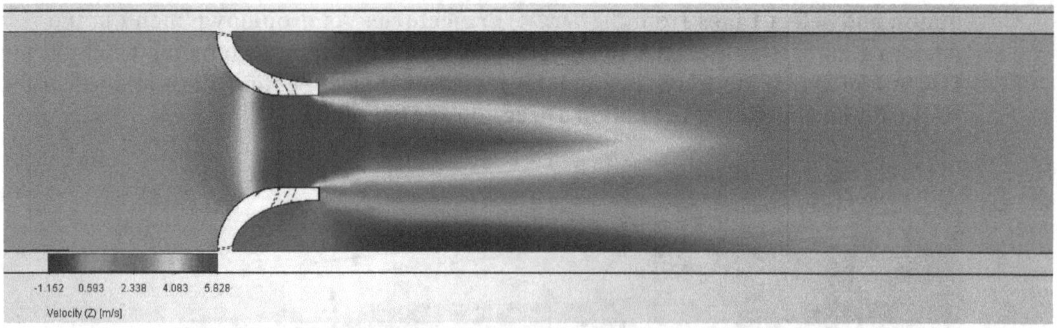

Figure 10.15b) Velocity (Z) distribution along long-radius flow nozzle

Figure 10.15c) Pressure distribution along long-radius flow nozzle

The discharge coefficient for the long radius nozzle is given by

$$C_d = 0.9975 - 6.53\sqrt{\frac{\beta}{Re}} \tag{10.6}$$

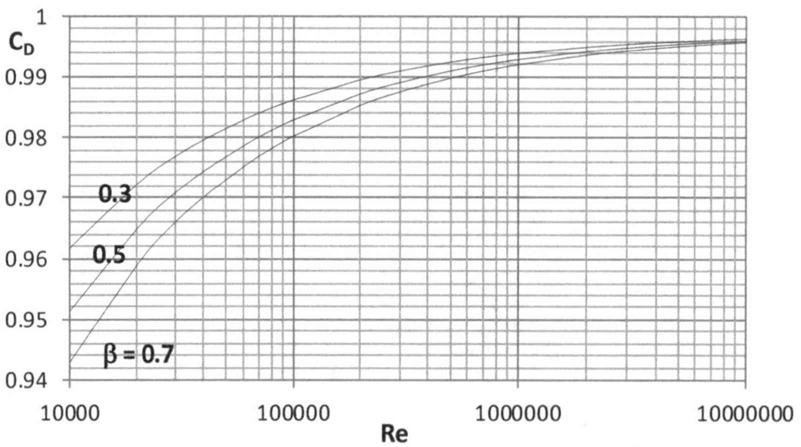

Figure 10.15d) Discharge coefficient versus Reynolds number for three different β ratios

The diameter ratio β = 21mm/50mm = 0.42 in the Flow Simulation calculations and the Reynolds *Re* number is 50,000, see equation (4). The pressure difference can be determined from data in Figure 10.15a) as $\Delta P = 112780\ Pa - 96949.1\ Pa = 15830.9\ Pa$. The discharge coefficient from Flow Simulation is

$$C_D = \frac{\dot{V}}{A_O V_O} = \frac{A_1 V_1}{A_O}\sqrt{\frac{\rho(1-\beta^4)}{2\Delta P}} = \frac{V_1}{\beta^2}\sqrt{\frac{\rho(1-\beta^4)}{2\Delta P}} = \frac{1m/s}{0.42^2}\sqrt{\frac{998kg/m^3(1-0.42^4)}{2\cdot 15830.9\text{ Pa}}} = 0.9907$$

The corresponding value from experiments, equation (6), is 0.979, a difference of 1.2 %.

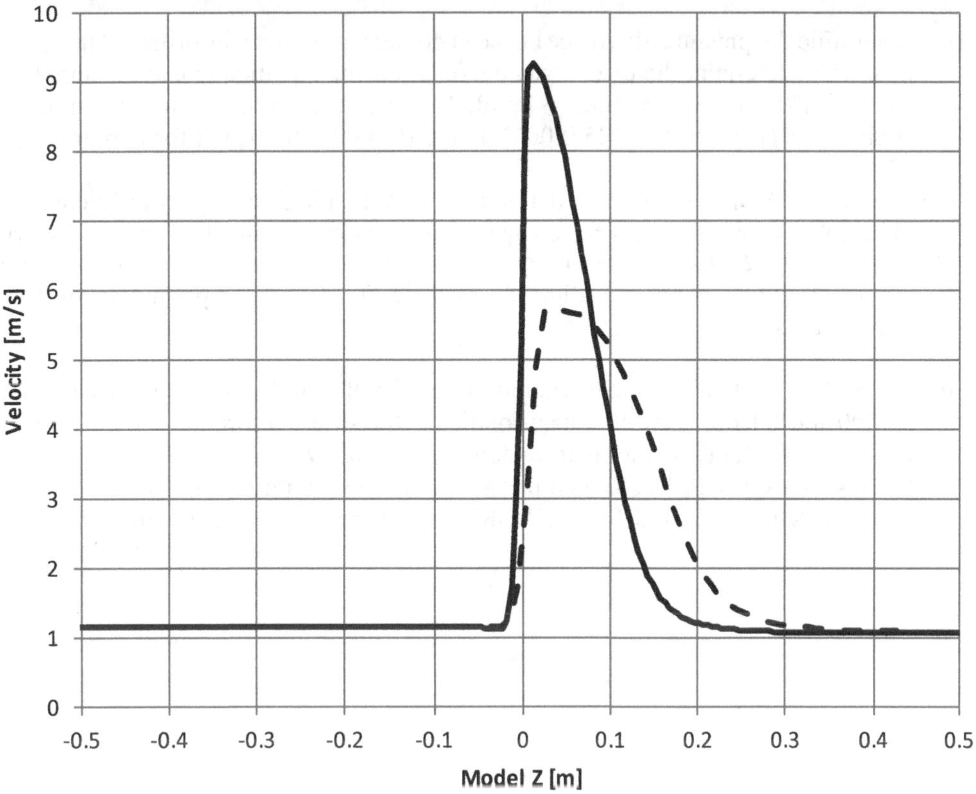

Figure 10.15e) A comparison of centerline velocity for orifice flow $\beta = 0.4$ (full line) and long-radius flow nozzle $\beta = 0.42$ (dashed line) at *Re* = 50,000

K. References

1. White, F. M., Fluid Mechanics, 4th Edition, McGraw-Hill, 1999.

L. Exercises

10.1 Change the mesh resolution in flow simulations and see how the mesh size affects the discharge coefficient in comparison with experimental values for the orifice plate and long radius nozzle.

10.2 Determine the pressure difference between corner taps (where the orifice plate meets the pipe wall), determine the discharge coefficient using equation (5), and compare with equation (3) using values for $A = B = 0$. The thickness of the orifice is 1 mm. Use coordinates $(x,y,z) = (0,0.025,0.001)$ m and $(0,0.025,-0.001)$ m for corner taps.

10.3 Use SOLIDWORKS Flow Simulation to determine the discharge coefficient for different Reynolds numbers and compare in graphs with figure 10.14a) for the orifice plate and figure 10.15d) for the long-radius nozzle. Use Re = 10,000; 25,000; 50,000, and 100,000. Plot graphs including both SOLIDWORKS and experimental data in the same graphs.

10.4 Use SOLIDWORKS Flow Simulation to keep the Reynolds number constant at Re = 50,000 and determine the discharge coefficient for different β ratios and compare with figure 10.14a) for the orifice plate and figure 10.15d) for the long-radius nozzle. Use β = 0.3, 0.4, 0.5, 0.6, and 0.7. Remember to change the minimum gap size for each case. Plot graphs including both SOLIDWORKS and experimental data in the same graphs.

CHAPTER 11. THERMAL BOUNDARY LAYER

A. Objectives

- Setting up a Flow Simulation projects for internal flow
- Inserting boundary conditions, creating goals and running the calculations
- Using cut plots and XY plots to visualize the resulting flow field
- Compare Flow Simulation results with theoretical and empirical data

B. Problem Description

In this chapter, we will use Flow Simulation to study the thermal two-dimensional laminar and turbulent boundary layer flow on a flat plate and compare with the theoretical boundary layer solution and empirical results. The inlet velocity for the 1 m long plate is 5 m/s and we will be using air as the fluid for laminar calculations and water to get a higher Reynolds number for turbulent boundary layer calculations. The temperature of the hot wall will be set to 393.2 K while the temperature of the approaching free stream is set to 293.2 K. We will determine the temperature profiles and plot the same profiles using the well-known boundary layer similarity coordinate. The variation of the local Nusselt number will also be determined.

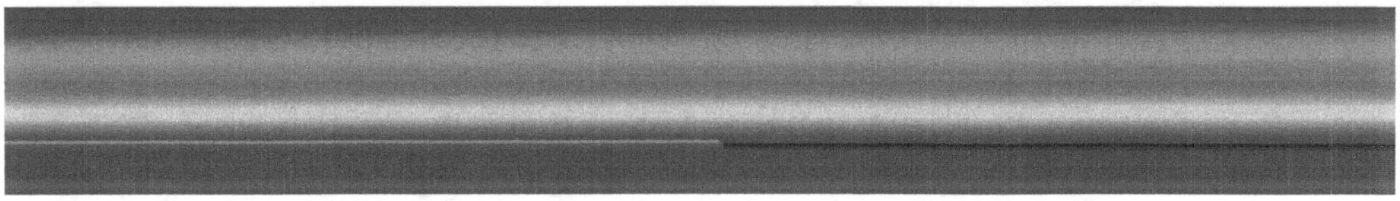
Figure 11.0 Thermal velocity boundary layer close to horizontal wall

C. Flow Simulation Project

1. Open the part named **Thermal Boundary Layer Part 2026**.

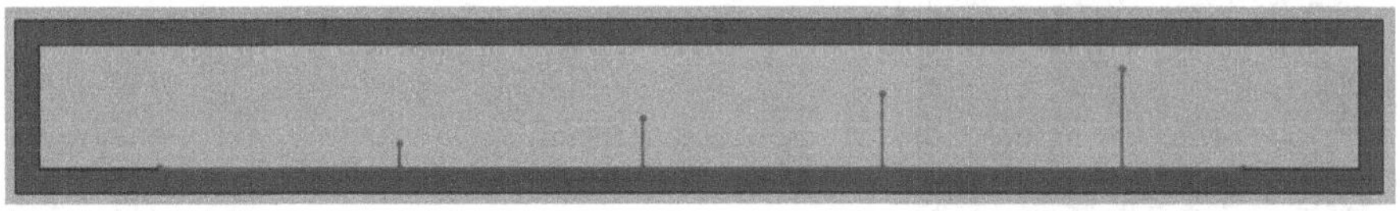
Figure 11.1 SOLIDWORKS model for thermal boundary layer

2. If Flow Simulation is not available in the menu, you can add it from SOLIDWORKS menu: **Tools>>Add Ins...** and check the corresponding **Flow Simulation** box. Select **Tools>>Flow Simulation>>Project>>Wizard...** to create a new Flow Simulation project. Create a new project named **Thermal Boundary Layer**. Click on the **Next >** button. Select the default **SI (m-kg-s)** unit system and click on the **Next>** button.

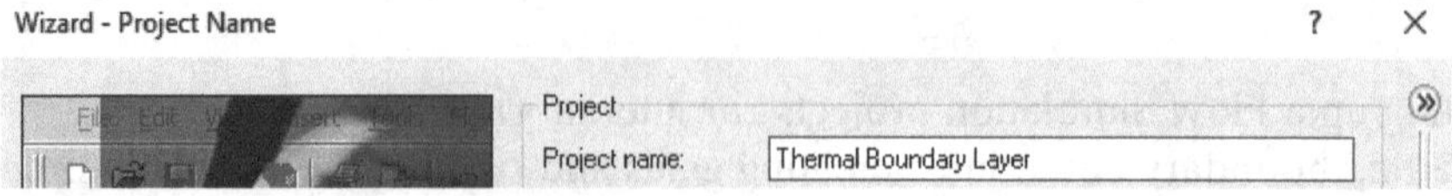

Figure 11.2 Name for the project

3. Use the **Internal Analysis type**. Click on the **Next >** button.

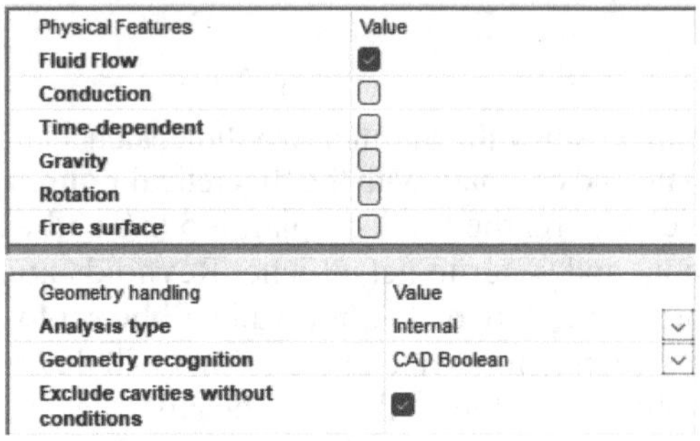

Figure 11.3 Analysis type window

4. Select **Air** from the **Gases** and add it as **Project Fluid**. Select **Laminar Only** from the **Flow Type** drop down menu. Click on the **Next >** button. Use the default **Wall Conditions** and **5 m/s** for **Velocity in X direction** as **Initial Condition**. Click on the **Finish** button. Select **Tools>>Flow Simulation>>Global Mesh....** Slide the **Level of initial mesh** to 7.

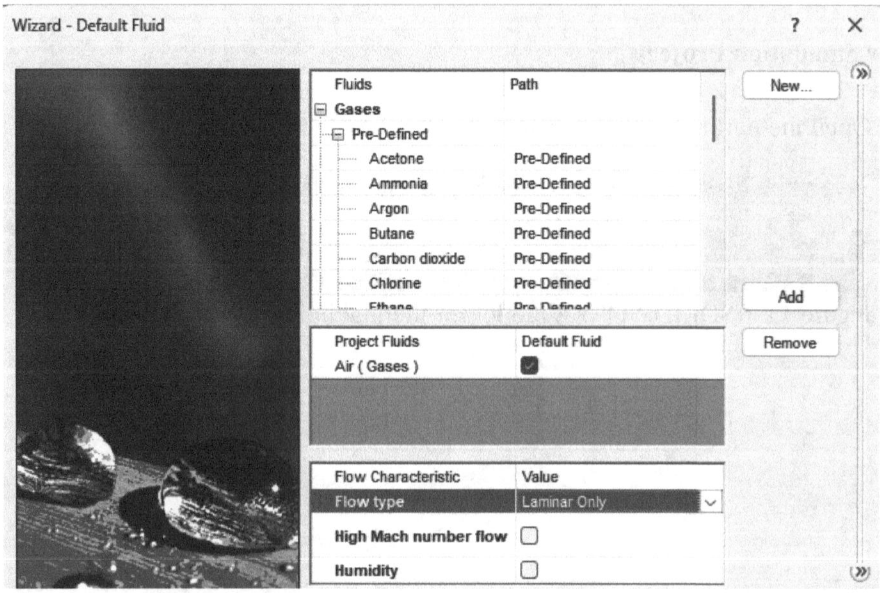

Figure 11.4 Selection of fluid for the project and flow type

5. Select **Tools>>Flow Simulation>>Computational Domain....** Click on the **2D simulation** button and select **XY plane**. Exit the **Computational Domain** window.

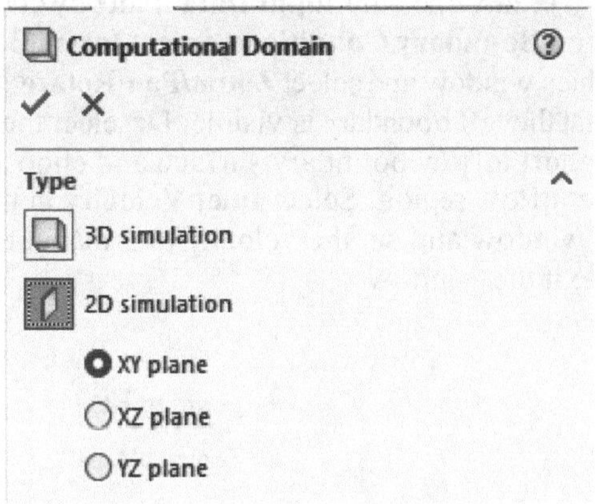

Figure 11.5 Selecting two-dimensional flow condition

6. Select **Tools>>Flow Simulation>>Global Mesh....** Check the **Manual setting** type. Change both the **Number of cells per X:** to **300** and the **Number of cells per Y:** to **200**. Click on the **OK** button to exit the **Initial Mesh** window.

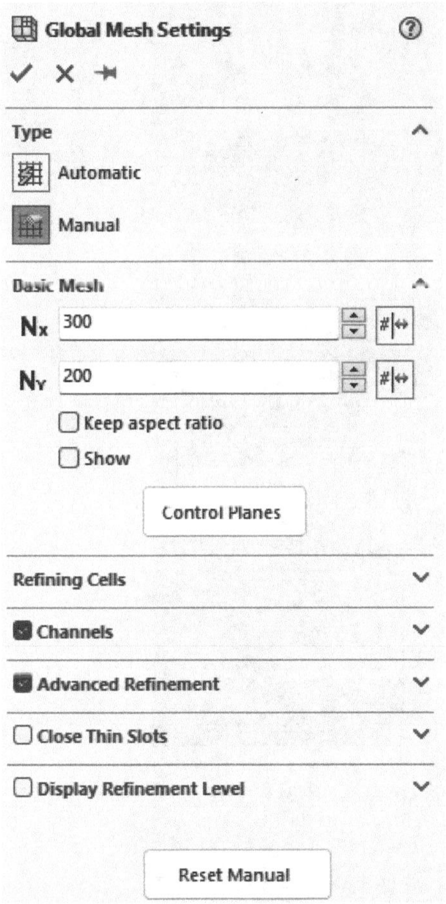

Figure 11.6 Number of cells in both directions

D. Boundary Conditions

7. Select the **Flow Simulation analysis tree** tab, open the **Input Data** folder by clicking on the plus sign next to it and right click on **Boundary Conditions**. Select **Insert Boundary Condition…**. Right click in the graphics window and select **Zoom/Pan/Rotate>>Rotate View**. Click and drag the mouse so that the left boundary is visible. Deselect the **Rotate View**. Zoom in and right click on the left inflow boundary surface and choose **Select Other**. Select the inner surface of the inflow region. Select **Inlet Velocity** in the **Type** portion of the **Boundary Condition** window and set the velocity to **5 m/s** in the **Flow Parameters** window. Click **OK** to exit the window.

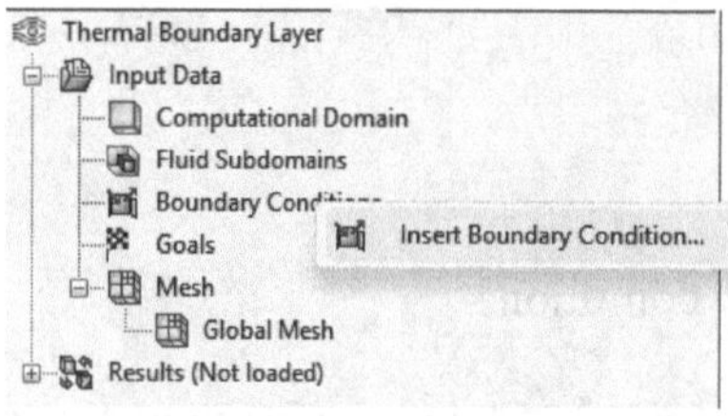

Figure 11.7a) Inserting boundary condition

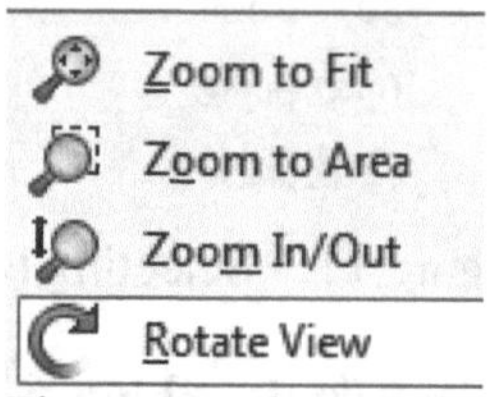

Figure 11.7b) Modifying view

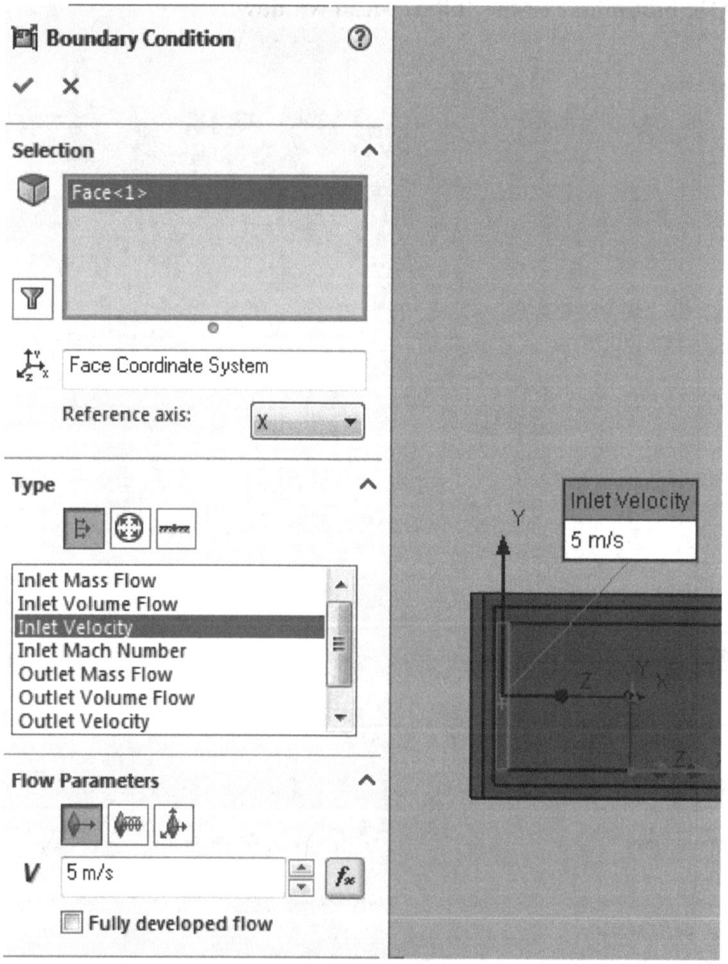

Figure 11.7c) Velocity boundary condition for the inflow

8. Right click again in the graphics window and select **Rotate View** once again to rotate the part and zoom in so that the inner right surface is visible in the graphics window. Right click and click on **Select**. Right click on **Boundary Conditions** in the **Flow Simulation analysis tree** and select **Insert Boundary Condition….** Right click on the outlet boundary and select **Select Other**. Select the outflow boundary of the model, see Figure 11.8. Click on the **Pressure Openings** button in the **Type** portion of the **Boundary Condition** window and select **Static Pressure**. Click **OK** to exit the window.

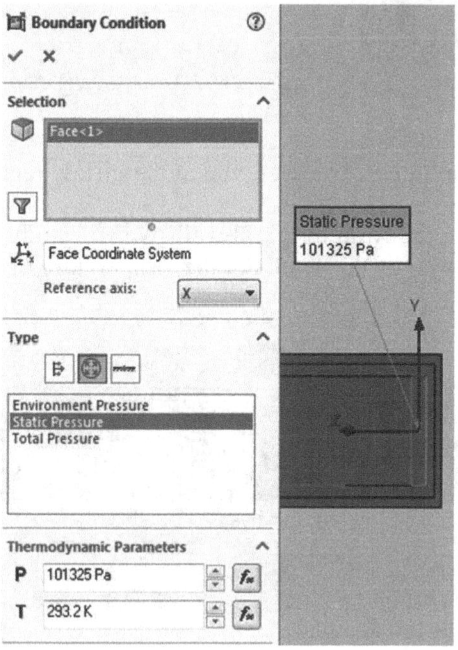

Figure 11.8 Selection of static pressure as boundary condition at the outlet

9. Insert the following boundary conditions: Ideal Wall for the upper wall and lower wall at the inflow region, see Figures 11.9a) and 11.9b). These will be adiabatic and frictionless walls.

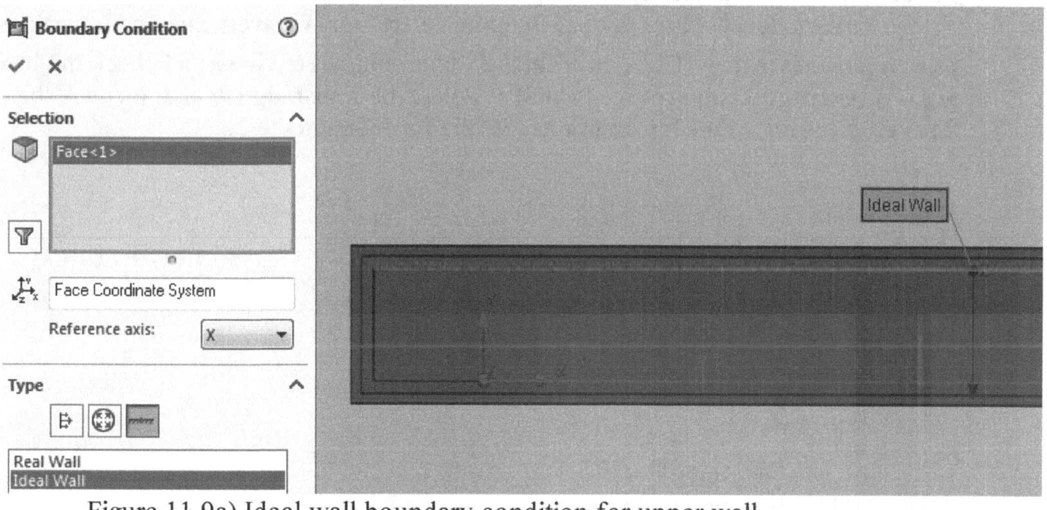

Figure 11.9a) Ideal wall boundary condition for upper wall

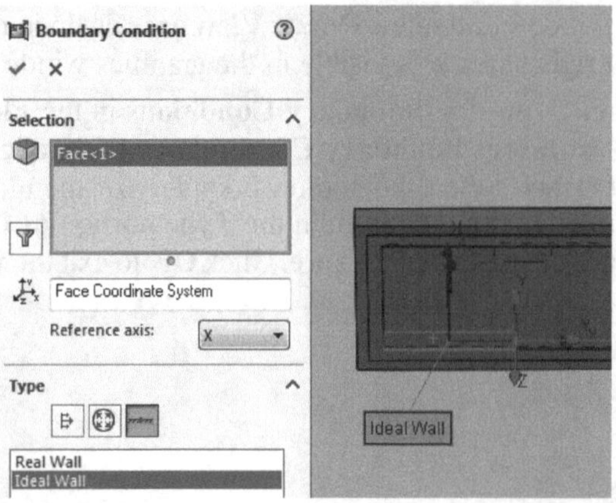

Figure 11.9b) Ideal wall boundary condition for lower wall at the inflow region

10. The last boundary condition will be in the form of a real wall. We will study the development of the thermal boundary layer on this wall. Set the temperature of the wall to **393.2 K**.

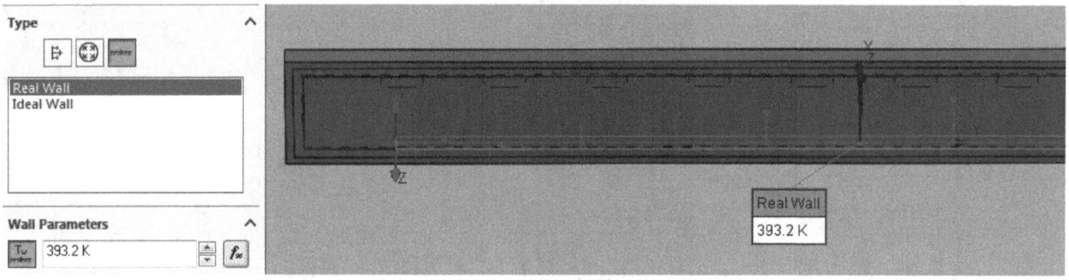

Figure 11.10 Real wall boundary condition for the flat plate

E. Goals and Calculation Controls

11. Right click on **Goals** in the **Flow Simulation analysis tree** and select **Insert Global Goals….** Select **Av Temperature (Fluid)** as global goal. Select **Tools>>Flow Simulation>>Calculation Control Options** from the menu. Select the **Refinement** tab. Set the **Value** to **level = 2** for **Global Domain**. Select **Goal Convergence** and **Iterations** as **Refinement strategy**. Click on ... in the **Value** column for **Goals** and check the box for **GG Average Temperature (Fluid) 1**. Select the **Finishing** tab and uncheck the **Travels** box under **Finish Conditions**. Set the **Refinements** to **2**.

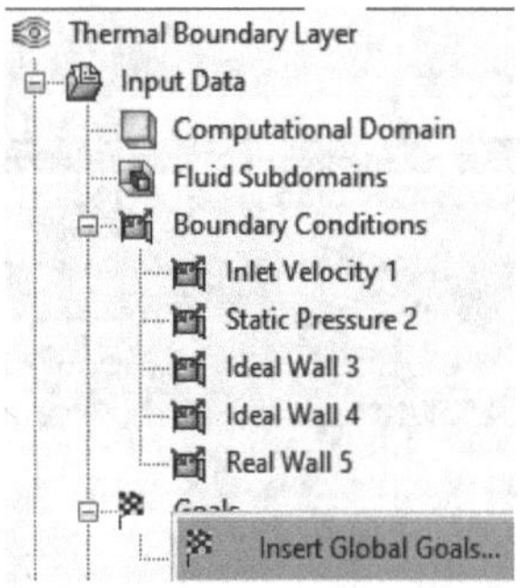

Figure 11.11a) Inserting global goals

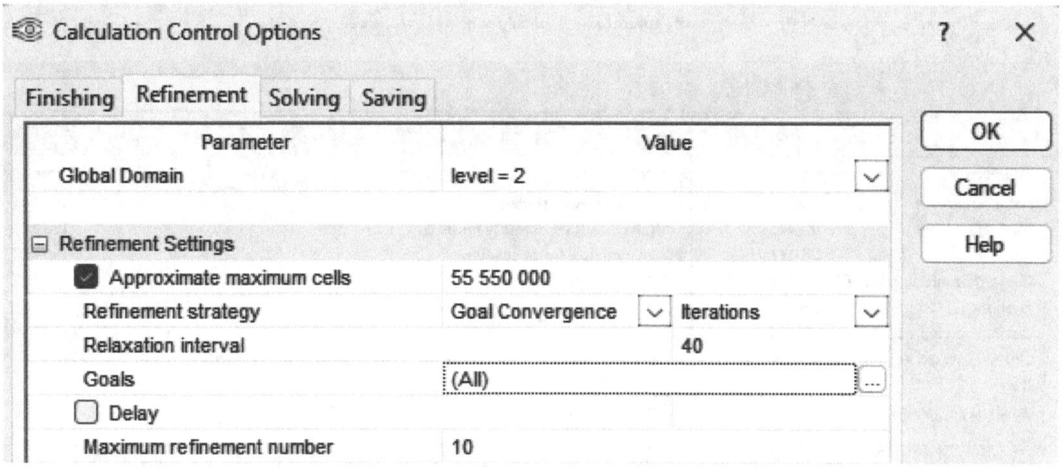

Figure 11.11b) Refinement settings for Calculation Control Options

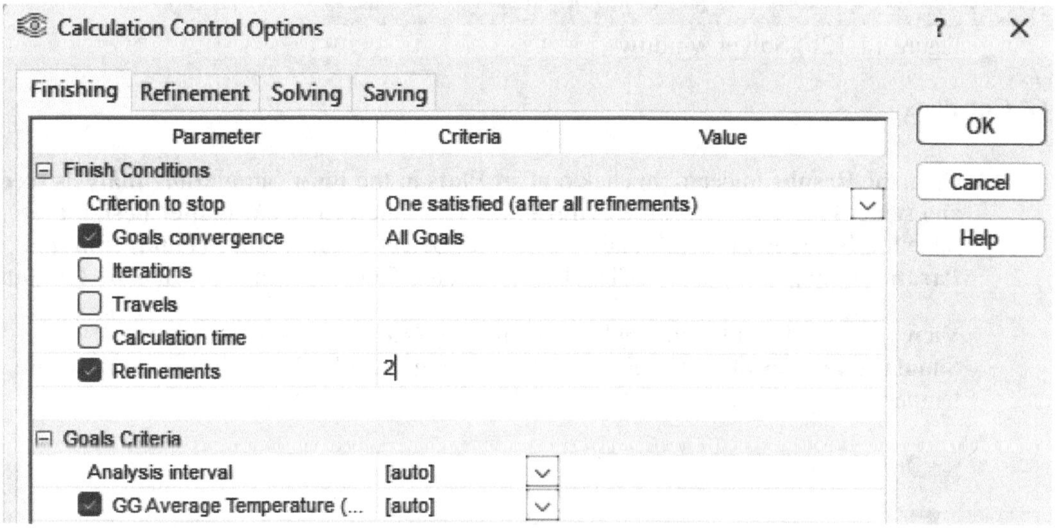

Figure 11.11c) Finishing settings for Calculation Control Options

F. Simulation for Low Reynolds Number

12. Select **Tools>>Flow Simulation>>Solve>>Run...** to start calculations. Click on the **Run** button in the **Run** window.

Figure 11.12a) Run window

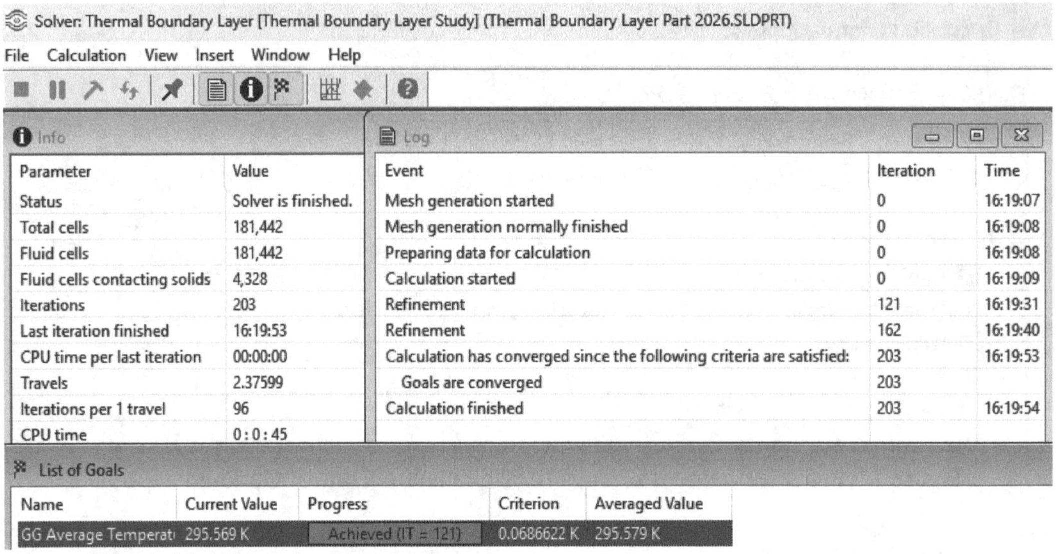

Figure 11.12b) Solver window

G. Cut-Plots

13. Open the **Results** folder, right click on **Cut Plots** in the **Flow Simulation analysis tree** and select **Insert...**. Select the **Front Plane** from the **FeatureManager design tree**. Slide the **Number of Levels** slide bar to **255**. Select **Temperature (Fluid)** from the **Parameter** drop down menu. Click **OK** to exit the **Cut Plot** window. Click on **Section View**  and exit the dialog box by clicking **OK**. Select **Tools>>Flow Simulation>>Results>>Display>>Lighting**. Figures 11.13b) and 11.13c) show the temperature gradient close to the heated wall of the flat plate.

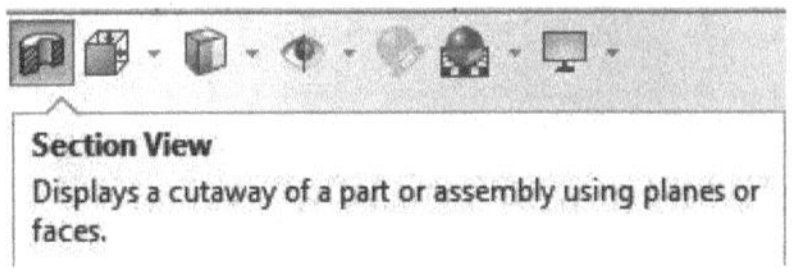

Figure 11.13a) Section view

Figure 11.13b) Thermal boundary layer along the flat plate

Figure 11.13c) Thermal boundary layer close to the wall

H. Plotting Temperature Profiles Using Templates

14. Place the file **"graph 11.14c)"** on the desktop. Click on the **FeatureManager design tree**. Click on the sketch **x = 0.2, 0.4, 0.6, 0.8 m**. Click on the **Flow Simulation analysis tree** tab. Right click **XY Plot** and select **Insert....** Check the **Temperature (Fluid)** box. Open the **Resolution** portion of the **XY Plot** window and slide the **Geometry Resolution** as far as it goes to the right. Click on the **Evenly Distribute Output Points** button and increase the number of points to **500.** Open the **Options** portion and check the **Display boundary layer** box. Select the **Excel Workbook (*.xlsx)** from the drop-down menu. Click on the **Export to Excel** button. Click **OK** to exit the **XY Plot** window. An Excel file will open with a graph of the temperature in the boundary layer at different streamwise positions.

    Double click on the **graph 11.14c)** file to open the file. Click on **Enable Editing** and **Enable Content** if you get a **Security Warning** that **Macros** have been disabled. If **Developer** is not available in the menu of the **Excel** file, you will need to do the following: Select **File>>Options** from the menu and click on the **Customize Ribbon** on the left-hand side. Check the **Developer** box on the right-hand side under **Main Tabs**. Click **OK** to exit the **Excel Options** window.

    Click on the **Developer** tab in the **Excel** menu for the **graph 11.14c)** file and select **Visual Basic** on the left-hand side to open the editor. Click on the plus sign next to **VBAProject (XY Plot 1.xlsx)** and click on the plus sign next to **Microsoft Excel Objects**. Right click on **Sheet2 (Plot Data)** and select **View Object**.

    Select **Macro** in the **Modules** folder under **VBAProject (graph 11.14c).xlsm)**. Select **Run>>Run Macro** from the menu of the **MVB for Applications** window. Click on the **Run** button in the **Macros** window. Figure 11.14c) will become available in **Excel** showing temperature ***T (K)*** versus wall normal coordinate ***y (m)***. Close the **XY Plot** window and the **graph 11.14c)** window in **Excel**. Exit the **XY Plot** window in **SOLIDWORKS Flow Simulation** and rename the inserted *xy*-plot in the **Flow Simulation analysis tree** to **Laminar Temperature Boundary Layer**.

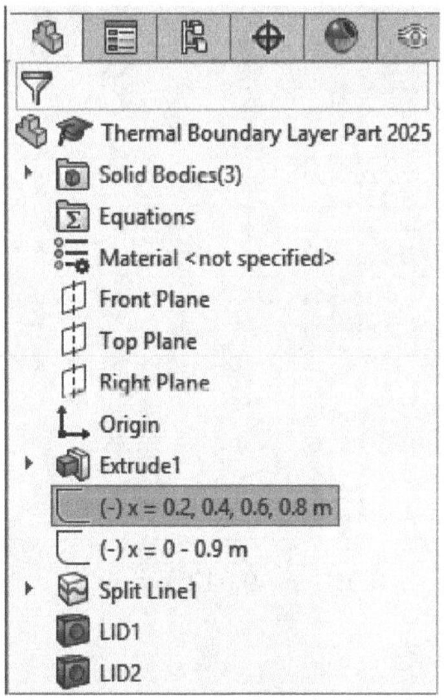

Figure 11.14a) Sketch for the XY Plot

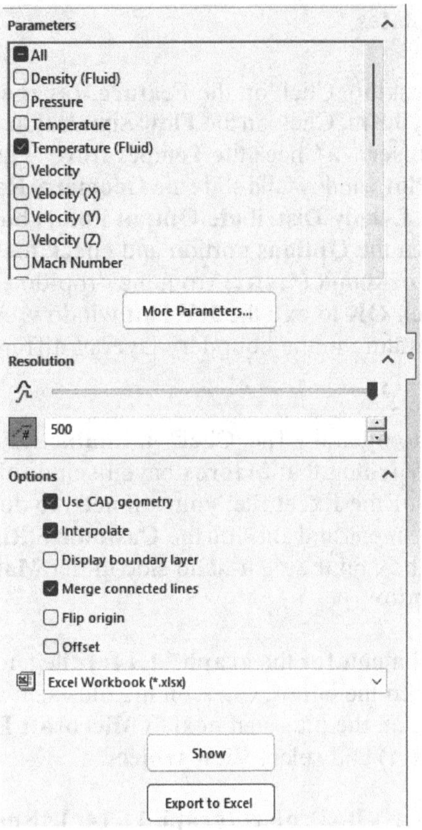

Figure 11.14b) Settings for the XY plot

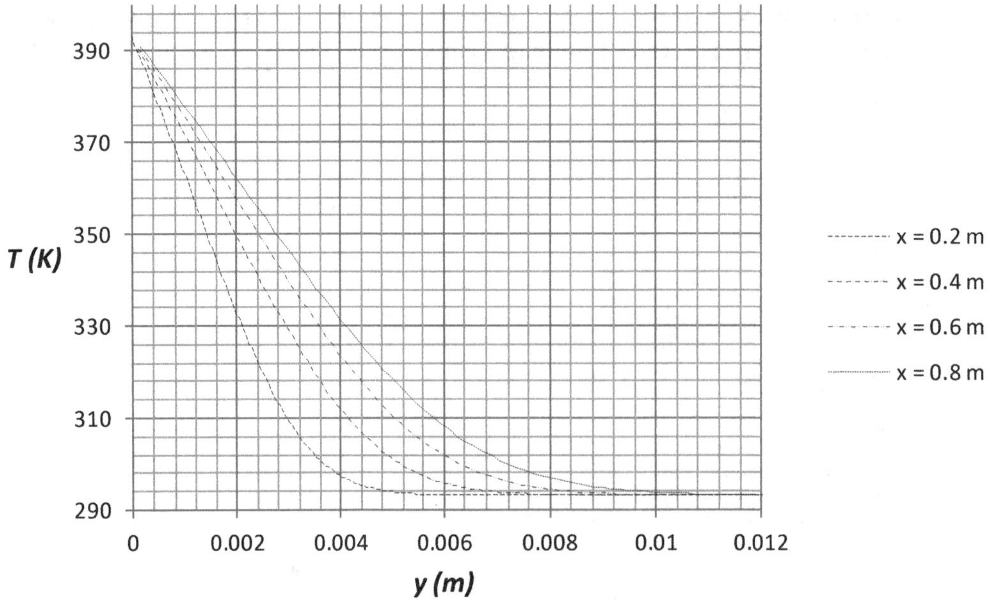

Figure 11.14c) Boundary layer temperature profiles on a flat plate

I. Theory

We now want to compare the temperature profiles with the theoretical temperature profile for laminar flow on a flat plate. First, we will normalize the temperature T in the boundary layer

$$\Theta = \frac{T - T_\infty}{T_w - T_\infty} \tag{11.1}$$

where T_∞ is the temperature in the free stream and T_w is the wall temperature. We will also transform the wall normal coordinate into the similarity coordinate for comparison with the theoretical profile. The similarity coordinate is described by

$$\eta = y\sqrt{\frac{U}{\upsilon x}} \tag{11.2}$$

where y (m) is the wall normal coordinate, U (m/s) is the free stream velocity, x (m) is the distance from the leading edge and υ (m^2/s) is the kinematic viscosity of the fluid. The fluid properties are evaluated at the film temperature $T_f = (T_w + T_\infty)/2$.

J. Plotting Non-Dimensional Temperature Profiles Using Templates

Place the file **graph 11.15** on the desktop. Repeat step **14** and select **graph 11.15** for the XY-plot. We see in Figure 11.15 that all profiles at different streamwise positions approximately collapse on the same curve when we use the boundary layer similarity coordinate. Exit the **XY Plot** window in **SOLIDWORKS Flow Simulation** and rename the inserted *xy*-plot in the **Flow Simulation analysis tree** to **Self-Similar Temperature Boundary Layer**.

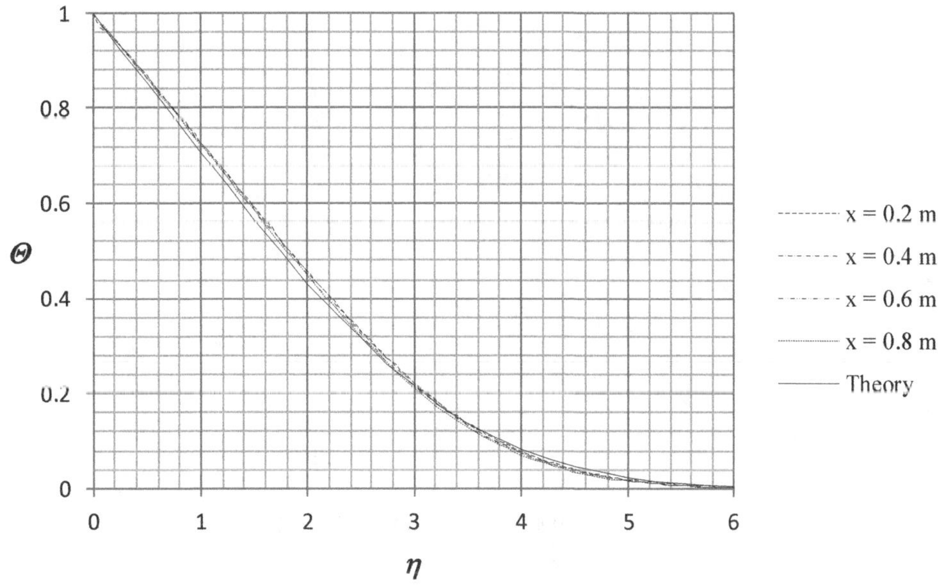

Figure 11.15 Temperature profiles in comparison with the theoretical profile (full line)

The Reynolds number for the flow on a flat plate is defined as

$$Re_x = \frac{Ux}{\nu} \tag{11.3}$$

The Reynolds number varies between $Re = 50{,}100$ at $x = 0.2$ m and $Re = 200{,}400$ at $x = 0.8$ m. We now want to study how the local Nusselt number varies along the plate. It is defined as the local convection coefficient h_x times the streamwise coordinate x divided by the thermal conductivity k:

$$Nu_x = \frac{h_x x}{k} \tag{11.4}$$

The theoretical local Nusselt number for laminar flow is given by

$$Nu_x = 0.332 Pr^{1/3} Re_x^{1/2} \qquad Pr > 0.6 \tag{11.5}$$

and for turbulent flow

$$Nu_x = 0.0296 Pr^{1/3} Re_x^{4/5} \qquad 5 \cdot 10^5 \leq Re_x \leq 10^7, 0.6 \leq Pr \leq 60 \tag{11.6}$$

K. Plotting Local Nusselt Number Using Templates

Place the file **"graph 11.16"** on the desktop. Repeat step **14** but this time choose the sketch **x = 0 – 0.9 m** and check the box for **Heat Transfer Coefficient**. An Excel file will open with a graph of the local Nusselt number versus the Reynolds number as compared with theoretical values for laminar thermal boundary layer flow, see figure 11.16. Exit the **XY Plot** window in **SOLIDWORKS Flow Simulation** and rename the inserted *xy*-plot in the **Flow Simulation analysis tree** to **Local Nusselt Number**.

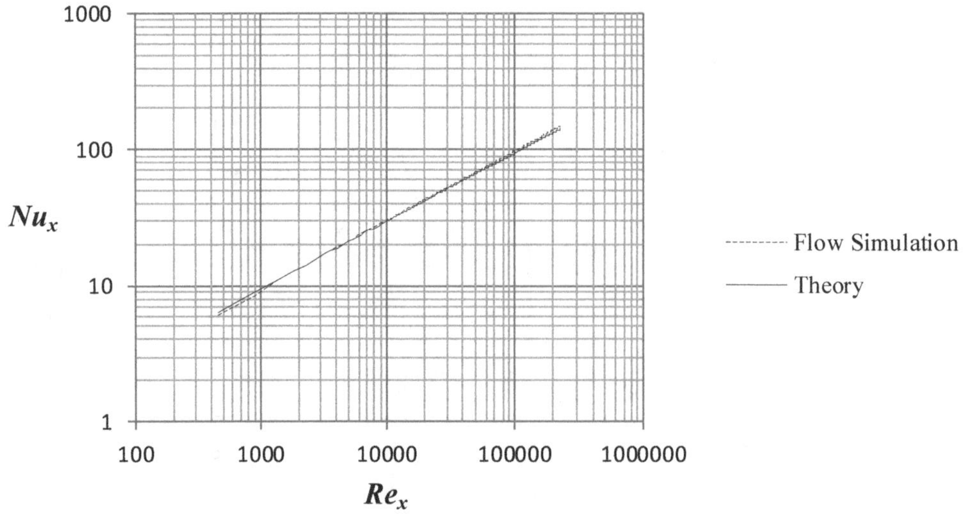

Figure 11.16 Local Nusselt number as a function of the Reynolds number

L. Simulations at a Higher Reynolds Number

15. In the next step, we will change the fluid to water to get higher Reynolds numbers. Start by selecting **Tools>>Flow Simulation>>Project>>Clone Project....** Enter the Project Name ***Thermal Boundary Layer Water***. Select **Tools>>Flow Simulation>>General Settings...** from the SOLIDWORKS menu. Click on **Fluids** in the **Navigator** portion and **Remove** air as the **Project Fluid**. Answer **OK** to the question that appears. Select **Water** from the **Liquids** and **Add** it as the **Project Fluid**. Change the **Flow type** to **Laminar and Turbulent**, see Figure 11.17. Click on **Apply** and **OK** to close the **General Setting** window.

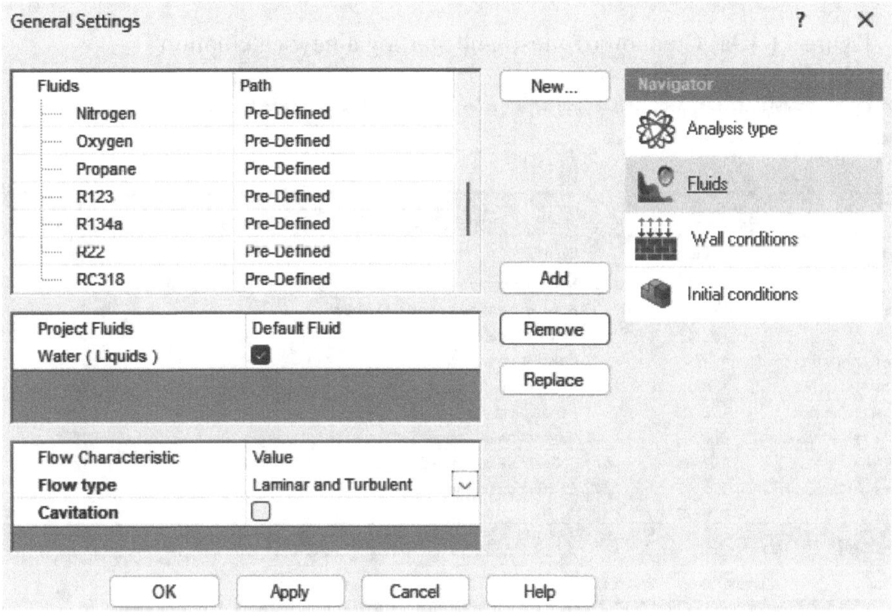

Figure 11.17 Selection of fluid and flow type

16. Right click the **Static Pressure 2 Boundary Condition** in the **Flow Simulation analysis tree** and select **Edit Definition....** Select **Turbulent Boundary Layer** in the **Boundary Layer** portion of the **Boundary Condition** window. Click **OK** to exit the **Boundary Condition** window.

    Right click the **Inlet Velocity 1 Boundary Condition** in the **Flow Simulation analysis tree** and select **Edit Definition....** Select **Laminar Boundary Layer**. Click **OK** to exit the **Boundary Condition** window.

    Right click the **Real Wall 4 Boundary Condition** in the **Flow Simulation analysis tree** and set the temperature of the wall to **353.2 K**. Click **OK** to exit the **Boundary Condition** window.

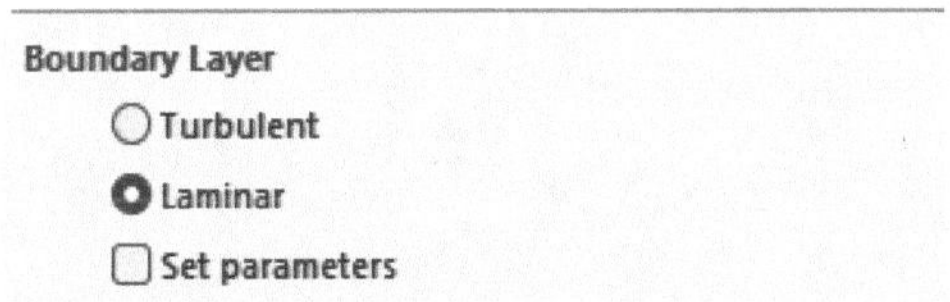

Figure 11.18 Selection of laminar boundary layer for inlet

17. Select **Tools>>Flow Simulation>>Solve>>Run...** to start calculations. Check the **Mesh** box and select **New calculation**. Click on the **Run** button in the **Run** window.

Figure 11.19a) Creation of mesh and starting a new calculation

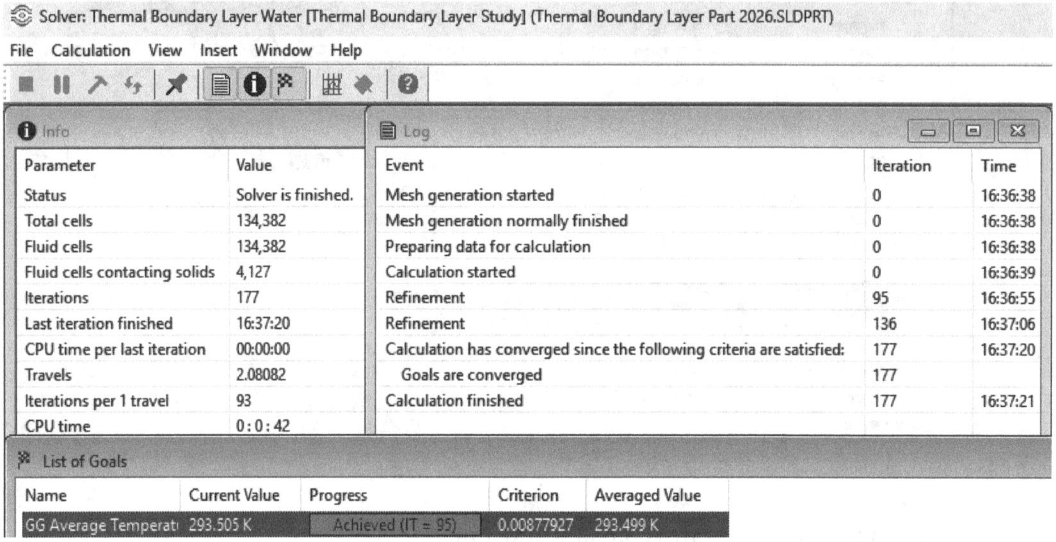

Figure 11.19b) Solver window for higher Reynolds number

18. Place the file **"graph 11.20"** on the desktop. Repeat step **16** but choose the file **"graph 11.20"**. An Excel file will open with a graph of the local Nusselt number versus the Reynolds number and compared with theoretical values for laminar and turbulent thermal boundary layer flow, see Figure 11.20.

Figure 11.20 is showing the Flow Simulation can capture the local Nusselt number in the laminar region in the Reynolds number range 40,000 – 300,000. Transition from laminar to turbulent flow occurs at a lower Reynolds number 300,000 in the simulations in comparison with theory that predict transition to occur at Reynolds number 500,000. In the turbulent region the Nusselt number is increasing again with a higher slope than in the laminar region. Exit the **XY Plot** window in **SOLIDWORKS Flow Simulation** and rename the inserted *xy*-plot in the **Flow Simulation analysis tree** to **Local Nusselt Number Water**.

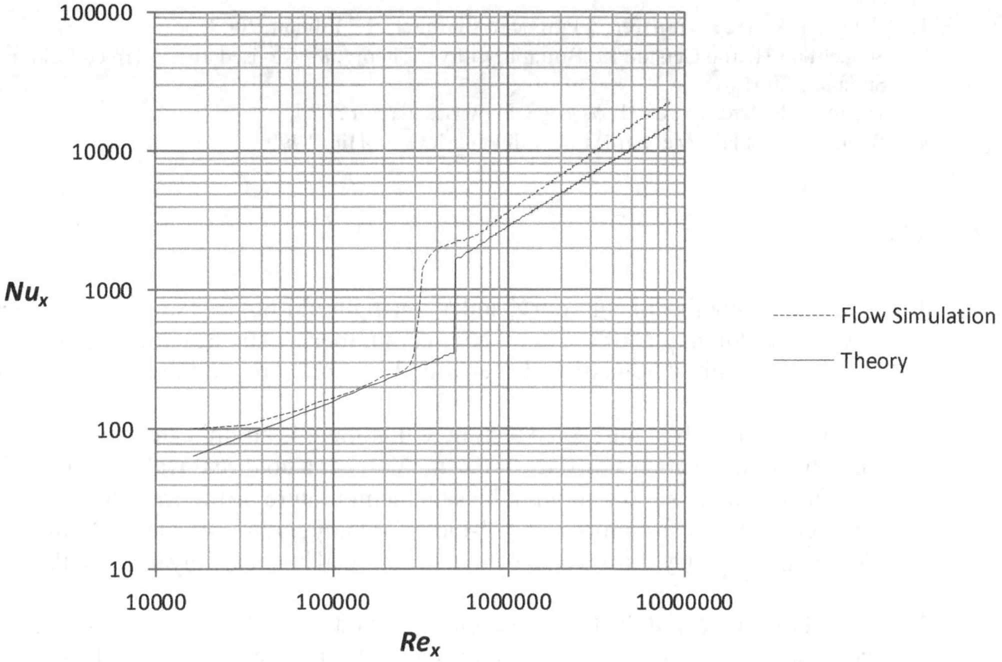

Figure 11.20 Comparison between Flow Simulation (dashed line) and theoretical laminar and empirical turbulent local Nusselt numbers

The average Nusselt number Nu over the entire length L of the plate for laminar flow is given by

$$Nu = 0.664 Pr^{1/3} Re_L^{1/2} \qquad Pr > 0.6,\ Re_L \leq 5 \cdot 10^5 \tag{11.7}$$

and for turbulent flow

$$Nu = 0.037 Pr^{1/3} Re_L^{4/5} \qquad 5 \cdot 10^5 \leq Re_L \leq 10^7, 0.6 \leq Pr \leq 60 \tag{11.8}$$

If the boundary layer is laminar on one part of the plate and turbulent on the remaining part the average Nusselt number is determined by

$$Nu = \left[0.664\sqrt{Re_{cr}} + 0.037\left(Re_L^{4/5} - Re_{cr}^{4/5}\right)\right] Pr^{1/3} \tag{11.9}$$

M. References

1. Çengel Y.A., Heat Transfer: A Practical Approach, 2nd Edition, 2003.
2. Schlichting H. and Gersten K., Boundary Layer Theory, 8th Revised and Enlarged Edition, Springer, 2001.
3. Technical Reference SOLIDWORKS Flow Simulation 2025.
4. White, F. M., Fluid Mechanics, 4th Edition, McGraw-Hill, 1999.

N. Exercise

11.1 Change the number of cells per X and Y, see figure 11.6b) for the laminar boundary layer and plot graphs of the local Nusselt number versus Reynolds number for different combinations of cells per X and Y. Compare with theoretical results.

11.2 Modify the length of the heated section so that there is an unheated starting length and the heated section starts at $x = 0.4$ m. You get a cold real wall section for the part upstream of $x = 0.4$ m with the same temperature as the free stream temperature. Use cut plots and XY-Plots for temperature profiles in Flow Simulation to study the development of the thermal boundary layer on the flat plate.

11.3 Modify the length of the heated section so that it ends at x = 0.6 m and you get a cold real wall section for the remaining part of the plate with the same temperature as the free stream temperature. Use cut plots and XY-Plots for temperature profiles in Flow Simulation to study the development of the thermal boundary layer after the heated section.

CHAPTER 12. FREE CONVECTION ON A VERTICAL PLATE AND A HORIZONTAL CYLINDER

A. Objectives

- Setting up Flow Simulation projects for external flow
- Creating goals
- Running the calculations
- Using cut plots, XY plots from templates and animations to visualize the resulting flow fields
- Compare Flow Simulation results with theoretical and empirical data

B. Problem Description

We will use Flow Simulation to study the thermal two-dimensional laminar flow on a vertical flat plate and compare with the theoretical boundary layer solution. We will be using air as the fluid for the flow calculations. The temperature of the vertical hot wall will be set to 296.2 K while the temperature of the surrounding air is 293.2 K. We will determine temperature and velocity profiles and plot the same profiles using similarity variables. The variation of the local Nusselt number will be determined. We will also look at free convection from a heated cylinder in air. The diameter of the cylinder is 20 mm and the temperature of the same cylinder will be set to 393.2 K.

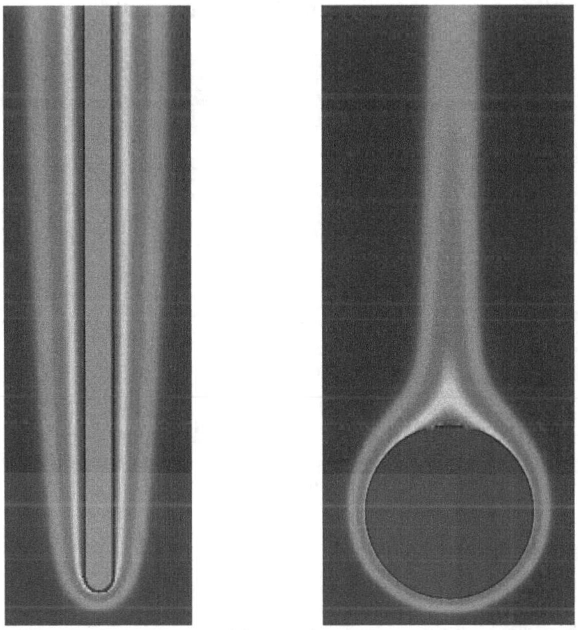

Figure 12.0 Thermal boundary layers on a vertical wall and around a horizontal cylinder

C. Flow Simulation Project

1. Open the part named **Free-Convection Boundary Layer Part 2026**.

Figure 12.1 SOLIDWORKS model for free-convection boundary layer

2. If Flow Simulation is not available in the menu, you can add it from SOLIDWORKS menu: **Tools>>Add Ins…** and check the corresponding **SOLIDWORKS Flow Simulation** box. Select **Tools>>Flow Simulation>>Project>>Wizard…** to create a new Flow Simulation project. Create a new project named **Free-Convection Boundary Layer Study**. Click on the **Next >** button. Select the default **SI (m-kg-s)** unit system and click on the **Next>** button once again.

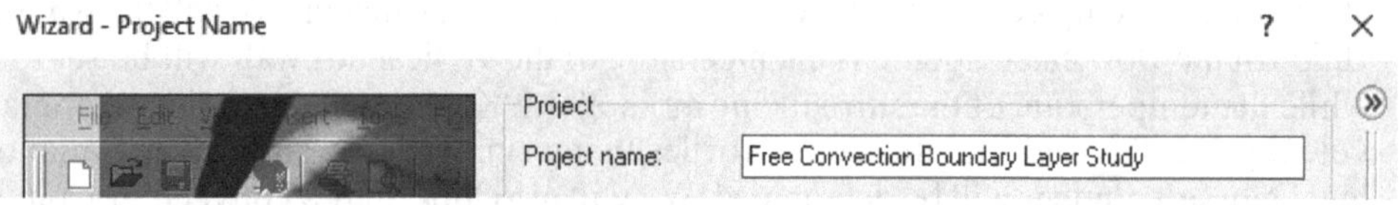

Figure 12.2 Creating a name for the project

3. Use the **External Analysis type** and check the box for **Gravity** as **Physical Feature**. Enter -9.81 m/s^2 as gravity for Y component. Click on the **Next >** button.

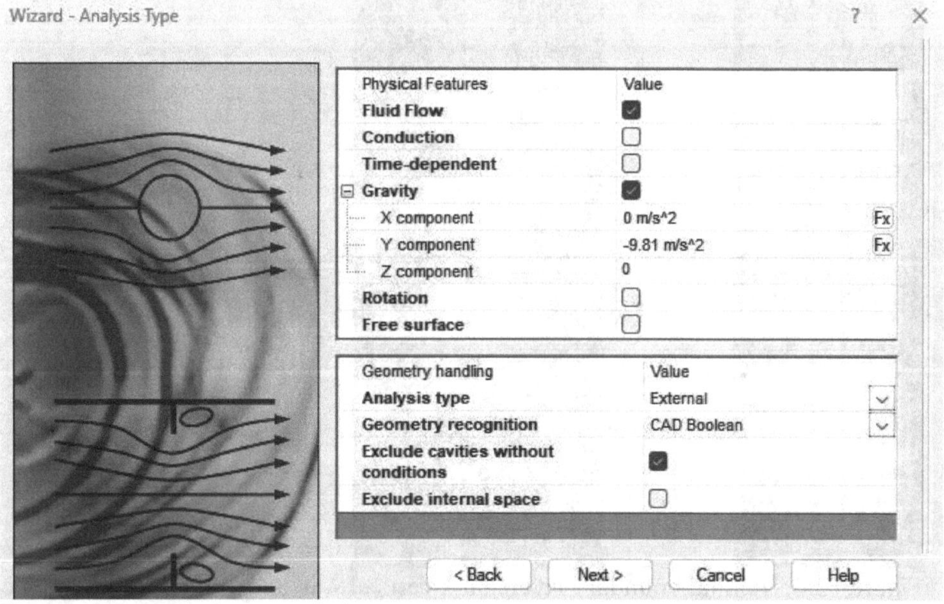

Figure 12.3 Analysis type window

4. Select **Air** from the **Gases** and add it as **Project Fluid**. Select **Laminar Only** from the **Flow Type** drop down menu. Click on the **Next >** button. Select **Wall temperature** from the **Default wall thermal condition Value** drop down menu. Set the **Wall temperature** to **296.2 K**. Click on the **Next >** button. Use default values for **Initial and Ambient Conditions**. Click on the **Finish** button. Select **Tools>>Flow Simulation>>Global Mesh**. Slide the **Level of initial mesh** to **7**.

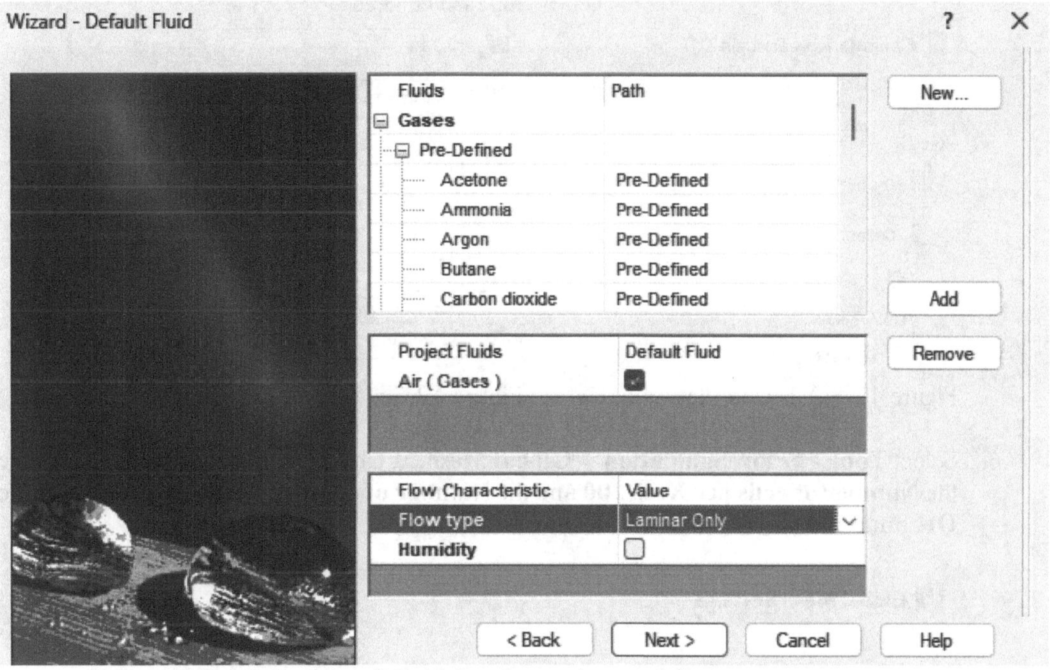

Figure 12.4a) Selection of fluid for the project and flow type

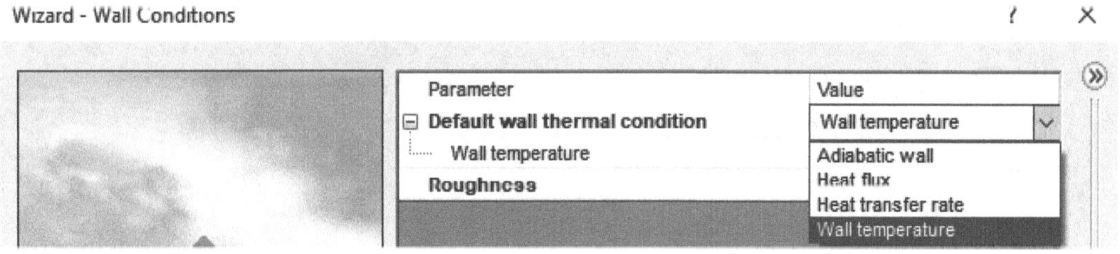

Figure 12.4b) Selection of wall temperature as thermal condition

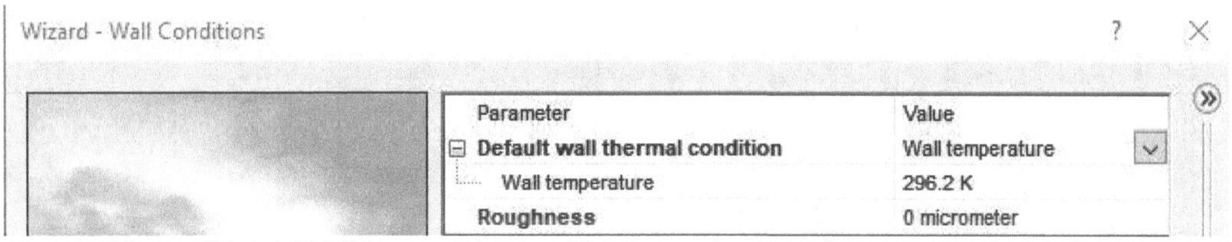

Figure 12.4c) Wall temperature setting

5. Select **Tools>>Flow Simulation>>Computational Domain…**. Click on the **2D simulation** button and select **XY plane**. Set the size of the computational domain as shown in Figure 12.5b). Click on the **OK** button to exit the **Computational Domain** window.

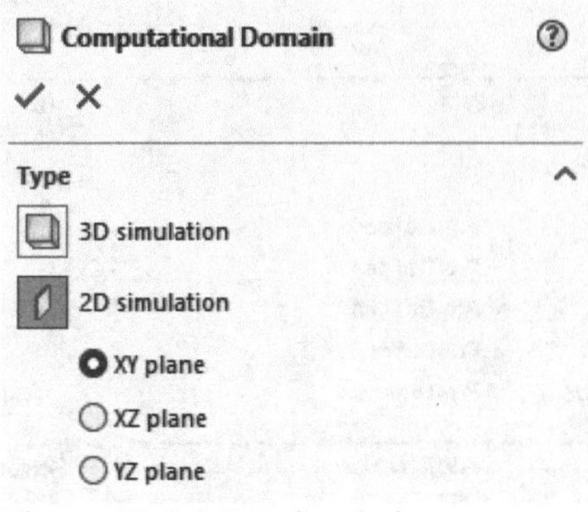

Figure 12.5a) 2D simulation

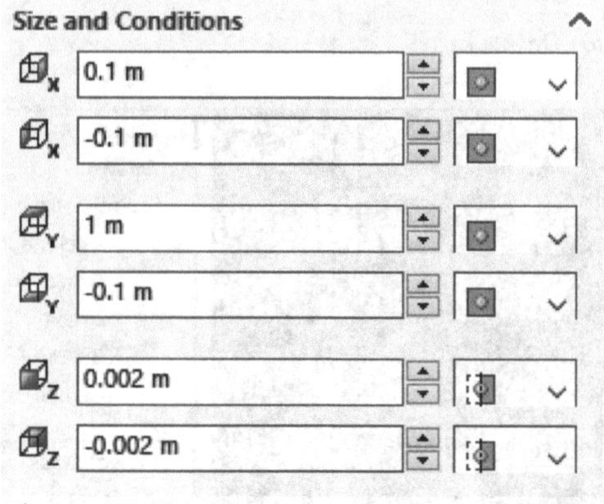

Figure 12.5b) Size of computational domain

6. Select **Tools>>Flow Simulation>>Global Mesh…**. Check the **Manual setting**. Change the **Number of cells per X:** to **200** and the **Number of cells per Y:** to **196**. Click on the **OK** button to exit the **Global Mesh** window.

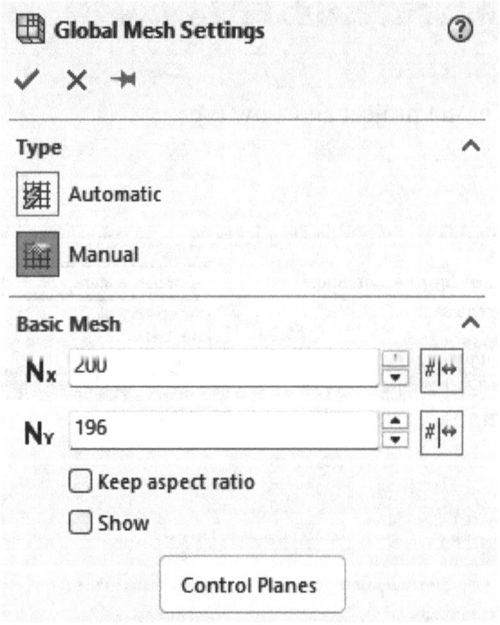

Figure 12.6 Number of cells in both directions

D. Goals and Calculation Controls

7. Open the **Input Data** folder and right click on **Goals** in the **Flow Simulation analysis tree** and select **Insert Global Goals….** Select global goals as shown in Figure 12.7b). Select **Tools>>Flow Simulation>>Calculation Control Options** from the menu. Select the **Refinement** tab. Set the **Value** to **level = 2** for **Global Domain**. Select **Goal Convergence** and **Iterations** as **Refinement strategy**. Click on [...] in the **Value** column for **Goals** and check the boxes for **GG Average Temperature (Fluid), GG Minimum Velocity (X)** and **GG Maximum Velocity (Y)**. Select the **Finishing** tab and uncheck the **Travels** box under **Finish Conditions**. Set the **Refinements** to **2**.

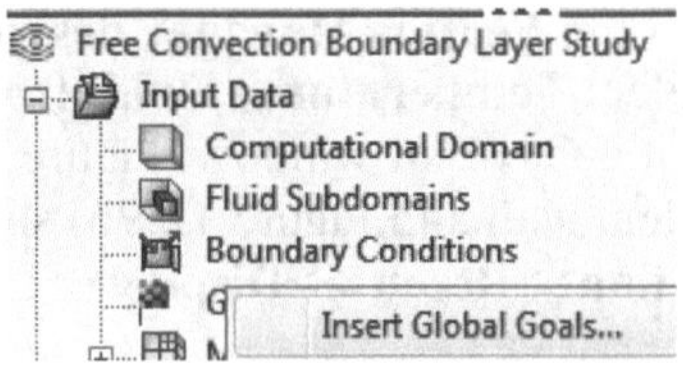

Figure 12.7a) Global goals

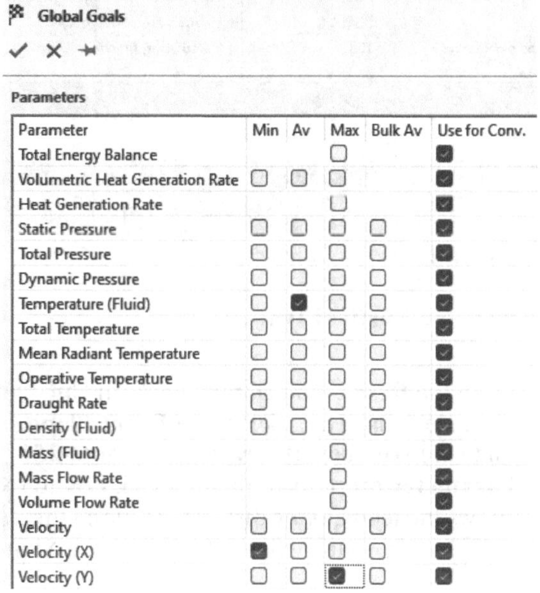

Figure 12.7b) Selection of temperature of fluid

E. Running Simulations for Vertical Plate

8. Select **Tools>>Flow Simulation>>Solve>>Run…** to start calculations. Click on the **Run** button in the **Run** window.

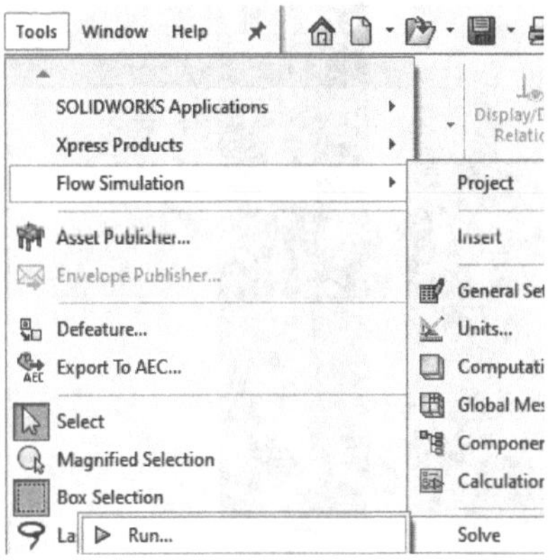

Figure 12.8a) Starting calculations

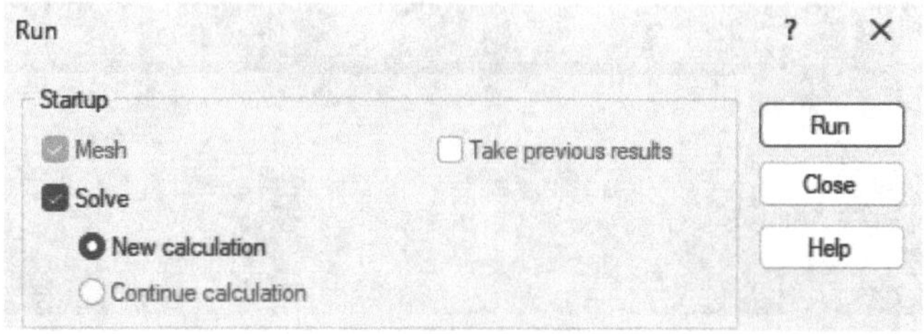

Figure 12.8b) Run window

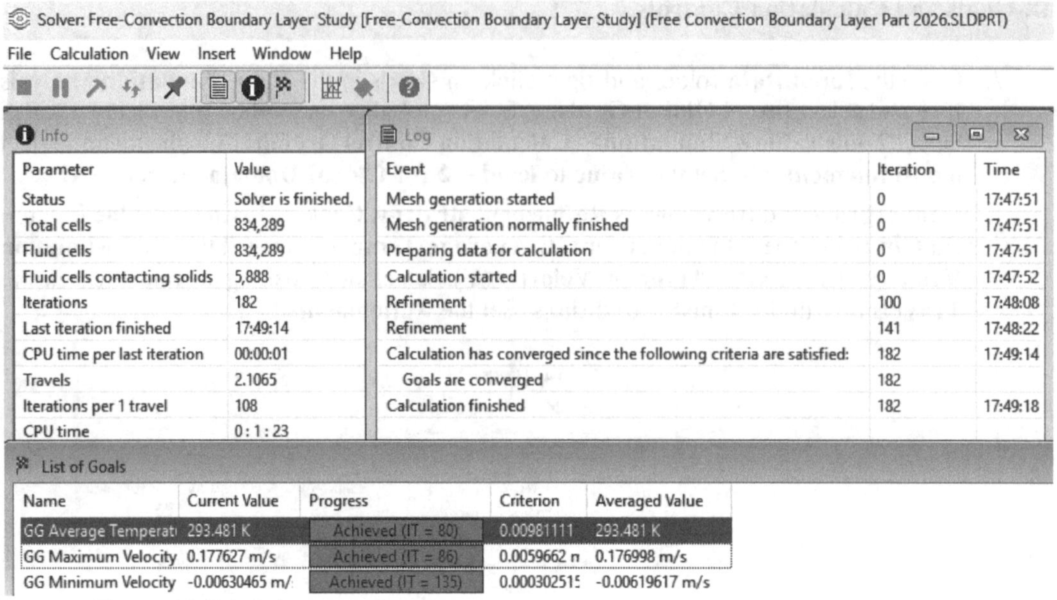

Figure 12.8c) Solver window

F. Cut-Plots for Vertical Wall

9. Open the **Results** folder, right click on **Cut Plots** in the **Flow Simulation analysis tree** and select **Insert….** Select the **Front Plane** from the **FeatureManager design tree.** Slide the **Number of Levels** slide bar to **255**. Select **Temperature (Fluid)** from the **Parameter** drop down menu. Click **OK** to exit the **Cut Plot** window. Figure 12.9a) shows the temperature distribution along the vertical wall and Figure 12.9b) shows the velocity distribution. Select **Tools>>Flow Simulation>>Results>>Display>>Lighting**.

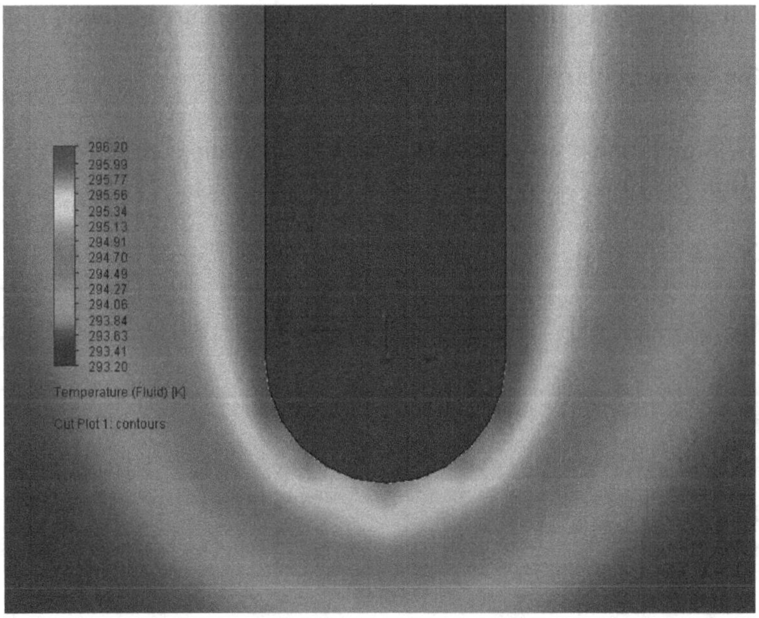

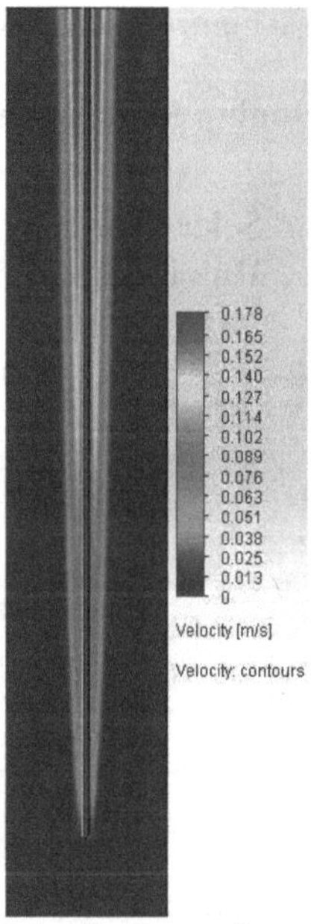

Figure 12.9a) Thermal boundary layer Figure 12.9b) Velocity boundary layer

G. Plotting Temperature and Velocity Profiles Using Templates

10. Place the files "**graph 12.10c)**" and "**graph 12.10d)**" on the desktop. Click on the **FeatureManager design tree**. Click on the sketch **y = 0.2, 0.4, 0.6, 0.8 m**. Click on the **Flow Simulation analysis tree** tab. Right click **XY Plot** and select **Insert...**. Check the **Temperature (Fluid)** box. Open the **Resolution** portion of the **XY Plot** window and slide the **Geometry Resolution** as far as it goes to the right. Click on the **Evenly Distribute Output Points** button and increase the number of points to **500**. Open the **Options** portion and check the **Display boundary layer** box. Select **Excel Workbook (*.xlsx)** from the drop-down menu. Click on the **Export to Excel** button. Click **OK** to exit the **XY Plot** window. An Excel file will open with a graph of the temperature in the boundary layer.

    Double click on **graph 12.10c)** file to open the file. Click on **Enable Editing** and **Enable Content** if you get a **Security Warning** that **Macros** have been disabled. If **Developer** is not available in the menu of the **Excel** file, you will need to do the following: Select **File>>Options** from the menu and click on the **Customize Ribbon** on the left-hand side. Check the **Developer** box on the right-hand side under **Main Tabs**. Click **OK** to exit the **Excel Options** window.

    Click on the **Developer** tab in the **Excel** menu for the **graph 12.10c)** file and select **Visual Basic** on the left-hand side to open the editor. Click on the plus sign next to **VBAProject (XY Plot 1.xlsx)** and click on the plus sign next to **Microsoft Excel Objects**. Right click on **Sheet2 (Plot Data)** and select **View Object**.

    Select **Macro** in the **Modules** folder under **VBAProject (graph 12.10c).xlsm)**. Select **Run>>Run Macro** from the menu of the **MVB for Applications** window. Click on the **Run** button in the **Macros** window. Figure 12.10c) will become available in **Excel** showing temperature ***T (K)*** versus wall normal coordinate ***x (m)***. Close the **XY Plot** window and the **graph 12.10c)** window in **Excel**. Exit the **XY Plot** window in **SOLIDWORKS Flow Simulation** and rename the inserted *xy*-plot in the **Flow Simulation analysis tree** to **Boundary Layer Temperature (Fluid) Profiles**.

    Repeat this step and select files "**graph 12.10d)**" and **Velocity (Y)** for the XY-plot, see Figure 12.10d). Exit the **XY Plot** window in **SOLIDWORKS Flow Simulation** and rename the inserted *xy*-plot in the **Flow Simulation analysis tree** to **Boundary Layer Velocity (Y) Profiles**.

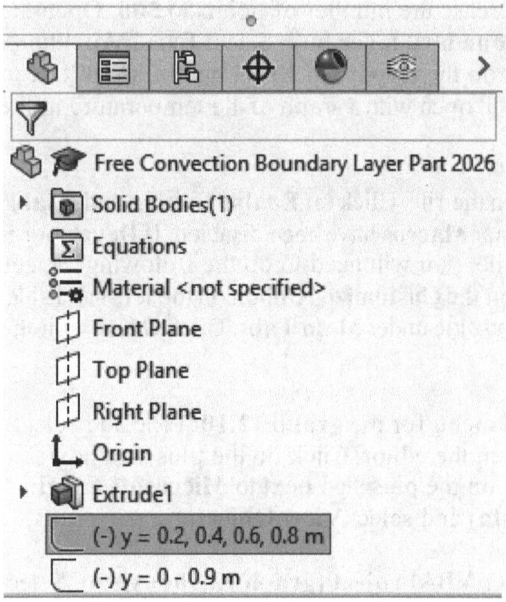

Figure 12.10a) Selecting the sketch

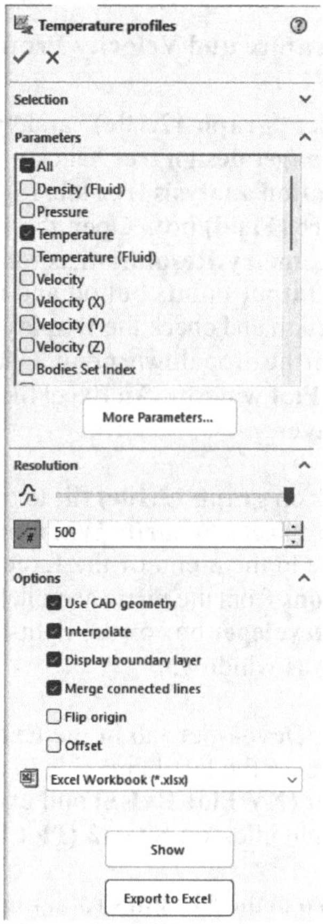

Figure 12.10b) Settings for the XY plot

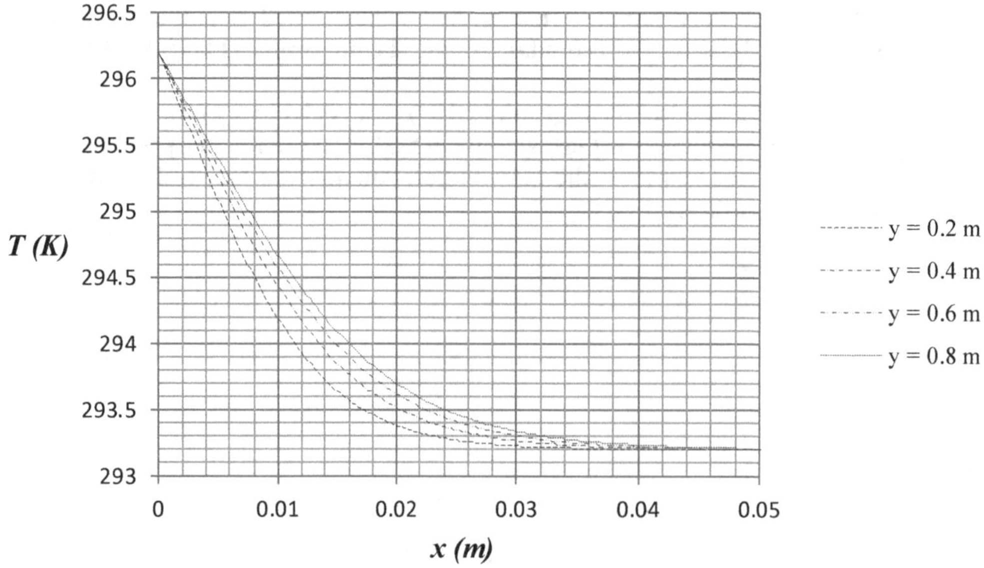

Figure 12.10c) Boundary layer temperature profiles on a vertical heated flat plate

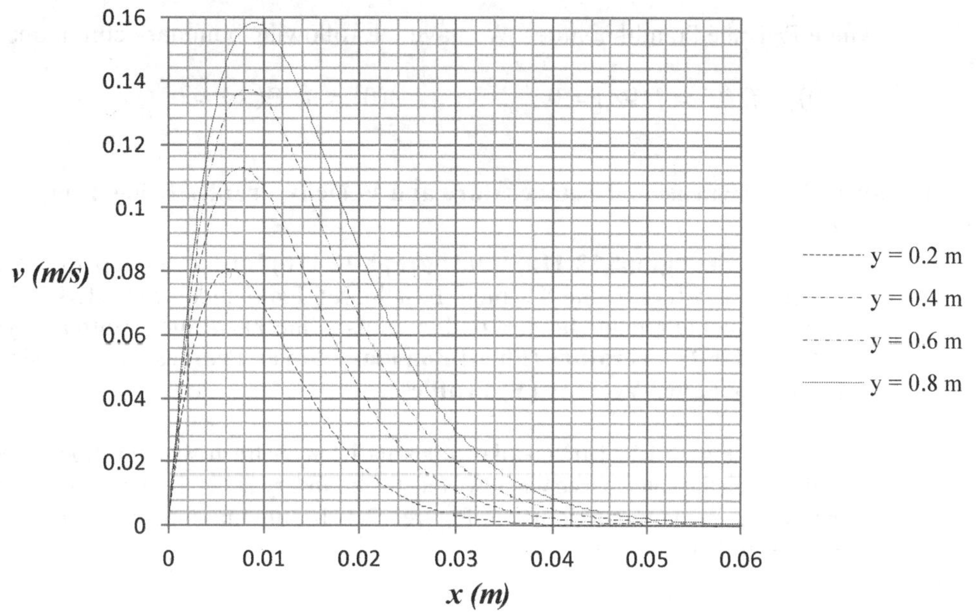

Figure 12.10d) Boundary layer velocity profiles on a vertical heated flat plate.

H. Theory

We now want to compare the temperature and velocity profiles with the theoretical profiles. First, we have to normalize the temperature T in the boundary layer

$$\Theta = \frac{T - T_\infty}{T_w - T_\infty} \tag{12.1}$$

where T_∞ is the ambient temperature and T_w is the wall temperature. We can also transform the wall normal coordinate into the similarity coordinate for comparison with the theoretical profile. The similarity coordinate is described by

$$\eta = \frac{x}{y} Ra^{1/4} \qquad Ra = \frac{\beta g (T_w - T_\infty) y^3}{\alpha v} \tag{12.2}$$

where Ra is the Rayleigh number, x is the wall normal coordinate, y is the coordinate along the vertical wall, g is acceleration due to gravity, α is the thermal diffusivity, β is the coefficient of volume expansion and v is the kinematic viscosity of the fluid. The fluid properties are evaluated at the film temperature $T_f = (T_w + T_\infty)/2$. The theoretical velocity component v in the y-direction is given by

$$v = -\frac{\alpha}{y} Ra^{1/2} f' \tag{12.3}$$

and there are two nonlinear coupled differential equations for f and Θ

$$4\mathrm{Pr}(f''' - \Theta) - 3ff'' + 2f'^2 = 0 \qquad 4\Theta'' - 3\Theta' f = 0 \qquad (12.4)$$

, where *Pr* is the Prandtl number. We have the following boundary conditions

$$f(0) = f'(0) = f'(\infty) = 0 \qquad \Theta(0) = 1,\ \Theta(\infty) = 0 \qquad (12.5)$$

I. Plotting Non-Dimensional Temperature and Velocity Profiles Using Templates

Place the files **"graph 12.11a)" and "graph 12.11b)"** on the desktop. Repeat step **10** and select the new files for the XY-plots. Exit the **XY Plot** window in **SOLIDWORKS Flow Simulation** and rename the inserted *xy*-plots in the **Flow Simulation analysis tree** to **Self-Similar Temperature (Fluid) Boundary Layer Profiles** and **Self-Similar Boundary Layer Velocity (Y) Profiles.**

We see in Figure 12.11a) that all profiles at different streamwise positions approximately collapse on the same curve when we use the boundary layer similarity coordinate. For the theoretical velocity maximum in Figure 12.11b), the maximum is slightly lower than Flow Simulation results.

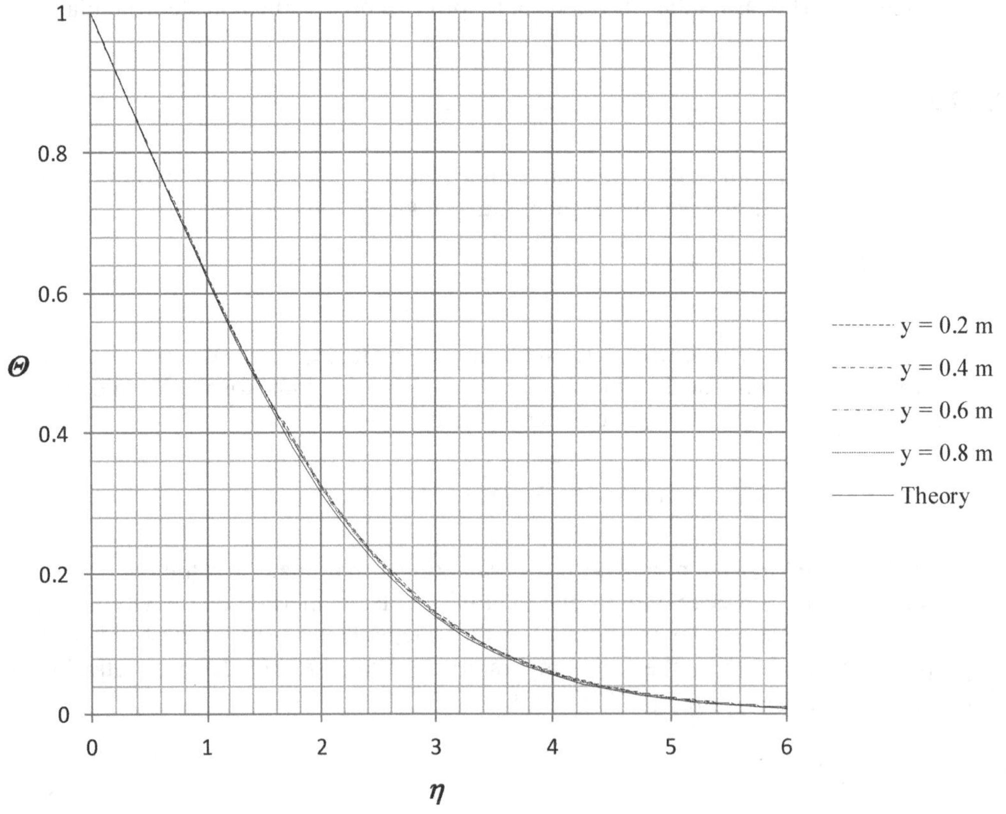

Figure 12.11a) Temperature profiles in comparison with the theoretical profile (full line)

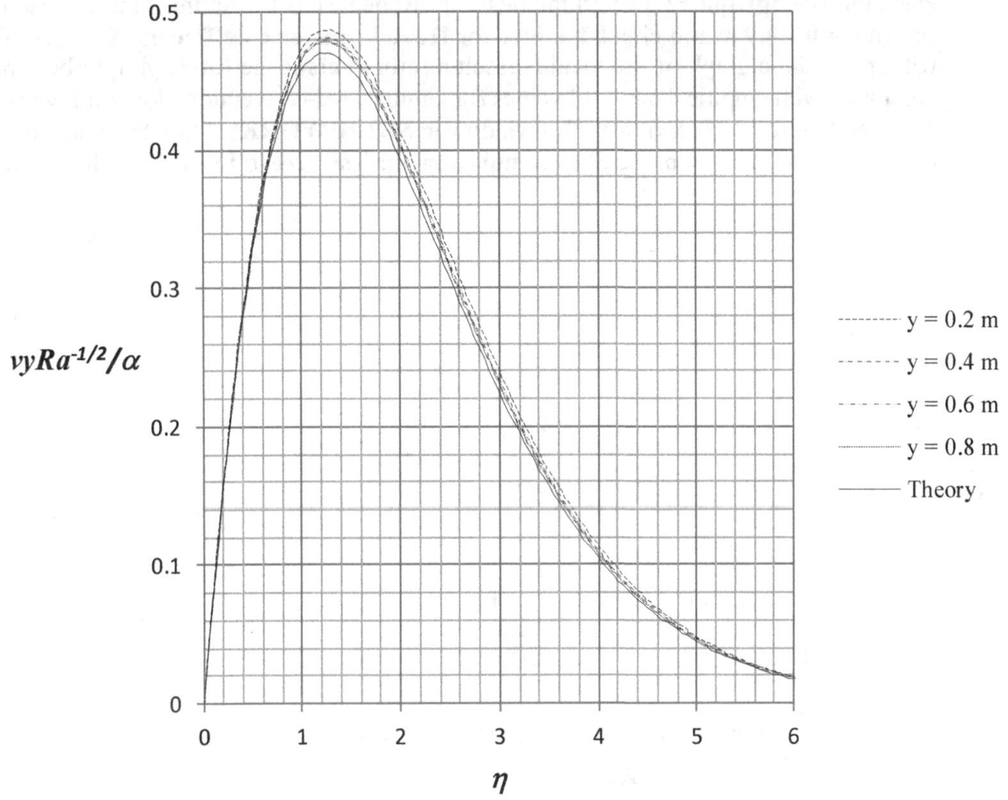

Figure 12.11b) Velocity profiles in comparison with the theoretical profile (full line)

We now want to study how the local Nusselt number varies along the vertical plate. It is defined as the local convection coefficient h_y times the vertical coordinate y divided by the thermal conductivity k:

$$Nu_y = \frac{h_y y}{k} \tag{12.6}$$

A curve-fit formula for local Nusselt number for laminar free-convection flow on a vertical flat wall is given by Churchill and Usagi

$$Nu_y = \frac{0.503Ra^{1/4}}{[1+\left(\frac{0.492}{\text{Pr}}\right)^{\frac{9}{16}}]^{4/9}} \qquad 10^5 < Ra < 10^9 \tag{12.7}$$

The overall Nusselt number for free-convection flow on a vertical plate is given by Churchill and Chu

$$Nu_L^{1/2} = 0.825 + \frac{0.387Ra_L^{1/6}}{[1+\left(\frac{0.492}{\text{Pr}}\right)^{\frac{9}{16}}]^{8/27}} \qquad Ra_L \leq 10^{12} \tag{12.8}$$

J. Plotting Local Nusselt Number Using Templates

Place the file **"graph 12.12"** on the desktop. Repeat step **10** but this time choose the sketch **y = 0 – 0.9 m** and check the box for **Heat Transfer Coefficient**. An Excel file will open with a graph of the local Nusselt number versus the Rayleigh number and compared with empirical curve-fit values for laminar free-convection flow on a vertical wall, see Figure 12.12. Exit **XY Plot** window in **SOLIDWORKS Flow Simulation** and rename inserted *xy*-plot in the **Flow Simulation analysis tree** to **Local Nusselt Number**.

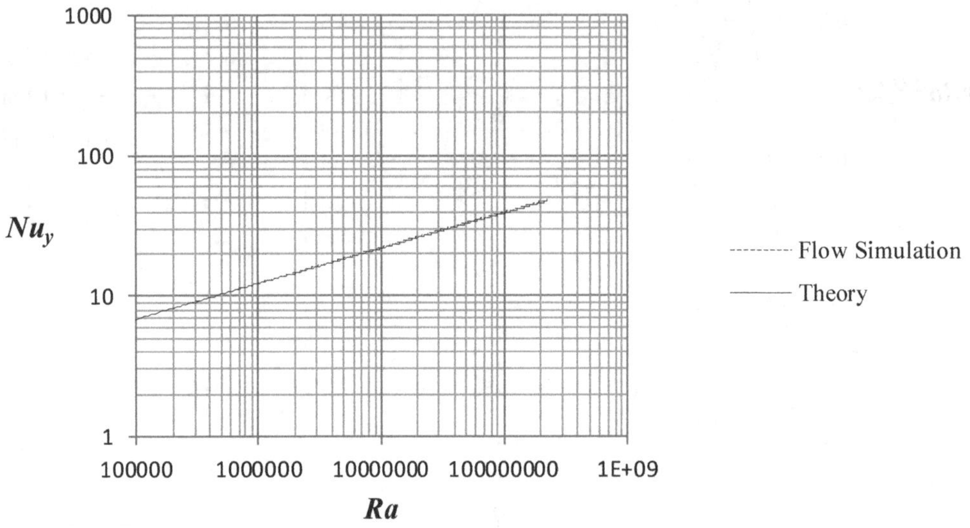

Figure 12.12 Local Nusselt number as a function of the Rayleigh number

K. Creating SOLIDWORKS Part for Free Convection from Horizontal Cylinder

11. Select **File>>New...** from the SOLIDWORKS menu. Select a new **Part** and click on the **OK** button. Select **Tools>>Options...** from the SOLIDWORKS menu. Click on the Document Properties tab and select **Units**. Select **MMGS** as your **Unit system**. Click on the **Front Plane** in the **FeatureManager design tree** to select the plane of the sketch. Select Front view from the **View Orientation** drop down menu in the graphics window. Select the **Circle** sketch tool from **Tools>>Sketch Entities** in the SOLIDWORKS menu.

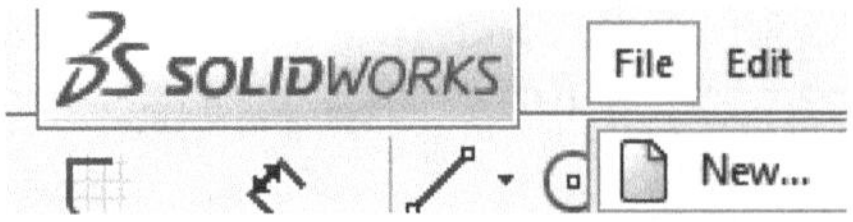

Figure 12.13a) SOLIDWORKS document

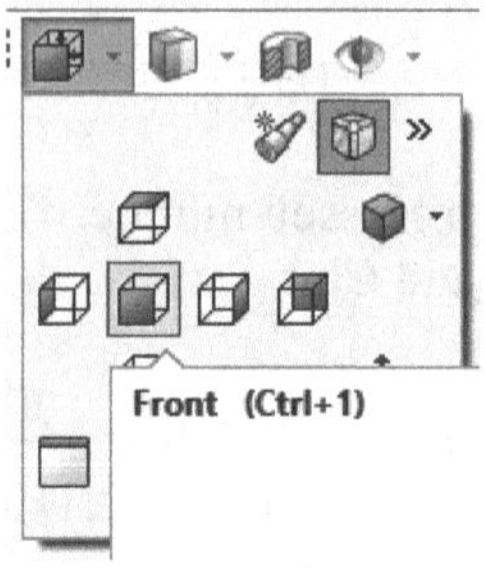

Figure 12.13b) Front view orientation

12. Draw a circle from the origin with a radius of **25.00 mm**. Close the **Circle** dialog box. Select **Insert>>Boss/Base>>Extrude...** from the SOLIDWORKS menu. Check the **Direction 2** box and exit the **Extrude** dialog box. Select **File>>Save As** and enter the name **Free Convection Horizontal Cylinder 2026** as the name for the SOLIDWORKS part.

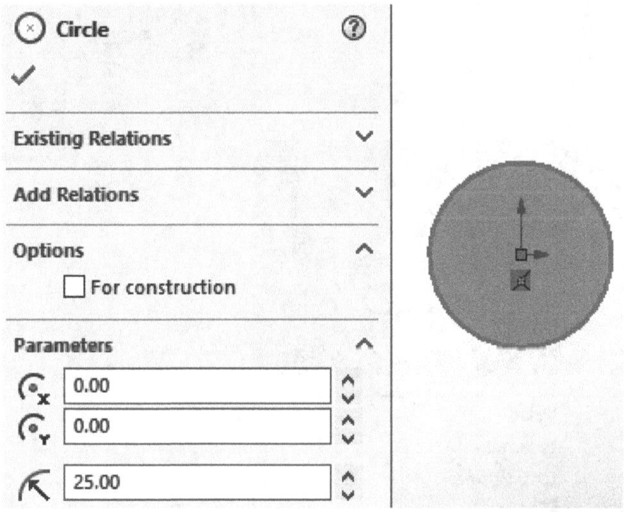

Figure 12.14 Sketch of a circle

L. Flow Simulation Project for Free Convection from Horizontal Cylinder

13. We create a project by selecting **Tools>>Flow Simulation>>Project>>Wizard...** from the menu. Create a new project and enter **Free Convection from a Horizontal Cylinder** as configuration name. Push the **Next>** button. We choose the **SI (m-kg-s)** unit system and click on the **Next>** button again.

    In the next step we select **External** as analysis type, check the boxes for **Time-dependent** flow and **Gravity**. Enter -9.81 m/s^2 for the **Gravity Y** component. Click on the **Next>** button. The **Default Fluid Wizard** will now appear. We are going to add **Air** as the **Project Fluid**. Start by clicking on the plus sign next to the **Gases** in the **Fluids** column. Scroll down the different gases and select **Air**. Next, click on the **Add** button so that **Air** will appear as the **Default Fluid**. Click on the **Next>** button.

    The next part of the wizard is about **Wall Conditions**. We will use an **Adiabatic wall** for the cylinder and use zero surface roughness. Next, we get the **Initial and Ambient Conditions** in the Wizard. Click on the **Finish** button. Select **Tools>>Flow Simulation>>Global Mesh**. Slide the **Level of initial mesh** to 7.

Figure 12.15a) Entering configuration name for project

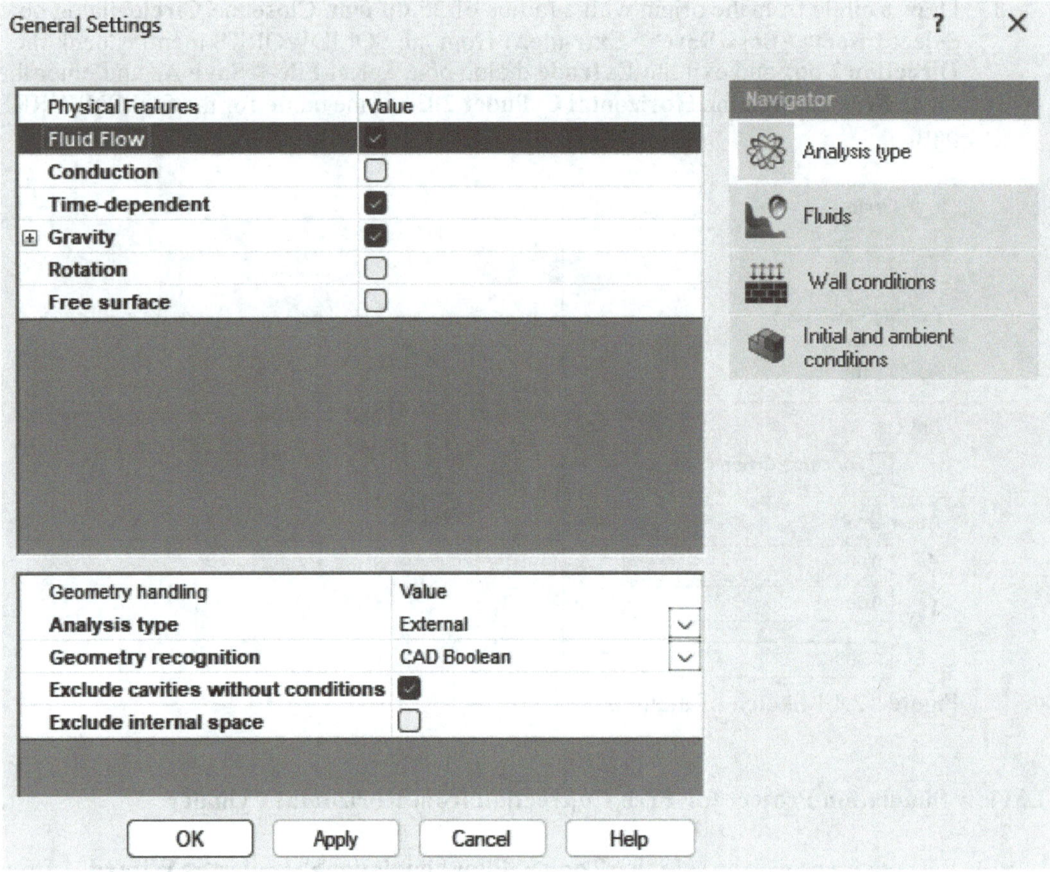

Figure 12.15b) Adding time-dependent flow and gravity to the project

M. Global Goal and 2D Flow for Free Convection from Horizontal Cylinder

14. We create a global goal for the project by selecting **Tools>>Flow Simulation>>Insert>>Global Goals…** from the SOLIDWORKS menu and check the box for **Max Heat Transfer Rate (Convective)**. Exit the global goals.

    Select **Tools>>Flow Simulation>>Computational Domain…** from the SOLIDWORKS menu. Select **2D Simulation** and **XY plane**, see Figure 12.16. Set the **Y max** to **1 m**. Click on the **OK** button to exit the **Computational Domain** window.

    Select **Tools>>Flow Simulation>>Global Mesh…** from the SOLIDWORKS menu. Check the **Manual settings**. Set the **Number of cells per X:** to **24** and the **Number of cells per Y:** to **20**. Click on the **OK** button.

    Select **Tools>>Flow Simulation>>Calculation Control Options…** from the SOLIDWORKS menu. Select the **Finishing** tab and set **Calculation time** to **45 s**. Click on the **OK** button.

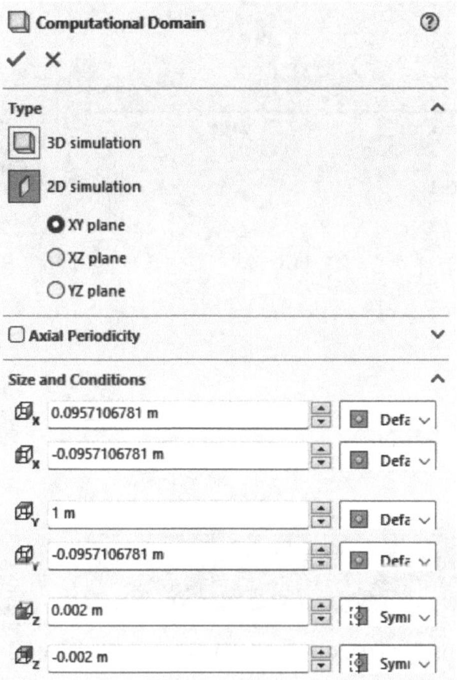

Figure 12.16 Computational domain for free convection from a horizontal cylinder

N. Tabular Saving for Free Convection from Horizontal Cylinder

15. Select **Tools>>Flow Simulation>>Calculation Control Options...** from the SOLIDWORKS menu. Select the **Saving** tab and check box next to **Periodic** under **Full Results**. Set the **Start Value** to iteration number **100** and the **Period Value** to **10**, see Figure 12.17a). Select the Finishing tab and use the settings as shown in Figure 12.17b). Click on the **OK** buttons to exit the **Calculation Control Options** windows.

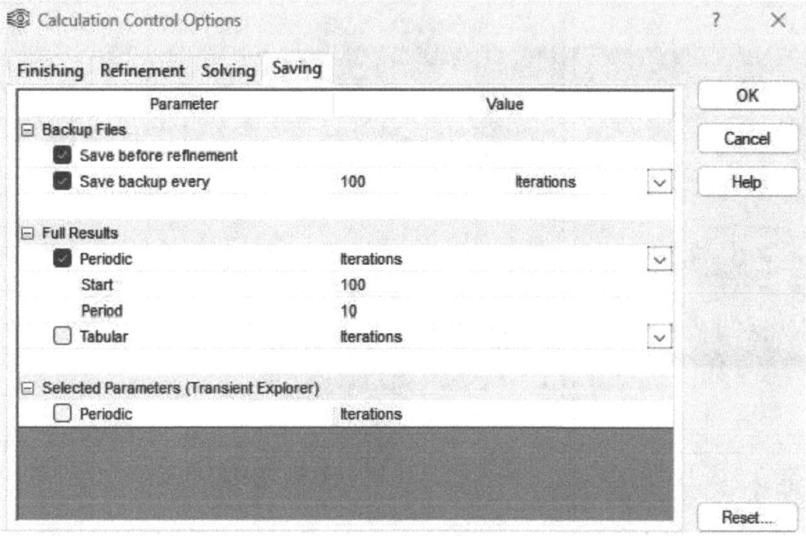

Figure 12.17a) Saving control options for free convection from a horizontal cylinder

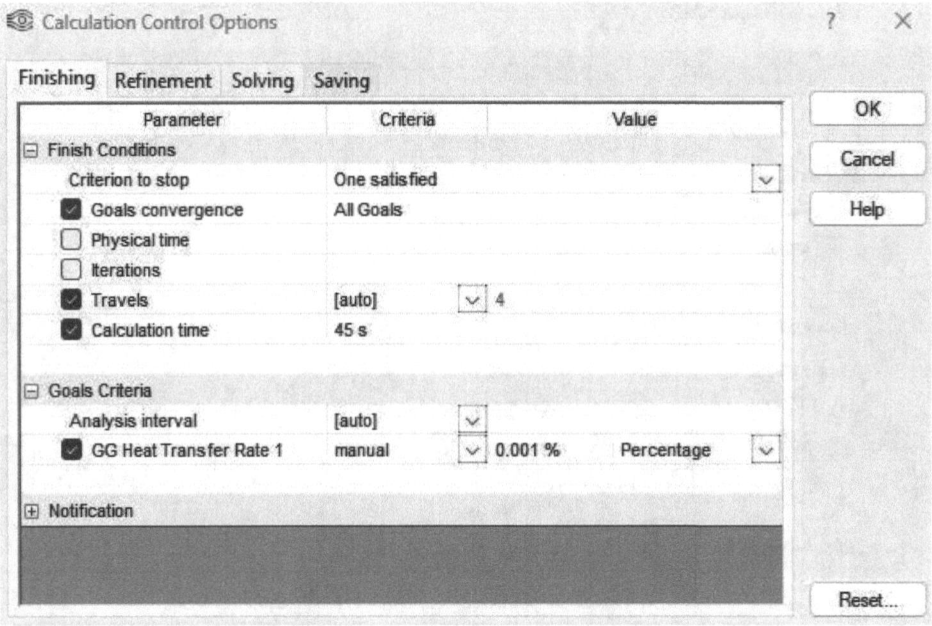

Figure 12.17b) Finishing control options for free convection from a horizontal cylinder

O. Boundary Condition for Free Convection from Horizontal Cylinder

16. Select **Isometric** view from the **View Orientation** drop down menu in the graphics window. Select **Tools>>Flow Simulation>>Insert>>Boundary Condition...** from the SOLIDWORKS menu. Select the cylindrical surface of the cylinder. Click on **Wall** button in the **Type** portion of the **Boundary Condition** window and select **Real Wall**. Adjust the **Wall Temperature** to **393.2 K** by clicking on the button and entering the numerical value in the **Wall Parameters** window. Click OK to exit the **Boundary Condition** window.

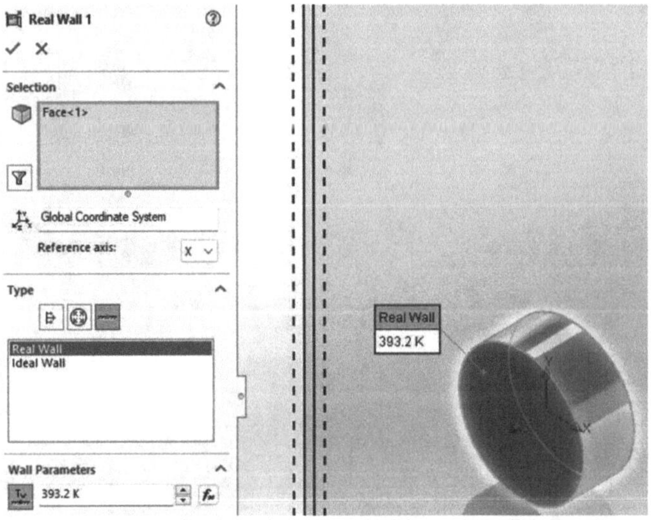

Figure 12.18 Cylindrical surface with real wall boundary condition at 393.2 K

P. Simulations for Free Convection from Horizontal Cylinder

17. Choose **Tools>>Flow Simulation>>Solve>>Run....** Click on the **Run** button in the window that appears. Click on the goals flag to **Insert Goals Table** in the **Solver** window. Click on **Insert Goals Plot** in the **Solver** window. Click on the **GG Heat Transfer Rate 1** check box followed by the OK button. Right click in the goals plot. Select **Physical time** from **X-axis units**. Slide the **Plot length** to **3** or enter 3 for Length Scale. In the Numerical settings, set Manual min to 0.4 and Manual max to 0.7. Click on the **OK** button.

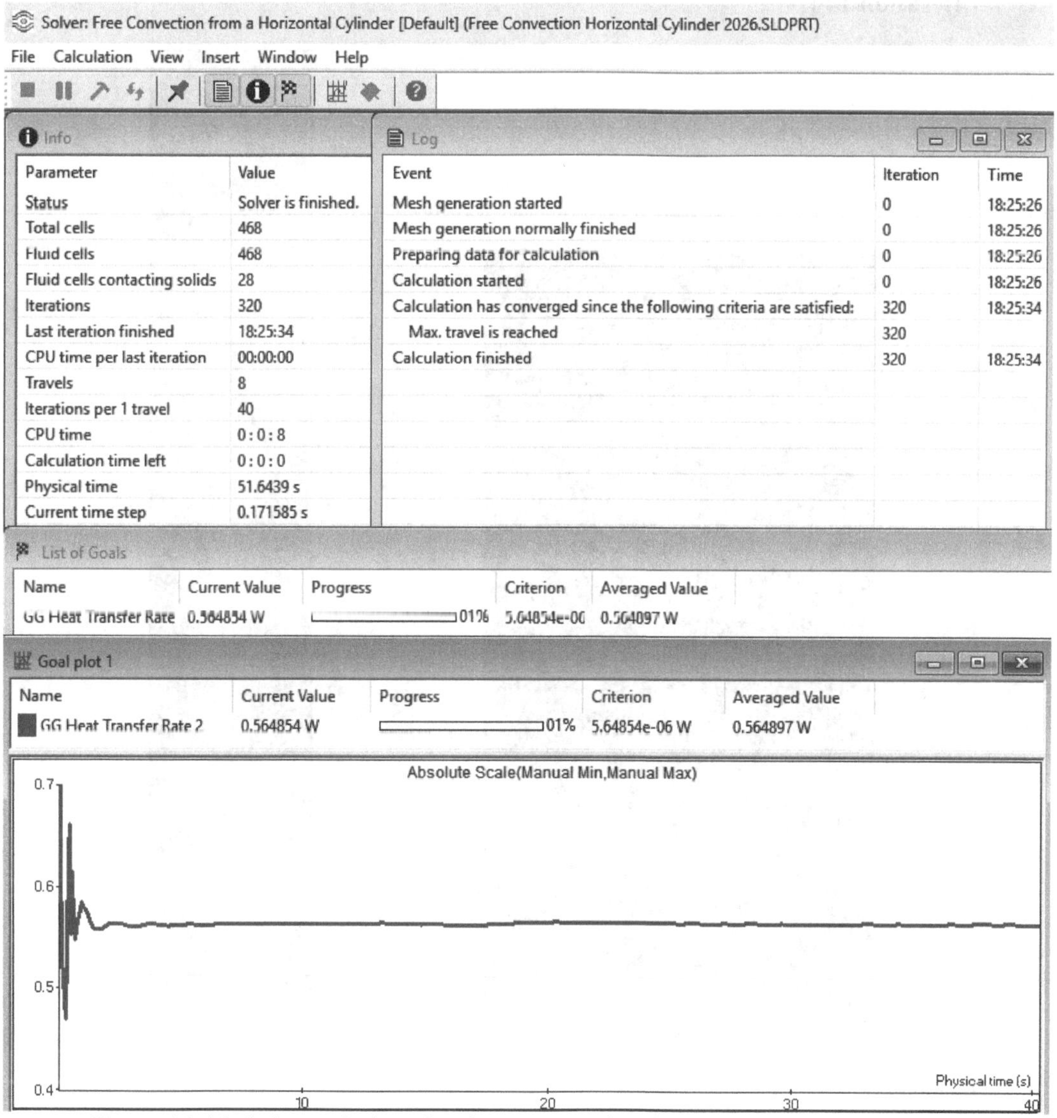

Figure 12.19 Solver window for free convection from a horizontal cylinder

Q. Cut-Plots for Free Convection from Horizontal Cylinder

18. Select **Tools>>Flow Simulation>>Results>>Load from File…** from the SOLIDWORKS menu. Open the file **r_000140.fld**. Open the **Results** folder and right click on **Cut Plots** in the **Flow Simulation analysis tree** and select **Insert…** and select **Temperature (Fluid)** from the **Contours** section. Slide the **Number of Levels** to **255**. Exit the cut plot dialog. Select front view from the view orientation drop down menu in the graphics window. Change the name of Cut Plot 1 to **Temperature (Fluid) at Iteration 140**. Select **Tools>>Flow Simulation>>Results>>Display>>Lighting**. Insert another cut plot and plot the velocity. Change the name of the cut plot to **Velocity at Iteration 140**.

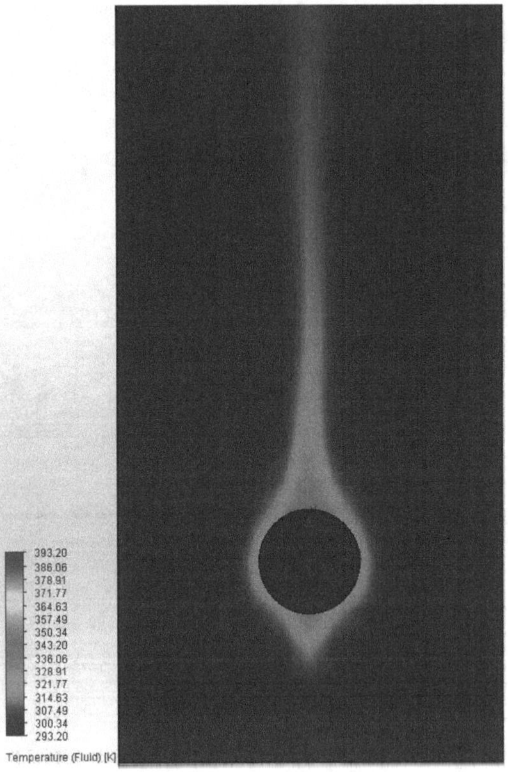

Figure 12.20a) Temperature field

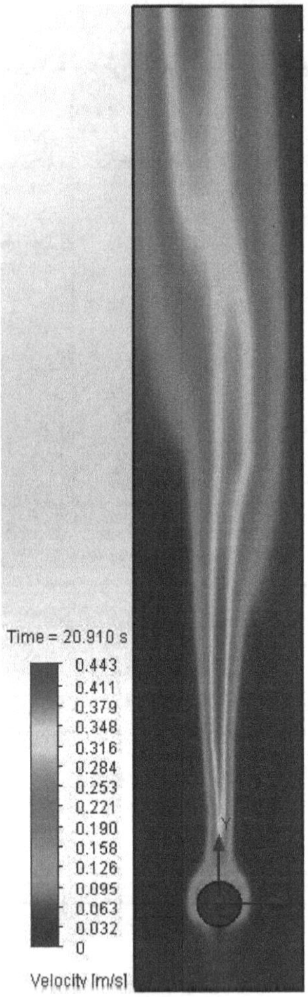

Figure 12.20b) Velocity field

R. References

1. Bejan A., Convection Heat Transfer, 3rd Edition, Wiley, 2004.
2. Sparrow E.M., Husar R.B. and Goldstein R.J., Observations and other characteristics of thermals. *J. Fluid Mech.,* **42**, 465 – 470, 1970.
3. White F. M., Viscous Fluid Flow, 2nd Edition, McGraw-Hill, 1991.

S. Exercises

12.1 Use Flow Simulation to study two-dimensional free-convection interaction between four heated horizontal cylinders arranged in a staggered grid, see figure E1. Make cut plots and animations of the temperature and velocity fields from the cylinders. Use a cylinder diameter of 20 mm and set the surface temperature of each cylinder to 393.2 K. Use air as the fluid. Set the center distance between the horizontal cylinders to H = 30 mm and the center distance between the vertical cylinders V = 60 mm.

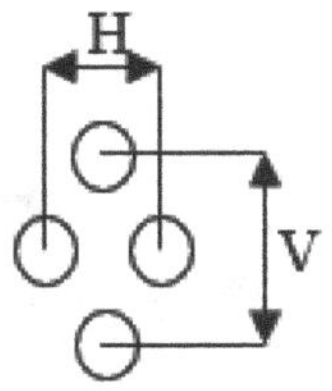

Figure E.1 Geometry for staggered grid of four horizontal cylinders

12.2 Use Flow Simulation to study free-convection on a vertical cylinder in air with a diameter of 20 mm and a length of 1 m. Set the surface temperature to 300 K and determine temperature and velocity profiles at different locations along cylinder.

12.3 Use Flow Simulation to study two-dimensional, time-dependent free-convection from a horizontal flat plate, use a 1 m wide plate but choose your own thickness of the plate. Set the temperature and roughness of the plate to different values and make cut plots and animations of the temperature and velocity fields in water to see if you can get Flow Simulation to generate intermittent rise of thermals as shown in experiments by Sparrow at al.[2]

Notes:

CHAPTER 13. SWIRLING FLOW IN A CLOSED CYLINDRICAL CONTAINER

A. Objectives

- Creating the SOLIDWORKS models needed for Flow Simulations
- Setting up Flow Simulation projects for internal flows
- Creating lids for boundary conditions and setting up boundary conditions
- Use of gravity as a physical feature and running the calculations
- Using cut plots and flow trajectories to visualize the resulting flow field

B. Problem Description

In this chapter we will study the swirling flow in a cylindrical container with a rotating lid. We will start by looking closer at the flow caused by a rotating top lid and we will use water as the fluid.

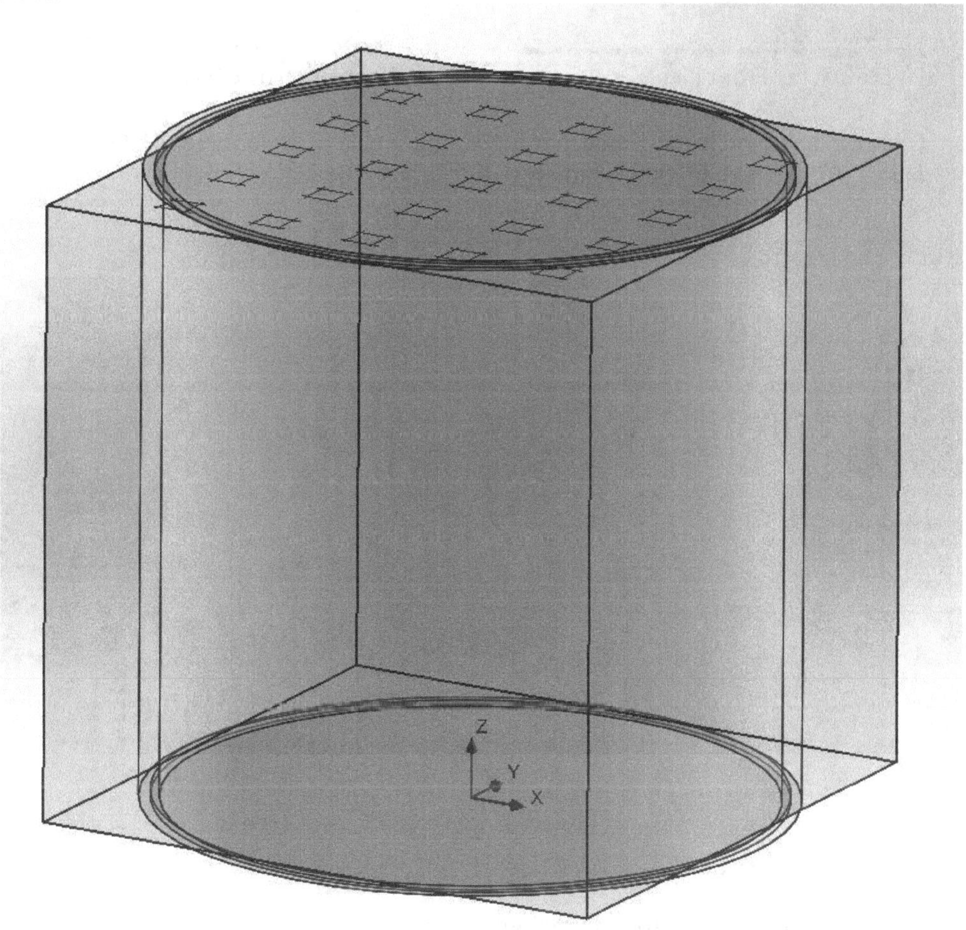

C. Modeling SOLIDWORKS Part

1. Start SOLIDWORKS and create a New Part. Select **Tools>>Options…** from the SOLIDWORKS menu. Click on the Document Properties tab and select **Units**. Select **MMGS** as your **Unit system**. Select the **Front** view from the **View Orientation** drop down menu in the graphics window and click on the **Front Plane** in the **FeatureManager design tree**. Next, select the **Basic Modeling Tools** tab and the **Circle** sketch tool.

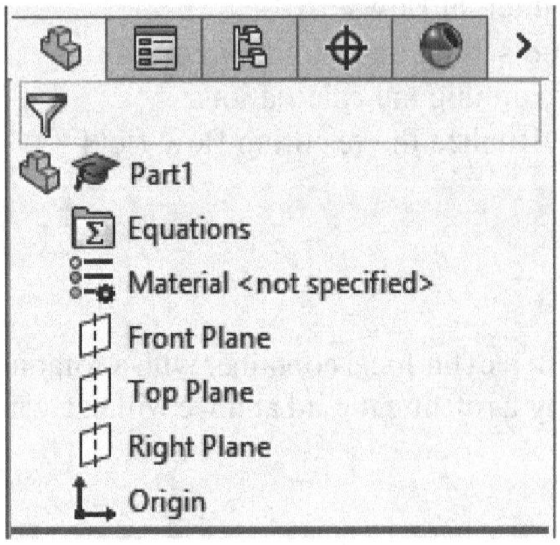

Figure 13.1a) Front Plane

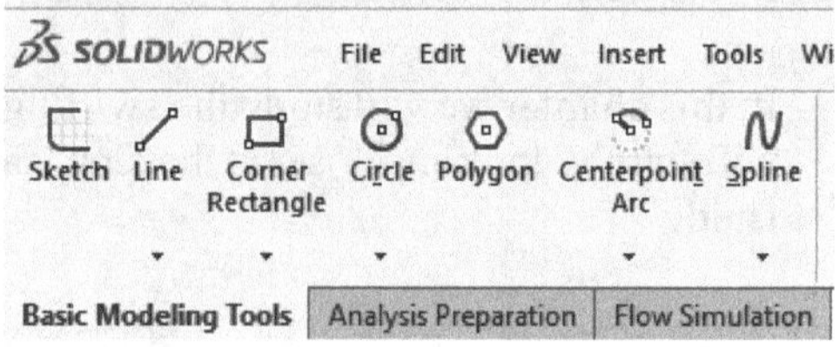

Figure 13.1b) **Circle** sketch tool

2. Click on the origin in the graphics window and create a circle. Enter **47.50 mm** for the radius of the circle in the **Parameters** box. Close the dialog box.

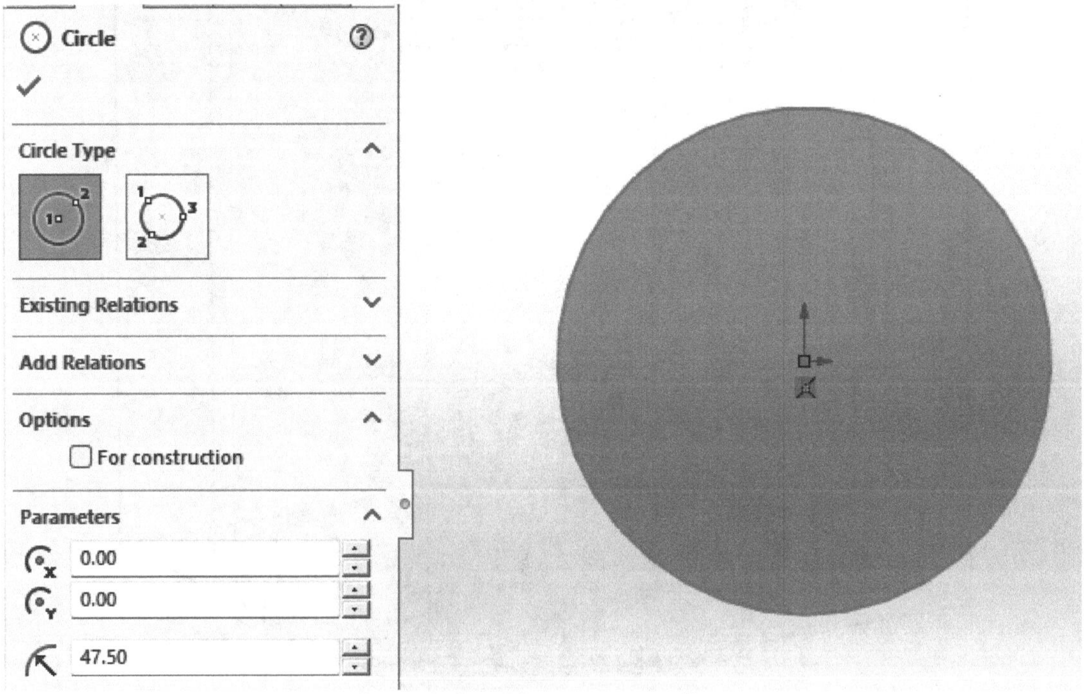

Figure 13.2 Parameters for a circle with 47.5 mm radius

3. Next, make an extrusion by selecting the **Analysis Preparation** tab and **Extruded Boss/Base**. Enter **95 mm** in **Direction 1** and check the **Thin Feature**. Enter **3.175 mm** for the thickness. Close the dialog box. Save the part with the name **Swirling Flow in Closed Cylindrical Container 2026**. Select the FeatureManager Design Tree and right click on **Material** and select **Edit Material**. Select **Acrylic (Medium-high impact)** from the **Plastics** folder. Click on the **Apply** button and Close the window.

Figure 13.3a) Entering data

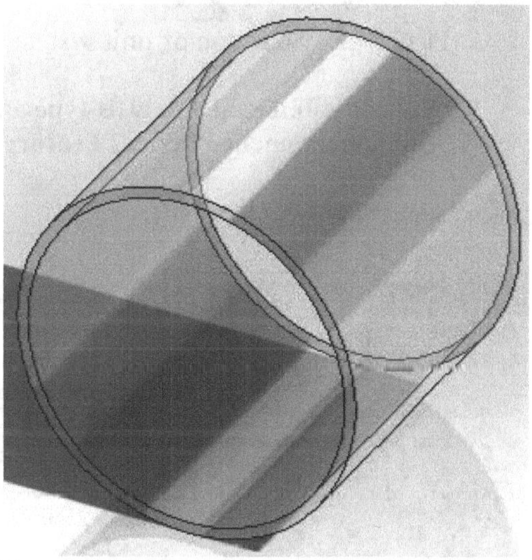
Figure 13.3b) Extruded acrylic cylinder

D. Flow Simulation Project

4. If Flow Simulation is not available in the SOLIDWORKS menu, select **Tools>>Add Ins...** and check the corresponding **SOLIDWORKS Flow Simulation** box. Start the **Flow Simulation Wizard** by selecting **Tools>>Flow Simulation>>Project>>Wizard...** from the SOLIDWORKS menu.

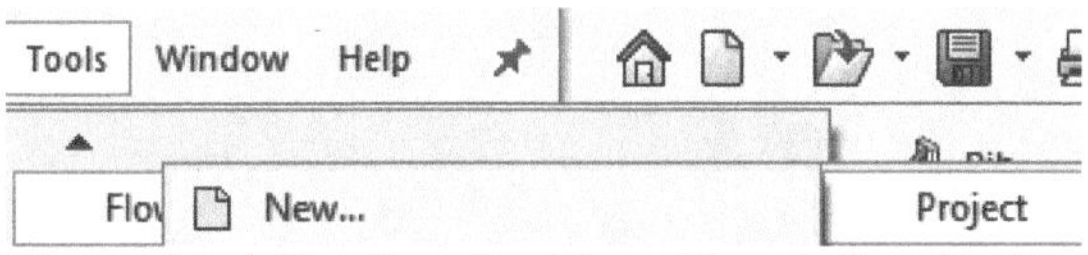

Figure 13.4 Starting the Flow Simulation Project Wizard

5. Create a new project with the following name: **Swirling Flow**. Click on Next >.

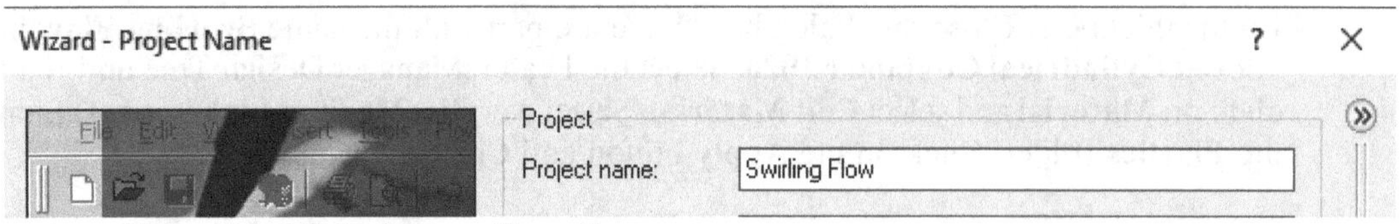

Figure 13.5 Entering configuration name

6. Select the SI unit system

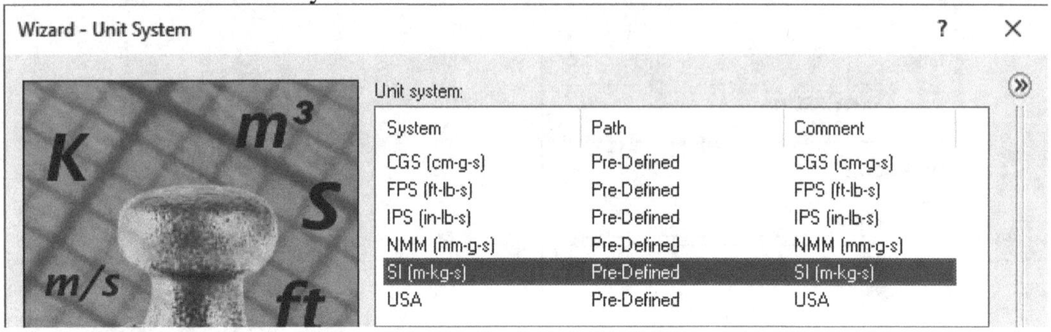

Figure 13.6 Selection of unit system

7. Select the **Internal Analysis type** and enter **-9.81 m/s^2** as **Gravity** for the **Z component** under **Physical Features**.

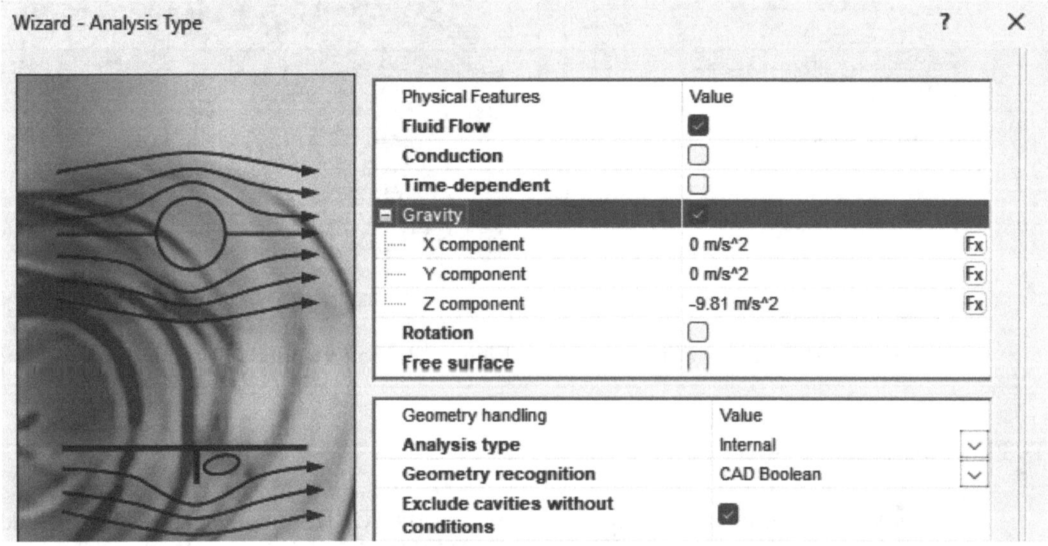

Figure 13.7 Enter gravity as physical feature

8. Add **Water** as the default **Project Fluid** by selection from **Liquids**. Choose default values for **Wall Conditions** and **Initial Conditions**. Finish the Wizard. Answer **Yes** to the question whether you want to open the Create Lids tool.

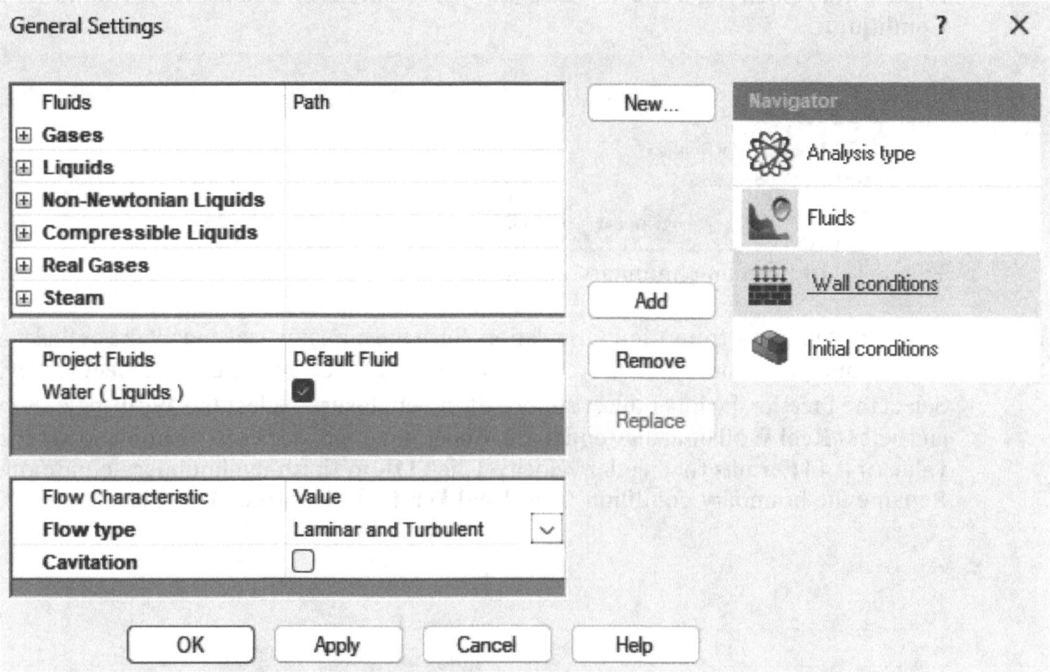

Figure 13.8 Adding water as the default fluid

E. Modeling Lids

9. Next, we will add a lid at both ends of the extrusion to create an enclosure. Select one of the two plane surfaces of the extrusion and set the thickness of the lid to **1.00 mm**. Click **OK** and answer **Yes** to the questions whether you want to reset the computational domain, mesh setting, and open the Create Lids tool that appears in the graphics window. Repeat this step for the other plane surface.

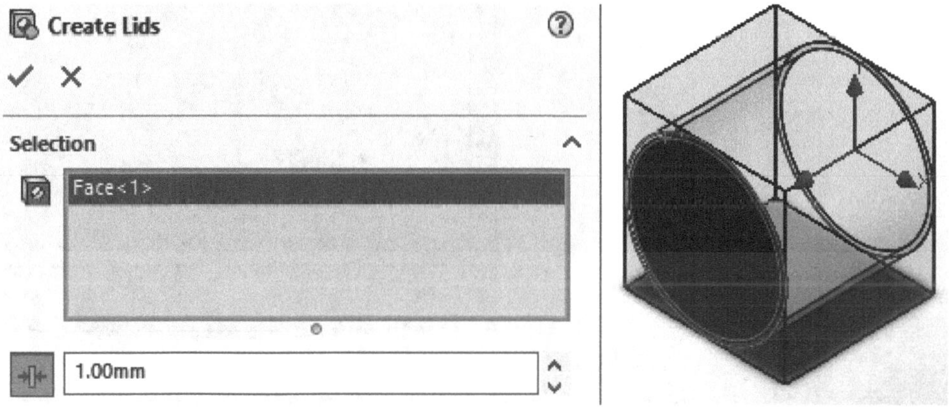

Figure 13.9 Selecting the face and thickness of the lid

F. Boundary Conditions

10. Click on the **Flow Simulation analysis tree** tab and click on the plus sign next to the **Input Data** folder. Right click on **Boundary Conditions** and select **Insert Boundary Condition...**

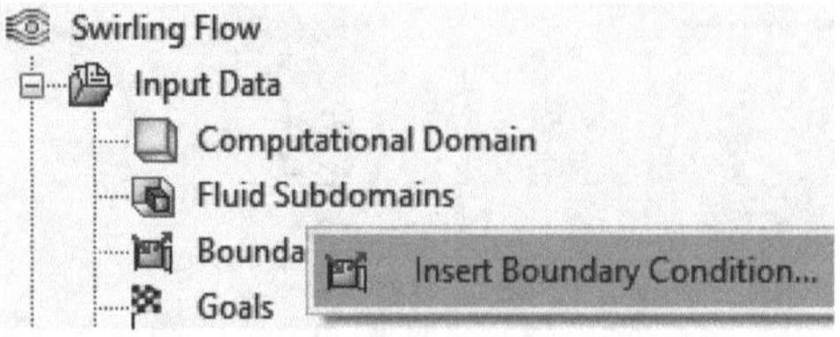

Figure 13.10 Selecting boundary conditions.

11. Select Bottom view from View Orientation. Push the mouse wheel and tilt the cylinder a little bit and position the cursor over the top lid, right-click and click on **Select Other**. Select the face for the inner upper surface of the enclosure. Select the **Wall** button and select **Real Wall** boundary condition. Check the box for **Wall Motion** and set the value of **0.4449 rad/s** for angular velocity. Click **OK** to finish the boundary condition. Rename the boundary condition from **Real Wall 1** to **Rotating Top Lid**.

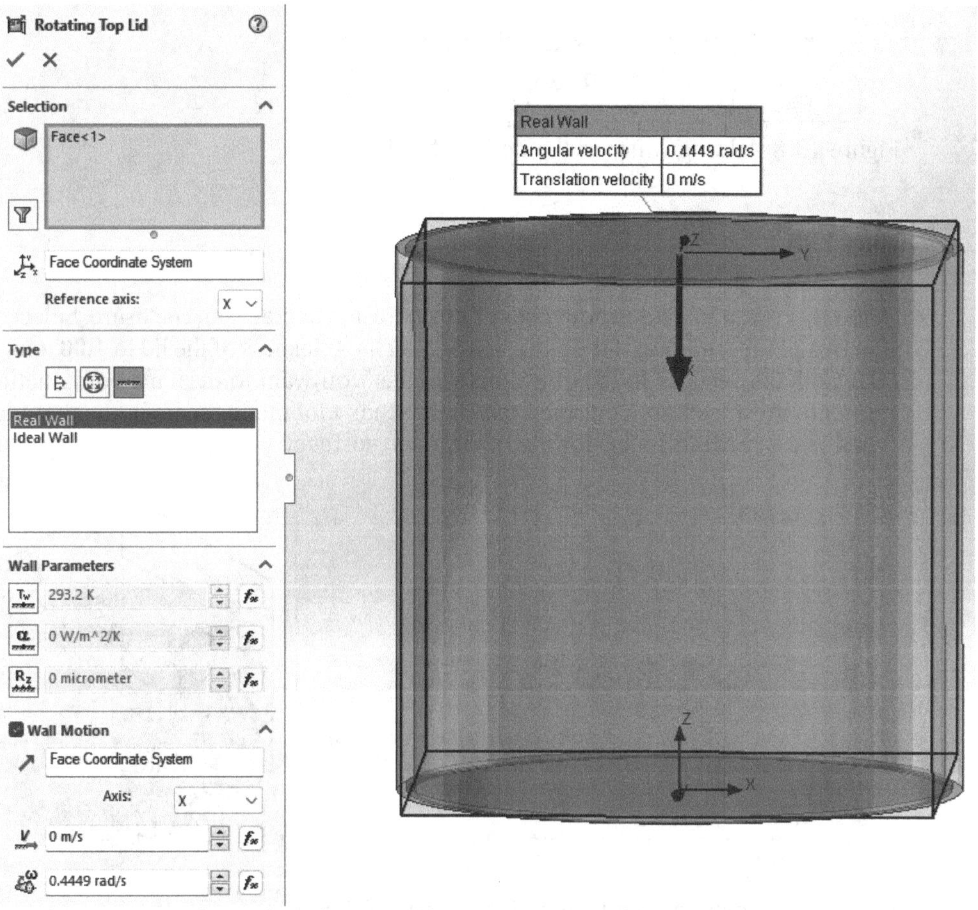

Figure 13.11 View of enclosure with upper rotating lid boundary condition

G. Global Goals

12. Right click on **Goals** in the **Flow Simulation analysis tree** and select **Insert Global Goals….** Check the boxes for **Min, Av** and **Max Velocity**.

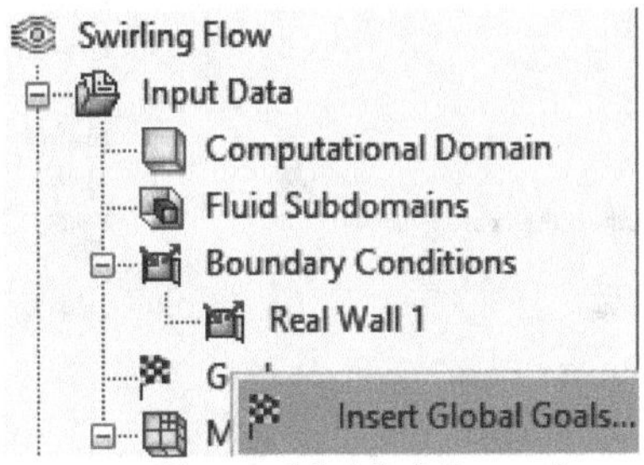

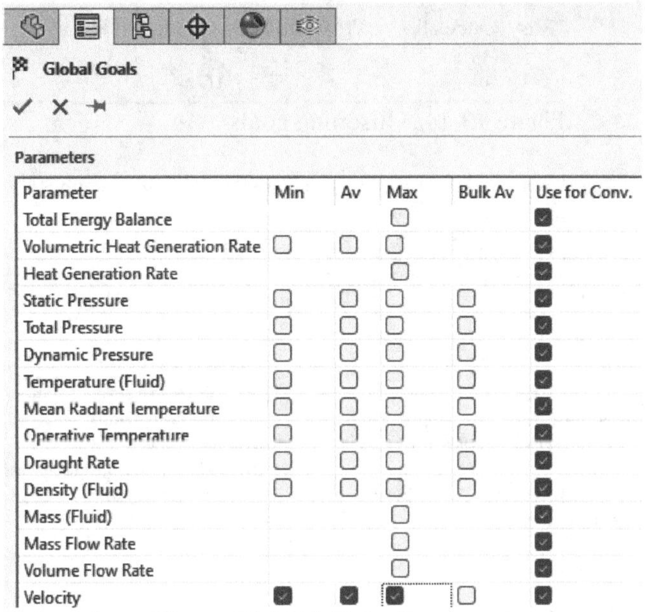

Figure 13.12a) Inserting global goals   Figure 13.12b) Velocity as goals

H. Running Simulations

13. Select **Tools>>Flow Simulation>>Solve>>Run….** Push the **Run** button in the window that appears.

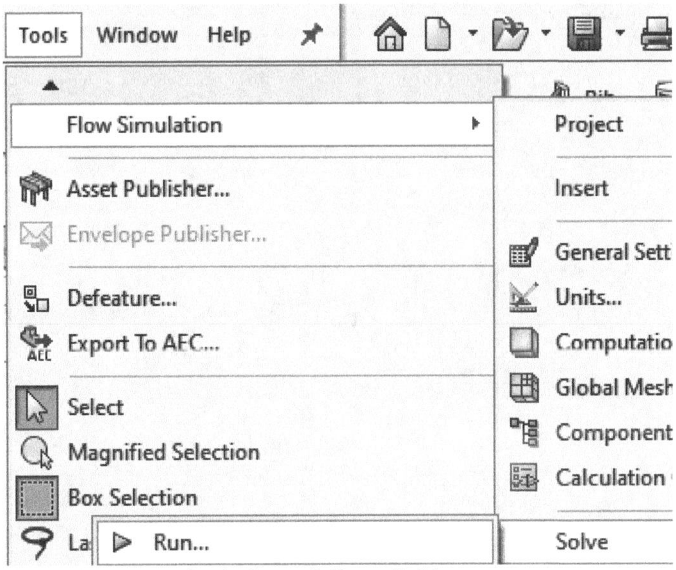

Figure 13.13 Calculation of flow field

14. Insert the goals table by clicking on the flag in the **Solver** as shown in Figure 13.14a).

Figure 13.14a) Inserting goals

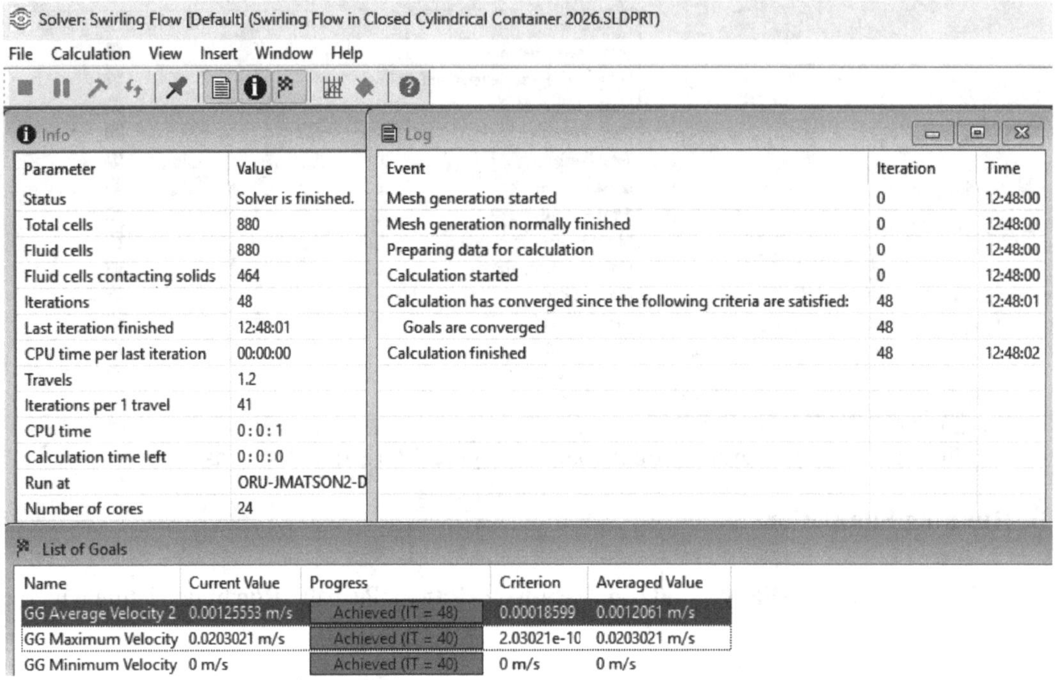

Figure 13.14b) Solver window

I. Flow Trajectories

15. Right click on **Flow Trajectories** in the **Flow Simulation analysis tree** under **Results** and select **Insert...**. Select the **Top Plane** from the **FeatureManager design tree**.

Check the **In-plane** box. Select Static Trajectories . Select to draw trajectories as **Lines** from the drop-down menu in the **Appearance** section. Select **Velocity** from the **Color by** drop down menu. Click **OK** to exit **Flow Trajectories.** Rename **Flow Trajectories 1** to **Streamlines.**

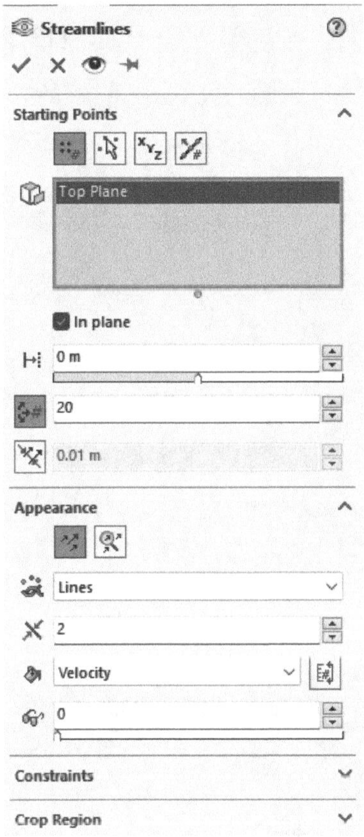

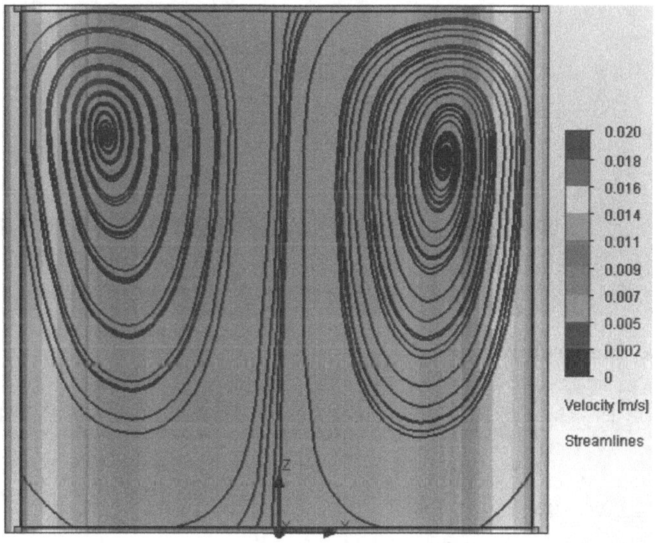

Figure 13.15a) Flow trajectories   Figure 13.15b) Streamlines, Re = 1,000 and H/R = 2

In figure 13.15b) we can see the streamlines for the first breakdown structure at the Reynolds number Re = 1,000 and H/R = 2. The fluid is rising in the center of the cylinder and flowing downward along the cylindrical wall.

J. Theory

16. We define the Reynolds number as

$$Re = \Omega R^2 / \nu \tag{13.1}$$

where Ω (rad/s) is the angular velocity of the lid, R (m) is the radius of the cylindrical container and ν (m^2/s) is kinematic viscosity. The aspect ratio of the cylindrical container is defined as

$$\lambda = H/R \tag{13.2}$$

where H (m) is the height of the cylindrical container.

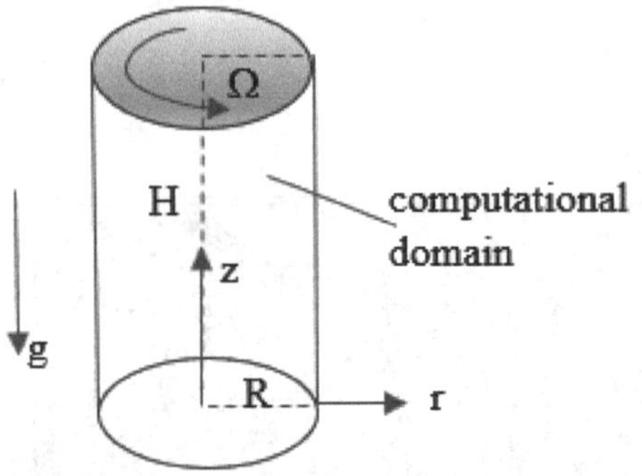

Figure 13.16 Geometry for cylinder with rotating lid

K. References

1. Granger R.A., Experiments in Fluid Mechanics, Holt, Rinehart and Winston, Inc., 1988.

L. Exercise

13.1 Run the flow case as described in this chapter for a different Reynolds number Re = 2494 and different height over radius ratio H/R = 2.5 to find the second breakdown structure, see Granger (1988).

CHAPTER 14. FLOW PAST A MODEL ROCKET

A. Objectives

- Creating the SOLIDWORKS model needed for Flow Simulations
- Setting up a Flow Simulation project for external flows
- Using cut plots to visualize the resulting flow field

B. Problem Description

In this chapter we will study the flow past a model rocket. The rocket that we will model is the Estes Firestreak SST.

C. Modeling SOLIDWORKS Parts

1. Start SOLIDWORKS and create a New Part. Select **Tools>>Options...** from the SOLIDWORKS menu. Click on the **Document Properties** tab and select **Units**. Select **MMGS** as your **Unit system**. Select the **Front** view from the **View Orientation** drop down menu in the graphics window and click on the **Front Plane** in the **FeatureManager design tree**.

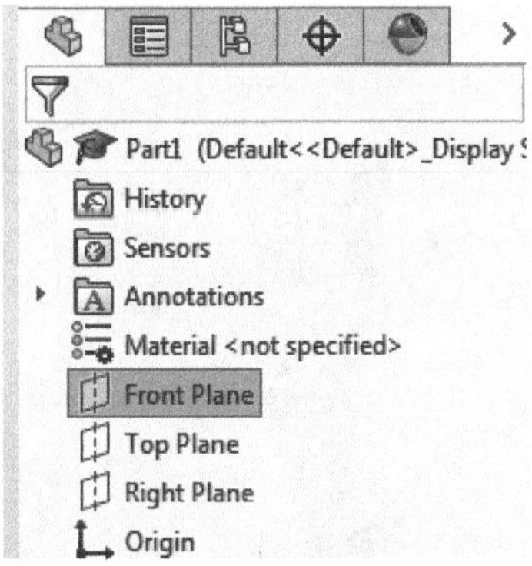

Figure 14.1 Front Plane

2. Next, select the **Sketch** tab and the **Line** sketch tool. Draw a horizontal line from the origin to the right with a length of **10.85 mm**. Next, draw a vertical line from the origin vertically downward with a length of **71.5 mm** followed by an **Equation Driven Curve** between the two open endpoints of the vertical and horizontal lines. Enter the Equation -71.5+((4*71.5*x^2)/21.7^2) and Parameters as shown in Figure 14.2b). Close the **Equation Driven Curve** dialog.

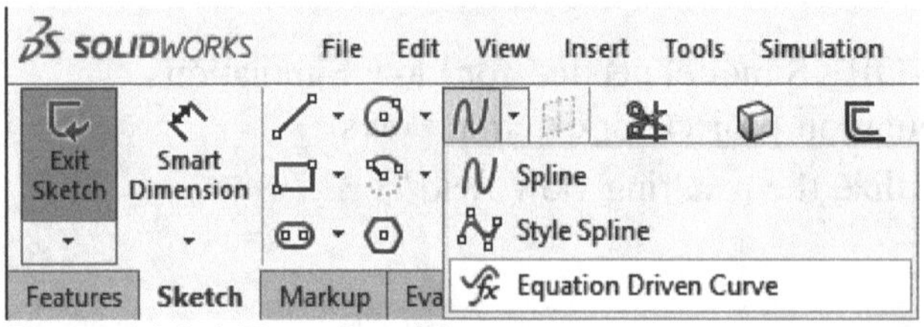

Figure 14.2a) Equation driven curve

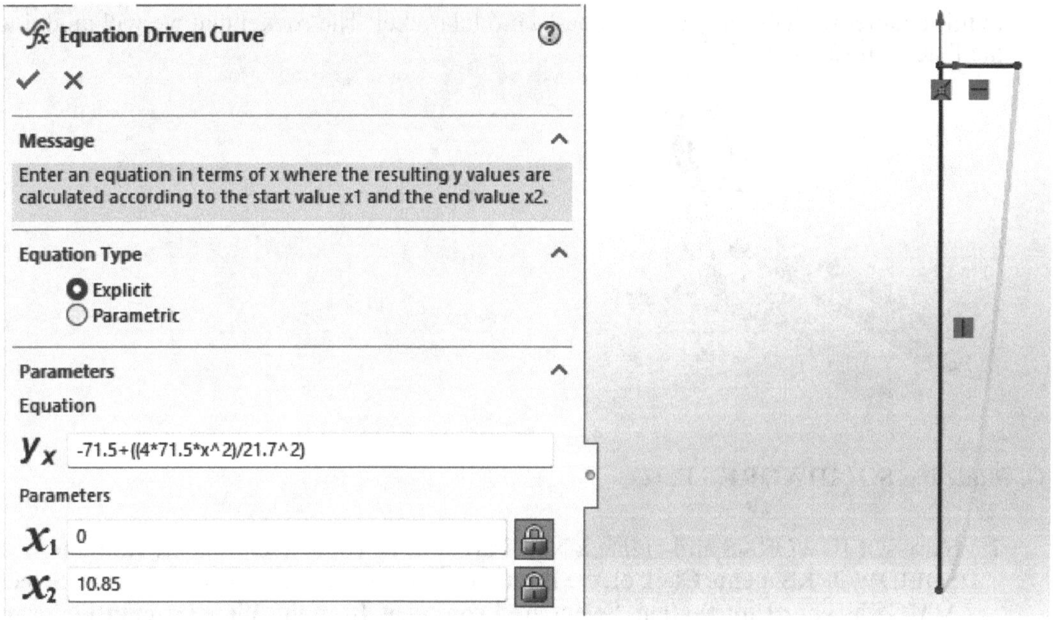

Figure 14.2b) Equation driven curve settings

3. Click on the **Features** tab and **Revolved Boss/Base** feature. Select the vertical line in the graphics window and exit the **Revolve** dialog.

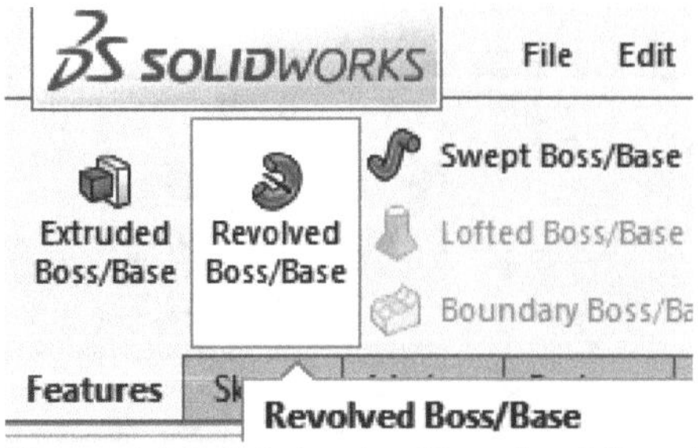

Figure 14.3a) Selecting Revolved Boss/Base

Figure 14.3b) Nose cone

4. Select the **Top Plane** in the **FeatureManager design tree**. Select **Normal To** from the **View Orientation** drop down menu. Draw a **Circle** from the origin with a radius of **10.85 mm**. Select **Extruded Boss/Base** from the **Features**. Make the extrusion **165 mm** in depth.

   Select **Insert>>Reference Geometry>>Plane...** from the menu and select the **Top Plane** as the first reference plane. The offset distance is **165 mm**. Draw a circle with a radius of **10.85 mm** in the new plane and select **Extruded Boss/Base** from the **Features**. The extrusion is set to a depth of **9.5 mm** and includes a **Draft** of **15.6 degrees**. Hide **Plane 1**.

Figure 14.4 Finished nose cone, tube and lock ring

5. Select the **Front** view from the **View Orientation** drop down menu in the graphics window and click on the **Front Plane** in the **FeatureManager design tree**. Next, select the **Sketch** tab and the **Line** sketch tool.

   Draw a **38.00 mm** long vertical line downward with the parameters as shown in Figure 14.5a).

   Next, draw a horizontal line from the lower endpoint of the former line. The second line will end at the edge of the tube. Next, draw an inclined line that is **60.00 mm** long starting from the endpoint of the **10.85 mm** long horizontal line, see Figure 14.5b). Set the angle to **50.00°** from the horizontal.

   Continue by drawing a **10.00 mm** long vertical line from the endpoint of the inclined line, see Figure 14.5b).

   Next, draw another inclined line with a length of **33.00 mm** starting from the top endpoint of the 10 mm long vertical line, see Figure 14.5b). Set the angle to **195.00°**.

Next, draw another inclined line to the intersection between the tube and the lock ring, see Figure 14.5b).

Finally, connect the two open end points with a 10.85 mm long horizontal line and close the **Line Properties** and **Insert Line** dialogues.

Make an extrusion by selecting the **Features** tab and **Extruded Boss/Base**. Enter **0.35 mm** for the depth of the extrusion in **Direction 1** and the same depth for **Direction 2**, see Figure 14.5c).

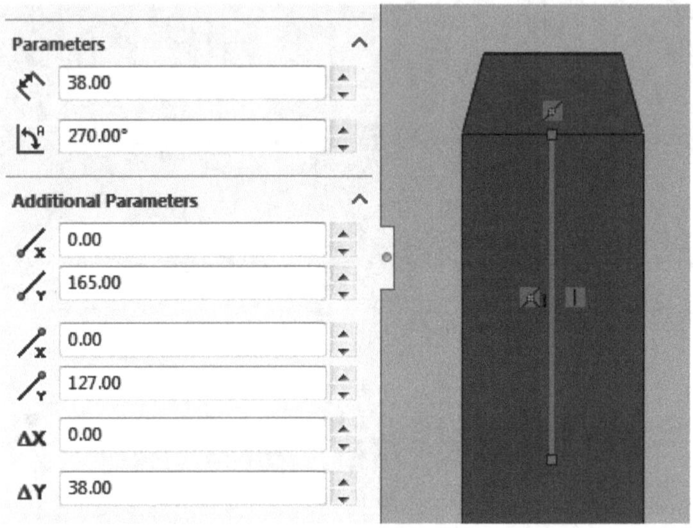

Figure 14.5a) First vertical line for fin

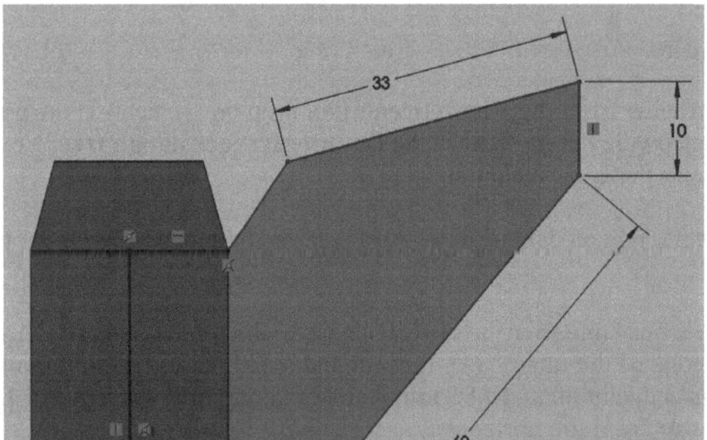

Figure 14.5b) Parameters for horizontal, inclined and vertical lines for fin

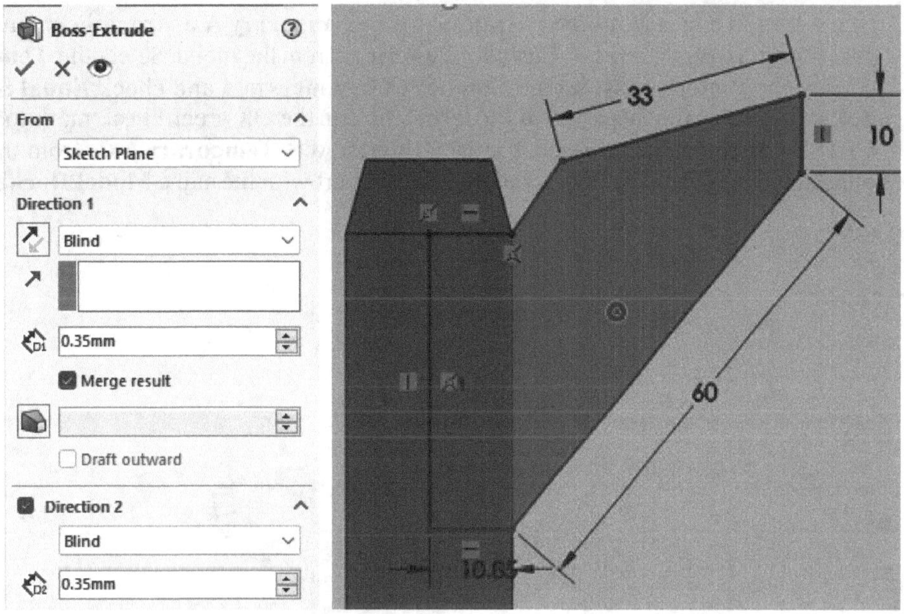

Figure 14.5c) Extrusion settings for fin

6. Rename the revolved feature and extrusions to Nose Cone, Body Tube, Engine Lock Ring, and Fin as shown in Figure 14.6.

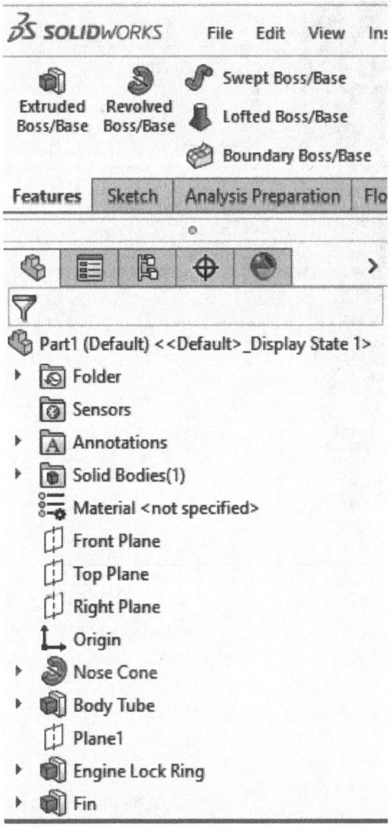

Figure 14.6 Renaming the revolved feature and extrusions

7. Select the Fin and select **View>>Hide/Show>>Temporary Axis** from the menu. Select **Insert>> Pattern/Mirror>>Circular Pattern...** from the menu. Select the **Temporary Axis** as the **Pattern Axis.** Set the **Number of Instances** to **4** and check **Equal Spacing**. Select the **Fin** as the **Features to Pattern**. Click on the OK green check mark to exit the **Circular Pattern** dialog. Select **View>>Hide/Show>>Temporary Axis** from the menu once again to hide the temporary axis. Save the part with the name **Model Rocket 2026**.

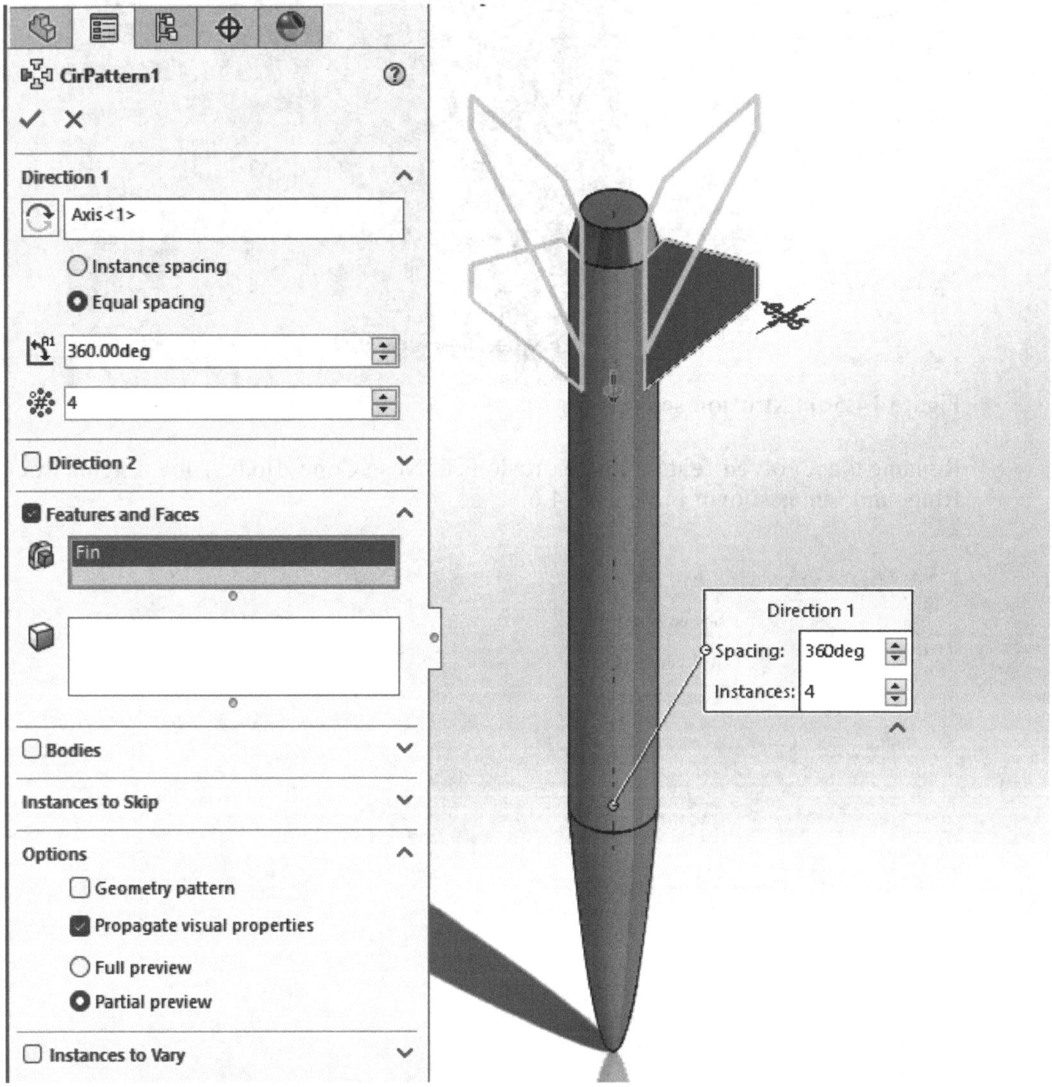

Figure 14.7 Circular pattern settings for fin

D. Flow Simulation Project

8. If Flow Simulation is not available in the SOLIDWORKS menu, select **Tools>>Add Ins...** and check the corresponding **SOLIDWORKS Flow Simulation** box. Start the **Flow Simulation Wizard** by selecting **Tools>>Flow Simulation>>Project>>Wizard** from the SOLIDWORKS menu. Create a new project with the following name: **Flow Past a Model Rocket**. Click on Next>.

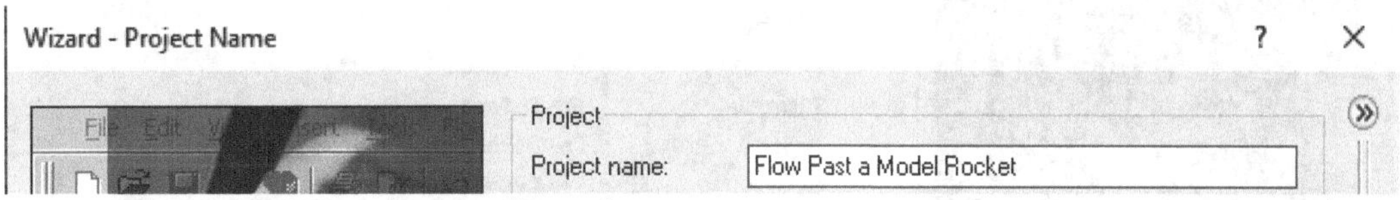

Figure 14.8 Entering configuration name

9. Select the **SI unit system.** Click on Next>.

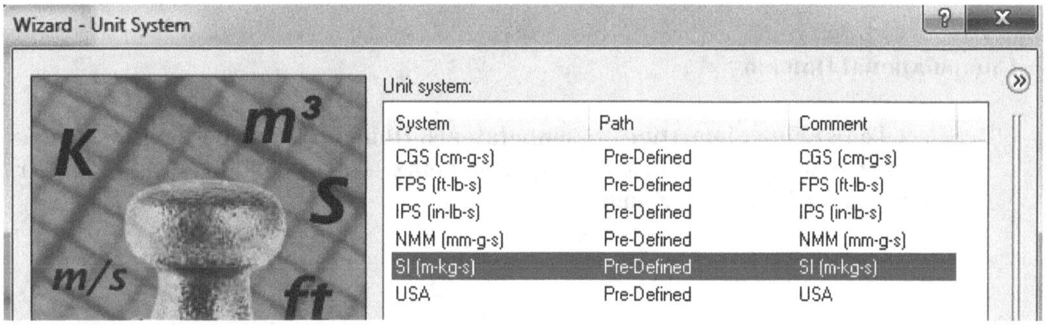

Figure 14.9 Selection of unit system

10. Select **External Analysis type**. Click on Next>.

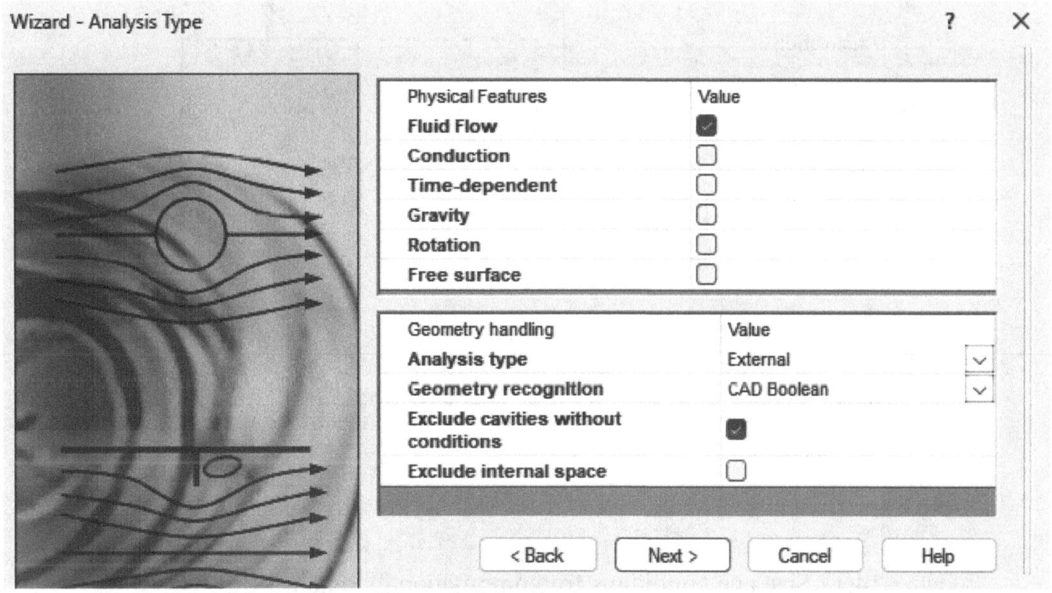

Figure 14.10 Selection of External Analysis type

11. Add **Air** as the default **Project Fluid** by selecting it from **Gases**. Click on Next. Choose default values for **Wall Conditions** and enter **10 m/s** as the **Velocity in Y direction** as **Initial Condition**. Finish the Wizard.

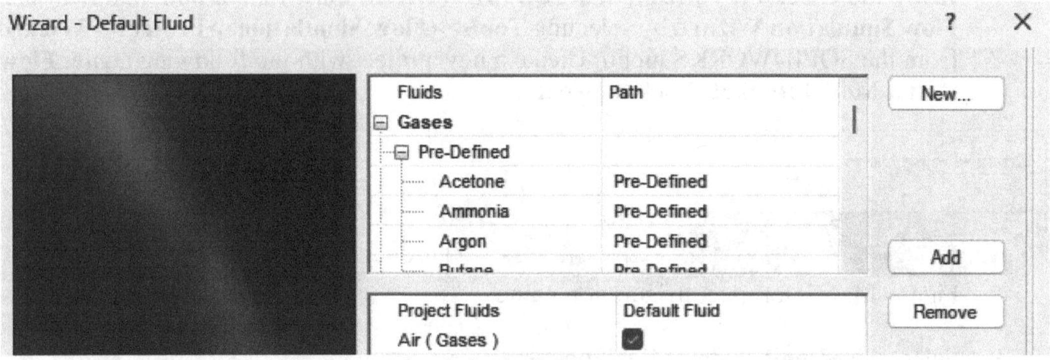

Figure 14.11 Adding air as the default fluid

E. Computational Domain

12. Select **Tools>Flow Simulation>>Computational Domain...** from the menu. Set **Xmax, Xmin** to **0.5, 0, Ymax, Ymin** to **0.5, -0.5** and **Zmax, Zmin** to **0.5, 0**. Select **Symmetry** conditions for **X min** and **Z min**.

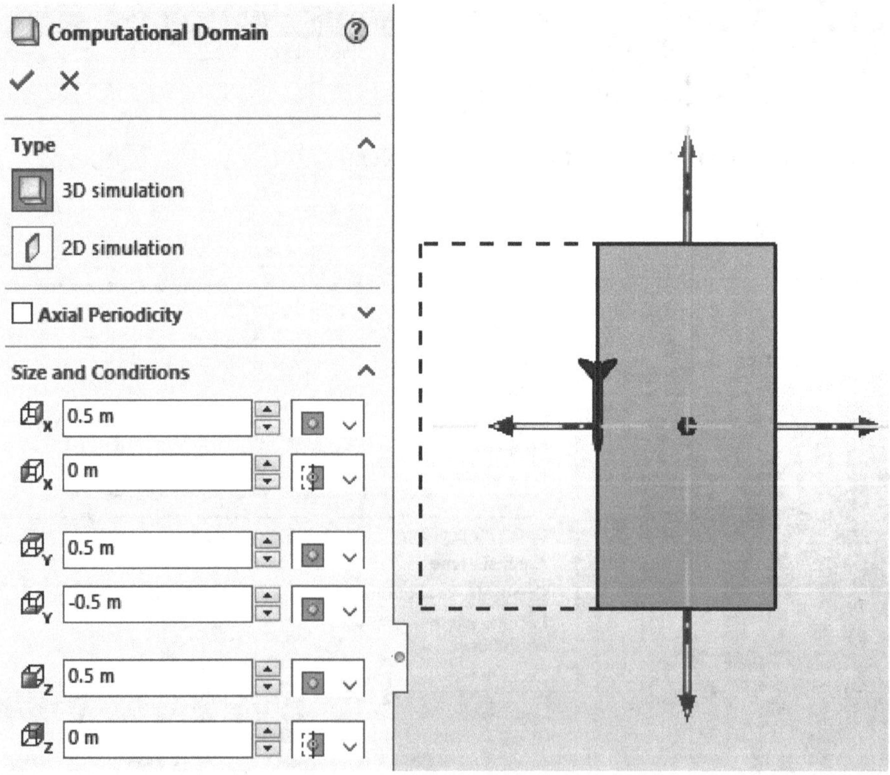

Figure 14.12 Size and conditions for computational domain

F. Goals

13. Right click on **Goals** in the **Flow Simulation analysis tree** and select **Insert Global Goals….** Check the box for **Force (Y).**

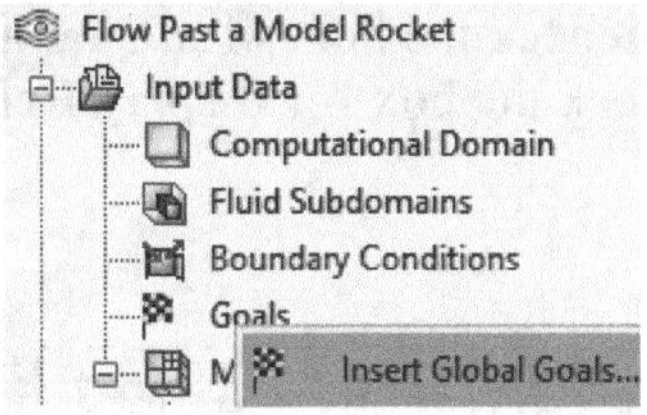

Figure 14.13a) Inserting global goals

Right click on **Goals** in the **Flow Simulation analysis tree** and select **Insert Equation Goal….** Click on **GG Force (Y) 1** in the Flow Simulation Analysis tree. Enter the **Expression** as shown in figure 14.13b):
{GG Force (Y) 1}/(0.5*1.225*10^2*(3.14*0.01085^2+4*0.0007*0.0386)/4)

Select **No unit** for **Dimensionality**. Enter **Drag Coefficient** as the name for the equation goal. Click on the OK button to exit the window. The drag coefficient is defined as drag force / (dynamic pressure * frontal area of the model rocket).

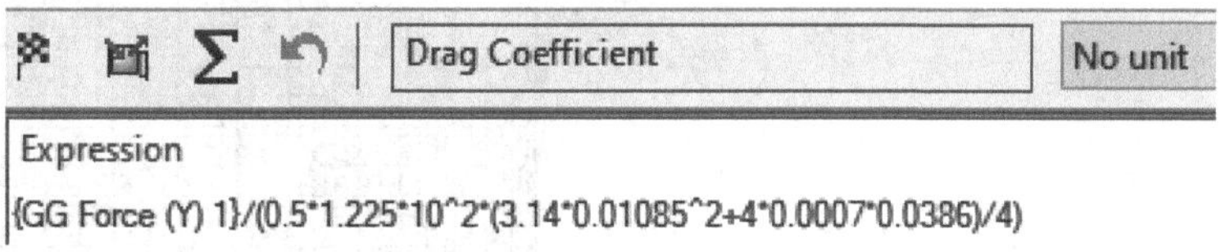

Figure 14.13b) Expression for equation goal

G. Global Mesh

14. Select **Tools>Flow Simulation>>Global Mesh…** from the menu. Set the **Level of initial mesh** to **4**. Check the box for **Show basic mesh** and exit the window.

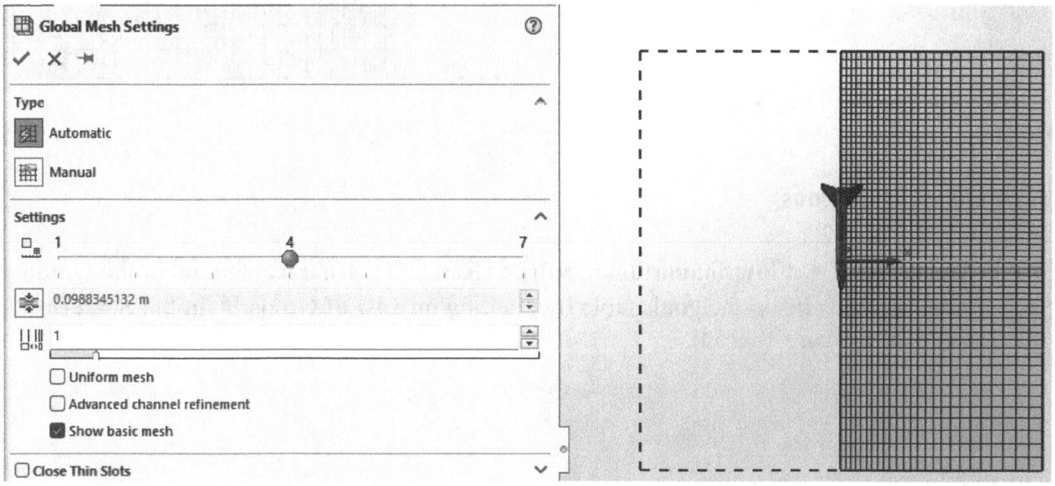

Figure 14.14 Global mesh settings

H. Local Mesh

15. Select **Tools>Flow Simulation>>Insert>>Local Mesh…** from the menu. Select **Region** under **Selection** and check **Cuboid.** Enter **0.06, 0** as **Xmax, Xmin, 0.2, -0.1** as **Ymax, Ymin** and **0.06, 0** as **Zmax, Zmin.** Set **Level of Refining Fluid Cells** to **1** and **Level of Refining Cells at Fluid/Solid Boundary** to **6.** Uncheck the boxes for **Channels, Advanced Refinement** and **Close Thin Slots.** Check the box for **Display Refinement Level.**

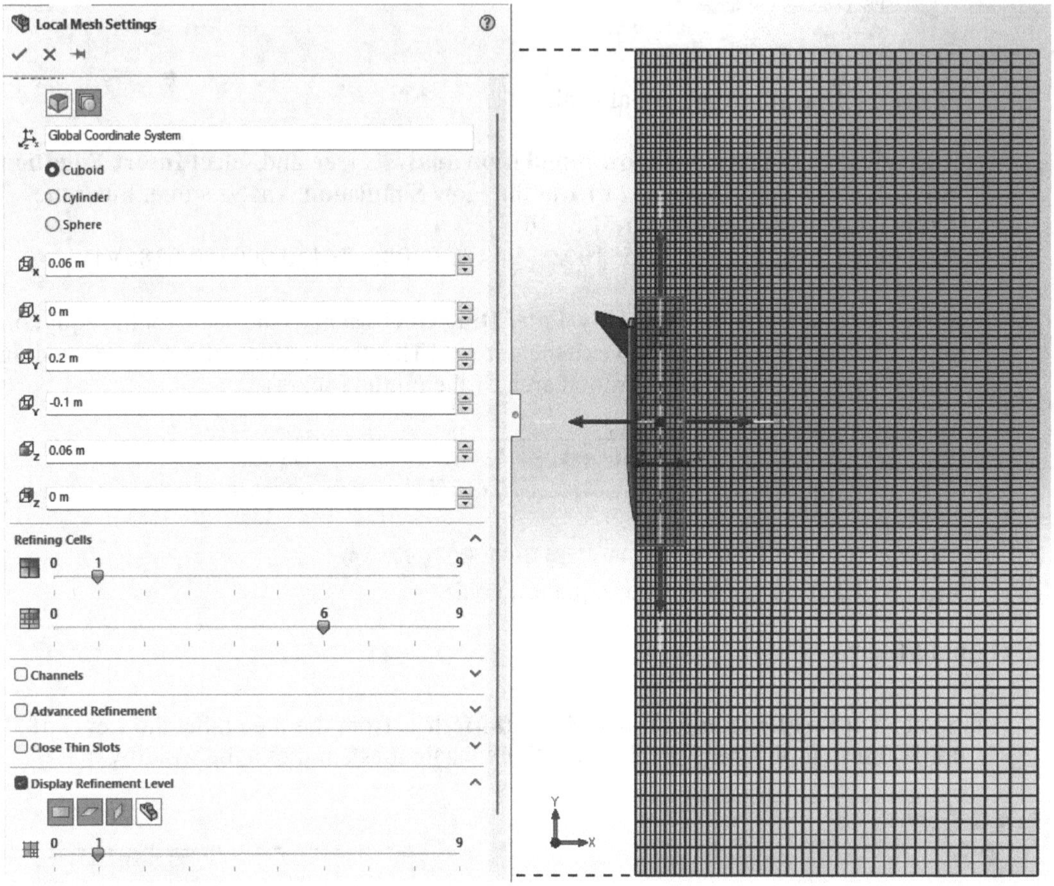

Figure 14.15 Local mesh settings

I. Running Simulations

1. Select **Tools>>Flow Simulation>>Solve>>Run….** Push the **Run** button in the window that appears. Insert the goals table by clicking on **List of Goals** in the **Solver** as shown in figure 14.16a).

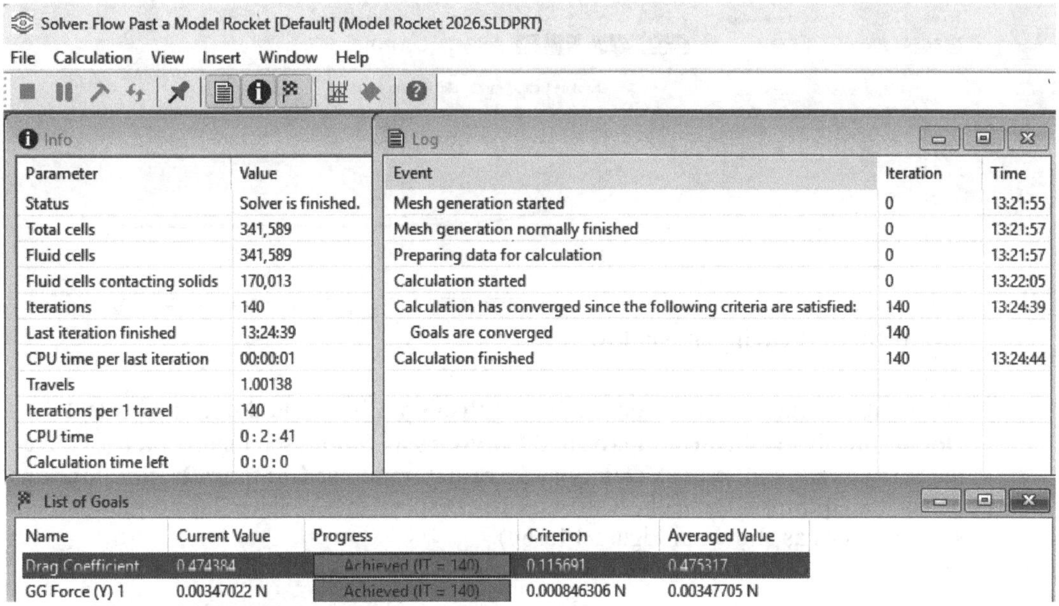

Figure 14.16a) Solver window

Click on the **Insert Goals Plot** in the **Solver** and check the box for **Drag Coefficient** in the **Add/Remove Goals** window, see Figure 14.16b). Right click in the **Goal plot 1** window, check the box for **Manual min:** and set the value to **0.4**. Set the corresponding value for Manual max to **0.6**. Set the **Length scale:** to **5**, see Figure 14.16c). Select **OK** to exit the **Goal Plot Settings** window.

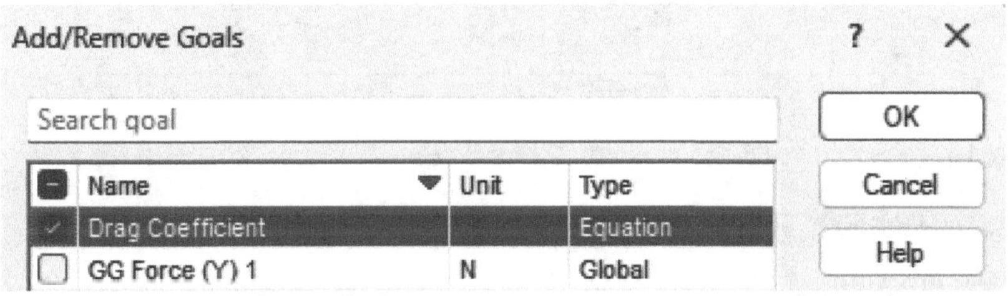

Figure 14.16b) Solver window

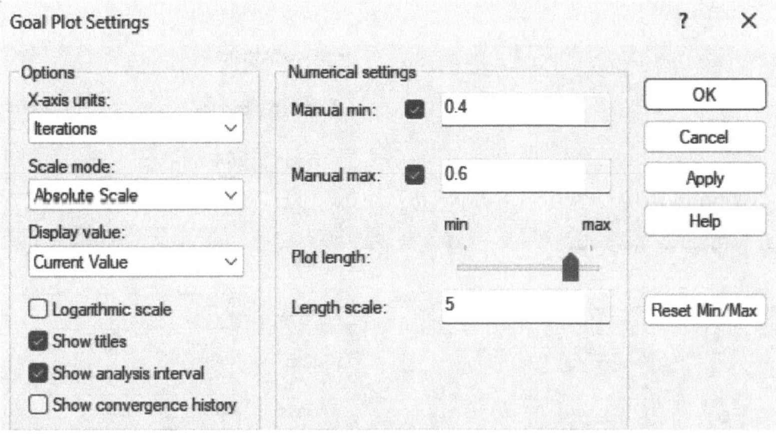

Figure 14.16c) Goal Plot settings

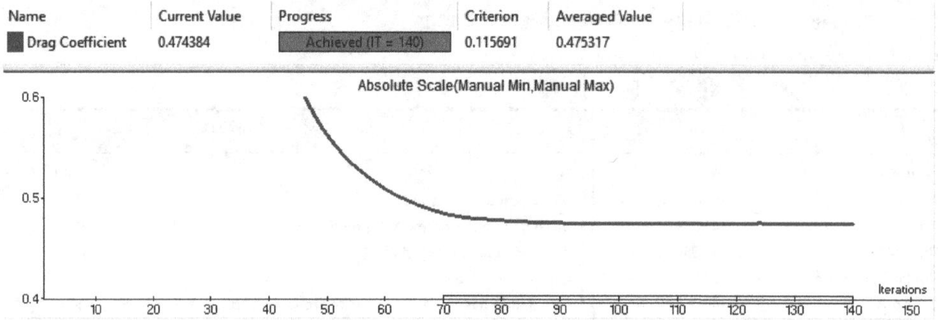

Figure 14.16d) Goal plot window

During the simulation, click on the **Insert Preview** in the **Solver** and select the **Definition** tab and the **Front Plane** and **Contours** as **Mode**, see Figure 14.16e). Select the **Settings** tab and select **Velocity** as **Parameter:** under **Contours/Isolines options**. Select the **Options** tab and check the box for **Display mesh**. Select the **Region** tab and set the values as shown in Figure 14.16e).

Figure 14.16e) Preview setting windows

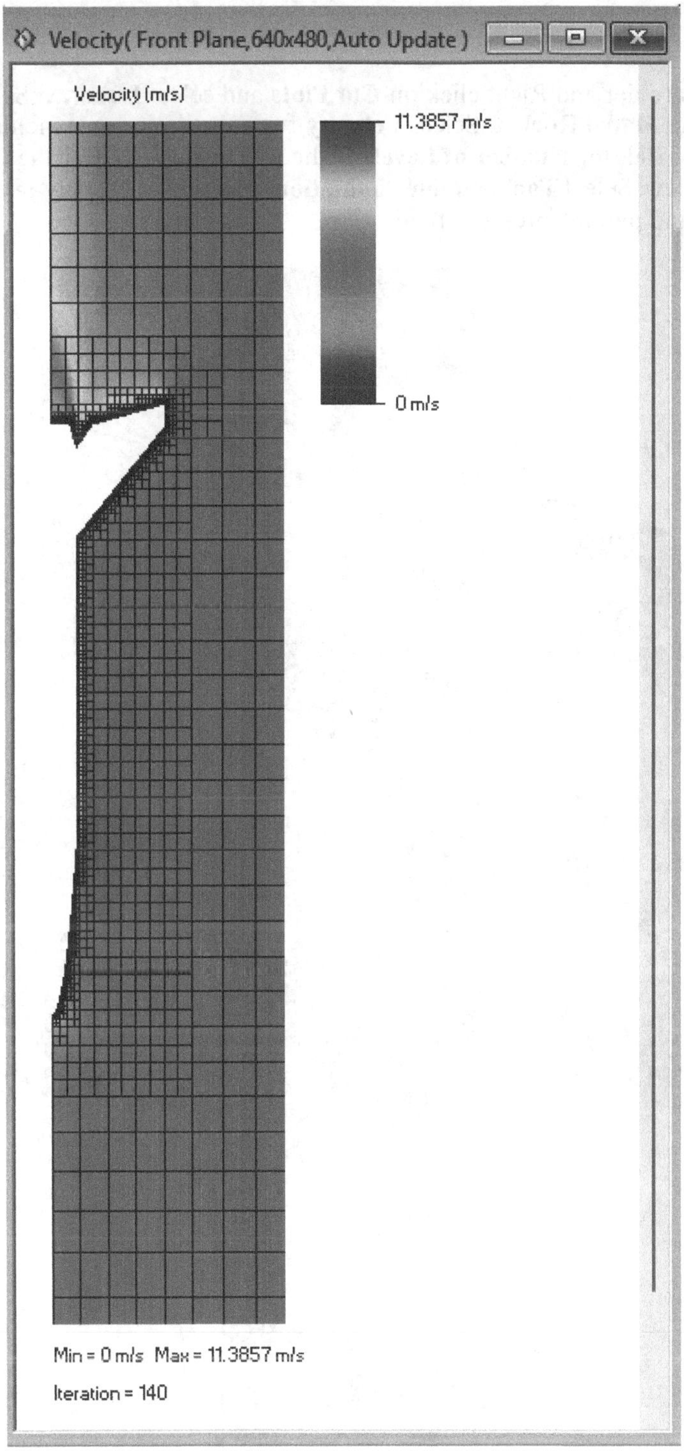

Figure 14.16f) Velocity contours with mesh during simulation

J. Cut-Plots

1. Open the **Results** folder and Right click on **Cut Plots** and select **Insert....** Select the **Right** plane of the **Model Rocket**. Select **Velocity** from the drop-down menu in the **Contours** section. Slide the **Number of Levels** all the way to the right. Exit the **Cut plot**. Select the Right view. Select **Tools>>Flow Simulation>>Results>>Display>>Lighting**. Repeat this step and plot the pressure field.

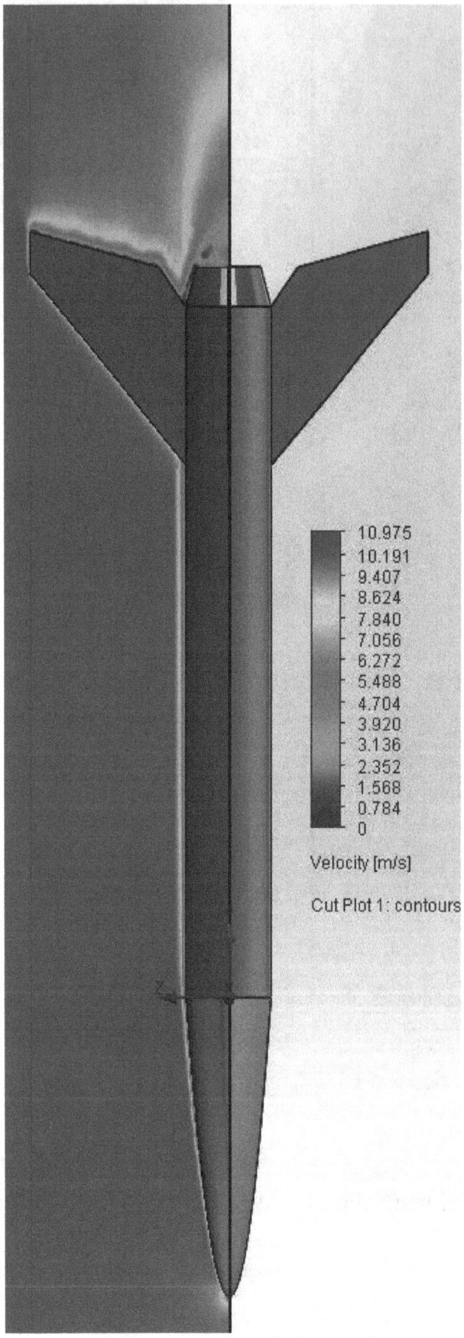

Figure 14.17a) Velocity field

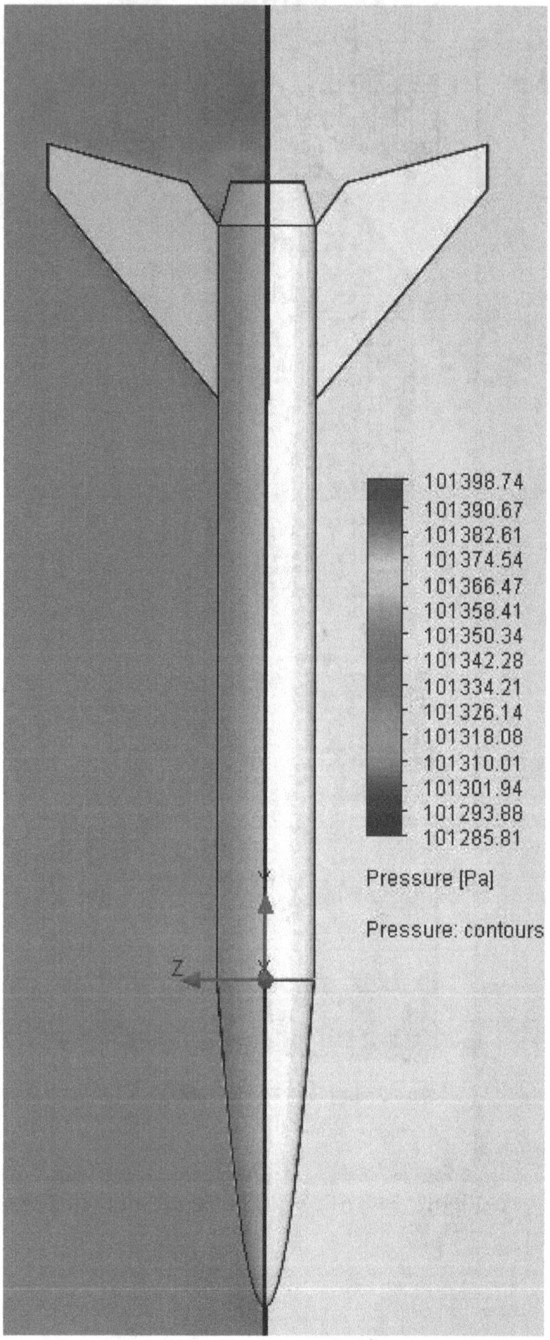

Figure 14.17b) Pressure field

K. Theory

2. The total drag-coefficient for a model rocket[2,3,6] can be expressed using equation (14.1).

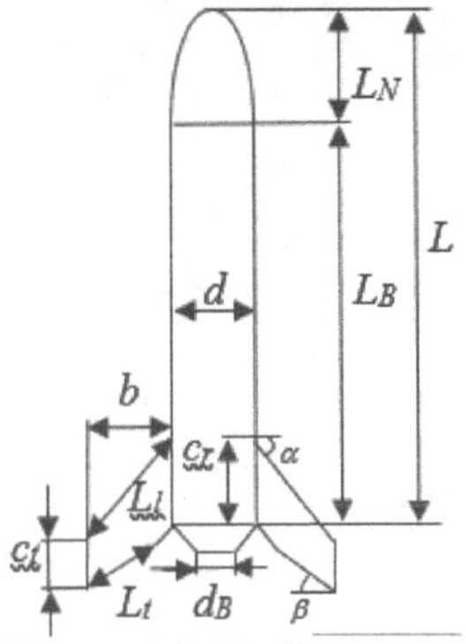

Figure 14.18 Geometry for model rocket

$$C_{D,T} = C_{D,NT} + C_{D,B} + C_{D,F} + C_{D,I} \tag{14.1}$$

, where

$$C_{D,NT} = 1.02 \frac{C_{f,turb} A_{w,NT}}{A_c} \left(1 + \frac{3}{2} \left(\frac{L}{d}\right)^{-3/2}\right) \tag{14.2}$$

$$C_{D,B} = \frac{0.029}{\sqrt{C_{D,NT}}} \left(\frac{d_b}{d}\right)^3 \tag{14.3}$$

$$C_{D,F} = \frac{2 C_{f,lam} A_{w,F}}{A_c} \left(1 + 2 \frac{t}{C_r}\right) \tag{14.4}$$

$$C_{D,I} = \frac{C_{f,lam} n d c_r}{A_c} \left(1 + 2 \frac{t}{c_r}\right) \tag{14.5}$$

The different drag coefficients and parameters are explained in Table 14.1. We define the Reynolds number for the nose cone and body tube as

$$Re_{NT} = \frac{UL\rho}{\mu} = \frac{10*0.2365*1.225}{0.000017894} = 161{,}905 \tag{14.6}$$

, and the Reynolds number for the fin as

$$Re_F = \frac{U c_{ave} \rho}{\mu} = \frac{10*0.0271525*1.225}{0.000017894} = 18{,}588 \tag{14.7}$$

, where $c_{ave} = \frac{S}{b} = \frac{S}{L_l \cos\alpha}$. The surface area for the fin can be determined from the geometry in Figure 14.16.

$$S = (c_t + L_l \sin\alpha) b - \frac{1}{2} \{L_l b \sin\alpha + L_t^2 \sin\beta \cos\beta + (b - L_t \cos\beta)(c_t - c_r + L_l \sin\alpha + L_t \sin\beta)\} \tag{14.8}$$

The skin friction coefficient can be approximated assuming fully turbulent flow on nose cone and body tube

$$C_{f,turb} = \frac{0.0315}{Re_{NT}^{1/7}} = 0.005677 \tag{14.9}$$

, and for a laminar boundary layer on the fin as

$$C_{f,lam} = \frac{1.328}{Re_F^{1/2}} = 0.00974 \tag{14.10}$$

For an ogive nose-cone we have the following relation

$$\frac{A_{w,NT}}{A_C} = \frac{8L_N + 12L_B}{3d} = 39.2012 \tag{14.11}$$

The different drag coefficient and the total value becomes

$$C_{D,NT} = 0.2365 \tag{14.12}$$

$$C_{D,B} = 0.0257 \tag{14.13}$$

$$C_{D,F} = 0.2288 \tag{14.14}$$

$$C_{D,I} = 0.0901 \tag{14.15}$$

$$C_{D,T} = 0.581 \tag{14.16}$$

The value for the total drag coefficient 0.581 according to the theory can be compared with the value 0.4879 from simulations, a difference of 16 %. The equation driven curve for the nose cone in a simple approximation for a tangent ogive is the following:

$$y = L_N \left(\frac{4x^2}{d^2} - 1\right) \tag{14.17}$$

An alternative expression for the nose cone curve is

$$y = \frac{2L_N^3}{d^2} - \frac{L_N}{2} - \frac{L_N}{2d^2}\sqrt{(d^2 + 4L_N^2)^2 - 64L_N^2 x^2} \tag{14.18}$$

A_c (m^2): cross sectional area for body tube 0.000369836 m^2
$A_{w,F}$ (m^2): total wetted surface area for all fins 0.00418879 m^2
$A_{w,NT}$ (m^2): wetted surface area for nose and body tube 0.014498 m^2
α : fin leading edge sweep angle 50°
β : fin trailing edge angle 15°
b (m): span for the fin 0.0385673 m
c_{ave} (m): average fin chord length 0.0271525 m
c_r (m): root fin chord length 0.038 m
c_t (m): tip fin chord length 0.010 m
$C_{D,NT}$: nose and body tube drag coefficient 0.2021
$C_{D,B}$: base-drag coefficient 0.0278
$C_{D,F}$: fin drag coefficient 0.1321
$C_{D,I}$: interference drag coefficient 0.0520
$C_{D,T}$: total drag coefficient 0.414

$C_{f,lam}$: skin friction coefficient for laminar boundary layer 0.00562365
$C_{f,turb}$: skin friction coefficient for turbulent boundary layer 0.00485255
$d\ (m)$: body tube diameter 0.0217 m
$d_b\ (m)$: base diameter 0.0164 m
$L\ (m)$: length of nose and body 0.2365 m
$L_B\ (m)$: length of body-tube 0.165 m
$L_l\ (m)$: length of leading edge of fin 0.060 m
$L_N\ (m)$: length of nose 0.0715 m
$L_t\ (m)$: length of trailing edge of fin 0.033 m
n: number of fins 4
Re_F: Reynolds number for the fin 55,765
Re_{NT}: Reynolds number for nose cone and body tube 485,714
$S\ (m^2)$: area for fin 0.0010472 m^2
$t\ (m)$: thickness of fin 0.0007 m
$U(m/s)$: free stream velocity 10 m/s
$\rho(kg/m^3)$: density of air 1.225 kg/m^3
$\mu(kg/ms)$: dynamic viscosity of air 0.000017894kg/m^3

Table 14.1 Drag coefficients and parameters

L. References

1. Stine G.H. and Stine B., Handbook of Model Rocketry, 7th Ed., John Wiley & Sons, Inc., 2004.
2. DeMar, J.S.,"Model Rocket Drag Analysis Using a Computerized Wind Tunnel", NARAM-37, 1995.
3. Gregorek, G.M., "Aerodynamic Drag of Model Rockets.", Estes Industries, Penrose, CO, 1970.
4. Cannon, B.,"Model Rocket Simulation with Drag Analysis", BYU, 2004.
5. Milligan, T.V, "Determining the Drag Coefficient of a Model Rocket Using Accelerometer Based Payloads", NARAM-54, 2012.
6. Matsson, J., "An Introduction to ANSYS Fluent 2024", SDC Publications, 2024.

M. Exercises

14.1 Run the flow case as described in this chapter for different free stream velocities as shown in Table 14.1. Compare with values from the theory section. What is the percent difference between Flow Simulation and theory for these higher Reynolds numbers?

U (m/s)	C_D Flow Sim.	Re, NT	Re, F	CD,NT	CD, B	CD, F	CD, I	C_D,T	% Diff.
10	0.4879	161,905	18,588	0.2365	0.0257	0.2288	0.0901	0.581	16
20									
30									
40									
50									

Table 14.1 Different free stream velocities

14.2 Run the flow case as described in this chapter U = 10m/s for different Levels of Refining Cells at Fluid/Solid Boundary from 1 to 6, see figure 14.15 for local mesh. Study how the drag coefficient will change with this parameter and determine as shown in table 14.2 the percent difference between Flow Simulation and theory for each case.

Level of Refining Cells at Fluid/Solid Boundary	No. Fluid Cells	No. Fluid Cells Contacting Solids	C_D Flow Sim.	C_D Theory	% Diff.
1				0.581	
2				0.581	
3				0.581	
4				0.581	
5				0.581	
6	344,679	171,678	0.4879	0.581	16

Table 14.2 Different levels of refining cells at fluid/solid boundary

14.3 Run the flow case as described in this chapter 10 m/s for different computational domain sizes to study how the drag coefficient will change. Use the following computational domain sizes as shown in table 14.3.

Xmin (m)	Xmax (m)	Ymin (m)	Ymax (m)	Zmin (m)	Zmax (m)	C_D Flow Sim.	C_D Theory	% Diff.
0	0.25	-0.25	0.25	0	0.25			
0	0.5	-0.5	0.5	0	0.5	0.4879	0.581	16
0	1	-1	1	0	1			
0	2	-2	2	0	2			
0	5	-5	5	0	5			

Table 14.3 Different sizes for computational domain

CHAPTER 15. DRAINING OF A CYLINDRICAL TANK

A. Objectives

- Creating the SOLIDWORKS models needed for Flow Simulations
- Setting up Flow Simulation projects for internal flows
- Modeling of a free surface
- Setting up boundary conditions
- Running the simulations
- Using cut plots and goal plots to visualize the resulting flow field

B. Problem Description

The problem of draining a tank has been frequently studied by many over the years. We will model a cylindrical tank with an inner diameter of 152.4 mm and a height of 304.8 mm. The free surface will be modeled at a height of 250 mm, and we will find the location of the free surface over time as the cylinder is drained.

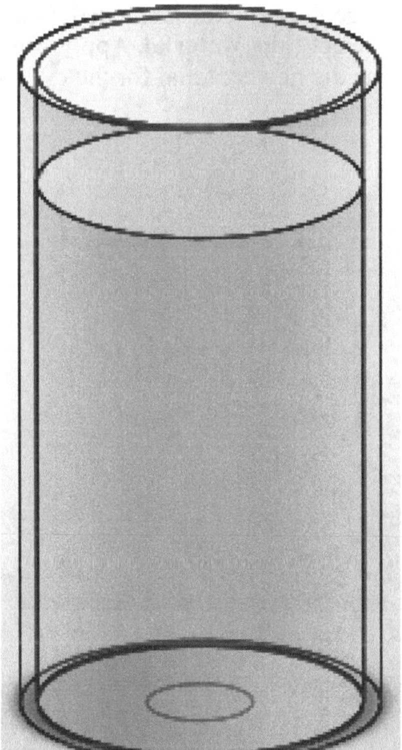

Figure 15.0 SOLIDWORKS model of cylindrical tank used to study drainage or water

C. Modeling SOLIDWORKS Part

1. We start by creating a new SOLIDWORKS part. Select **File>>New** from the menu, select the Part Template and click OK. Select **Tools>>Options…** from the SOLIDWORKS menu. Click on the **Document Properties** tab and select **Units**. Select **MMGS** as your **Unit system**. Select the **Top Plane** and draw a circle with a radius of **76.2 mm**.

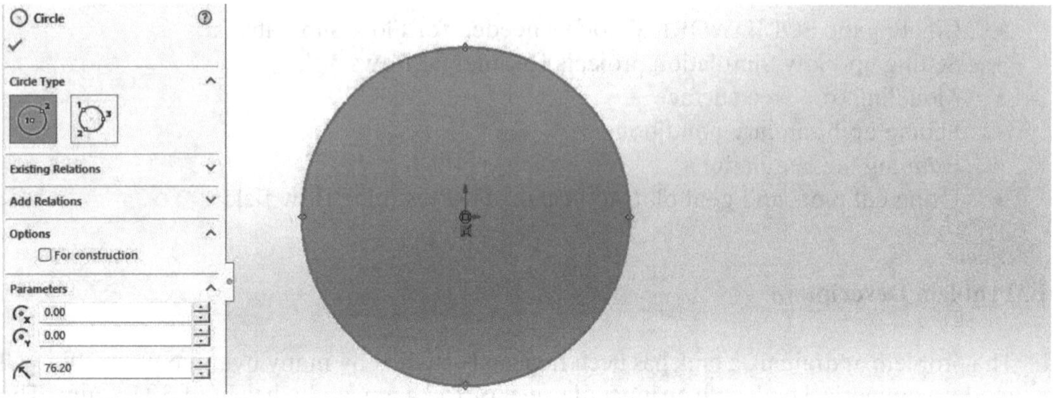

Figure 15.1 Circle in the Top plane

2. Select **Extruded Boss/Base** from the **Features** tab and use the **Thin Feature** to model a **304.8 mm** high cylinder with wall thickness of **8 mm**. Cap both ends of the cylinder with a wall thickness of **1.4 mm**, see Figure 15.2. Change the name of **Extruded-Thin1** to **Cylinder**. Right click on Material in the tree and select **Edit Material**. Apply **Acrylic (Medium-high impact)** from the **Plastics** folder as the new material for the cylinder.

Figure 15.2 Extruded thin wall cylinder with capped ends

3. Model another circle in the **Top Plane** with a radius of **76.2 mm.** Extrude the circle with a height of **250 mm**. Make sure to uncheck the box for **Merge results**. Change the name for **Boss-Extrude1** to **Water**.

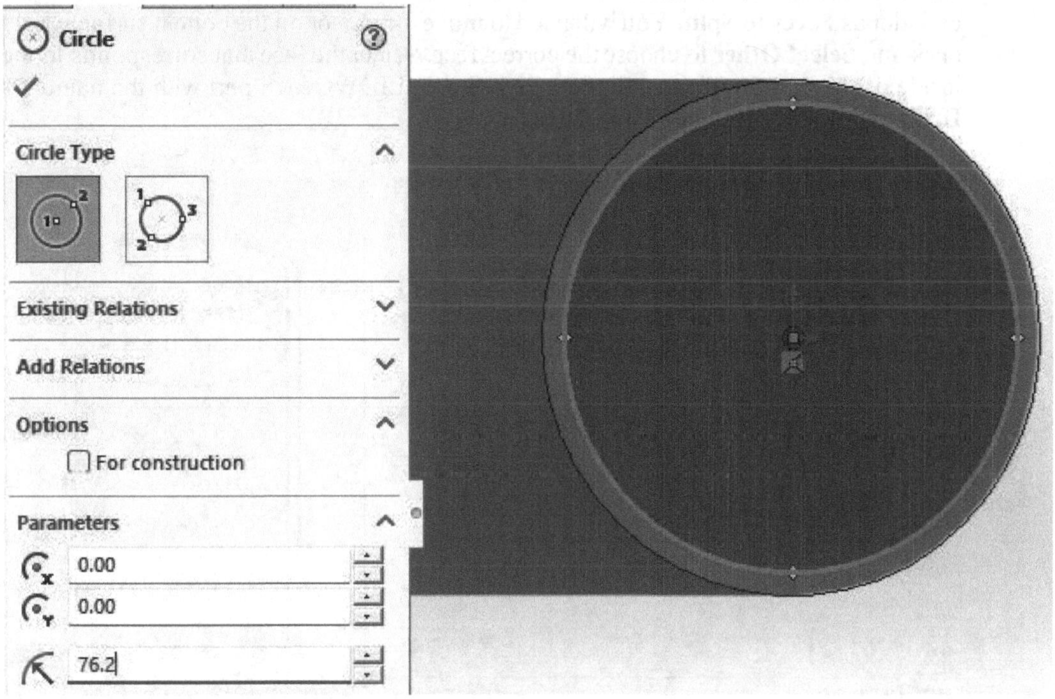

Figure 15.3a) Creation of the second circle in the top plane

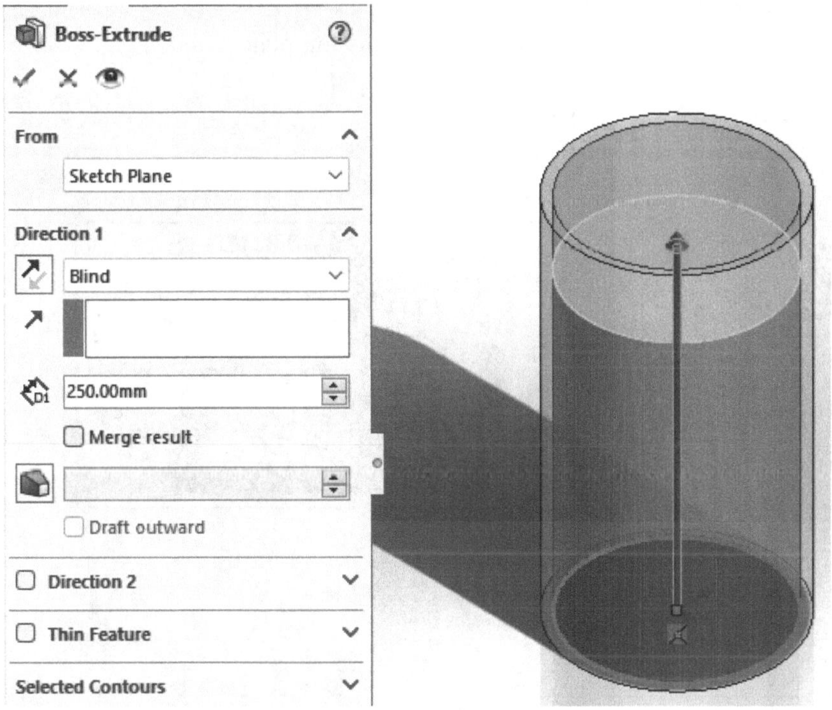

Figure 15.3b) Second extrusion from the top plane

4. Select the **Top Plane** and select **Insert>>Reference Geometry>>Plane...** from the menu. Set the **Offset Distance** to **1.4 mm** and exit the window. Model another circle in the new **Plane1** with a radius of **25 mm**. Select **Insert>>Curve>>Split Line...** from the menu. Select **Sketch3** as **Sketch to Project** and select the inside bottom surface of the cylinder as **Faces to Split**. You will need to move the cursor on the bottom surface, right click and **Select Other** to choose the correct face. Select the face that corresponds to the inside of the bottom of the cylinder. Save the SOLIDWORKS part with the name **Draining of a Cylindrical Tank 2026**.

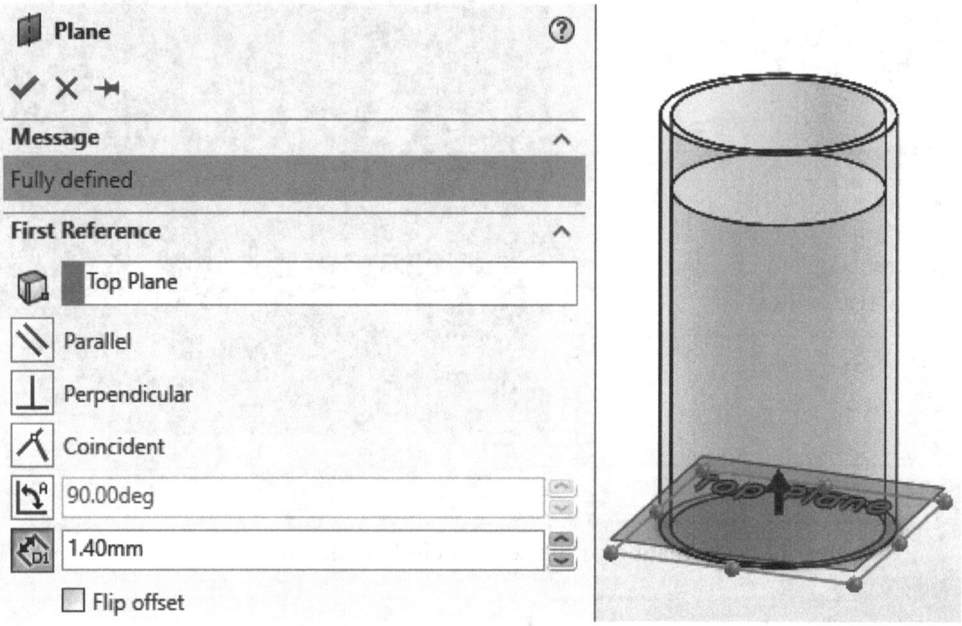

Figure 15.4a) Creation of the third circle in the top plane

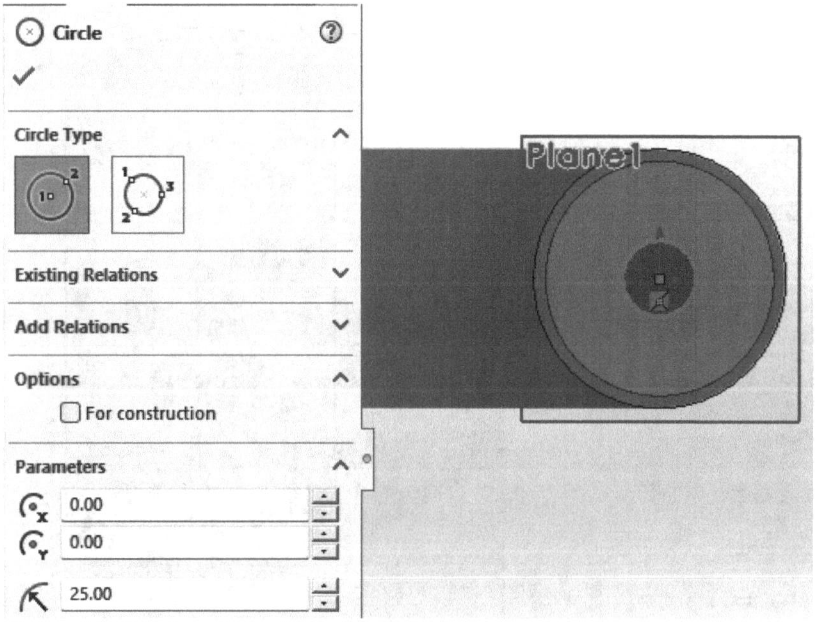

Figure 15.4b) Creation of the third circle in the top plane

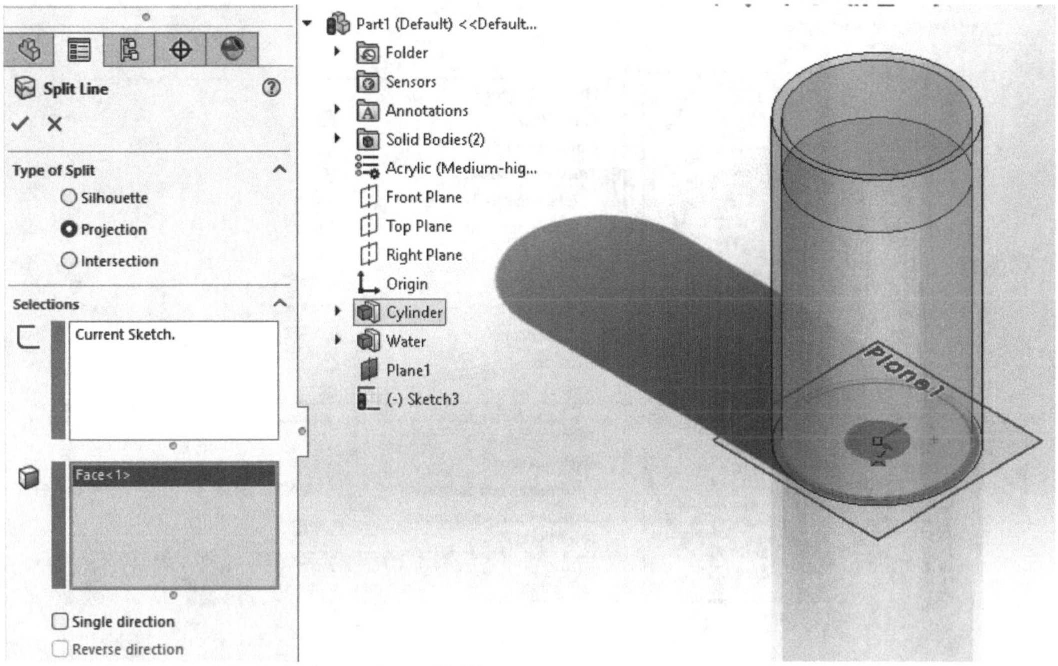

Figure 15.4c) Creation of a split line

D. Flow Simulation Project

5. Start a new Flow Simulation project by selecting **Tools>>Flow Simulation >>Project>>Wizard…** from the menu. Enter the Project name: **Draining of a Cylindrical Tank**. Click on **Next>**. Select the default SI unit system and click on **Next>**.

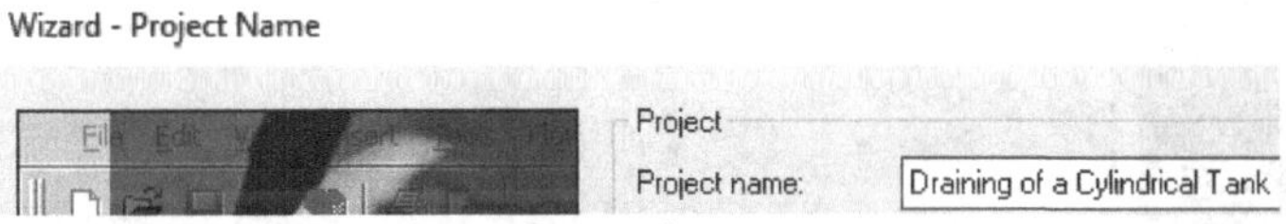

Figure 15.5a) Creation of a project name

Use **Internal** as **Analysis Type**. Check the boxes for **Time-dependent**, **Gravity** and **Free Surface**. Enter **3 seconds** as **Total analysis time**. Enter **X component 0, Y component -9.81 m/s^2** and **Z component 0** for gravity. Click on **Next>**.

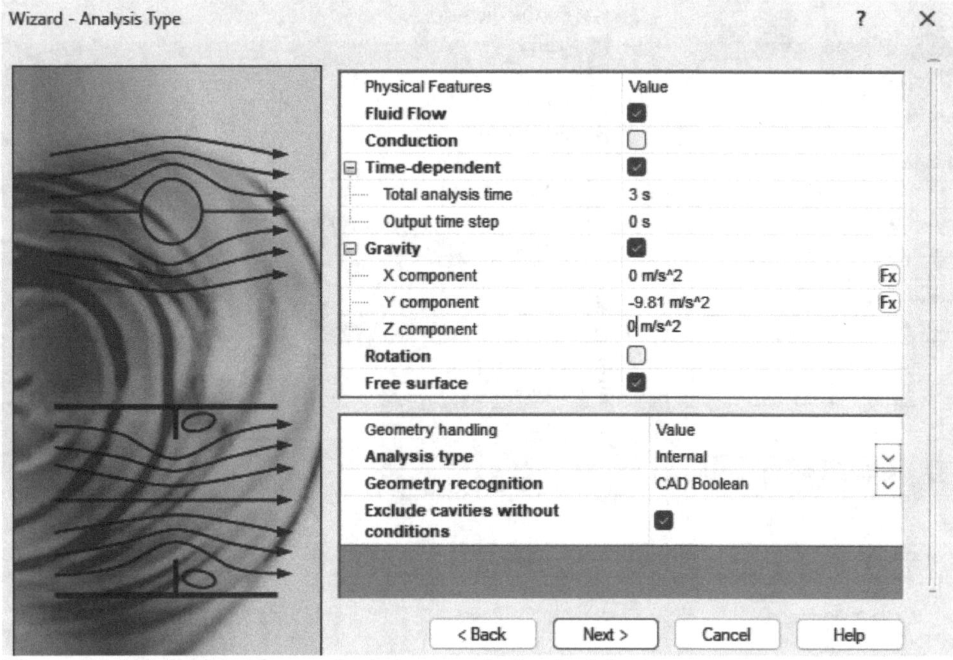

Figure 15.5b) Settings for analysis type and physical features

6. Add **Air** from **Gases** and **Water** from **Liquids** as **Project Fluids**. The **Default fluid type** is **Immiscible Mixture**. Select **Laminar Only** as **Flow Type**. Click on **Next>** twice and **Finish** the wizard.

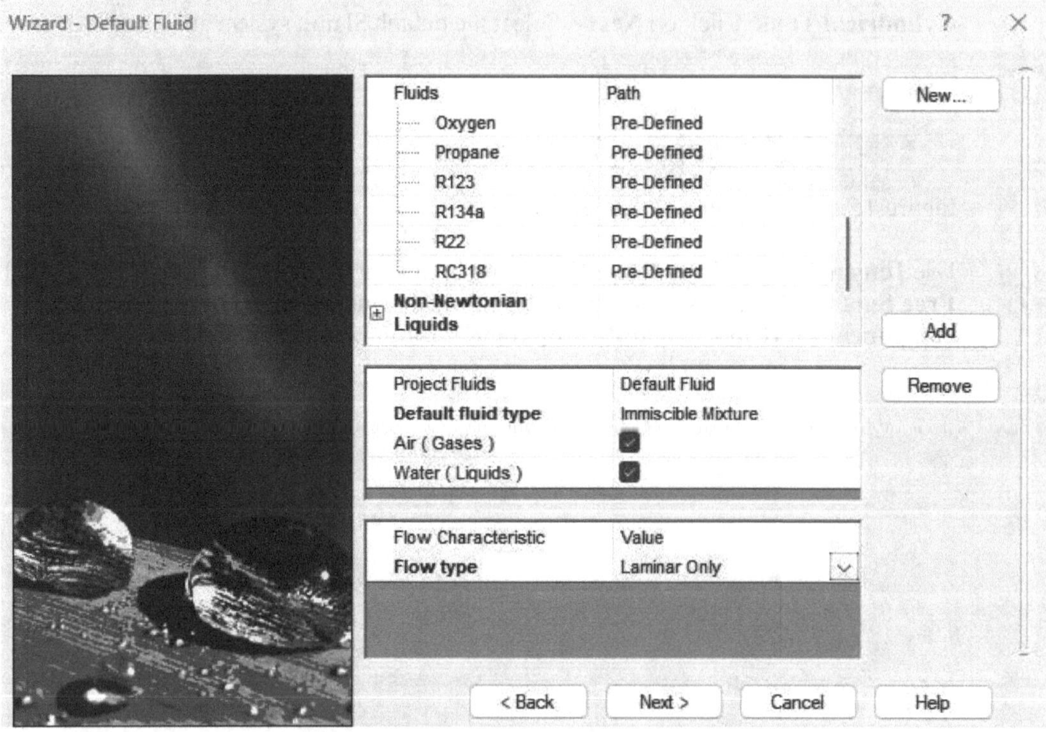

Figure 15.6 Creation of a default fluid

E. Computational Domain, Initial Condition and Boundary Conditions

7. Right click on **Computational Domain** under **Input Data** and select **Edit Definition....** Set **Y min** to **0.00135 m** and close the window, see Figure 15.7a).

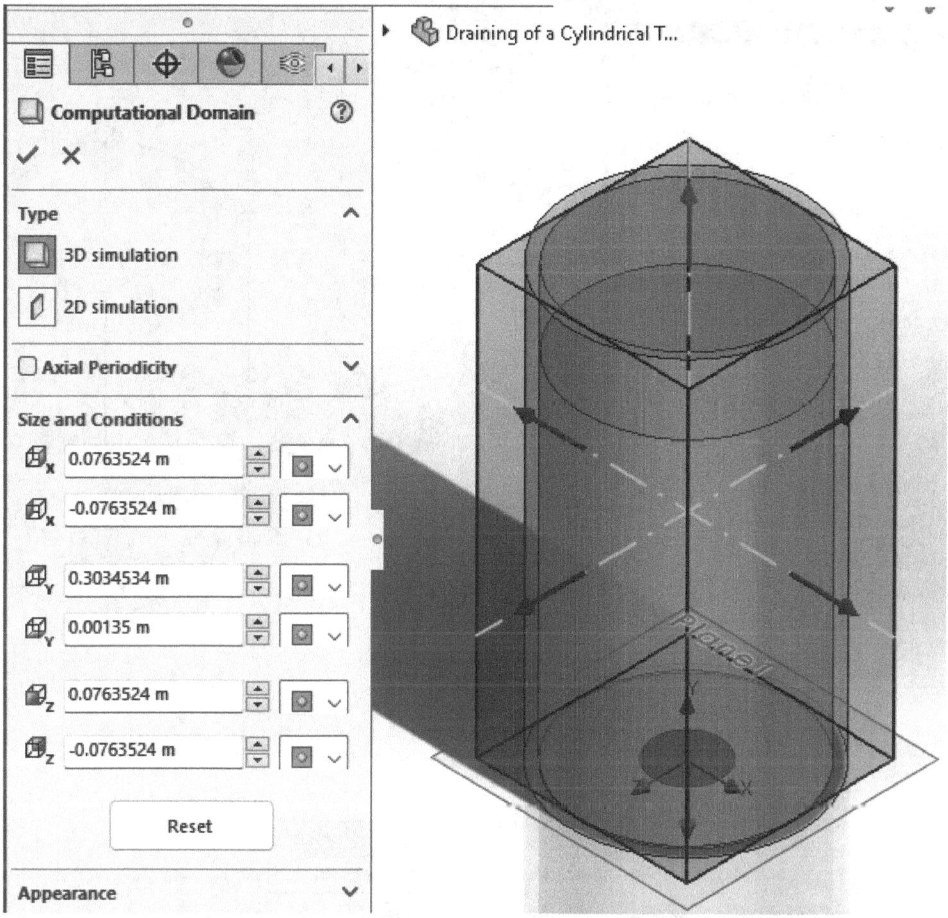

Figure 15.7a) Setting the size of the computational domain

Right click on **Water** under **Solid Bodies(2)** in the **FeatureManager Design Tree** and select **Hide**. Select **Tools>>Flow Simulation>>Insert>>Initial Condition...** from the menu. Select **Water** under **Solid Bodies(2)** as **Components /Faces to Apply Initial Condition**, see Figure 15.7b). Check the box for **Disable solid components**. Select **Water** as **Initial fluid** under **Substance Concentrations**. Select the green checkmark to exit the Initial Condition.

Right click on **Water** under **Solid Bodies(2)** in the **FeatureManager Design Tree** and select **Show**. Right click on **Boundary Conditions** in the **Flow Simulation Analysis** tree and select **Insert Boundary Conditions....** Move the cursor on the top lid of the cylinder, right click and **Select Other**. Select the face corresponding to the inside plane face of the upper lid, see Figure 15.7c). Select **Static Pressure** as **Type** and exit the window. Repeat this step and select static pressure for the opening in the bottom lid.

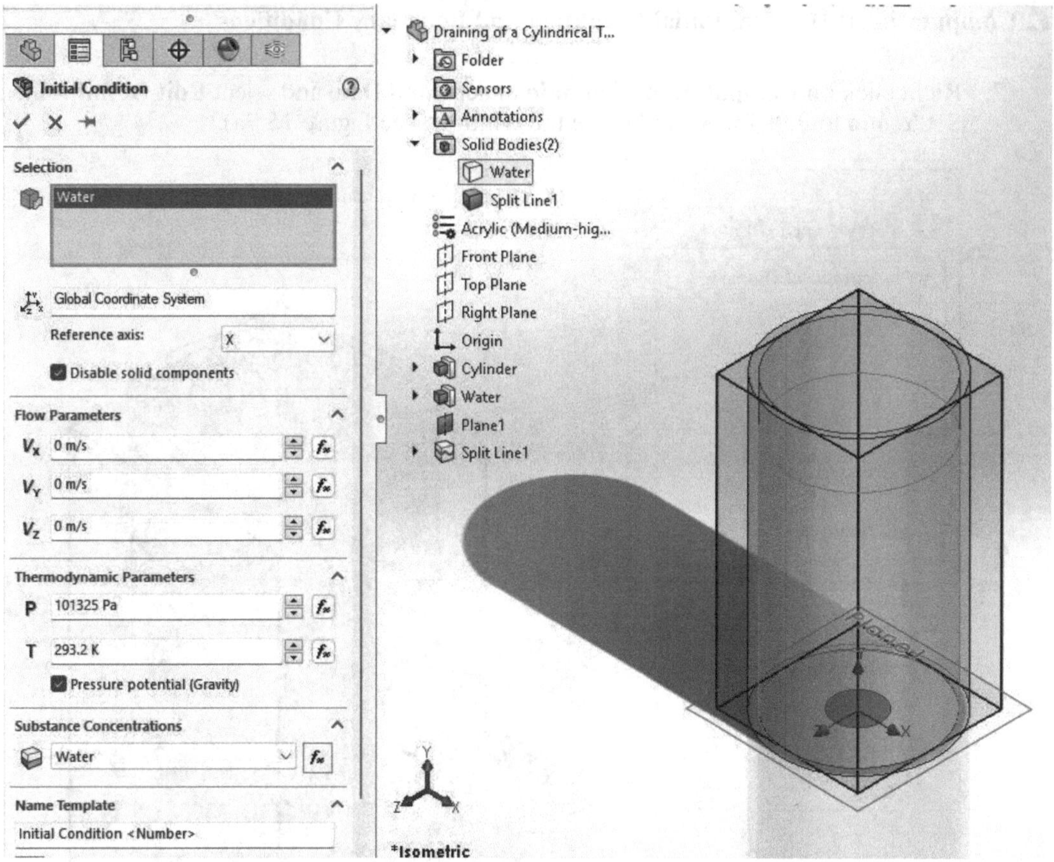

Figure 15.7b) Initial condition settings

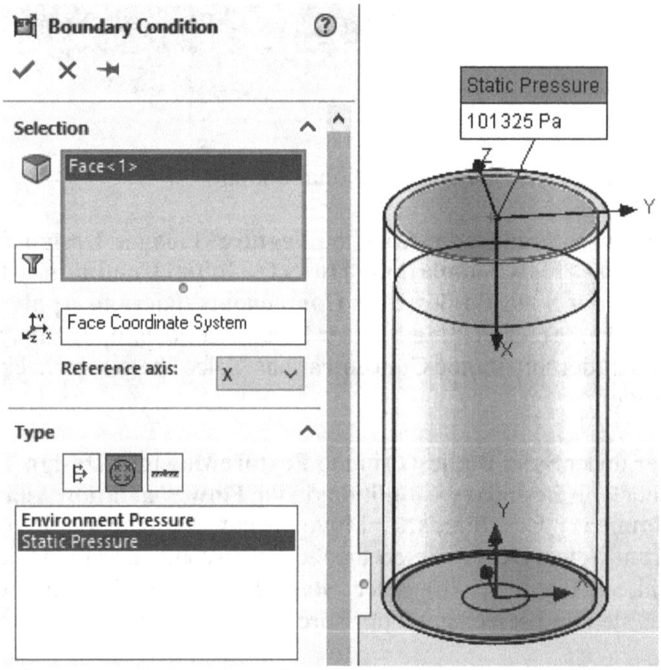

Figure 15.7c) Creation of static pressure on upper lid

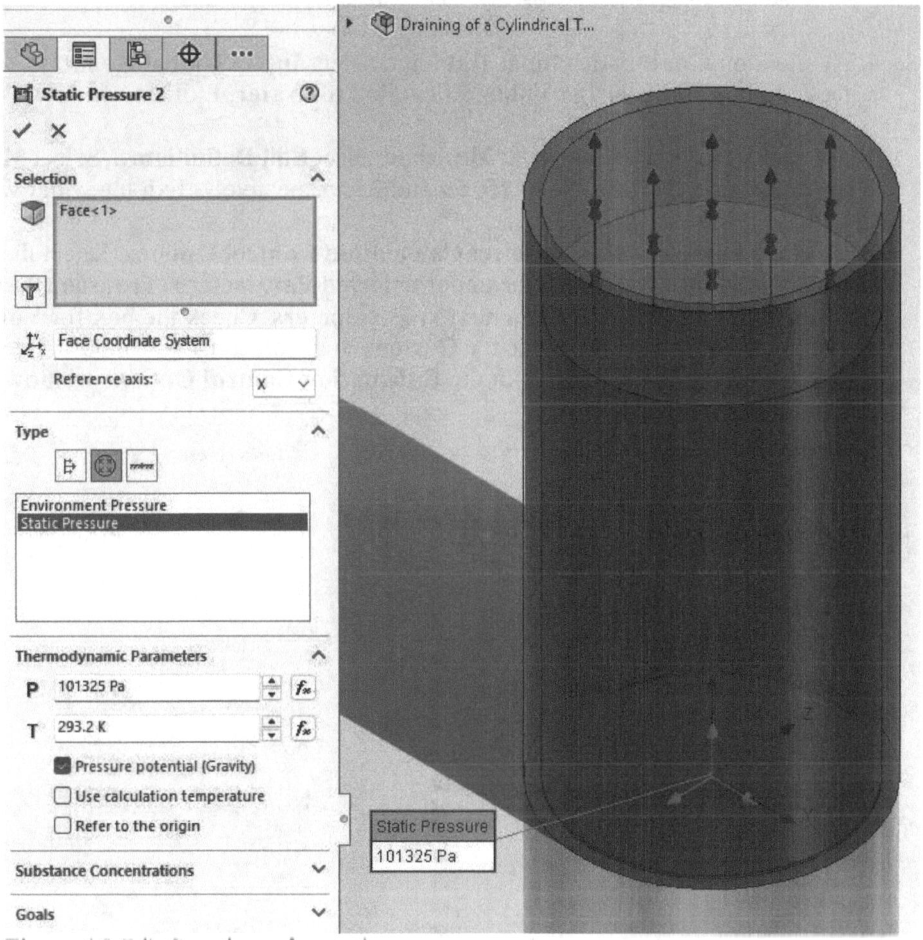

Figure 15.7d) Creation of a static pressure on lower opening

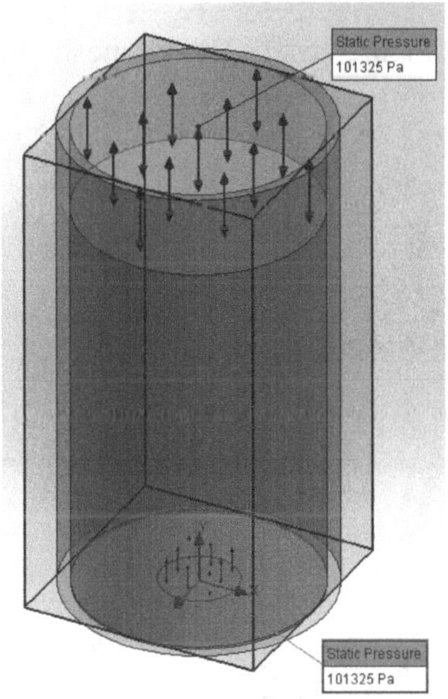

Figure 15.7e) Static pressure on upper lid and lower opening

F. Goal, Global Mesh and Calculation Control Options

8. Right click on **Goals** under **Input Data** and select **Insert Global Goals.** Check the box for **Average Volume Fraction of Water**. Exit the window.

   Right click on **Global Mesh** under **Mesh** and select **Edit Definition….** Select **Manual** as **Type** and set **Nx, Ny** and **Nz** to **25, 50** and **25**, respectively. Exit the window.

   Right click on **Input Data** and select **Calculation Control Options**. Select the **Saving** tab and check the box for **Periodic** under **Selected Parameters (Transient Explorer).** Click on **…** in the **Value** column next to **Parameters**. Check the box for **Volume Fraction of Water** under **Main** in the **Customize Parameter List** window. Select **OK** to exit the window. Click **OK** to exit the **Calculation Control Options** window.

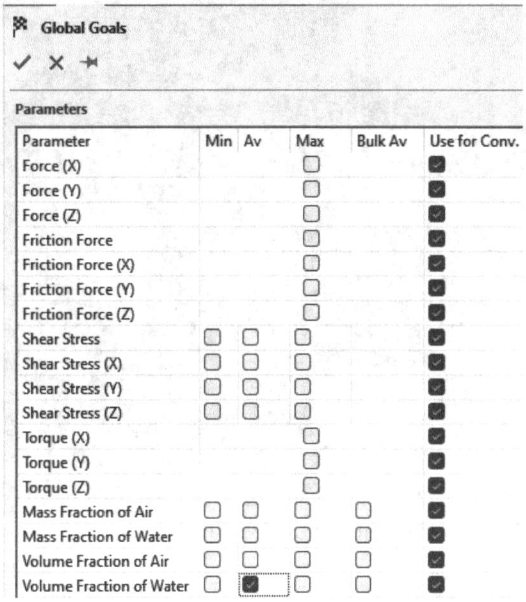

Figure 15.8a) Global goal

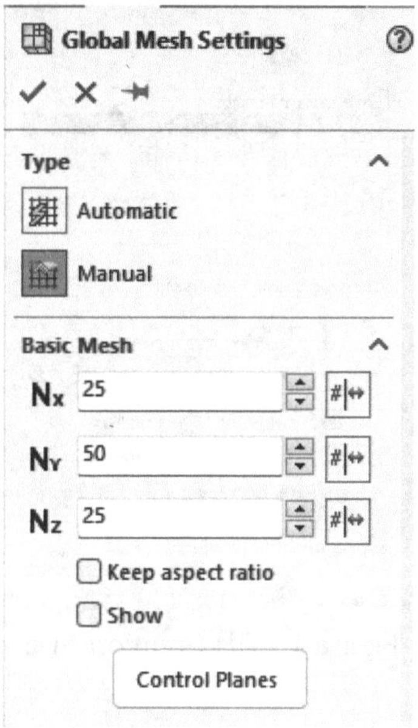

Figure 15.8b) Global mesh

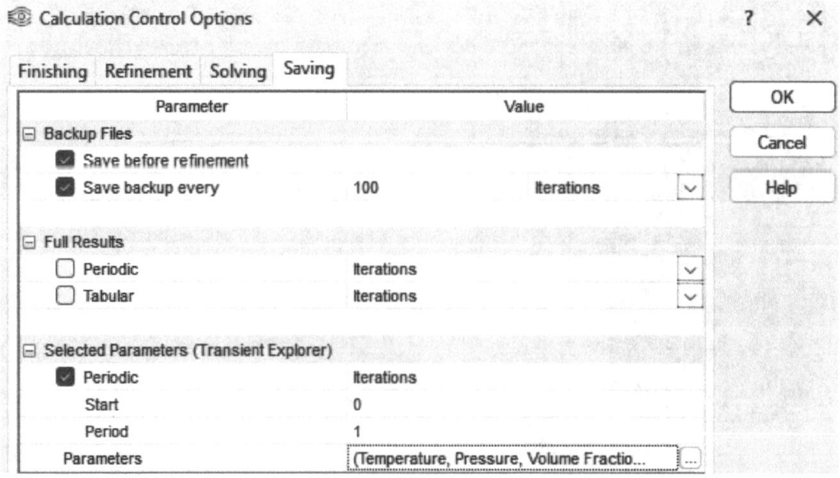

Figure 15.8c) Calculation control options

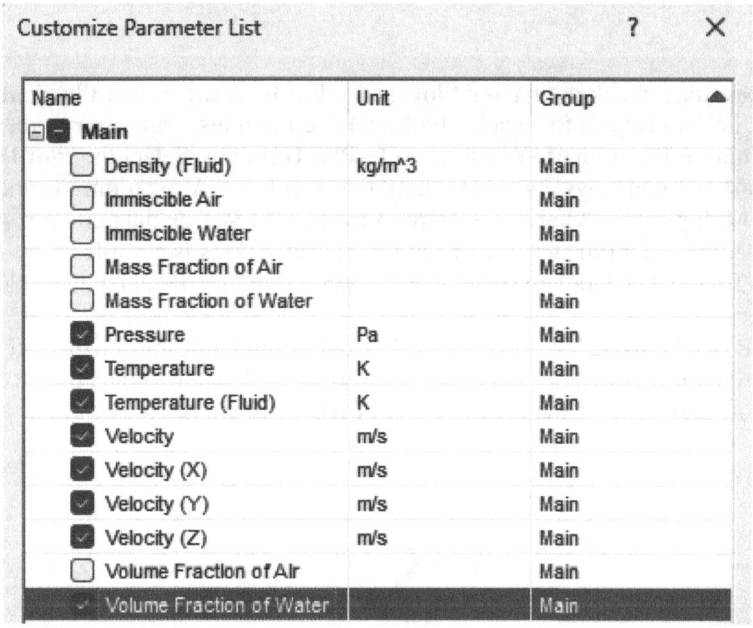

Figure 15.8d) Customize parameter list

G. Running the Flow Simulation

9. Select **Tools>>Flow Simulation>>Solve >>Run…** from the menu and click on the **Run** button.

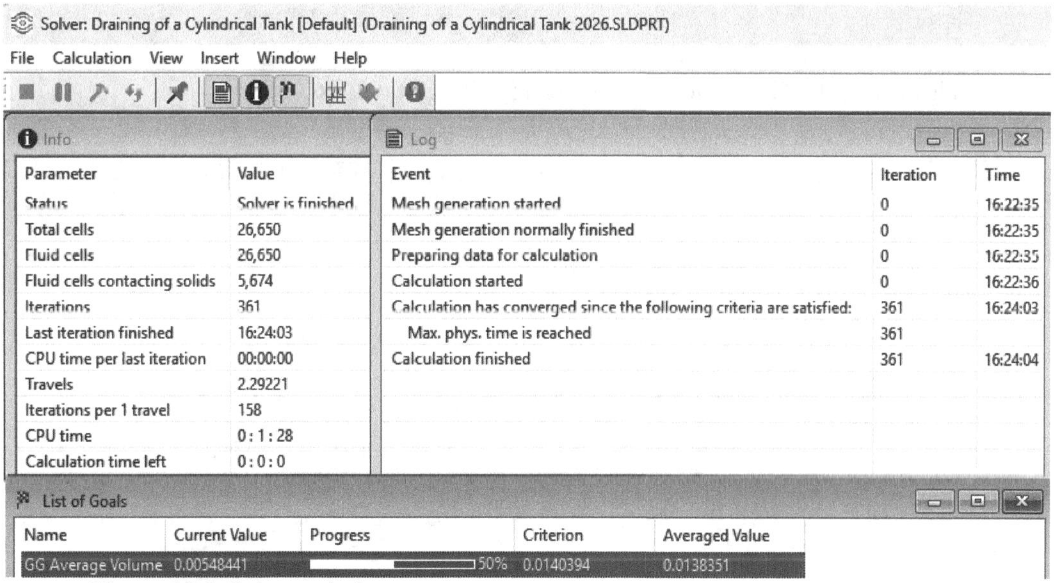

Figure 15.9 Solver window

H. Goal Plots

10. Open the **Results**, right click on **Goal Plots** and select **Insert....** Select **Physical time** as **Abscissa**. Click on Export to Excel. The Excel file includes a **Summary** tab, a **GG Average Volume Fraction of Water** tab and a **Plot Data** tab. Select the **Plot Data** tab. Delete rows 1 – 3 and rows 2 – 9 after that. Copy column A to column C and delete column A. Multiply **GG Average Volume Fraction of Water** data column A with **0.3048** to get the height of water *h* (m) in the cylinder. This is completed by entering =0.3048*A2 in cell C2. Drag this cell down the whole column of data. Label column C as *h* (m). Enter =0.25*(SQRT(0.23)*B2-2*SQRT(0.256))^2 in cell D2 and drag the cell down the whole column of data. Label column D as *h* (m), Theory. Plot height versus physical time, include theoretical solution and second order polynomial curve fit, see Figure 15.10c).

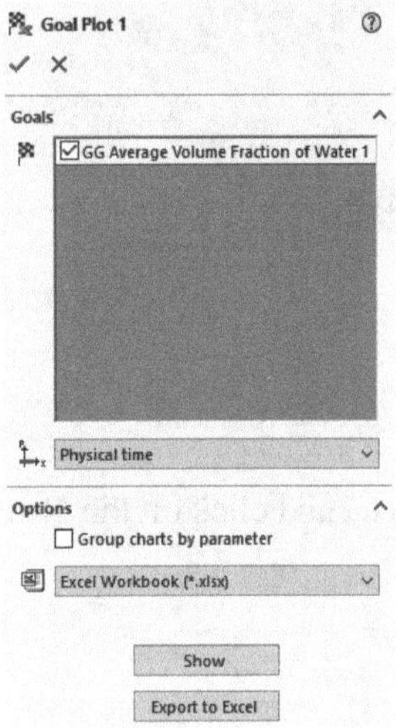

	A	B	C	D
1	GG Average Volume Fraction of Water 1	Physical time [s]	*h* (m).	*h* (m), Theory
2	0.840127477	0.005265655	0.256071	0.254723872
3	0.839920753	0.007354524	0.256008	0.25421852
4	0.839592124	0.009511864	0.255908	0.253697129
5	0.839230565	0.011261838	0.255797	0.253274585
6	0.838796038	0.012995498	0.255665	0.252856327
7	0.838048234	0.015637932	0.255437	0.252219486
8	0.837200716	0.018339888	0.255179	0.25156913
9	0.836405624	0.020732272	0.254936	0.250993987
10	0.835671326	0.022924193	0.254713	0.250467616
11	0.834991099	0.024978004	0.254505	0.249974911
12	0.833995886	0.027933176	0.254202	0.249266824
13	0.833016076	0.030737458	0.253903	0.248595819
14	0.83206863	0.033401293	0.253615	0.247959259
15	0.831101623	0.035952971	0.25332	0.247350265
16	0.830091552	0.03843296	0.253012	0.246759098
17	0.828490368	0.042069889	0.252524	0.245893425
18	0.826779467	0.045636462	0.252002	0.245045975
19	0.82500598	0.049113075	0.251462	0.244221309
20	0.823189594	0.052527043	0.250908	0.243412855

Figure 15.10a) Goals plot Figure 15.10b) Data in Excel file

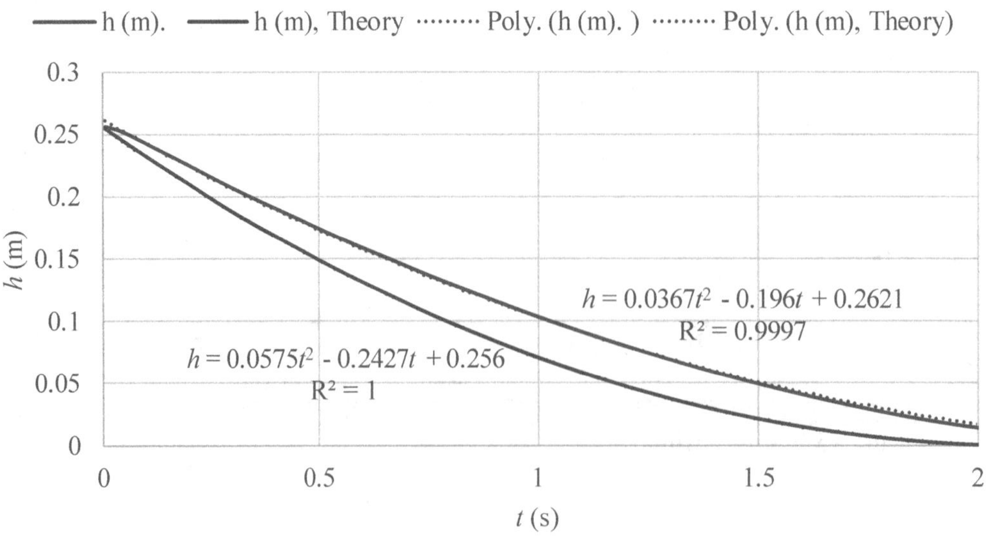

Figure 15.10c) Water height *h* (m) versus time *t* (s) for draining of a cylindrical tank

I. Transient Explorer

11. Right click on **Cut Plots** under Results and select the **Insert....** Select **Front Plane** and select **Contours** of **Volume Fraction of Water** and slide the **Number of Levels** to **255**. Exit the **Cut Plot** and select **Front View**. Select **Tools>>Flow Simulation>>Results>>Display>>Lighting.** Right click on **Results** and select **Transient Explorer**. Click on Play to see draining of water from the cylindrical tank.

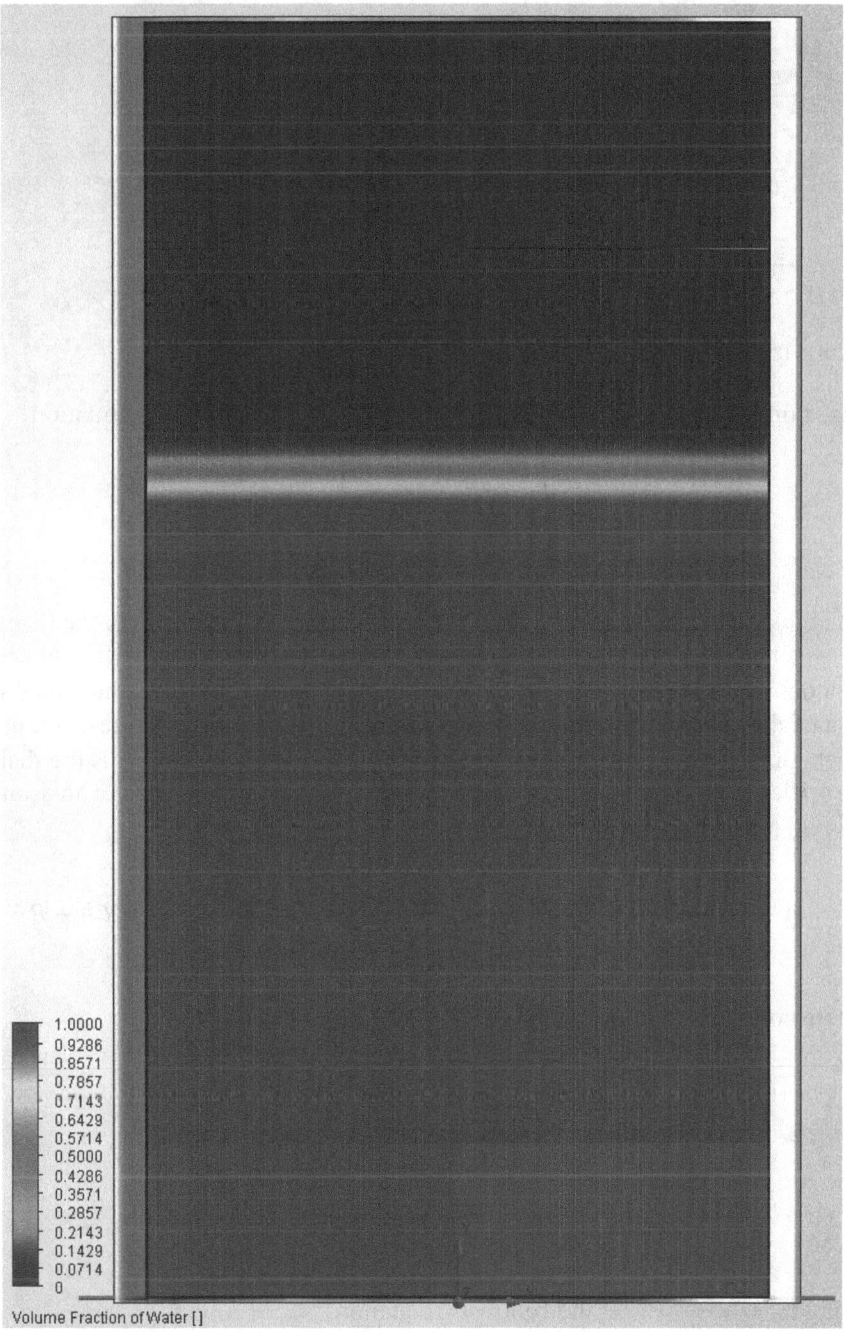

Figure 15.11 Volume fraction of water at $t = 0.36$ s.

J. Theory

12. The geometry for the problem studied in this chapter is shown in Figure 15.12.

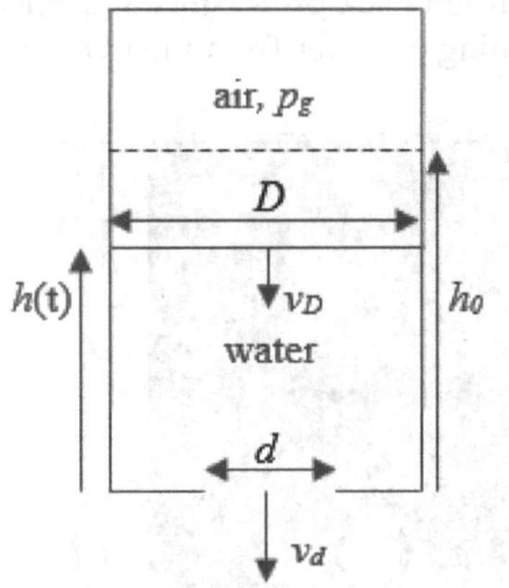

Figure 15.12 Geometry for draining water cylinder

Based on the equation of continuity for the fluid and Bernoulli's equation

$$v_d A_d = v_D A_D = v_{d,a} A_{d,a} \tag{15.1}$$

$$\frac{1}{2}\rho v_d^2 = \frac{1}{2}\rho v_D^2 + \rho g h + p_g = \frac{1}{2}\rho v_{d,a}^2 \tag{15.2}$$

where v_D is the theoretical velocity of the free surface, v_d is the theoretical velocity of the water jet, $v_{d,a}$ is the actual velocity of the jet, A_D is the cross-sectional area of the cylinder, A_d is the cross-sectional area of the orifice, $A_{d,a}$ is the actual cross sectional area of the water jet due to the vena contracta, p_g is the air gage pressure, h(t) is the height of the free surface, h_0 is the initial height of the free surface, d is the diameter of the orifice and D is the diameter of the cylinder. We get the following expression for the velocity v_D of the free surface

$$v_D^2 = v_d^2 - 2gh - \frac{2p_g}{\rho} = v_D^2 \frac{A_D^2}{A_d^2} - 2gh - \frac{2p_g}{\rho} \quad \text{or} \quad v_D^2 = \frac{2gh + \frac{2p_g}{\rho}}{\frac{A_D^2}{A_d^2} - 1} = Ch + B \tag{15.3}$$

where constants

$$C = \frac{2g}{\frac{A_D^2}{A_d^2} - 1} \tag{15.4}$$

$$B = \frac{2p_g}{\rho\left(\frac{A_D^2}{A_d^2} - 1\right)} \tag{15.5}$$

Using $v_D = -\frac{dh}{dt}$, we get the following equation

$$(\frac{dh}{dt})^2 = Ch + B \qquad \text{or} \qquad \frac{dh}{dt} = \sqrt{Ch + B} \quad \text{with} \quad h(0) = h_0 \tag{15.6}$$

with the solution $h(t) = h_0 + \frac{t}{4}\left(Ct - 4\sqrt{B + Ch_0}\right)$ with $t_{empty} = \frac{2(\sqrt{B+Ch_0}-\sqrt{B})}{C}$

where t_{empty} is the time it takes to empty the water in the cylinder. For atmospheric air pressure we get

$$h(t) = \frac{1}{4}\left(\sqrt{C}t - 2\sqrt{h_0}\right)^2 = \frac{1}{4}Ct^2 - \sqrt{Ch_0}t + h_0 \tag{15.7}$$

$$t_{empty} = 2\sqrt{\frac{h_0}{C}} \tag{15.8}$$

Comparing equation 15.7 with the second order polynomial trend line in Figure 15.10b), we find that C_a = 0.1468m/s^2, $h_{0,a}$ = 0.2609 m, $t_{empty,a}$ = 2.67 s from SOLIDWORKS Flow Simulation. The corresponding values from theory are C = 0.23 m/s^2, h_0 = 0.256 m, t_{empty} = 2.1 s. The effect of the vena contracta can be expressed using the coefficient of discharge C_d and equations 15.1 and 15.2

$$C_d = \frac{actual\,mass\,flow\,rate}{theoretical\,mass\,flow\,rate} = C_c C_v = \frac{A_{d,a}}{A_d}\frac{v_{d,a}}{v_d} = \frac{A_{d,a}}{A_d}\sqrt{\frac{A_D^2 - A_d^2}{A_D^2 - A_{d,a}^2}} \tag{15.9}$$

where C_c is the coefficient of contraction and C_v is the coefficient of velocity. From equation 15.4 we get

$$A_{d,a} = \frac{A_D}{\sqrt{\frac{2g}{C_a}+1}} \tag{15.10}$$

and we find that C_d = 0.760.

K. References

1. Hicks A. and Slaton W., Determining the Coefficient of Discharge for a Draining Container, *The Physics Teacher* **52**, 43, 2014.
2. Guerra D. *et al.*, A Bernoulli's lab in a bottle, *The Physics Teacher* **34**, 456-459, 2005.
3. Guerra D. *et al.*, An introduction to dimensionless parameters in the study of viscous fluid flows, *The Physics Teacher* **49**, 175-179, 2011.
4. Lienhard, J.H., Velocity coefficients for free jets from sharp-edges orifices, *J. Fluids Eng.*, **106**, 13-17, 1984.
5. Libii J.N., Mechanics of the slow draining of a large tank under gravity, *Am. J. Phys.*, **71**, 1204-1207, 2003.
6. Saleta M.E. *et al.*, Experimental study of Bernoulli's equation with losses, *Am. J. Phys.*, **73** (7), 598-602, 2005.

L. Exercises

15.1 Run flow simulations as shown in this chapter for different time steps and different basic mesh size to study how this affects the solution. Set the time step in calculation control options under the solving tab.

Nx	Ny	Nz	Time Step (s)	h0 (m)	d (m)	D (m)	β = d/D	C_d
25	50	25	automatic	0.25	0.05	0.1524	0.328	0.768
20	40	20	0.01	0.25	0.05	0.1524	0.328	
30	60	30	0.005	0.25	0.05	0.1524	0.328	
40	80	40	0.002	0.25	0.05	0.1524	0.328	
50	100	50	0.001	0.25	0.05	0.1524	0.328	

Table 15.1 Basic mesh size and time step for Exercise 15.1

15.2 Run flow simulations for different ratios of the orifice diameter to cylinder diameter $\beta = d/D$ as shown in tables 15.1 and 15.2.

Nx	Ny	Nz	Time Step (s)	h0 (m)	d (m)	D (m)	β = d/D	C_d
25	50	25	automatic	0.25	0.00892	0.1524	0.059	
25	50	25	automatic	0.25	0.0125	0.1524	0.082	
25	50	25	automatic	0.25	0.025	0.1524	0.164	
25	50	25	automatic	0.25	0.03	0.1524	0.197	
25	50	25	automatic	0.25	0.05	0.1524	0.328	0.768

Table 15.2 Settings for Exercise 15.2

15.3 Run flow simulations with the orifice offset from the center. The offset is determined by $\alpha = 2a/(D - d)$ where a is the distance from the center of the orifice to the center of the cylinder.

Nx	Ny	Nz	Time Step (s)	h0 (m)	d (m)	D (m)	β = d/D	a (m)	α = 2a/(D-d)	C_d
25	50	25	automatic	0.25	0.05	0.1524	0.328	0	0	0.768
25	50	25	automatic	0.25	0.05	0.1524	0.328	0.01024	0.2	
25	50	25	automatic	0.25	0.05	0.1524	0.328	0.02048	0.4	
25	50	25	automatic	0.25	0.05	0.1524	0.328	0.03072	0.6	
25	50	25	automatic	0.25	0.05	0.1524	0.328	0.04096	0.8	
25	50	25	automatic	0.25	0.05	0.1524	0.328	0.0512	1	

Table 15.3 Settings for Exercise 15.3

15.4 Run flow simulations with the orifice offset from the center and different number of orifices N spaced at equal angles in between them around the circumference. The offset is determined by $\alpha = 2a/(D - d)$ where a is the distance from the center of the hole to the center of the cylinder.

Nx	Ny	Nz	Time Step (s)	h0 (m)	d (m)	D (m)	β = d/D	a (m)	α = 2a/(D-d)	N	C_d
25	50	25	automatic	0.25	0.05	0.1524	0.328	0.0512	1	1	
25	50	25	automatic	0.25	0.05	0.1524	0.328	0.0512	1	2	
25	50	25	automatic	0.25	0.05	0.1524	0.328	0.0512	1	3	
25	50	25	automatic	0.25	0.05	0.1524	0.328	0.0512	1	4	

Table 15.4 Settings for Exercise 15.4

CHAPTER 16. AHMED BODY

A. Objectives

- Creating the SOLIDWORKS model needed for Flow Simulations
- Setting up a Flow Simulation project for external flows
- Using cut plots to visualize the resulting flow field
- Use a Local Mesh
- Use Flow Trajectories

B. Problem Description

We will in this chapter study the flow past the Ahmed body. The Ahmed body is a simple geometry for the body of a car, and this flow case is useful as a benchmark test case for CFD codes.

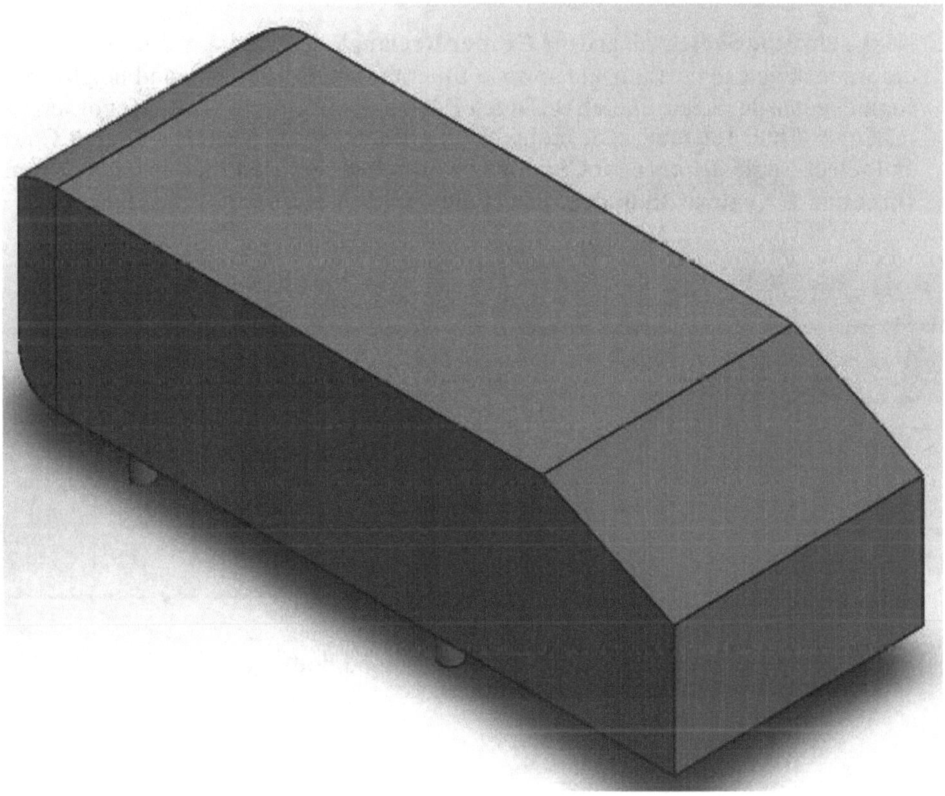

C. Modeling SOLIDWORKS Part

1. Start SOLIDWORKS and create a New Part. Select **Tools>>Options...** from the SOLIDWORKS menu. Click on the **Document Properties** tab and select **Units**. Select **MMGS** as your **Unit system**. Select the **Front** view from the **View Orientation** drop down menu in the graphics window and click on the **Front Plane** in the **FeatureManager design tree**.

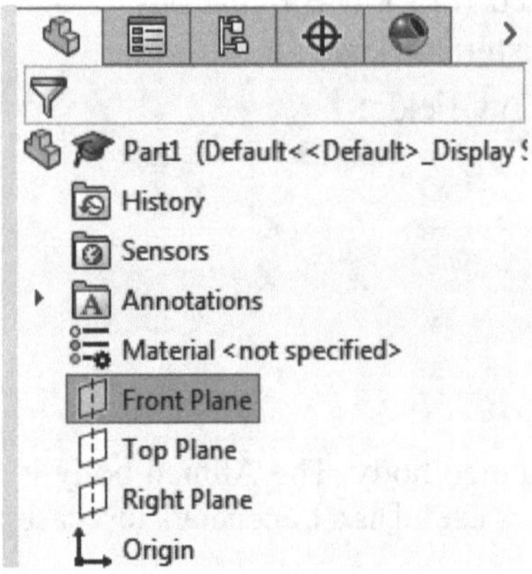

Figure 16.1 Front Plane

2. Next, select the **Sketch** tab and the **Corner Rectangle** sketch tool. Start at the origin and draw a rectangle to the right and upward. Enter the length **1044 mm** and height **288 mm** for the rectangle. Select **Sketch>>Sketch Fillet** and click on the two left corners of the rectangle. Enter **100 mm** as the radius for the fillets. Select **Sketch>>Sketch Chamfer** and select **Angle-distance** for **Chamfer Parameters**. Set **Distance 1** to **201.2 mm** and **Direction 1 Angle** to **25.00deg**. Select the upper right corner of the rectangle.

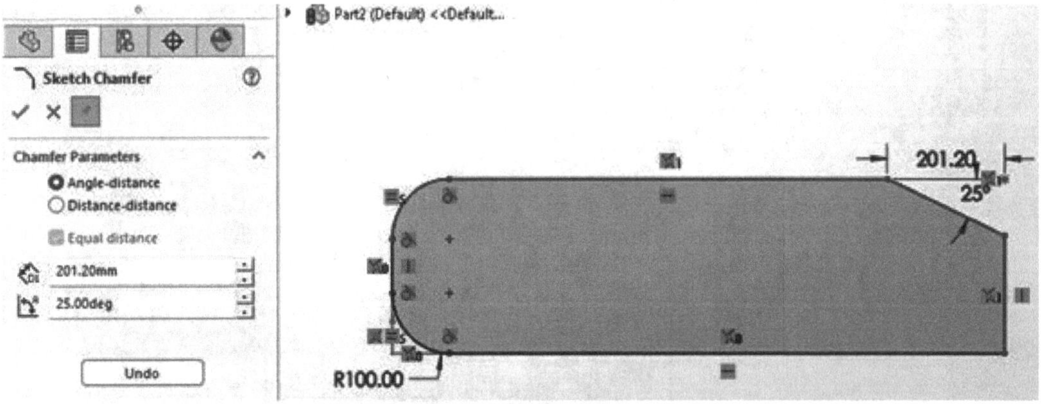

Figure 16.2 Corner radius and chamfer for Ahmed body

3. Select the **Features** tab and **Extruded Boss/Base**. Set the **End Condition** to **Mid Plane** in **Direction 1** and enter **389 mm** as the **Depth** of the extrusion.

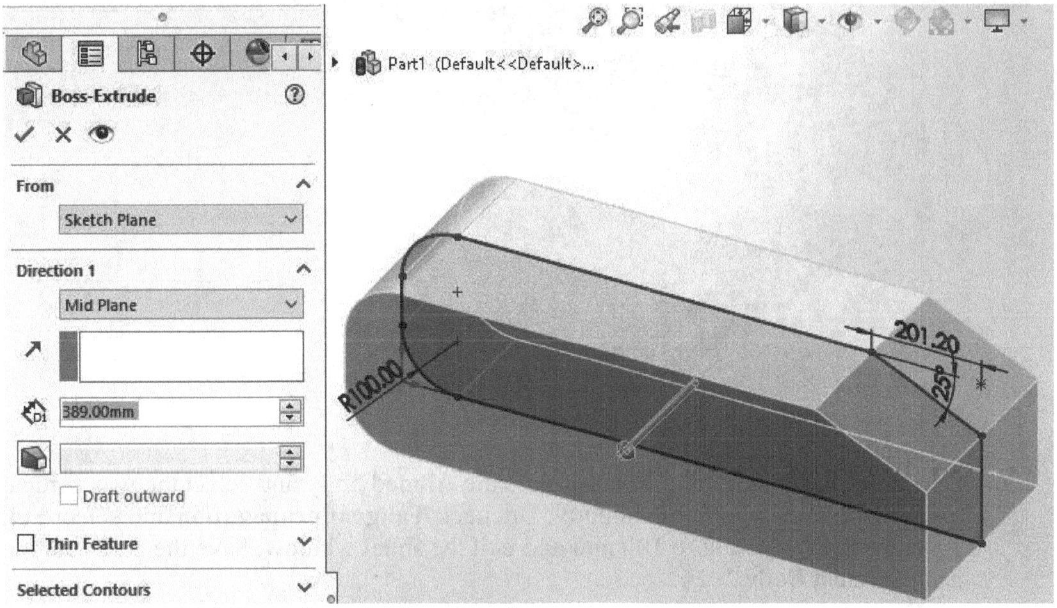

Figure 16.3 Extrusion of Ahmed body

4. Select the **Bottom** view. Sketch a circle with a 15 mm radius on the bottom plane of the Ahmed body and position the circle at X -202.00, Y 163.50. Create another circle with the same radius at X -202.00, Y -163.50 and two more circles with the same radius at X -672.00, Y -163.50 and X -672.00, Y 163.50.

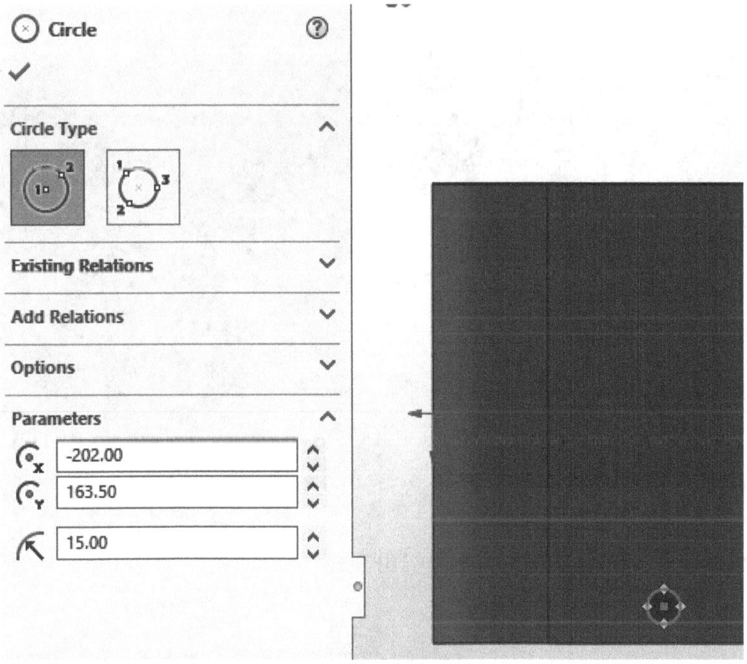

Figure 16.4 Circle on the bottom of the Ahmed body

5. Select the **Features** tab and **Extruded Boss/Base**. Set the **End Condition** to **Blind** in **Direction 1** and enter **50 mm** as the **Depth** of the extrusion.

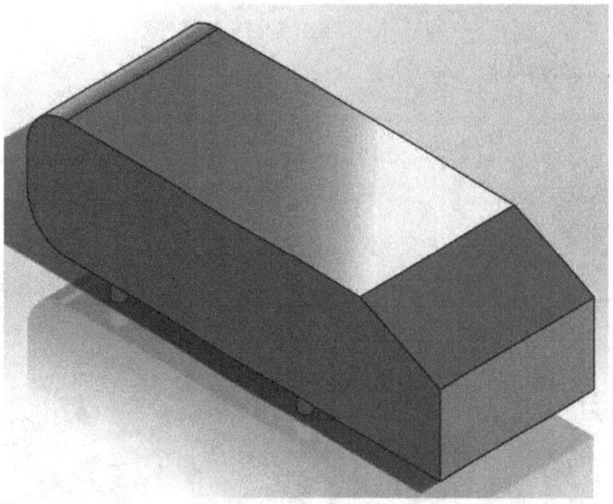

Figure 16.5 Ahmed body with extruded feet

6. Select the **Features** tab and **Fillet**. Rotate the Ahmed body and select the two vertical edges at the front of the Ahmed body. Uncheck **Tangent propagation** and select **Full preview**. Set the **Radius** to **100 mm** and exit the **Fillet** window. Save the part with the name **Ahmed Body 2026**.

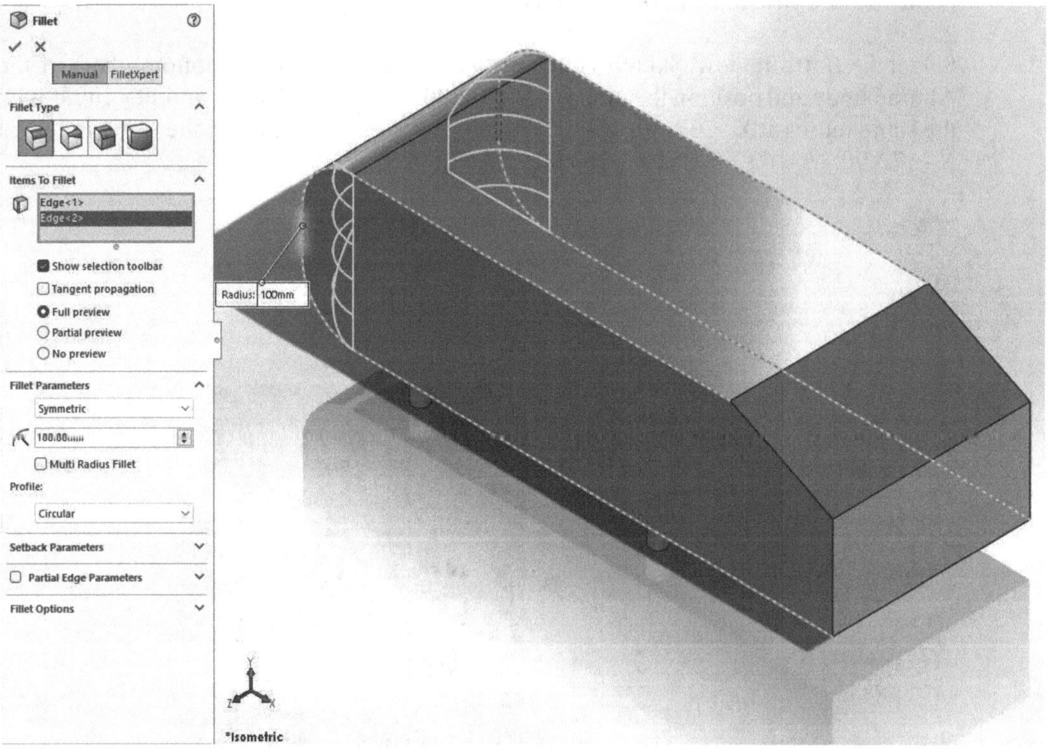

Figure 16.6a) Settings and selections for fillet

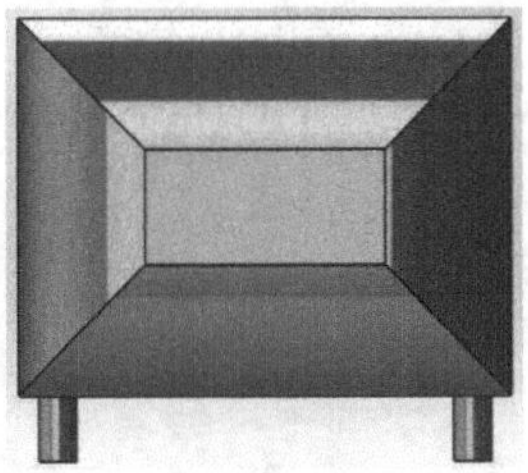

Figure 16.6b) View of the front of the finished Ahmed body

D. Flow Simulation Project

7. If Flow Simulation is not available in the SOLIDWORKS menu, select **Tools>>Add Ins…** and check the corresponding **SOLIDWORKS Flow Simulation** box. Start the **Flow Simulation Wizard** by selecting **Tools>>Flow Simulation>>Project>>Wizard…** from the SOLIDWORKS menu. Create a new project with the name **Flow Past Ahmed Body**. Click on Next>.

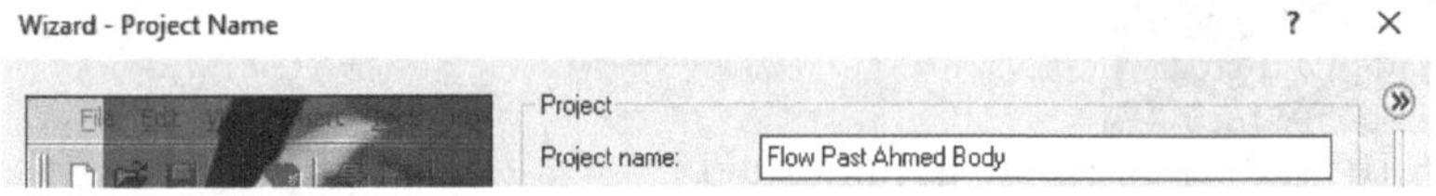

Figure 16.7 Entering configuration name

8. Select the **SI unit system.** Click on Next>.

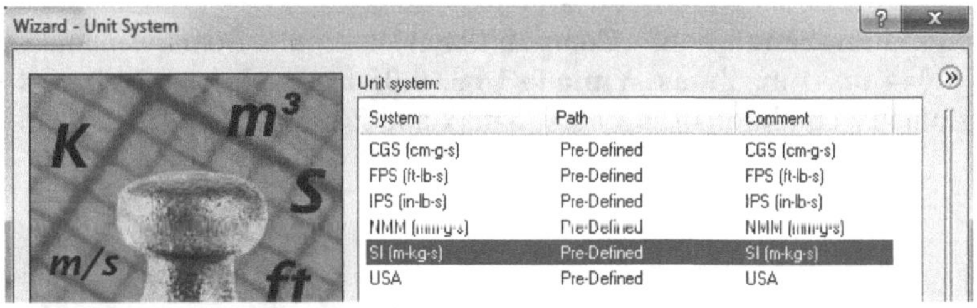

Figure 16.8 Selection of unit system

9. Select **External Analysis type**. Click on Next>.

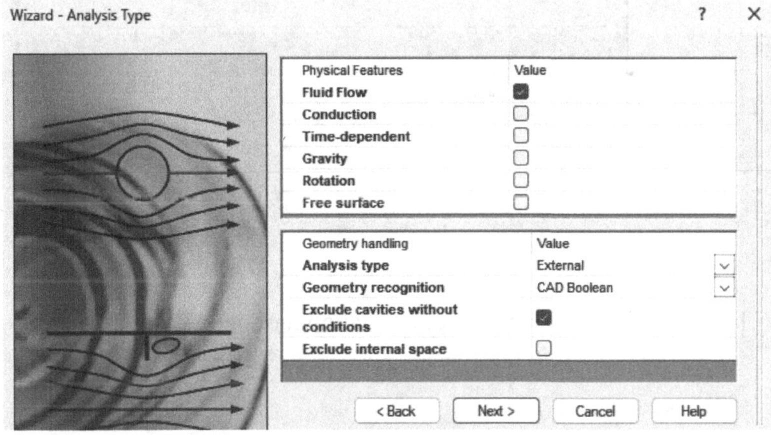

Figure 16.9 Selection of External Analysis type

10. Add **Air** as the default **Project Fluid** by selecting it from **Gases**. Click on Next. Choose default values for **Wall Conditions** and enter **30 m/s** as the **Velocity in X direction** as **Initial Condition**. Finish the Wizard.

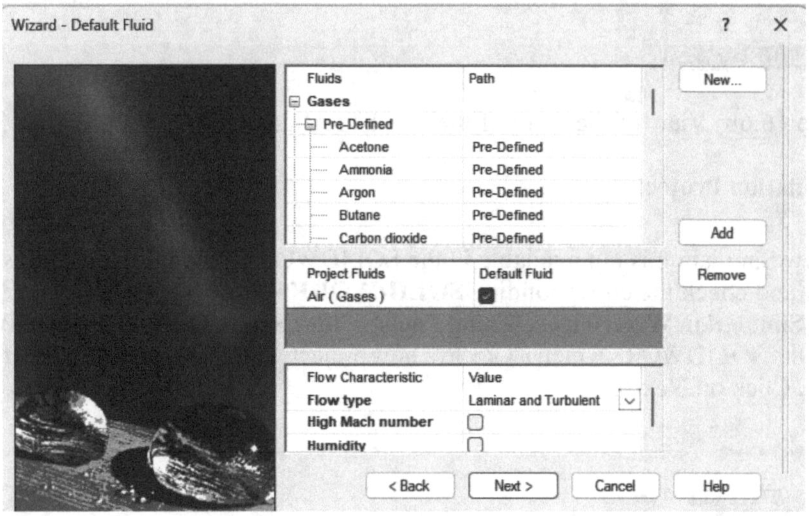

Figure 16.10 Adding air as the default fluid

E. Computational Domain

11. Select **Tools>Flow Simulation>>Computational Domain…** from the menu. Set **Xmax, Xmin** to **6.044 m, -1 m, Ymax, Ymin** to **1 m, -0.05 m** and **Zmax, Zmin** to **1 m, 0 m**. Select Symmetry conditions for **Ymax, Zmax** and **Zmin.**

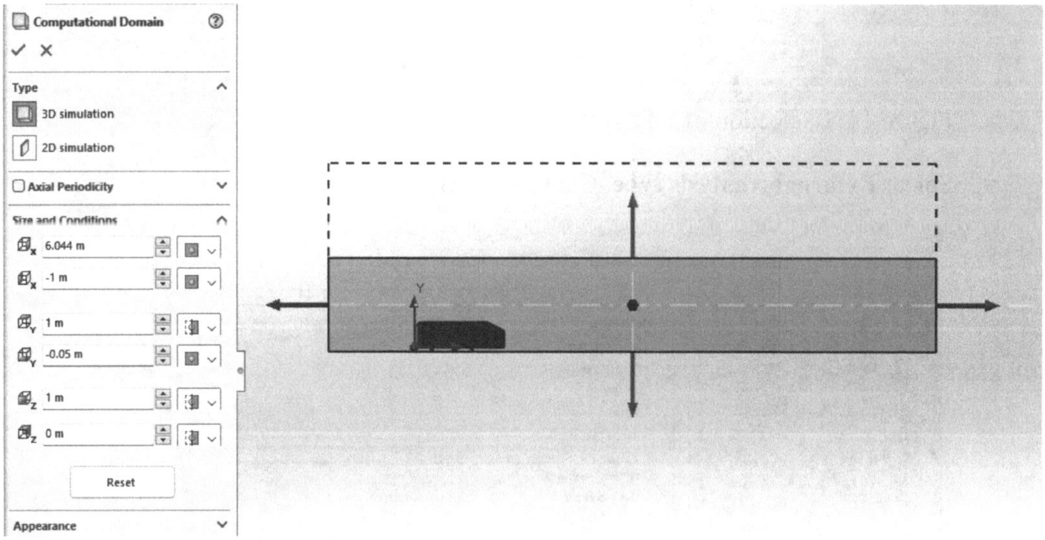

Figure 16.11 Size and conditions for computational domain

F. Goals

12. Right click on **Goals** in the **Flow Simulation analysis tree** and select **Insert Global Goals....** Check the box for **Force (X)**. Right click on **Goals** in the **Flow Simulation analysis tree** and select **Insert Equation Goal....** Click on **GG Force (X) 1** in the Flow Simulation Analysis tree. Enter the **Expression** as shown in figure 16.12:
{GG Force (X) 1}/(0.5*1.225*30^2*0.112/2)

    Select **No unit** for **Dimensionality**. Enter **Drag Coefficient** as the name for the equation goal. Click on the OK button to exit the window. The drag coefficient is defined as drag force / (dynamic pressure * frontal area of the Ahmed body).

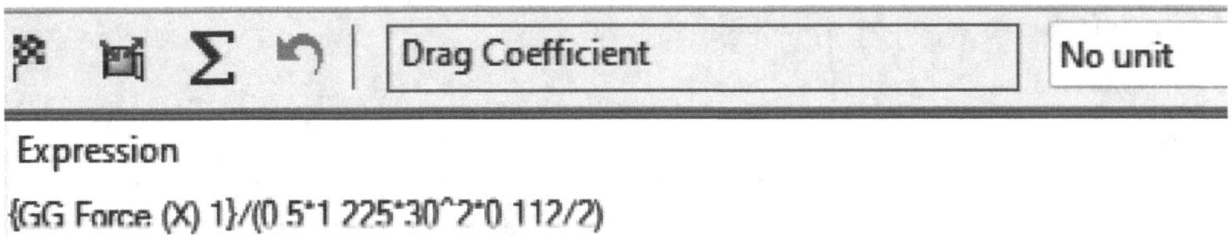

Figure 16.12 Expression for equation goal

G. Global Mesh

13. Select **Tools>Flow Simulation>>Global Mesh...** from the menu. Set the **Level of initial mesh** to **4**. Check the box for **Show basic mesh** and exit the window.

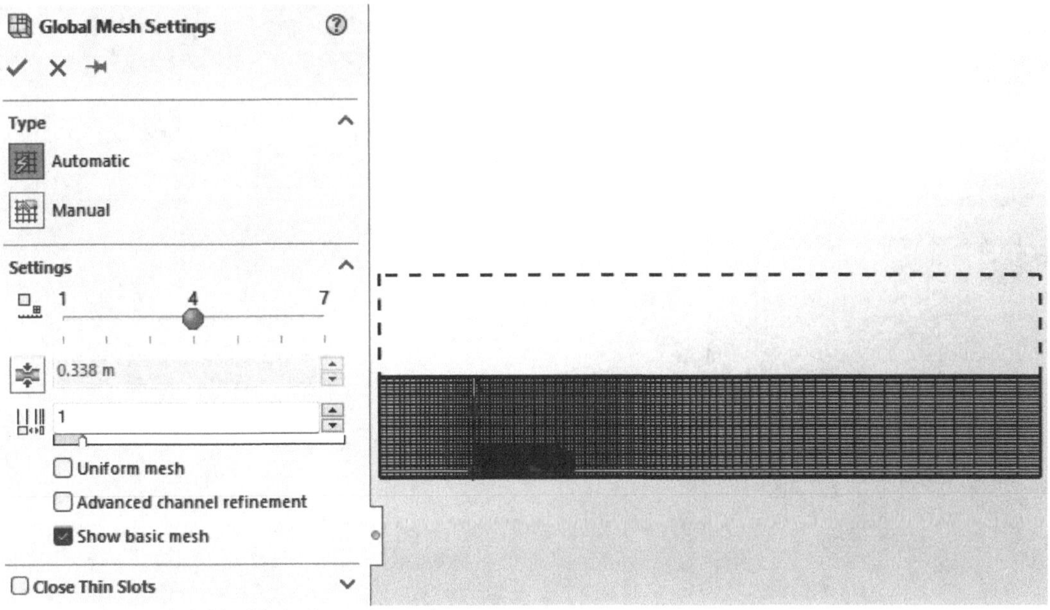

Figure 16.13 Global mesh settings

H. Local Mesh

14. Select **Tools>Flow Simulation>>Insert>>Local Mesh...** from the menu. Select **Region** under **Selection** and check **Cuboid.** Enter **2.148 m, -0.552 m** as **Xmax, Xmin, 0.85 m, -0.05 m** as **Ymax, Ymin** and **0.45 m, 0 m** as **Zmax, Zmin**. Set **Level of Refining Fluid Cells** to **1** and **Level of Refining Cells at Fluid/Solid Boundary** to **2**. Uncheck the boxes for **Channels, Advanced Refinement** and **Close Thin Slots**. Check the box for **Display Refinement Level.**

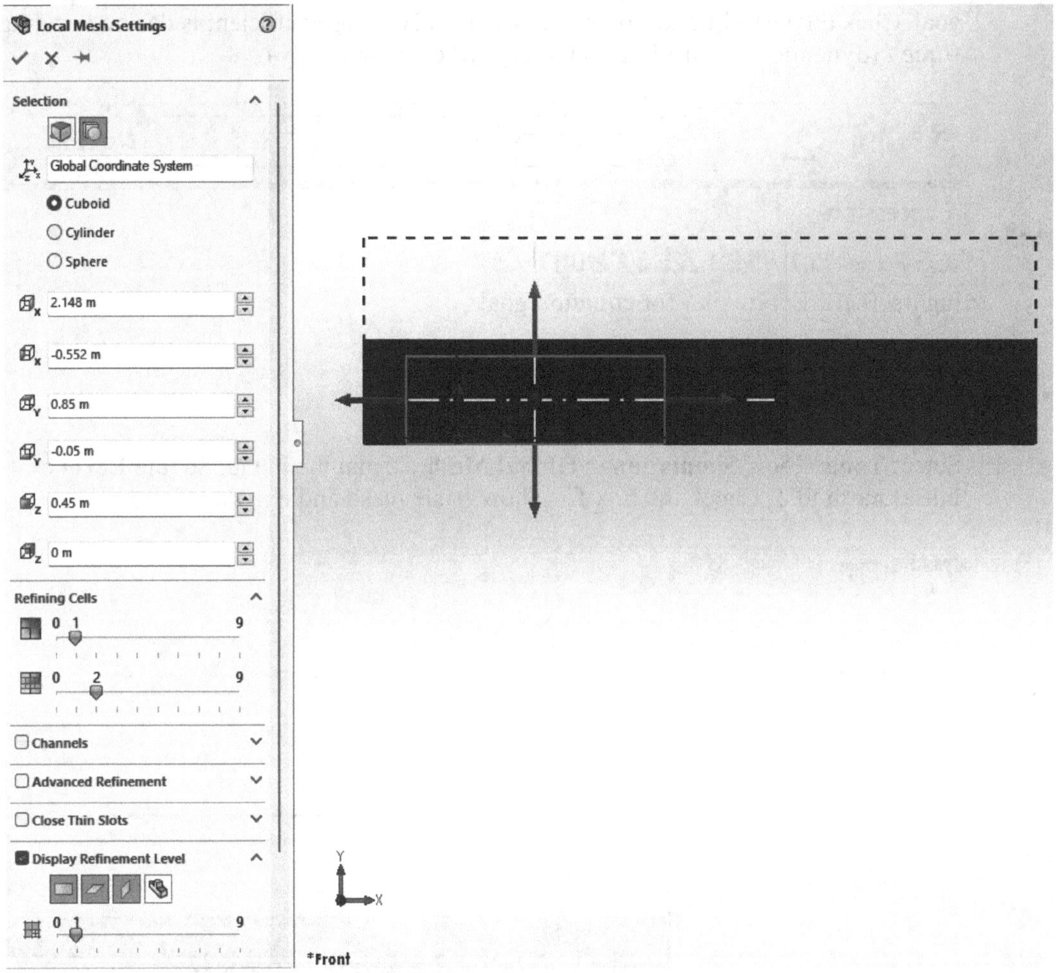

Figure 16.14 Local mesh settings

I. Running Simulations

15. Select **Tools>>Flow Simulation>>Solve>>Run….** Push the **Run** button in the window that appears. Insert the goals table by clicking on **List of Goals** in the **Solver** as shown in figure 16.15a).

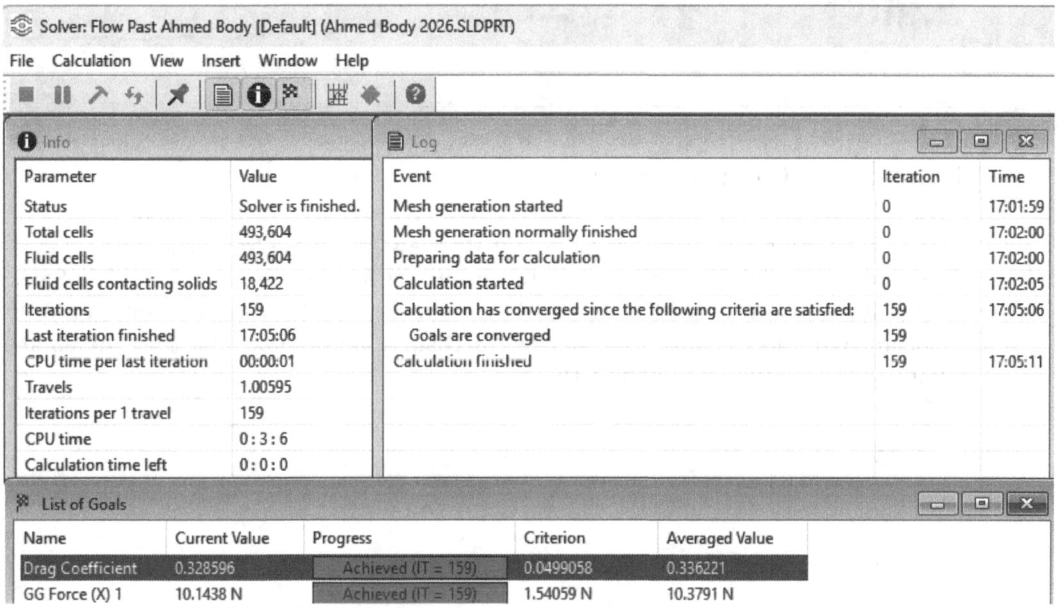

Figure 16.15a) Solver window

Click on the **Insert Goals Plot** in the **Solver** and check the box for **Drag Coefficient** in the **Add/Remove Goals** window, see Figure 16.15b). Right click in the **Goal plot 1** window, check the box for **Manual min:** and set the value to **0.2**. Set the corresponding value for **Manual max** to **0.5**. Set the **Length scale:** to **5**, see Figure 16.15c). Select **OK** to exit the **Goal Plot Settings** window.

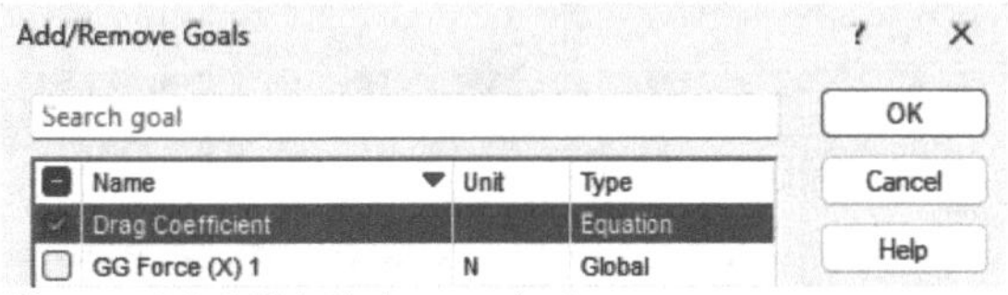

Figure 16.15b) Solver window

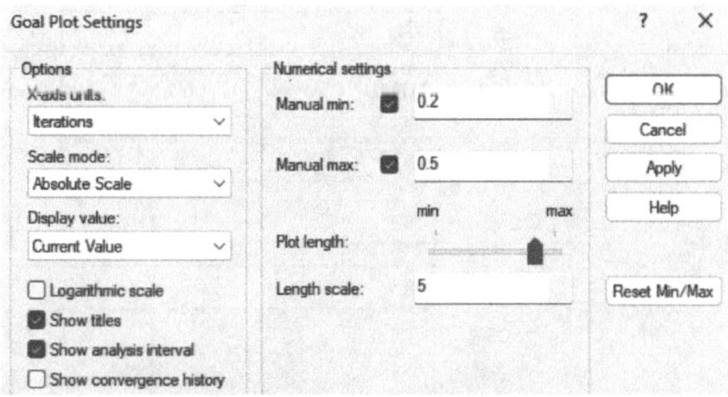

Figure 16.15c) Goal Plot settings

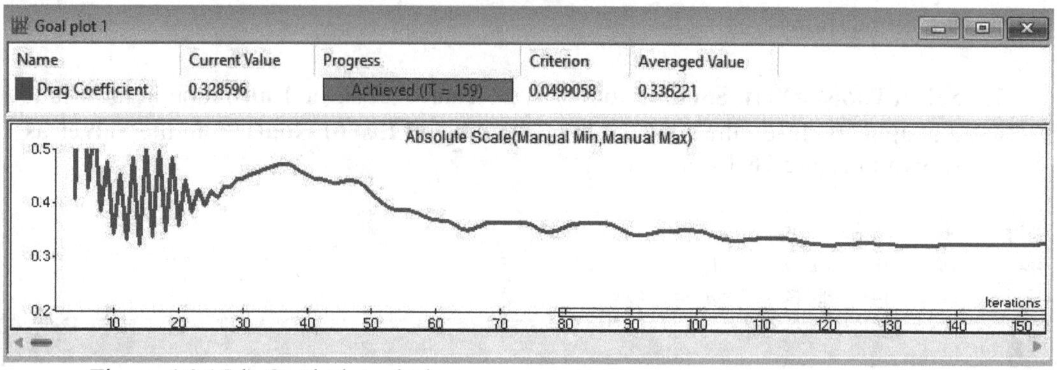

Figure 16.15d) Goal plot window

During the simulation, click on the **Insert Preview** in the **Solver** and select the **Definition** tab and the **Front Plane** and **Contours** as **Mode**, see Figure 16.15e). Select the **Settings** tab and select **Velocity** as **Parameter:** under **Contours/Isolines options**. Select the **Options** tab and check the box for **Display mesh**. Select the **Region** tab and set the values as shown in Figure 16.15e).

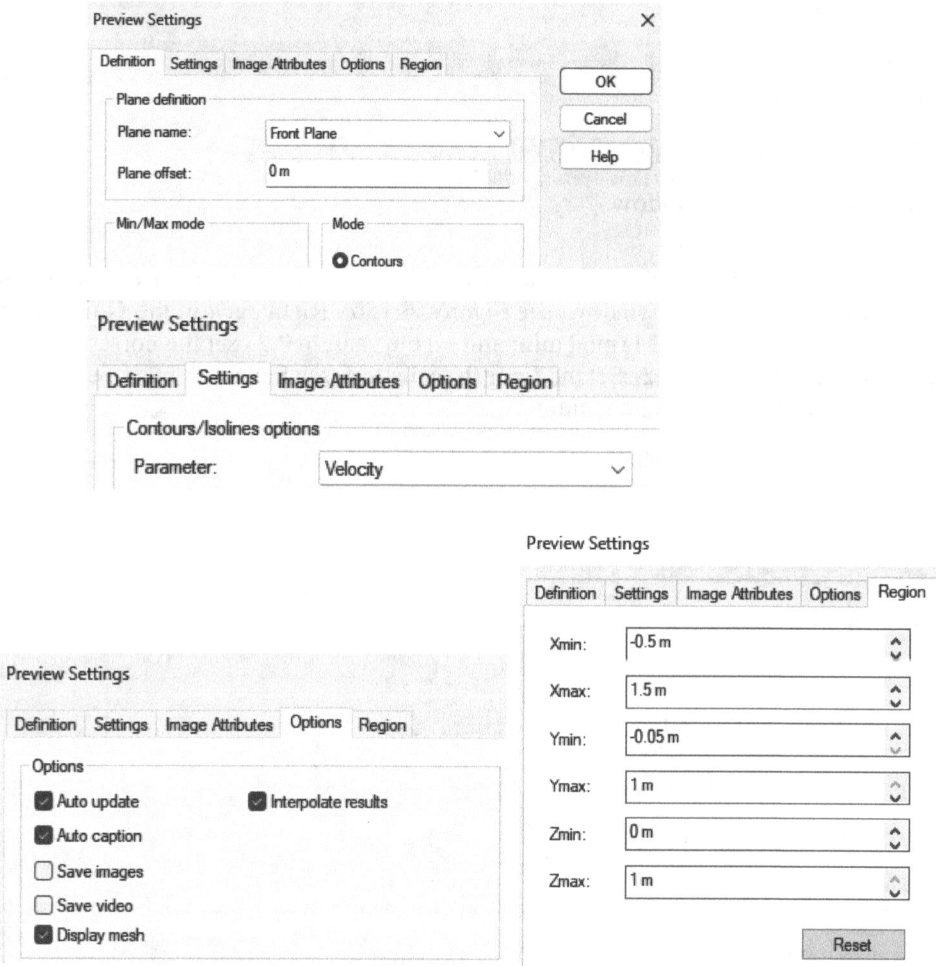

Figure 16.15e) Preview setting windows

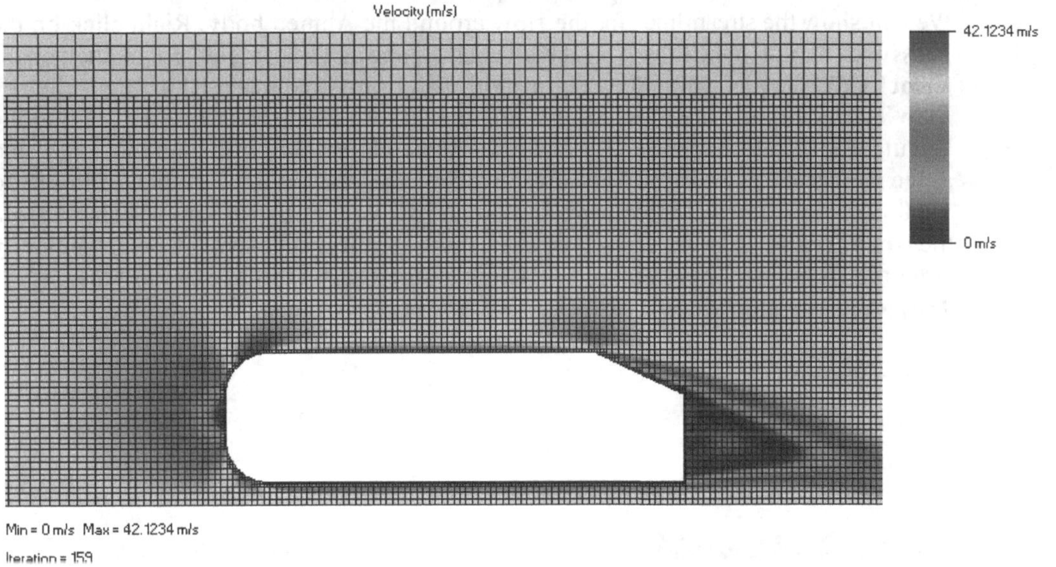

Figure 16.15f) Velocity contours with mesh during simulation

J. Cut-Plots and Flow Trajectories

16. Open the **Results** folder and Right click on **Cut Plots** and select **Insert….** Select the **Front Plane** of the **Ahmed Body**. Select **Velocity (X)** from the drop-down menu in the **Contours** section. Slide the **Number of Levels** all the way to the right. Exit the **Cut plot**. Select **Tools>>Flow Simulation>>Results>>Display>>Lighting**. Select the Front view. Repeat this step and plot the pressure field.

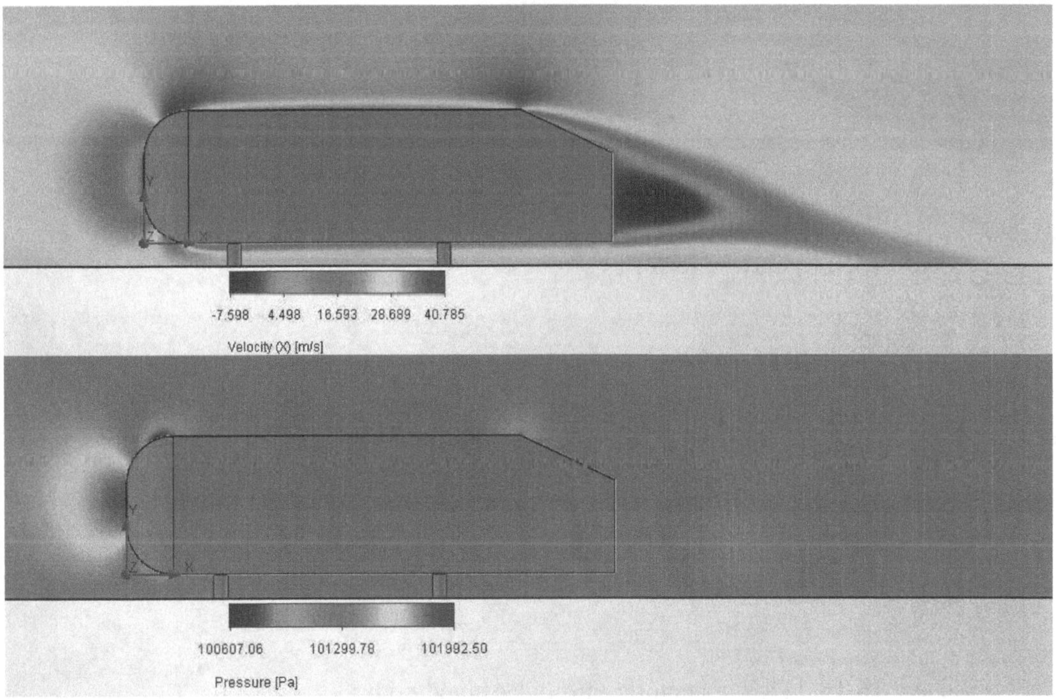

Figure 16.16a) Velocity (X) and Pressure fields in mid-plane

We will show the streamlines for the flow around the Ahmed body. Right click on the **Pressure** cut plot in the Flow Simulation analysis tree and select **Hide**. Right click on the **Velocity (X)** cut plot in the Flow Simulation analysis tree and select **Hide**. Right click on **Flow Trajectories** in the Flow Simulation analysis tree and select **Insert…**. Go to the FeatureManager design tree and click on the **Front Plane**. The front plane will be listed as the **Reference** plane in the **Flow Trajectories** window. Set the **Number of Points** to **1000**. Select the **Static Trajectories** button and select **Lines** with **Lines Width 1** from the **Draw Trajectories As** drop-down menu in the **Appearance** section. Select **Velocity** from the **Color by** drop down menu. Click on the **OK** button to exit the **Flow Trajectories** window.

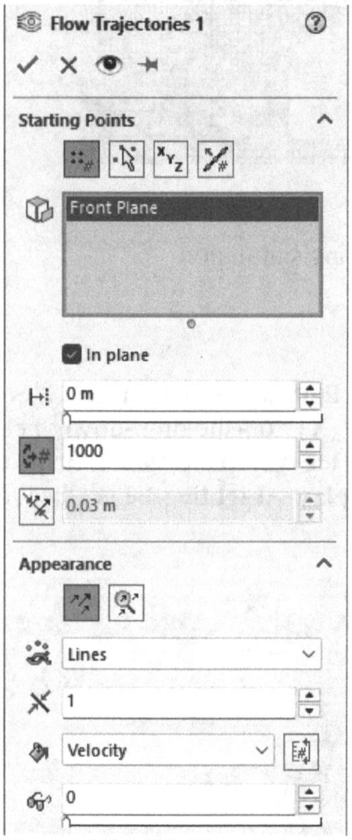

Figure 16.16b) Flow trajectories settings

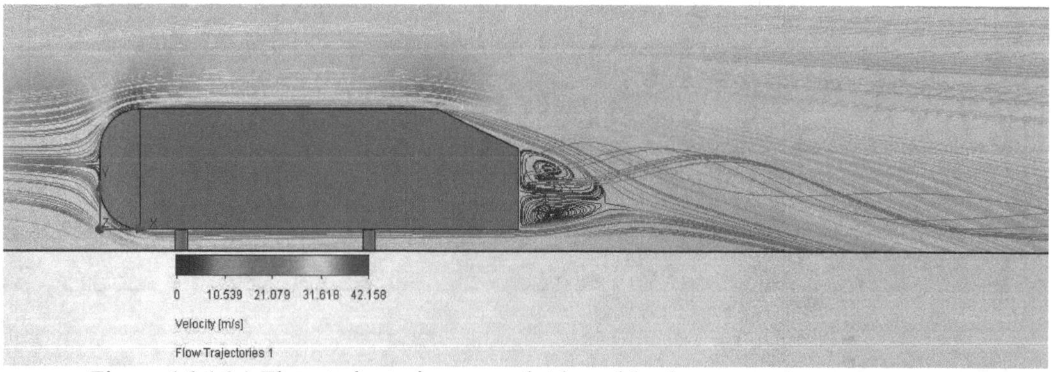

Figure 16.16c) Flow trajectories around Ahmed body

K. Theory

17. The Reynolds number is defined as

$$Re = \frac{UL\rho}{\mu} \quad (16.1)$$

where U (m/s) is inlet velocity, L (m) is the length of the Ahmed body, ρ (kg/m^3) is the density of the fluid and μ (m^2/s) is dynamic viscosity of the fluid. We define the drag coefficient C_d as

$$C_d = \frac{F_d}{\frac{1}{2}\rho U^2 A} \quad (16.2)$$

where F_d(N) is the drag force and A (m^2) is the frontal area of the Ahmed body. Meile *et al.*[(6)] determined the following relationship between the drag coefficient and the Reynolds number for the Ahmed body.

$$C_d = 0.2788 + 0.0915e^{-Re/1797100} \quad (16.3)$$

L. References

1. Ahmed, S.R., Ramm, G.,"Some Salient Features of the Time-Averaged Ground Vehicle Wake", *SAE-Paper 840300*, 1984.
2. Dogan, T., Conger, M., Kim, D-H., Mousaviraad, M., Xing, T., Stern, F.,"Simulation of Turbulent Flow over the Ahmed Body", *ME: 5160 Intermediate Mechanics of Fluids CFD Lab 4*, (2016).
3. Kalyan, D.K., Paul, A.R., "Computational Study of Flow around a Simplified 2D Ahmed Body", *International Journal of Engineering Science and Innovative Technology (IJESIT)*, **2**, 3, (2013).
4. Khan, R.S, Umale, S.,"CFD Aerodynamic Analysis of Ahmed Body", *International Journal of Engineering Trends and Technology (IJETT)*, **18**, 7, (2014).
5. Lienhart, H., Stoots, C. and Becker, S.,"Flow and Turbulence Structures in the Wake of a Simplified Car Model (Ahmed Model)", *Notes on Numerical Fluid Mechanics*, **77**, 6, (2002).
6. Meile, W., Brenn, G., Reppenhagen, A., Lechner, B., Fuchs, A., "Experiments and numerical simulations on the aerodynamics of the Ahmed body", *CFD Letters*, **3**, 1, (2011).

M. Exercises

16.1 Run the flow case as described in this chapter U = 30m/s for different Levels of Refining Cells at Fluid/Solid Boundary from 1 to 5, see Figure 16.14 for local mesh. Study how the drag coefficient will change with this parameter and determine as shown in Table 16.2 the percent difference between Flow Simulation and theory for each case.

Level of Refining Cells at Fluid/Solid Boundary	No. Fluid Cells	No. Fluid Cells Contacting Solids	C_D Flow Sim.	C_D Theory	% Diff.
1	493,604	18,422		0.30655	1.3
2					
3					
4					
5					

Table 16.2 Different levels of refining cells at fluid/solid boundary

16.2 Run the flow case as described in this chapter U = 30 m/s for different computational domain sizes to study how the drag coefficient will change. Use the following computational domain sizes as shown in Table 16.3. See Figure 16.11 for computational domain.

Xmin (m)	Xmax (m)	Ymin (m)	Ymax (m)	Zmin (m)	Zmax (m)	C_D Flow Sim.	C_D Theory	% Diff.
-1	6.044	-0.05	1	0	1		0.30655	1.3
-2	7.044	-0.05	1	0	1			
-3	8.044	-0.05	1	0	1			
-1	6.044	--0.05	2	0	1			
-1	6.044	-0.05	3	0	1			
-1	6.044	-0.05	1	0	2			
-1	6.044	-0.05	1	0	3			

Table 16.3 Different sizes for computational domain

16.3 Run the flow case as described in this chapter U = 30 m/s for different local mesh computational domain sizes to study how the drag coefficient will change. Use the following local mesh computational domain sizes as shown in Table 16.4. See Figure 16.14 for local mesh.

Xmin (m)	Xmax (m)	Ymin (m)	Ymax (m)	Zmin (m)	Zmax (m)	C_D Flow Sim.	C_D Theory	% Diff.
-0.552	2.148	-0.05	0.85	0	0.45		0.30655	1.3
-0.252	1.648	-0.05	0.85	0	0.45			
-0.052	1.148	-0.05	0.85	0	0.45			
-0.552	2.148	--0.05	0.65	0	0.45			
-0.552	2.148	-0.05	0.45	0	0.45			
-0.552	2.148	-0.05	0.85	0	0.35			
-0.552	2.148	-0.05	0.85	0	0.25			

Table 16.3 Different sizes for computational domain

CHAPTER 17. SAVONIUS WIND TURBINE

A. Objectives

- Creating the SOLIDWORKS model needed for the Vertical Axis Wind Turbine
- Setting up a Flow Simulation project for External Flows
- Using cut plots to visualize the resulting flow field
- Use a Rotating Region

B. Problem Description

We will in this chapter create the model for and study the flow past a Savonius Turbine.

C. Modeling SOLIDWORKS Part and Rotating Domain

1. Start SOLIDWORKS and create a New Part. Select **Tools>>Options...** from the SOLIDWORKS menu. Click on the **Document Properties** tab and select **Units**. Select **MMGS** as your **Unit system**. Select the **Top** view from the **View Orientation** drop down menu in the graphics window and click on the **Top Plane** in the **FeatureManager design tree**.

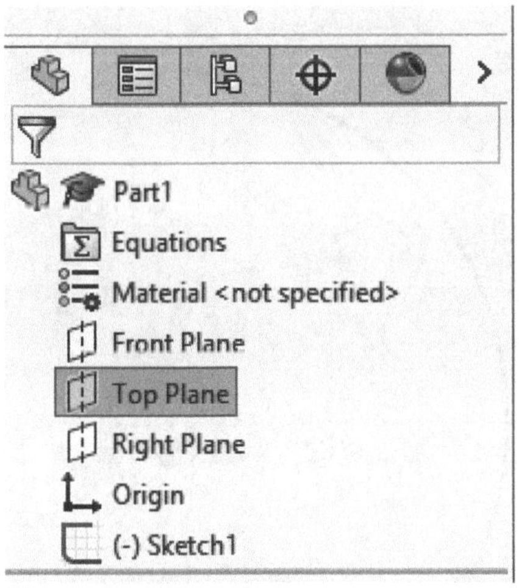

Figure 17.1 Top Plane

2. Select the **Basic Modeling Tools** tab and the **Centerpoint Arc** tool. Make sure you get a vertical dashed line when you move the cursor above the origin. Create a half-circle as shown in Figure 17.2a). Select the green check mark to exit the Arc window. Select the top end-point of the half circle and set **X** to **0** and **Y** to **250**. Click on Fix under Add Relation. Select the green check mark. Click on the bottom end-point of the half circle and set **X** to **0** and **Y** to **-60.5**. Click on Fix under Add Relation. Select the green check mark. Click on the center point of the half circle and set **X** to **0** and **Y** to **94.75**. Click on Fix under Add Relation, see Figure 17.2a). Select the green check mark to exit the Point window. Select Rebuild from the menu.

   Right click on Sketch1 and select Edit Sketch. Create the second half-circle as shown in Figure 17.2b). Click on the top end-point of the lower half circle and set **X** to **0** and **Y** to **60.5**. Click on Fix under Add Relation. Select the green check mark. Click on the bottom end-point of the lower half circle and set **X** to **0** and **Y** to **-250**. Click on Fix under Add Relation. Select the green check mark. Click on the center point for the half circle and set **X** to **0** and **Y** to **-94.75**. Click on Fix under Add Relation, see Figure 17.2b). Select the green check mark to exit the Point window. Select Rebuild from the menu.

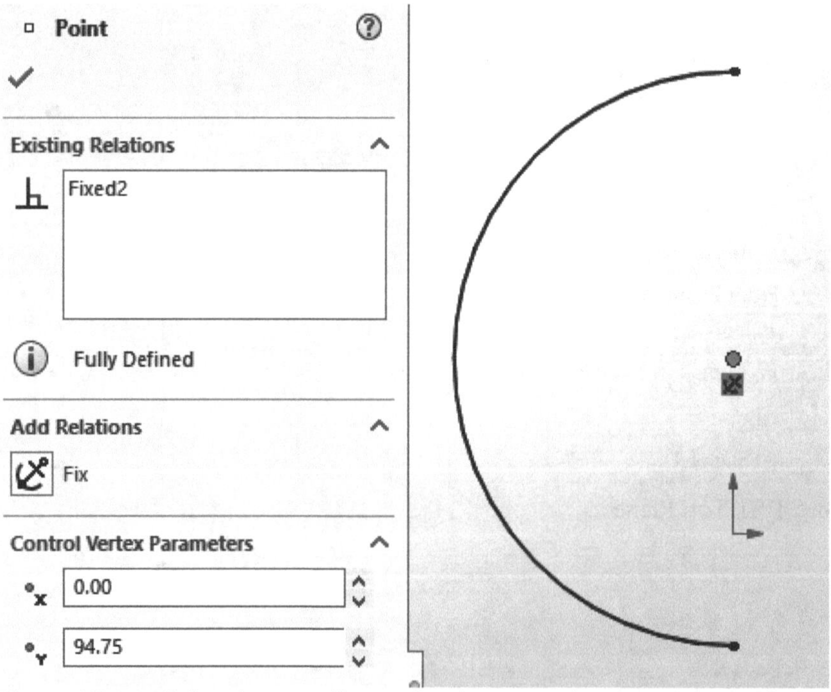

Figure 17.2a) Fixing the coordinates for the top end point of the half circle.

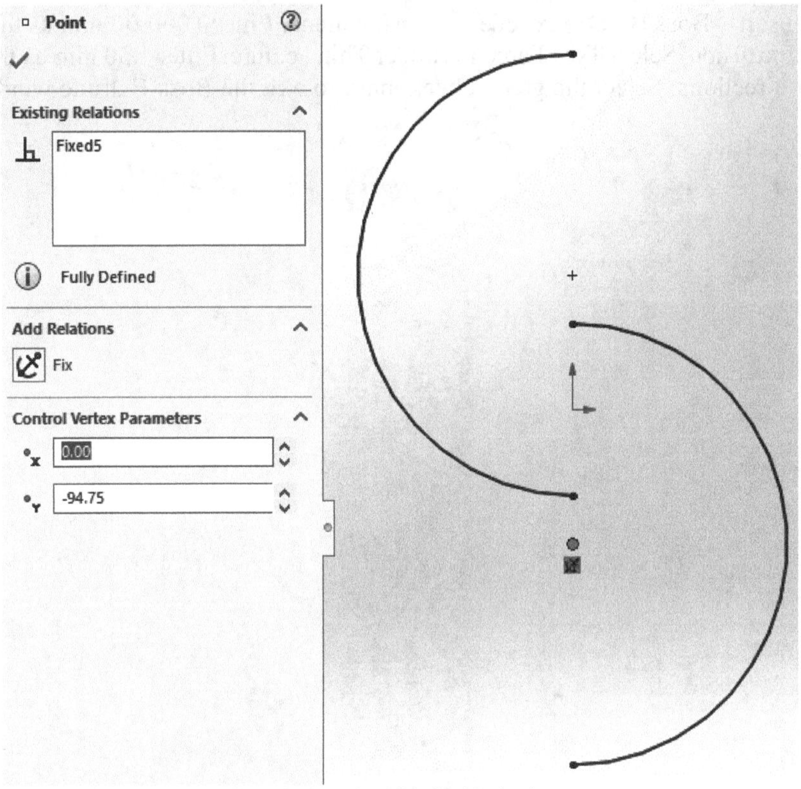

Figure 17.2b) Completed sketch with half circles

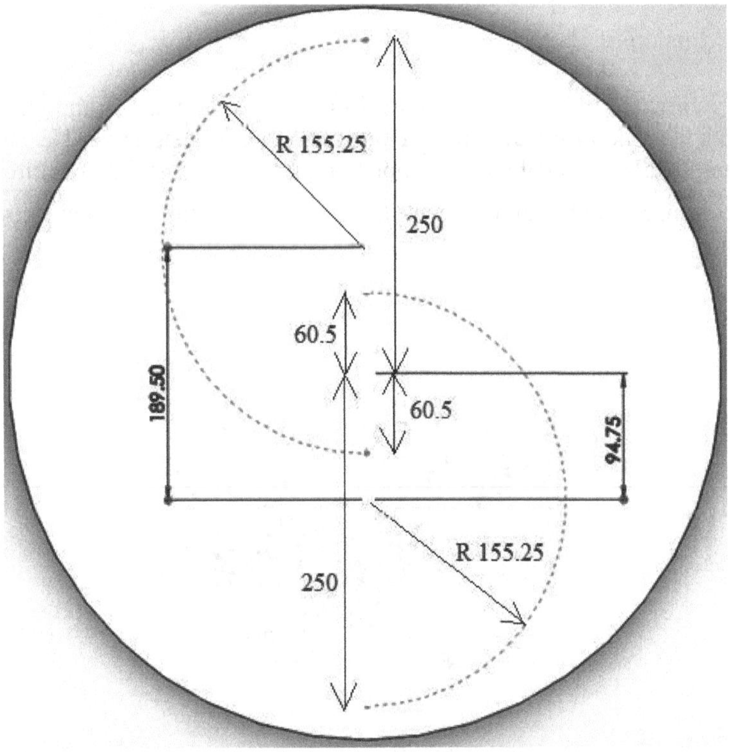

Figure 17.2c) Completed sketch with dimensions

3. Select Insert>>Boss/Base>>Extrude… from the menu. Enter 1000.00 mm as the Depth for the Extrusion. Select Two-Direction under Thin Feature. Enter 1.50 mm as thickness in both directions. Select the green check mark to exit the Boss-Extrude window.

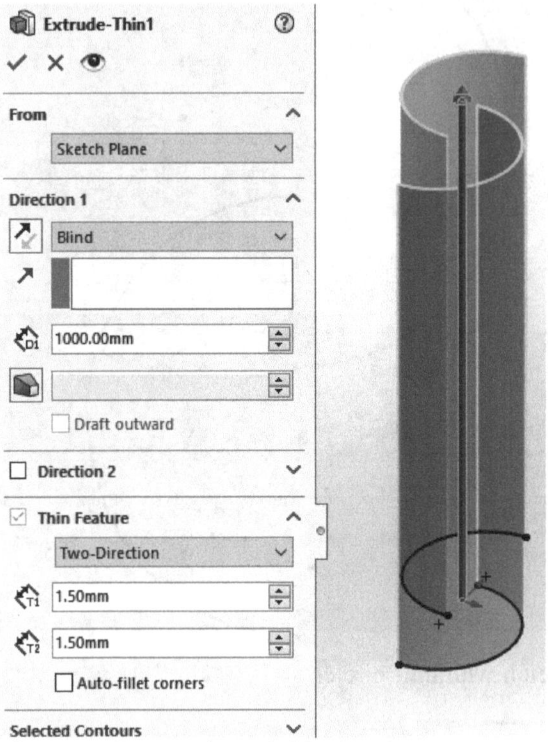

Figure 17.3 Extrusion of sketch

4. Select the **Top** view from the **View Orientation** drop down menu in the graphics window and click on the **Top Plane** in the **FeatureManager design tree**. Next, select the **Basic Modeling Tools** tab and the **Circle** tool. Start at the origin and draw a circle with a **radius** of **275 mm**. Select the green check mark to exit the circle. Select Rebuild from the menu.

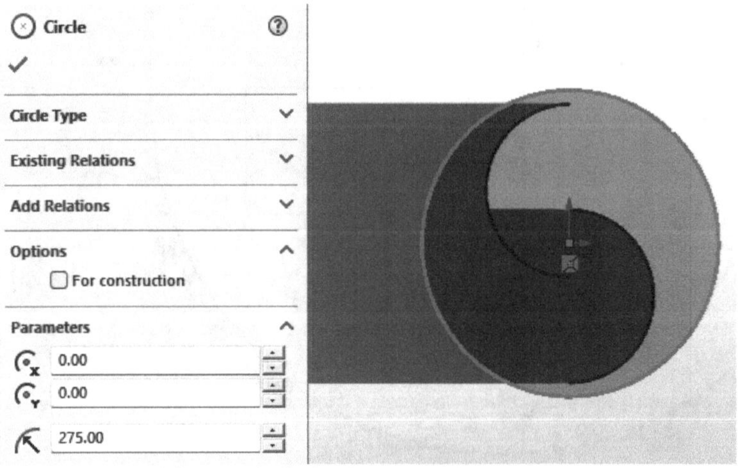

Figure 17.4 Adding a circle in the top plane

5. Select Trimetric view in the graphics window by selecting View Orientation and Trimetric. Select Sketch2 and select the Analysis Preparation tab and Extruded Boss/Base. Select Mid Plane under Direction 1, set the thickness to 2 mm and check the box for Merge results. Choose Selected bodies under Feature Scope. Select the green check mark to exit the Boss-Extrude window.

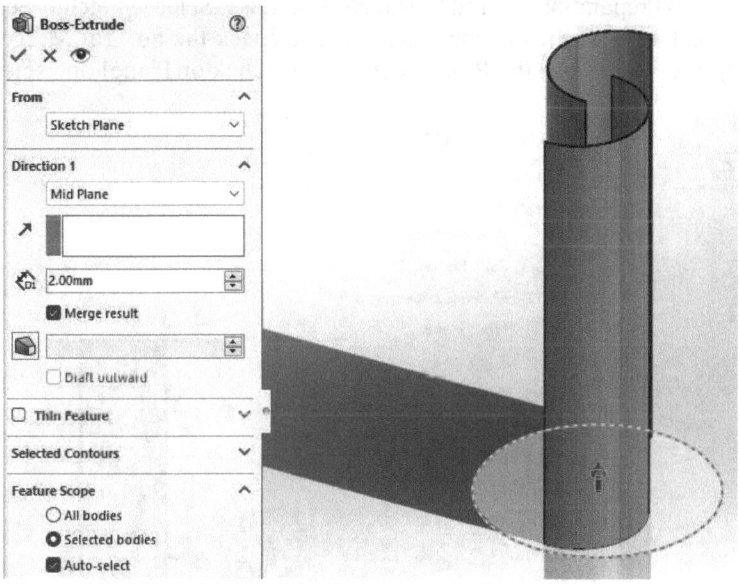

Figure 17.5 Extrusion of the bottom end plate

6. Select Insert>>Reference Geometry>>Plane… from the menu. Select Top Plane as First Reference and set the Offset Distance to 1000 mm.

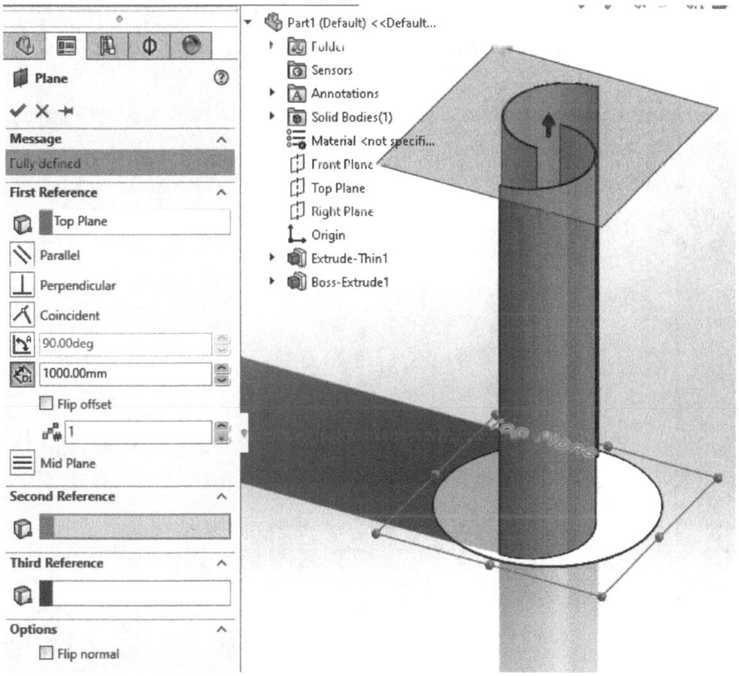

Figure 17.6 Insertion of a reference plane

7. Select the **Top** view from the **View Orientation** drop down menu in the graphics window and select **Plane1** in the **FeatureManager design tree**. Next, select the **Basic Modeling Tools** tab and the **Circle** tool. Start at the origin and draw a circle with a **radius** of **275 mm**. Exit the Circle window and select Rebuild from the menu. Select Trimetric view in the graphics window by selecting View Orientation and Trimetric. Select the Analysis Preparation tab and Extruded Boss/Base. Select Sketch3. Select Mid Plane under Direction 1, set the thickness to 2 mm and check the box for Merge results. Select green check mark to exit the Boss-Extrude. Right click on Plane1 and select Hide.

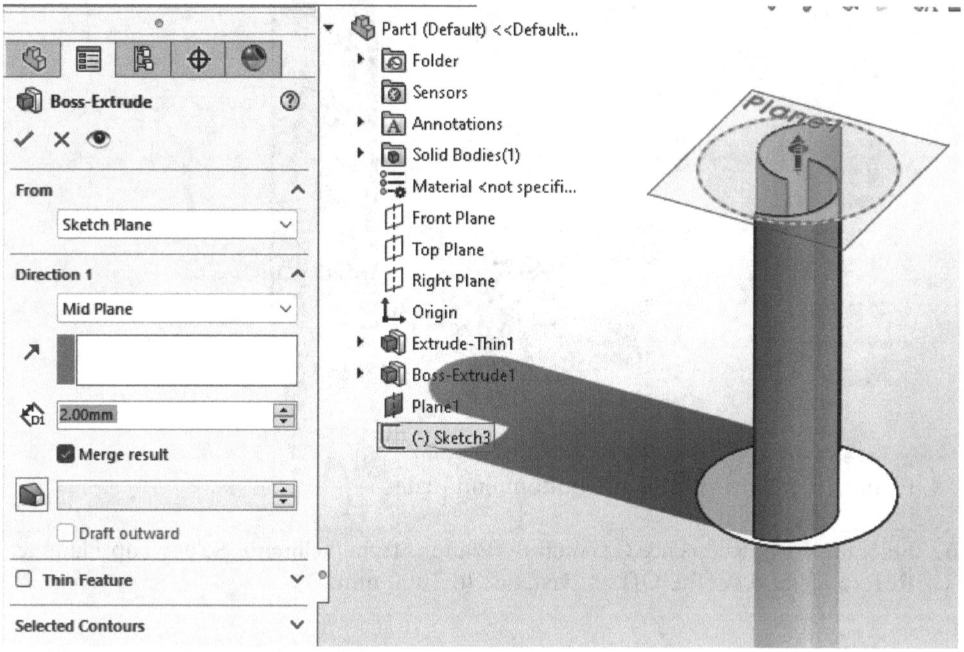

Figure 17.7a) Extrusion of the top end plate

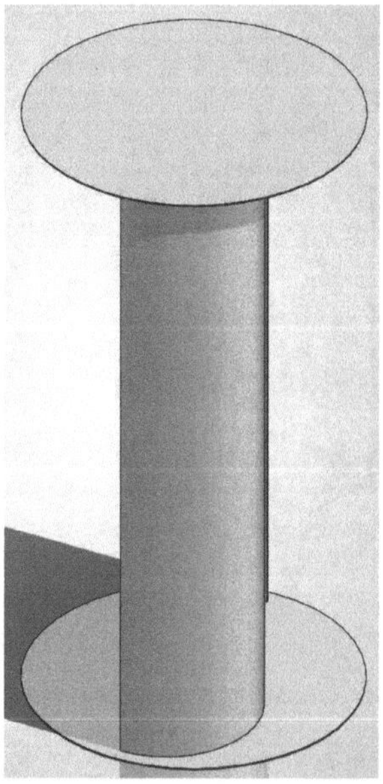

Figure 17.7b) Finished Savonius Wind Turbine

8. Select the **Top** view from the **View Orientation** drop down menu in the graphics window and click on the **Top Plane** in the **FeatureManager design tree**. Select Wireframe Display Style. Right click on Material and select Edit Material. Select ABS under Plastics. Select Units: SI – N/m^2 (Pa) and click on Apply in the Material window. The density of ABS is 1020 kg/m^3. Close the Material window.
Next, select the **Top Plane**, select the **Basic Modeling Tools** tab and the **Circle** tool. Start at the origin and draw a circle with a **radius** of **302.5mm**. Exit the Circle and select Rebuild from the menu. Select **Trimetric** view in the graphics window by selecting **View Orientation** and **Trimetric**. Select the **Analysis Preparation** tab and **Extruded Boss/Base**. Select **Sketch4**. Select **Blind** under **Direction 1**, set the depth to **1050 mm** and uncheck the box for **Merge results**. Check the box for **Direction 2** and enter **50 mm** as the depth. Select the green checkmark to exit the **Boss-Extrude window**.
Rename **Extrude-Thin1** to **Rotors** and **Sketch1** to **Rotor Profiles**.
Rename **Boss-Extrude1** to **Bottom End Plate** and **Sketch2** to **Bottom End Plate Sketch**.
Rename **Boss-Extrude2** to **Top End Plate** and **Sketch3** to **Top End Plate Sketch**.
Rename **Boss-Extrude3** to **Rotating Region** and **Sketch4** to **Rotating Region Sketch**.
Save the part with the name ***Savonius Wind Turbine 2026***.

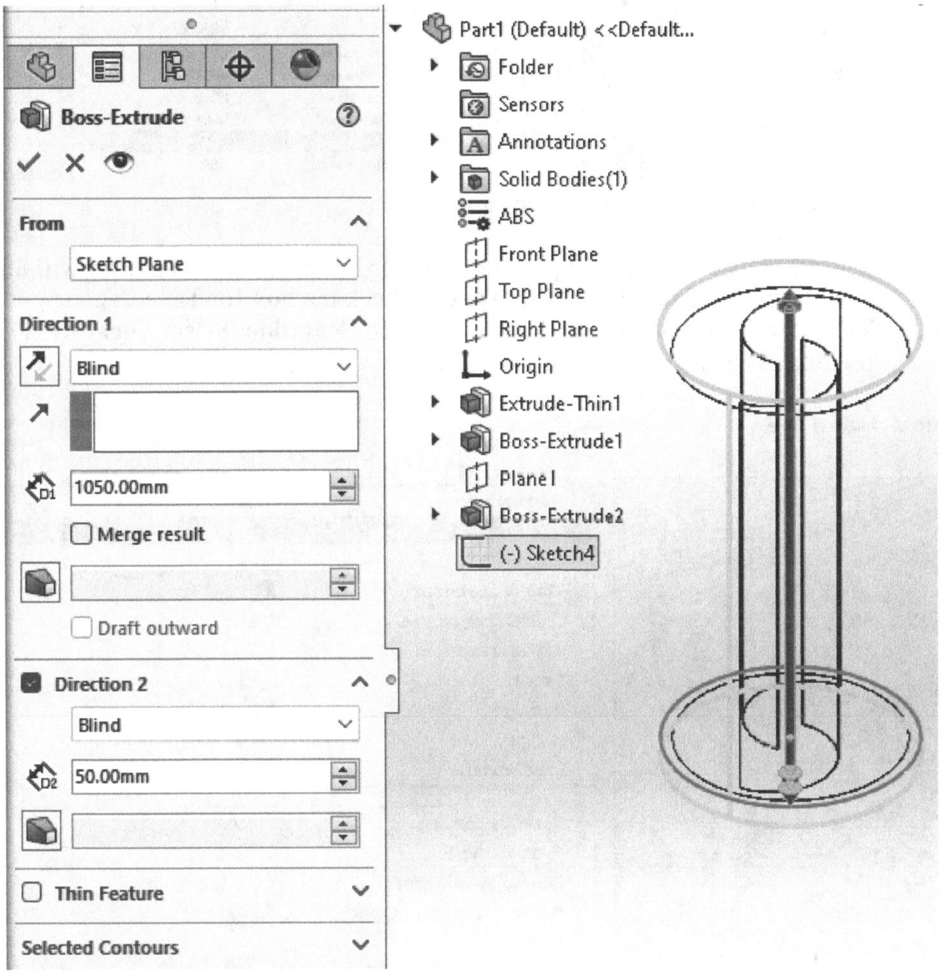

Figure 17.8 Extrusion for rotating region.

D. Flow Simulation Project

9. If Flow Simulation is not available in the SOLIDWORKS menu, select **Tools>>Add Ins…** and check the corresponding **SOLIDWORKS Flow Simulation** box. Start the **Flow Simulation Wizard** by selecting **Tools>>Flow Simulation>>Project>>Wizard…** from the SOLIDWORKS menu. Create a new project with the following name: **Flow Past Savonius Wind Turbine**. Click on Next>.

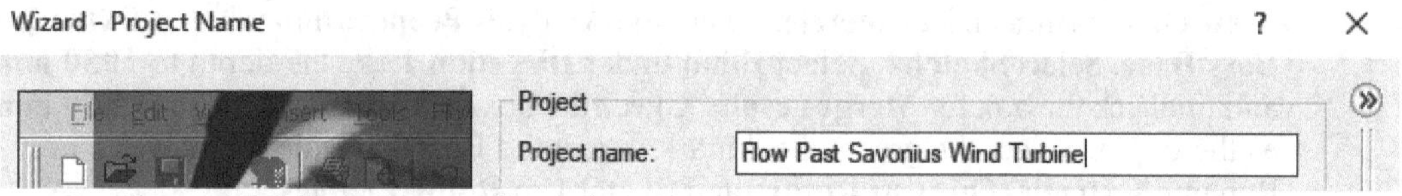

Figure 17.9 Entering configuration name

10. Select the **SI unit system.** Click on Next>.

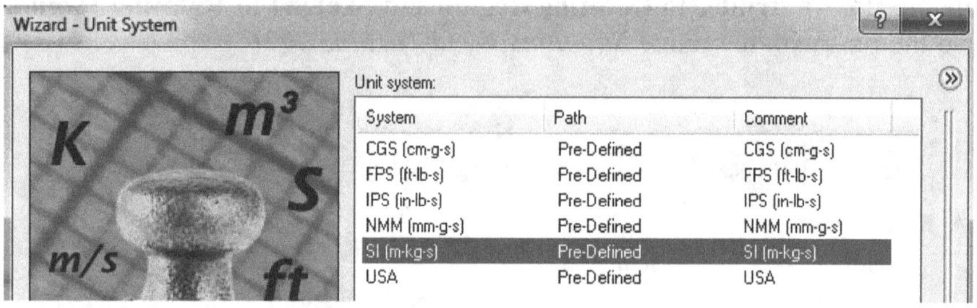

Figure 17.10 Selection of unit system

11. Select **External Analysis type**. Check the boxes for **Exclude cavities without flow conditions** and **Exclude internal space**. Check the box for Time-dependent. Set the **Total Analysis time** to **2 s**. Check the box for **Rotation**. Select **Local Region(s) (Sliding)** as **Type** under **Rotation**. Click on Next>.

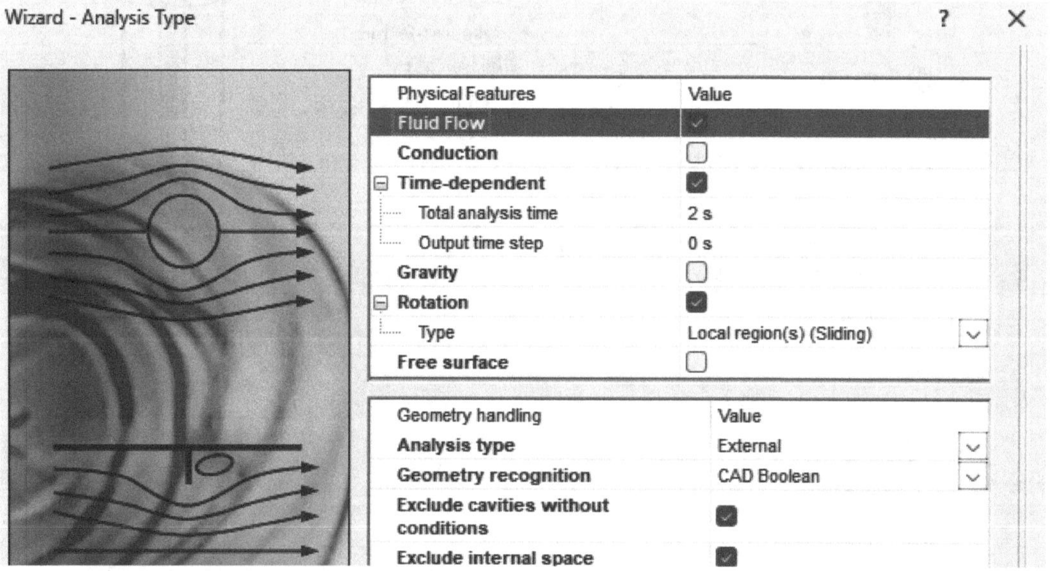

Figure 17.11 Selection of Analysis type

12. Add **Air** as the default **Project Fluid** by selecting it from **Gases**. Click on Next. Choose default values for **Wall Conditions** and enter **5 m/s** as the **Velocity in X direction** as **Initial Condition**. Finish the Wizard.

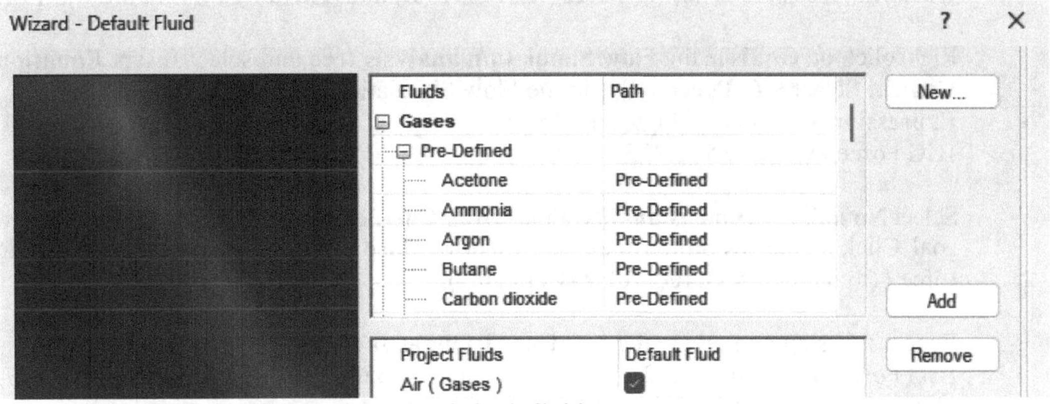

Figure 17.12 Adding air as the default fluid

E. Computational Domain

13. Select **Tools>Flow Simulation>>Computational Domain...** from the menu. Select 2D simulation and XZ plane. Select the green check mark to exit the window.

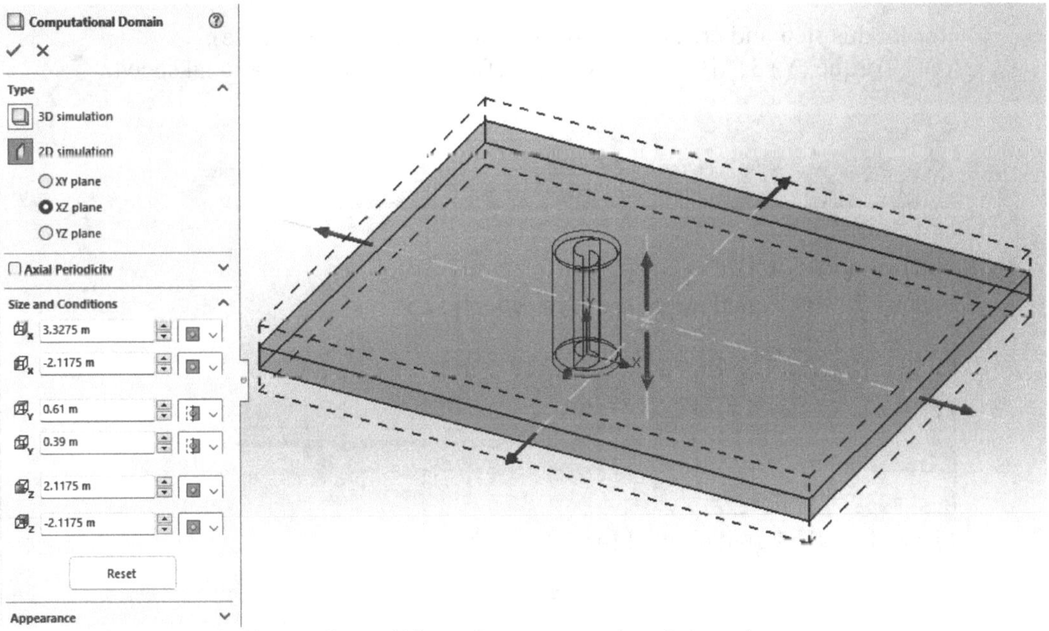

Figure 17.13 Size and conditions for computational domain

F. Goals

14. Right click on **Goals** in the **Flow Simulation analysis tree** and select **Insert Global Goals….** Check the boxes for **Force (X), Force (Z)** and **Torque (Y).** Exit the window.

    Right click on **Goals** in the **Flow Simulation analysis tree** and select **Insert Equation Goal….** Select **GG Force (X) 1** in the Flow Simulation Analysis tree. Enter the **Expression** as shown in Figure 17.14a):
    {GG Force (X) 1}/(0.5*1.225*5^2*0.5)

    Select **No unit** for **Dimensionality**. Enter **Drag Coefficient** as the name for the equation goal. Click on the OK button to exit the window. The drag coefficient is defined as drag force / (dynamic pressure * rotor swept area).

    Repeat this step and create the **Lift Coefficient** as shown in Figure 17.14b):
    {GG Force (Z) 2}/(0.5*1.225*5^2*0.5). The lift coefficient is defined as lift force / (dynamic pressure * rotor swept area).

    Repeat this step and create the **Torque Coefficient** as shown in Figure 17.14c):
    {GG Torque (Y) 3}/(0.5*1.225*5^2*0.5*0.25). The torque coefficient is defined as torque / (dynamic pressure * rotor swept area * rotor radius).

    Repeat this step and create the **Power Coefficient** as shown in Figure 17.14d):
    {Torque coefficient}*10*0.25/5. The power coefficient is defined as torque coefficient * tip speed ratio = torque coefficient * rotational speed * rotor radius/free stream velocity.

    Repeat this step and create the **Power** as shown in Figure 17.14e):
    {GG Torque (Y) 3}*10. The power is defined as torque * rotational speed.

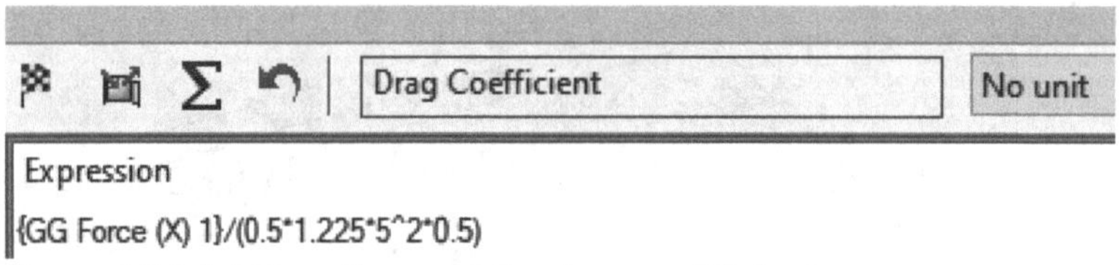

Figure 17.14a) Equation goal for drag coefficient

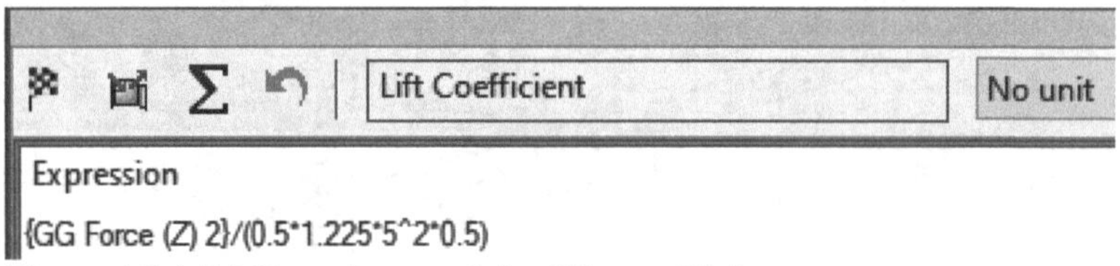

Figure 17.14b) Equation goal for lift coefficient

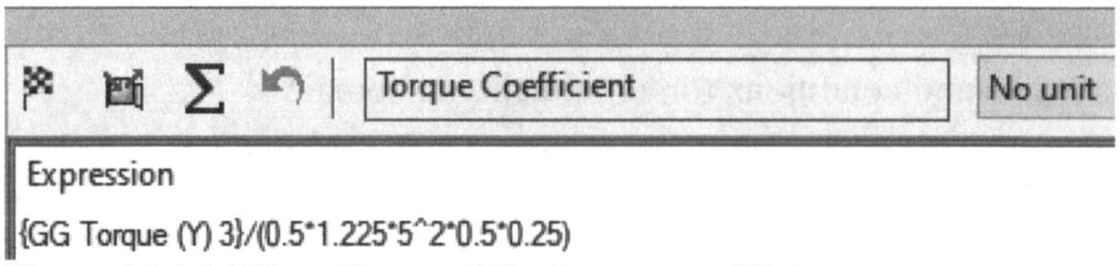

Figure 17.14c) Equation goal for torque coefficient

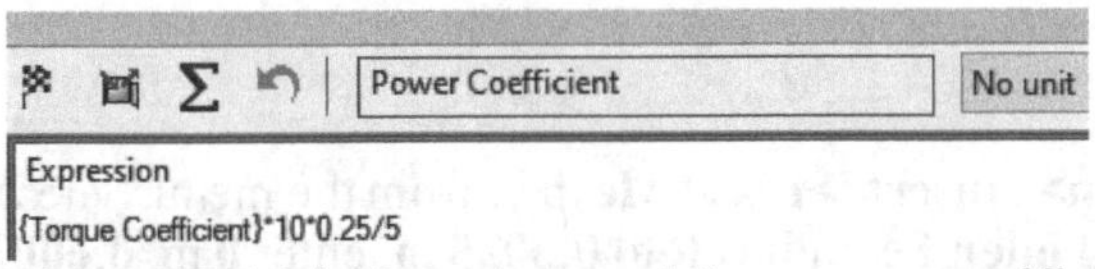

Figure 17.14d) Equation goal for power coefficient

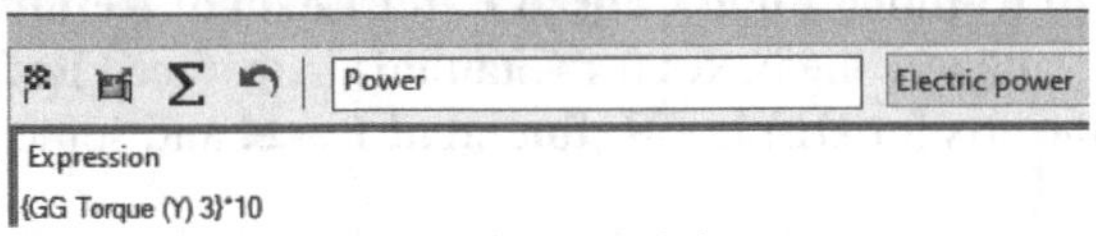

Figure 17.14e) Equation goal for power

G. Rotating Region

15. Right click on **Rotating Regions** under **Input Data**. Select **Insert Rotating Region....** Select the cylindrical rotating region in the graphics window. Set the **Angular Velocity** to **10 rad/s**. Select the green check mark to exit the window.

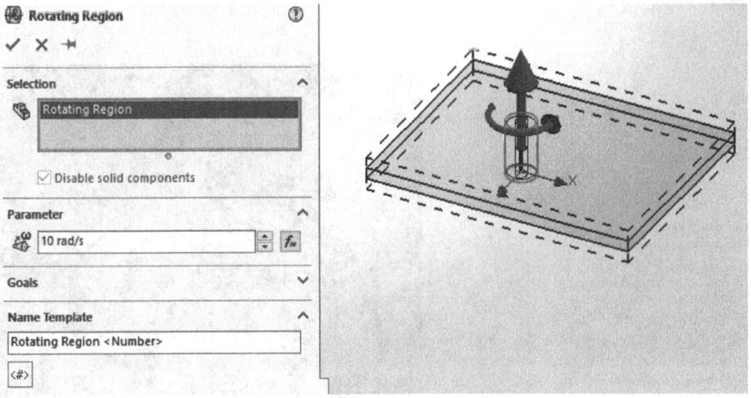

Figure 17.15 Rotating region

H. Global Mesh

16. Select **Tools>Flow Simulation>>Global Mesh...** from the menu. Set the **Level of initial mesh** to 7. Check the box for **Show basic mesh** and exit the window.

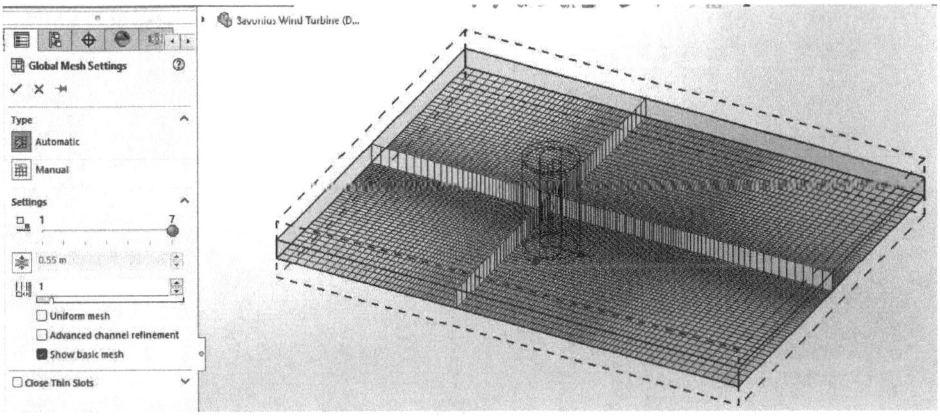

Figure 17.16 Global mesh settings

I. Local Mesh

17. Select **Tools>Flow Simulation>>Insert>>Local Mesh...** from the menu. Select **Region** under **Selection** and check **Cylinder**. Set radius **R** to **0.3025 m**, enter **0 m**, **0.6002 m** and **0 m** as **Xmax**, **Ymax**, **Zmax**, respectively, and **0 m**, **0.3998 m** and **0 m** as **Xmin**, **Ymin**, **Zmin**, respectively. Set **Level of Refining Fluid Cells** to **1** and **Level of Refining Cells at Fluid/Solid Boundary** to **2**. Uncheck the boxes for **Channels**, **Advanced Refinement** and **Close Thin Slots**. Check the box for **Display Refinement Level** and set level to **1**.

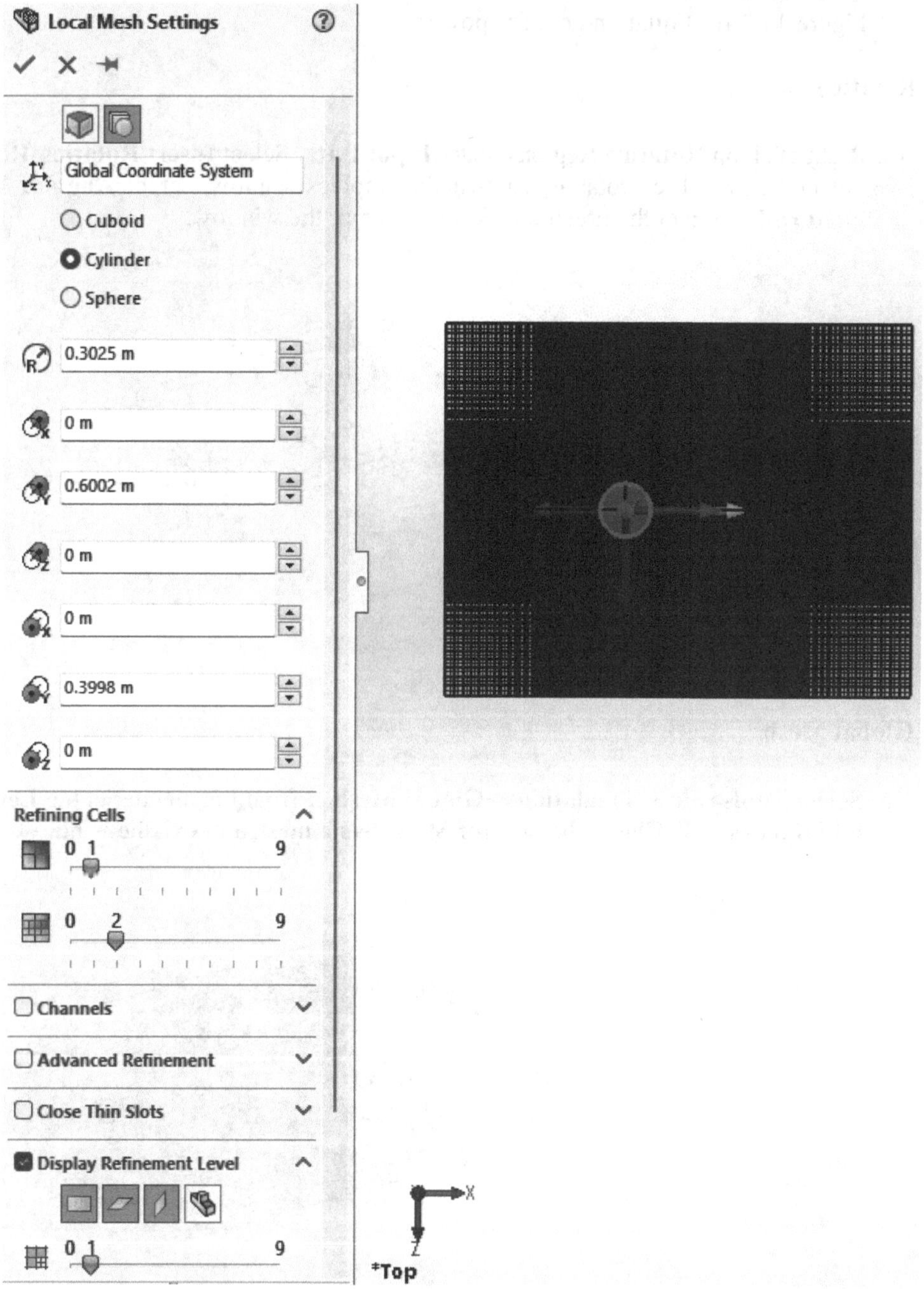

Figure 17.17 Local mesh setting

J. Running Simulations

18. Select **Tools>>Flow Simulation>>Solve>>Run....** Push the **Run** button in the window that appears. Insert the goals table by clicking on **List of Goals** in the **Solver** as shown in Figure 17.18a).

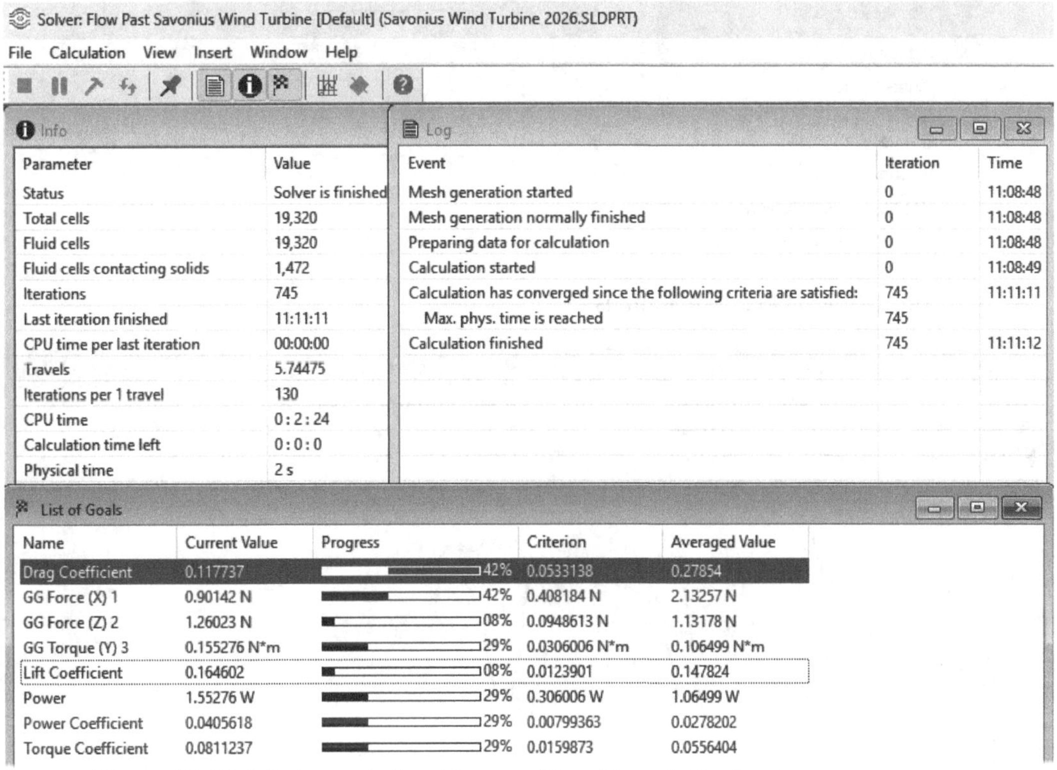

Figure 17.18a) Solver window for $\omega = 10$ rad/s and $V = 5$ m/s.

Click on the **Insert Goals Plot** in the **Solver** and check the box for **Drag Coefficient** and **Lift Coefficient** in the **Add/Remove Goals** window, see Figure 17.18b). Right click in the **Goal plot 1** window, check the box for **Manual min:** and set the value to **0**. Set the corresponding value for **Manual max** to **0.4**. Set the **X-axis units:** to **Physical time** and set the **Scale Mode:** to **Absolute Scale**. Set the **Length scale:** to **0.6**, see Figure 17.18c). Select **OK** to exit the **Goal Plot Settings** window. Repeat this step and create a goals plot for the Power. Set the value for **Manual min:** to 0 and **Manual max** to **3.**

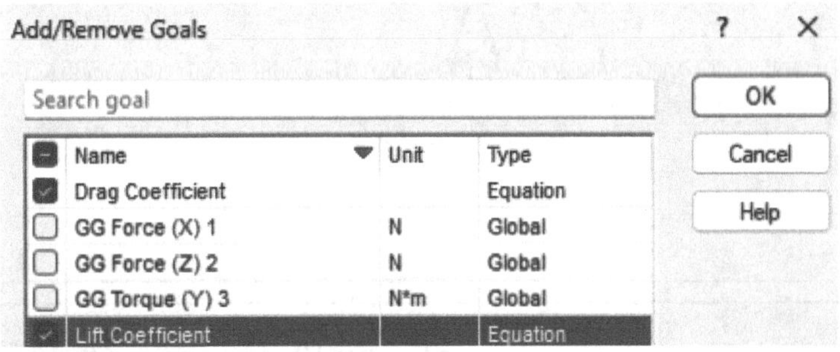

Figure 17.18b) Solver window

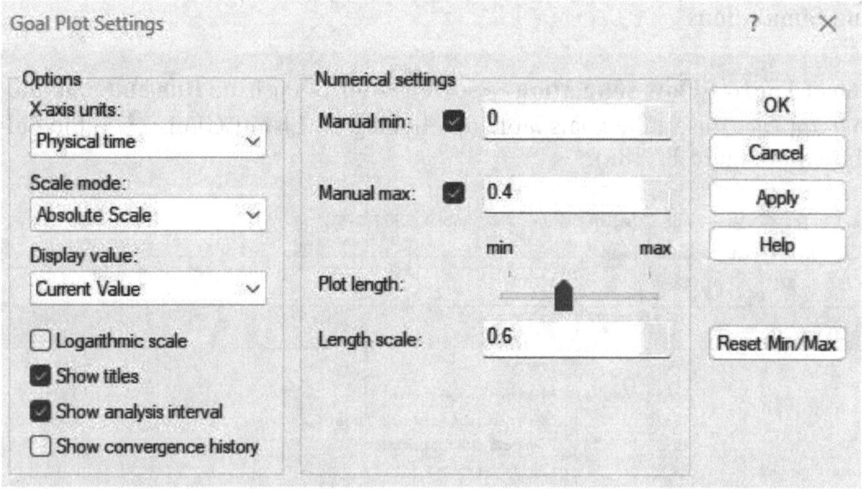

Figure 17.18c) Goal Plot settings

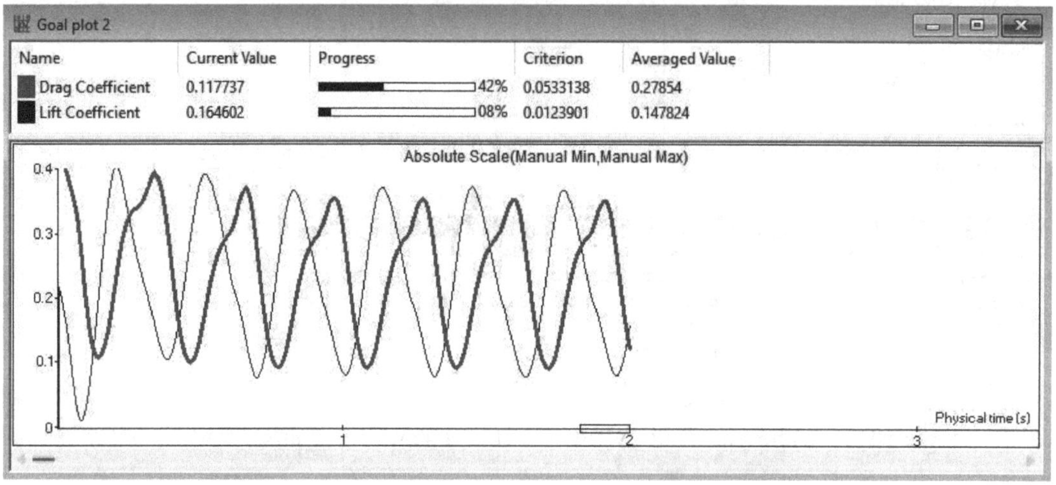

Figure 17.18d) Drag and lift coefficients for $\omega = 10$ rad/s and $V = 5$ m/s

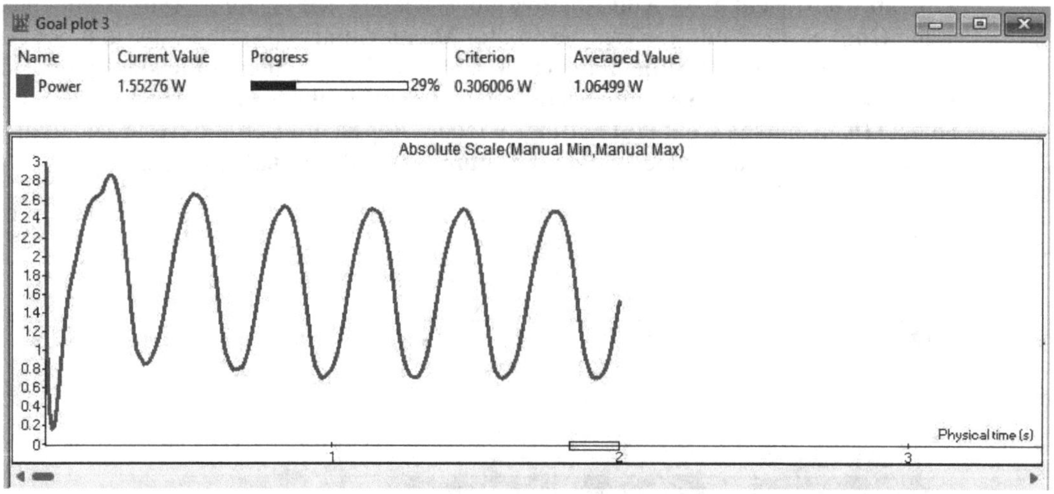

Figure 17.18e) Goal plot window for power for $\omega = 10$ rad/s and $V = 5$ m/s

K. Cut-Plots, Flow Trajectories and Goals Plot

19. Select the **FeatureManager Design Tree**, right click on **Rotors** and select **Hide**. Select **Flow Simulation Analysis**, open the **Results** folder and Right click on **Cut Plots** and select **Insert**. Select the **Top Plane** for the **Savonius Wind Turbine**. Select **Velocity** from drop-down menu in the **Contours** section. Slide the **Number of Levels** all the way to the right. Exit the **Cut plot**. Select Top view. Repeat this step and plot **Pressure** field.

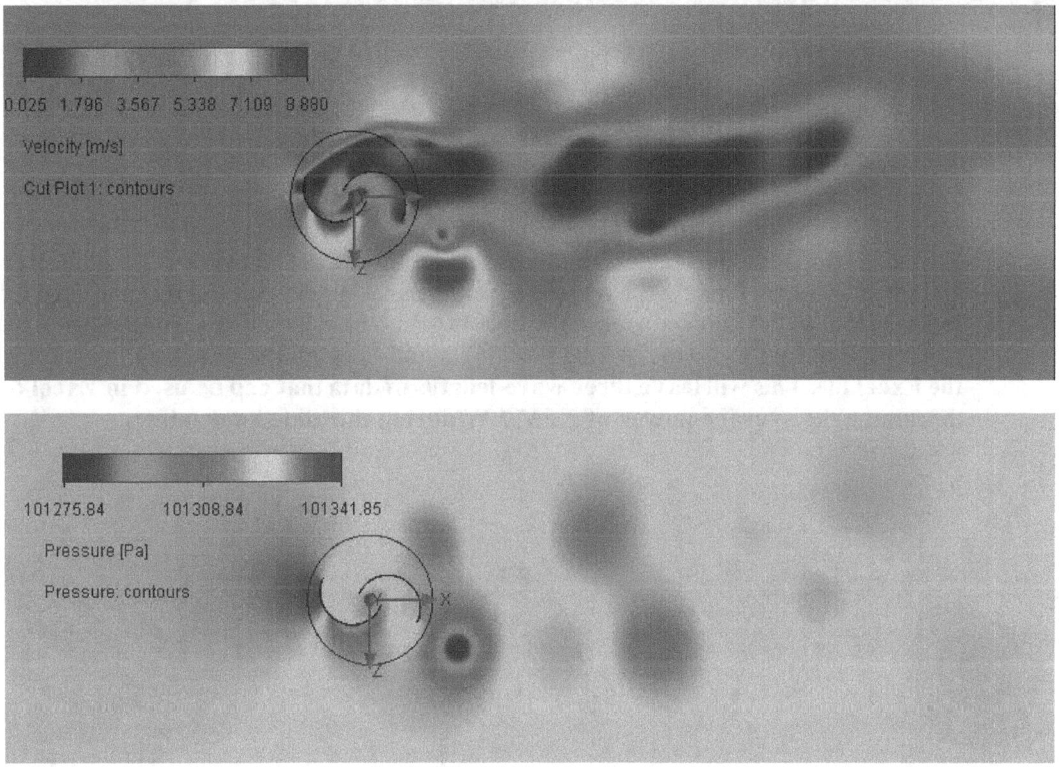

Figure 17.19a) Velocity and Pressure fields at $t = 5$ s for $\omega = 10$ rad/s and $V = 5$ m/s.

We will now show the streamlines of the flow for the Savonius wind turbine. Right click on the **Pressure** cut plot in the Flow Simulation analysis tree and select **Hide**. Right click on the **Velocity** cut plot in the Flow Simulation analysis tree and select **Hide**. Right click on **Flow Trajectories** in the Flow Simulation analysis tree and select **Insert....** Go to the FeatureManager design tree and click on the **Top Plane**. The top plane will be listed as the **Reference** plane in the **Flow Trajectories** window. Set the **Number of Points** to **1000**. Select the **Static Trajectories** button and select **Lines** with **Lines Width 1** in the **Appearance** section. Select **Velocity** from the **Color by** drop down menu. Click on the **OK** button to exit the **Flow Trajectories** window.

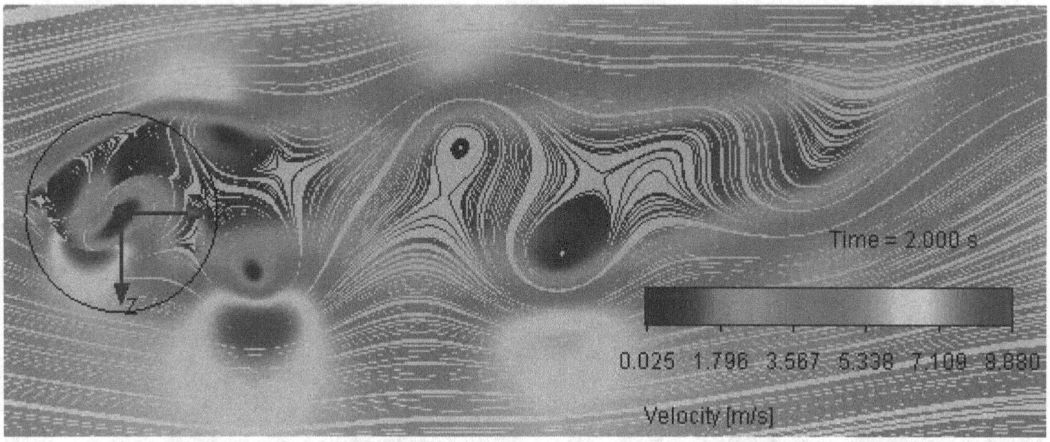

Figure 17.19b) Flow trajectories around Savonius turbine for $\omega = 10$ rad/s and $V = 5$ m/s.

Right click on **Goal Plots** under **Results** and select **Insert…**. Check the box for **Power** and select **Physical time** for the **Abscissa**. Select **Excel Workbook (*.xlsx)** and **Export to Excel**. Select the **Plot Data** tab at the bottom of the Excel window. Plot the two data columns. **Delete rows up to $t_1 = 1.051466062$ s and keep all the data up to $t_2 = 2$ s in the Excel file. This will leave three wave-lengths of data that can be used in Excel to determine the average power of 1.5577 W during this time interval.**

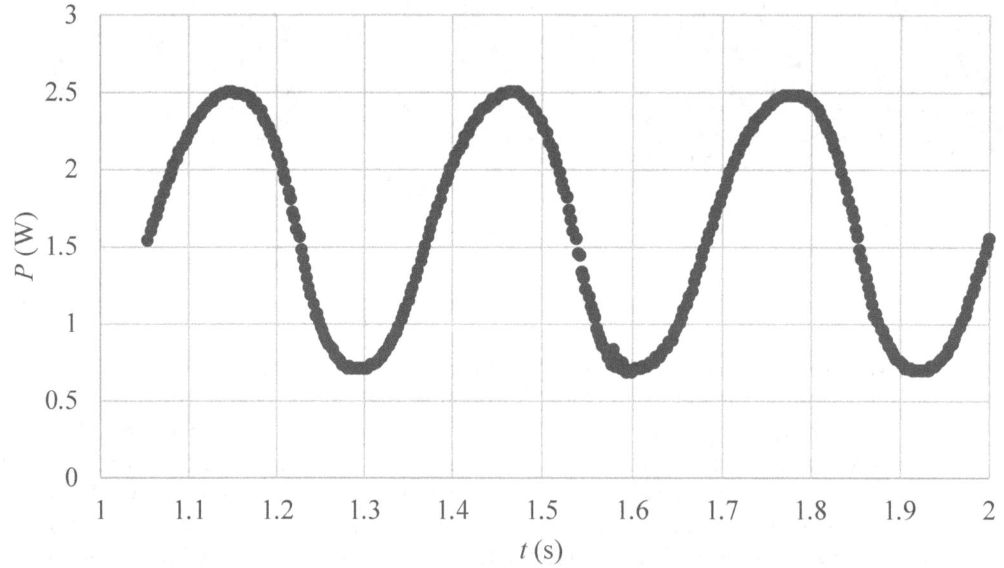

Figure 17.19c) Time series for power of Savonius turbine at $\omega = 10$ rad/s and $V = 5$ m/s.

L. Cloning of Project

20. Select **Tools>>Flow Simulation>>Project>>Clone Project....** Create a cloned project with the name **Savonius Wind Turbine Angular Velocity 5 radps**. Exit the **Clone Project** window. Change the **Rotating Region** to include **5 rad/s** instead of 10 rad/s for the **Angular Velocity**. Also, change the expressions for **Power Coefficient** and **Power Goals** to include **5 rad/s** instead of 10 rad/s for the **Angular Velocity**.

    Power Coefficient = {Torque Coefficient}***Angular Velocity***0.25/5

    Power = {GG Torque (Y) 3}***Angular Velocity**

    Select **Tools>>Flow Simulation>>Calculation Control Options....** Set **Physical time** to **3 s**.

    Repeat step **20** and change angular velocity and physical time as shown in Table 17.1.

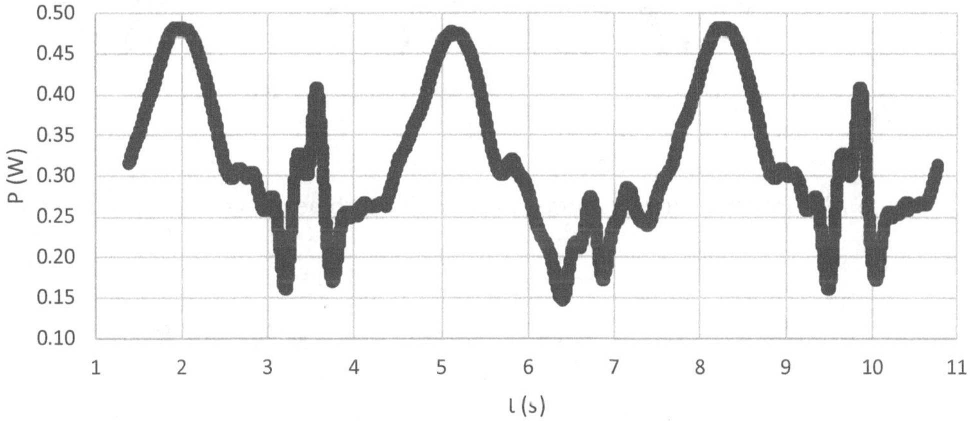

Figure 17.20a) Time series for power of Savonius turbine at $\omega = 1$ rad/s and $V = 5$ m/s

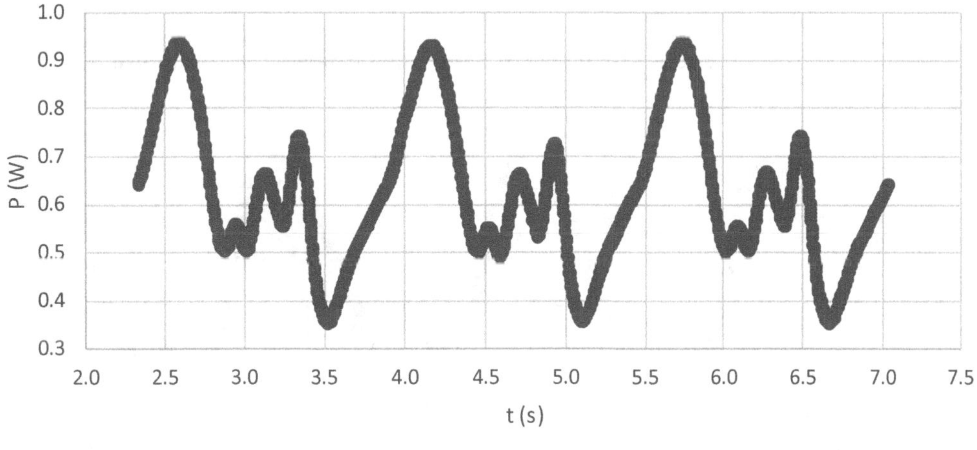

Figure 17.20b) Time series for power of Savonius turbine at $\omega = 2$ rad/s and $V = 5$ m/s

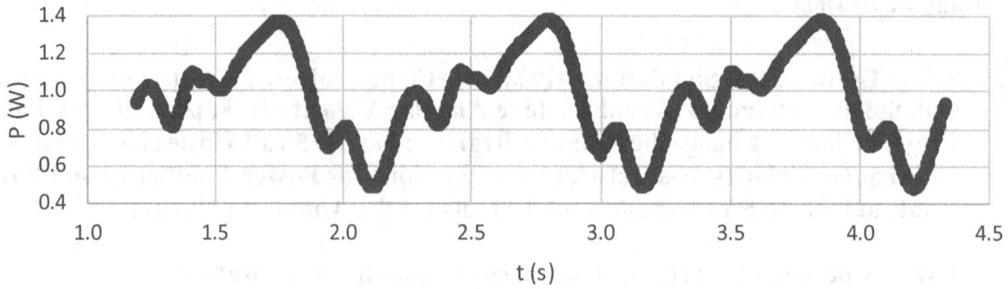

Figure 17.20c) Time series for power of Savonius turbine at $\omega = 3$ rad/s and $V = 5$ m/s.

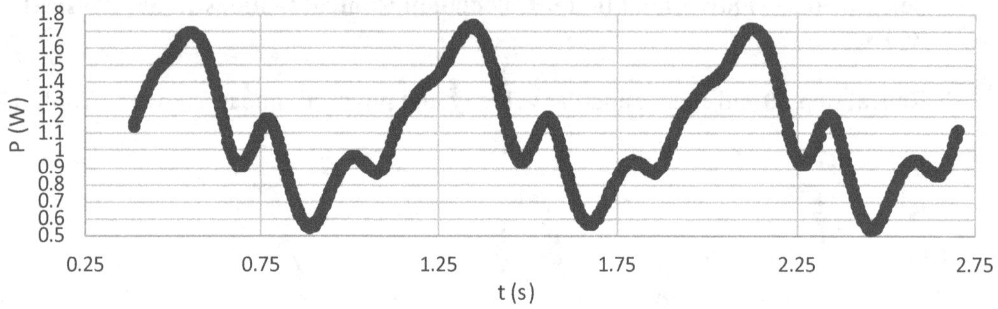

Figure 17.20d) Time series for power of Savonius turbine at $\omega = 4$ rad/s and $V = 5$ m/s.

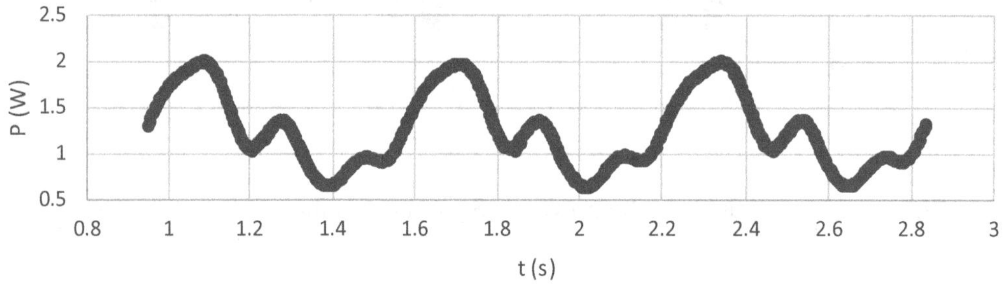

Figure 17.20e) Time series for power of Savonius turbine at $\omega = 5$ rad/s and $V = 5$ m/s.

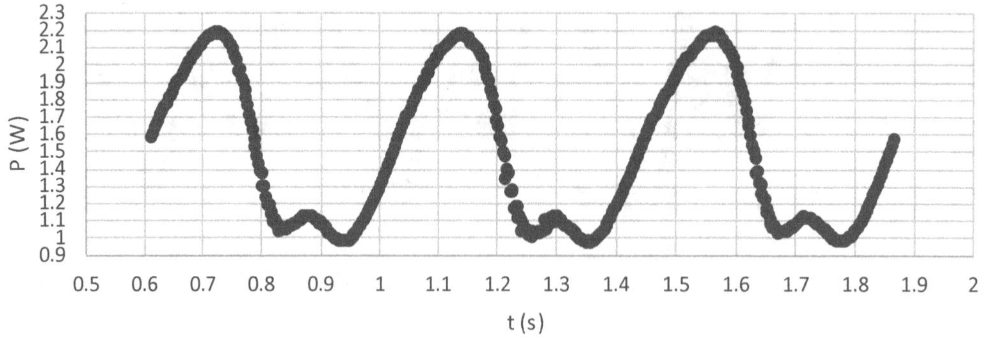

Figure 17.20f) Time series for power of Savonius turbine at $\omega = 7.5$ rad/s and $V = 5$ m/s.

M. Creating a Batch Run

21. Select **Tools>>Flow Simulation>>Solve>>Batch Run…**. Make sure to check all boxes as shown in figure 17.21a). Click on the **Run** button to start the calculations.

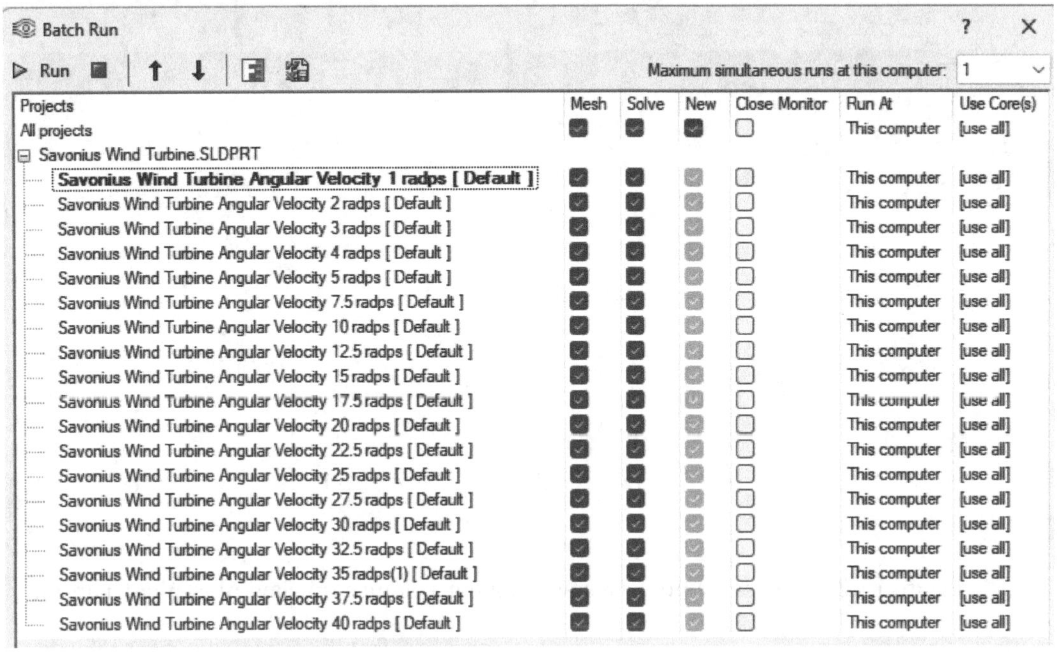

Figure 17.21a) Settings for the batch run

ω (rad/s)	*Physical time* (s)	*TSR*	*P (W)*	*T (Nm)*	t_1 (s)	t_2 (s)
1	15	0.05	0.3221	0.3221	1.3597	10.7844
2	7.5	0.1	0.6285	0.3143	2.3299	7.0363
3	5	0.15	0.9655	0.3218	1.1902	4.3316
4	4	0.2	1.1176	0.2794	0.3879	2.7023
5	3	0.25	1.2592	0.2518	0.9486	2.8356
7.5	2.5	0.375	1.4680	0.1957	0.6100	1.8672
10	2	0.5	1.5577	0.1558	1.0515	2.0000
12.5	1.75	0.625	1.7102	0.1368	0.5883	1.3419
15	1.5	0.75	1.8710	0.1247	0.7019	1.3316
17.5	1.25	0.875	1.9989	0.1142	0.6019	1.1426
20	1	1	2.0689	0.1034	0.5229	0.9964
22.5	0.9375	1.125	2.0379	0.0906	0.4621	0.8843
25	0.875	1.25	2.0298	0.0812	0.4165	0.7934
27.5	0.8125	1.375	1.9767	0.0719	0.3776	0.7204
30	0.75	1.5	1.8382	0.0613	0.3458	0.6594
32.5	0.6875	1.625	1.5699	0.0483	0.3184	0.6089
35	0.625	1.75	1.1951	0.0341	0.2962	0.5664
37.5	0.5625	1.875	0.7123	0.0190	0.2778	0.5290
40	0.5	2	0.1570	0.0039	0.2600	0.4953

Table 17.1 Angular velocity, physical time, tip speed ratio and average power and average torque for $V = 5$ m/s

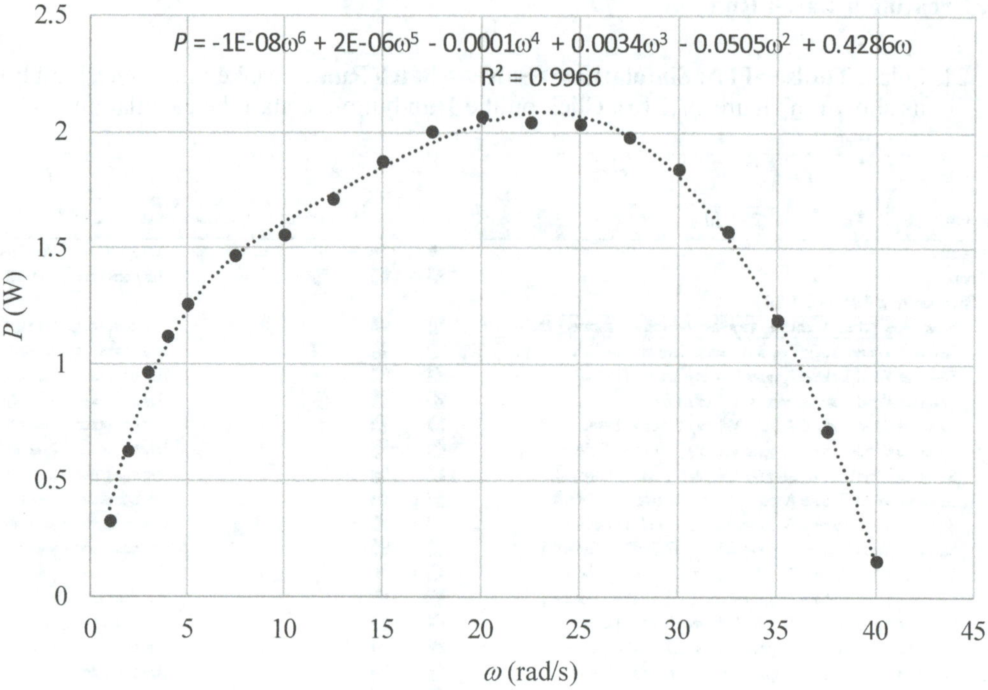

Figure 17.21b) Average power versus angular velocity for Savonius Wind Turbine

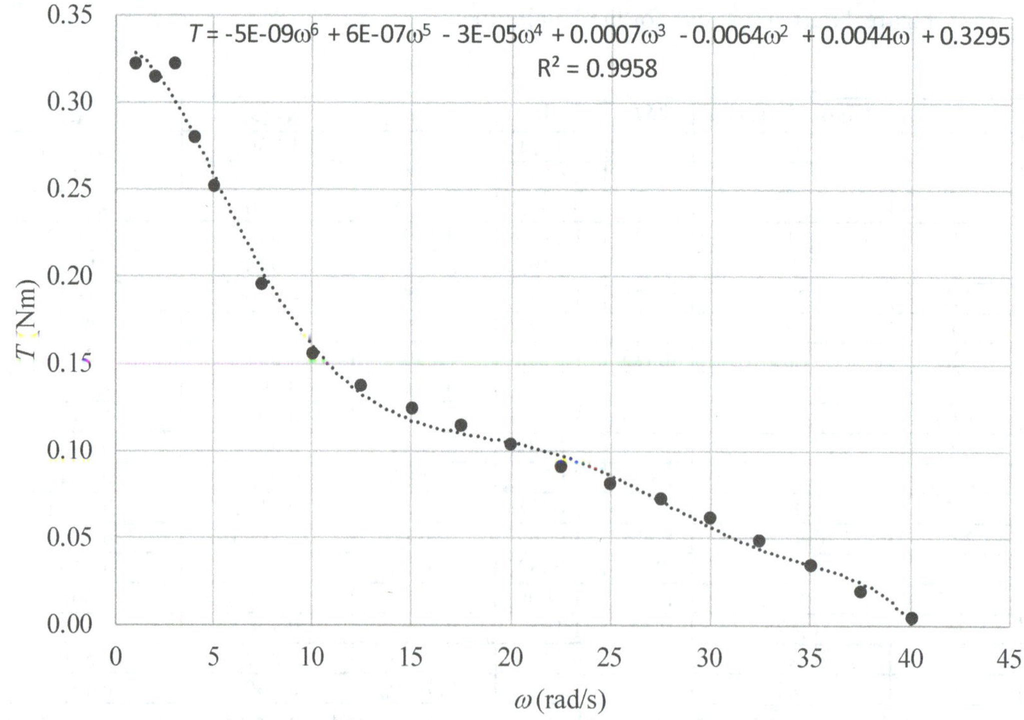

Figure 17.21c) Average torque versus angular velocity for Savonius Wind Turbine

N. Theory

22. In defining the geometry, we follow the approach by Rogowski and Maronski[3]. The cross-sectional geometry of the rotor is shown in Figure 17.22.

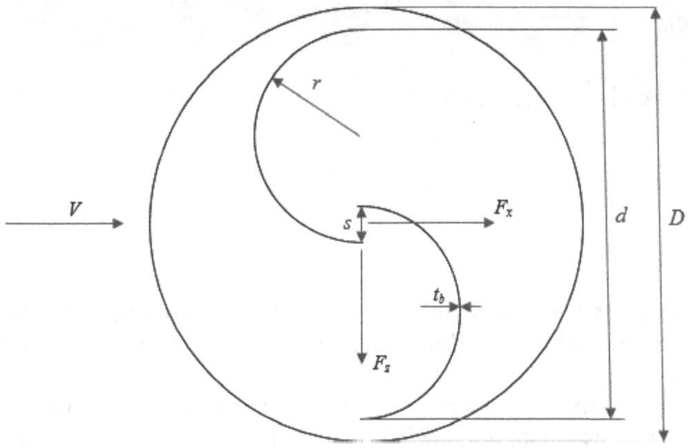

Figure 17.22 Cross sectional geometry for the Savonius rotor

The bucket gap width s is 0.121 m and the bucket thickness t_b is 3 mm. The bucket radius r is 0.15525 m and the rotor diameter $d = 4r - s = 0.5$ m. The overlap ratio is s/d = 0.242. The end plate diameter D is 0.55 m and the end plate thickness t_e is 2 mm. The free stream velocity is V (m/s). The downwind drag force is F_x (N) and the side force or lift force is F_z (N). The rotor swept area is defined as

$$A_s = (4r - s)h \tag{17.1}$$

where $h = 1$ m is the height of the rotor. We define the rotor tip speed v (m/s) and the tip speed ratio TSR as

$$v = \omega d/2 \tag{17.2}$$

$$TSR = \frac{\omega d}{2V} = \frac{v}{V} \tag{17.3}$$

where ω (rad/s) is the rotational speed of the turbine. The turbine rotational speed N (rpm) is then given by

$$N = \frac{30\omega}{\pi} = \frac{60v}{\pi d} \tag{17.4}$$

The drag and lift coefficients can be defined as

$$C_{F_x} = \frac{F_x}{\frac{1}{2}\rho V^2 A_s} \tag{17.5}$$

$$C_{F_z} = \frac{F_z}{\frac{1}{2}\rho V^2 A_s} \tag{17.6}$$

where ρ (kg/m^3) is air density. We can also define the torque coefficient

$$C_T = \frac{T}{\frac{1}{2}\rho V^2 A_s \frac{d}{2}} \tag{17.7}$$

where T (Nm) is the turbine torque. We define the turbine power coefficient as

$$C_P = C_T * TSR \tag{17.8}$$

and turbine power P (W) is defined as

$$P = T\omega \tag{17.9}$$

O. References

1. Zakaria, A. and Ibrahim, M.S.N., "Analysis of Savonius Rotor Performance Operating at Low Wind Speeds Using Numerical Study.", International Journal of Engineering & Technology, 7, 1549-1552, 2018.
2. Zakaria, A. and Ibrahim, M.S.N., "Numerical Performance Evaluation of Savonius Rotors by Flow-Driven and Sliding-Mesh Approaches.", International Journal of Advanced Trends in Computer Science and Engineering, **8**, No. 1, 2019.
3. Rogowski, K and Maronski, R, "CFD Computation of the Savonius rotor.", Journal of Theoretical and Applied Mechanics, **53**, 37-45, 2015.
4. Blackwell, B.F., Sheldahl, R.E. and Feltz, L.V., "Wind Tunnel Performance Data for Two- and Three-Bucket Savonius Rotors, Sandia Laboratories", Report SAND76-0131, 1977.

P. Exercises

17.1 Run the simulations in this chapter for the Savonius rotor at the different free stream velocities as shown in Table 17.2. Fill out the table and plot drag and lift coefficients versus tip speed ratio.

V (m/s)	ω (rad/s)	TSR	P (W)	T (Nm)	F_x (N)	C_{F_x}	F_z (N)	C_{F_z}
2	20							
3	20							
4	20							
5	20							
6	20							

Table 17.2 Average power, torque, drag and lift versus free stream velocity.

17.2 Run the simulations in this chapter for the Savonius wind turbine at the different aspect ratios *h/d* as shown in Table 17.3. Fill out the table and plot drag and lift coefficients versus tip speed ratio.

h/d	V (m/s)	ω (rad/s)	TSR	F_x (N)	C_{F_x}	F_z (N)	C_{F_z}
2	5	20					
8	5	20					
32	5	20					

Table 17.3 Input data and results from SOLIDWORKS Flow Simulations

h/d	A_s (m^2)	h (m)	d (m)	D (m)	s (m)
2	0.5	1	0.5	0.55	0.121
8	0.5	2	0.25	0.275	0.0605
32	0.5	4	0.125	0.1375	0.03025

Table 17.4 Input data for SOLIDWORKS Flow Simulation

CHAPTER 18. SPINNING PROPELLER

A. Objectives

- Model Geometry and Mesh
- Run Simulations for Turbulent Flow
- Determine Thrust
- Visualize Flow Around Propeller

B. Problem Description

We will study the flow generated by a spinning propeller. The propeller is an RAF6 Durand Propeller C, see Durand[2-3]. The file *Propeller.IGS* for this chapter can be downloaded from *sdcpublications.com*. The size of the rotating sliding mesh region that encloses the propeller is given by Kutty and Rajendran[6]. The diameter of the rotating mesh region is 10% larger than the propeller diameter and the thickness of the sliding mesh region is 40% of the propeller diameter.

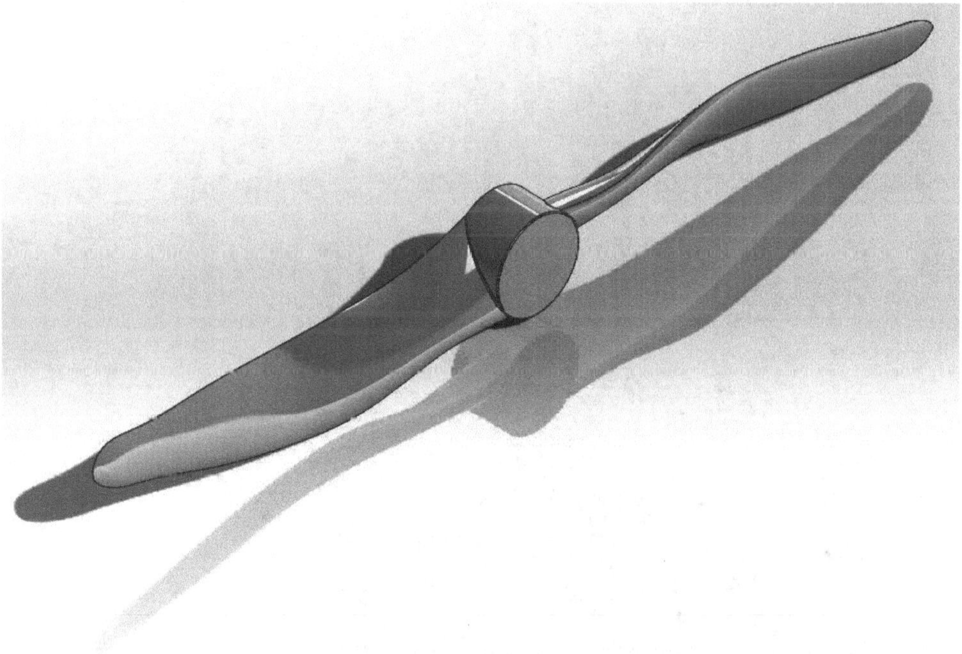

C. Flow Simulation Project

1. Start SOLIDWORKS and open the file ***Propeller.IGS*** in SOLIDWORKS. Do not run import diagnostics. Select **Tools>>Options...** from the SOLIDWORKS menu. Click on the **Document Properties** tab and select **Units.** Select **MMGS** as your **Unit system.** Save the document with the name ***Propeller 2026.sldprt.*** Select the **Right** view from the **View Orientation** drop down menu in the graphics window and click on the **Right Plane** in the **FeatureManager design tree.** Right click on Material and select Edit Material. Select ABS under Plastics. Select Units: SI – N/m^2 (Pa) and click on Apply in the Material window. The density of ABS is 1020 kg/m^3. Close the Material window.

   Next, select the **Right Plane**, select the **Sketch** tab and the **Circle** tool. Start at the origin and draw a circle with a **radius** of **500mm**. Exit the Circle and select Rebuild from the menu. Select **Trimetric** view in the graphics window by selecting **View Orientation** and **Trimetric**. Select the **Features** tab and **Extruded Boss/Base**. Select **Sketch1**. Select **Blind** under **Direction 1**, set the depth to **200 mm** and uncheck the box for **Merge results**. Check the box for **Direction2** and enter **200 mm** as the depth. Select the green checkmark to exit the **Boss-Extrude window**. Right-click on **Boss-Extrude1** and select **Change Transparency**.

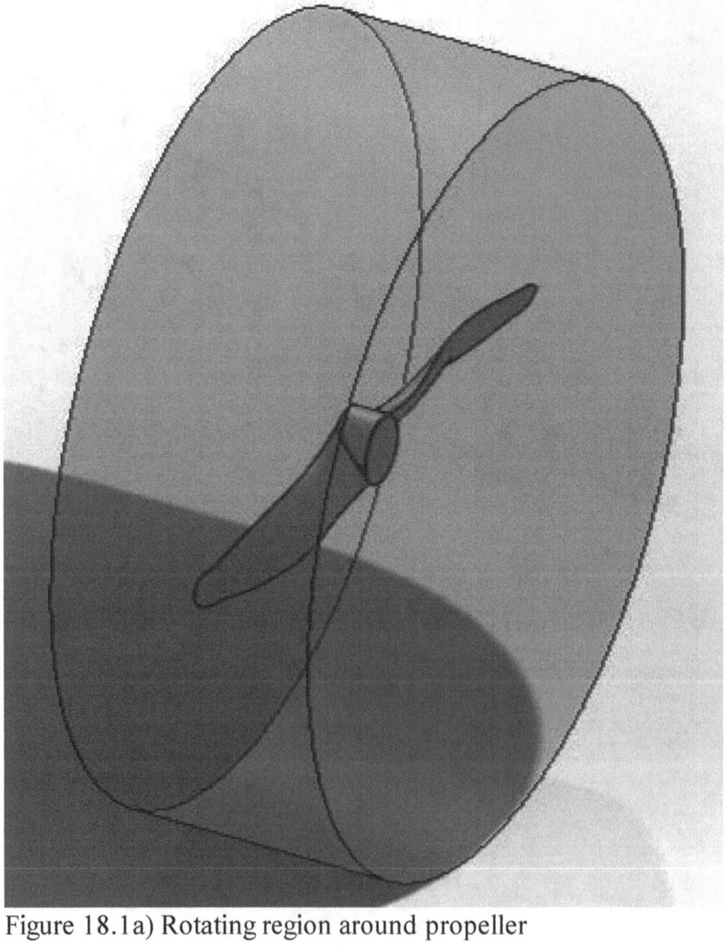

Figure 18.1a) Rotating region around propeller

If Flow Simulation is not available in the SOLIDWORKS menu, select **Tools>>Add Ins…** and check the corresponding **SOLIDWORKS Flow Simulation** box. Start the **Flow Simulation Wizard** by selecting **Tools>>Flow Simulation>>Project>>Wizard…** from the SOLIDWORKS menu. Create a new project with the following name: **Flow Past Propeller**. Click on Next>.

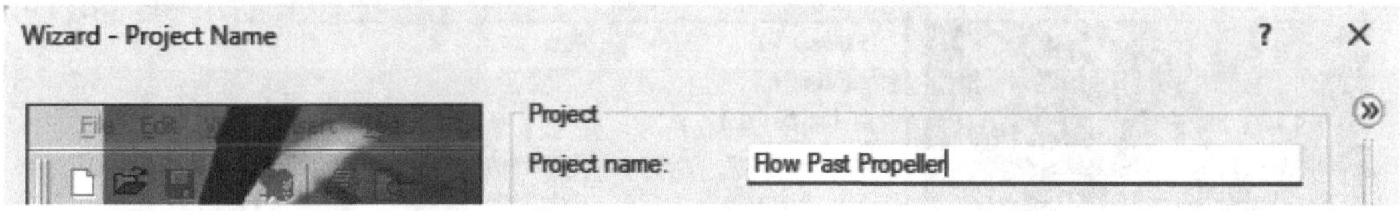

Figure 18.1b) Entering configuration name

2. Select the **SI unit system.** Click on Next>.

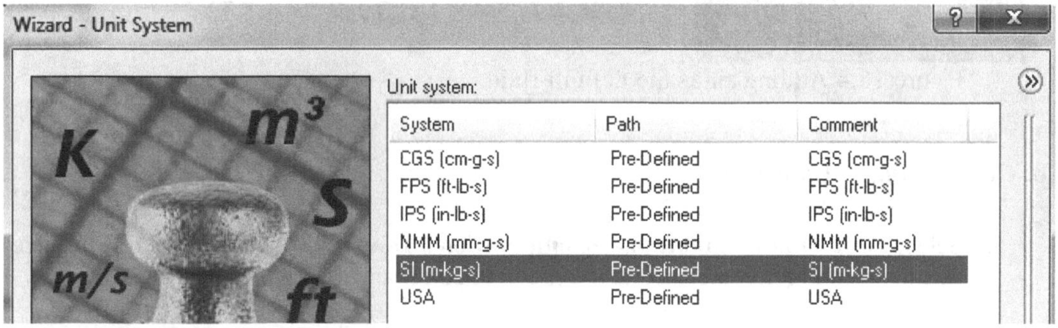

Figure 18.2 Selection of unit system

3. Select **External Analysis type**. Check the boxes for **Exclude cavities without flow conditions** and **Exclude internal space**. Check the box for **Rotation**. Select **Local Region(s) (Averaging)** as **Type** under **Rotation**. Click on Next>.

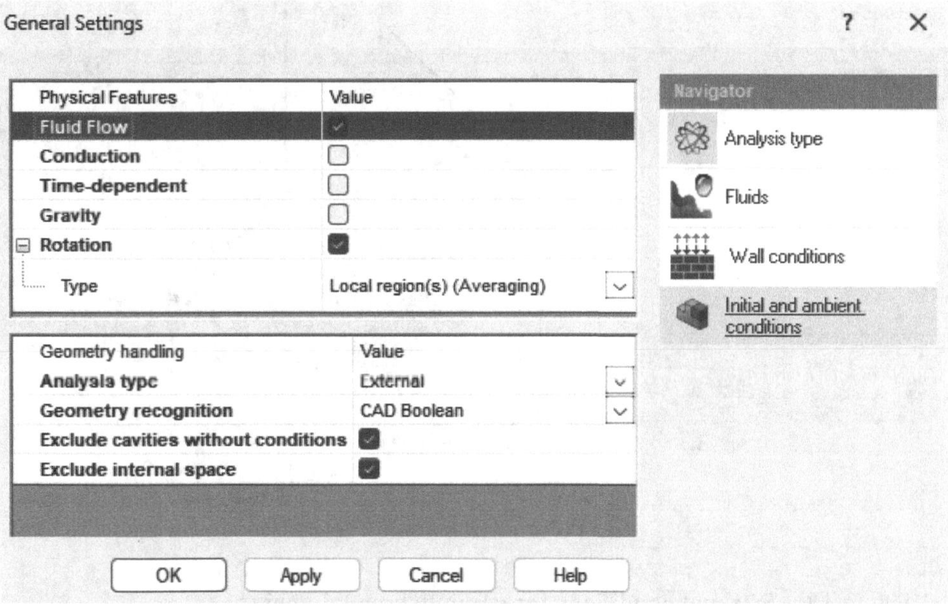

Figure 18.3 Selection of Analysis type

4. Add **Air** as the default **Project Fluid** by selecting it from **Gases**. Click on Next. Choose default values for **Wall Conditions** and enter **-17.88 m/s** as the **Velocity in X direction** as **Initial Condition**. Finish the Wizard.

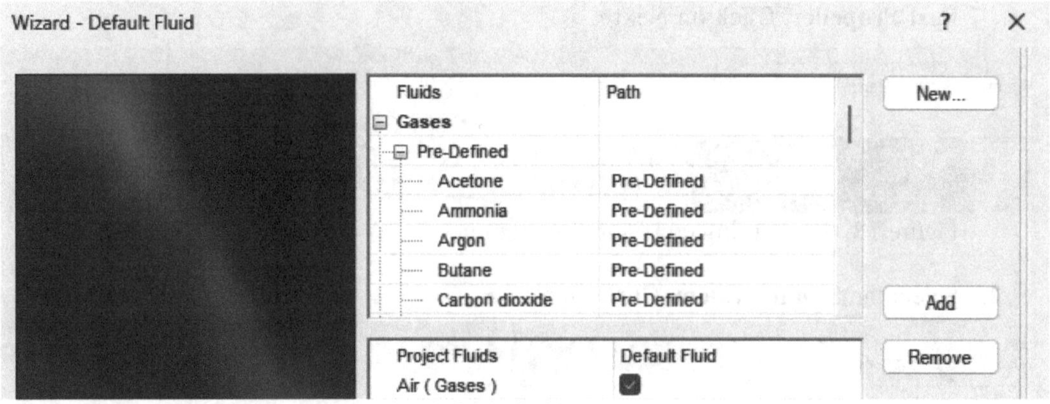

Figure 18.4 Adding air as the default fluid

D. Computational Domain

5. Select **Tools>Flow Simulation>>Computational Domain** from the menu. Use the sizes as shown in Figure 18.5. Select the green check mark to exit the window.

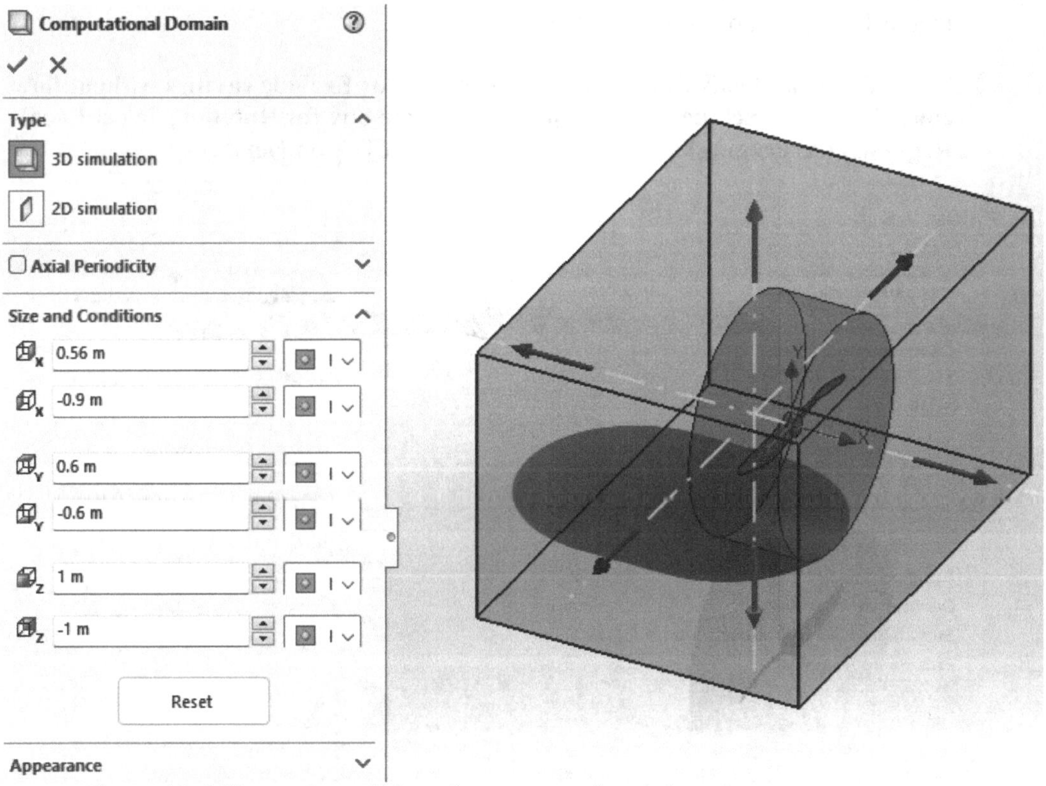

Figure 18.5 Size and conditions for computational domain

E. Goals

6. Right click on **Goals** in the **Flow Simulation analysis tree** and select **Insert Global Goals….** Check the boxes for **Force (X)** and **Torque (X).** Exit the window.

   Right click on **Goals** in the **Flow Simulation analysis tree** and select **Insert Equation Goal….** Select **GG Force (X) 1** in the Flow Simulation Analysis tree. Enter the **Expression** as shown in Figure 18.6a):
   {GG Force (X) 1}*3600/(1.2304*1800^2*0.9144^4)

   Select **No unit** for **Dimensionality**. Enter **Thrust Coefficient** as the name for the equation goal. Click on the OK button to exit the window.

   Repeat this step and create the **Torque Coefficient** as shown in Figure 18.6b):
   -{GG Torque (X) 2}*3600/(1.2304*1800^2*0.9144^5)

   Repeat this step and create the **Efficiency** as shown in Figure 18.6c):
   {GG Force (X) 1}*30*(-17.88)/(3.14159265*1800*{GG Torque (X) 2})

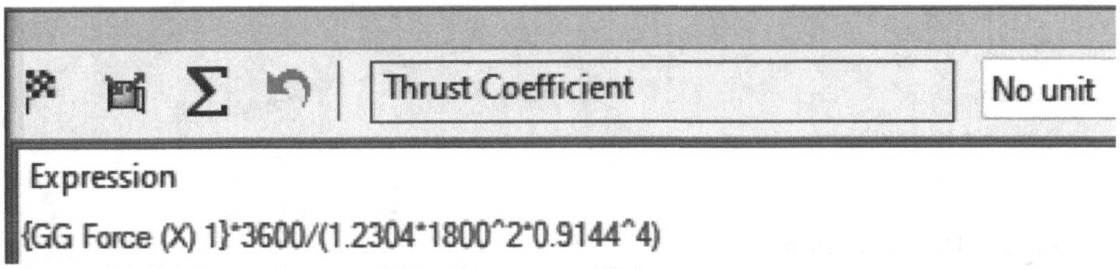

Figure 18.6a) Equation goal for thrust coefficient

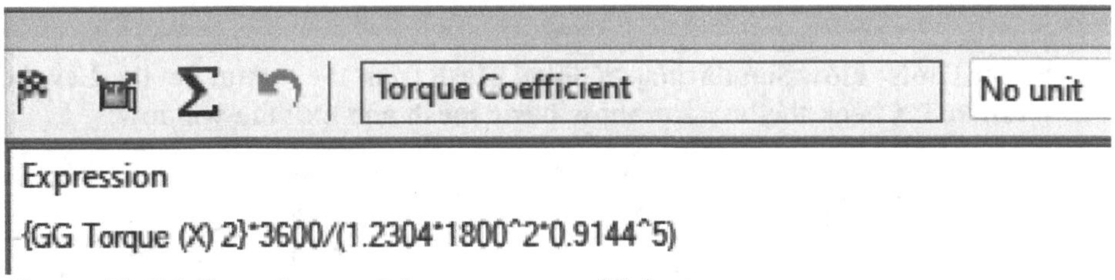

Figure 18.6b) Equation goal for torque coefficient

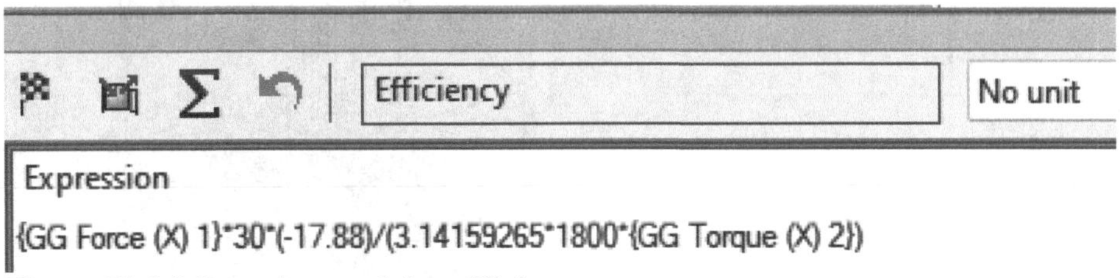

Figure 18.6c) Equation goal for efficiency

F. Rotating Region

7. Right click on **Rotating Regions** under **Input Data**. Select **Insert Rotating Region....** Select the rotating cylindrical region in the graphics window. Set the **Angular Velocity** to **188.4956 rad/s**. Select the green check mark to exit the window.

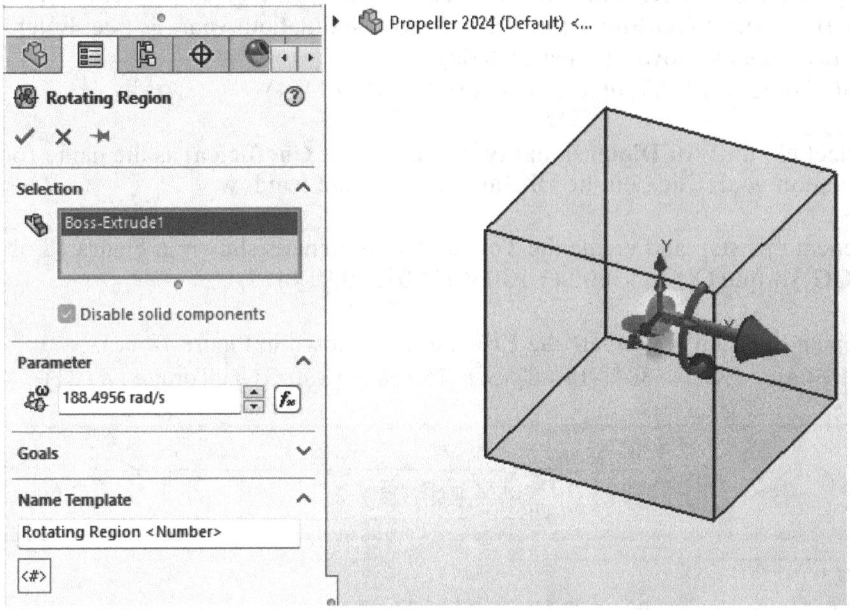

Figure 18.7 Rotating region

G. Global Mesh

8. Select **Tools>Flow Simulation>>Global Mesh** from the menu. Set the **Level of initial mesh** to **3**. Check the box for **Show basic mesh** and exit the window.

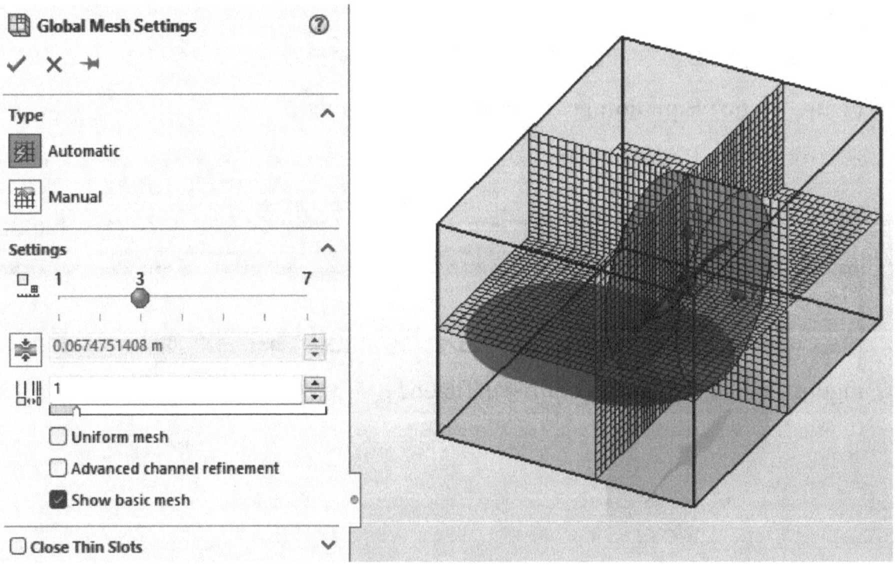

Figure 18.8 Global mesh settings

H. Local Mesh

9. Select **Tools>Flow Simulation>>Insert>>Local Mesh…** from the menu. Select **Region** under **Selection** and check **Cylinder**. Set radius **R** to **0.5 m**, enter **0.2 m**, **0 m** and **0 m** as **Xmax**, **Ymax**, **Zmax**, respectively, and **-0.2 m**, **0 m** and **0 m** as **Xmin**, **Ymin**, **Zmin**, respectively. Set **Level of Refining Fluid Cells** to **2** and **Level of Refining Cells at Fluid/Solid Boundary** to **2**. Uncheck the boxes for **Channels**, **Advanced Refinement** and **Close Thin Slots**.

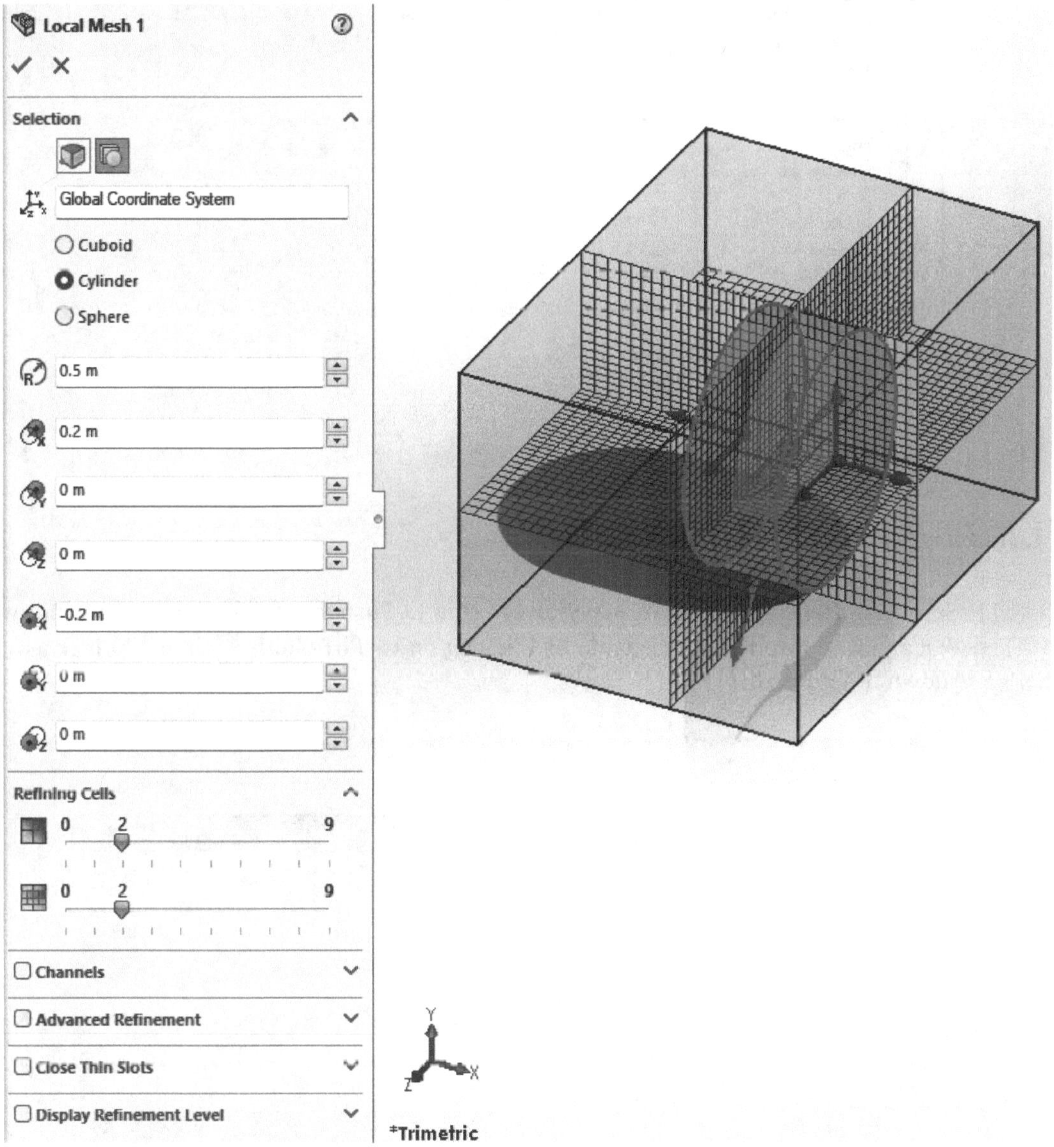

Figure 18.9 Local mesh setting

I. Calculation Control Options

10. Select **Tools>Flow Simulation>>Calculation Control Options...** from the menu. Use the settings as shown in Figure 18.10 for the **Finishing** tab. Open Goals Criteria and uncheck all the boxes as shown in Figure 18.10.

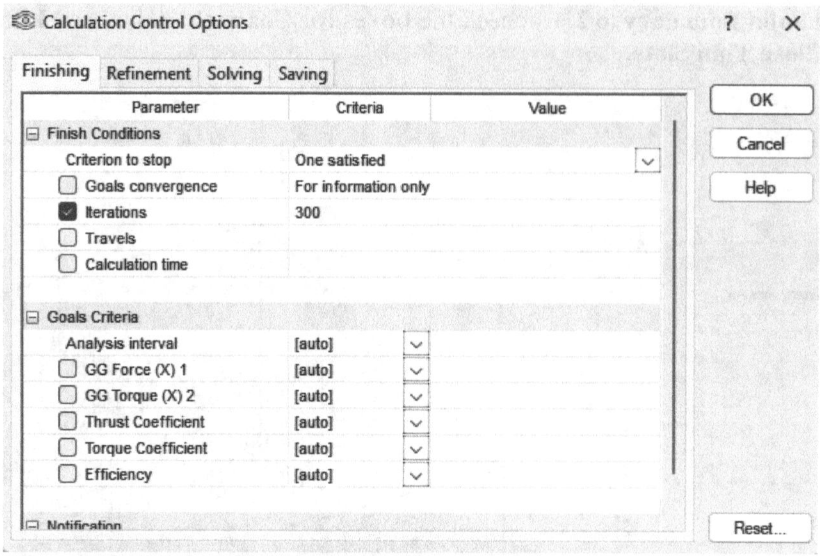

Figure 18.10 Calculation control options

J. Running Simulations

11. Select **Tools>>Flow Simulation>>Solve>>Run....** Push the **Run** button in the window that appears. Insert the goals table by clicking on **List of Goals** in the **Solver** as shown in figure 18.11a).

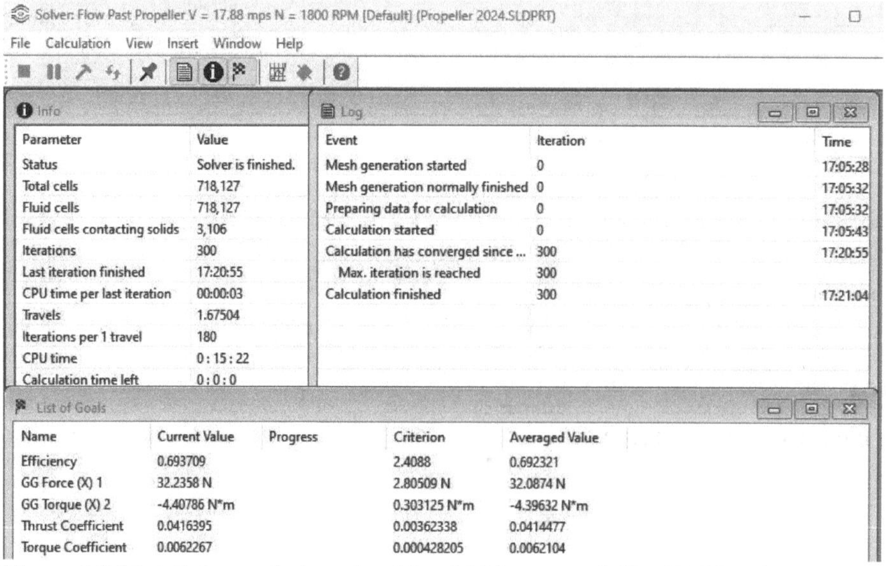

Figure 18.11a) Solver window for N = 1800 rpm and V = 17.88 m/s.

Click on the **Insert Goals Plot** in the **Solver** and check the box for **Efficiency** in the **Add/Remove Goals** window, see Figure 18.11b). Right click in the **Goal plot 1** window, check the box for **Manual min:** and set the value to **0.6**. Set the corresponding value for **Manual max:** to **0.8**. Set the **X-axis units:** to **Iterations** and set the **Scale Mode:** to **Absolute Scale**. Set the **Length scale:** to **2.5**, see Figure 18.11c). Select **OK** to exit the **Goal Plot Settings** window.

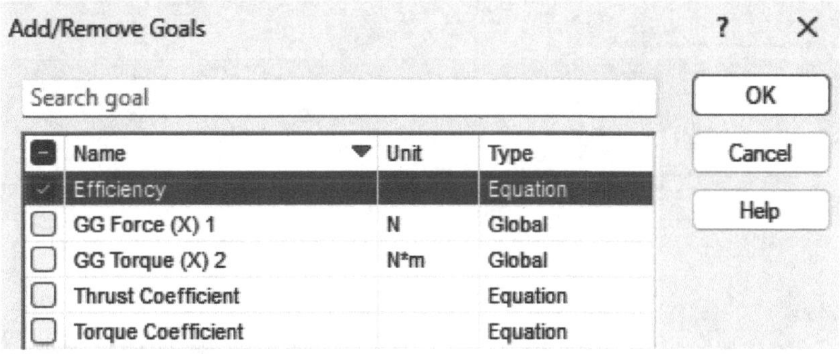

Figure 18.11b) Goals window

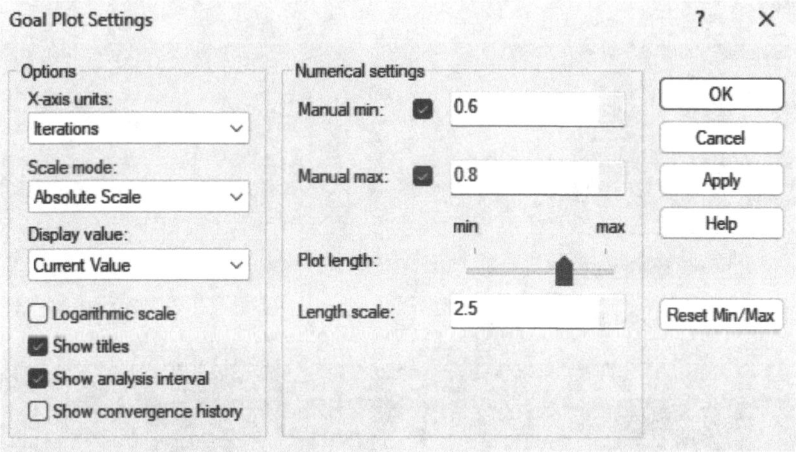

Figure 18.11c) Goal plot settings

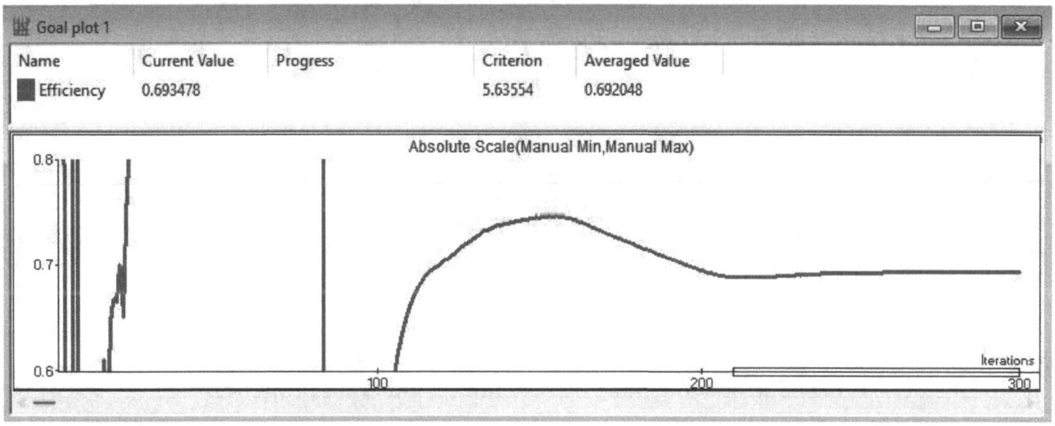

Figure 18.11d) Goal plot

Insert a Surface plot from the Results folder. Check Use all faces under Selection in the Surface Pot window. Select Contours of Pressure and slide the Number of Levels to 255. Repeat this step and create a surface plot for velocity.

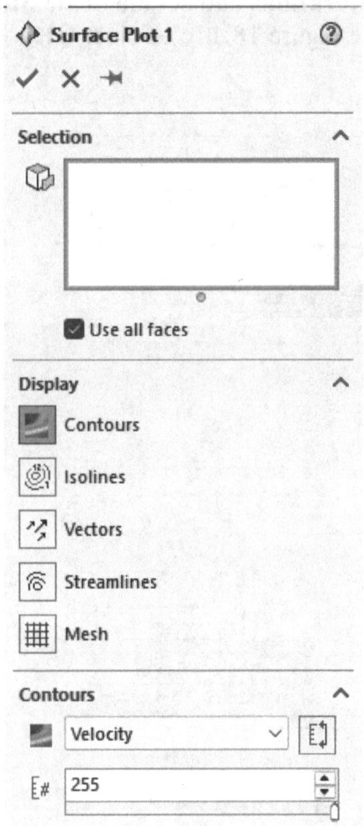

Figure 18.11e) Surface plot settings

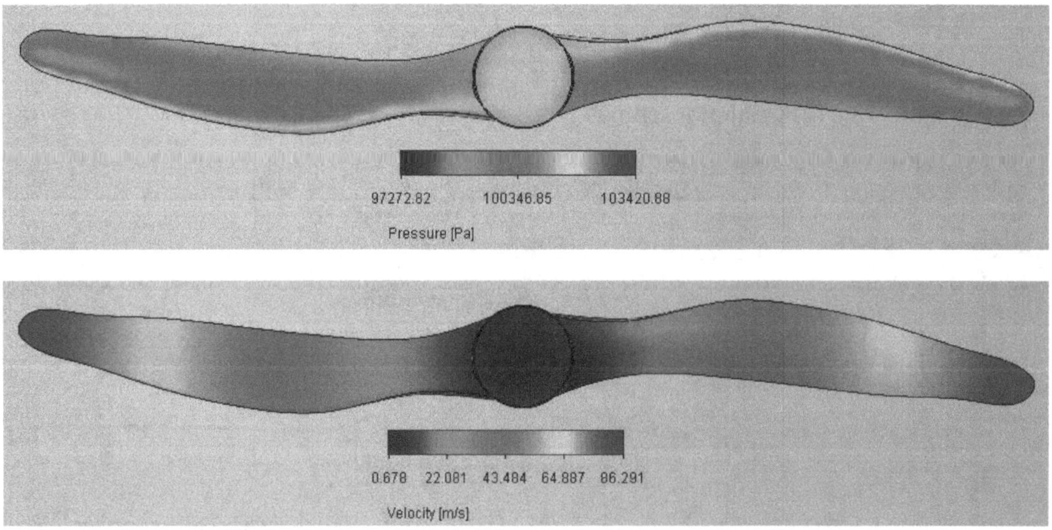

Figure 18.11f) Surface plots of pressure and velocity on propeller.

K. Cloning of Project and Creating a Batch Run

12. Select **Tools>>Flow Simulation>>Project>>Clone Project….** Create a cloned project with the name **Flow Past Propeller V = 0 mps N = 1800 RPM**. Exit the **Clone Project** window. Select **Tools>>Flow Simulation>>General Settings….** Select **Initial and ambient conditions** under **Navigator** and change **Velocity in X direction** from -17.88 m/s to **0 m/s**. Click on **Apply** and **OK** to close the **General Settings** window. Open the **Goal** for **Efficiency**. Change the **Velocity** from -17.88 m/s to **0 m/s**.

    {GG Force (X) 1}*30*(**Velocity**)/(3.14159265*1800*{GG Torque (X) 2})

    Repeat step **12** and change the velocity as shown in Figure 18.12a) and Table 18.1. Select **Tools>>Flow Simulation>>Solve>>Batch Run….** Make sure to check all boxes as shown in figure 18.12a). Click on the **Run** button to start the calculations.

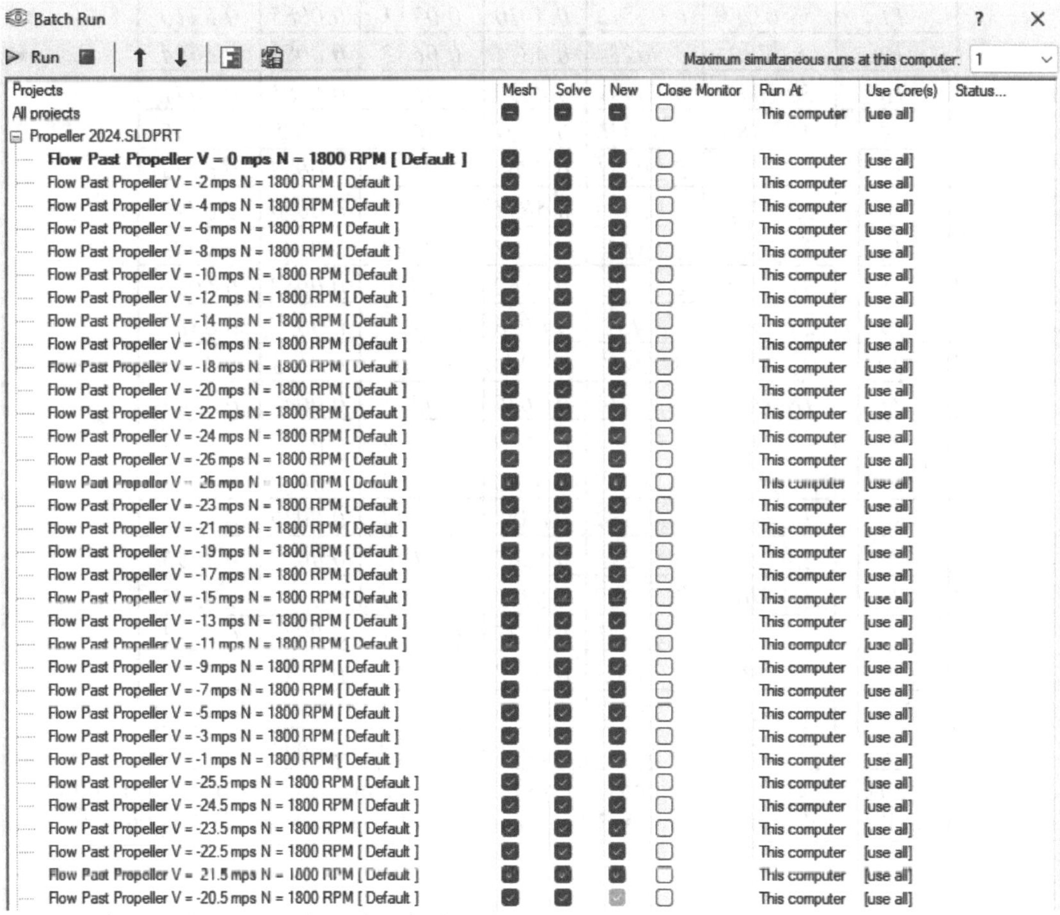

Figure 18.12a) Settings for the batch run

V (m/s)	T (N)	τ (Nm)	J	C_T	C_τ	η
0	45.6017	5.17781	0.0000	0.0589	0.0073	0.0000
-1	102.521	9.13905	0.0365	0.1324	0.0129	0.0595
-2	65.8664	6.4309	0.0729	0.0851	0.0091	0.1087
-3	52.6713	5.85187	0.1094	0.0680	0.0083	0.1433
-4	63.884	6.64941	0.1458	0.0825	0.0094	0.2039
-5	64.5234	6.62813	0.1823	0.0833	0.0094	0.2582
-6	65.392	6.66933	0.2187	0.0845	0.0094	0.3121
-7	63.7664	6.61673	0.2552	0.0824	0.0093	0.3579
-8	61.9052	6.49283	0.2916	0.0800	0.0092	0.4047
-9	58.2691	6.257	0.3281	0.0753	0.0088	0.4446
-10	57.002	6.18144	0.3645	0.0736	0.0087	0.4892
-11	55.0107	6.04512	0.4010	0.0711	0.0085	0.5310
-12	52.789	5.90234	0.4374	0.0682	0.0083	0.5694
-13	50.2317	5.73499	0.4739	0.0649	0.0081	0.6041
-14	47.1386	5.52336	0.5104	0.0609	0.0078	0.6339
-15	44.2265	5.29781	0.5468	0.0571	0.0075	0.6643
-16	39.8545	4.97729	0.5833	0.0515	0.0070	0.6797
-17	35.8617	4.68174	0.6197	0.0463	0.0066	0.6908
-18	31.7436	4.37105	0.6562	0.0410	0.0062	0.6935
-19	27.5449	4.0432	0.6926	0.0356	0.0057	0.6867
-20	23.2739	3.72457	0.7291	0.0301	0.0053	0.6630
-21	18.9372	3.39916	0.7655	0.0245	0.0048	0.6207
-22	14.6465	3.08604	0.8020	0.0189	0.0044	0.5539
-22.5	12.5164	2.93079	0.8202	0.0162	0.0041	0.5098
-23	10.4102	2.77584	0.8384	0.0134	0.0039	0.4576
-23.5	8.43291	2.63295	0.8567	0.0109	0.0037	0.3993
-24	6.22468	2.47299	0.8749	0.0080	0.0035	0.3205
-24.5	3.70346	2.28041	0.8931	0.0048	0.0032	0.2111
-25	1.65862	2.13203	0.9113	0.0021	0.0030	0.1032
-25.5	-0.39371	1.98472	0.9296	-0.0005	0.0028	-0.0268
-26	-2.43721	1.8376	0.9478	-0.0031	0.0026	-0.1829

Table 18.1 Free stream velocity V (m/s), T (N), τ (Nm), J, C_T, C_τ and η for spinning propeller at $N = 1800$ rpm, $n = 30$ rps, $d = 0.9144$ m and $\rho = 1.2304$ kg/m^3

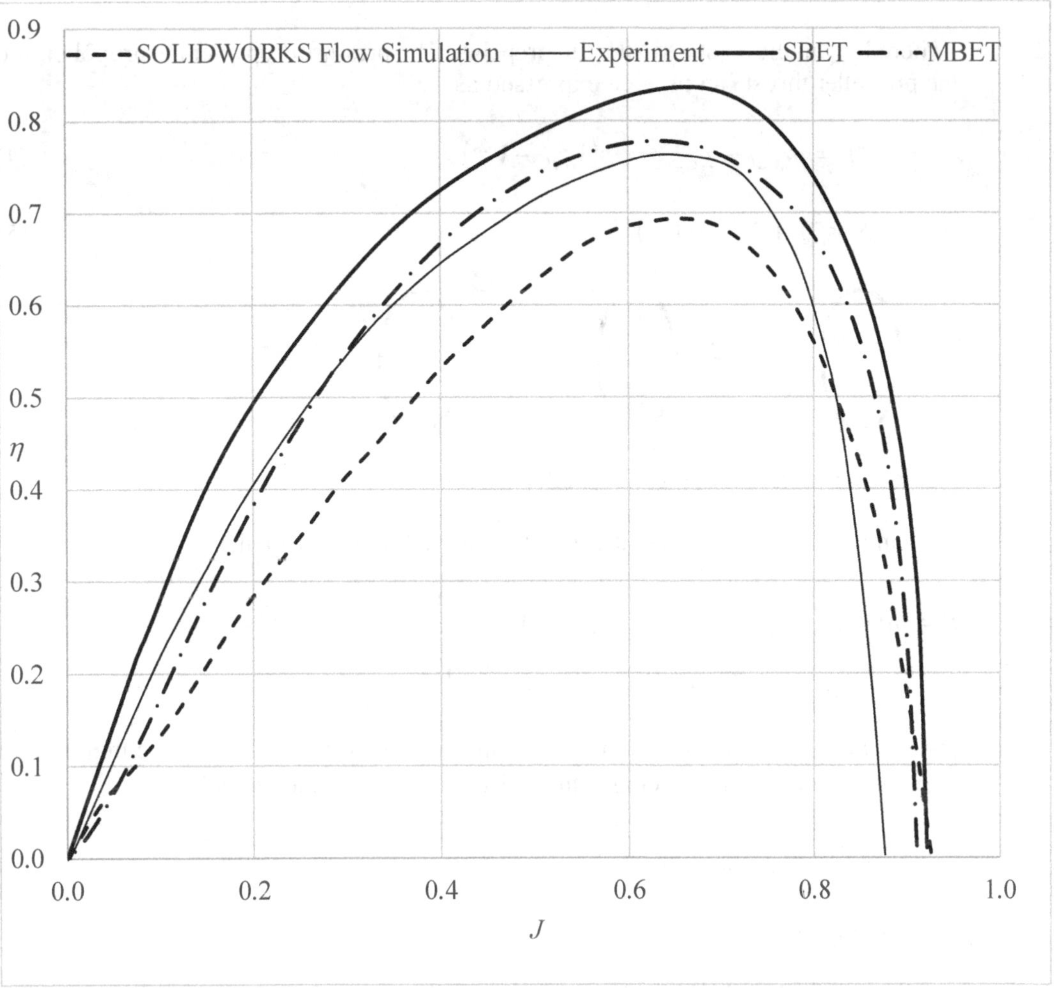

Figure 18.12b) Propeller efficiency versus forward ratio for experiments, SOLIDWORKS Flow Simulations, Simple Blade Element Theory and Modified Blade Element Theory, see Weick[2].

L. Theory

13. The thrust F generated by the propeller is equal to the pressure drop Δp over the propeller times the area A of the propeller disk.

$$F = \Delta pA \tag{1}$$

In front of the propeller we have the total pressure $p_{t,in}$ expressed as

$$p_{t,in} = p + \frac{1}{2}\rho V_{in}^2 \tag{2}$$

, where V_{in} in the incoming air speed, p is static pressure, $\frac{1}{2}\rho V_{in}^2$ is dynamic pressure and ρ is air density. Behind the propeller we have the total pressure $p_{t,out}$ expressed as

$$p_{t,out} = p + \frac{1}{2}\rho V_{out}^2 \tag{3}$$

, where V_{out} in the air speed after the propeller. The pressure drop over the propeller and the propeller thrust can now be expressed as

$$\Delta p = p_{t,out} - p_{t,in} = \frac{1}{2}\rho\left(V_{out}^2 - V_{in}^2\right) \tag{4}$$

$$F = \frac{1}{2}\rho A\left(V_{out}^2 - V_{in}^2\right) \tag{5}$$

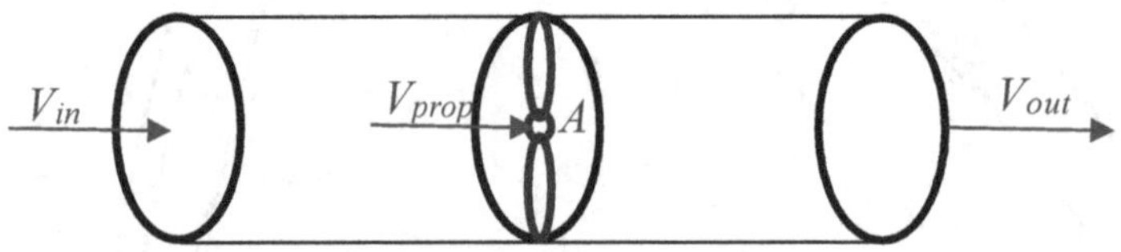

Figure 18.13a) Geometry for propeller

We can alternatively express the thrust generated by the propeller as

$$F = \dot{m}(V_{out} - V_{in}) = \rho V_{prop} A(V_{out} - V_{in}) = \frac{1}{2}\rho A\left(V_{out}^2 - V_{in}^2\right) = \\ = \frac{1}{2}\rho A(V_{out} - V_{in})(V_{out} + V_{in}) \tag{6}$$

, where $\dot{m}$ is mass flow rate and V_{prop} is air velocity at propeller. We see that the propeller velocity is the average value of the inlet and outlet velocities.

$$V_{prop} = \frac{1}{2}(V_{out} + V_{in}) \tag{7}$$

Blade Element Theory

We consider an infinitesimal blade element at distance r from the axis of rotation with length dr and blade chord length c as shown in Figure 18.13b). The length of the blade or tip radius is R. We define V as axial flow velocity past blade element, ωr is circumferential flow velocity past blade element related to propeller rotation and V_r is the resultant flow velocity past the blade element, see Figure 18.13c). The blade element has a pitch blade angle β and angle of attack α. The difference between β and α is $\phi = \beta - \alpha$.

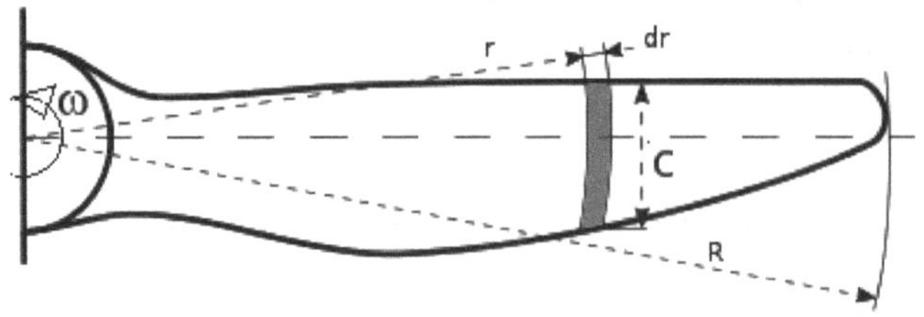

Figure 18.13b) Geometry for a blade element, see Weick[2].

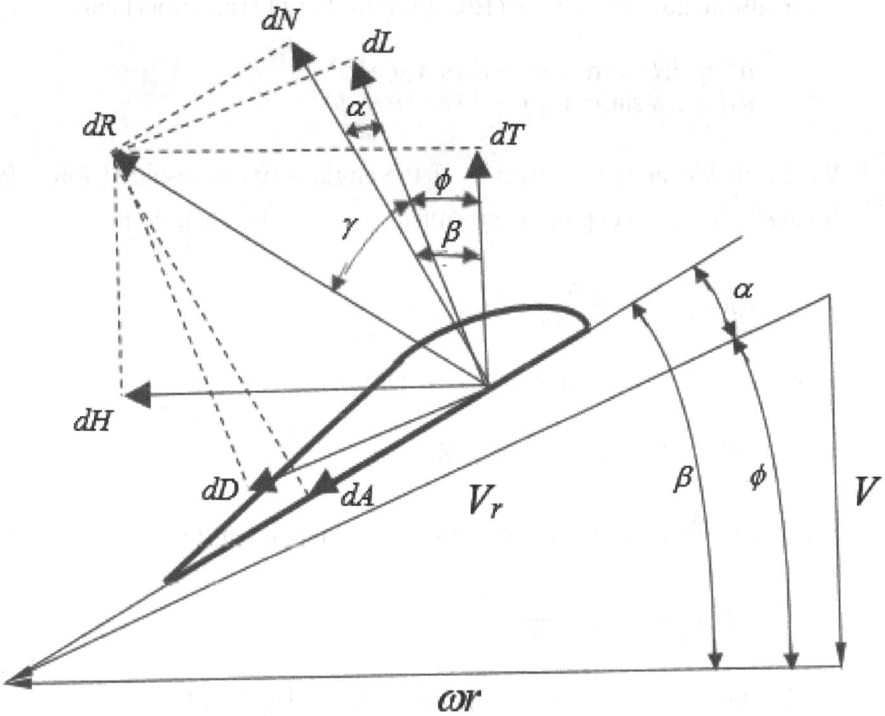

Figure 18.13c) Forces on a blade element, see Weick[2].

The normal and axial forces *dN, dA* on the blade element are

$$dN = \frac{1}{2}\rho V_r^2 S C_N \tag{8}$$
$$dA = \frac{1}{2}\rho V_r^2 S C_A \tag{9}$$

, where C_N is the normal force coefficient, C_A is the axial force coefficient and $S = c{\cdot}dr$ is the planform area of the *2D* airfoil section. Similarly, we can define the lift and drag forces *dL, dD* on the blade element

$$dL = \frac{1}{2}\rho V_r^2 S C_L \tag{10}$$

$$dD = \frac{1}{2}\rho V_r^2 S C_D \tag{11}$$

, where C_L is the lift coefficient and C_D is the drag coefficient. The relation between the force pairs *dN, dA* and *dL, dD* are

$$dL = dN\cos\alpha - dA\sin\alpha \tag{12}$$
$$dD = dN\sin\alpha + dA\cos\alpha \tag{13}$$

The thrust *dT* and horizontal force *dH* related to torque on the blade element is given by

$$dT = dL\cos\phi - dD\sin\phi \tag{14}$$
$$dH = dL\sin\phi + dD\cos\phi \tag{15}$$

After substitution of equations (10), (11) into (12), (13) and from Figure 35.12c) we find

$$dT = dN\cos(\alpha+\phi) - dA\sin(\alpha+\phi) \tag{16}$$
$$dH = dN\sin(\alpha+\phi) + dA\cos(\alpha+\phi) \tag{17}$$

We define the angle $\gamma = atan\frac{dD}{dL}$ as the angle between resultant force dR and lift force dL. Next, we express the resultant force on the blade element

$$dR = \frac{dL}{\cos\gamma} = \frac{\frac{1}{2}\rho V_r^2 SC_L}{\cos\gamma} \tag{18}$$

Using $S = c{\cdot}dr$ and the geometry in Figure 18.13c), we can express the thrust dT

$$dT = dR\cos(\gamma+\phi) = \frac{1}{2}\rho V_r^2 cC_L\frac{\cos(\gamma+\phi)}{\cos\gamma}dr \tag{19}$$

Since $V_r = \frac{V}{\sin\phi}$, we can alternatively express the thrust force on the blade element as

$$dT = \frac{1}{2}\rho V^2 cC_L\frac{\cos(\gamma+\phi)}{\sin^2\phi\,\cos\gamma}dr \tag{20}$$

The total thrust force T for a propeller with n_b blades will be

$$T = \frac{1}{2}n_b\rho V^2\int_0^R cC_L\frac{\cos(\gamma+\phi)}{\sin^2\phi\,\cos\gamma}\,dr \tag{21}$$

Again, using the the geometry in Figure 18.13c), we can express the horizontal force dH

$$dH = dR\sin(\gamma+\phi) = \frac{1}{2}\rho V_r^2 cC_L\frac{\sin(\gamma+\phi)}{\cos\gamma}dr \tag{22}$$

and the corresponding torque $d\tau$ on the blade element

$$d\tau = rdH = rdR\sin(\gamma+\phi) = \frac{1}{2}\rho V_r^2 cC_L\frac{\sin(\gamma+\phi)}{\cos\gamma}rdr = \frac{1}{2}\rho V^2 cC_L\frac{\sin(\gamma+\phi)}{\sin^2\phi\,\cos\gamma}rdr \tag{23}$$

The total torque τ for a propeller with n_b blades will be

$$\tau = \frac{1}{2}n_b\rho V^2\int_0^R cC_L\frac{\sin(\gamma+\phi)}{\sin^2\phi\,\cos\gamma_L}\,rdr \tag{24}$$

We can express the efficiency η of a blade element as the ratio of the useful power of thrust times velocity or $dP_T = VdT$ divided by the power related to torque or $dP_\tau = \omega d\tau$

$$\eta = \frac{dP_T}{dP_\tau} = \frac{VdT}{\omega d\tau} = \frac{V\,dR\cos(\gamma+\phi)}{\omega r\,dR\sin(\gamma+\phi)} = \frac{\tan\phi}{\tan(\gamma+\phi)} \tag{25}$$

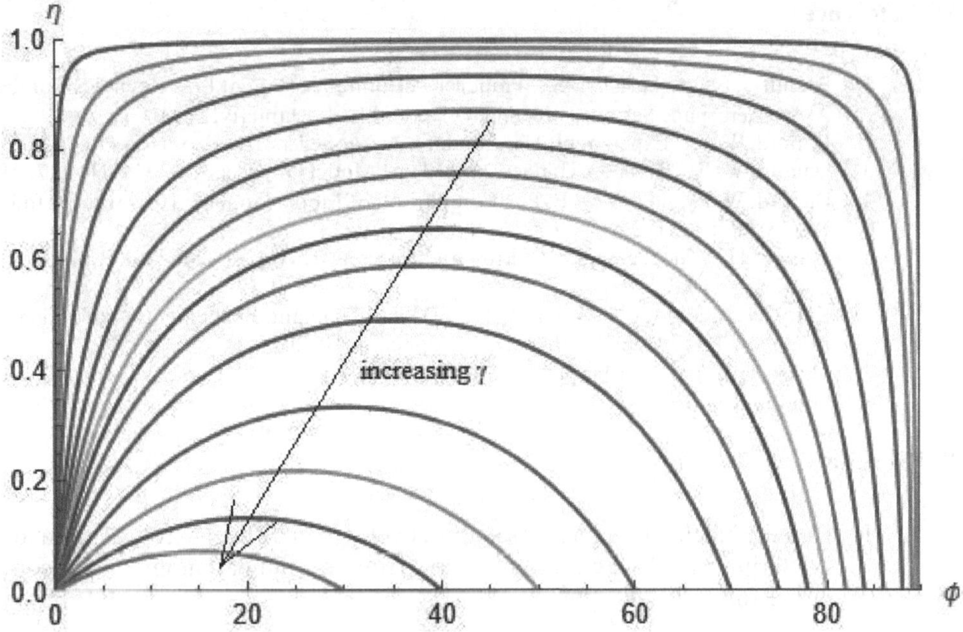

Figure 18.13d) Efficiency diagram for $\gamma = 0.1°,\ 0.5°,\ 1°,\ 2°,\ 4°,\ 6°,\ 8°,\ 10°,\ 12°,\ 15°,\ 20°,\ 30°,\ 40°,\ 50°,\ 60°$. Maximum efficiency for $\phi = 45° - \frac{\gamma}{2}$

We can define the advance ratio J as

$$J = \frac{V}{nd} \tag{26}$$

where $d = 2R$ is propeller diameter and $n = \frac{\omega}{2\pi} = \frac{N}{60}$ is the propeller angular rotation rate with units rev/s or RPS. N is the propeller revolutions per minute or RPM.

Next, we define the thrust coefficient C_T for the propeller as

$$C_T = \frac{T}{\rho n^2 d^4} = \frac{3600T}{\rho N^2 d^4} \tag{27}$$

, the torque coefficient C_τ as

$$C_\tau = \frac{\tau}{\rho n^2 d^5} \tag{28}$$

and we can then define the efficiency η

$$\eta = \frac{J}{2\pi}\frac{C_T}{C_\tau} = \frac{V}{2\pi nd}\frac{\frac{T}{\rho n^2 d^4}}{\frac{\tau}{\rho n^2 d^5}} = \frac{V}{2\pi n}\frac{T}{\tau} \tag{29}$$

Finally, the blade passing frequency is defined as

$$BPF = n_b n \tag{30}$$

M. References

1. Brandt, J. B. and Selig, M. S., "Propeller Performance Data at Low Reynolds Numbers.", 49th AIAA Aerospace Sciences Meeting, Orlando, FL, 4-7 January, 2011.
2. Durand, W. F., "Experimental Research on Air Propellers", NACA-TR-141, 1923.
3. Durand, W. F., "Tests on Thirteen Navy Type Model Propellers", NACA-TR-237, 1927.
4. Durand, W. F. and Lesley, E. P., "Comparison of Model Propeller Tests with Airfoil Theory", NACA-TR-196, 1925.
5. Glauert, H., "The Elements of Airfoil and Airscrew Theory", Second Ed., University Press, Cambridge, 1948.
6. Kutty, H. A. and Rajendran, P., "3D CFD Simulation and Experimental Validation of Small APC Slow Flyer Propeller Blade.", Aerospace, **4**, 10, 2017.
7. Weick, F.E., "Aircraft Propeller Design", McGraw-Hill Book Company, Inc., New York and London, 1930.

N. Exercise

1. Run the batch job simulations in this chapter for a different propeller rotation rate $N =$ 3600 rpm and plot the efficiency curve from the simulation in comparison with the curve for $N = 1800$ rpm.

2. Create a SOLIDWORKS model for a different propeller than Durand Propeller C as shown in this chapter and run the batch job simulation for the propeller of your choice Durand Propeller A – M and compare the efficiency curve with the curve for Duran Propeller C for propeller speed $N = 1800$ RPM.

CHAPTER 19. SUPERSONIC FLOW OVER A CONE

A. Objectives

- Creating the SOLIDWORKS model needed for the cone
- Setting up a Flow Simulation project for External Flows
- Using cut plots to visualize the resulting flow field

B. Problem Description

We will in this chapter create the model for and study the supersonic flow past a cone with an incoming Mach number equal to 2.

C. Modeling SOLIDWORKS Part

1. Start SOLIDWORKS and create a New Part. Select **Tools>>Options...** from the SOLIDWORKS menu. Click on the **Document Properties** tab and select **Units**. Select **MMGS** as your **Unit system**. Select the **Front** view from the **View Orientation** drop down menu in the graphics window and click on the **Front Plane** in the **FeatureManager design tree**. User the **Centerline** sketch tool and draw a horizontal line from the origin to the right with a length of **2000 mm** and add a **Fix** relation. Next, draw an inclined **Line** in the first quadrant from the origin. Set the length of the line to **2128.35554495 mm**, set the angle to **20 degrees** and add a **Fix** relation. Draw a vertical line downward from the endpoint of the inclined line to the centerline. Use the **Revolved Boss/Base** feature to create the cone. Answer Yes to the question if you would like the sketch to be automatically closed. Insert a Sketch in the Front Plane and draw a vertical **Line** from the base of the cone vertically upward with the **Length 1271.93640421 mm** and **Start Y Coordinate 727.94046853 mm** and add a **Fix** relation, see Figure 19.1. Save the model with the name **Cone 2026**.

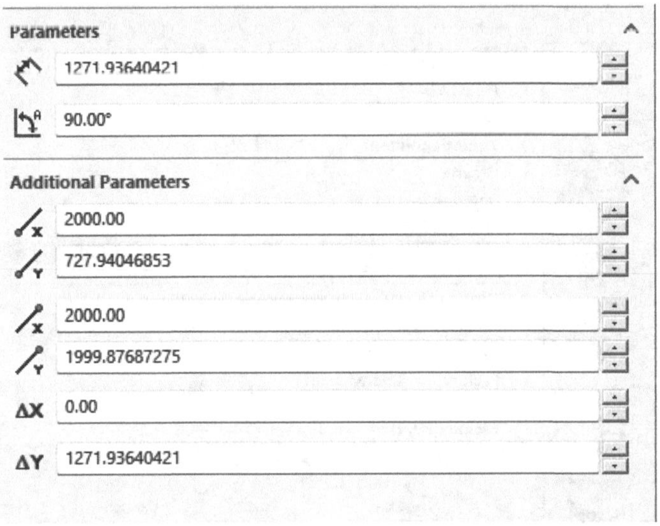

Figure 19.1 SOLIDWORKS model of 20-degree cone and Sketch2

D. Flow Simulation Project

2. If Flow Simulation is not available in the SOLIDWORKS menu, select **Tools>>Add Ins…** and check the corresponding **SOLIDWORKS Flow Simulation** box. Start the **Flow Simulation Wizard** by selecting **Tools>>Flow Simulation>>Project>>Wizard…** from the SOLIDWORKS menu. Create a new project with the following name: **Supersonic Flow Past Cone**. Click on Next>.

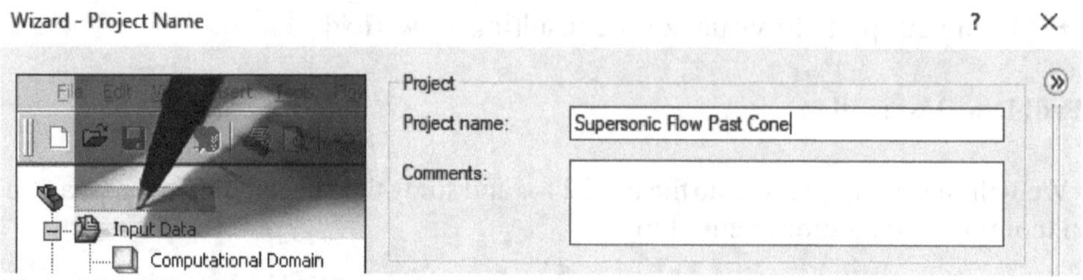

Figure 19.2 Entering configuration name

3. Select the **SI unit system.** Click on Next>.

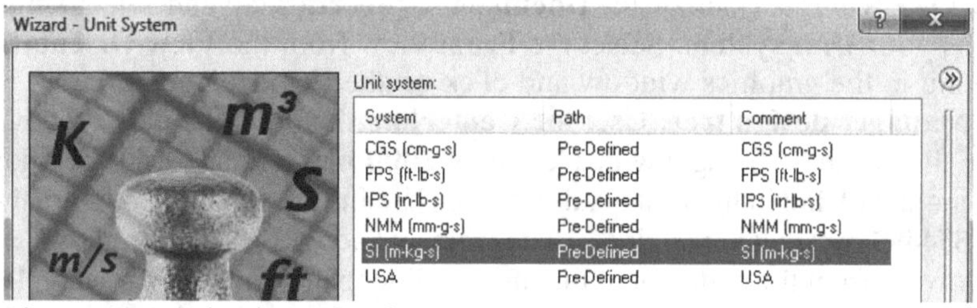

Figure 19.3 Selection of unit system

4. Select **External Analysis type**. Check the box for **Exclude cavities without flow conditions**. Click on Next>.

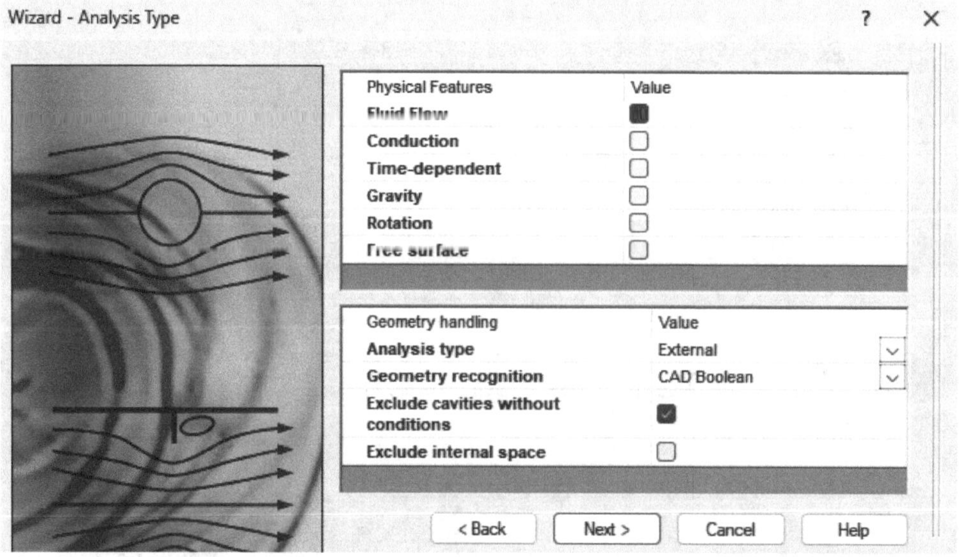

Figure 19.4 Selection of Analysis type

5. Add **Air** as the default **Project Fluid** by selecting it from **Gases**. Check the box for **High Mach number flow**. Click on Next. Choose default values for **Wall Conditions** and set the **Initial and Ambient Conditions** as shown in figure 19.5b) and finish the Wizard.

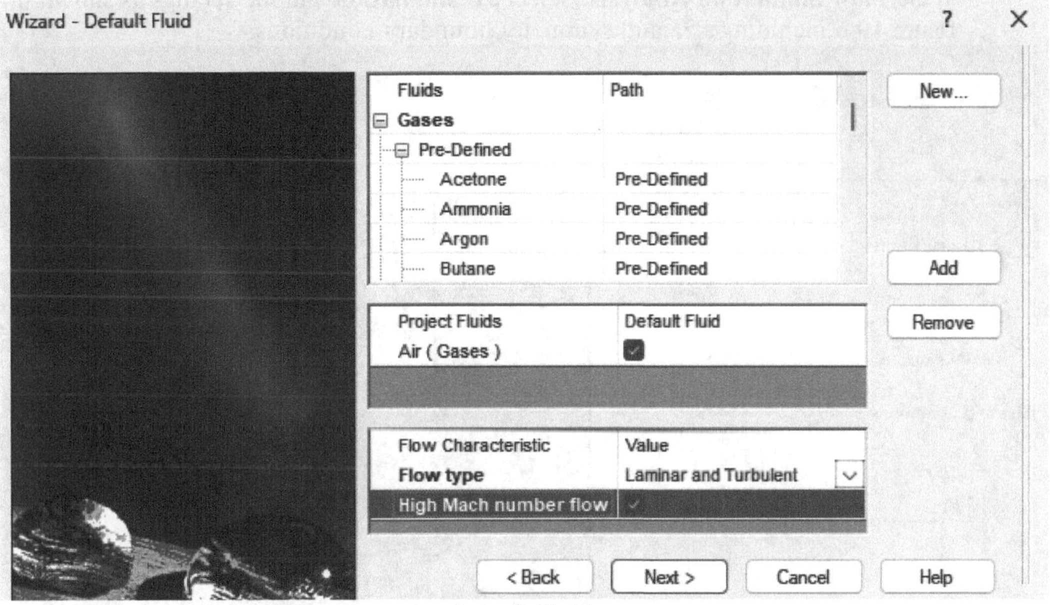

Figure 19.5a) Adding air as the default fluid

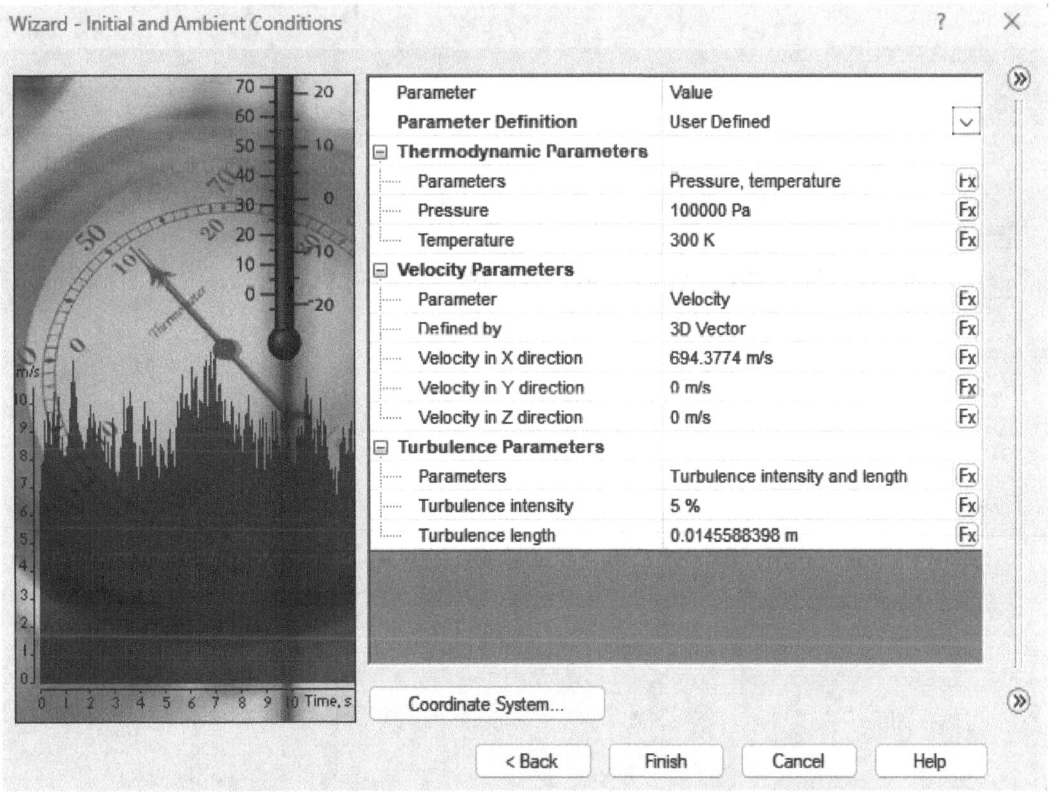

Figure 19.5b) Initial and ambient conditions

E. Computational Domain

6. Right-click on **Computational Domain** and select **Edit Definition...** under **Input Data** in the **Flow Simulation Analysis**. Select **3D simulation** and the settings as shown in figure 19.6 including size and symmetry boundary conditions.

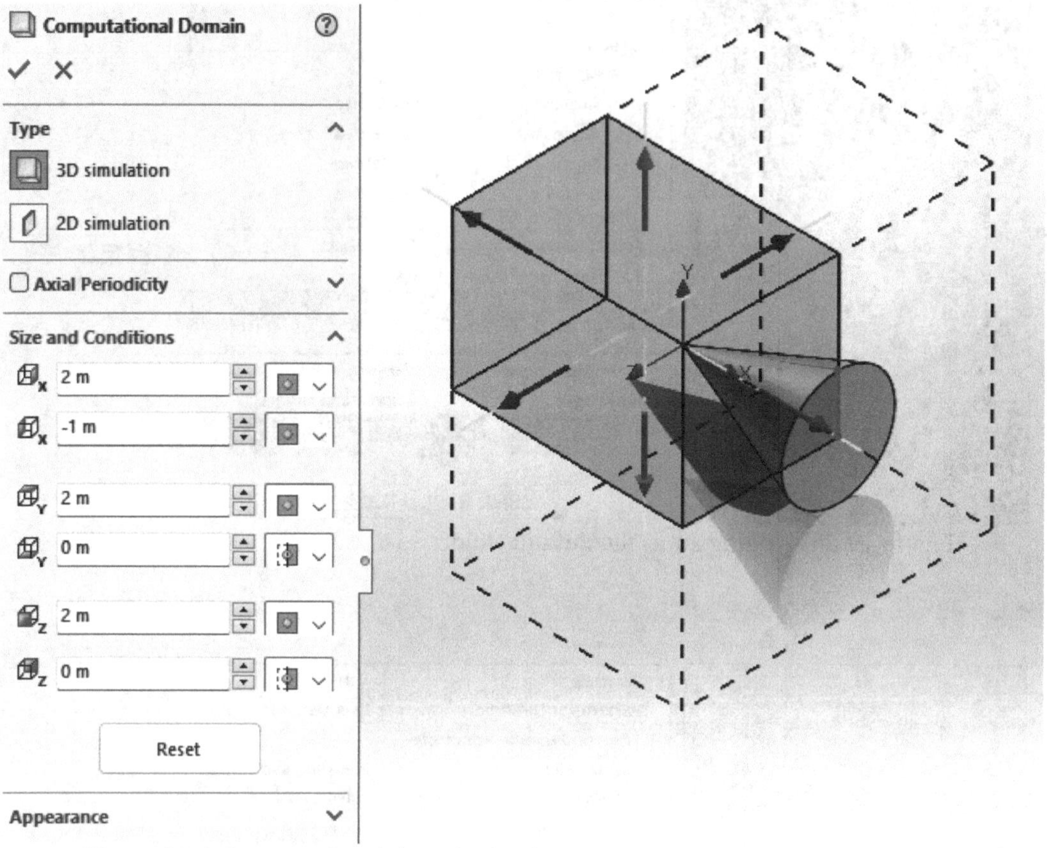

Figure 19.6 Computational domain for flow past a cone

F. Global Mesh

7. Select **Tools>>Flow Simulation>>Global Mesh...** from the SOLIDWORKS menu, select **Manual Type** and select the settings in figure 19.7.

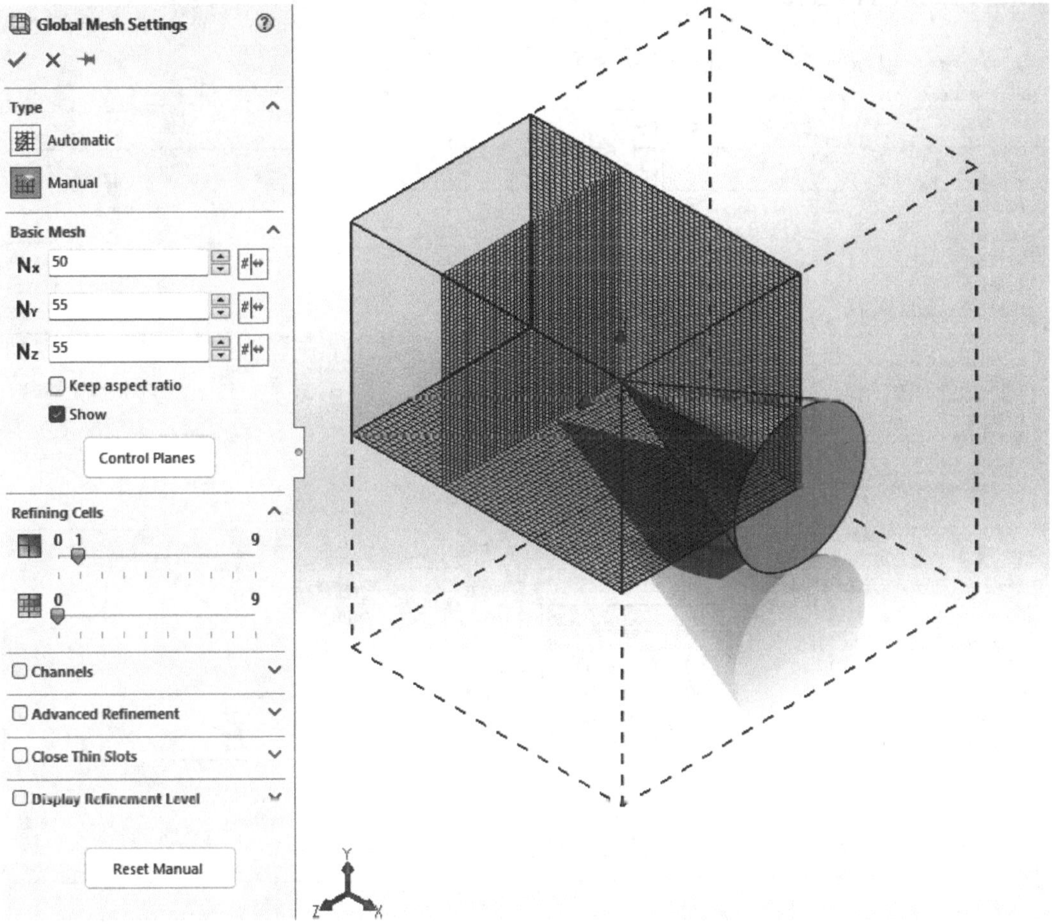

Figure 19.7 Global mesh settings

G. Goals

8. Right-click on **Goals** under **Input Data** and select **Insert Global Goals**. Check the boxes for **Min, Av and Max Static Pressure** and **Min, Av and Max Mach Number**.

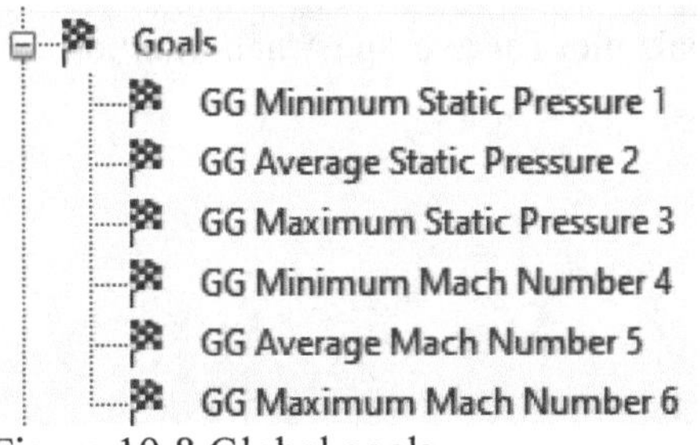

Figure 19.8 Global goals

H. Running Simulations

9. Select **Tools>>Flow Simulation>>Solve>>Run**. Push the **Run** button in the window that appears. Insert the goals table by clicking on **List of Goals** in the **Solver** as shown in figure 19.9a).

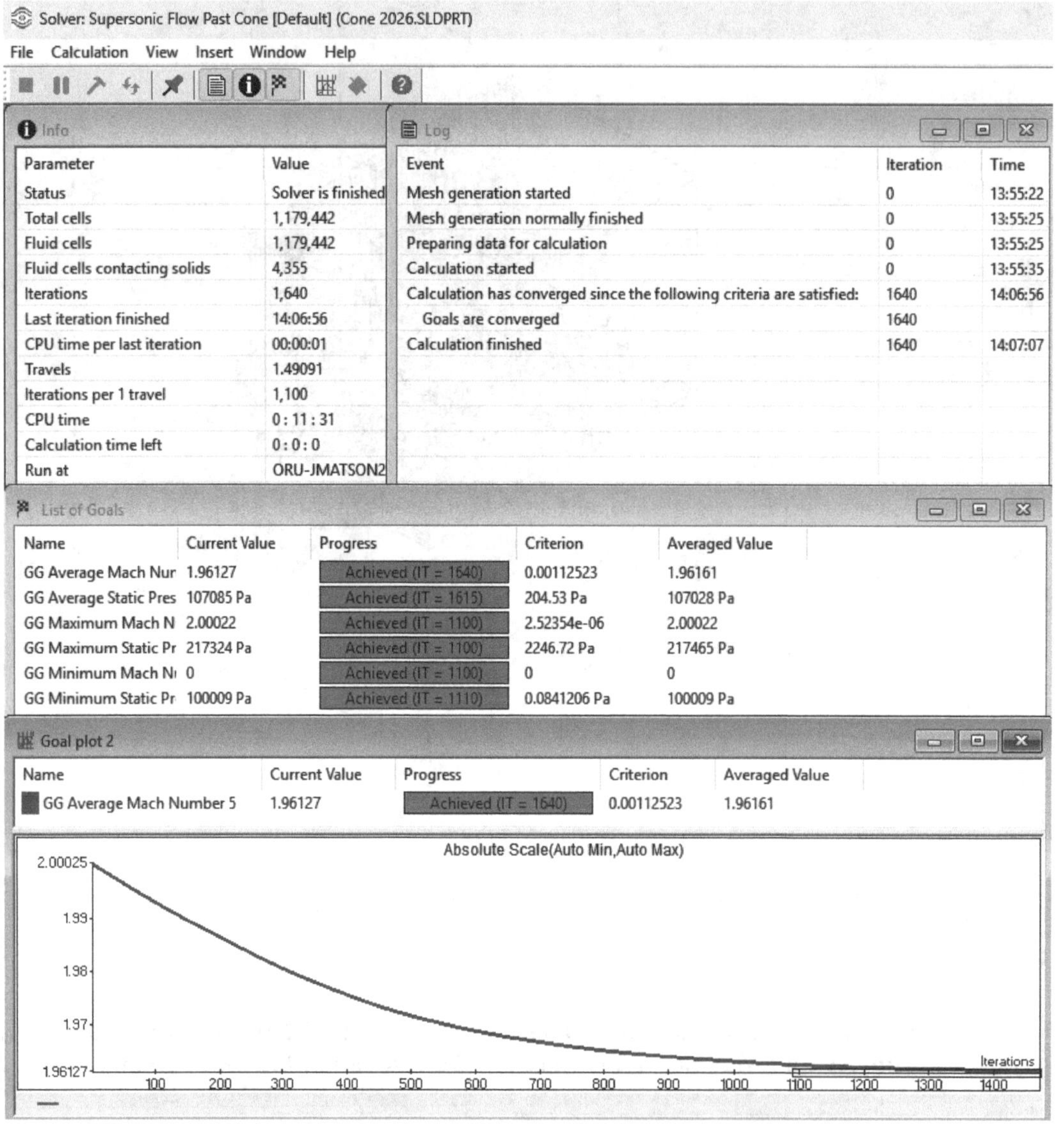

Figure 19.9 Solver information and goals plot for average Mach number

I. Cut Plots

10. Right click on **Cut Plots** under **Results** and select **Insert….** Select **Front Plane**, **Contours** and **Contours** of **Mach Number**. Set Number of Levels to 255. Continue with contour plots of density (fluid), pressure and temperature (fluid).

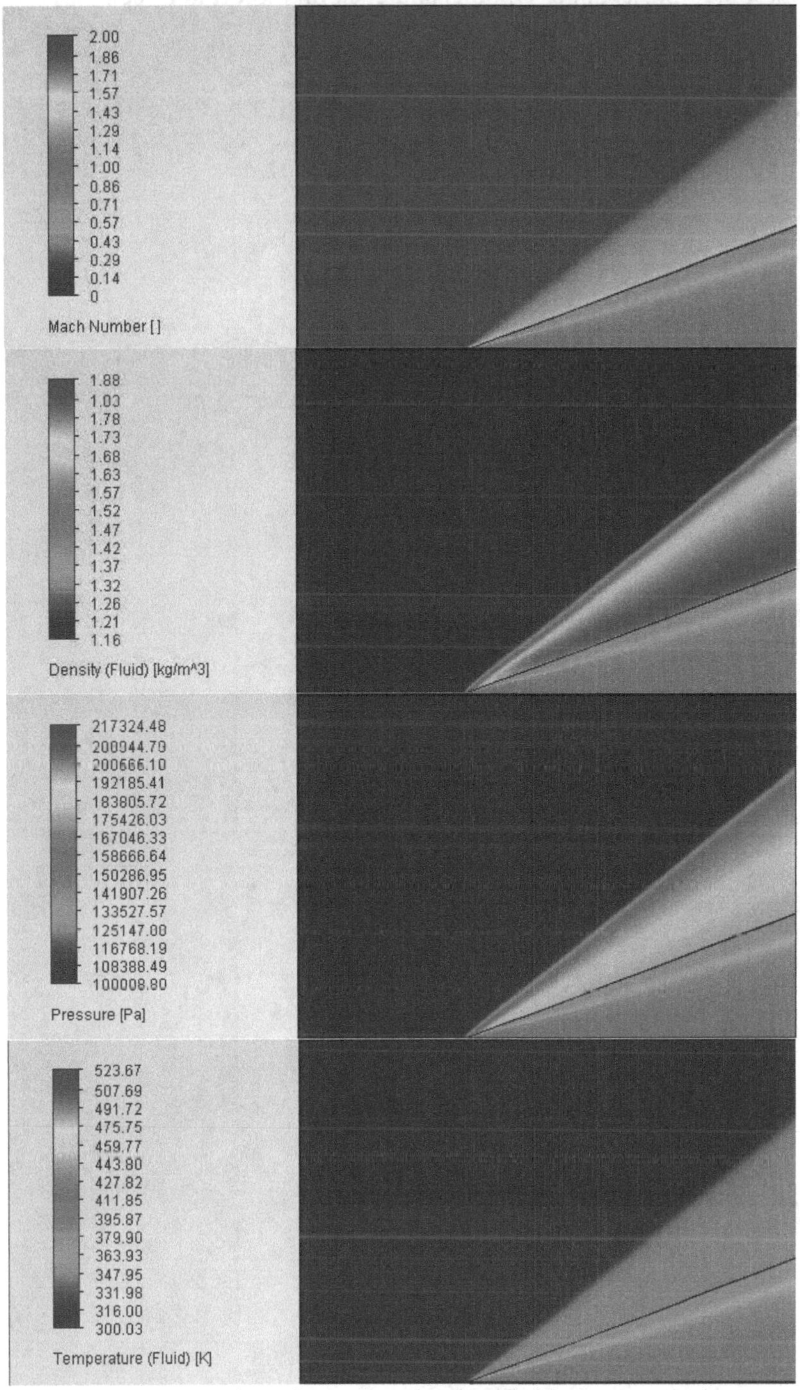

Figure 19.10 Contours of Mach number, density (fluid), pressure and temperature (fluid)

J. Cut Plots

11. Right click on **XY Plots** under **Results** and select **Insert…**. Select **Sketch2**, **Model Y** as **Abscissa** and check the boxes for Density (Fluid), Pressure, Temperature (Fluid) and Mach Number. Slide the Geometry Resolution all the way to the right. Select Excel Workbook (*.xlsx) under Options and click on Export to Excel.

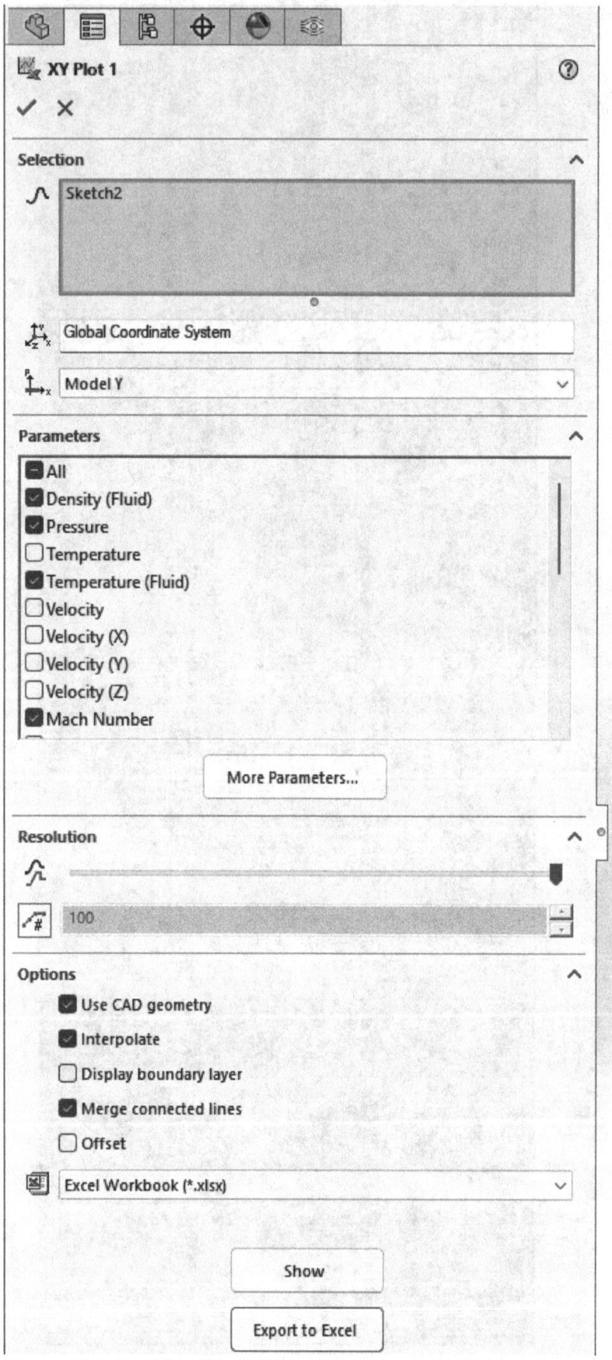

Figure 19.11 XY Plot settings

K. Plotting Density

12. Select the Plot Data tab at the bottom of the Excel sheet. Copy column A to column C and delete column A. Delete the first three rows. Select columns A and B and create a Scatter plot. We will now focus our attention on the three data points as shown encircled in Figure 19.12 and delete all the other data.

    Clear contents of the 12 last rows in the Excel file. Take the average of the remaining last three data points in the Model Y column which we define as the *y*-coordinate for the shock wave at the outlet. The average *Y*-coordinate is 1.56614 m. We use this value as the location for the shockwave, and we can determine the shock angle as =180*ATAN(1.56614/2)/PI(). The shock angle is 38.0634 degrees. This value can be compared with the wave angle that we can determine at the following web address: *https://devenport.aoe.vt.edu/aoe3114/calc.html*

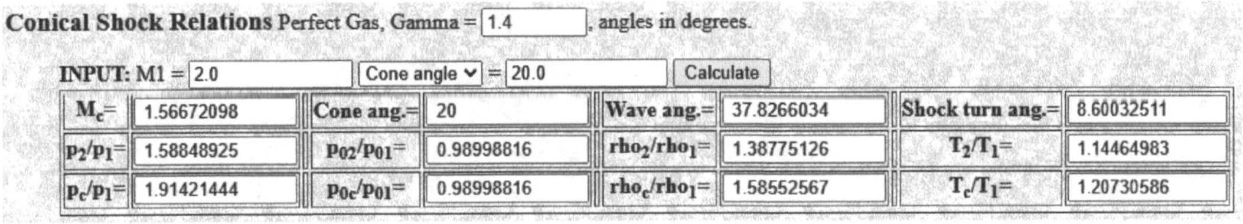

Conical Shock Relations Perfect Gas, Gamma = 1.4, angles in degrees.

INPUT: M1 = 2.0 | Cone angle = 20.0 | Calculate

M_c=	1.56672098	Cone ang.=	20	Wave ang.=	37.8266034	Shock turn ang.=	8.60032511
p_2/p_1=	1.58848925	p_{02}/p_{01}=	0.98998816	rho_2/rho_1=	1.38775126	T_2/T_1=	1.14464983
p_c/p_1=	1.91421444	p_{0c}/p_{01}=	0.98998816	rho_c/rho_1=	1.58552567	T_c/T_1=	1.20730586

Figure 19.12a) Conical shock wave relations, from Davenport[2]

The wave angle from this web site is 37.8266 degrees. The difference of this value from the corresponding angle determined in SOLIDWORKS Flow Simulation is 0.5 %.

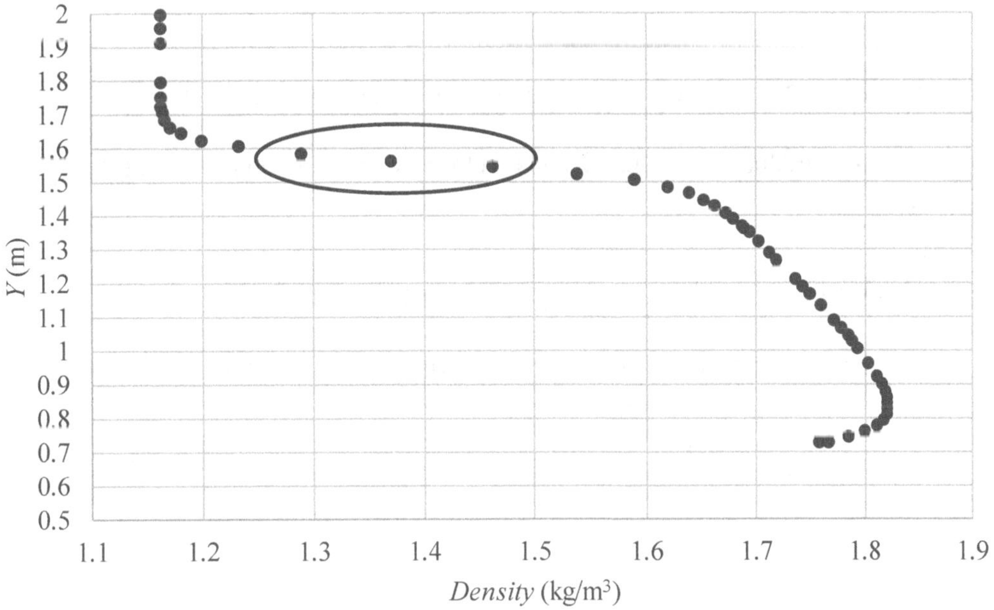

Figure 19.12b) Scatter plot for density (fluid)

L. Theory

13. Supersonic flow over a cone can be found theoretically assuming inviscid flow and a sharp semi-infinite cone that extends to infinity in the streamwise direction. The theoretical solution is called Taylor-Maccoll equation and is given by Anderson[1]. This is an ordinary differential equation with one dependent variable. Solution to this equation is shown in Figure 19.13b) from Lassaline[2].

$$\frac{\gamma-1}{2}\left[V_{max}^2 - V_r^2 - \left(\frac{dV_r}{d\theta}\right)^2\right]\left[2V_r + \frac{dV_r}{d\theta}\cot\theta + \frac{d^2V_r}{d\theta^2}\right] - \left(\frac{dV_r}{d\theta}\right)^2\left[V_r + \frac{d^2V_r}{d\theta^2}\right] = 0 \qquad (18.1)$$

where $V_r = f(\theta)$ is the radial component of velocity and V_{max} is the maximum theoretical velocity. The normal component of velocity $V_\theta = \frac{dV_r}{d\theta}$

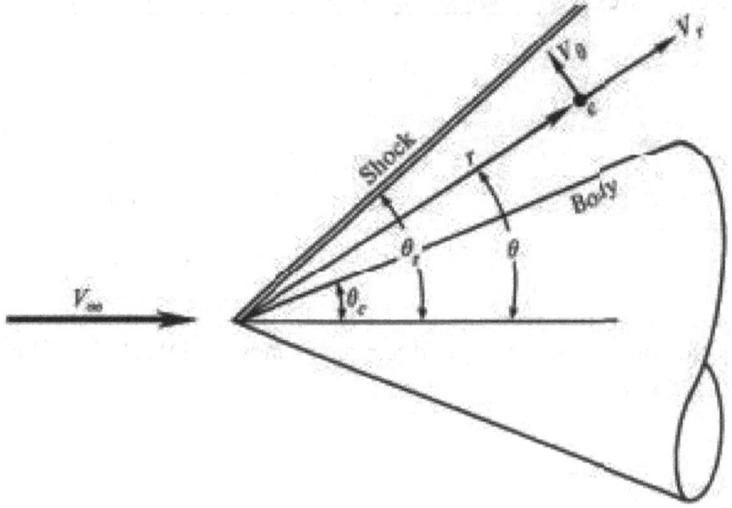

Figure 19.13a) Spherical coordinate system for a cone, from Anderson[1]

We can introduce a non-dimensional velocity $V' = \frac{V}{V_{max}}$ and equation (18.1) can be written as

$$\frac{\gamma-1}{2}\left[1 - V'^2_r - \left(\frac{dV'_r}{d\theta}\right)^2\right]\left[2V'_r + \frac{dV'_r}{d\theta}\cot\theta + \frac{d^2V'_r}{d\theta^2}\right] - \left(\frac{dV'_r}{d\theta}\right)^2\left[V'_r + \frac{d^2V'_r}{d\theta^2}\right] = 0 \qquad (18.2)$$

It can be shown that the non-dimensional velocity is a function of the Mach number

$$V' = \frac{1}{\sqrt{1+\frac{2}{(\gamma-1)M^2}}} \qquad (18.3)$$

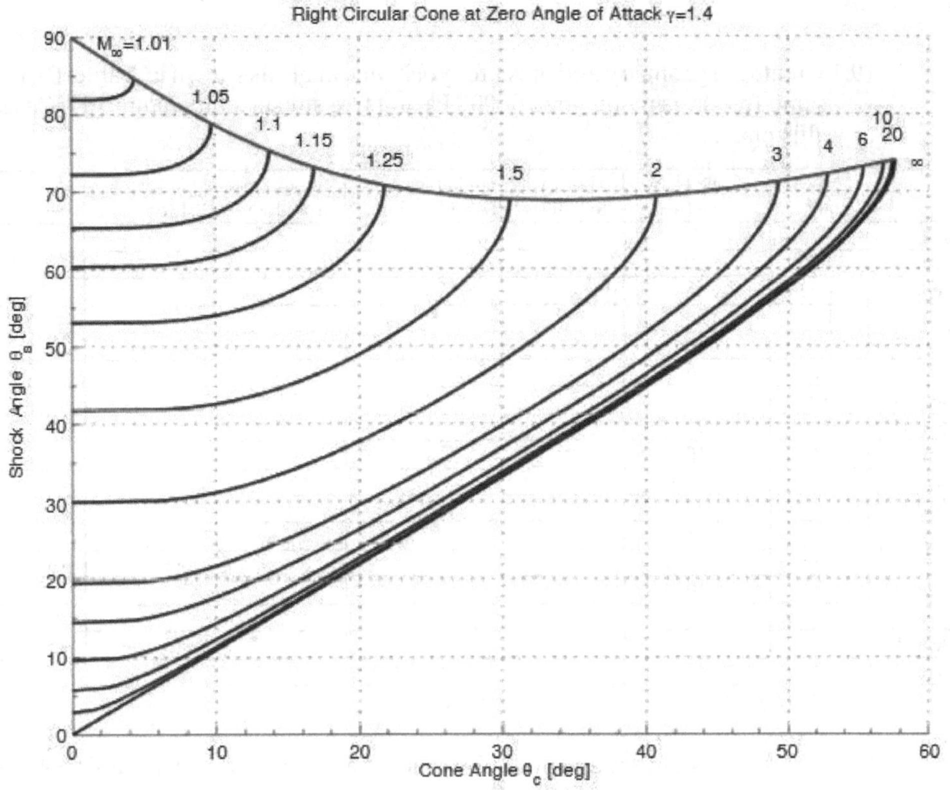

Figure 19.13b) Shock angle versus half cone angle, from Lassaline[3]

We define the Reynolds number *Re* over the cone as

$$Re - \frac{V_2 L \rho_2}{\mu_2} \tag{18.4}$$

where V_2 is the free stream velocity after the shock wave, L is the slant height of the cone, ρ_2 is the density after the shock wave and μ_2 is the dynamic viscosity after the shock wave. The Mach numbers are defined as

$$M_\infty = \frac{V_\infty}{a_\infty},\ M_2 = \frac{V_2}{a_2} \tag{18.5}$$

Where ∞ is related to conditions before the shock and *2* is after the shock wave.

M. References

1. Anderson, J.D., "Fundamentals of Aerodynamics", McGraw-Hill Education, 6th Ed., 2011.
2. Davenport, W.J., "Compressible Aerodynamics Calculator 3.2", Department of Aerospace and Ocean Engineering, Virginia Tech.
3. Lassaline, J.V., "Supersonic Right Circular Cone at Zero Angle of Attack", Ryerson University, 2009.

N. Exercises

19.1 Create the geometry and mesh for your cone angle as shown in Table 19.1. Use the same free stream pressure 100000 Pa and free stream temperature 300 K as shown in this chapter.

	Mach number	Cone Half-Angle (deg.)	Shock wave angle (deg.) SOLIDWORKS Flow Sim.	Shock wave angle (deg.) from Figure 18.13b)	Percent difference
Student A	1.25	5			
Student B	1.25	10			
Student C	1.25	15			
Student D	1.25	20			
Student E	1.5	10			
Student F	1.5	15			
Student G	1.5	20			
Student H	1.5	25			
Student I	2	10			
Student J	2	20			
Student K	2	30			
Student L	2	35			
Student M	3	10			
Student N	3	20			
Student O	3	30			
Student P	3	40			
Student Q	3	45			

Table 19.1 Student data for Exercise 19.1.

19.2 Create the geometry and mesh for your cone angle as shown in Table 19.2. Use the free stream pressure 25000 Pa and free stream temperature 100 K.

	Mach number	Cone Half-Angle (deg.)	Shock wave angle (deg.) SOLIDWORKS Flow Sim.	Shock wave angle (deg.) from Figure 33.9	Percent difference
Student A	1.25	20			
Student B	1.5	20			
Student C	1.75	20			
Student D	2	20			
Student E	2.25	20			
Student F	2.5	20			
Student G	2.75	20			
Student H	3	20			
Student I	3.25	20			
Student J	3.5	20			
Student K	3.75	20			
Student L	4	20			
Student M	4.25	20			
Student N	4.5	20			

Table 19.2 Student data for Exercise 19.2.

CHAPTER 20. ROTATING PLANE CHANNEL FLOW

A. Objectives

- Creating the SOLIDWORKS models needed for Flow Simulations
- Setting up Flow Simulation projects for internal flows
- Creating lids for boundary conditions and setting up boundary conditions
- Use of gravity as a physical feature and running the calculations
- Using cut plots and surface plots to visualize the resulting flow field
- Compare results with linear stability theory

B. Problem Description

In this chapter we will study the appearance of streamwise vortices for the flow in a narrow gap rotating plane channel with rectangular cross section. The height of the rectangular cross section is 100 mm and the channel width is 10 mm. The length of the channel is 1000 mm. The Coriolis force due to spanwise system rotation will cause the appearance of counter-rotating vortices and transition to turbulent flow at much lower Reynolds numbers as compared with the non-rotating plane channel flow case.

C. Creating SOLIDWORKS Part for Rotating Plane Channel Flow

1. Start SOLIDWORKS and create a New Part. Select **Tools>>Options...** from the SOLIDWORKS menu. Click on the Document Properties tab and select **Units**. Select **MMGS** as your **Unit system**. Select the **Right** view from the **View Orientation** drop down menu in the graphics window and click on the **Right Plane** in the **FeatureManager design tree**. Next, select the **Center Rectangle** sketch tool from the **Basic Modeling Tools** tab in the menu. Click on the origin in the graphics window and create a rectangle with the dimensions as shown in Figure 20.1. Draw another larger center-rectangle with dimensions as shown in Figure 20.1. Close the dialog box.

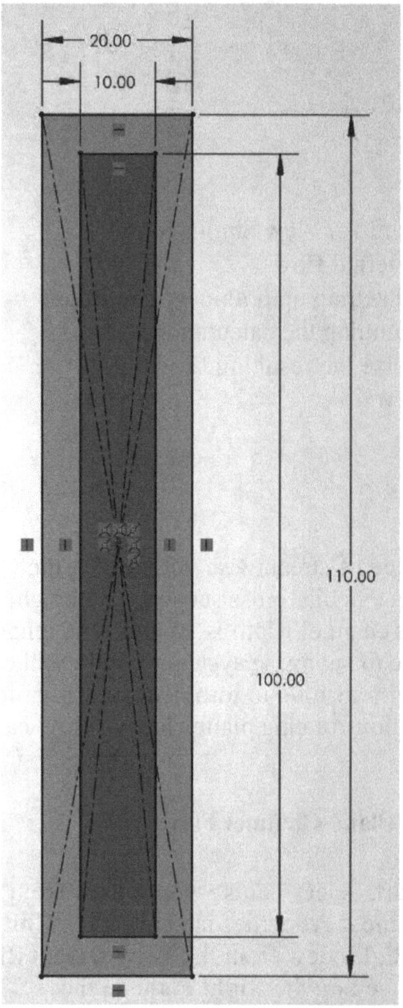

Figure 20.1 Two center rectangles with dimensions

2. Click on **Sketch 1** in the **FeatureManager design tree** followed by the selection of **Extruded Boss/Base** from the **Analysis Preparation** tab in the menu. Enter a depth of **1000 mm**. Click on OK. Save the part with the name **Rotating Plane Channel 2026**.

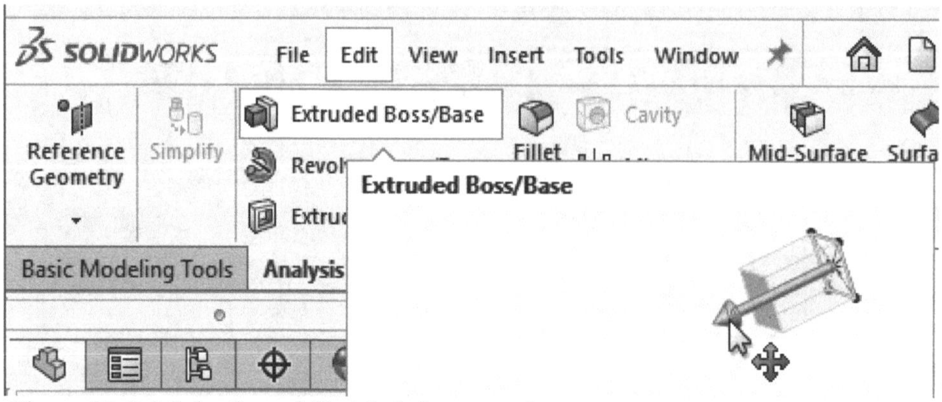

Figure 20.2a) Selection of Sketch 1 for extrusion

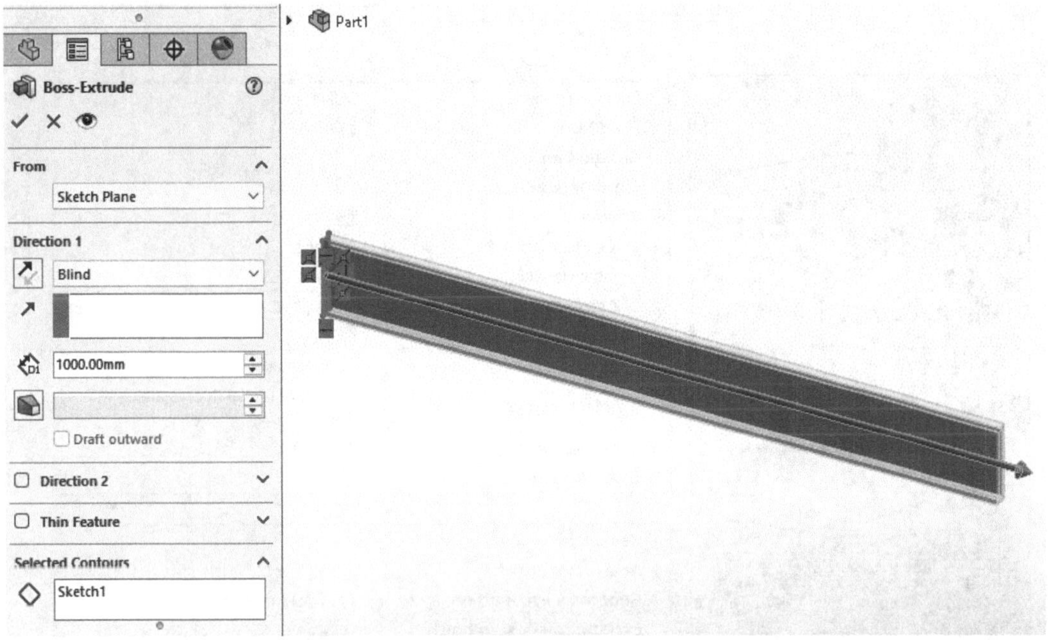

Figure 20.2b) Entering depth of extrusion

D. Flow Simulation Project for Rotating Plane Channel Flow

3. If Flow Simulation is not available in the SOLIDWORKS menu, select **Tools>>Add Ins...** and check the corresponding **SOLIDWORKS Flow Simulation** box. Start the Flow Simulation Wizard by selecting **Tools>>Flow Simulation>>Project>>Wizard....** Enter Project name: **Instabilities in Rotating Plane Channel Flow**.

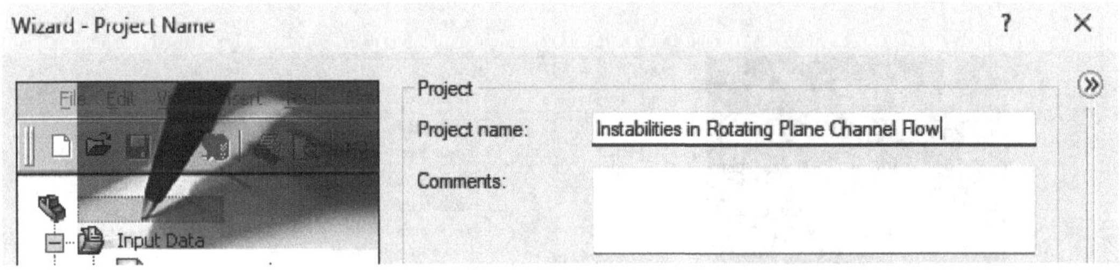

Figure 20.3 Creating a new project name

4. Select the **SI unit system** in the next step followed by selection of the **Internal Analysis type** in the following step. Check the boxes for Gravity and Rotation under Physical Features. Set the values and choose the selections as shown in Figure 20.4a).

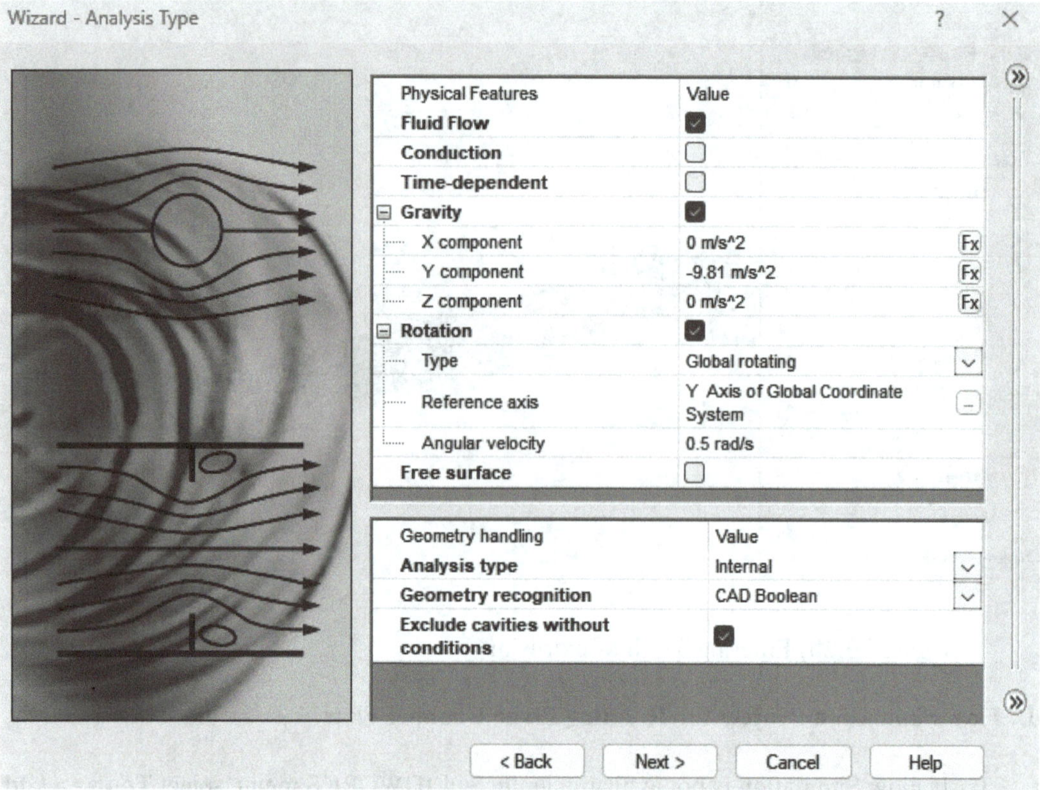

Figure 20.4a) Settings for physical features

In the next step, add **Water** as the **Project Fluid** and select **Laminar Only** as **Flow type**.

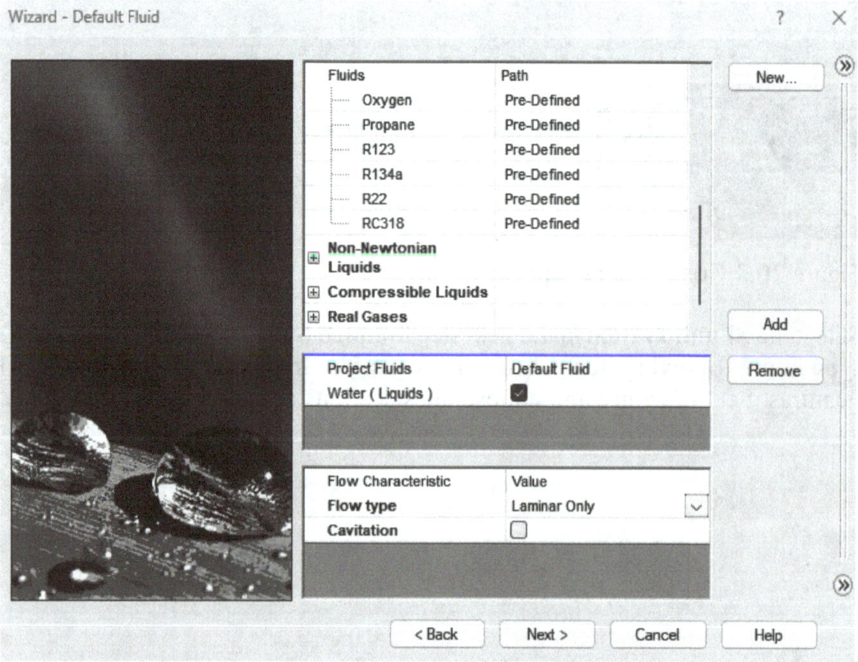

Figure 20.4b) Settings for project fluid and flow type

Use default values of wall conditions and initial conditions in the following two steps. Enter **0.05 m/s** as **Velocity in X direction** under **Velocity Parameters** in the **Initial Conditions** window. Select **Finish** to close the wizard.

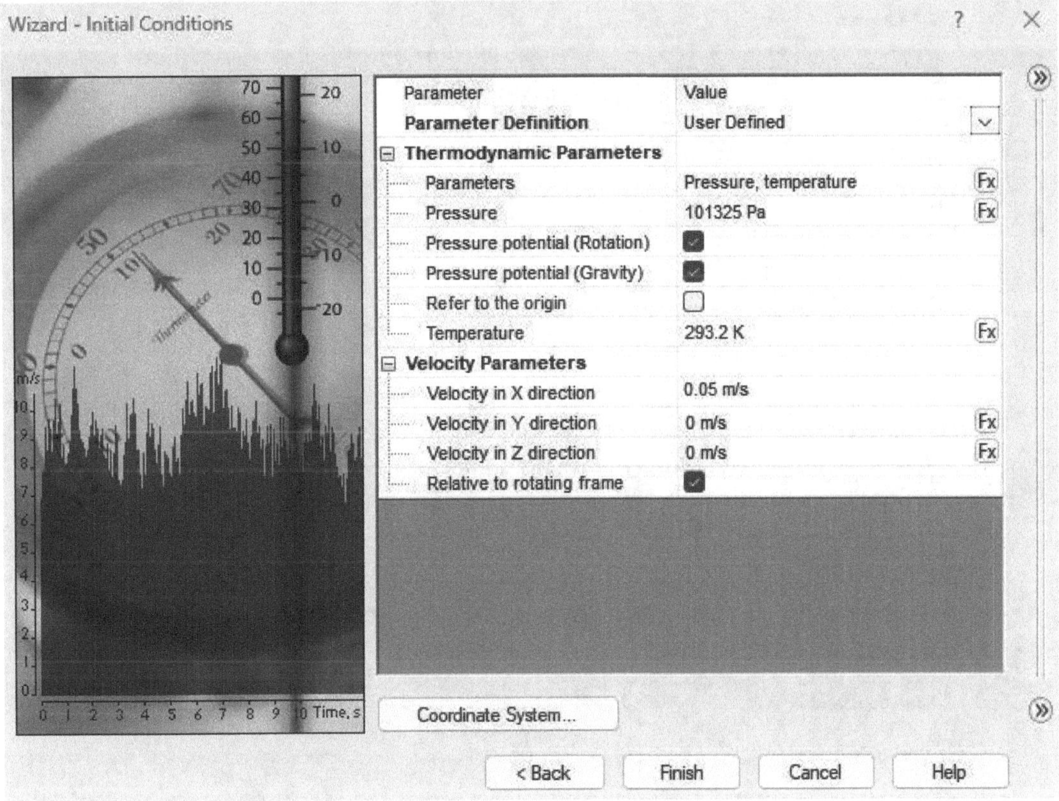

Figure 20.4c) Settings for initial conditions

You will get a fluid volume recognition failure message. Answer **Yes** to this question and create lids at the two ends of the model. Select the face at one of the ends of the channel for the lid and click OK. Answer **Yes** to the questions whether you want to reset the computational domain, mesh settings and the Create Lids tool will open.

Next, right click in the graphics window and select **Zoom/Pan/Rotate>>Rotate View**. Rotate the plane channel model around and deselect **Rotate View**. Select the other end face and create the second lid. Answer "**Yes**" when asked to reset computational domain and mesh settings.

Select **Tools>>Flow Simulation>>Global Mesh...** from the SOLIDWORKS menu. Select **Manual settings**. Set the number of cells in all three directions X, Y and Z to **128**, **128**, and **32**. Make sure to use the same settings as shown in Figure 20.4d). Click on the **OK** button to exit the **Global Mesh Settings** window.

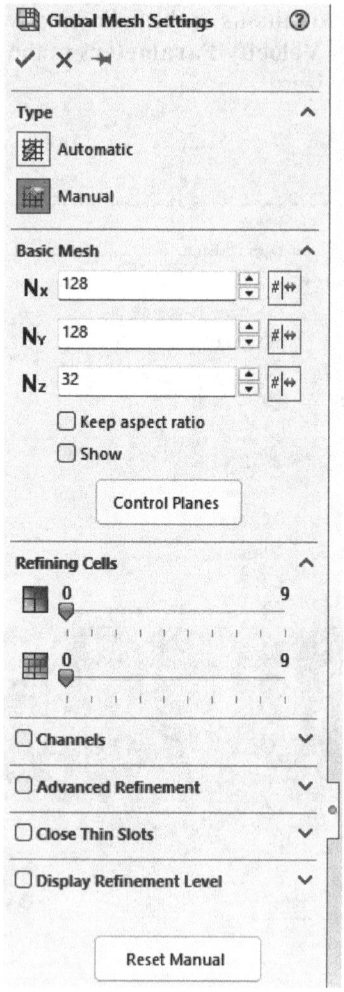

Figure 20.4d) Global mesh settings

Select **Tools>>Flow Simulation>>Calculation Control Options...** from the SOLIDWORKS menu. Click on the **Refinement** tab and select **level = 1** for the **Value** of the **Refinement Parameter**. Click on the **OK** button to exit the **Calculation Control Options** window.

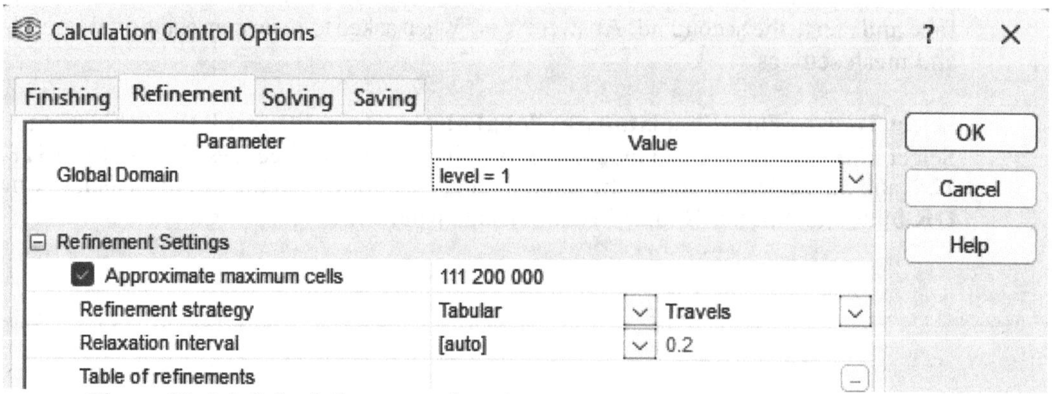

Figure 20.4e) Calculation control options

Select **Hidden Lines Visible** from the **Display Type** drop down menu in the graphics window and **Trimetric** view from the **View Orientation** drop down menu.

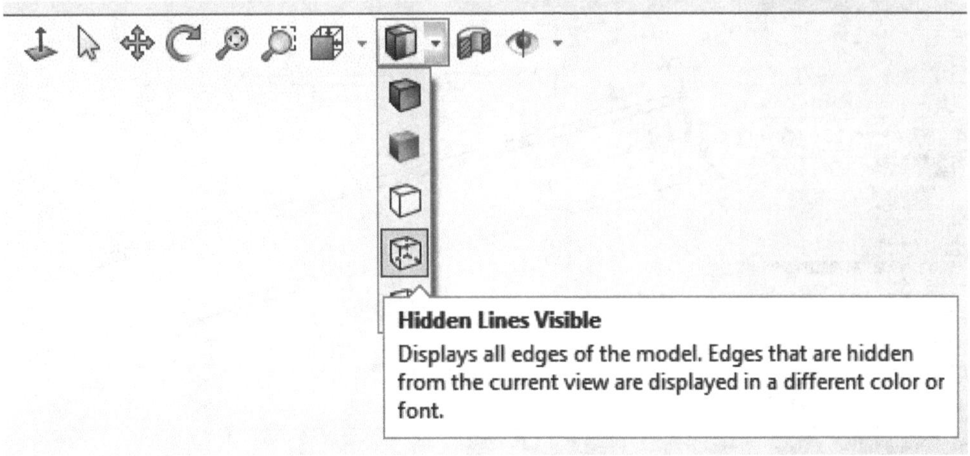

Figure 20.4f) Showing hidden lines

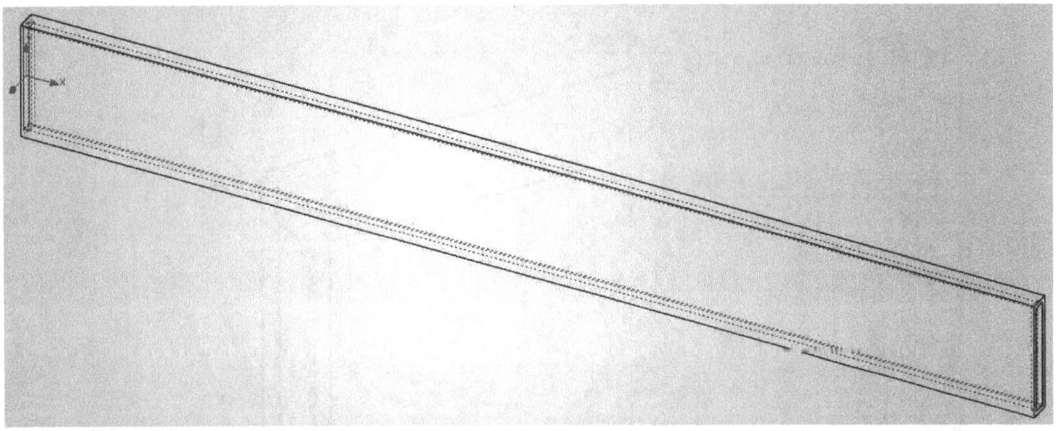

Figure 20.4g) Lids added to the plane channel

E. Boundary Conditions for Rotating Plane Channel Flow

5. Click on the **Flow Simulation analysis tree** tab and click on the plus sign next to the **Input Data** folder. Right click on **Boundary Conditions** and select **Insert Boundary Condition…** Move the cursor over the left end of the plane channel, right click and select **Select Other**. Select the face for the inner rectangular surface of the inflow domain, see Figures 20.5a).

   Select the **Inlet Velocity** boundary condition and set the value of **0.05 m/s** for the inlet velocity in the **X Axis direction.** Click OK to finish the boundary condition. Insert another boundary condition for the other end of the plane channel, select the **Pressure Openings** and **Static Pressure** boundary condition.

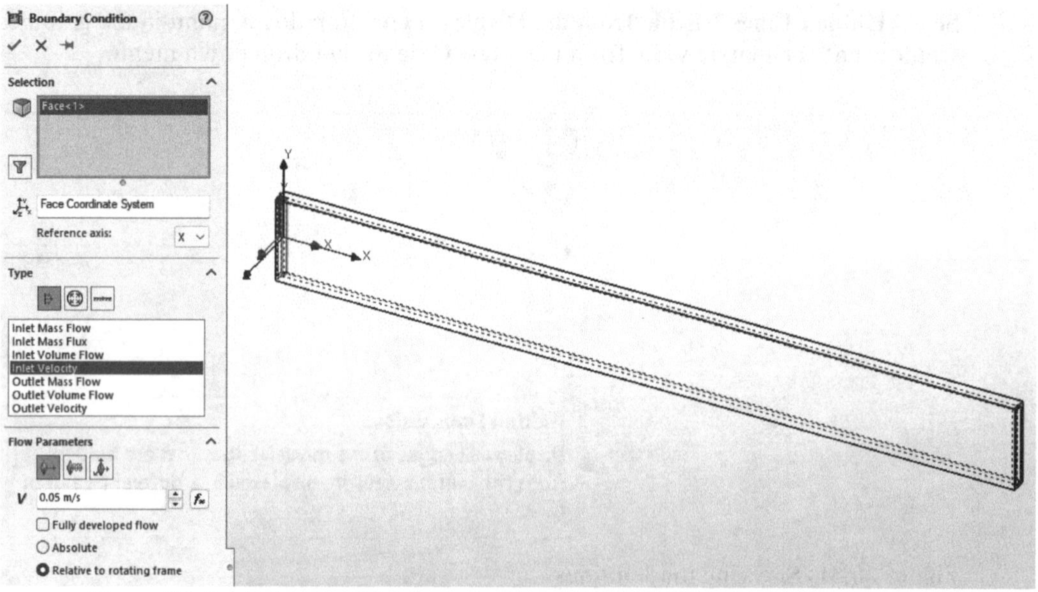

Figure 20.5a) Selection of inlet boundary condition for plane channel

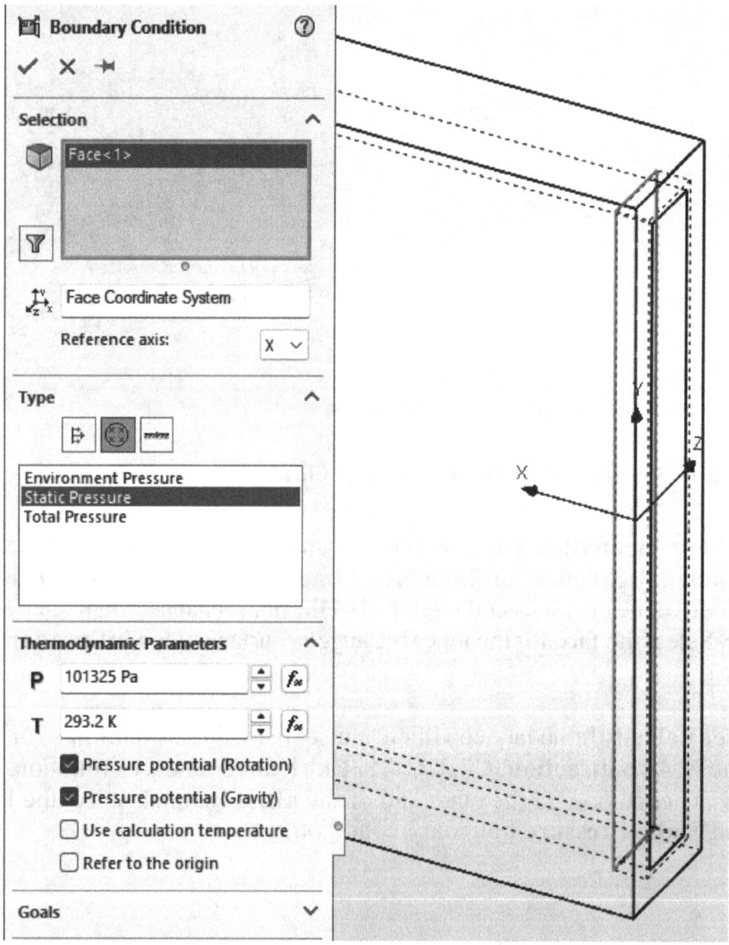

Figure 20.5b) Selection of outlet boundary condition for plane channel

F. Global Goal and Simulations for Rotating Plane Channel Flow

6. Right click on **Goals** in the **Flow Simulation analysis tree** and select **Insert Global Goals….** Check the boxes for **Min, Av** and **Max Velocity** and exit the window. Select **Tools>>Flow Simulation>>Solve>>Run….** Push the **Run** button in the window that appears.

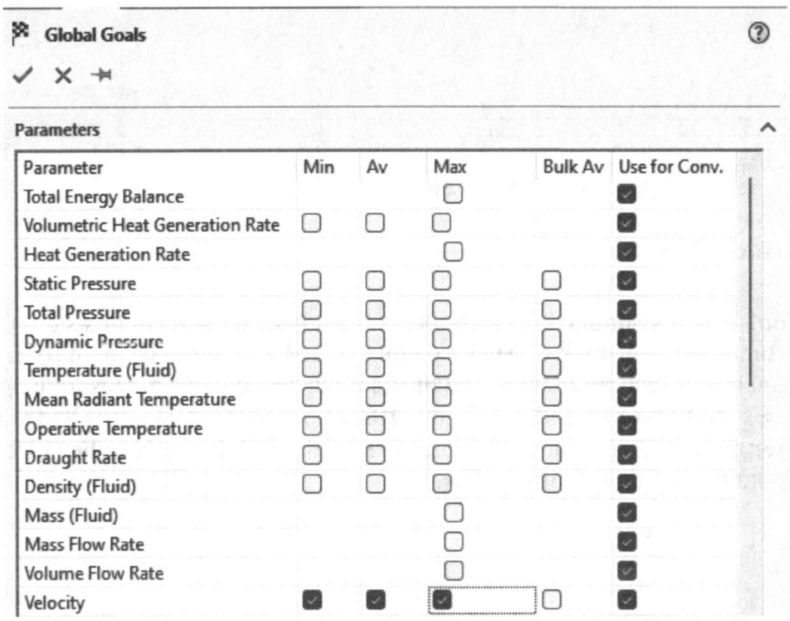

Figure 20.6a) Selecting minimum, average and maximum velocities as global goal

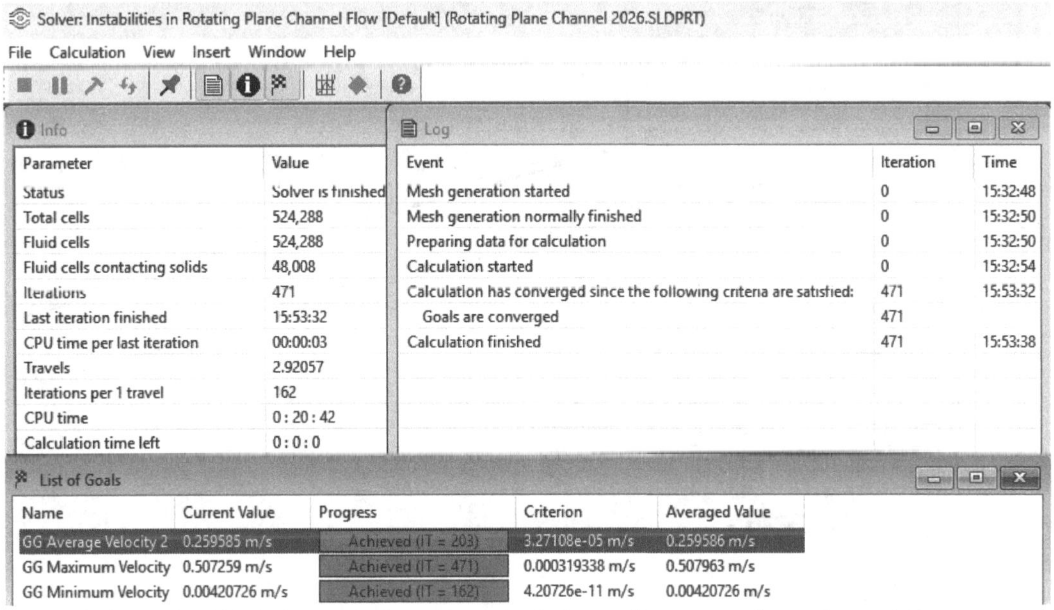

Figure 20.6b) Solver window for calculations of rotating plane channel flow

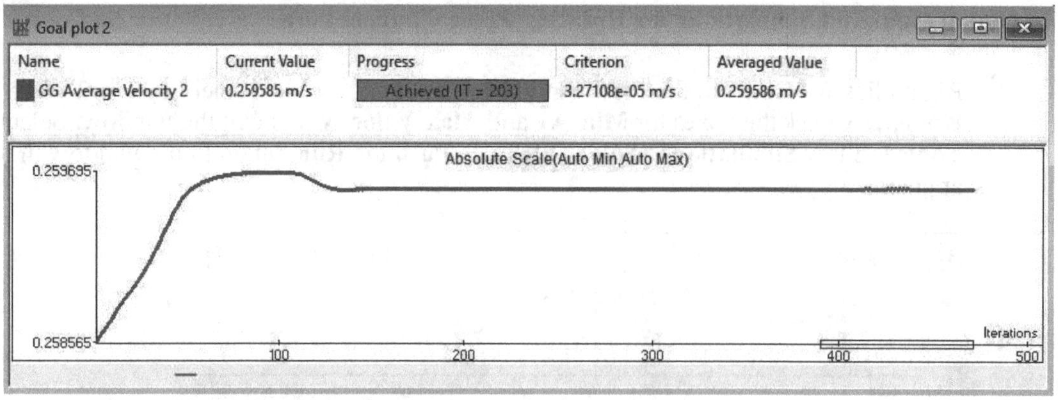

Figure 20.6c) Goal plot for average velocity

G. Inserting Surface Plots

7. Select **Tools>>Flow Simulation>>Results>>Load/Unload.** Repeat this step. Open the **Results** folder and right click on **Surface Plots** in the **Flow Simulation analysis tree** and select **Insert....** Select the face of one of the inner rectangular planes in the graphics window. Expand **Options** and check the **Offset** box. Select **Velocity (X)** from the **Parameter** drop down menu in the **Contours** section. Slide the **Number of Levels** to **255** and exit the **Surface Plot** window.

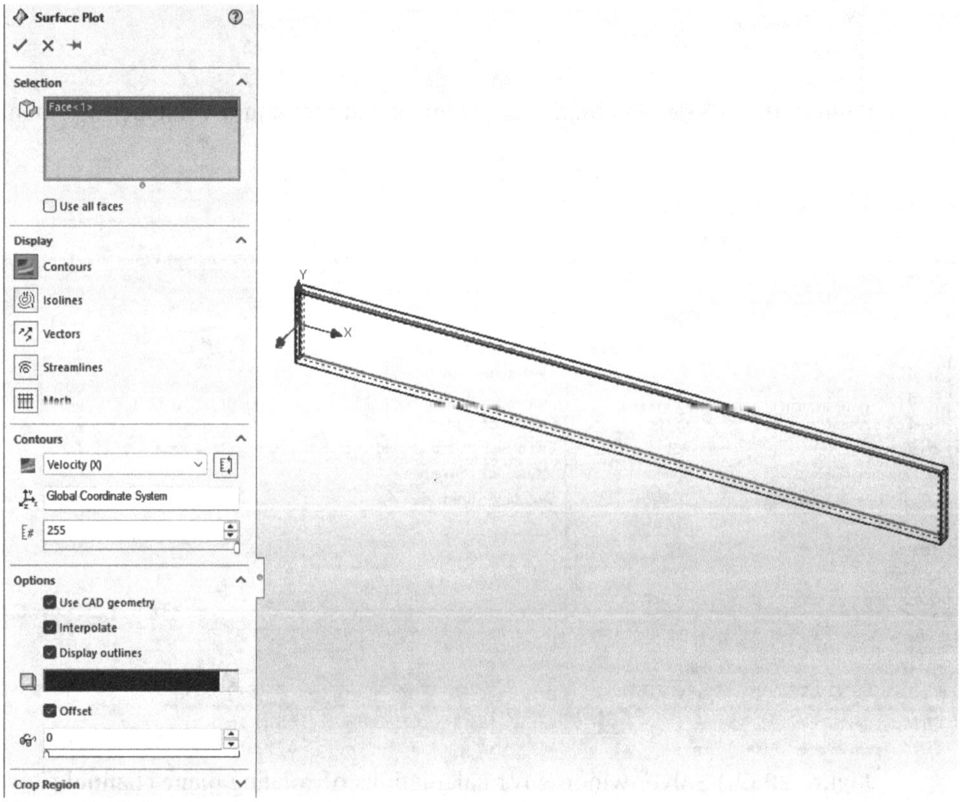

Figure 20.7 Surface plot settings.

8. Select **Tools>>Flow Simulation>>Results>>Display>>Lighting** from the SOLIDWORKS menu. Select **Trimetric** view from the **View Orientation** drop down menu in the graphics window. Rename the surface plot to **Velocity (X)**.

   Click on **Section View**. Exit the **Section View** window. The velocity field is shown in Figure 20.8c). Alternating bands of high and low velocity are shown in the spanwise *Z*-direction indicating the presence of streamwise vortices. It should be emphasized that the surface plot is not located on the channel walls but offset in the *Z* direction.

   Right click on **Computational Domain** in the **Input Data** folder and select **Hide**. Right click on **Instabilities in Rotating Plane Channel Flow** and select **Hide Global Coordinate System**.

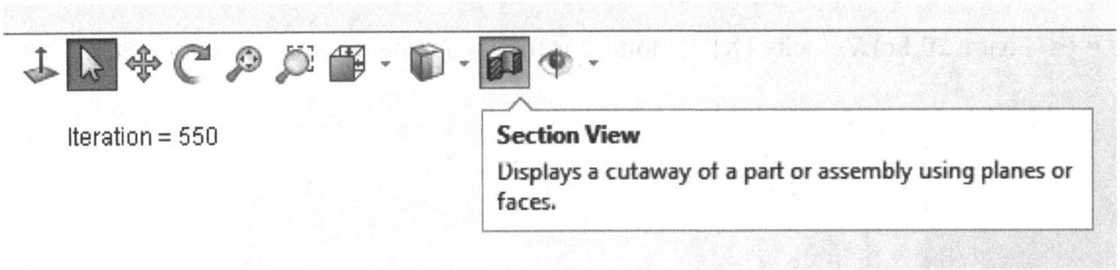

Figure 20.8a) Section view

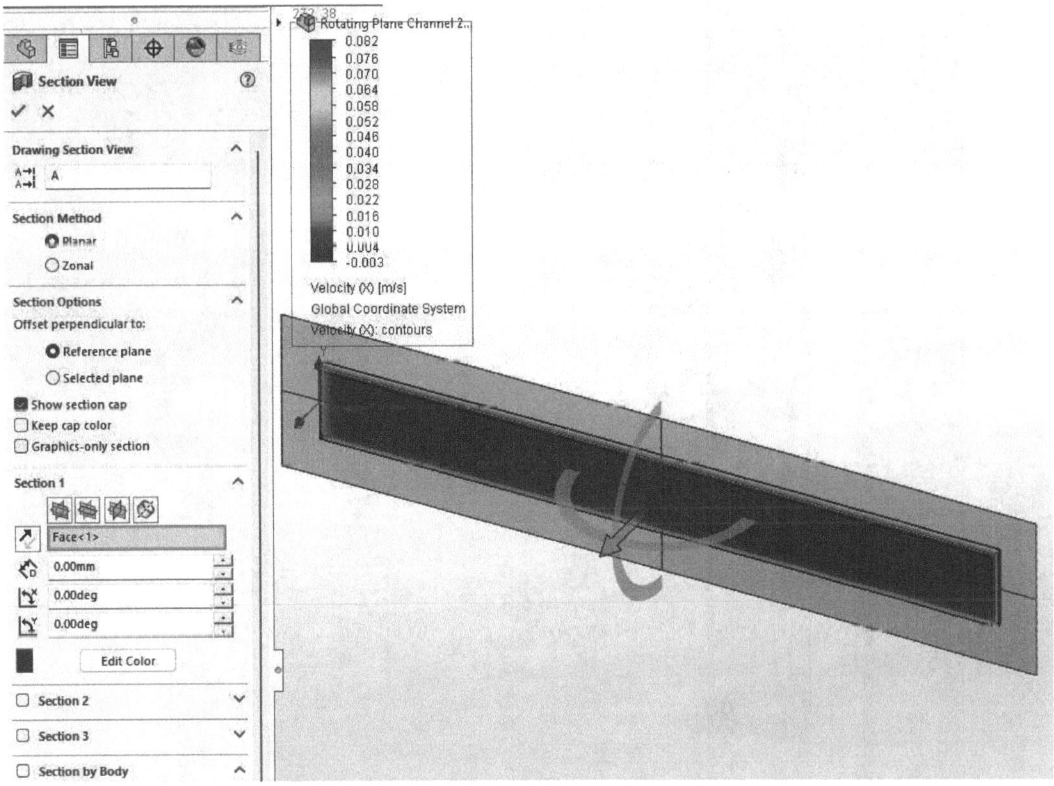

Figure 20.8b) Section view settings for plane channel

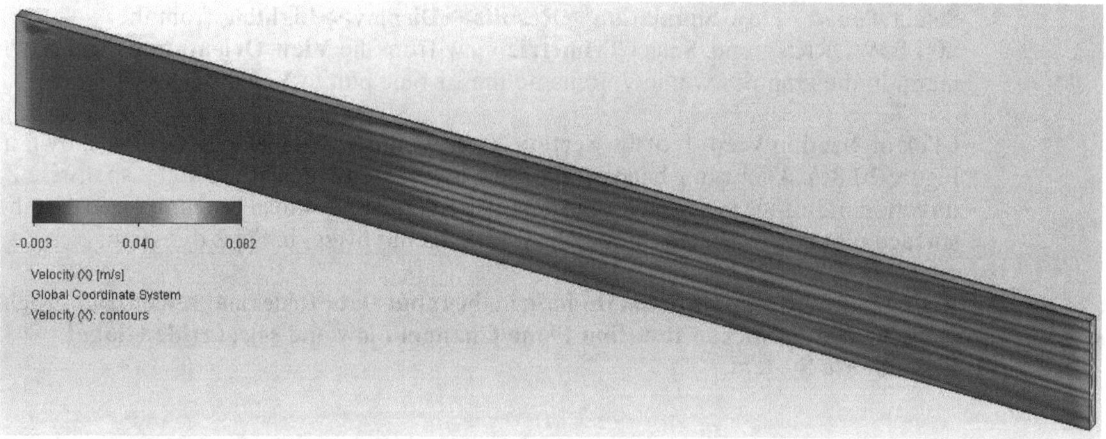

Figure 20.8c) Velocity (X) contours for rotating plane channel flow, isometric view

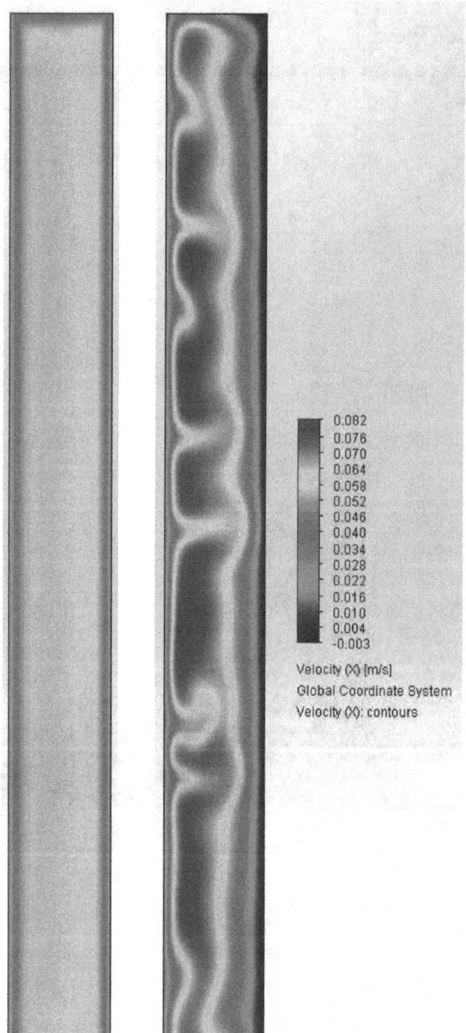

Figure 20.8d) Velocity (X) contours, rotating plane channel flow, inlet and outlet views

H. Theory

9. The Coriolis instability for the flow in a plane channel with system rotation is governed by the Reynolds number *Re* and the rotation number *Ro*.

$$Re = \frac{U_b d}{\nu} \tag{20.1}$$

$$Ro = \frac{\Omega d}{U_b} \tag{20.2}$$

where U_b is the bulk flow velocity in the channel, d is the channel width, Ω is the rotation rate and ν is the kinematic viscosity of the fluid. The critical Reynolds number Re_{crit} is 5770 caused by Tollmien-Schlichting waves without rotation. Roll cell instabilities will develop below this Reynolds number due to the Coriolis force. The non-dimensional wave number α of the Coriolis instability is determined by

$$\alpha = \frac{2\pi d}{\lambda} \tag{20.3}$$

where λ is the spanwise wave-length of the instability. From Figure 20.9, the wave number can be determined to be

$$\alpha = \frac{2\pi \cdot 0.010}{0.01033} = 6.08 \tag{20.4}$$

Figure 20.9 Velocity (X) contours, rotating plane channel flow, front view

To determine the wave-length that is used to determine the wave number in equation (20.3), you can measure the total length in the vertical spanwise direction for seven successive streaks in Figure 20.9. Next, you take this vertical length and divide by seven to get the average wave-length in the vertical spanwise direction. To get the scale for Figures 20.9, use the total height of the channel in the vertical direction in Figure 20.9 that corresponds to 100 mm.

Reynolds and rotation numbers in the SOLIDWORKS Flow Simulations is

$$Re = \frac{U_b d}{\nu} = \frac{0.05*0.01}{10^{-6}} = 1000 \tag{20.5}$$

$$Ro = \frac{\Omega d}{U_b} = \frac{0.5*0.01}{0.05} = 0.1 \tag{20.6}$$

I. References

1. Alfredsson, P.H. and Persson, H., Instabilities in channel flow with system rotation. *J. Fluid Mech.,* **202**, 543, (1989).
2. Chandrasekhar, S., Hydrodynamic and Hydromagnetic Stability, Dover, 1981.
3. Hart, J.E., Instability and secondary motion in a rotating channel flow. *J. Fluid Mech.,* **45**, 341, (1971).
4. Lezius, D.K. and Johnston, J.P., The structure and stability of turbulent boundary layers in rotating channel flow. *J. Fluid Mech.,* **77**, 153, (1976).
5. Speziale, C.G. and Thangam, S., Numerical study of secondary flows and roll-cell instabilities in rotating channel flow. *J. Fluid Mech.,* **130**, 377, (1983).

J. Exercises

1. Run the calculations for the flow in the rotating channel in this chapter but use bulk flow velocities: 0.03, 0.06, 0.09 and 0.12 m/s and determine the Reynolds number, rotation number and the spanwise wave number for each velocity.

2. Run the calculations for the flow in the rotating channel as shown in this chapter at Re = 500 for different rotation numbers Ro = 0.2, 0.3, 0.4 and 0.5. Determine the spanwise wave number for each case and compare with the critical value.

CHAPTER 21. CURVED CHANNEL FLOW

A. Objectives

- Creating the SOLIDWORKS models needed for Flow Simulations
- Setting up Flow Simulation projects for internal flows
- Creating lids for boundary conditions and setting up boundary conditions
- Use of gravity as a physical feature and running the calculations
- Using cut plots and surface plots to visualize the resulting flow field
- Compare results with linear stability theory

B. Problem Description

In this chapter we will study the appearance of streamwise vortices for the flow in a narrow gap curved channel with rectangular cross section. The height of the rectangular cross section is 100 mm, and the channel width is 10 mm. The mean radius of the channel is 400 mm. The centrifugal force due to curvature will cause the appearance of counter-rotating vortices and transition to turbulent flow at much lower Reynolds numbers as compared with the non-rotating plane channel flow case.

C. Creating SOLIDWORKS Part for Curved Channel Flow

1. Start SOLIDWORKS and create a New Part. Select **Tools>>Options...** from the SOLIDWORKS menu. Click on the Document Properties tab and select **Units**. Select **MMGS** as your **Unit system**. Select the **Top** view from the **View Orientation** drop down menu in the graphics window and click on the **Top Plane** in the **FeatureManager design tree**. Next, select the **Centerpoint Arc** sketch tool from the **Basic Modeling Tools** tab in the menu. Click on the origin in the graphics window and create two 180-degree arcs with radii 395 mm and 405 mm as shown in Figure 21.1. Connect the end points of the two arcs as shown in Figure 21.1. Close the dialog box.

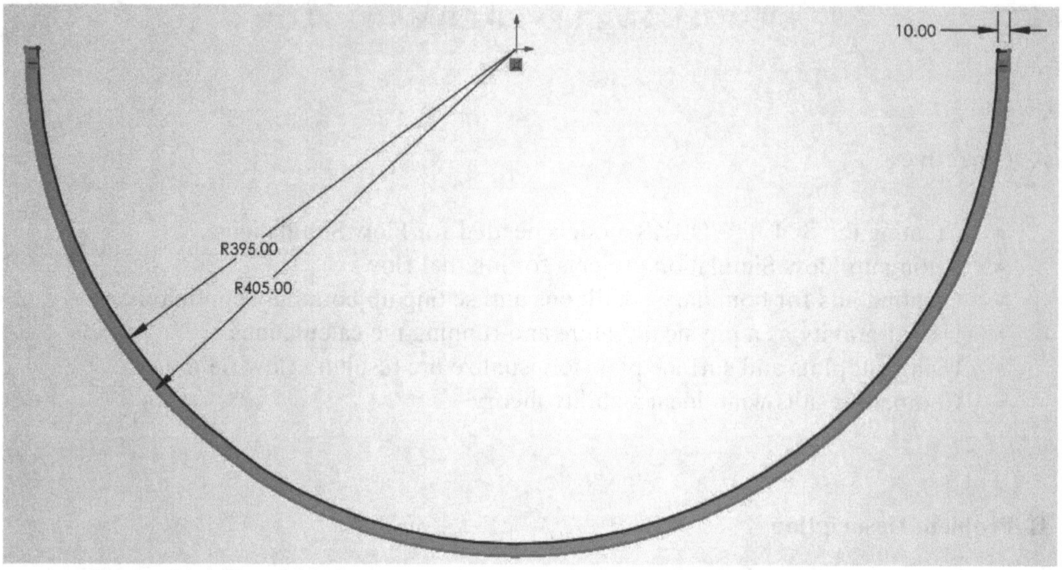

Figure 21.1 Two 180-degree center arcs and connecting lines with dimensions

2. Click on **Sketch 1** in the **FeatureManager design tree** followed by the selection of **Extruded Boss/Base** from the **Analysis Preparation** tab in the menu. Enter a depth of **100 mm** in both directions. Check the box for **Thin Feature** and enter **5 mm** as thickness. Check the box for **Cap ends** and enter **5 mm** as thickness. Click on OK. Save the part with name **Curved Channel 2026**.

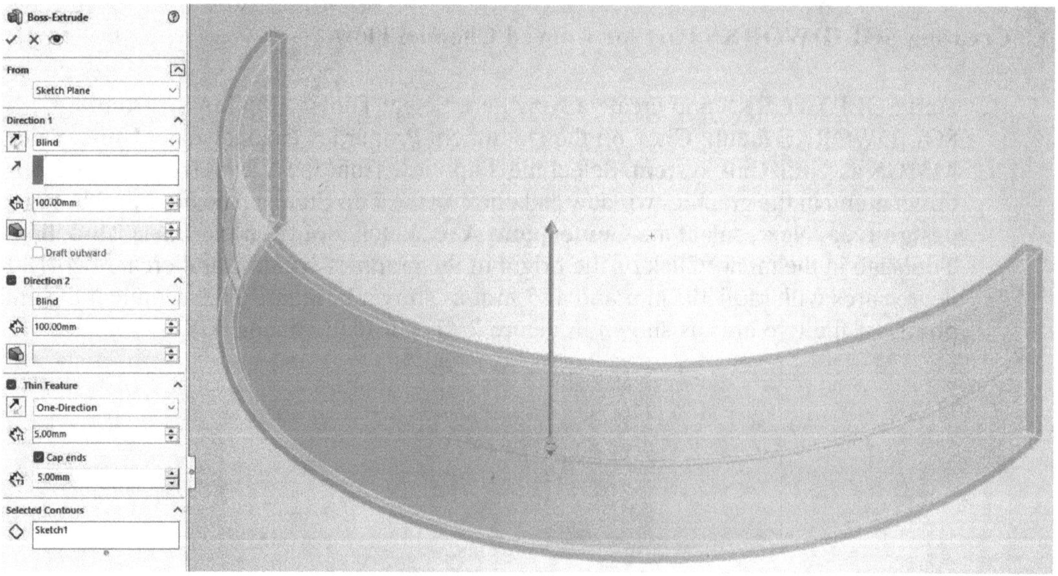

Figure 21.2 Entering depths of extrusion, thin feature and capped ends.

D. Flow Simulation Project for Curved Channel Flow

3. If Flow Simulation is not available in the SOLIDWORKS menu, select **Tools>>Add Ins...** and check the corresponding **SOLIDWORKS Flow Simulation** box. Start the Flow Simulation Wizard by selecting **Tools>>Flow Simulation>>Project>>Wizard....** Enter Project name: **Instabilities in Curved Channel Flow.**

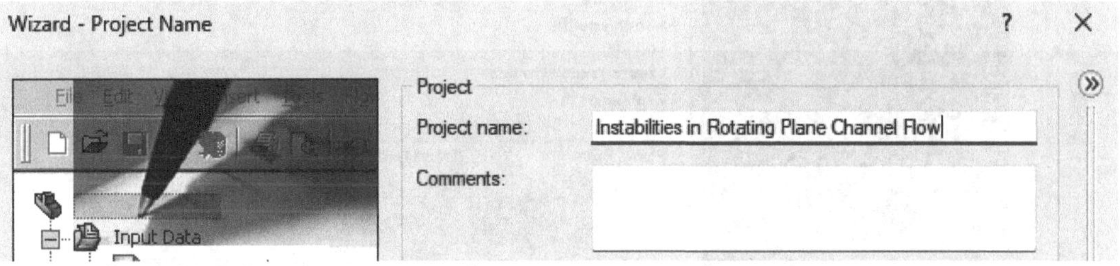

Figure 21.3 Creating a new project name

4. Select the **SI unit system** in the next step followed by selection of the **Internal Analysis type** in the following step. Check the boxes for Gravity under Physical Features. Set the values and choose the selections as shown in Figure 21.4a).

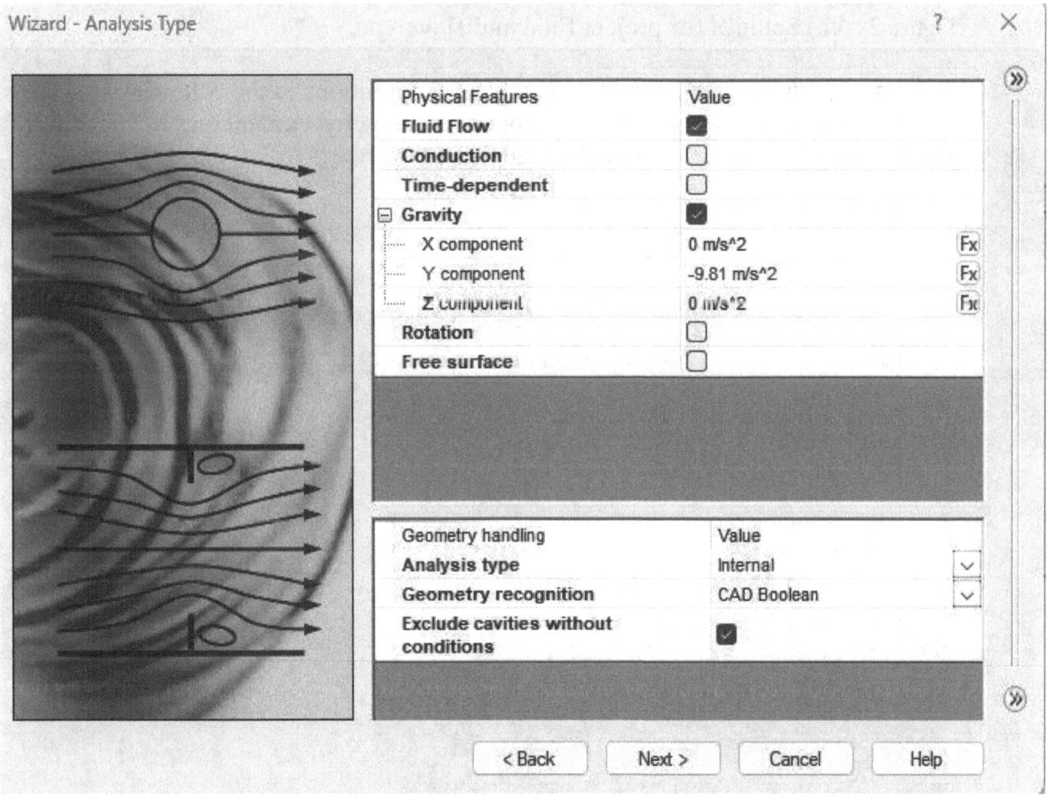

Figure 21.4a) Settings for physical features

In the next step, add **Water** as the **Project Fluid** and select **Laminar Only** as **Flow type**.

Figure 21.4b) Settings for project fluid and flow type

Use default values of wall conditions and initial conditions in the following two steps. Enter **0.1 m/s** as **Velocity in X direction** under **Velocity Parameters** in the **Initial Conditions** window. Select **Finish** to close the wizard.

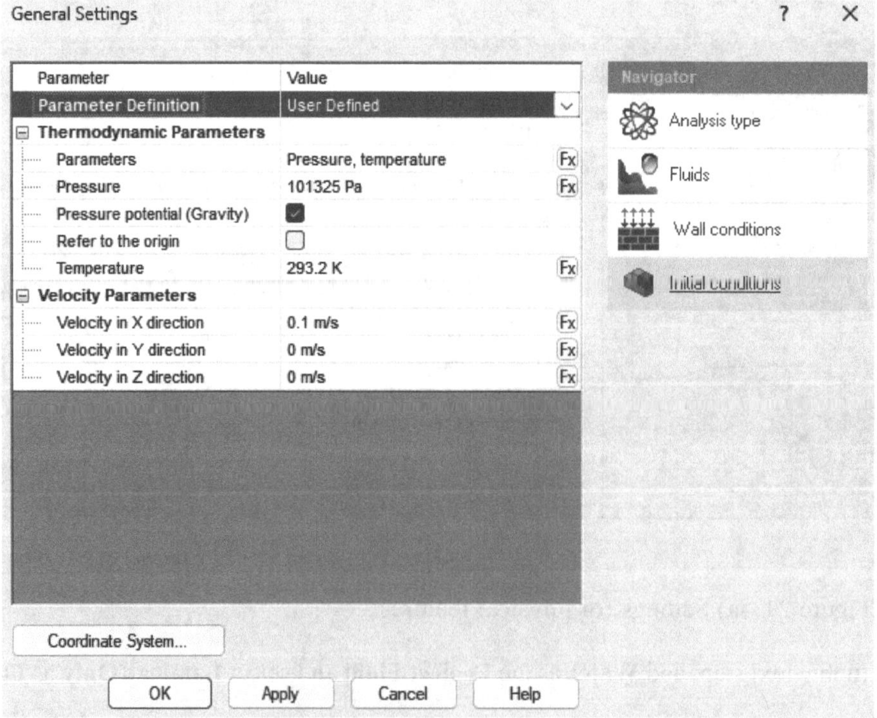

Figure 21.4c) Settings for initial conditions

Select **Tools>>Flow Simulation>>Global Mesh...** from the SOLIDWORKS menu. Select **Manual settings**. Set the number of cells in all three directions X, Y and Z to **500**, **50**, and **250**. Make sure to use the same settings as shown in Figure 21.4d). Click on the **OK** button to exit the **Global Mesh Settings** window.

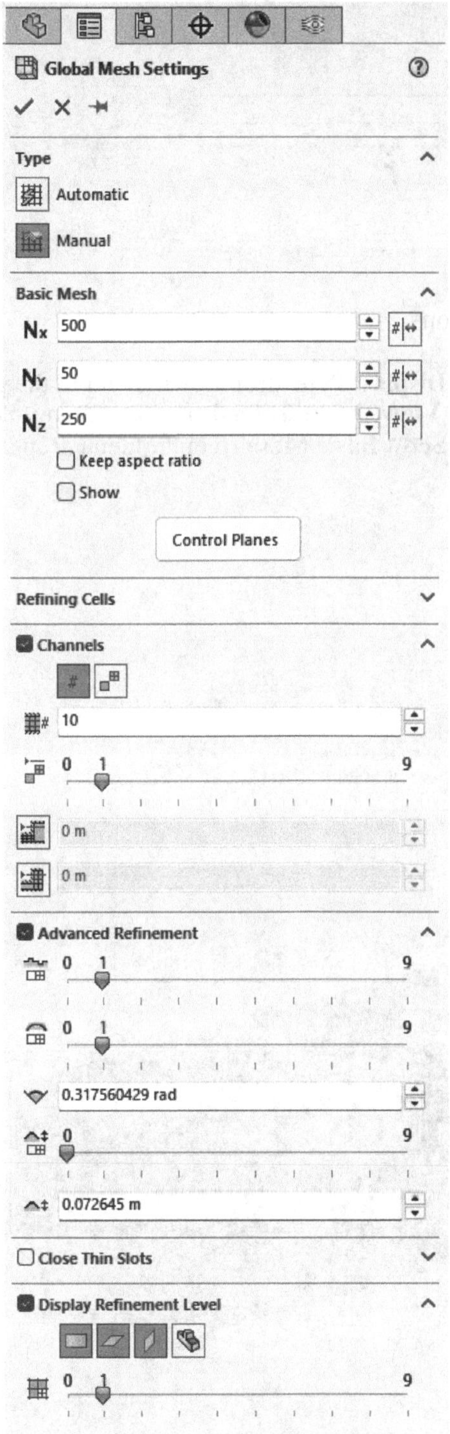

Figure 21.4d) Global mesh settings

Select **Tools>>Flow Simulation>>Calculation Control Options…** from the SOLIDWORKS menu. Click on the **Refinement** tab and select **level = 1** for the **Value** of the **Refinement Parameter**. Click on the **OK** button to exit the **Calculation Control Options** window.

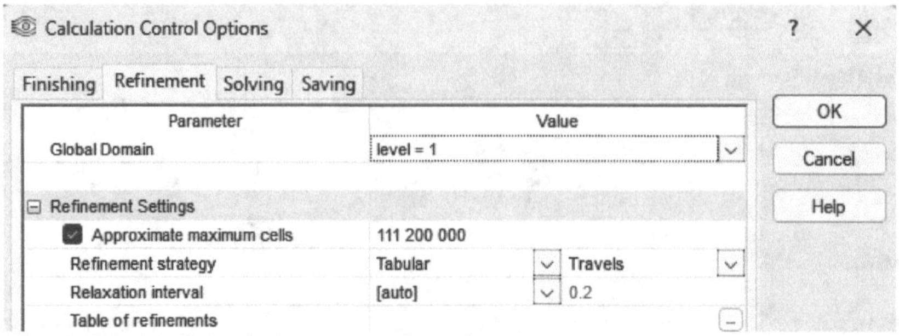

Figure 21.4e) Calculation control options

Select **Hidden Lines Visible** from the **Display Type** drop down menu in the graphics window and **Isometric** view from the **View Orientation** drop down menu. Select **Tools>>Flow Simulation>>Project>>Show Basic Mesh** from the menu. Repeat this to hide the mesh.

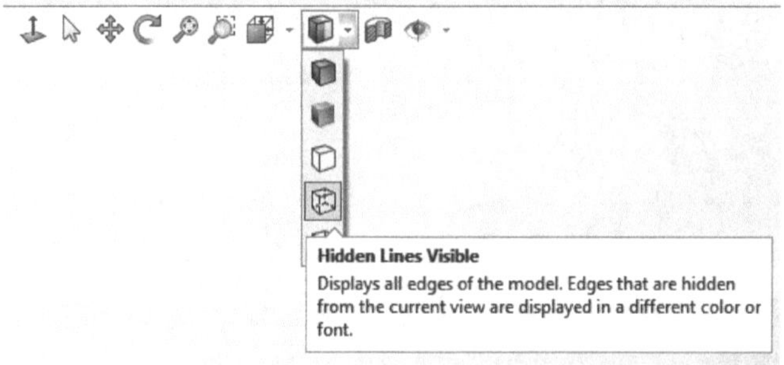

Figure 21.4f) Showing hidden lines

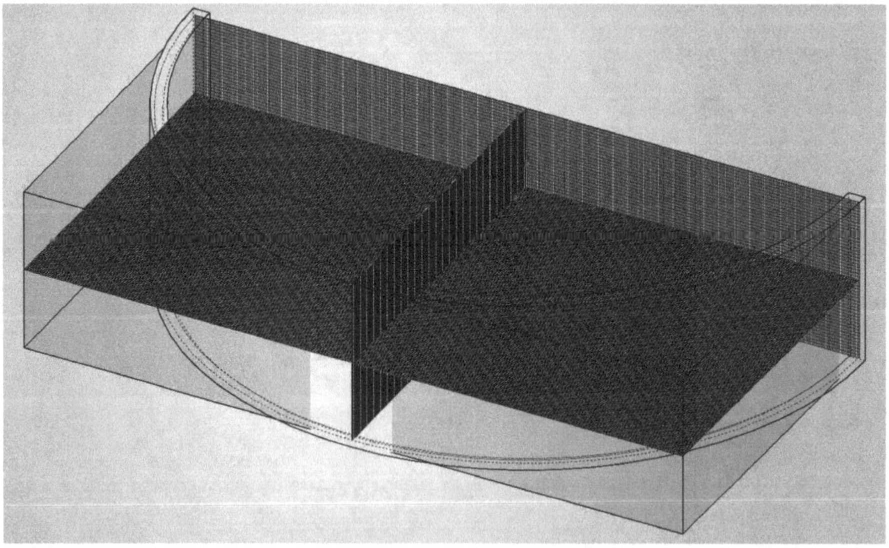

Figure 21.4g) Computational domain with basic mesh for curved channel flow

E. Boundary Conditions for Curved Channel Flow

5. Click on the **Flow Simulation analysis tree** tab and click on the plus sign next to the **Input Data** folder. Right click on **Boundary Conditions** and select **Insert Boundary Condition….** Zoom in and move the cursor over the left end of the curved channel, right click and select **Select Other**. Select the face for the inner rectangular surface of the inflow domain, see Figures 21.5a).

   Select the **Inlet Velocity** boundary condition and set the value of **0.1 m/s** for the inlet velocity in the **X Axis direction**. Check the box for Fully developed flow in Flow Parameters. Click OK to finish the boundary condition. Insert another boundary condition for the other end of the curved channel, select the **Pressure Openings** and **Static Pressure** boundary condition.

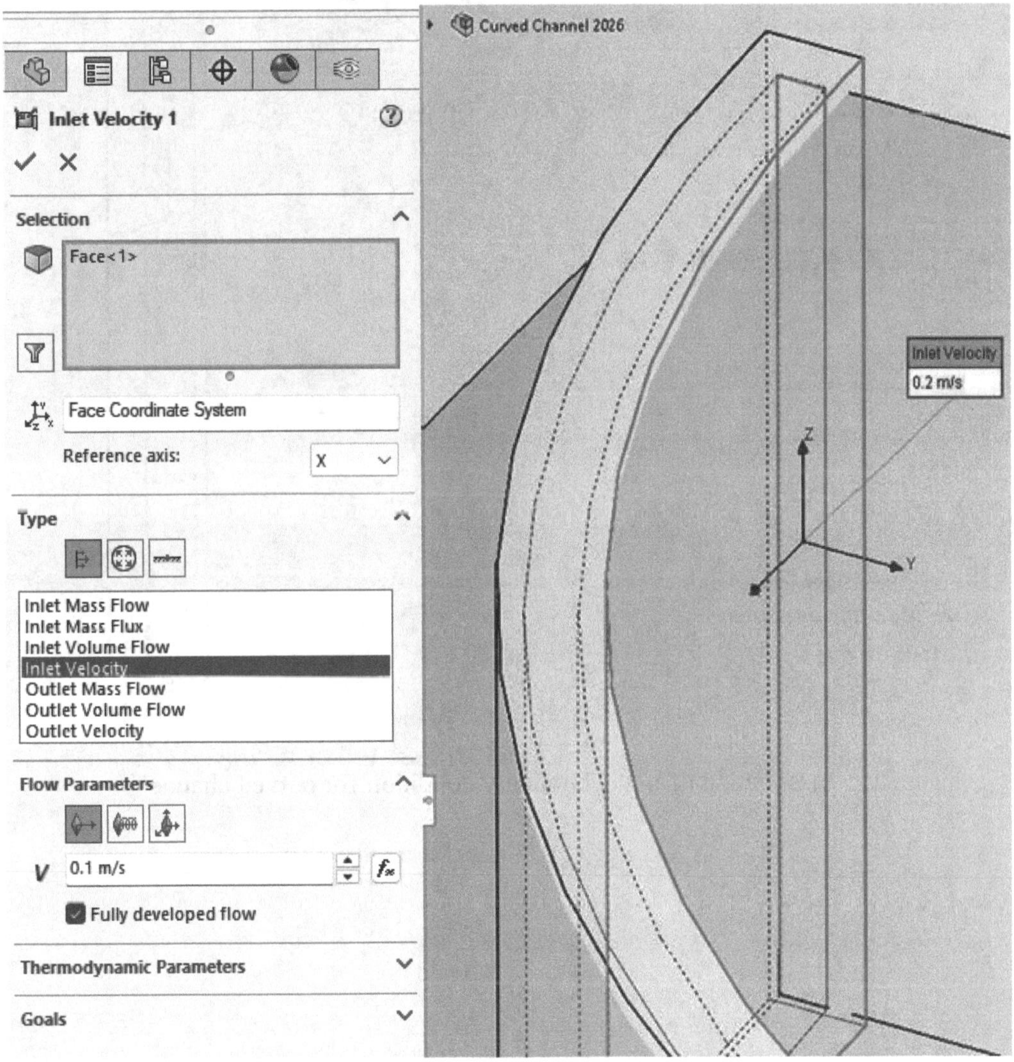

Figure 21.5a) Selection of inlet boundary condition for curved channel

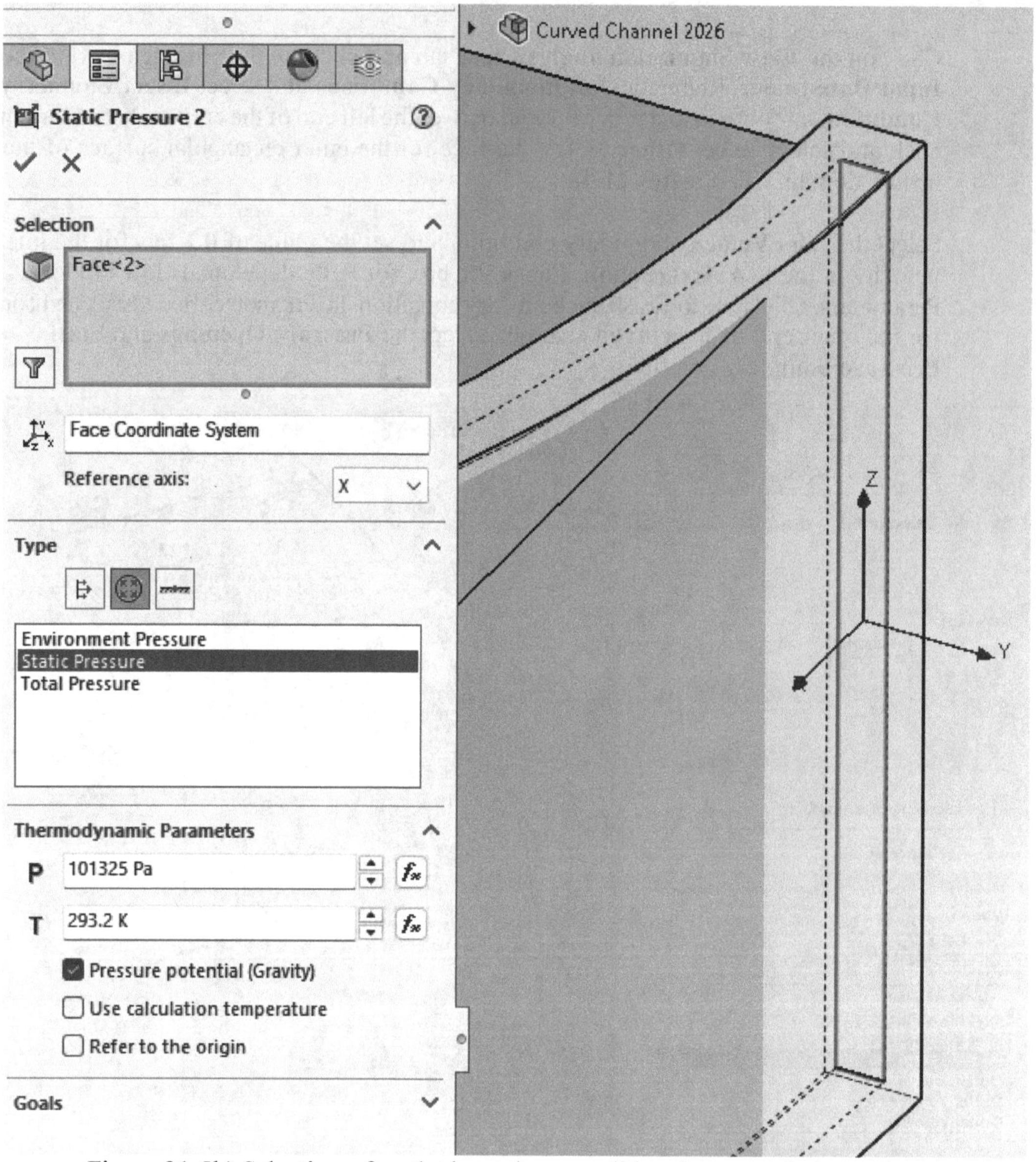

Figure 21.5b) Selection of outlet boundary condition for curved channel

F. Global Goal and Simulations for Curved Channel Flow

6. Right click on **Goals** in the **Flow Simulation analysis tree** and select **Insert Global Goals….** Check the boxes for **Min, Av** and **Max Velocity** and exit the window. Select **Tools>>Flow Simulation>>Solve>>Run….** Push the **Run** button in the window that appears.

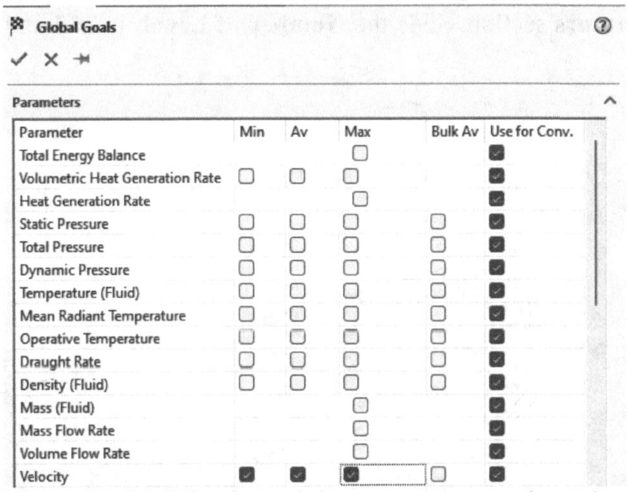

Figure 21.6a) Selecting minimum, average and maximum velocities as global goals

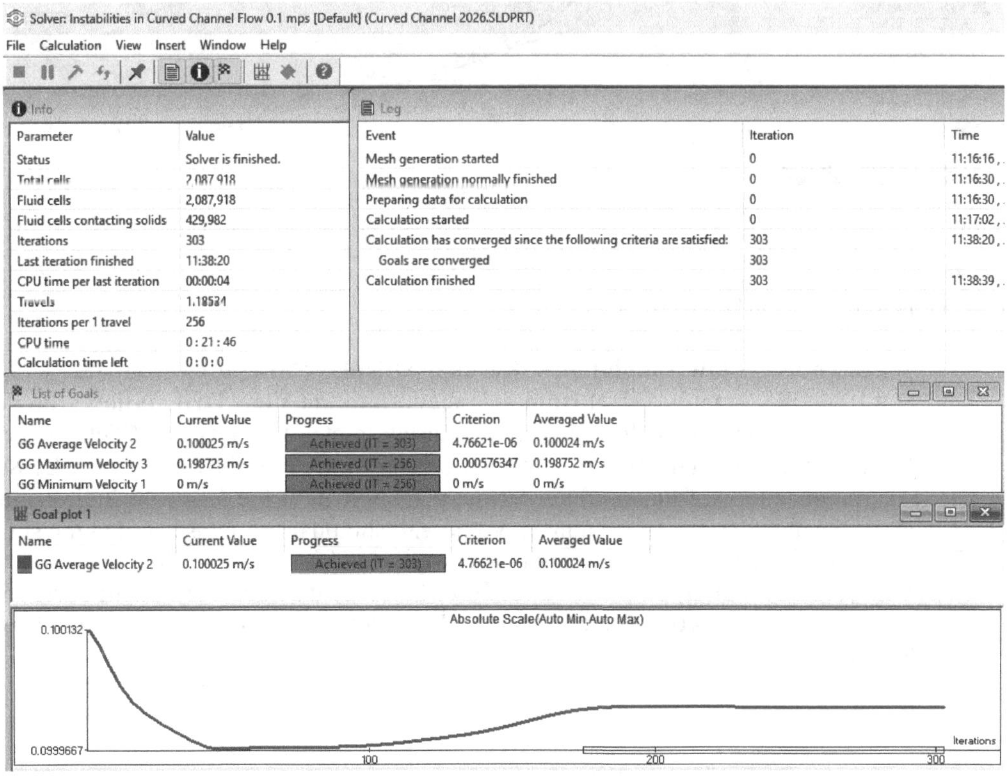

Figure 21.6b) Solver window for calculations of curved channel flow

G. Inserting Surface Plots

7. Select **Tools>>Flow Simulation>>Results>>Load/Unload.** Open the **Results** folder and right click on **Surface Plots** in the **Flow Simulation analysis tree** and select **Insert....** Move the mouse pointer on the curved channel, right click and select Select Other. Select the face of the outer curved channel wall that is in touch with the fluid. Expand **Options** and check the **Offset** box. Select **Velocity (X)** from the **Parameter** drop down menu in the **Contours** section. Slide the **Number of Levels** to **255** and exit the **Surface Plot** window.

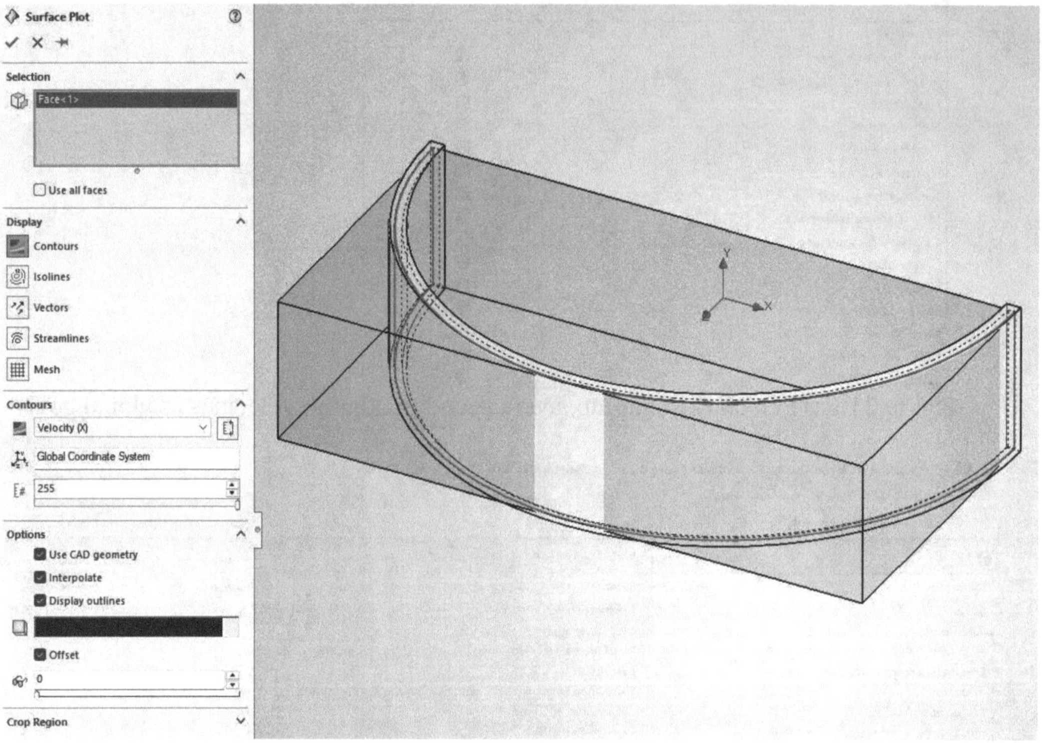

Figure 21.7 Surface plot settings

8. Select **Tools>>Flow Simulation>>Results>>Display>>Lighting** from the SOLIDWORKS menu. Select **Isometric** view from the **View Orientation** drop down menu in the graphics window. Rename the surface plot to **Velocity (Y)**. Click on **Section View**. Exit the **Section View** window. The velocity field is shown in Figure 21.8c). Alternating bands of high and low velocity are shown in the spanwise Z direction indicating the presence of streamwise vortices. It should be emphasized that the surface plot is not located on the curved channel wall but offset into the fluid. Right click on **Computational Domain** in the **Input Data** folder and select **Hide**. Right click on **Instabilities in Rotating Plane Channel Flow** and select **Hide Global Coordinate System.**

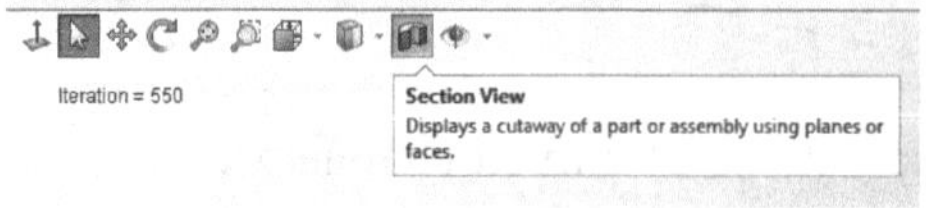

Figure 21.8a) Section view

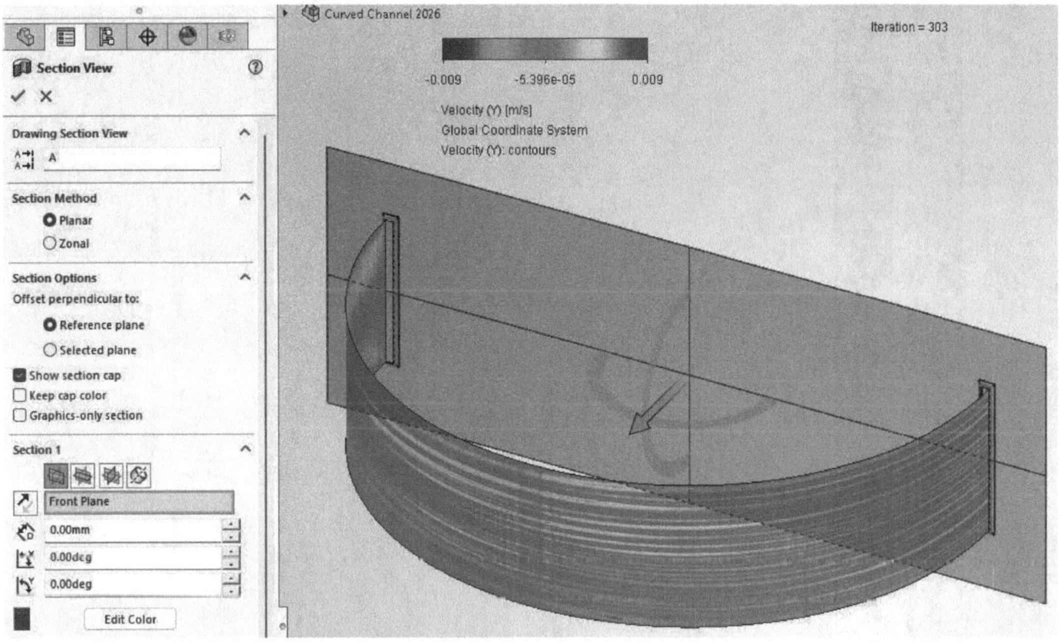

Figure 21.8b) Section view settings for curved channel

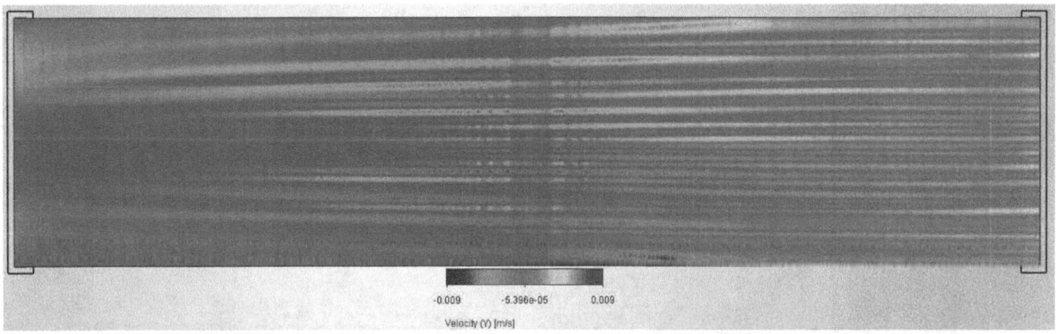

Figure 21.8c) Velocity (Y) contours for curved channel flow, front view

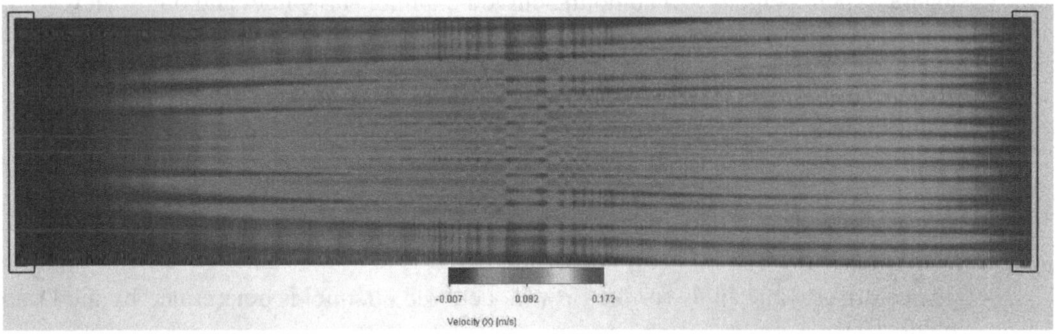

Figure 21.8d) Velocity (X) contours for curved channel flow, front view

Figure 21.8e) Velocity (Z) contours, curved channel flow, inlet and outlet views

In Figures 21.8b) – e), you can see distinct streaks along the vertical direction of the channel. The streaks indicate the presence of streamwise counter rotating vortices with a wavelength in the spanwise direction that can be determined from the figures.

H. Theory

9. The centrifugal instability for the flow in a curved channel is determined by the Dean number *De*.

$$De = Re\sqrt{\gamma} = \frac{U_b d}{\nu}\sqrt{\frac{d}{R}} \tag{21.1}$$

where U_b is the bulk flow velocity in the curved channel, d is the channel width, R its radius of curvature at the channel centerline and ν is the kinematic viscosity of the fluid.

Below the critical $De_{crit} = 36$, the flow is stable, but instabilities will develop above this Dean number[1,2]. The non-dimensional wave number α of the centrifugal instability is determined by

$$\alpha = \frac{2\pi d}{\lambda} \tag{21.2}$$

where λ is the spanwise wave-length of the instability. The critical wave numbers $\alpha_{crit} = 3.96$. From Figure 21.6a), the wave number can be determined to be

$$\alpha = \frac{2\pi \cdot 0.010}{0.015363} = 4.09 \tag{21.3}$$

To determine the wave-length that is used for the wave number in equation (21.3), you can measure the total length in the vertical spanwise direction for 12 yellow successive bands in figure 21.6a). Next, you take this vertical length and divide by 12 to get the average wave-length in the vertical spanwise direction. To get the scale for figure 21.9a), use the total height of the curved channel in the vertical direction in figure 21.9a) that corresponds to 200 mm.

The Dean number in the Ansys Fluent simulations is

$$De = Re\sqrt{\gamma} = \frac{0.1 * 0.01}{10^{-6}}\sqrt{\frac{0.01}{0.4}} = 158 \tag{21.4}$$

The neutral stability curve to the first approximation[4], see Figure 21.8.

$$De = \frac{1}{6\alpha}\left[\frac{(\pi^2+\alpha^2)(4\pi^2+\alpha^2)}{(A-B-C)(D+E-F)}\right]^{1/4} \tag{21.5}$$

where

$$A = \frac{2(640-48\pi^2)}{27\pi^4(\alpha^2+\pi^2)^2} + \frac{64(9\pi^2-56)}{27\pi^2(\alpha^2+\pi^2)^3} - \frac{256(\alpha^2-5\pi^2)}{9\pi^2(\alpha^2+\pi^2)^4} \tag{21.6}$$

$$B = \frac{64\pi^2[16\alpha\pi^6+24\alpha\pi^4(\alpha^2+3)+\alpha^3\pi^2(9\alpha^2-38)+\alpha^5(\alpha^2-2)]}{(\alpha^2+4\pi^2)^3(\alpha^2+\pi^2)^4(\sinh\alpha+\alpha)} \tag{21.7}$$

$$C = \frac{64\pi^2\{(24\pi^4-34\alpha^2\pi^2-22\alpha^4)\alpha\cosh\alpha+[16\pi^4(\pi^2+3)+4\alpha^2\pi^2(8\pi^2-21)+\alpha^4(19\pi^2+36)+3\alpha^6]\sinh\alpha\}}{(\alpha^2+4\pi^2)^3(\alpha^2+\pi^2)^4(\sinh\alpha+\alpha)} \tag{21.8}$$

$$D = \frac{2(640-48\pi^2)}{27\pi^4(\alpha^2+4\pi^2)^2} - \frac{64(9\pi^2-104)}{27\pi^2(\alpha^2+4\pi^2)^3} - \frac{256(\alpha^2-20\pi^2)}{9\pi^2(\alpha^2+4\pi^2)^4} \tag{21.9}$$

$$E = \frac{64\pi^2[4\alpha\pi^6+9\alpha\pi^4(\alpha^2+8)+2\alpha^3\pi^2(3\alpha^2+59)+\alpha^5(\alpha^2-2)]}{(\alpha^2+4\pi^2)^4(\alpha^2+\pi^2)^3(\sinh\alpha-\alpha)} \tag{21.10}$$

$$F = \frac{64\alpha\pi^2\{(24\pi^4-46\alpha^2\pi^2-22\alpha^4)\alpha\cosh\alpha+[4\pi^4(\pi^2+12)+\alpha^2\pi^2(17\pi^2-156)+4\alpha^4(4\pi^2+9)+3\alpha^6]\sinh\alpha\}}{(\alpha^2+4\pi^2)^4(\alpha^2+\pi^2)^3(\sinh\alpha-\alpha)} \tag{21.11}$$

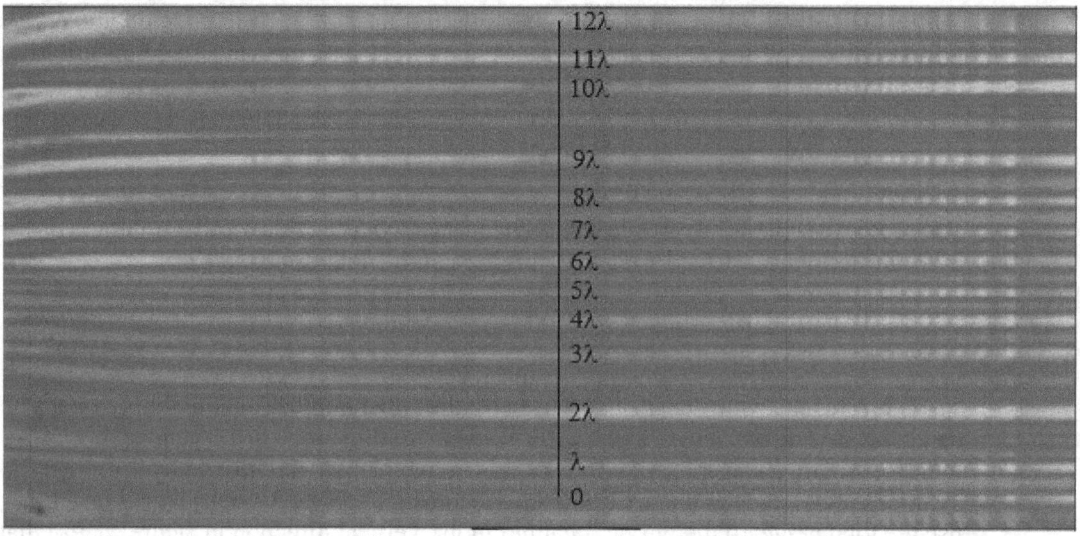

Figure 21.9a) Velocity (Y) contours for curved channel flow, right view

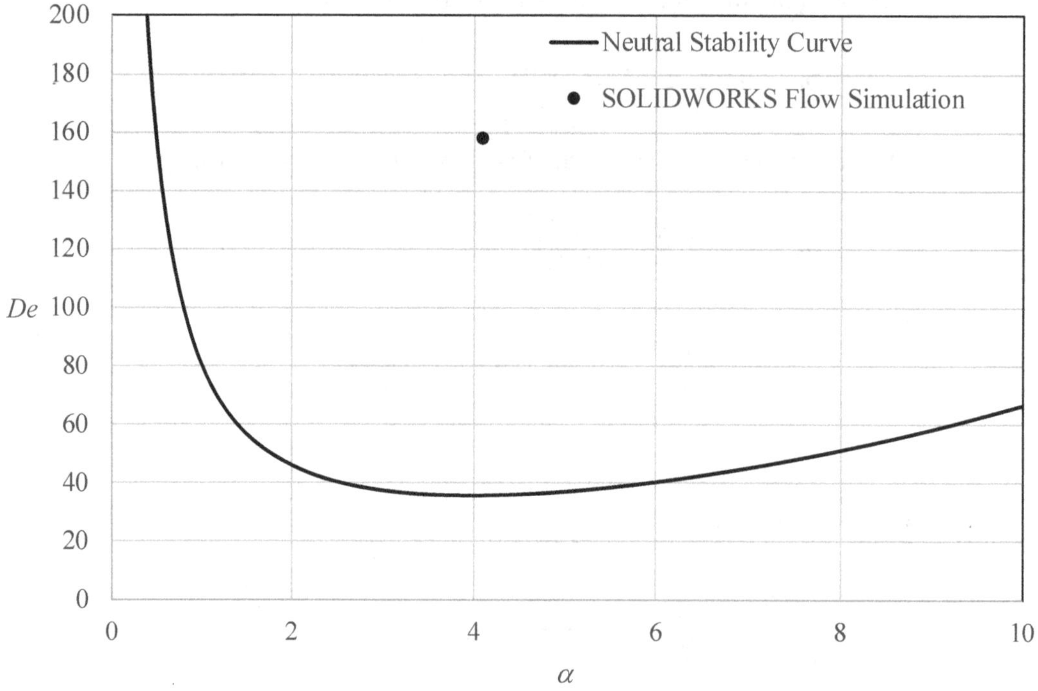

Figure 21.9b) Neutral stability curve for Dean flow in a curved channel. The filled circle represents results from SOLIDWORKS Flow Simulation.

I. References

1. Chandrasekhar, S., Hydrodynamic and Hydromagnetic Stability, Dover, 1981.
2. Dean, W.R., Fluid motion in a curved channel. *Proc. Roy. Soc.* A**121**, 402, 1928.
3. Matsson, J.E. and Alfredsson, P.H., Curvature- and rotation induced instabilities in channel flow. *J. Fluid Mech.* **210**, 537, (1990).
4. Reid, W.H., On the stability of viscous flow in a curved channel. Proc. Roy. Soc. A, **244**, 1237, (1958).

J. Exercises

21.1 Run the calculations for the flow in the curved channel but use the following velocities: 0.05, 0.15, 0.2 and 0.25 m/s and determine the Dean number and the spanwise wave number for each velocity. Include your results in Figure 21.6b).

21.2 Run the calculations for the flow in the curved channel as shown in this chapter for different mesh sizes as shown in the table below. Determine the spanwise wave number for each case. Include your results in Figure 21.6b).

No. Cells X	*No. Cells Y*	*No. Cells Z*
250	25	125
500	50	250
750	75	375
1000	100	500

Notes:

INDEX